59th Annual Meeting of the Association for Computational Linguistics and the 11th International Joint Conference on Natural Language Processing (ACL-IJCNLP 2021)

Student Research Workshop

Online
5-6 August 2021

ISBN: 978-1-7138-3311-6

Printed from e-media with permission by:

Curran Associates, Inc.
57 Morehouse Lane
Red Hook, NY 12571

Some format issues inherent in the e-media version may also appear in this print version.

Association for Computational Linguistics
209 N. Eighth Street
Stroudsburg, Pennsylvania 18360

Phone: 1-570-476-8006
Fax: 1-570-476-0860

acl@aclweb.org

Additional copies of this publication are available from:

Curran Associates, Inc.
57 Morehouse Lane
Red Hook, NY 12571 USA
Phone: 845-758-0400
Fax: 845-758-2633
Email: curran@proceedings.com
Web: www.proceedings.com

ACL-IJCNLP 2021

The 59th Annual Meeting of the Association for Computational Linguistics and the 11th International Joint Conference on Natural Language Processing

Proceedings of the Student Research Workshop

August 5-6, 2021
Bangkok, Thailand (online)

Introduction

Welcome to the ACL-IJCNLP 2021 Student Research Workshop!

The ACL-IJCNLP 2021 Student Research Workshop (SRW) is a forum for student researchers in computational linguistics and natural language processing. The workshop provides a unique opportunity for student participants to present their work and receive valuable feedback from the international research community as well as from faculty mentors.

Following the tradition of the previous student research workshops, we have two tracks: research papers and thesis proposals. The research paper track is a venue for Ph.D. students, Masters students, and advanced undergraduates to describe completed work or work-in-progress along with preliminary results. The thesis proposal track is offered for advanced Masters and Ph.D. students who have decided on a thesis topic and are interested in feedback on their proposal and ideas about future directions for their work.

This year, the student research workshop has again received wide attention. We received 114 submissions including 109 research papers and 5 thesis proposals. The submissions included 68 long papers and 46 short papers. Following withdrawals and desk rejects, 45 were accepted for an acceptance rate of 39%. Excluding non-archival papers, 36 papers appear in these proceedings. All the accepted papers will be presented virtually in three sessions during the course of August 3rd.

Mentoring is at the heart of the SRW. In keeping with previous years, we had a pre-submission mentoring program before the submission deadline. A total of 36 papers participated in the pre-submission mentoring program. This program offered students the opportunity to receive comments from an experienced researcher to improve the writing style and presentation of their submissions.

We are deeply grateful to the Swiss National Science Foundation (SNSF) for providing funds that covered student registrations. We thank our program committee members for their careful reviews of each paper and all of our mentors for donating their time to provide feedback to our student authors. Thank you to our faculty advisors, Jing Jiang, Rico Sennrich, Derek F. Wong and Nianwen Xue, for their essential advice and guidance, and to the ACL-IJCNLP 2021 organizing committee for their support. Finally, thank you to our student participants!

Organizers:

Jad Kabbara, McGill University and the Montreal Institute for Learning Algorithms (MILA)
Haitao Lin, Institute of Automation, Chinese Academy of Sciences
Amandalynne Paullada, University of Washington
Jannis Vamvas, University of Zurich

Faculty Advisors:

Jing Jiang, Singapore Management University
Rico Sennrich, University of Edinburgh
Derek F. Wong, University of Maca
Nianwen Xue, Brandeis University

Pre-submission Mentors:

Duygu Ataman, University of Zürich
Valerio Basile, University of Turin
Eduardo Blanco, University of North Texas
David Chiang, University of Notre Dame
Marta R. Costa-Jussà, Universitat Politècnica de Catalunya
Lucia Donatelli, Saarland University
Greg Durrett, UT Austin
Sarah Ebling, University of Zurich
Yansong Feng, Peking University
Orhan Firat, Google AI
Lea Frermann, Melbourne University
Shujian Huang, National Key Laboratory for Novel Software Technology, Nanjing University
Kentaro Inui, Tohoku University / Riken
Robin Jia, Facebook AI Research
Katharina Kann, University of Colorado Boulder
Mamoru Komachi, Tokyo Metropolitan University
Parisa Kordjamshidi, Michigan State University
Jindřich Libovický, Ludwig Maximilian University of Munich
Pengfei Liu, Carnegie Mellon University
Vincent Ng, University of Texas at Dallas
Sai Krishna Rallabandi, Carnegie Mellon University
Masoud Rouhizadeh, Johns Hopkins University
Dipti Sharma, IIIT, Hyderabad
Manish Shrivastava, International Institute of Information Technology Hyderabad
Sunayana Sitaram, Microsoft Research India
Gabriel Stanovsky, The Hebrew University of Jerusalem
Amanda Stent, Bloomberg
Hanna Suominen, The Australian National University, Data61/CSIRO, and University of Turku
Mihai Surdeanu, University of Arizona
Masashi Toyoda, The University of Tokyo
Chen-Tse Tsai, Bloomberg LP
Bonnie Webber, University of Edinburgh
Yujiu Yang, tsinghua.edu.cn
Arkaitz Zubiaga, Queen Mary University of London

Program Committee:

Assina Abdussaitova, Suleyman Demirel University
Ibrahim Abu Farha, University of Edinburgh
Oshin Agarwal, University of Pennsylvania
Piush Aggarwal, University of Duisburg-Essen, Language Technology Lab
Roee Aharoni, Google
Miguel A. Alonso, Universidade da Coruña
Malik Altakrori, McGill University /Mila
Rami Aly, University of Cambridge
Bharat Ram Ambati, Apple Inc.
Aida Amini, University of Washington
Maria Antoniak, Cornell University
Tal August, University of Washington
Vidhisha Balachandran, Carnegie Mellon University
Anusha Balakrishnan, Microsoft Semantic Machines
Jorge Balazs, Amazon
Roberto Basili, University of Roma, Tor Vergata
Rachel Bawden, Inria
Chris Biemann, Universität Hamburg
Tatiana Bladier, Heinrich Heine University Düsseldorf
Nikolay Bogoychev, University of Edinburgh
Avishek Joey Bose, Mila/McGill
Ruken Cakici, METU
Ronald Cardenas, University of Edinburgh
Arlene Casey, University of Edinburgh
Aishik Chakraborty, McGill University
Jonathan P. Chang, Cornell University
Jifan Chen, UT Austin
Sihao Chen, University of Pennsylvania
Elizabeth Clark, University of Washington
Xiang Dai, University of Copenhagen
Siddharth Dalmia, Carnegie Mellon University
Samvit Dammalapati, Indian Institute of Technology Delhi
Alok Debnath, Factmata
Louise Deléger, INRAE - Université Paris-Saclay
Pieter Delobelle, KU Leuven, Department of Computer Science
Dorottya Demszky, Stanford University
Etienne Denis, McGill
Chris Develder, Ghent University
Anne Dirkson, Leiden University
Radina Dobreva, University of Edinburgh
Zi-Yi Dou, UCLA
Hicham El Boukkouri, LIMSI, CNRS, Université Paris-Saclay
Carlos Escolano, Universitat Politècnica de Catalunya
Luis Espinosa Anke, Cardiff University
Tina Fang, University of Waterloo
Murhaf Fares, University of Oslo
Amir Feder, Technion - Israel Institute of Technology
Jared Fernandez, Carnegie Mellon University

Dayne Freitag, SRI International
Daniel Fried, UC Berkeley
Yoshinari Fujinuma, University of Colorado Boulder
David Gaddy, University of California, Berkeley
Diana Galvan-Sosa, RIKEN AIP
Marcos Garcia, Universidade de Santiago de Compostela
Arijit Ghosh Chowdhury, Manipal Institute of Technology
Liane Guillou, The University of Edinburgh
Sarah Gupta, University of Washington
Hardy Hardy, The University of Sheffield
Mareike Hartmann, University of Copenhagen
Junxian He, Carnegie Mellon University
Jack Hessel, Allen AI
Christopher Homan, Rochester Institute of Technology
Junjie Hu, Carnegie Mellon University
Jeff Jacobs, Columbia University
Aaron Jaech, Facebook
Labiba Jahan, Florida International University
Tomoyuki Kajiwara, Ehime University
Zara Kancheva, IICT-BAS
Sudipta Kar, Amazon Alexa AI
Alina Karakanta, Fondazione Bruno Kessler (FBK), University of Trento
Najoung Kim, Johns Hopkins University
Philipp Koehn, Johns Hopkins University
Allison Koenecke, Stanford University
Mandy Korpusik, Loyola Marymount University
Jonathan K. Kummerfeld, University of Michigan
Kemal Kurniawan, University of Melbourne
Yash Kumar Lal, Stony Brook University
Ian Lane, Carnegie Mellon University
Alexandra Lavrentovich, Amazon Alexa
Lei Li, Peking University
Yiyuan Li, University of North Carolina, Chapel Hill
Jasy Suet Yan Liew, School of Computer Sciences, Universiti Sains Malaysia
Lucy Lin, University of Washington
Kevin Lin, Microsoft
Fangyu Liu, University of Cambridge
Di Lu, Dataminr
Chunchuan Lyu, The University of Edinburgh
Debanjan Mahata, Bloomberg
Valentin Malykh, Huawei Noah's Ark Lab / Kazan Federal University
Emma Manning, Georgetown University
Courtney Mansfield, University of Washington
Pedro Henrique Martins, Instituto de Telecomunicações, Instituto Superior Técnico
Bruno Martins, IST and INESC-ID
Rui Meng, University of Pittsburgh
Antonio Valerio Miceli Barone, The University of Edinburgh
Tsvetomila Mihaylova, Instituto de Telecomunicações
Farjana Sultana Mim, Tohoku University
Sewon Min, University of Washington
Koji Mineshima, Keio University

Gosse Minnema, University of Groningen
Amita Misra, IBM
Omid Moradiannasab, Saarland University
Nora Muheim, University of Bern
Masaaki Nagata, NTT Corporation
Aakanksha Naik, Carnegie Mellon University
Denis Newman-Griffis, University of Pittsburgh
Dat Quoc Nguyen, VinAI Research
Vincent Nguyen, Australian National University & CSIRO Data61
Shinji Nishimoto, CiNet
Yasumasa Onoe, The University of Texas at Austin
Silviu Oprea, University of Edinburgh
Naoki Otani, Carnegie Mellon University
Ashwin Paranjape, Stanford University
Archita Pathak, University at Buffalo (SUNY)
Viviana Patti, University of Turin, Dipartimento di Informatica
Siyao Peng, Georgetown University
Ian Porada, Mila, McGill University
Jakob Prange, Georgetown University
Adithya Pratapa, Carnegie Mellon University
Yusu Qian, New York University
Long Qiu, Onehome (Beijing) Network Technology Co. Ltd.
Ivaylo Radev, IICT-BAS
Sai Krishna Rallabandi, Carnegie Mellon University
Vikas Raunak, Microsoft
Lina M. Rojas Barahona, Orange Labs
Guy Rotman, Faculty of Industrial Engineering and Management, Technion, IIT
Maria Ryskina, Carnegie Mellon University
Farig Sadeque, Educational Testing Service
Jin Sakuma, University of Tokyo
Elizabeth Salesky, Johns Hopkins University
Younes Samih, University of Düsseldorf
Ramon Sanabria, The University Of Edinburgh
Michael Sejr Schlichtkrull, University of Amsterdam
Sebastian Schuster, New York University
Olga Seminck, CNRS
Indira Sen, GESIS
Vasu Sharma, Carnegie Mellon University
Sina Sheikholeslami, KTH Royal Institute of Technology
A.B. Siddique, University of California, Riverside
Kevin Small, Amazon
Marco Antonio Sobrevilla Cabezudo, University of São Paulo
Katira Soleymanzadeh, Ege University
Swapna Somasundaran, Educational Testing Service
Sandeep Soni, Georgia Institute of Technology
Richard Sproat, Google, Japan
Makesh Narsimhan Sreedhar, Mila, Universite de Montreal
Tejas Srinivasan, Microsoft
Vamshi Krishna Srirangam, International Institute of Information Technology, Hyderabad
Marija Stanojevic, Center for Data Analytics and Biomedical Informatics, Temple University
Shane Steinert-Threlkeld, University of Washington

Alane Suhr, Cornell University
Shabnam Tafreshi, The George Washington University
Wenyi Tay, RMIT University
Uthayasanker Thayasivam, University of Moratuwa
Trang Tran, Institute for Creative Technologies, University of Southern California
Sowmya Vajjala, National Research Council
Emiel van Miltenburg, Tilburg University
Dimitrova Vania, University of Leeds
Rob Voigt, Northwestern University
Ivan Vulić, University of Cambridge
Adina Williams, Facebook, Inc.
Jiacheng Xu, University of Texas at Austin
Yumo Xu, University of Edinburgh
Rongtian Ye, Aalto University
Olga Zamaraeva, University of Washington
Meishan Zhang, Tianjin University, China
Justine Zhang, Cornell University
Ben Zhang, NYU Langone
Shiyue Zhang, The University of North Carolina at Chapel Hill
Ben Zhou, University of Pennsylvania
Zhong Zhou, Carnegie Mellon University

Table of Contents

Conference Program

An Adaptive Learning Method for Solving the Extreme Learning Rate Problem of Transformer
Jianbang Ding, Xuancheng Ren, Ruixuan Luo, Xu Sun and Xiaozhe REN

Investigation on Data Adaptation Techniques for Neural Named Entity Recognition
Evgeniia Tokarchuk, David Thulke, Weiyue Wang, Christian Dugast and Hermann Ney

Using Perturbed Length-aware Positional Encoding for Non-autoregressive Neural Machine Translation
Yui Oka, Katsuhito Sudoh and Satoshi Nakamura

Stage-wise Fine-tuning for Graph-to-Text Generation
Qingyun Wang, Semih Yavuz, Xi Victoria Lin, Heng Ji and Nazneen Rajani

Transformer-Based Direct Hidden Markov Model for Machine Translation
Weiyue Wang, Zijian Yang, Yingbo Gao and Hermann Ney

AutoRC: Improving BERT Based Relation Classification Models via Architecture Search
Wei Zhu

How Low is Too Low? A Computational Perspective on Extremely Low-Resource Languages
Rachit Bansal, Himanshu Choudhary, Ravneet Punia, Niko Schenk, Émilie Pagé-Perron and Jacob Dahl

On the Relationship between Zipf's Law of Abbreviation and Interfering Noise in Emergent Languages
Ryo Ueda and Koki Washio

Long Document Summarization in a Low Resource Setting using Pretrained Language Models
Ahsaas Bajaj, Pavitra Dangati, Kalpesh Krishna, Pradhiksha Ashok Kumar, Rheeya Uppaal, Bradford Windsor, Eliot Brenner, Dominic Dotterrer, Rajarshi Das and Andrew McCallum

Attending Self-Attention: A Case Study of Visually Grounded Supervision in Vision-and-Language Transformers
Jules Samaran, Noa Garcia, Mayu Otani, Chenhui Chu and Yuta Nakashima

Video-guided Machine Translation with Spatial Hierarchical Attention Network
Weiqi Gu, Haiyue Song, Chenhui Chu and Sadao Kurohashi

Stylistic approaches to predicting Reddit popularity in diglossia
Huikai Chua

Investigation on Data Adaptation Techniques for Neural Named Entity Recognition

Evgeniia Tokarchuk*, David Thulke†, Weiyue Wang†, Christian Dugast†, and Hermann Ney†

*Informatics Institute, University of Amsterdam
†Human Language Technology and Pattern Recognition Group
Computer Science Department
RWTH Aachen University
e.tokarchuk@uva.nl
{thulke,wwang,dugast,ney}@cs.rwth-aachen.de

Abstract

Data processing is an important step in various natural language processing tasks. As the commonly used datasets in named entity recognition contain only a limited number of samples, it is important to obtain additional labeled data in an efficient and reliable manner. A common practice is to utilize large monolingual unlabeled corpora. Another popular technique is to create synthetic data from the original labeled data (data augmentation). In this work, we investigate the impact of these two methods on the performance of three different named entity recognition tasks.

1 Introduction

Recently, deep neural network models have emerged in various fields of natural language processing (NLP) and replaced the mainstream position of conventional count-based methods (Lample et al., 2016; Vaswani et al., 2017; Serban et al., 2016). In addition to providing significant performance improvements, neural models often require high hardware conditions and a large amount of clean training data. However, there is usually only a limited amount of cleanly labeled data available, so techniques such as data augmentation and self-training are commonly used to generate additional synthetic data.

Significant progress has been made in recent years in designing data augmentations for computer vision (CV) (Krizhevsky et al., 2012), automatic speech recognition (ASR) (Park et al., 2019), natural language understanding (NLU) (Hou et al., 2018) and machine translation (MT) (Wang et al., 2018) in supervised settings. In addition, semi-supervised approaches using self-training techniques (Blum and Mitchell, 1998) have shown promising performance in conventional named entity recognition (NER) systems (Kozareva et al., 2005; Daumé III, 2008; Täckström, 2012). In this work, the effectiveness of self-training and data augmentation techniques on neural NER architectures is explored.

To cover different data situations, we select three different datasets: The English CoNLL 2003 (Tjong Kim Sang and De Meulder, 2003) dataset, which is the benchmark on which almost all NER systems report results, it is very clean and the baseline models achieve an F1 score of around 92.6%; The English W-NUT 2017 (Derczynski et al., 2017) dataset, which is generated by users and contains inconsistencies, baseline models get an F1 score of around 52.7%; The GermEval 2014 (Benikova et al., 2014) dataset, a fairly clean German dataset with baseline scores of around 86.3%[1]. We observe that the baseline scores on clean datasets such as CoNLL and GermEval can hardly be improved by data adaptation techniques, while the performance on the W-NUT dataset, which is relatively small and inconsistent, can be significantly improved.

2 Related Work

2.1 State-of-the-art Techniques in NER

Collobert et al. (2011) advance the use of neural networks (NN) for NER, who propose an architecture based on temporal convolutional neural networks (CNN) over the sequence of words. Since then, many articles have suggested improvements to this architecture. Huang et al. (2015) propose replacing the CNN encoder in Collobert et al. (2011) with a bidirectional long short-term memory (LSTM) encoder, while Lample et al. (2016) and Chiu and Nichols (2016) introduce a hierarchy into the architecture by replacing artificially designed features

*Work completed while studying at RWTH Aachen University.

[1]From here on, for the sake of simplicity, we omit the annual information of the datasets.

Proceedings of the Joint Conference of the 59th Annual Meeting of the Association for Computational Linguistics and the 11th International Joint Conference on Natural Language Processing: Student Research Workshop, pages 1–15
August 5–6, 2021.

with additional bidirectional LSTM or CNN encoders. In other related work, Mesnil et al. (2013) have pioneered the use of recurrent neural networks (RNN) to decode tags.

Recently, various pre-trained word embedding techniques have offered further improvements over the strong baseline achieved by the neural architectures. Akbik et al. (2018) suggest using pre-trained character-level language models from which to extract hidden states at the start and end character positions of each word to embed any string in a sentence-level context. In addition, the embedding generated by unsupervised representation learning (Peters et al., 2018; Devlin et al., 2019; Liu et al., 2019; Taillé et al., 2020) has been used successfully for NER, as well as other NLP tasks. In this work, the strongest model for each task is used as the baseline model.

2.2 Data Adaptation in NLP

In NLP, generating synthetic data using forward or backward inference is a commonly used approach to increase the amount of training data. In strong MT systems, synthetic data that is generated by back-translation is often used as additional training data to improve translation quality (Sennrich et al., 2016). A similar approach using backward inference is also successfully used for end-to-end ASR (Hayashi et al., 2018). In addition, back-translation, as observed by Yu et al. (2018), can create various paraphrases while maintaining the semantics of the original sentences, resulting in significant performance improvements in question answering.

In this work, synthetic annotations, which are generated by forward inference of a model that is trained on annotated data, are added to the training data. The method of generating synthetic data by forward inference is also called self-training in semi-supervised approaches. Kozareva et al. (2005) use self-training and co-training to recognize and classify named entities in the news domain. Täckström (2012) uses self-training to adapt a multi-source direct transfer named entity recognizer to different target languages, "relexicalizing" the model with word cluster features. Clark et al. (2018) propose cross-view training, a semi-supervised learning algorithm that improves the representation of a bidirectional LSTM sentence encoder using a mixture of labeled and unlabeled data.

In addition to the promising pre-trained embedding that is successfully used for various NLP tasks, the masked language modeling (MLM) can also be used for data augmentation. Kobayashi (2018) and Wu et al. (2019) propose to replace words with other words that are predicted using the language model at the corresponding position, which shows promising performance on text classification tasks. Recently, Kumar et al. (2020) discussed the effectiveness of such different pre-trained transformer-based models for data augmentation on text classification tasks. And for neural MT, Gao et al. (2019) suggest replacing randomly selected words in a sentence with a mixture of several related words based on a distribution representation. In this work, we explore the use of MLM-based contextual augmentation approaches for various NER tasks.

3 Self-training

Though, the amount of annotated training data is limited for many NLP tasks, additional unlabeled data is available in most situations. Semi-supervised learning approaches make use of this additional data. A common way to do this is self-training (Kozareva et al., 2005; Täckström, 2012; Clark et al., 2018).

At a high level, it consists of the following steps:

1. An initial model is trained using the labeled data.
2. This model is used to annotate the additional unlabeled data.
3. A subset of this data is selected and used in addition to the labeled data to retrain the model.

For the performance of the method it is critical to find a heuristic to select a good subset of the automatically labeled data. The selected data should not introduce too many errors, but at the same time they should be informative, i.e. they should be useful to improve the decision boundary of the final model. One selection strategy (Drugman et al., 2016) is to calculate a confidence measure for all unlabeled sentences and to randomly sample sentences above a certain threshold.

We consider two different confidence measures in this work. The first, hereinafter referred to as c_1, is the posterior probability of the tag sequence y given the word sequence x:

$$c_1(y, x) = p(y \mid x) = \frac{e^{s(x,y)}}{\sum_{y'} e^{s(x,y')}} \quad (1)$$

whereby $s(x, y)$ is the unnormalized log score assigned by the model to the sequence, consisting of an emission model q_i^E and transition model q^T:

$$s(x, y_1^T) = \sum_{i=1}^{T} q_i^E(y_i \mid x) + q^T(y_i \mid y_{i-1})$$

For the second confidence measure, we take into account the normalized tag scores at each position. To get a confidence score for the entire sequence, we take the minimum tag score of all positions. Thus, c_2 is defined as follows:

$$c_2(y, x) = \min_i \frac{q_i^E(y_i \mid x) + q^T(y_i \mid y_{i-1})}{\sum_{y_i'} q_i^E(y_i' \mid x) + q^T(y_i' \mid y_{i-1})} \quad (2)$$

4 MLM-based Data Augmentation

Instead of using additional unlabeled data, we apply MLM-based data augmentation specifically for NER by masking and replacing original text tokens while maintaining labels.

For each masked token x_i:

$$\hat{x}_i = \arg\max_w p(x_i = w|\tilde{\mathbf{x}}) \quad (3)$$

where $\hat{x}_i$ is the predicted token, $w \in V$ is the token from the model vocabulary and $\tilde{\mathbf{x}}$ is the original sentence with $x_i =$ `[MASK]`.

There are several configurations that can affect the performance of the data augmentation method: Techniques of selecting the tokens to be replaced, the order of token replacement in case of multiple replacement and the criterion for selecting the best tokens from the predicted ones. This section studies the effect of these configurations.

4.1 Sampling

Entity spans (entities of arbitrary length) make the training sentences used in NER tasks special. Since there is no guarantee that a predicted token belongs to the same entity type as an original token, it is important to ensure that the masked token is not in the middle of the entity span and that the existing label is not damaged. In this work, we propose three different types of token selection inside and outside of entity spans:

- **Entity replacement**: Collect entity spans of length one in the sentence and randomly select the entity span to be replaced. In this case, exactly one entity in the sentence is replaced. The sentences without entities or with longer entity spans are skipped.
- **Context replacement**: We consider tokens with the label "O" as context and alternate between two setups: (1) Select only context tokens before and after entities, and (2) select a random subset of context tokens among all context tokens.
- **Mixed**: Select uniformly at random the number of masked tokens between two and the sentence length among all tokens in the sentence.

The first approach allows only one entity to be generated and thus benefits from conditioning to the full sequence context. However, it does not guarantee the correct labeling for the generated token. The disadvantage of the second approach is that we do not generate new entity information, but only generate a new context for the existing entity spans. Even if a new entity type is generated, it has the original "O" label without a NER classification pipeline. The disadvantage of the third approach is that the token may be selected in the middle of the entity span and the label is no longer relevant. The sampling approaches depicted on the Figure 1. In addition, the number of replaced tokens should be properly tuned to avoid inadequate generation. In this work, we do not set any boundaries for maximum token replacement and leave such investigation to future work.

4.2 Order of Generation

In our method, we predict exactly one mask token per time. Our sampling approaches allow multiple tokens to be replaced. Therefore we have two possible options for the generation order:

- **Independent**: Each consecutive masking and prediction is made on top of the original sequence.
- **Conditional**: Each consecutive masking and prediction is made on top of the prediction of the previous step.

4.3 Criterion

The criterion is an important part of the generation process. On the one hand, we want our synthetic sequence to be reliable (highest token probability), on the other hand, it should differ as much as possible from the original sequence (high distance). We

[2]Given example is taken from `https://artificialintelligence-news.com`

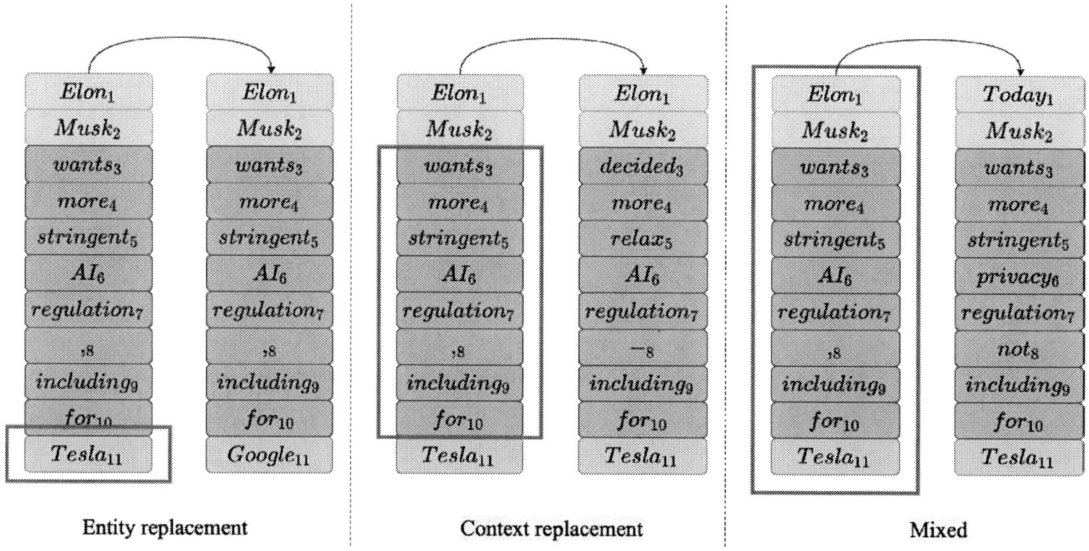

Figure 1: Sampling approaches example[2] for the MLM data augmentation. Gray color refers to the tokens with the entity type "O" (context), green color refers to the PER entity type and purple color refers to the ORG entity type. Red square represents the subset of tokens which is used for replacement.

propose two criteria for choosing the best token from the five-best predictions:

- **Highest probability (top token)**: Choose the target token only based on the MLM probability for that token.
- **Highest probability and distance (joint criterion)**: Choose the target token based on the product of the MLM probability for the token and Levenshtein distance (Levenshtein, 1966) between the original sentence and the sentence with the new token.

Regardless of the combination of the parameters, the sentences must be changed. As a result, we guarantee that there is no duplication in our synthetic data with the original dataset.

4.4 Discussion

The main disadvantage of using a language model (LM) for the augmentation of NER datasets is that the LM does not take into account the labeling of the sequence and the prediction of the masked token, which only depends on the surrounding tokens. As a result, we lose important information for decision-making. Incorporating label information as described in Wu et al. (2019) into the MLM would be the way to tackle this problem.

Another way to reduce the noise in the generated dataset is to apply a filtering step to the generation pipeline. One way to incorporate filtering into the augmentation process is to set the threshold for the MLM token probabilities: If the probability of the predicted token is less than a threshold, we ignore such prediction. However, the problem of misaligning token labels is not resolved. Therefore, we adapt our proposed confidence measure from Section 3 for filtering.

In this work, we do not discuss the selection of the MLM itself as well as the effects of fine-tuning on the specific task.

5 Experiments

5.1 Datasets

We test our data adaptation approaches with three different NER datasets: CoNLL (Tjong Kim Sang and De Meulder, 2003), W-NUT (Derczynski et al., 2017) and GermEval (Benikova et al., 2014).

All datasets have the original labeling scheme as BIO, but following Lample et al. (2016) we convert it to the IOBES scheme for training and evaluation. For our baseline models, we do not use any additional data apart from the provided training data. Development data is only used for validation. For CoNLL we skip all document boundaries. The statistics for the datasets are shown in Table 1.[3]

[3]Further details on the used datasets can be found in Appendix A

Dataset	train	dev	test
CoNLL	14041	3250	3453
W-NUT	3394	1008	1287
GermEval	24001	2199	5099

Table 1: Dataset sizes in number of sentences.

5.2 Model Description

The Bidirectional LSTM - Conditional Random Field (BiLSTM-CRF) model (Lample et al., 2016) is a widely used architecture for NER tasks. Together with pre-trained word embeddings, it surpasses other neural architectures. We use the BiLSTM-CRF model implemented in the *Flair*[4] framework version 0.5, which delivers the state-of-the-art performance.

The BiLSTM-CRF model consists of 1 hidden layer with 256 hidden states. Following Reimers and Gurevych (2017), we set the initial learning rate to 0.1 and the mini-batch size to 32. For each task, we select the best performing embedding from all embedding types in *Flair*. For training models with CoNLL data, we use pre-trained *GloVE* (Pennington et al., 2014) word embedding (Grave et al., 2018) together with the Flair embedding (Akbik et al., 2018) as input into the model. For W-NUT experiments, we use *roberta-large* embedding provided by *Transformers* library (Wolf et al., 2019). German *dbmdz/bert-base-german-cased* embedding is used for experiments with the GermEval dataset.

5.3 Unlabeled Data

Additional unlabeled data is required for self-training. To match the domain of the test data, we collect the data from the sources mentioned in the individual task descriptions.

W-NUT Like the test data, the data for W-NUT consists of user comments from Reddit, which were created in April 2017[5] (comments in the test data were created from January to March 2017), as well as titles, posts and comments from StackExchange, which were created from July to December 2017[6] (the content of the test data was created from January to May 2017). The documents are filtered according to length and community as described in the task description paper and tokenized with the *TweetTokenizer* from *nltk*[7].

CoNLL The data was sampled from news articles in the Reuters corpus from October and November 1996. The sentences are tokenized using *spaCy*[8] and filtered (by removing common patterns like the date of the article, sentences that do not contain words and sentences with more than 512 characters as this is the length of the longest sentence in the CoNLL training data).

GermEval We randomly sampled additional data from sentences extracted from news and Wikipedia articles provided by the Leipzig Corpora Collection[9]. In addition to tokenizing the sentences using spaCy, we do not do any additional preprocessing or filtering.

5.4 Self-training

Before applying the approach described in Section 3, we need to find the thresholds t for the confidence measures c_1 and c_2 for each corpus. We evaluate both confidence measures on the development sets of the three corpora. One way to evaluate confidence measures is to calculate the confidence error rate (CER). It is defined as the number of misassigned labels (i.e. confidence is above the threshold and the prediction of the model is incorrect or the confidence is below the threshold and the prediction is correct) divided by the total number of samples.

Figure 2 shows the CER of c_1 and c_2 on the development set of W-NUT for different threshold values t. For the threshold of 0.0 or 1.0 the CER degrades to the percentage of incorrect or correct predictions as either all or no confidence values are above the threshold. For c_2 there is a clear optimum at $\hat{t}_2 = 0.42$ and for larger and smaller thresholds the CER rises rapidly.

In contrast, the optimum for c_1 at $\hat{t}_1 = 0.57$ is not as pronounced. This motivated us not only to choose the best value in terms of CER, but also a lower threshold $t'_1 = 0.42$ with slightly worse CER. In this way, we include more sentences where the model is less confident without introducing too many additional errors. The threshold values for

[4] https://github.com/zalandoresearch/flair/

[5] https://files.pushshift.io/reddit/comments/

[6] https://archive.org/download/stackexchange

[7] https://www.nltk.org/api/nltk.tokenize.html

[8] https://github.com/explosion/spaCy

[9] https://wortschatz.uni-leipzig.de/de/download

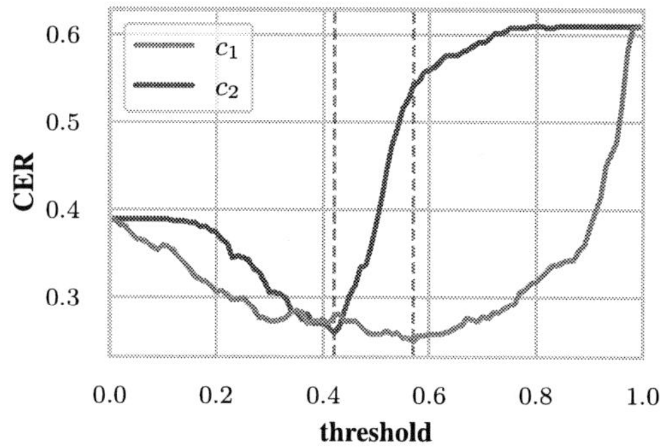

Figure 2: CERs for c_1 (orange) and c_2 (blue) with different threshold values on the W-NUT development set. Vertical dashed lines represent $\hat{t}_1$ and $\hat{t}_2$.

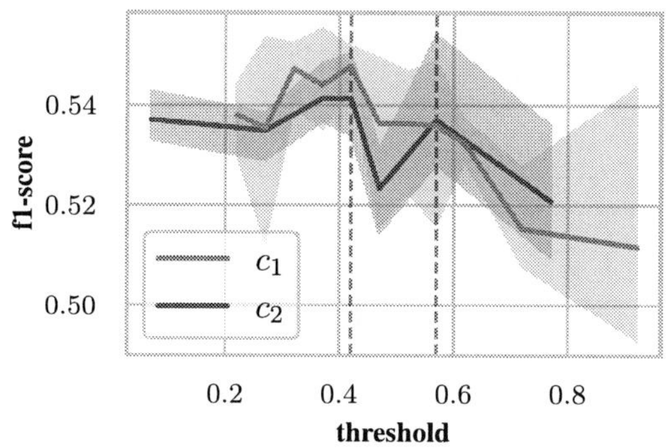

Figure 3: Average F1 scores and standard deviation (shaded area) of 3 runs on the test set of W-NUT after retraining the model on additional data selected using different confidence measures (color) and thresholds.

	W-NUT	CoNLL	GermEval
$\hat{t}_1$	0.57	0.83	0.63
t'_1	0.42	0.70	0.50
$\hat{t}_2$	0.42	0.50	0.47

Table 2: Selected confidence threshold values.

CoNLL and GermEval are selected analogously. Table 2 provides an overview of all threshold values that are used in all subsequent experiments.

The unlabeled data is annotated using the baseline models described in Section 3 (we choose the best runs based on the score on the development set) and is filtered based on the different confidence thresholds. Then we sample a random subset of size k from these remaining sentences. For tasks where the data comes from different sources, e.g. news and Wikipedia for GermEval, we uniformly sample from the different sources to avoid that a particular domain is overrepresented. The selected additional sentences are then appended to the original set of training sentences to create a new training set that is used to retrain the model from scratch.

To validate our selection strategy, we test our pipeline with different confidence thresholds for both confidence measures. Figure 3 shows the results on the test set of W-NUT. For each threshold, 3394 sentences are sampled, i.e. the size of the training set is doubled. The results confirm our selection strategy. t'_1 and $\hat{t}_2$ give the best results of all tested threshold values. In particular, t'_1 performs better than $\hat{t}_1$.

Table 3 shows the results of self-training on all three datasets. For each of them, we test the three selection strategies by sampling new sentences in the size of 0.5 times, 1 times and 2 times the size of the original training data. For W-NUT we get up to 2% of the absolute improvements in the F1 score over the baseline. On larger datasets like CoNLL and GermEval these effects disappear and we only get improvements of up to 0.1% and in some cases even deterioration.

5.5 MLM-based Data Augmentation

We follow the approach explained in Section 4 and generate synthetic data using pre-trained models from the Transformers library. We concatenate original and synthetic data and train the NER model on the new dataset. We test all possible combinations of the augmentation parameters from Section 4 on the W-NUT dataset. Table 4 shows the result of the augmentation. When sampling with one entity, there is no difference between independent and conditional generation, since only one token in a sentence is masked. We therefore only carry out an independent generation for this type of sampling. We report an average result among 3 runs along with a standard deviation of the model with different random seeds.

W-NUT and CoNLL datasets are augmented using a pre-trained English BERT model[10] and GermEval with a pre-trained German BERT model[11] respectively. We do not fine-tune these models.

Sampling from the context of the entity spans shows significant improvements on W-NUT test set. First of all, it includes implicit filtering: Only the sentences with the entities are selected and re-

[10] https://huggingface.co/bert-large-cased-whole-word-masking

[11] https://huggingface.co/bert-base-german-cased

		W-NUT		CoNLL		GermEval	
		Δ sen.	**F1**	**Δ sen.**	**F1**	**Δ sen.**	**F1**
1	baseline	+0%	52.7 ± 2.48	+0%	92.6 ± 0.18	+0%	86.3 ± 0.06
2	$c_1 \geq \hat{t}_1$	+50%	54.2 ± 0.35	+50%	92.5 ± 0.06	+50%	86.0 ± 0.08
3	$c_1 \geq \hat{t}_1$	+100%	53.6 ± 1.41	+100%	92.5 ± 0.12	+100%	86.1 ± 0.26
4	$c_1 \geq \hat{t}_1$	+200%	53.5 ± 0.53	+200%	92.4 ± 0.08	+200%	86.3 ± 0.14
5	$c_1 \geq t'_1$	+50%	53.7 ± 1.95	+50%	92.5 ± 0.02	+50%	86.1 ± 0.21
6	$c_1 \geq t'_1$	+100%	$\mathbf{54.8 \pm 0.33}$	+100%	92.6 ± 0.09	+100%	86.2 ± 0.12
7	$c_1 \geq t'_1$	+200%	53.5 ± 0.29	+200%	92.5 ± 0.06	+200%	$\mathbf{86.4 \pm 0.03}$
8	$c_2 \geq \hat{t}_2$	+50%	54.6 ± 0.42	+50%	$\mathbf{92.7 \pm 0.04}$	+50%	86.0 ± 0.16
9	$c_2 \geq \hat{t}_2$	+100%	54.2 ± 0.98	+100%	92.6 ± 0.06	+100%	$\mathbf{86.4 \pm 0.15}$
10	$c_2 \geq \hat{t}_2$	+200%	54.5 ± 0.43	+200%	$\mathbf{92.7 \pm 0.02}$	+200%	86.3 ± 0.05

Table 3: Results of self-training.

placed. Therefore, compared to other methods, we add less new sentences (except when replacing entities). Second of all, since replacing tokens with a language model should result in the substitution with similar words, the label is less likely to be destroyed while context tokens are replaced.

On the other hand, the mixed sampling strategy performs the worst among all methods. We believe that this is the effect when additional noise is included in the dataset (by noise we mean all types of noise, e.g. incorrect labeling, grammatical errors, etc). Allowing masking of words up to sequence in some cases destroys the sentence, e.g. incorrect and multiple occurrences of the same words can occur. In Appendix B we present the examples of augmented sentences for each augmentation approach and each dataset. Additionally, we report the average number of masked token.

To analyze the resulting models, we plot the average confidence scores of the test set as well as the number of errors per sentence for the best baseline model and best augmented model. We use the best baseline system with 54.6% F1 score and the best model corresponding to the setup of line 8 in Table 4 with 57.4% F1 score. We count the error every time the model predicts a correct label with low confidence or an incorrect label with high confidence. We set high and low confidence to be 0.6 and 0.4 respectively. Figure 4 shows that the augmented model makes a more reliable prediction than the best baseline system model.

We repeat the promising MLM generation pipeline on the CoNLL and GermEval datasets. These datasets contain more entities in the original data. In addition, even though the entity replacement sampling did not work well on W-NUT

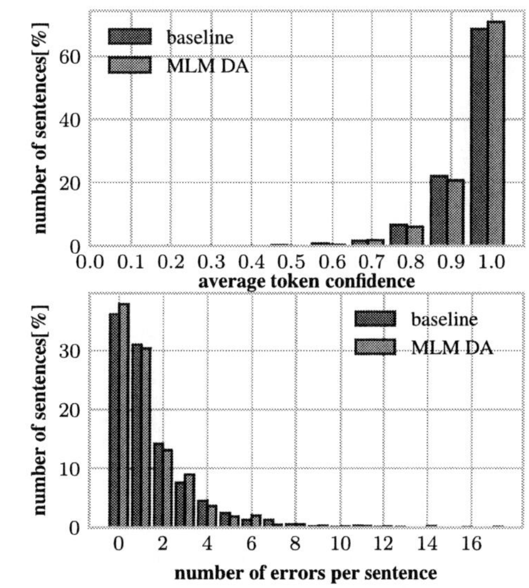

Figure 4: Average confidence score and the error per sentence on W-NUT test data. `MLM DA` refers to the setup of line 8 in Table 4

dataset, we repeat these experiments, since generating new entities is the most interesting scenario for using the MLM augmentation.

Although the MLM-based data augmentation leads to improvements of up to 3.6% F1 score on the W-NUT dataset, Table 5 shows that such effect disappears when we apply our method to larger and cleaner datasets such as CoNLL and GermEval. We believe there are several reasons for that. First, our MLM-based data augmentation method does not guarantee the accuracy of the labeling after augmentation. So for larger datasets, there are many more possibilities to increase the noise of the corpus. Moreover, we do not study

		sampling	generation	criterion	Δ sen.	F1
1	baseline	-	-	-	$+0.0\%$	52.7 ± 2.48
2	MLM DA	entity	independent	top token	$+24.4\%$	53.7 ± 0.91
3				joint	$+24.7\%$	54.6 ± 0.50
4		mixed	conditional	top token	$+98.7\%$	52.3 ± 1.25
5				joint	$+99.7\%$	51.7 ± 1.36
6			independent	top token	$+98.6\%$	53.7 ± 0.89
7				joint	$+99.7\%$	53.3 ± 0.61
8		context	conditional	top token	$+33.8\%$	$\mathbf{56.3 \pm 1.21}$
9				joint	$+35.8\%$	$\mathbf{55.6 \pm 1.12}$
10			independent	top token	$+33.8\%$	$\mathbf{55.0 \pm 1.16}$
11				joint	$+35.8\%$	$\mathbf{56.0 \pm 0.06}$
12		random context	conditional	top token	$+96.8\%$	$\mathbf{54.9 \pm 0.40}$
13				joint	$+99.7\%$	54.5 ± 1.21
14			independent	top token	$+96.9\%$	53.7 ± 0.93
15				joint	$+99.7\%$	53.5 ± 2.40

Table 4: Results of the MLM-based augmentation on the W-NUT dataset. `entity` refers to the sampling tokens from entity spans of length one, `mixed` means sampling from the complete sequence, `context` indicates sampling from the entity span context, `random context` denotes sampling from random context labels. `conditional` refers to the conditional generation and `independent` refers to the independent generation type. The `top token` criterion selects the token based on the highest probability, and the `joint` criterion takes into account the token probability and the Levenshtein distance.

how well pre-trained models suit the specific task, which might be crucial for the DA. Besides, for GermEval augmentation, we use the BERT model with three times fewer parameters than for W-NUT and CoNLL.

5.5.1 Filtering of Augmented Data

As discussed in Section 4, an additional data filtering step can be applied on top of the augmentation process. We report results on two different filtering methods: First, we set a threshold for the probability of the predicted token (in our experiments we use the probability 0.5); Second, we filter sentences by minimum confidence scores as discussed in Section 3. We set the minimum confidence score according to Table 2. We apply filtering to the worst and best-performing model according to the numbers in Table 4. The filtering results on W-NUT are shown in Table 6.

In the case of the worst model, filtering based on the token probability improve the performance of the model by 2.6% compared to the unfiltered one. Filtering by confidence score does not improve the performance, but significantly reduces the standard deviation of the score. The results are expected, since by using token probability we increase the sentence reliability and completely change the synthetic data, while using the confidence score we filter on the same synthetic data. In the case of the better model, we see the opposite trend. Here filtering leads to performance degradation and an increase in the standard deviation.

We apply the same filtering techniques for CoNLL and GermEval. Table 7 shows the results for 3 different models. We choose the best, the worst and the model with the highest number of additional sentences for filtering. In the case of the worst model, the performance is improved by 1.1% F1 score with the minimum confidence filtering for CoNLL and 0.5% F1 score for GermEval compared to the unfiltered version. However, for the best model, the results remain at the same level and the baseline systems are not improved.

Although we do not achieve significant improvements compared to the baseline system, we see a potential in the MLM-based augmentation with the combination with filtering.

6 Discussion and Future Work

In this work, we present results of data adaptation methods on various NER tasks. We show that MLM-based data augmentation and self-training approaches lead to improvements on the small and noisy W-NUT dataset.

We propose two different confidence measures for self-training and empirically estimate the best

		sampling	generation	criterion	CoNLL Δ sen.	CoNLL F1	GermEval Δ sen.	GermEval F1
1	baseline	-	-	-	+0.0%	**92.6 ± 0.18**	0.0%	**86.3 ± 0.06**
3	MLM DA	entity	independent	joint	+57.9%	91.5 ± 0.10	+47.9%	85.9 ± 0.06
8		context	conditional	top token	+65.7%	92.4 ± 0.12	+51.4%	86.1 ± 0.26
9				joint	+72.2%	92.3 ± 0.06	+58.5%	86.0 ± 0.15
10			independent	top token	+65.7%	92.5 ± 0.06	+51.4%	86.1 ± 0.15
11				joint	+72.2%	92.2 ± 0.17	+58.5%	86.0 ± 0.20
12		rand. cont.	conditional	top token	+85.1%	92.1 ± 0.15	+94.1%	86.1 ± 0.10

Table 5: Results of the MLM-based data augmentation on CoNLL and GermEval datasets. The row numbers refer to the row numbers of the Table 4.

	Δ sen.	filtering	F1
5	+99.7%	-	51.7 ± 1.36
	+86.3%	token prob.	**54.3 ± 0.31**
	+59.5%	min. conf.	51.2 ± 0.60
9	+33.8%	-	**56.3 ± 1.21**
	+13.8%	token prob.	53.3 ± 2.00
	+10.4%	min. conf.	51.7 ± 2.10

Table 6: F1 scores of using filtered augmented data on W-NUT. The row numbers refer to the row numbers of the Table 4.

	filtering	CoNLL Δ sen.	CoNLL F1	GermEval Δ sen.	GermEval F1
3	none	+57.9%	91.5 ± 0.10	+47.9%	85.9 ± 0.06
	tok. prob.	+7.8%	92.4 ± 0.15	+13.1%	86.1 ± 0.29
	min. conf.	+13.5%	92.6 ± 0.15	+13.9%	**86.4 ± 0.12**
10	none	+65.7%	92.5 ± 0.06	+51.5%	86.1 ± 0.15
	tok. prob.	+22.5%	92.5 ± 0.15	+34.5%	**86.3 ± 0.21**
	min. conf.	+52.1%	**92.6 ± 0.20**	+23.9%	86.1 ± 0.10
12	none	+85.1%	92.1 ± 0.15	+94.1%	86.1 ± 0.10
	tok. prob.	+42.5%	**92.8 ± 0.06**	+76.1%	86.1 ± 0.00
	min. conf.	+58.9%	**92.6 ± 0.12**	+62.3%	86.0 ± 0.21

Table 7: F1 scores of using filtered augmented data on CoNLL and GermEval. The first line represents the augmentation method from Table 4.

thresholds. Our results on the W-NUT dataset show the effectiveness of the selection strategies based on those confidence measures.

For MLM-based data augmentation, we suggest multiple ways of generating synthetic NER data. Our results show that even without generating new entity spans we are able to achieve better results.

For future work, we would like to incorporate label information into the augmentation pipeline by either conditioning the token predictions on labels or adding additional classification steps on top of the token prediction. Another important question is the choice of the MLM and the impact of task-specific fine-tuning. Further investigations into the filtering step should also be carried out.

For both self-training and MLM-based data augmentation we would like to improve the integration in the training process. The contribution of the original training data to the loss function could be increased or additional data could be weighted by their confidence. Finally, we would like to test whether we can combine the two methods to achieve additional improvements.

Acknowledgements

This work has received funding from the European Research Council (ERC) under the European Union's Horizon 2020 research and innovation programme (grant agreement No 694537, project "SEQCLAS"). The work reflects only the authors' views and the European Research Council Executive Agency (ERCEA) is not responsible for any use that may be made of the information it contains.

References

Alan Akbik, Duncan Blythe, and Roland Vollgraf. 2018. Contextual string embeddings for sequence labeling. In *Proceedings of the 27th International Conference on Computational Linguistics (COLING)*, pages 1638–1649, Santa Fe, NM, USA.

Darina Benikova, Chris Biemann, Max Kisselew, and Sebastian Padó. 2014. Germeval 2014 named entity recognition: Companion paper. *Proceedings of the KONVENS GermEval Shared Task on Named Entity Recognition, Hildesheim, Germany*, pages 104–112.

Avrim Blum and Tom M. Mitchell. 1998. Combining labeled and unlabeled data with co-training. In *Proceedings of the Eleventh Annual Conference on Computational Learning Theory, COLT 1998, Madison, Wisconsin, USA, July 24-26, 1998*, pages 92–100. ACM.

Jason P.C. Chiu and Eric Nichols. 2016. Named entity recognition with bidirectional LSTM-CNNs. *Transactions of the Association for Computational Linguistics*, 4:357–370.

Kevin Clark, Minh-Thang Luong, Christopher D. Manning, and Quoc Le. 2018. Semi-supervised sequence modeling with cross-view training. In *Proceedings of the 2018 Conference on Empirical Methods in Natural Language Processing*, pages 1914–1925, Brussels, Belgium. Association for Computational Linguistics.

Ronan Collobert, Jason Weston, Léon Bottou, Michael Karlen, Koray Kavukcuoglu, and Pavel P. Kuksa. 2011. Natural language processing (almost) from scratch. *J. Mach. Learn. Res.*, 12:2493–2537.

Hal Daumé III. 2008. Cross-task knowledge-constrained self training. In *Proceedings of the 2008 Conference on Empirical Methods in Natural Language Processing*, pages 680–688, Honolulu, Hawaii. Association for Computational Linguistics.

Leon Derczynski, Eric Nichols, Marieke van Erp, and Nut Limsopatham. 2017. Results of the WNUT2017 shared task on novel and emerging entity recognition. In *Proceedings of the 3rd Workshop on Noisy User-generated Text*, pages 140–147, Copenhagen, Denmark. Association for Computational Linguistics.

Jacob Devlin, Ming-Wei Chang, Kenton Lee, and Kristina Toutanova. 2019. BERT: Pre-training of deep bidirectional transformers for language understanding. In *Proceedings of the 2019 Conference of the North American Chapter of the Association for Computational Linguistics: Human Language Technologies, Volume 1 (Long and Short Papers)*, pages 4171–4186, Minneapolis, Minnesota. Association for Computational Linguistics.

Thomas Drugman, Janne Pylkkönen, and Reinhard Kneser. 2016. Active and semi-supervised learning in asr: Benefits on the acoustic and language models. In *Interspeech 2016*, pages 2318–2322.

Fei Gao, Jinhua Zhu, Lijun Wu, Yingce Xia, Tao Qin, Xueqi Cheng, Wengang Zhou, and Tie-Yan Liu. 2019. Soft contextual data augmentation for neural machine translation. In *Proceedings of the 57th Annual Meeting of the Association for Computational Linguistics*, pages 5539–5544, Florence, Italy. Association for Computational Linguistics.

Edouard Grave, Piotr Bojanowski, Prakhar Gupta, Armand Joulin, and Tomas Mikolov. 2018. Learning word vectors for 157 languages. In *Proceedings of the International Conference on Language Resources and Evaluation (LREC 2018)*, pages 3483–3487, Miyazaki, Japan.

Tomoki Hayashi, Shinji Watanabe, Yu Zhang, Tomoki Toda, Takaaki Hori, Ramón Fernández Astudillo, and Kazuya Takeda. 2018. Back-translation-style data augmentation for end-to-end ASR. In *2018 IEEE Spoken Language Technology Workshop, SLT 2018, Athens, Greece, December 18-21, 2018*, pages 426–433. IEEE.

Yutai Hou, Yijia Liu, Wanxiang Che, and Ting Liu. 2018. Sequence-to-sequence data augmentation for dialogue language understanding. In *Proceedings of the 27th International Conference on Computational Linguistics, COLING 2018, Santa Fe, New Mexico, USA, August 20-26, 2018*, pages 1234–1245. Association for Computational Linguistics.

Zhiheng Huang, Wei Xu, and Kai Yu. 2015. Bidirectional LSTM-CRF models for sequence tagging. *CoRR*, abs/1508.01991.

Sosuke Kobayashi. 2018. Contextual augmentation: Data augmentation by words with paradigmatic relations. In *Proceedings of the 2018 Conference of the North American Chapter of the Association for Computational Linguistics: Human Language Technologies, Volume 2 (Short Papers)*, pages 452–457, New Orleans, Louisiana. Association for Computational Linguistics.

Zornitsa Kozareva, Boyan Bonev, and Andres Montoyo. 2005. Self-training and co-training applied to spanish named entity recognition. In *Proceedings of the 4th Mexican International Conference on Artificial Intelligence*, pages 770–779, Monterrey, Mexico.

Alex Krizhevsky, Ilya Sutskever, and Geoffrey E. Hinton. 2012. Imagenet classification with deep convolutional neural networks. In *Advances in Neural Information Processing Systems 25: 26th Annual Conference on Neural Information Processing Systems 2012. Proceedings of a meeting held December 3-6, 2012, Lake Tahoe, Nevada, United States*, pages 1106–1114.

Varun Kumar, Ashutosh Choudhary, and Eunah Cho. 2020. Data augmentation using pre-trained transformer models. *arXiv preprint arXiv:2003.02245.*

Guillaume Lample, Miguel Ballesteros, Sandeep Subramanian, Kazuya Kawakami, and Chris" Dyer. 2016. Neural Architectures for Named Entity Recognition. In *Proceedings of the 2016 Conference of the North American Chapter of the Association for Computational Linguistics: Human Language Technologies (NAACL-HLT)*, pages 260–270, San Diego, CA, USA.

Vladimir I Levenshtein. 1966. Binary codes capable of correcting deletions, insertions, and reversals. In *Soviet physics doklady*, volume 10, pages 707–710.

Yinhan Liu, Myle Ott, Naman Goyal, Jingfei Du, Mandar Joshi, Danqi Chen, Omer Levy, Mike Lewis, Luke Zettlemoyer, and Veselin Stoyanov. 2019. Roberta: A robustly optimized BERT pretraining approach. *CoRR*, abs/1907.11692.

Grégoire Mesnil, Xiaodong He, Li Deng, and Yoshua Bengio. 2013. Investigation of recurrent-neural-network architectures and learning methods for spoken language understanding. In *INTERSPEECH 2013, 14th Annual Conference of the International*

Speech Communication Association, Lyon, France, August 25-29, 2013, pages 3771–3775. ISCA.

Daniel S. Park, William Chan, Yu Zhang, Chung-Cheng Chiu, Barret Zoph, Ekin D. Cubuk, and Quoc V. Le. 2019. Specaugment: A simple data augmentation method for automatic speech recognition. In *Interspeech 2019, 20th Annual Conference of the International Speech Communication Association, Graz, Austria, 15-19 September 2019*, pages 2613–2617. ISCA.

Jeffrey Pennington, Richard Socher, and Christopher D. Manning. 2014. Glove: Global vectors for word representation. In *Proceedings of the Conference on Empirical Methods in Natural Language Processing (EMNLP)*, pages 1532–1543, Doha, Qatar.

Matthew Peters, Mark Neumann, Mohit Iyyer, Matt Gardner, Christopher Clark, Kenton Lee, and Luke Zettlemoyer. 2018. Deep contextualized word representations. In *Proceedings of the 2018 Conference of the North American Chapter of the Association for Computational Linguistics: Human Language Technologies, Volume 1 (Long Papers)*, pages 2227–2237, New Orleans, Louisiana. Association for Computational Linguistics.

Nils Reimers and Iryna Gurevych. 2017. Reporting score distributions makes a difference: Performance study of LSTM-networks for sequence tagging. In *Proceedings of the 2017 Conference on Empirical Methods in Natural Language Processing (EMNLP)*, pages 338–348, Copenhagen, Denmark. Association for Computational Linguistics.

Rico Sennrich, Barry Haddow, and Alexandra Birch. 2016. Improving neural machine translation models with monolingual data. In *Proceedings of the 54th Annual Meeting of the Association for Computational Linguistics (Volume 1: Long Papers)*, pages 86–96, Berlin, Germany. Association for Computational Linguistics.

Iulian V. Serban, Alessandro Sordoni, Yoshua Bengio, Aaron Courville, and Joelle Pineau. 2016. Building End-to-end Dialogue Systems Using Generative Hierarchical Neural Network Models. In *Proceedings of the Thirtieth AAAI Conference on Artificial Intelligence*, pages 3776–3783, Phoenix, AZ, USA.

Oscar Täckström. 2012. Nudging the envelope of direct transfer methods for multilingual named entity recognition. In *Proceedings of the NAACL-HLT Workshop on the Induction of Linguistic Structure*, pages 55–63, Montréal, Canada. Association for Computational Linguistics.

Bruno Taillé, Vincent Guigue, and Patrick Gallinari. 2020. Contextualized embeddings in named-entity recognition: An empirical study on generalization. In *Advances in Information Retrieval*, pages 383–391, Cham. Springer International Publishing.

Erik F. Tjong Kim Sang and Fien De Meulder. 2003. Introduction to the conll-2003 shared task: Language-independent named entity recognition. In *Proceedings of the Seventh Conference of the North American Chapter of the Association for Computational Linguistics: Human Language Technologies (NAACL-HLT)*, pages 142–147, Edmonton, Canada.

Ashish Vaswani, Noam Shazeer, Niki Parmar, Jakob Uszkoreit, Llion Jones, Aidan N. Gomez, Lukasz Kaiser, and Illia Polosukhin. 2017. Attention Is All You Need. In *Proceedings of the 31st Conference on Neural Information Processing Systems (NIPS 2017)*, pages 5998–6008, Long Beach, CA, USA.

Xinyi Wang, Hieu Pham, Zihang Dai, and Graham Neubig. 2018. SwitchOut: an efficient data augmentation algorithm for neural machine translation. In *Proceedings of the 2018 Conference on Empirical Methods in Natural Language Processing*, pages 856–861, Brussels, Belgium. Association for Computational Linguistics.

Thomas Wolf, Lysandre Debut, Victor Sanh, Julien Chaumond, Clement Delangue, Anthony Moi, Pierric Cistac, Tim Rault, R'emi Louf, Morgan Funtowicz, and Jamie Brew. 2019. Huggingface's transformers: State-of-the-art natural language processing. *ArXiv*, abs/1910.03771.

Xing Wu, Shangwen Lv, Liangjun Zang, Jizhong Han, and Songlin Hu. 2019. Conditional BERT contextual augmentation. In *Computational Science - ICCS 2019 - 19th International Conference, Faro, Portugal, June 12-14, 2019, Proceedings, Part IV*, volume 11539 of *Lecture Notes in Computer Science*, pages 84–95. Springer.

Adams Wei Yu, David Dohan, Minh-Thang Luong, Rui Zhao, Kai Chen, Mohammad Norouzi, and Quoc V. Le. 2018. Qanet: Combining local convolution with global self-attention for reading comprehension. In *6th International Conference on Learning Representations, ICLR 2018, Vancouver, BC, Canada, April 30 - May 3, 2018, Conference Track Proceedings*. OpenReview.net.

A Data Description

In our work we use three NER datasets:

- CoNLL 2003 (Tjong Kim Sang and De Meulder, 2003) contains news articles from the Reuters[12] corpus. The annotation contains 4 entity types `person`, `location`, `organization`, `miscellaneous`. We remove the document boundary information for our experiments.

- W-NUT 2017 (Derczynski et al., 2017) contains texts from Twitter (training data), YouTube (development data), StackExchange and Reddit (test data). The annotation contains 6 entity types: `person`, `location`, `corporation`, `product`, `creative-work`, `group`

- GermEval 2014 (Benikova et al., 2014): contains the data from the German Wikipedia and news Corpora. The annotation contains 12 entity types: `location`, `organization`, `person`, `other`, `location deriv`, `location part`, `organization deriv`, `organization part`, `person deriv`, `person part`, `other deriv`, `other part`.

Table 8 shows detailed statistics of those datasets. Together with number of entities, tokens and sentences we report the percentage of the labelled tokens among all the tokens.

Dataset		train	dev	test
CoNLL	#sentences	14041	3250	3453
	#entities	23500	5943	5649
	#tokens	203621	51362	46435
	#entity types	4	4	4
	%labelled	16.7	16.8	17.5
W-NUT	#sentences	3394	1008	1287
	#entities	1976	836	1080
	#tokens	62730	15723	23394
	#entity types	6	6	6
	%labelled	5.0	7.9	7.4
GermEval	#sentences	24001	2199	5099
	#entities	29077	2674	6178
	#tokens	452790	41635	96475
	#entity types	12	12	12
	%labelled	9.3	9.5	9.3

Table 8: Dataset sizes in number of sentences, tokens and entities. Here, entity means the entity span, e.g. `European Union` is considered as one entity.

[12] `https://trec.nist.gov/data/reuters/reuters.html`

B MLM-based Data Augmentation

B.1 Data statistics

The number of masked tokens solely depends on the augmentation strategy discussed in section 4. Table 9 reports the average number of masked tokens in the sentence on W-NUT dataset for each augmentation strategy. Table 10 and Table 11 show the average number of masked tokens in the sentence for the most promising augmentation strategies for CoNLL and GermEval tasks.

sampling	generation	criterion	Δ sen.	Masked
entity	independent	top token	+24.4%	1.2
		joint	+24.7%	1.2
mixed	conditional	top token	+98.7%	7.4
		joint	+99.7%	8.8
	independent	top token	+98.6%	7.0
		joint	+99.7%	8.8
context	conditional	top token	+33.8%	4.4
		joint	+35.8%	4.5
	independent	top token	+33.8%	4.3
		joint	+35.8%	4.5
random context	conditional	top token	+96.8%	7.1
		joint	+99.7%	8.1
	independent	top token	+96.9%	6.9
		joint	+99.7%	8.1

Table 9: Average number of masked tokens for each augmentation strategy on W-NUT dataset.

sampling	generation	criterion	Δ sen.	Masked
entity	independent	joint	+57.9%	1.1
context	conditional	top token	+65.7%	3.4
		joint	+72.2%	6.4
	independent	top token	+65.7%	3.4
		joint	+72.2%	6.4
random context	conditional	top token	+85.1%	4.5

Table 10: Average number of masked tokens on CoNLL dataset.

sampling	generation	criterion	Δ sen.	Masked
entity	independent	joint	+47.9%	1.0
context	conditional	top token	+51.4%	4.4
		joint	+58.5%	5.7
	independent	top token	+51.4%	4.3
		joint	+58.5%	5.3
random context	conditional	top token	+94.1%	6.0

Table 11: Average number of masked tokens on GermEval dataset.

B.2 Data Examples

We show the data examples on different dataset by varying one augmentation parameter while keeping others unchanged. Table 12 shows the examples on W-NUT dataset. In Table 13 and Table 14 we collect the examples for GermEval and CoNLL.

Parameter	Value	Example
Sampling	-	RT @Quotealicious: Today, I saw a guy driving a <corporation>Pepsi</corporation> truck, drinking a <product>Coke</product>. MLIA #Quotealicious
	entity	RT @Quotealicious: Today, I saw a guy driving a <corporation>Pepsi</corporation> truck, drinking a **<product>beer</product>** MLIA #Quotealicious
	context	RT @Quotealicious : Today, I saw a guy driving a <corporation>Pepsi</corporation> **car**, drinking a <product>Coke</product>. MLIA #Quotealicious
	random context	**m me:** Today, I saw a **man** driving a <corporation>Pepsi</corporation> truck, **buying** a <product>Coke</product>. MLIA #Quotealicious
	mixed	**m** @Quotealicious **Earlier** Today, I saw a guy driving a <corporation>Pepsi</corporation> truck, drinking a <product>Coke</product>. MLIA #Quotealicious
Order	-	What is everyone watching this weekend? <group>Twins</group>? <group>Vikings</group>? anyone going to see <creativework>Friday Night Lights</creativework>?
	independent	What is everyone watching this weekend? <group>Twins</group>? <group>Vikings</group>? anyone going to see <creativework>**the** Night Lights</creativework>?
	conditional	What is **he** doing this weekend with **<group>the</group> ##ing** <group>Vikings</group>? anyone going to install <creativework>Friday Night **lights**</creativework>?
Criterion	-	<person>Oscar</person>'s new favorite pass time is running as fast as he can from one end of the house to another yelling BuhBYYYYYE
	top token	**<person>Jack</person>**'s new favorite pass time is running as fast as he can from one end of the house to another yelling BuhBYYYYYE
	joint	**<person>Ben</person>**'s new favorite pass time is running as fast as he can from one end of the house to another yelling BuhBYYYYYE

Table 12: Data examples of W-NUT augmentation.

Parameter	Value	Example
Sampling	-	Zu einer Gebietsveränderung kam es 1822, als das vorher selbständige <LOC>Champsigna</LOC> nach <LOC>Soucia</LOC> eingemeindet wurde.
	entity	Zu einer Gebietsveränderung kam es 1822, als das vorher selbständige <LOC>Champsigna</LOC> nach **<LOC>Paris</LOC>** eingemeindet wurde.
	context	Zu einer Gebietsveränderung kam es 1822, als das vorher selbständige <LOC>Champsigna</LOC> nach <LOC>Soucia</LOC> **verlegt** wurde.
	random context	Zu einer Gebietsveränderung kam es 1822, als das **damals** selbständige <LOC>Champsigna</LOC> nach <LOC>Soucia</LOC> eingemeindet wurde.
	mixed	Zu einer **Eingemeindung** kam es 1822, als **die damals** selbständige **<LOC>Dorf</LOC>** nach **<LOC>Turin</LOC> verlegt** wurde.
Order	-	Aus diesem Grund wurde er Anfang Januar auch nach nur wenigen Tagen aus dem Klinikum <LOC>Jena</LOC> in eine Reha-Einrichtung am <LOC>Bodensee</LOC> verlegt.
	independent	**Zu** diesem Grund wurde er Anfang Januar **und** nach nur **zwei** Tagen aus dem Klinikum <LOC>Jena</LOC> in **die** Reha-Einrichtung am **<LOC> Boden </LOC>** verlegt.
	conditional	Aus diesem Grund **wo ich** Anfang Januar auch nach nur wenigen Tagen aus dem Klinikum <LOC>Jena</LOC> in **die** Reha-Einrichtung am <LOC>Bodensee</LOC> verlegt.
Criterion	-	Mit ihm der gleichen Meinung sind <PER>Pyrrhon</PER> und <PER>Erillus</PER> von <LOC>Karthago</LOC>.
	top token	Mit ihm der gleichen Meinung sind <PER>Pyrrhon</PER> und **<PER>Gregor</PER>** von <LOC>Karthago</LOC>.
	joint	Mit ihm der gleichen Meinung sind **<PER>Alexander</PER>** und <PER>Erillus</PER> von <LOC>Karthago</LOC>.

Table 13: Data examples of GermEval augmentation.

Parameter	Value	Example
Sampling	-	<PER>Christopher Reeve</PER> -- <PER>Reeve</PER> was best known for playing the comic book hero <PER>Superman</PER> in four movies but his greatest heroics came in real life.
	entity	<PER>Christopher Reeve</PER> -- <PER>Reeve</PER> was best known for playing the comic book hero **<PER>Batman</PER>** in four movies but his greatest heroics came in real life .
	context	<PER>Christopher Reeve</PER> **The** <PER>Reeve</PER> **is** best known for playing the comic book superhero <PER>Superman</PER> in four movies but his greatest heroics came in real life.
	random context	<PER>Christopher Reeve</PER> -- <PER>Reeve</PER> **popular** best known for **popular popular popular** book hero <PER>Superman</PER> in four movies but his popular heroics came in real **popular popular**
	mixed	<PER>Christopher Reeve</PER> **The** **<PER>He</PER> is** best known for playing the comic book superhero <PER>Superman</PER> in **the films** but his greatest heroics came in real life.
Order	-	Four weeks ago <ORG>Stagecoach </ORG> said it had agreed the deal in principle, and it expected to pay 110 million stg-plus for the firm, with <ORG>Swebus</ORG>' current owner, the state railway company.
	independent	Four **days** ago <ORG>it</ORG> said it had **made** the deal in principle, and it expected to **raise** 110 million **euros to** the **operation contract including** <ORG>Swebus</ORG> ' current **employer being** the state railway company.
	conditional	**Two years** ago <ORG>Stagecoach</ORG> said it had **made** the deal in principle, and **was** expected to pay 110 million **marks** for the **operation**, with <ORG>Swebus</ORG>**'s** owner, the **Swedish** railway company.
Criterion	-	<ORG>ZDF</ORG> said <LOC> Germany </LOC> imported 47,600 sheep from <LOC> Britain </LOC> last year, nearly half of total imports.
	top token	**<ORG>He</ORG>** said **<LOC> they </LOC>** imported **more goods** from **<LOC> Germany </LOC> that** year, nearly half of **all number.**
	joint	<ORG>ZDF</ORG> **this <LOC> this </LOC> this** 47,600 sheep **this <LOC> this </LOC> this** year **this** nearly half of **this** imports.

Table 14: Data examples of CoNLL augmentation.

Stage-wise Fine-tuning for Graph-to-Text Generation

Qingyun Wang[1]*, **Semih Yavuz**[2], **Xi Victoria Lin**[3],
Heng Ji[1], **Nazneen Fatema Rajani**[2]
[1] University of Illinois at Urbana-Champaign[2] Salesforce Research [3] Facebook AI
syavuz,nazneen.rajani@salesforce.com
victorialin@fb.com
{qingyun4,hengji}@illinois.edu

Abstract

Graph-to-text generation has benefited from pre-trained language models (PLMs) in achieving better performance than structured graph encoders. However, they fail to fully utilize the structure information of the input graph. In this paper, we aim to further improve the performance of the pre-trained language model by proposing a structured graph-to-text model with a two-step fine-tuning mechanism which first fine-tunes the model on Wikipedia before adapting to the graph-to-text generation. In addition to using the traditional token and position embeddings to encode the knowledge graph (KG), we propose a novel tree-level embedding method to capture the interdependency structures of the input graph. This new approach has significantly improved the performance of all text generation metrics for the English WebNLG 2017 dataset.[1]

1 Introduction

In the graph-to-text generation task (Gardent et al., 2017), the model takes in a complex KG (an example is in Figure 1) and generates a corresponding faithful natural language description (Table 1). Previous efforts for this task can be mainly divided into two categories: sequence-to-sequence models that directly solve the generation task with LSTMs (Gardent et al., 2017) or Transformer (Castro Ferreira et al., 2019); and graph-to-text models (Trisedya et al., 2018; Marcheggiani and Perez-Beltrachini, 2018) which use a graph encoder to capture the structure of the KGs. Recently, Transformer-based PLMs such as GPT-2 (Radford et al., 2019), BART (Lewis et al., 2020),

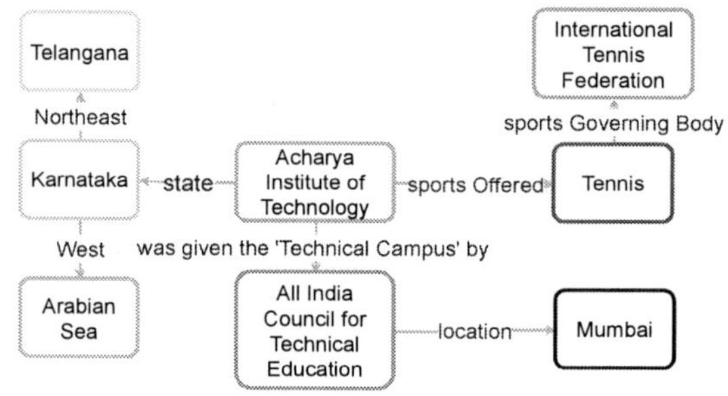

Figure 1: Input RDF Knowledge Graph

and T5 (Raffel et al., 2020) have achieved state-of-the-art results on WebNLG dataset due to factual knowledge acquired in the pre-training phase (Harkous et al., 2020; Ribeiro et al., 2020b; Kale, 2020; Chen et al., 2020a).

Despite such improvement, PLMs fine-tuned only on the clean (or labeled) data might be more prone to hallucinate factual knowledge (e.g., *"Visvesvaraya Technological University"* in Table 1). Inspired by the success of domain-adaptive pre-training (Gururangan et al., 2020), we propose a novel two-step fine-tuning mechanism graph-to-text generation task. Unlike (Ribeiro et al., 2020b; Herzig et al., 2020; Chen et al., 2020a) which directly fine-tune the PLMs on the training set, we first fine-tune our model over noisy RDF graphs and related article pairs crawled from Wikipedia before final fine-tuning on the clean/labeled training set. The additional fine-tuning step benefits our model by leveraging triples not included in the training set and reducing the chances that the model fabricates facts based on the language model.

Meanwhile, the PLMs might also fail to cover all relations in the KG by creating incorrect or missing facts. For example, in Table 1, although the T5-large with Wikipedia fine-tuning successfully removes the unwanted contents, it still ignores the *"sports Governing Body"* relation and incorrectly

*This research was conducted during the author's internship at Salesforce Research.

[1]The programs, data and resources are publicly available for research purpose at: https://github.com/EagleW/Stage-wise-Fine-tuning

Proceedings of the Joint Conference of the 59th Annual Meeting of the Association for Computational Linguistics and the 11th International Joint Conference on Natural Language Processing: Student Research Workshop, pages 16–22
August 5–6, 2021. ©2021 Association for Computational Linguistics

Category	Output
Reference	The Acharya Institute of Technology in Karnataka state was given Technical Campus status by All India Council for Technical Education in Mumbai. The school offers tennis which is governed by the International Tennis Federation. Karnataka has the Arabian Sea to its west and in the northeast is Telangana.
T5-large	The state of Karnataka is located southwest of Telangana and east of the Arabian Sea. It is the location of the Acharya Institute of Technology which was granted the Technical Campus status by the All India Council for Technical Education in Mumbai. The Institute is affiliated with the *Visvesvaraya Technological University* and offers the sport of tennis. [International Tennis Federation]
T5-large + Wiki	The Acharya Institute of Technology is located in the state of Karnataka. It was given the Technical Campus status by the All India Council for Technical Education which is located in Mumbai. The institute offers tennis and **has Telangana to its northeast and the Arabian Sea to its west**. [International Tennis Federation]
T5-large + Position	The Acharya Institute of Technology is located in the state of Karnataka which has Telangana to its northeast and the Arabian Sea to its west. It was given the Technical Campus status by the All India Council for Technical Education in Mumbai. The Institute offers tennis which is governed by the International Tennis Federation.
T5-large + Wiki + Position	The Acharya Institute of Technology in Karnataka was given the 'Technical Campus' status by the All India Council for Technical Education in Mumbai. Karnataka has Telangana to its northeast and the Arabian Sea to its west. One of the sports offered at the Institute is tennis which is governed by the International Tennis Federation.

Table 1: Human and System Generated Description in Figure 1. We use the color box to frame each entity out with the same color as the corresponding entity in Figure 1. We highlight *fabricated facts*, [missed relations], and **incorrect relations** with different color.

links the university to both *"Telangana"* and *"Arabian Sea"*. To better capture the structure and interdependence of facts in the KG, instead of using a complex graph encoder, we leverage the power of Transformer-based PLMs with additional position embeddings which have been proved effective in various generation tasks (Herzig et al., 2020; Chen et al., 2020a,b). Here, we extend the embedding layer of Transfomer-based PLMs with two additional *triple role* and *tree-level* embeddings to capture graph structure.

We explore the proposed stage-wise fine-tuning and structure-preserving embedding strategies for graph-to-text generation task on WebNLG corpus (Gardent et al., 2017). Our experimental results clearly demonstrate the benefit of each strategy in achieving the state-of-the-art performance on most commonly reported automatic evaluation metrics.

2 Method

Given an RDF graph with multiple relations $G = \{(s_1, r_1, o_1), (s_2, r_2, o_2), ..., (s_n, r_n, o_n)\}$, our goal is to generate a text faithfully describing the input graph. We represent each relation with a triple $(s_i, r_i, o_i) \in G$ for $i \in \{1, ..., n\}$, where s_i, r_i, and o_i are natural language phrases that represent the subject, type, and object of the relation, respectively. We augment our model with addi-

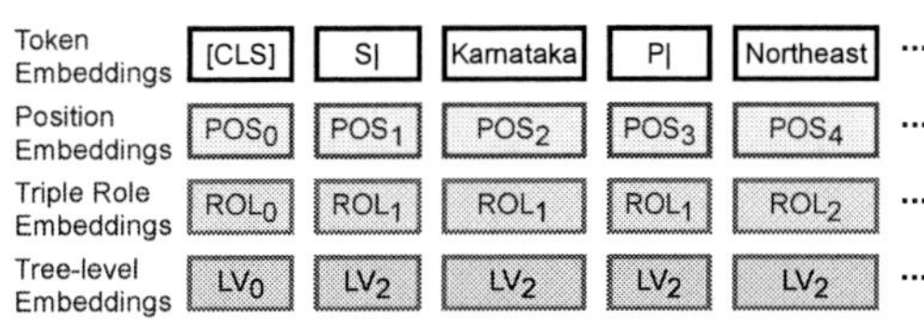

Figure 2: Position Embeddings for the KG in Figure 1

tional position embeddings to capture the structure of the KG. To feed the input for the large-scale Transformer-based PLM, we flatten the graph as a concatenation of linearized triple sequences:

$$|S\ s_1\ |P\ r_1\ |O\ o_1\ ...\ |S\ s_n\ |P\ r_n\ |O\ o_n$$

following Ribeiro et al. (2020b), where $|S$, $|P$, $|O$ are special tokens prepended to indicate whether the phrases in the relations are subjects, relations, or objects, respectively. Instead of directly fine-tuning the PLM on the WebNLG dataset, we first fine-tune our model on a noisy, but larger corpus crawled from Wikipedia, then we fine-tune the model on the training set.

Positional embeddings Since the input of the WebNLG task is a small KG which describes properties of entities, we introduce additional positional

Model		BLEU(%)↑			METEOR↑			TER↓		
		Seen	Unseen	All	Seen	Unseen	All	Seen	Unseen	All
Without Pretrained LM	Gardent et al. (2017)	54.52	33.27	45.13	0.41	0.33	0.37	0.40	0.55	0.47
	Moryossef et al. (2019) [2]	53.30	34.41	47.24	0.44	0.34	0.39	0.47	0.56	0.51
	Zhao et al. (2020)	64.42	38.23	52.78	0.45	0.37	0.41	0.33	0.53	0.42
With Pretrained LM	Nan et al. (2021)	52.86	37.85	45.89	0.42	0.37	0.40	0.44	0.59	0.51
	Kale (2020)	63.90	52.80	57.10	**0.46**	0.41	**0.44**	-	-	-
	Ribeiro et al. (2020b)	64.71	53.67	59.70	**0.46**	**0.42**	**0.44**	-	-	-
Our model	T5-large + Wiki + Position	**66.07**	**53.87**	**60.56**	**0.46**	**0.42**	**0.44**	**0.32**	**0.41**	**0.36**

Table 2: System Results on WebNLG Test Set Evaluated by BLEU, METEOR, and TER with Official Scripts

embeddings to enhance the flattened input of pre-trained Transformer-based sequence-to-sequence models such as BART and TaPas (Herzig et al., 2020). We extend the input layer with two position-aware embeddings in addition to the original position embeddings[3] as shown in the Figure 2:

- Position ID, which is the same as the original position ID used in BART, is the index of the token in the flattened sequence $|S\ s_1\ |P\ r_1\ |O\ o_1\ ...\ |S\ s_n\ |P\ r_n\ |O\ o_n$.
- Triple Role ID takes 3 values for a specific triple (s_i, r_i, o_i): 1 for the subject s_i, 2 for the relation r_i, and 3 for the object o_i.
- Tree level ID calculates the distance (the number of relations) from the root which is the source vertex of the RDF graph.

Two-step Fine-tuning To get better domain adaptation ability (Gururangan et al., 2020; Herzig et al., 2020), following TaPas and Wikipedia Person and Animal Dataset (Wang et al., 2018), we perform intermediate pre-training by coupling noisy English Wikipedia data with Wikidata triples, both of which are crawled in March 2020. We select 15 related categories (Astronaut, University, Monument, Building, ComicsCharacter, Food, Airport, SportsTeam, WrittenWork, Athlete, Artist, City, MeanOfTransportation, CelestialBody, Politician) that appear in the WebNLG dataset (Gardent et al., 2017) and collect 542,192 data pairs. For each Wikipedia article, we query its corresponding WikiData triples and remove sentences which contain no values in the Wikidata triples to form graph-text pairs. Unlike (Chen et al., 2020a) which focuses on individual entity-sentence pairs for distant supervision, our pre-training corpus, on the other hand, is designed to better adapt to translating deeper graph structure into text. We remove triples and description pairs that have already appeared in the WebNLG dataset. After intermediate pre-training on this noisy corpus, we continue with fine-tuning our model on the WebNLG dataset.

3 Experiments

3.1 Dataset and Implementation details

Model	BLEU↑	P↑	R↑	F1↑
BART-base	57.8	68.7	68.9	67.0
+ Wikipedia	**59.7**	**69.6**	**70.7**	**68.4**
+ Position	58.8	68.7	69.9	67.6
+ Wiki + Position	57.3	67.8	69.0	66.6
BART-large	58.3	67.9	69.4	66.8
+ Wikipedia	59.0	68.0	**70.4**	**67.4**
+ Position	58.1	67.6	69.4	66.6
+ Wiki + Position	**60.0**	**68.6**	69.2	67.1
distill-BART-xsum	59.1	69.9	70.6	68.5
+ Wikipedia	59.8	69.7	**71.1**	**68.8**
+ Position	59.2	69.8	70.2	68.3
+ Wiki + Position	**59.9**	**70.1**	70.1	68.7
T5-base	**61.2**	72.3	72.0	70.6
+ Wikipedia	60.9	72.0	71.8	70.2
+ Position	60.8	**72.4**	**72.4**	**70.8**
+ Wiki + Position	60.3	72.2	72.0	70.5
T5-large	60.0	71.6	72.1	70.2
+ Wikipedia	61.3	72.2	72.0	70.5
+ Position	60.6	72.1	72.4	70.6
+ Wiki + Position	**61.9**	**72.8**	**73.5**	**71.6**

Table 3: Results with both Wikipedia Fine-tuning and Positional Embedding for Various Pre-trained Models over All Categories on Development Set Evaluated by average of PARENT[4]precision, recall, F1 and BLEU (%)

We use the original version of English WebNLG2017 (Gardent et al., 2017) dataset which contains 18,102/2,268/4,928 graph-description pairs for training, validation, and testing set respectfully. For this task, we investigate a variety of the BART and T5 models with our novel tree-

[2]For this baseline, we use the results reported from Zhao et al. (2020) who also use official evaluation scripts.

[3]For T5 models, we only keep the Triple Role and Tree-level embeddings.

[4]https://github.com/KaijuML/parent

level embeddings. The statistics and more details of those models are listed in Appendix A.

Model	P↑	R↑	F1↑
Gardent et al. (2017)	88.35	90.22	89.23
Moryossef et al. (2019)	85.77	89.34	87.46
Nan et al. (2021)	89.49	92.33	90.83
Ribeiro et al. (2020b)	89.36	91.96	90.59
T5-large + Wiki + Position	**96.36**	**96.13**	**96.21**

Table 4: System Results on WebNLG Test Set Evaluated by BERTScore precision, recall, F1 (%)

3.2 Results and Analysis

We use the standard NLG evaluation metrics to report results: BLEU (Papineni et al., 2002), METEOR (Lavie and Agarwal, 2007), and TER (Snover et al., 2006) , as shown in Table 2. Because Castro Ferreira et al. (2020) has found that BERTScore (Zhang* et al., 2020) correlates with human evaluation ratings better, we use BERTscore to evaluate system results[5] as shown in Table 4. When selecting the best models, we also evaluate each model with PARENT (Dhingra et al., 2019) metric which measures the overlap between predictions and both reference texts and graph contents. Dhingra et al. (2019) show PARENT metric has better human rating correlations. Table 3 shows the pre-trained models with 2-step fine-tuning and position embeddings achieve better results.[6] We conduct paired t-test between our proposed model and all the other baselines on 10 randomly sampled subsets. The differences are statistically significant with $p \leq 0.008$ for all settings.

Results with Wikipedia fine-tuning. The Wikipedia fine-tuning helps the model handle unseen relations such as *"inOfficeWhileVicePresident"*, and *"activeYearsStartYear"* by stating *"**His vice president** is Atiku Abubakar."* and *"**started playing** in 1995"* respectively. It also combines relations with the same type together with correct order, e.g., given two death places of a person, the model generates: *"died in **Sidcup, London**"* instead of generating two sentences or placing the city name ahead of the area name.

Results with positional embeddings. For the KG with multiple triples, additional positional embeddings help reduce the errors introduced by pronoun ambiguity. For instance, for a KG which has *"leaderName"* relation to both country's leader and university's dean, position embeddings can distinguish these two relations by stating *"**Denmark's** leader is Lars Løkke Rasmussen"* instead of *"**its** leader is Lars Løkke Rasmussen"*. The tree-level embeddings also help the model arrange multiple triples into one sentence, such as combining the city, the country, the affiliation, and the affiliation's headquarter of a university into a single sentence: *"The School of Business and Social Sciences at the Aarhus University in **Aarhus, Denmark** is affiliated to **the European University Association** in **Brussels**"*.

3.3 Remaining Challenges

However, pre-trained language models also generate some errors as shown in Table 5. Because the language model is heavily pre-trained, it is biased against the occurrence of patterns that would enable it to infer the right relation. For example, for the *"activeYearsStartYear"* relation, the model might confuse it with the birth year. For some relations that do not have a clear direction, the language model is not powerful enough to consider the deep connections between the subject and the object. For example, for the relation *"doctoralStudent"*, the model mistakenly describes a professor as a Ph.D. student. Similarly, the model treats an asteroid as a person because it has an epoch date. For KGs with multiple triples, the generator still has a chance to miss relations or mixes the subject and the object of different relations, especially for the unseen category. For instance, for a soccer player with multiple clubs, the system might confuse the subject of one club's relation with another club.

4 Related Work

The WebNLG task is similar to Wikibio generation (Lebret et al., 2016; Wang et al., 2018), AMR-to-text generation (Song et al., 2018) and ROTOWIRE (Wiseman et al., 2017; Puduppully et al., 2019). Previous methods usually treat the graph-to-text generation as an end-to-end generation task. Those models (Trisedya et al., 2018; Gong et al., 2019; Shen et al., 2020) usually first lineralize the knowledge graph and then use attention mechanism to generate the description sentences. While the linearization of input graph may sacrifice the inter-dependency inside input graph, some papers (Ribeiro et al., 2019, 2020a; Zhao et al., 2020)

[5]We only use BERTScore to evaluate baselines which have results available online.

[6]For more examples, please check Appendix for reference.

Category	Output
T5-large	Andrew White *(born in 2003)* is a musician who is associated with the band Kaiser Chiefs and Marry Banilow. He is also associated with the label Polydor Records and is signed to B-Unique Records. S| Aleksandra Kovač P| activeYearsStartYear O| 1990
T5-large	Walter Baade was born in the German Empire and graduated from the University of Gottingen. **He was the doctoral student of Halton Arp and Allan Sandage** and was the discoverer of 1036 Ganymed. S| Walter Baade P| doctoralStudent O| Halton Arp; S| Walter Baade P| doctoralStudent O| Allan Sandage
T5-large +Wiki	11264 Claudiomaccone was *born on the 26th of November, 2005*. He has an orbital period of 1513.722 days, a periapsis of 296521000.0 kilometres and an apoapsis of 475426000.0 kilometres. S| 11264 Claudiomaccone P| epoch O| 2005-11-26; S| Aleksandr Prudnikov P| club O| FC Amkar Perm
T5-large +Position	The chairman of FC Spartak Moscow is Sergey Rodionov. Aleksandr Prudnikov plays for FC Spartak Moscow and *manages FC Amkar Perm*. [S| FC Amkar Perm P| manager O| Gadzhi Gadzhiyev; S| Aleksandr Prudnikov P| club O| FC Amkar Perm]

Table 5: System Error Examples. We highlight *fabricated facts*, [missed relations], **incorrect relations**, and ground truth relations with different color.

use graph encoder such as GCN (Duvenaud et al., 2015) and graph transformer (Wang et al., 2020a; Koncel-Kedziorski et al., 2019) to encode the input graphs. Others (Shen et al., 2020; Wang et al., 2020b) try to carefully design loss functions to control the generation quality. With the development of computation resources, large scale PLMs such as GPT-2 (Radford et al., 2019), BART (Lewis et al., 2020) and T5 (Raffel et al., 2020) achieve state-of-the-art results even with simple linearized graph input (Harkous et al., 2020; Chen et al., 2020a; Kale, 2020; Ribeiro et al., 2020b). Instead of directly fine-tuning the PLMs, we propose a two-step fine-tuning mechanism to get better domain adaptation ability. In addition, using positional embeddings as an extension for PLMs has shown its effectiveness in table-based question answering (Herzig et al., 2020), fact verification (Chen et al., 2020b), and graph-to-text generation (Chen et al., 2020a). We capture the graph structure by enhancing the input layer with the triple role and tree-level embeddings.

5 Conclusions and Future Work

We propose a new two-step structured generation task for the graph-to-text generation task based on a two-step fine-tuning mechanism and novel tree-level position embeddings. In the future, we aim to address the remaining challenges and extend the framework for broader applications.

Acknowledgement

This work is partially supported by Agriculture and Food Research Initiative (AFRI) grant no. 2020-67021-32799/project accession no.1024178 from the USDA National Institute of Food and Agriculture, and by the Office of the Director of National Intelligence (ODNI), Intelligence Advanced Research Projects Activity (IARPA), via contract # FA8650-17-C-9116. The views and conclusions contained herein are those of the authors and should not be interpreted as necessarily representing the official policies, either expressed or implied of the U.S. Government. The U.S. Government is authorized to reproduce and distribute reprints for governmental purposes notwithstanding any copyright annotation therein.

References

Thiago Castro Ferreira, Claire Gardent, Nikolai Ilinykh, Chris van der Lee, Simon Mille, Diego Moussallem, and Anastasia Shimorina. 2020. The 2020 bilingual, bi-directional WebNLG+ shared task: Overview and evaluation results (WebNLG+ 2020). In *Proceedings of the 3rd International Workshop on Natural Language Generation from the Semantic Web (WebNLG+)*, pages 55–76, Dublin, Ireland (Virtual). Association for Computational Linguistics.

Thiago Castro Ferreira, Chris van der Lee, Emiel van Miltenburg, and Emiel Krahmer. 2019. Neural data-to-text generation: A comparison between pipeline and end-to-end architectures. In *Proceedings of the 2019 Conference on Empirical Methods in Natural Language Processing and the 9th International Joint Conference on Natural Language Processing (EMNLP-IJCNLP)*, pages 552–562, Hong Kong, China. Association for Computational Linguistics.

Wenhu Chen, Yu Su, Xifeng Yan, and William Yang Wang. 2020a. KGPT: Knowledge-grounded pretraining for data-to-text generation. In *Proceedings of the 2020 Conference on Empirical Methods in Natural Language Processing (EMNLP)*, pages 8635–8648, Online. Association for Computational Linguistics.

Wenhu Chen, Hongmin Wang, Jianshu Chen, Yunkai Zhang, Hong Wang, Shiyang Li, Xiyou Zhou, and William Yang Wang. 2020b. Tabfact: A large-scale dataset for table-based fact verification. In *Proceedings of the 8th International Conference on Learning Representations*.

Bhuwan Dhingra, Manaal Faruqui, Ankur Parikh, Ming-Wei Chang, Dipanjan Das, and William Cohen. 2019. Handling divergent reference texts when evaluating table-to-text generation. In *Proceedings of the 57th Annual Meeting of the Association for Computational Linguistics*, pages 4884–4895, Florence, Italy. Association for Computational Linguistics.

David K Duvenaud, Dougal Maclaurin, Jorge Iparraguirre, Rafael Bombarell, Timothy Hirzel, Alan Aspuru-Guzik, and Ryan P Adams. 2015. Convolutional networks on graphs for learning molecular fingerprints. In C. Cortes, N. D. Lawrence, D. D. Lee, M. Sugiyama, and R. Garnett, editors, *Advances in Neural Information Processing Systems 28*, pages 2224–2232. Curran Associates, Inc.

Claire Gardent, Anastasia Shimorina, Shashi Narayan, and Laura Perez-Beltrachini. 2017. The WebNLG challenge: Generating text from RDF data. In *Proceedings of the 10th International Conference on Natural Language Generation*, pages 124–133, Santiago de Compostela, Spain. Association for Computational Linguistics.

Heng Gong, Xiaocheng Feng, Bing Qin, and Ting Liu. 2019. Table-to-text generation with effective hierarchical encoder on three dimensions (row, column and time). In *Proceedings of the 2019 Conference on Empirical Methods in Natural Language Processing and the 9th International Joint Conference on Natural Language Processing (EMNLP-IJCNLP)*, pages 3143–3152, Hong Kong, China. Association for Computational Linguistics.

Suchin Gururangan, Ana Marasović, Swabha Swayamdipta, Kyle Lo, Iz Beltagy, Doug Downey, and Noah A. Smith. 2020. Don't stop pretraining: Adapt language models to domains and tasks. In *Proceedings of the 58th Annual Meeting of the Association for Computational Linguistics*, pages 8342–8360, Online. Association for Computational Linguistics.

Hamza Harkous, Isabel Groves, and Amir Saffari. 2020. Have your text and use it too! end-to-end neural data-to-text generation with semantic fidelity. In *Proceedings of the 28th International Conference on Computational Linguistics*, pages 2410–2424, Barcelona, Spain (Online). International Committee on Computational Linguistics.

Jonathan Herzig, Pawel Krzysztof Nowak, Thomas Müller, Francesco Piccinno, and Julian Eisenschlos. 2020. TaPas: Weakly supervised table parsing via pre-training. In *Proceedings of the 58th Annual Meeting of the Association for Computational Linguistics*, pages 4320–4333, Online. Association for Computational Linguistics.

Mihir Kale. 2020. Text-to-text pre-training for data-to-text tasks. *Computation and Language Repository*, arXiv:2005.10433. Version 2.

Rik Koncel-Kedziorski, Dhanush Bekal, Yi Luan, Mirella Lapata, and Hannaneh Hajishirzi. 2019. Text Generation from Knowledge Graphs with Graph Transformers. In *Proceedings of the 2019 Conference of the North American Chapter of the Association for Computational Linguistics: Human Language Technologies, Volume 1 (Long and Short Papers)*, pages 2284–2293, Minneapolis, Minnesota. Association for Computational Linguistics.

Alon Lavie and Abhaya Agarwal. 2007. METEOR: An automatic metric for MT evaluation with high levels of correlation with human judgments. In *Proceedings of the Second Workshop on Statistical Machine Translation*, pages 228–231, Prague, Czech Republic. Association for Computational Linguistics.

Rémi Lebret, David Grangier, and Michael Auli. 2016. Neural text generation from structured data with application to the biography domain. In *Proceedings of the 2016 Conference on Empirical Methods in Natural Language Processing*, pages 1203–1213, Austin, Texas. Association for Computational Linguistics.

Mike Lewis, Yinhan Liu, Naman Goyal, Marjan Ghazvininejad, Abdelrahman Mohamed, Omer Levy, Veselin Stoyanov, and Luke Zettlemoyer. 2020. BART: Denoising sequence-to-sequence pre-training for natural language generation, translation, and comprehension. In *Proceedings of the 58th Annual Meeting of the Association for Computational Linguistics*, pages 7871–7880, Online. Association for Computational Linguistics.

Diego Marcheggiani and Laura Perez-Beltrachini. 2018. Deep graph convolutional encoders for structured data to text generation. In *Proceedings of the 11th International Conference on Natural Language Generation*, pages 1–9, Tilburg University, The Netherlands. Association for Computational Linguistics.

Amit Moryossef, Yoav Goldberg, and Ido Dagan. 2019. Step-by-step: Separating planning from realization in neural data-to-text generation. In *Proceedings of the 2019 Conference of the North American Chapter of the Association for Computational Linguistics: Human Language Technologies, Volume 1 (Long and Short Papers)*, pages 2267–2277, Minneapolis, Minnesota. Association for Computational Linguistics.

Linyong Nan, Dragomir Radev, Rui Zhang, Amrit Rau, Abhinand Sivaprasad, Chiachun Hsieh, Xiangru Tang, Aadit Vyas, Neha Verma, Pranav Krishna, Yangxiaokang Liu, Nadia Irwanto, Jessica

Pan, Faiaz Rahman, Ahmad Zaidi, Mutethia Mutuma, Yasin Tarabar, Ankit Gupta, Tao Yu, Yi Chern Tan, Xi Victoria Lin, Caiming Xiong, Richard Socher, and Nazneen Fatema Rajani. 2021. DART: Open-domain structured data record to text generation. In *Proceedings of the 2021 Conference of the North American Chapter of the Association for Computational Linguistics: Human Language Technologies*, pages 432–447, Online. Association for Computational Linguistics.

Kishore Papineni, Salim Roukos, Todd Ward, and Wei-Jing Zhu. 2002. Bleu: a method for automatic evaluation of machine translation. In *Proceedings of the 40th Annual Meeting of the Association for Computational Linguistics*, pages 311–318, Philadelphia, Pennsylvania, USA. Association for Computational Linguistics.

Ratish Puduppully, Li Dong, and Mirella Lapata. 2019. Data-to-text generation with content selection and planning. In *Proceedings of the AAAI Conference on Artificial Intelligence*, volume 33, pages 6908–6915.

Alec Radford, Jeffrey Wu, Rewon Child, David Luan, Dario Amodei, and Ilya Sutskever. 2019. Language models are unsupervised multitask learners. *OpenAI blog*, 1(8):9.

Colin Raffel, Noam Shazeer, Adam Roberts, Katherine Lee, Sharan Narang, Michael Matena, Yanqi Zhou, Wei Li, and Peter J. Liu. 2020. Exploring the limits of transfer learning with a unified text-to-text transformer. *Journal of Machine Learning Research*, 21(140):1–67.

Leonardo F. R. Ribeiro, Claire Gardent, and Iryna Gurevych. 2019. Enhancing AMR-to-text generation with dual graph representations. In *Proceedings of the 2019 Conference on Empirical Methods in Natural Language Processing and the 9th International Joint Conference on Natural Language Processing (EMNLP-IJCNLP)*, pages 3183–3194, Hong Kong, China. Association for Computational Linguistics.

Leonardo F. R. Ribeiro, Yue Zhang, Claire Gardent, and Iryna Gurevych. 2020a. Modeling global and local node contexts for text generation from knowledge graphs. *Transactions of the Association for Computational Linguistics*, 8:589–604.

Leonardo FR Ribeiro, Martin Schmitt, Hinrich Schütze, and Iryna Gurevych. 2020b. Investigating pretrained language models for graph-to-text generation. *arXiv preprint arXiv:2007.08426*.

Xiaoyu Shen, Ernie Chang, Hui Su, Cheng Niu, and Dietrich Klakow. 2020. Neural data-to-text generation via jointly learning the segmentation and correspondence. In *Proceedings of the 58th Annual Meeting of the Association for Computational Linguistics*, pages 7155–7165, Online. Association for Computational Linguistics.

Matthew Snover, Bonnie Dorr, Richard Schwartz, Linnea Micciulla, and Ralph Weischedel. 2006. A study of translation error rate with targeted human annotation. In *In Proceedings of the Association for Machine Transaltion in the Americas (AMTA 2006)*.

Linfeng Song, Yue Zhang, Zhiguo Wang, and Daniel Gildea. 2018. A graph-to-sequence model for AMR-to-text generation. In *Proceedings of the 56th Annual Meeting of the Association for Computational Linguistics (Volume 1: Long Papers)*, pages 1616–1626, Melbourne, Australia. Association for Computational Linguistics.

Bayu Distiawan Trisedya, Jianzhong Qi, Rui Zhang, and Wei Wang. 2018. GTR-LSTM: A triple encoder for sentence generation from RDF data. In *Proceedings of the 56th Annual Meeting of the Association for Computational Linguistics (Volume 1: Long Papers)*, pages 1627–1637, Melbourne, Australia. Association for Computational Linguistics.

Qingyun Wang, Xiaoman Pan, Lifu Huang, Boliang Zhang, Zhiying Jiang, Heng Ji, and Kevin Knight. 2018. Describing a knowledge base. In *Proceedings of the 11th International Conference on Natural Language Generation*, pages 10–21, Tilburg University, The Netherlands. Association for Computational Linguistics.

Tianming Wang, Xiaojun Wan, and Hanqi Jin. 2020a. AMR-to-text generation with graph transformer. *Transactions of the Association for Computational Linguistics*, 8:19–33.

Zhenyi Wang, Xiaoyang Wang, Bang An, Dong Yu, and Changyou Chen. 2020b. Towards faithful neural table-to-text generation with content-matching constraints. In *Proceedings of the 58th Annual Meeting of the Association for Computational Linguistics*, pages 1072–1086, Online. Association for Computational Linguistics.

Sam Wiseman, Stuart Shieber, and Alexander Rush. 2017. Challenges in data-to-document generation. In *Proceedings of the 2017 Conference on Empirical Methods in Natural Language Processing*, pages 2253–2263, Copenhagen, Denmark. Association for Computational Linguistics.

Tianyi Zhang*, Varsha Kishore*, Felix Wu*, Kilian Q. Weinberger, and Yoav Artzi. 2020. Bertscore: Evaluating text generation with bert. In *International Conference on Learning Representations*.

Chao Zhao, Marilyn Walker, and Snigdha Chaturvedi. 2020. Bridging the structural gap between encoding and decoding for data-to-text generation. In *Proceedings of the 58th Annual Meeting of the Association for Computational Linguistics*, pages 2481–2491, Online. Association for Computational Linguistics.

Transformer-Based Direct Hidden Markov Model for Machine Translation

Weiyue Wang **Zijian Yang** **Yingbo Gao** **Hermann Ney**
Human Language Technology and Pattern Recognition Group
Computer Science Department
RWTH Aachen University
{wwang|zyang|ygao|ney}@cs.rwth-aachen.de

Abstract

The neural hidden Markov model has been proposed as an alternative to attention mechanism in machine translation with recurrent neural networks. However, since the introduction of the transformer models, its performance has been surpassed. This work proposes to introduce the concept of the hidden Markov model to the transformer architecture, which outperforms the transformer baseline. Interestingly, we find that the zero-order model already provides promising performance, giving it an edge compared to a model with first-order dependency, which performs similarly but is significantly slower in training and decoding.

1 Introduction

Recently, significant improvements have been made to neural machine translations (NMT). Regardless of whether a recurrent neural network with long short-term memory (Hochreiter and Schmidhuber, 1997) (LSTM-RNN) (Bahdanau et al., 2015) or a convolutional neural network (CNN) (Gehring et al., 2017) or a self-attentive transformer network (Vaswani et al., 2017) is used, the attention mechanism is always one of the key components that all state-of-the-art NMT systems contain.

Several attempts have been made to explore alternative architectures that do not use an attention mechanism (Wang et al., 2017, 2018; Bahar et al., 2018; Press and Smith, 2018). However, either the performance of those systems is significantly worse than that of the LSTM-RNN-based approaches, or the time and memory complexity is much higher. Since the transformer architecture has upgraded the state-of-the-art to an even higher standard, fewer studies are being carried out in this direction.

Despite the promising translation performance of the transformer architecture, recent studies have found that the quality of the word alignments produced by the multi-head cross-attention weights is quite poor, and various techniques are proposed to address this problem (Alkhouli et al., 2018; Garg et al., 2019; Zenkel et al., 2020). While these works focus on extracting promising alignment information from the transformer architecture, we aim to improve the translation performance of the baseline model by introducing alignment components while keeping the system monolithic. To this end, the possibilities are studied to apply the transformer architecture to the direct hidden Markov model (HMM), which is not as straightforward as in the case of LSTM-RNN due to the cross-attention through all decoder layers. Experimental results show that the zero-order direct HMM already outperforms the baseline transformer model in terms of TER scores (Snover et al., 2006), while the first-order dependency with higher computational complexity offers no further improvements.

2 Related Work

The attention component is introduced by Bahdanau et al. (2015) in NMT to simulate the alignment between the source and target sentence, which leads to significant improvements compared to the pure sequence-to-sequence model (Sutskever et al., 2014). Wang et al. (2018) present a LSTM-RNN-based HMM that does not employ an attention mechanism. This work aims to build a similar model with the transformer architecture. While they perform comparable to the LSTM-RNN-based attention baseline with a much slower model, our model outperforms the transformer baseline in terms of TER scores.

The derivation of neural models for translation on the basis of the HMM framework is also studied in Yu et al. (2017) and Alkhouli et al. (2018). In Yu et al. (2017), alignment-based neural models are used to model alignment and translation from the target to the source side (inverse direction), and

Proceedings of the Joint Conference of the 59th Annual Meeting of the Association for Computational Linguistics and the 11th International Joint Conference on Natural Language Processing: Student Research Workshop, pages 23–32
August 5–6, 2021.

a language model is included in addition. And Alkhouli et al. (2018) rely on alignments generated by statistical systems that serve as supervision for the training of the neural systems. By contrast, the model proposed in this work does not require any additional language model or alignment information and thus keeps the entire system monolithic.

Several works have been carried out to change attention models to capture more complex dependencies. Cohn et al. (2016) introduce structural biases from word-based alignment concepts such as fertility and Markov conditioning. Arthur et al. (2016) incorporate lexical probabilities to influence attention. These changes are based on the LSTM-RNN-based attention model. Garg et al. (2019) and Zenkel et al. (2020) try to generate translation and high-quality alignment jointly using an end-to-end neural training pipeline. By contrast, our work focuses more on improving the translation quality using the alignment information generated by the self-contained model.

3 Direct HMM

The goal of machine translation is to find the target language sentence $e_1^I = e_1, e_2, \cdots, e_I$ that is the translation of a particular source language sentence $f_1^J = f_1, f_2, \cdots, f_J$ with the maximum likelihood ($\arg\max_{I,e_1^I} \{\Pr(e_1^I|f_1^J)\}$). In the direct HMM, an alignment from target to source ($i \rightarrow j = b_i$) is introduced into the translation probability:

$$\Pr(e_1^I|f_1^J) = \sum_{b_1^I} \Pr(e_1^I, b_1^I|f_1^J) \tag{1}$$

$$= \sum_{b_1^I} \prod_{i=1}^{I} \Pr(b_i, e_i|b_0^{i-1}, e_0^{i-1}, f_1^J) \tag{2}$$

$$= \sum_{b_1^I} \prod_{i=1}^{I} \underbrace{\Pr(e_i|b_0^i, e_0^{i-1}, f_1^J)}_{\text{lexicon probability}} \cdot \underbrace{\Pr(b_i|b_0^{i-1}, e_0^{i-1}, f_1^J)}_{\text{alignment probability}} \tag{3}$$

The term "direct" refers to the modeling of $p(e|f)$ instead of $p(f|e)$ as in the conventional HMM (Vogel et al., 1996). In Wang et al. (2018), two LSTM-RNN based neural networks are used to model the lexicon and the alignment probability separately. In this work they are modeled with a single transformer-based network.

4 Direct HMM in Transformer

This section describes in detail how we modify the transformer model so that both the alignment and the lexicon probability can be generated. While the lexicon model in the direct HMM has a zero-order dependency on the current alignment position b_i:

$$\Pr(e_i|b_0^i, e_0^{i-1}, f_1^J) := p(e_i|b_i, e_0^{i-1}, f_1^J) \tag{4}$$

we implement zero- and first-order dependencies for the alignment model.

4.1 Zero-order Architecture

In the zero-order architecture, the alignment model is defined as follows:

$$\Pr(b_i|b_0^{i-1}, e_0^{i-1}, f_1^J) := p(b_i|e_0^{i-1}, f_1^J) \tag{5}$$

To obtain the alignment probability we change the order of the weighted sum and the activation function at each decoder layer in the transformer:

$$c_i^{(l+1)} = \boxed{\sum_{j=1}^{J} \alpha^{(l+1)}(j|i)} W_1 \max\left(0, W_2 h_j + W_3 s_i^{(l)}\right) \tag{6}$$

l: index of the decoder layer $\in \{1, 2. \cdots, L\}$
c_i: context vector, input to the next layer
h_j: source hidden state (key and value)
s_i: target hidden state (query)
W_n: weight matrices
$\alpha(j|i)$: softmax($A[s_i, h_j]$) cross-attention weights

The arrow indicates that the weighted sum with the cross-attention is moved outside of the ReLU activation function. Before the ReLU function is employed, the target hidden state s_{i-1} is projected and added to the projected source hidden state h_j in order to include information from the target side to the context vector, which can also be considered as a substitution for the residual layer in the standard transformer architecture. As the outputs of the last decoder layer (and the entire network) we have a lexicon probability:

$$p(e_i|j, e_0^{i-1}, f_1^J) = \text{softmax}\left(W_4 \cdot \max\left(0, W_5 \cdot h_j + W_6 \cdot s_i^{(L)}\right)\right) \tag{7}$$

and an alignment probability:

$$p(j|e_0^{i-1}, f_1^J) = \alpha^{(L)}(j|i) \tag{8}$$

The output probability for the current word is:

$$p(e_i|e_0^{i-1}, f_1^J) = \sum_{j=1}^{J} p(j|e_0^{i-1}, f_1^J) \cdot p(e_i|j, e_0^{i-1}, f_1^J) \tag{9}$$

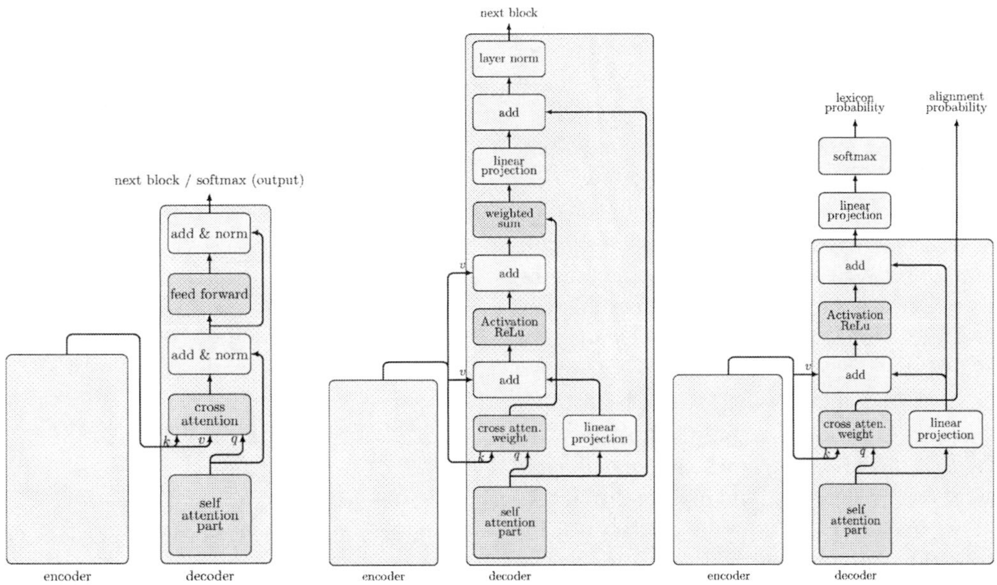

(a) standard transformer (b) first decoder layers of direct HMM (c) the last decoder layer of direct HMM

Figure 1: Visualized comparison between the direct HMM and the standard transformer architecture.

And the sentence probability is then:

$$p(e_1^I|f_1^J) = \prod_{i=1}^{I} p(e_i|e_0^{i-1}, f_1^J) \tag{10}$$

Due to the redefinition of the context vector, layer normalization, residual connection and linear projection are also modified accordingly. Detailed changes to the architecture are shown in Figure 1. Note that all modifications are made to decoder layers while encoder layers remain unchanged.

4.2 First-order Architecture

In the first-order architecture, the alignment model is defined as follows:

$$\Pr(b_i|b_0^{i-1}, e_0^{i-1}, f_1^J) := p(b_i|b_{i-1}, e_0^{i-1}, f_1^J) \tag{11}$$

The lexicon probability remains the same as in the zero-order model (Equation 4). To consider the dependency on the previous source position ($j' = b_{i-1}$), we change the cross-attention weights:

$$\alpha^{(L)}(j|i,j') = \text{softmax}\left(A\left[s_i^{(L-1)}, W \cdot [h_j^{(L)}, h_{j'}^{(L)}]\right]\right) \tag{12}$$

where $[h_j^{(L)}, h_{j'}^{(L)}]$ denotes the concatenation of the source hidden states at positions j and j'.

Changing the architecture from the zero-order model to the first-order model is straightforward, but the main challenge is in the training process. Due to the first-order dependency, the complexity of the brute-force search (forward path) becomes exponential (confirm Equation 3). To address this problem, we apply a dynamic programming algorithm to find the probability of the entire sentence:

$$Q(i,j) = \sum_{j'} p(e_i, j|j', f_1^J, e_0^{i-1}) \cdot Q(i-1, j') \tag{13}$$

$$p(e_1^I|f_1^J) = Q(I) = \sum_{j} Q(I,j) \tag{14}$$

where Q denotes the recursive function. For given sentence pairs (F_r, E_r), the training criterion is then the maximization of the log-likelihood function $\arg\max_\theta \sum_r \log p(E_r|F_r, \theta)$.

In previous work on the neural HMM, the forward-backward algorithm is implemented to calculate the posterior probability as the golden truth to guide the training of the lexicon and the alignment models (referred to as "manual differentiation"). But actually it is not necessary. As long as the forward path is implemented according to a recursive function of dynamic programming, as shown in Equation 13, the frameworks can handle the backward path automatically (referred to as "automatic differentiation"). Intuitively, the recursive equation is nothing more than a sum of products that should be easy to work with the automatic differentiation toolkit. Theoretically, the mathematical proof for this is presented in Eisner (2016). And practically, our experimental results of the automatic differentiation and the manual differentiation are the same as long as label smoothing (Szegedy et al., 2016) is not applied.

Without an explicitly implemented forward-backward algorithm, applying label smoothing is not straightforward as it should be applied to the words while the automatic differentiation is performed after the forward path has been done for the entire sentence. To solve this problem, we apply label smoothing to the lexicon probability $p(e_i|j, e_0^{i-1}, f_1^J)$ at each step of the forward path. Although in this case the type of label smoothing is different for the automatic and manual differentiation, experimental results are quite similar ($< 0.1\%$ differences). The automatic differentiation has an advantage in terms of memory and time complexity and is therefore used for all subsequent experiments.

5 Experiments

5.1 Translation Performance

In order to test the performance of the direct HMM, we carry out experiments on the WMT 2019[1] German→English (de-en), WMT 2019 Chinese→English (zh-en) and WMT 2018[2] English→Turkish (en-tr) tasks. These three tasks represent different amounts of training data, from hundreds of thousands to tens of millions. Detailed data statistics are shown in Appendix A.

The proposed approaches are completely implemented in fairseq (Ott et al., 2019). The standard transformer base model (Vaswani et al., 2017) implemented in the fairseq framework is used as our baseline and we follow the standard setup for hyperparameters. Translation performance is measured by case-insensitive BLEU (Papineni et al., 2002) and TER (Snover et al., 2006) scores with SACREBLEU toolkit (Post, 2018). The results are shown in Table 1.

The results show that the direct HMMs achieve comparable performance to the transformer baselines in terms of BLEU scores and outperform the baseline systems in terms of TER scores. The TER metric is known to favor shorter hypotheses, but from the length ratio results we can conclude that the improvements are not due to it. In addition, it can be seen that the first-order dependency could not provide further improvements over the zero-order model. To find the possible reasons for this, we try to extract alignment heat maps with regard to the dependencies between the current position j and the predecessor position j'.

[1] http://www.statmt.org/wmt19/

[2] http://www.statmt.org/wmt18/

BLEU [%]	de-en	zh-en	en-tr
transformer base	**38.7**	**31.5**	17.4
zero-order HMM	38.5	**31.5**	17.6
first-order HMM	**38.7**	31.3	**17.7**
TER [%]	de-en	zh-en	en-tr
transformer base	48.2	56.6	71.9
zero-order HMM	**47.7**	55.7	71.4
first-order HMM	47.9	**55.4**	**71.2**
length ratio [%]	de-en	zh-en	en-tr
transformer base	97.3	**94.1**	**99.7**
zero-order HMM	97.7	94.0	**99.7**
first-order HMM	**98.0**	93.9	99.5

Table 1: Experimental results on the WMT news translation tasks.

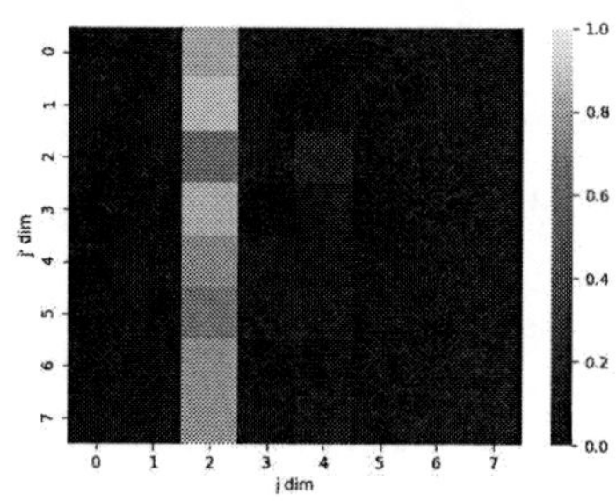

Figure 2: Alignment heat map for $p(j|j', e_0^{i-1}, f_1^J)$ with fixed target position i. The heat map is extracted when the training is almost converging.

As shown in Figure 2, the target position j with the maximum probability is often the same for different predecessor positions j', which indicates that the training of the model tends to "forget" the explicit first-order dependency. We checked a lot of heat maps and this happens quite often, in fact, for short sentences it almost always happens. This essentially explains why the first-order model fails to make improvements. To benefit from the first-order dependency, constraints or other techniques might be used during training.

Here the results of the RNN-based direct HMM are not included as one of the baselines, as the performance of the RNN-based approaches is significantly surpassed by the transformer-based approaches. We believe this work will outperform the system proposed in (Wang et al., 2018), but that is mainly due to the transformer architecture rather than refinements we made.

Compared to the baseline transformer model, the direct HMM only has about 2% more free parameters. While the first-order model has a clear disadvantage in terms of training and decoding speed compared to the baseline system due to the inevitable loop over the target position i, the decoding speed of the zero-order model is only slightly slower than that of the transformer baseline. Details of time usage are given in Appendix B.

5.2 Alignment Quality

In addition to improvements in the TER scores, we believe that the direct HMM also provides better alignment quality than the standard cross-attention. To verify this assumption, we compute the alignment error rate (AER) (Och and Ney, 2000) on the RWTH German-English Golden Alignments corpus (Vilar et al., 2006), which provides 505 manually word-aligned sentence pairs extracted from the Europarl corpus. We take the argmax of the alignment probability output of our model as an estimated alignment. In addition, as with the conventional HMM, the argmax of the posterior probability can also be used as an estimated alignment, which explicitly includes the lexicon information and should lead to a better quality. As baselines, we take the argmax of the average of the attention heads in the fifth and sixth decoder layers, since Garg et al. (2019) claim that the cross-attention weights in the fifth layer produce more accurate alignment information than the last layer. All models are trained in both directions to get bidirectional alignments. These bidirectional alignments are then merged using the grow diagonal heuristic (Koehn et al., 2005).

model	alignment from	AER
transformer	fifth layer	39.1
	sixth layer	55.7
direct HMM	alignment prob.	31.8
	posterior prob.	27.4

Table 2: Experimental results on the German-English alignment task in AER [%].

From the results shown in Table 2, we can observe that the alignment generated by the direct HMM has a significantly better quality than that extracted directly from the transformer attention weights. The posterior probability that contains the lexicon information indeed provides better alignments, which can be seen as a further advantage of the direct HMM, since it cannot be calculated in the standard transformer architecture without an explicit alignment probability. In terms of AER performance, our model stands behind GIZA++ (Och and Ney, 2003) as well as the approaches proposed in Garg et al. (2019) and Zenkel et al. (2020). Note, however, that our zero-order model does not include the future target word information in estimating alignments, and we do not use additional loss for alignment training, since the original goal of this work is to improve translation quality by applying HMM factorization.

In addition to the AER results, Appendix C shows heat maps extracted for the alignment probability from direct HMM compared to those extracted for cross-attention weights from the standard transformer model.

6 Conclusion

This work exhibits the use of the transformer architecture in a direct HMM for machine translation, which significantly improves TER scores. In addition, we show that the proposed system tends to "refuse" to learn first-order dependency during training. The zero-order model achieves a good compromise between performance and decoding speed, which is much faster than previous work on the direct HMM. In order to benefit from the predecessor alignment information, further techniques should be carried out. Another future work would be to combine the attention mechanism with the alignment information to further improve performance.

Acknowledgments

This work has received funding from the European Research Council (ERC) under the European Union's Horizon 2020 research and innovation programme (grant agreement No 694537, project "SEQCLAS"). The work reflects only the authors' views and the European Research Council Executive Agency (ERCEA) is not responsible for any use that may be made of the information it contains.

References

Tamer Alkhouli, Gabriel Bretschner, and Hermann Ney. 2018. On the alignment problem in multi-head attention-based neural machine translation. In *Proceedings of the Third Conference on Machine Translation: Research Papers*, pages 177–185, Brussels, Belgium. Association for Computational Linguistics.

Philip Arthur, Graham Neubig, and Satoshi Nakamura. 2016. Incorporating discrete translation lexicons into neural machine translation. In *Proceedings of the 2016 Conference on Empirical Methods in Natural Language Processing*, pages 1557–1567, Austin, Texas. Association for Computational Linguistics.

Parnia Bahar, Christopher Brix, and Hermann Ney. 2018. Towards two-dimensional sequence to sequence model in neural machine translation. In *Proceedings of the 2018 Conference on Empirical Methods in Natural Language Processing*, pages 3009–3015, Brussels, Belgium. Association for Computational Linguistics.

Dzmitry Bahdanau, Kyunghyun Cho, and Yoshua Bengio. 2015. Neural machine translation by jointly learning to align and translate. In *3rd International Conference on Learning Representations, ICLR 2015, San Diego, CA, USA, May 7-9, 2015, Conference Track Proceedings*.

Trevor Cohn, Cong Duy Vu Hoang, Ekaterina Vymolova, Kaisheng Yao, Chris Dyer, and Gholamreza Haffari. 2016. Incorporating structural alignment biases into an attentional neural translation model. In *Proceedings of the 2016 Conference of the North American Chapter of the Association for Computational Linguistics: Human Language Technologies*, pages 876–885, San Diego, California. Association for Computational Linguistics.

Jason Eisner. 2016. Inside-outside and forward-backward algorithms are just backprop (tutorial paper). In *Proceedings of the Workshop on Structured Prediction for NLP*, pages 1–17, Austin, TX. Association for Computational Linguistics.

Sarthak Garg, Stephan Peitz, Udhyakumar Nallasamy, and Matthias Paulik. 2019. Jointly learning to align and translate with transformer models. In *Proceedings of the 2019 Conference on Empirical Methods in Natural Language Processing and the 9th International Joint Conference on Natural Language Processing (EMNLP-IJCNLP)*, pages 4453–4462, Hong Kong, China. Association for Computational Linguistics.

Jonas Gehring, Michael Auli, David Grangier, Denis Yarats, and Yann N. Dauphin. 2017. Convolutional sequence to sequence learning. In *Proceedings of the 34th International Conference on Machine Learning, ICML 2017, Sydney, NSW, Australia, 6-11 August 2017*, volume 70 of *Proceedings of Machine Learning Research*, pages 1243–1252. PMLR.

Sepp Hochreiter and Jürgen Schmidhuber. 1997. Long short-term memory. *Neural Computation*, 9(8):1735–1780.

Philipp Koehn, Amittai Axelrod, Alexandra Birch, Chris Callison-Burch, Miles Osborne, and David Talbot. 2005. Edinburgh system description for the 2005 IWSLT speech translation evaluation. In *Proceedings of the International Workshop on Spoken Language Translation (IWSLT)*, pages 68–75, Pittsburgh, PA, USA.

Ruixuan Luo, Jingjing Xu, Yi Zhang, Xuancheng Ren, and Xu Sun. 2019. Pkuseg: A toolkit for multi-domain chinese word segmentation. *CoRR*, abs/1906.11455.

Franz Josef Och and Hermann Ney. 2000. Improved statistical alignment models. In *Proceedings of the 38th Annual Meeting of the Association for Computational Linguistics*, pages 440–447, Hong Kong. Association for Computational Linguistics.

Franz Josef Och and Hermann Ney. 2003. A systematic comparison of various statistical alignment models. *Computational Linguistics*, 29(1):19–51.

Myle Ott, Sergey Edunov, Alexei Baevski, Angela Fan, Sam Gross, Nathan Ng, David Grangier, and Michael Auli. 2019. fairseq: A fast, extensible toolkit for sequence modeling. In *Proceedings of the 2019 Conference of the North American Chapter of the Association for Computational Linguistics (Demonstrations)*, pages 48–53, Minneapolis, Minnesota. Association for Computational Linguistics.

Kishore Papineni, Salim Roukos, Todd Ward, and Wei-Jing Zhu. 2002. Bleu: a method for automatic evaluation of machine translation. In *Proceedings of the 40th Annual Meeting of the Association for Computational Linguistics*, pages 311–318, Philadelphia, Pennsylvania, USA. Association for Computational Linguistics.

Matt Post. 2018. A call for clarity in reporting BLEU scores. In *Proceedings of the Third Conference on Machine Translation: Research Papers*, pages 186–191, Brussels, Belgium. Association for Computational Linguistics.

Ofir Press and Noah A. Smith. 2018. You may not need attention. *CoRR*, abs/1810.13409.

Rico Sennrich, Barry Haddow, and Alexandra Birch. 2016. Neural machine translation of rare words with subword units. In *Proceedings of the 54th Annual Meeting of the Association for Computational Linguistics (Volume 1: Long Papers)*, pages 1715–1725, Berlin, Germany. Association for Computational Linguistics.

Matthew Snover, Bonnie Dorr, Richard Schwartz, Linnea Micciulla, and John Makhoul. 2006. A study of translation edit rate with targeted human annotation. In *In Proceedings of Association for Machine Translation in the Americas*, pages 223–231, Cambridge, MA, USA.

Ilya Sutskever, Oriol Vinyals, and Quoc V. Le. 2014. Sequence to sequence learning with neural networks. In *Advances in Neural Information Processing Systems 27: Annual Conference on Neural Information Processing Systems 2014, December 8-13 2014, Montreal, Quebec, Canada*, pages 3104–3112.

C. Szegedy, V. Vanhoucke, S. Ioffe, J. Shlens, and Z. Wojna. 2016. Rethinking the inception architecture for computer vision. In *2016 IEEE Conference on Computer Vision and Pattern Recognition (CVPR)*, pages 2818–2826, Los Alamitos, CA, USA. IEEE Computer Society.

Ashish Vaswani, Noam Shazeer, Niki Parmar, Jakob Uszkoreit, Llion Jones, Aidan N. Gomez, Lukasz Kaiser, and Illia Polosukhin. 2017. Attention is all you need. In *Advances in Neural Information Processing Systems 30: Annual Conference on Neural Information Processing Systems 2017, 4-9 December 2017, Long Beach, CA, USA*, pages 5998–6008.

David Vilar, Maja Popović, and Hermann Ney. 2006. AER: Do we need to "improve" our alignments? In *Proceedings of the International Workshop on Spoken Language Translation (IWSLT)*, pages 205–212, Kyoto, Japan.

Stephan Vogel, Hermann Ney, and Christoph Tillmann. 1996. HMM-based word alignment in statistical translation. In *COLING 1996 Volume 2: The 16th International Conference on Computational Linguistics*.

Weiyue Wang, Tamer Alkhouli, Derui Zhu, and Hermann Ney. 2017. Hybrid neural network alignment and lexicon model in direct HMM for statistical machine translation. In *Proceedings of the 55th Annual Meeting of the Association for Computational Linguistics (Volume 2: Short Papers)*, pages 125–131, Vancouver, Canada. Association for Computational Linguistics.

Weiyue Wang, Derui Zhu, Tamer Alkhouli, Zixuan Gan, and Hermann Ney. 2018. Neural hidden Markov model for machine translation. In *Proceedings of the 56th Annual Meeting of the Association for Computational Linguistics (Volume 2: Short Papers)*, pages 377–382, Melbourne, Australia. Association for Computational Linguistics.

Lei Yu, Phil Blunsom, Chris Dyer, Edward Grefenstette, and Tomás Kociský. 2017. The neural noisy channel. In *5th International Conference on Learning Representations, ICLR 2017, Toulon, France, April 24-26, 2017, Conference Track Proceedings*. OpenReview.net.

Thomas Zenkel, Joern Wuebker, and John DeNero. 2020. End-to-end neural word alignment outperforms GIZA++. In *Proceedings of the 58th Annual Meeting of the Association for Computational Linguistics*, pages 1605–1617, Online. Association for Computational Linguistics.

A Data Statistics

WMT 2019 German→English	train		valid		test	
	source	target	source	target	source	target
# sentence pairs	5.9M		2169		2000	
# original vocabulary	2.1M	932k	12.2k	10.7k	10.8k	9.5k
# vocabulary after BPE	45.1k	33.2k	10.5k	8.2k	9.3k	7.3k
# running words	137M	144M	38.2k	40.8k	31.1k	34.4k
# running BPE sub-words	160M	157M	54.8k	53.1k	44.7k	43.4k
WMT 2019 Chinese→English	**train**		**valid**		**test**	
	source	target	source	target	source	target
# sentence pairs	26.0M		2002		2000	
# vocabulary	1.3M	651k	9.2k	8.7k	9.5k	8.5k
# vocabulary after BPE	47.0k	32.2k	9.2k	9.2k	9.3k	8.8k
# running words	555M	606M	53.7k	59.8k	62.7k	82.2k
# running BPE sub-words	588M	658M	58.7k	65.1k	69.2k	87.2k
WMT 2018 English→Turkish	**train**		**valid**		**test**	
	source	target	source	target	source	target
# sentence pairs	208k		3007		3000	
# vocabulary	70.6k	160k	8.7k	15.1k	9.4k	16.4k
# vocabulary after BPE	7280	7324	4944	5437	5093	5592
# running words	5.16M	4.61M	68.3k	55.0k	70.5k	56.8k
# running BPE sub-words	6.72M	7.45M	98.0k	101k	101k	107k

For the German→English task, joint byte pair encoding (BPE) (Sennrich et al., 2016) with 32k merge operations is used. The `newstest2015` dataset is used as the validation set and `newstest2019` as the test set.

The Chinese data are segmented using the pkuseg toolkit[3] (Luo et al., 2019). The vocabulary size and number of running words are calculated after segmentation. Separate BPE with 32k merge operations is used for Chinese and English data. The `newsdev2017` dataset is used as the validation set and `newstest2019` as the test set.

For the English→Turkish task, separate BPE with 8k merge operations is used. The `newstest2017` dataset is used as the validation set and `newstest2018` as the test set.

[3] https://github.com/lancopku/pkuseg-python

B Training and Decoding Speed

Training and decoding are performed on one NVIDIA GeForce RTX 1080 Ti with 11 GB of GPU memory. Table 3 shows the training and decoding speed on the WMT 2019 German→English dataset. Compared to the baseline system, the disadvantages of the zero-order HMM on training speed are mainly due to the limited GPU memory. Since the largest tensor of the proposed model has a dimension of batch size × length of the source sentence × length of the target sentence × vocabulary size (in the standard transformer the dimension of "length of the source sentence" is not required), the batch size must be reduced to fit in the GPU memory. Although gradient accumulation can be used to guarantee performance, the reduced batch size still linearly slows the training speed. The influence on the decoding speed is rather small. By introducing the first-order dependency, however, a `for` loop over every target position is inevitable, so that the training and decoding speeds are greatly slowed down. This is also reported by the previous work.

model	# parameters	training		decoding	
		tokens/sec	time	tokens/sec	time
transformer baseline	84.2M	10.2k	5d	108.2	6.9min
zero-order HMM	86.1M	2.2k	20d	84.0	8.9min
first-order HMM	88.0M	0.4k	54d	31.7	23.5min

Table 3: Comparison of training and decoding speed.

C Heat Maps of Attention Weights and Alignments

Figure 3 demonstrates the heat maps of some sentence pairs that are randomly selected from the German→English training data after the training has almost converged. Note that here the x and y axes indicate the source and target positions (j and i), which differs from Figure 2, where they indicate the current and previous source positions (j and j'). We can observe that the alignment paths are much more focused than the attention weights. Since our main goal is to propose an alternative technique to improve translation performance rather than alignment quality, alignment error rates are not calculated in this work.

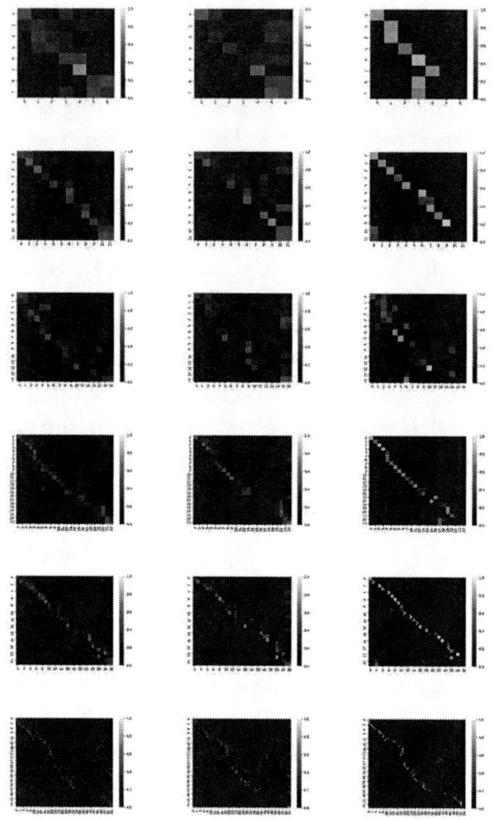

Figure 3: Heat maps of attention weights and alignments. The source sentence goes from left to right and the target sentence goes from top to bottom. The first column shows the attention weight heat maps (average of the multi-head cross-attention) for the 4th decoder layer. The second column shows the attention weight heat maps (average of the multi-head cross-attention) for the 6th (last) decoder layer. The third column shows the alignment heat maps taken from the proposed direct HMM.

AutoRC: Improving BERT Based Relation Classification Models via Architecture Search

Wei Zhu[1] *

[1] East China Normal University, China

Abstract

Although BERT based relation classification (RC) models have achieved significant improvements over the traditional deep learning models, it seems that no consensus can be reached on what is the optimal architecture, since there are many design choices available. In this work, we design a comprehensive search space for BERT based RC models and employ a modified version of efficient neural architecture search (ENAS) method to automatically discover the design choices mentioned above. Experiments on eight benchmark RC tasks show that our method is efficient and effective in finding better architectures than the baseline BERT based RC models. Ablation study demonstrates the necessity of our search space design and the effectiveness of our search method. We also show that our framework can also apply to other entity related tasks like coreference resolution and span based named entity recognition (NER).

1 Introduction

The task of relation classification (RC) is to predict semantic relations between pairs of entities inside a context. It is an important NLP task since it serves as an intermediate step in variety of NLP applications. There are many works that apply deep neural networks (DNN) to relation classification (Socher et al., 2012; Zeng et al., 2014; Shen and Huang, 2016). With the rise of pre-trained language models (PLMs) (Devlin et al., 2018), a series of literature have incorporated PLMs such as BERT in RC tasks (Baldini Soares et al., 2019; Wu and He, 2019; Eberts and Ulges, 2019; Peng et al., 2019), and shows significant improvements over the traditional DNN models.

Despite great success, there is yet no consensus reached on how to represent the entity pair and their contextual sentence for a BERT based RC model. First, Baldini Soares et al. (2019) and Peng et al. (2019) use different entity identification methods. Second, Baldini Soares et al. (2019) and Wu and He (2019) use different aggregation methods of entity representations and contexts. Third, choosing which features should be considered for the classfication layer should also be determined (Eberts and Ulges, 2019). In addition, previous literature does not consider the interactions between the feature vectors.

In this work, we experiment on making the design choices in the BERT based RC model automatically, so that one can obtain an architecture that better suits the task at hand (Figure 1). Throughout this work, we will refer to our framework as *AutoRC*, which includes our search space and search method. Firstly, a comprehensive search space for the design choices that should be considered in a BERT based RC model is established. Second, to navigate on our search space, we employ reinforcement learning (RL) strategy following ENAS (Pham et al., 2018). That is, a controller generates new RC architectures, receives rewards, and updates its policy via policy gradient method. To stabilize and improve the search results, three non-trivial modifications to ENAS are proposed: a) heterogeneous parameter sharing, which is to share parameters more deeply than ENAS if the modules play similar role, and not to share if not; b) maintain multiple copies of the shared parameters which will be drawn randomly to the child models; c) search warm-ups, which is to generate and update child models without updating the controller at the beginning of the search stage.

Experiments on eight benchmark RC tasks show that our method can outperform the standard BERT based RC models. Transfer of the learned architecture across different tasks is investigated, which shows the transferred architectures can outperform

Contact: 52205901018@stu.ecnu.edu.cn.

Proceedings of the Joint Conference of the 59th Annual Meeting of the Association for Computational Linguistics and the 11th International Joint Conference on Natural Language Processing: Student Research Workshop, pages 33–43
August 5–6, 2021.

the baseline models but cannot outperform the architecture learned on this task. Ablation study of the search space demonstrates the validity of the search space design. In addition, ablation studies on the search space show the validity of our search space design, and experiments show that our proposed modifications to ENAS are effective. We also show our framework can work effectively on other entity related tasks like coreference resolution and span based NER.

The contributions of the paper can be summarized as:

- We develop a comprehensive search space and improve the BERT based RC models, in which alternatives of the input formats and the aggregation layers are applicable to other tasks.

- As far as we know, we are the first to introduce NAS for BERT based models. Our proposed methods for improving search results are effective and universally applicable.

2 Related Work

Our work is closely related to the literature on neural architecture search (NAS). The field of NAS has attracted a lot of attentions in the recent years. The goal is to find automatic mechanisms for generating new neural architectures to replace conventional handcrafted ones, or automatically deciding optimal design choices instead of manually tuning (Bergstra et al., 2011). Recently, it has been widely applied to computer vision tasks, such as image classification (Cai et al., 2018), semantic segmentation (Liu et al., 2019), object detection (Ghiasi et al., 2019), super-resolution (Ahn et al., 2018), etc. However, NAS is less well studied in the field of natural language processing (NLP), especially in information extraction (IE). Recent works (Zoph and Le, 2017; Pham et al., 2018; Liu et al., 2018) search new recurrent cells for the language modeling (LM) tasks. The evolved transformer (So et al., 2019) employs an evolution-based search algorithm to generate better transformer architectures for machine translation tasks. Zhu et al. (2021) develops a novel search space which incorporates cross-sentence attention mechanism and are able to find novel architectures for natural language understanding (NLU) tasks. In this work, we design a method that incorporate NAS to improve BERT based relation extraction models.

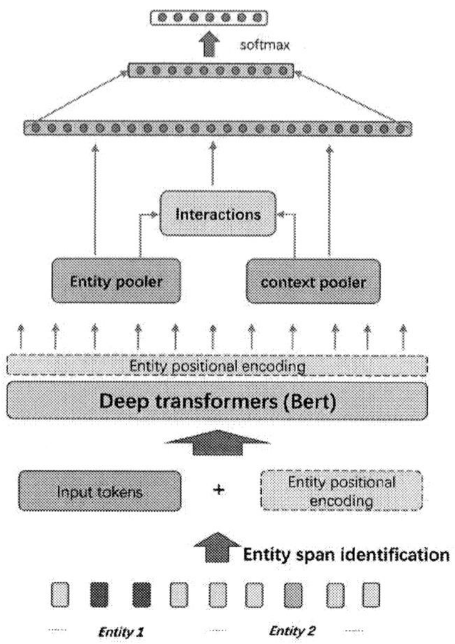

Figure 1: General architecture for a RC model.

Our work is closely related to literatures on relation extraction, especially the recent ones that take advantages of the pre-trained language models (PLMs). In terms of entity span identification, Baldini Soares et al. (2019) argues that adding entity markers to the input tokens works best, while Peng et al. (2019) shows that some RC tasks are in favor of replace entity mentions with special tokens. For feature selection, Baldini Soares et al. (2019) shows that aggregating the entity representations via start pooling works best across a panel of R-C tasks. Meanwhile, Wu and He (2019) chooses average pooling for entity features. In addition, it argues that incorporating the representation of the [CLS] token is beneficial. Eberts and Ulges (2019) shows that the context between two entities serves as a strong signal on some RC task. Zhu (2020) shows that pre-training with entity spans can benefit the downstream tasks. In this work, we provide a more comprehensive overview of the design choices in BERT based RC models, and provide a solution for efficient and task-specific architecture discovery, thus alleviating NLP practitioner in the field of RE from manually or simple heuristic model tuning.

3 Search space for RC model

An overall architecture design for a RC model is shown in Figure 1. Following its bottom-up work-

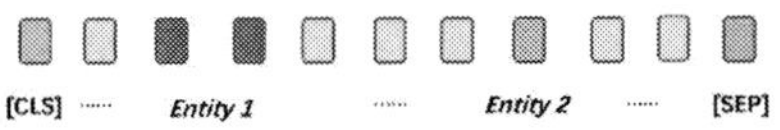

(a) standard input

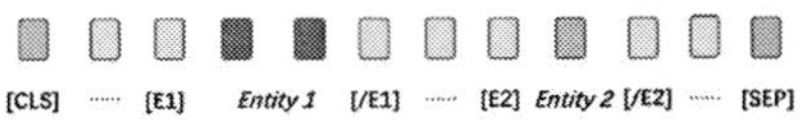

(b) entity_markers

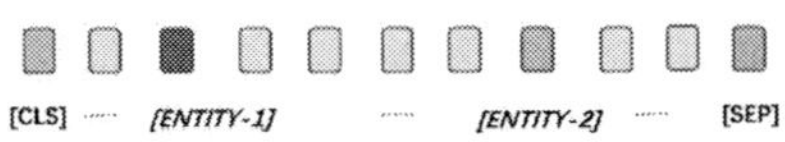

(c) entity_tokens

Figure 2: How to make changes to the input sequence for entity span identification.

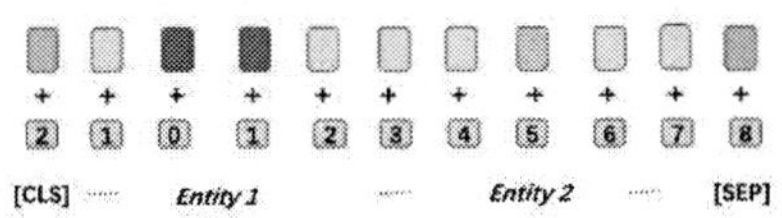

Figure 3: An example of the entity positional encoding.

flow, we will define the search space for $AutoRC$.

3.1 Formal definition of task

In this paper, we focus on learning mappings from relation statements to relation representations. Formally, let $x = [x_0, ..., x_n]$ be a sequence of tokens, and entity 1 (e_1) and entity 2 (e_2) to be the entity mentions, which is depicted at the bottom of Figure 1. The position of e_i in x is denoted by the start and end position, $s_i = (e_i^s, e_i^e)$. A relation statement is a triple $r = (x, e_1, e_2)$. Our goal is to learn a function f_θ that maps the relation statement to a fixed-length vector $h_r = f_\theta(r) \in R^d$ that represents the relation expressed in r.

Note that the two entities divide the sentence into five parts, e_1 and e_2 as entity mentions, and three contextual pieces, denoted as c_0, c_1 and c_2.

3.2 Entity span identification

In this work, we employ BERT (Devlin et al., 2018) as the encoder for the input sentences. The BERT encoder may need to distinguish the entity mentions from the context sentence to properly model the semantic representations of a relation statement. We present three different options for getting information about the entity spans s_1 and s_2 into our BERT encoder, which are depicted in Figure 2.

standard, that is, not to make any change to the input sentence (Figure 2(a)).

entity_markers. We add special tokens at the start and end of the entities to inform BERT where the two entities are in the sentence, as depicted by Figure 2(b). Formally, the sentence x becomes $[[CLS], x_0...[E1]...[/E1]...[E2]...[/E2] ...x_n, [SEP]]$.

entity_tokens. This approach (Figure 2(c)) replaces the entity mentions in the sentence with special tokens. Formally, x becomes $[[CLS]...[ENTITY - 1]...[ENTITY - 2]...[SEP]]$.

3.3 Entity positional encoding

To make up for the standard input's lack of entity identification, or to further address the position of entities, one can add special entity positional encoding accompany input sequence x. As is shown in Figure 3, for entity 1, the entity positional encoding will be the distance to entity 1's starting token. [1]

Now there are two design choices. First is whether to use entity positional encoding at all. Second, as is shown in Figure 1 if using entity positional encoding, do we add this extra embedding to the embedding layer of the BERT (denoted as add_to_embedding), or do we concatenate this embedding to the output of BERT encoder (denoted as concat_to_output)?

3.4 Pooling layer

How to aggregate the entities' and contexts' hidden representations into fixed length feature vectors, i.e., what kind of poolers are used becomes the core part of the RC model architecture. In this work, we investigate 5 different poolers: average pooling (avg_pool), max pooling (denoted as max_pool), self-attention pooling (denoted as self_attn_pool), dynamic routing pooling (dr_pool) (Gong et al., 2018), and start pooling (start_pool), which is to use the reprsentation of the starting token as in Baldini Soares et al. (2019).

3.5 Output features

To select appropriate features for classifying relation types, there are many design choices. First, whether the two entity vectors should be used as features. Second, whether each contextual piece

[1] Entity positional encoding corresponds to two (one for either entity) entity positional embedding modules in the RC model, and they are randomly initialized and fine-tuned during BERT fine-tuning.

(c_0, c_1, c_2) should be added as features (Eberts and Ulges, 2019; Wu and He, 2019).

We notice that the literature does not consider the interactions of the features from different parts of the sentence, which proves to be useful in other tasks such as natural language inference (NLI) (Chen et al., 2016). Here, we consider the interaction between the two entities, and their interactions with contextual pieces. The interaction can be dot product (denoted as dot) or absolute difference (denoted as minus) between two feature vectors.

3.6 Search space

Now we are ready to define the search space formally. The search space is as follows:

- entity span identification = entity_markers, entity_tokens, standard;
- how to use entity positional embedding = null, add_to_embedding, concat_to_output;
- poolers for entity or contextual piece = avg_pool, max_pool, self_attn_pool, dr_pool, start_pool;
- whether to use the representation of entity e_i = True, False, where $i = 1, 2$;
- whether to use the representation of context c_i = True, False, where $i = 0, 1, 2$;
- Interaction between the two entities = dot, minus, null, where null means no interaction;
- Interaction between entity and contextual piece c_i = dot, minus, null, where null means no interaction, and $i = 0, 1, 2$.

Our search space contains 1.64e+8 combinations of design choices, which makes manually fine-tuning or random search impractical.

4 Search method

In this section, we first formally formulate the problem of architecture search with reinforcement learning. Then, , we discuss the search algorithm based on policy gradient. At the last part, we discuss our modifications to stabilize the search outputs.

4.1 Problem formulation

Given a search space $\mathcal{M}$ of neural architectures, and a dataset split into train set $\mathcal{D}_{train}$ and $\mathcal{D}_{valid}$, we aim to find the best architecture $m^* \in \mathcal{M}$ that

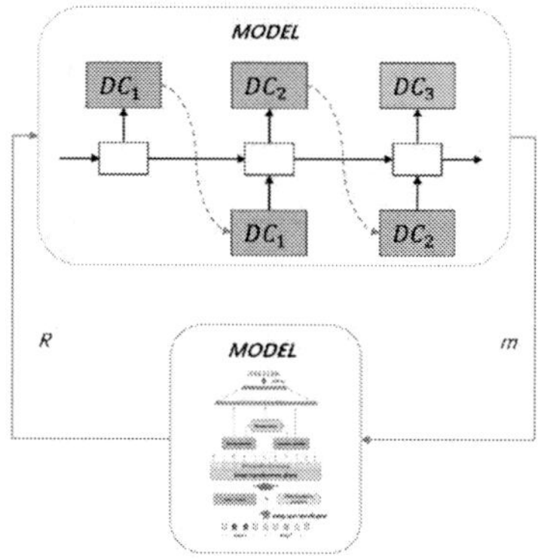

Figure 4: An illustration of the RL mechanism for architecture search.

maximizes the expected reward $\mathrm{E}[\mathcal{R}_{\mathcal{D}_{valid}}(m)]$ on the validation set $\mathcal{D}_{valid}$, i.e.,

$$m^* = \arg\max_{m \in \mathcal{M}} \mathrm{E}[R_{\mathcal{D}_{valid}}(m)]. \tag{1}$$

Figure 4 shows the reinforcement learning framework used to solve Eq 1 by continuously sampling architectures $m \in \mathcal{M}$ and evaluating the reward (performance score) $\mathcal{R}$ on the validation set $\mathcal{D}_{valid}$. First, the recurrent network generates a network description $m \in \mathcal{M}$ that corresponds to a RC model. Then, the generated model m is trained on $\mathcal{D}_{train}$ and tested on the validation set $\mathcal{D}_{valid}$. The test result is taken as a reward signal R to update the controller.

4.2 Search and evaluation

The whole procedure for model search can be divided into the search phase and evaluation phase. The search phase updates the shared parameters and the parameters for the controller in an interleaving manner, while the evaluation phase obtains multiple top-ranked models from the controller and train them till convergence on the task dataset for proper evaluations of the learned architectures.

Parameter sharing. In order to avoid training from scratch to obtain reward signals, parameter sharing is applied. The same operator is re-used for a child model if it is chosen. Specific to our architecture, the BERT encoder and the final classifier are shared for all child models. We denote the collection of all the parameters shared as Φ.

Search phase. Now we describe the interleaving optimization procedure. First, an architecture is sampled by the controller, and its network parameters are initialized with Φ. It is trained for n_c steps (which is usually a small integer), during which Φ is updated. Then, the reward of this model is obtained on $\mathcal{D}_{valid}$. With n reward signals receive, Θ is updated using policy gradients following REINFORCE (Williams, 1992):

$$\nabla_\Theta \hat{J}(\Theta) = \frac{1}{n}\sum_{i=1}^{n} \nabla_\Theta \log \pi(a_i, \Theta)(R(\Theta) - b), \tag{2}$$

where b denotes a moving average of the past rewards and it is used to reduce the variance of gradient approximation. In this work, we find $n = 1$ already works quite well. Repeating this interleaving optimization procedure for N times till the controller is well trained, then we generate k candidate architectures, evaluate them using the shared parameters, and then select the top-ranked k_e models for architecture evaluation.

Evaluation phase. In this phase, the top-ranked models are trained with the whole train set, and validated on the dev set to select the best checkpoint for prediction on the test set. Note that the shared parameters Φ are discarded in this phase, and the learned architecture is trained from scratch. To fully evaluate each architecture, we run a grid search for the optimal hyper-parameters including learning rate, batch size and warm-up steps. After the optimal combination of hyper-parameters is selected, the model is run several times to ensure replication.

4.3 Improving search

Now we propose a few methods to stabilize the search results and improve the search performance.

Heterogeneous parameter sharing. First, the reward signals directly relies on the parameter sharing mechanism, thus we should think deeper into how to design proper parameter sharing strategies for RC model search. Parameter sharing in ENAS is unconditional. Note that to much or too little parameter sharing can generate un-reliable reward signals, guiding the controller to wrong directions. Thus based on our extensive experiments, we now present our parameter sharing strategies, which we will call heterogeneous parameter sharing, since our idea is to share parameters among modules that plays similar roles in the model architectures. The details are as follows: (a) first, note that the entity span identification method entity_tokens significantly alter the original sentence, thus, it is natural for it to use a different BERT encoder in the child models. (b) since entities and contexts play quite different roles in the RC tasks, the aggregators for entities and contexts will not share parameters. Note that start_pooler and dr_pooler have a common component, which is a linear layer followed by a non-linear module, thus the linear layer will be shared in these two aggregators for entities or for contexts. However, we will use the linear layer of the BERT pooler to initialize all the linear layers of start_pooler and dr_pooler.

Multiple copies of shared parameters. Note that all child models have a BERT encoder and a classifier layer, thus parameters in these modules may over-fit quickly. Thus, during search training, we maintain multiple copies of these modules, and each time we initialize a child model, a copy of BERT encoder and classifier layer will be randomly selected from shared parameters Φ. After updating, these copies will be stored back to Φ.

Search warm-ups At the beginning of training, the shared parameters are not trained, thus reward signals generated are unreliable. Thus, at the first few epochs, the controller will generate child models to train on the dataset, but it will not be updated.

5 Experiments

Due to resource limitations, we assign up to 2 NVIDIA V100 GPU cards to each tasks.

5.1 Datasets

We run experiments on 8 different benchmark datasets, semeval10 (Hendrickx et al., 2009),[2] tacred (Zhang et al., 2017), kbp37 (Zhang and Wang, 2015), wiki80 (Han et al., 2019), deft2020 (Spala et al., 2019), i2b2 (zlem et al., 2011), ddi (Herrero-Zazo et al., 2013), chemprot (Krallinger et al., 2017). These tasks are from various domains and are different in the respects of dataset sizes, sentence length, entity mention length, etc, to demonstrate that our method is robust for various RC tasks. Detailed descriptions and statistics are provided in the Appendix.

5.2 Search protocol

During search phase, the interleaving optimization process is run 100 epochs. Throughout this work, we use the base uncased version of BERT (Devlin et al., 2018) as the sentence encoder, and its

[2]This dataset does not establish a default split for development, so for this work we adopt the same train/dev split with that provided by OpenNRE (Han et al., 2019). Thus, we cannot adopt the reported results for semeval10 on Table 1 of Baldini Soares et al. (2019).

parameters are fine-tuned to better adjust to downstream tasks. During search, 4 copies of BERT model checkpoints are maintained, 2 for method entity_tokens and 2 for the other two entity span identifiers, so each time we initialize a child model, a BERT checkpoint is randomly selected and its parameters can be updated. If the entity position embedding is concatenated after the BERT output, its size is set to be 12.

During search, each child model is trained with 4 batches of training data and evaluated on a single batch of valid data, and the evaluation batch size is 4 times the training batch size. The learning rate for the controller is set at 1e-4, and the learning rate and batch size for the sampled architectures are manually tuned to obtain better search results. During search, the number of warm-up steps for the BERT encoders is set to be equal to 0.8 of a epoch, and the warm-up steps for search is set to be 1.5 epochs.

5.3 Architecture evaluation protocol

In this work, we differentiate between a NAS method's performance and that of a learned model. We obtain the former by running architecture search 5 times. The best learned model's performance will be regarded as the NAS method's performance in each run. The best learned model in each search is also run for 10 times.

To make our results more reproducible, each learned model or each baseline model is trained for 10 times, and the mean and variance of the performance will be reported. And for evaluating the search method, after the search phase, 30 model architectures are sampled from the trained controller, and they are ranked via their performance on the valid data when they are initialized using the shared parameters. Then the top-ranked 5 models are trained from scratch till convergence on the whole training data of the task to formally evaluate their performances. The best learned model's performance of a search run is regarded as the search method's performance. In this work, we will report the mean and standard deviation of the search method performances in 5 independent runs.

To compare our methods with random search, for each task, we randomly samples 10 different models with a randomly initialized controller, since the GPU time for training 10 models is guaranteed to be larger than an entire search and evaluation process described above.

To thoroughly evaluate a learned model or a baseline model, we run a random search of 10 times on the following space for the optimal combination of the following key hyper-parameters:

- learning rate = 1e-4, 5e-5, 2e-5, 1e-5;
- training batch size = 128, 64, 32;
- warm-up steps = 0.8, 1.0 of the number of steps in an epoch.

The hyper-params for the baseline models are reported in the Appendix.

5.4 Baseline models

In this work, we select two strong baselines for comparison. The first one is **BERT-entity**, the best model from Baldini Soares et al. (2019). The second is **R-BERT** by Wu and He (2019). **BERT-entity** and **R-BERT** are implemented by OpenNRE (Han et al., 2019). The two models are special cases in our search space. The baseline models also have to go through the above reproducibility protocols. We will not compare with traditional deep-learning based model in the pre-BERT era, since **BERT-entity** significantly outperforms them.[3]

5.5 Results on Benchmark datasets

The results on the 8 benchmarks RC datasets are reported in Table 1. We report both the performance of the search methods and the performance of the best model learned on each task using *AutoRC*. For all eight tasks, *AutoRC* successfully obtains higher average scores than the baseline models. In addition, we find that *AutoRC* outperforms naive ENAS and random search and its results are more stable. In addition, we can see that the best learned model outperforms the baseline models significantly. One observation can be made is that the test results of the search architectures are consistently stable than the baseline, which also validates that our method are efficient in finding a task-specific model for the task at hand.

Figure 5, 6 and 7 report the best searched architectures for the deft2020, i2b2 and kbp37 tasks. We can see that learned architectures can be quite

[3]This work only considers the effects of architecture design, thus some of the SOTAs may not provide fair comparison. KnowBert (Peters et al., 2019) explicitly incorporates external KGs. Tao et al. (2019) take advantage of syntactic priors. Before submission, we run the REDN (Li and Tian, 2020) model (by using their code and re-implement by our self), but the results are not comparable to the results in their paper.

Model	semeval10	tacred	kbp37	wiki80	deft2020	i2b2	ddi	chemprot
R-BERT	88.19±0.234	69.63±0.178	64.15±0.285	85.38±0.158	60.12±0.875	81.88±0.547	75.73±0.786	66.77±0.336
BERT-entity	88.35±0.159	69.97 ± 0.198	64.20±0.273	85.35±0.141	60.19±0.723	81.94±0.691	75.66±0.712	66.86±0.393
random search	87.61±0.316	69.15±0.376	63.90±0.516	83.46±0.378	58.19±1.968	81.33±1.364	74.23±0.653	66.04±0.873
naive ENAS	88.23±0.256	69.98±0.267	64.25±0.412	85.38±0.286	61.57±0.727	82.18±0.632	75.57±0.598	66.94±0.453
AutoRC	88.53±0.212	70.06±0.242	64.32±0.414	85.46±0.143	62.87±0.632	82.76±0.587	75.72±0.532	67.15±0.367
$AR_{semeval10}$	**88.89**±0.165	-	-	-	-	-	-	-
AR_{tacred}	-	**70.87**±0.167	-	-	-	-	-	-
AR_{kbp37}	-	-	**64.96**±0.185	85.63±0.175	-	81.87±0.778	75.58±0.704	-
AR_{wiki80}	-	-	64.58±0.169	**85.98**±0.134	-	82.32±0.604	75.89±0.633	-
$AR_{deft2020}$	-	-	-	-	**63.82**±0.593	-	-	-
AR_{i2b2}	-	-	64.43±0.166	85.46±0.164	-	**83.59**±0.478	76.05±0.658	-
AR_{ddi}	-	-	64.37±0.172	85.39±0.159	-	82.92±0.454	**76.73**±0.475	-
$AR_{chemprot}$	-	-			-	-	-	**67.95**±0.283

Table 1: Test results for eight relation classification tasks. The performance metric is micro F1 for all tasks except for deft2020 which uses macro F1. Results from the baseline model are obtained with the help of OpenNRE (Han et al., 2019).

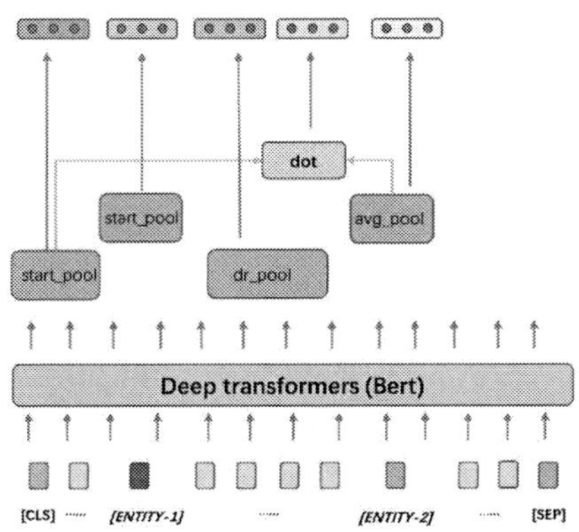

Figure 5: $AR_{deft2020}$, the best learned architecture on deft2020.

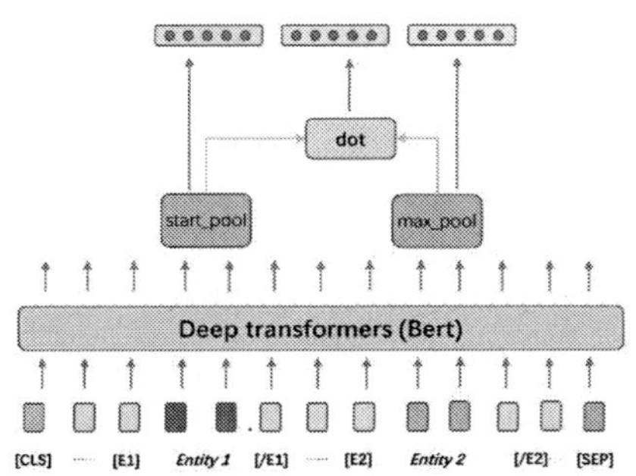

Figure 6: AR_{i2b2}, the best learned architecture on i2b2.

different, thus validating the necessity of task specificity. The learned models are different in the following three aspects. First, $AR_{deft2020}$ choose to replace entity mentions with entity tokens. We hypothesis that in deft-2020, the entities are often quite long, thus replacing entity mentions with entity tokens is beneficial for the model to understand

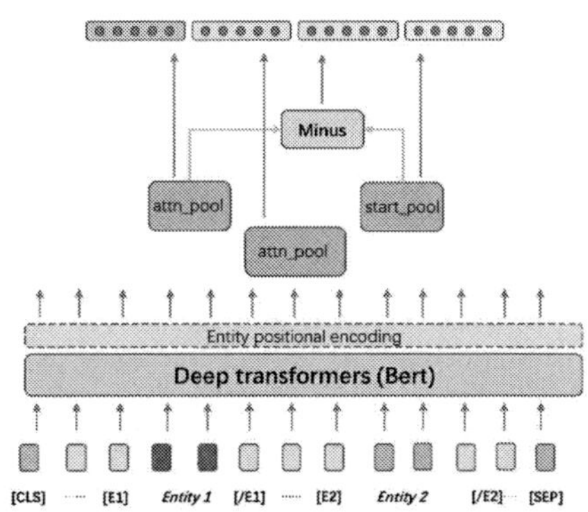

Figure 7: AR_{kbp37}, the best learned architecture on kbp37.

the contexts' structural patterns. Second, note that $AR_{deft2020}$ uses start_pool to aggregate context piece c_0, which is the representation of [CLS] token. In addition, it includes the representation of context c_1, which is also used in AR_{kbp37}. Third, $AR_{deft2020}$ incorporates the interaction between context c_0 and the two entities, while AR_{i2b2} and AR_{kbp37} include the interaction between the two entities. Differences in the learned architectures for different tasks indicate the necessity of task specific architectures, which is challenging without the help of NAS. We believe there are two aspects that can affect the learned models. First, different domains have different contexts, which may lead to different models. Second, the formulation of data. For example, in deft-2020, some extended definitions of scientific concepts are annotated as entities. Thus, the avg entity mention length (18.5) is quite different from other tasks (2.3 in "ddi").

In Table 1, we also study how does an architecture learned on one task performs on another.

Search space	deft2020	i2b2
$\mathcal{M}$	**63.82** ± 0.593	**83.59** ± 0.478
$\mathcal{M}_1$	63.45 ± 0.698	83.22 ± 0.514
$\mathcal{M}_2$	62.31 ± 0.423	82.68 ± 0.483
$\mathcal{M}_3$	61.78 ± 0.893	82.35 ± 0.558
BERT-entity	60.19 ± 0.723	81.94 ± 0.691

Table 2: Results of ablation study on the search space.

Note that when evaluated on a different task, an architecture's hyper-parameters are tuned again, following the procedure described in subsection 5.3. The architecture learned on kbp37, which is an open-domain dataset, AR_{kbp37}, transfer well on wiki80. But it does not perform well on the two tasks of medical domain, i2b2 and ddi. However, the learned architectures learned on i2b2 and ddi transfer well on each other and perform comparably well. The above results demonstrate that the learned models have certain ability for task transfer, but its suitability is significantly affected by the domains of the tasks.

5.6 Ablation study on the search space

We further investigate the specific contributions by the different components of the search space. For this purpose, we create three smaller search space. The first one, denoted as $\mathcal{M}_1$, which does not allow any interactions among entity features and context features. The second one, $\mathcal{M}_2$ further reduce $\mathcal{M}_1$ by limiting that the pooling operation available is the start pooling operation. The third one, $\mathcal{M}_3$, further forbid contextual features. If further limit the entity span identification method to be entity markers, the search space is reduced to the baseline **BERT-entity** model. The search and evaluation protocols on the reduced search space strictly follow the previous subsections.

Ablation study for the search space is done on deft2020 and i2b2. Results are reported in Table 2. For deft2020, alternating the method for span identification provides significant performance gain on deft2020, and interaction among features is also important. For i2b2, the most significant performance drop occurs when the pooling operations are limited, indicating that even for powerful bi-directional context encoder like BERT, considering different pooling operations are beneficial.

5.7 Ablations on the modifications for search method

In this subsection, we will show that our modifications to the search method, i.e., the naive ENAS, are indeed effective and necessary. Here we use $AutoRC$ to denote our method, which is the combination of ENAS and our proposed modifications. We now experiment on three variations to $AutoRC$. First, $AutoRC_1$ drops heterogeneous parameter sharing, that is, all input formats share the same BERT encoder, and all context and all entity representations share the same aggregators. The second variant, $AutoRC_2$, is to maintain single copies of shared weights. The third variant, $AutoRC_3$, is the one that drops search warm-ups.

Search Method	deft2020	i2b2
naive ENAS	61.57 ± 0.727	82.18 ± 0.632
$AutoRC$	**62.87** ± 0.632	**82.76** ± 0.587
$AutoRC_1$	62.38 ± 0.689	82.42 ± 0.616
$AutoRC_2$	62.53 ± 0.672	82.56 ± 0.595
$AutoRC_3$	62.49 ± 0.708	82.61 ± 0.614

Table 3: Ablation study on the search methods.

The average search performance, which is the average score of the best learned model at each search run, and their standard deviations are reported on Table 3. From the results, dropping any of three strategies we propose results in performance drop and increased variance in results. And changing the parameter sharing strategies cause the most significant performance drops on both tasks. The above results demonstrate that our proposed modifications make the reward signal during search more reliable, thus resulting in better searched architectures.

Method	OntoNotes	CoNLL04
SpanBERT	85.3	-
SpERT	-	88.94
$AutoRC$	86.1	89.87

Table 4: Experiments on the coreference resolution and span based NER.

5.8 Applications to other entity related tasks

In Table 4, we apply our $AutoRC$ framework to the other two entity related tasks, i.e., coreference resolution and span based NER. $AutoRC$ can directly apply to coreference resolution since it essentially asks the model to determine whether an expression refers to an entity. It can also be applied to span based NER since it asks the model to determine whether a span in the sentence is an entity.

We experiment on the OntoNotes coreference resolution benchmark (Pradhan et al., 2012). The metric is MUC F1 and we choose the state-of-the-art (SOTA) SpanBERT (Joshi et al., 2019) as baseline. The results show that our $AutoRC$ framework can effectively improve the performances of the SpanBERT checkpoint.

We experiment on the NER task of CoNLL04 (Roth and tau Yih, 2004), which uses entity level F1 as metric. Eberts and Ulges (2020) provides a SOTA baseline. The results show that performance improves via $AutoRC$.

6 Conclusion

In this work, we first construct a comprehensive search space to include many import design choices for a BERT based RC model. Then we design an efficient search method with the help of RL to navigate on this search space. To improve the search results, parameter sharing strategies different from ENAS are designed. To avoid over-fitting, we maintain multiple copies of shared weights during search. To stabilize the reward signal, search warm-ups are applied. Experiments on eight benchmark RC tasks show that our method can outperform the standard BERT based RC model significantly. Ablation study shows our search space design and proposed modifications are effective.

References

Namhyuk Ahn, Byungkon Kang, and Kyung-Ah Sohn. 2018. Fast, accurate, and lightweight super-resolution with cascading residual network. In *ECCV*.

Livio Baldini Soares, Nicholas FitzGerald, Jeffrey Ling, and Tom Kwiatkowski. 2019. Matching the blanks: Distributional similarity for relation learning. In *Proceedings of the 57th Annual Meeting of the Association for Computational Linguistics*, pages 2895–2905, Florence, Italy. Association for Computational Linguistics.

James S Bergstra, Rémi Bardenet, Yoshua Bengio, and Balázs Kégl. 2011. Algorithms for hyper-parameter optimization. In *Advances in neural information processing systems*, pages 2546–2554.

Han Cai, Ligeng Zhu, and Song Han. 2018. Proxylessnas: Direct neural architecture search on target task and hardware. *arXiv preprint arXiv:1812.00332*.

Qian Chen, Xiaodan Zhu, Zhenhua Ling, Si Wei, Hui Jiang, and Diana Inkpen. 2016. Enhanced lstm for natural language inference. *arXiv preprint arXiv:1609.06038*.

Jacob Devlin, Ming-Wei Chang, Kenton Lee, and Kristina Toutanova. 2018. Bert: Pre-training of deep bidirectional transformers for language understanding. *arXiv preprint arXiv:1810.04805*.

Markus Eberts and A. Ulges. 2020. Span-based joint entity and relation extraction with transformer pre-training. In *ECAI*.

Markus Eberts and Adrian Ulges. 2019. Span-based Joint Entity and Relation Extraction with Transformer Pre-training. *arXiv e-prints*, page arXiv:1909.07755.

Golnaz Ghiasi, Tsung-Yi Lin, and Quoc V. Le. 2019. Nas-fpn: Learning scalable feature pyramid architecture for object detection. In *CVPR*.

Jingjing Gong, Xipeng Qiu, Shaojing Wang, and Xuanjing Huang. 2018. Information aggregation via a dynamic routing for sequence encoding. *arXiv preprint arXiv:1806.01501*.

Xu Han, Tianyu Gao, Yuan Yao, Deming Ye, Zhiyuan Liu, and Maosong Sun. 2019. OpenNRE: An open and extensible toolkit for neural relation extraction. In *Proceedings of EMNLP-IJCNLP: System Demonstrations*, pages 169–174.

Xu Han, Hao Zhu, Pengfei Yu, Ziyun Wang, Yuan Yao, Zhiyuan Liu, and Maosong Sun. 2018. FewRel: A large-scale supervised few-shot relation classification dataset with state-of-the-art evaluation. In *Proceedings of the 2018 Conference on Empirical Methods in Natural Language Processing*, pages 4803–4809, Brussels, Belgium. Association for Computational Linguistics.

Iris Hendrickx, Su Nam Kim, Zornitsa Kozareva, Preslav Nakov, Diarmuid Ó Séaghdha, Sebastian Padó, Marco Pennacchiotti, Lorenza Romano, and Stan Szpakowicz. 2009. Semeval-2010 task 8: Multi-way classification of semantic relations between pairs of nominals. In *Proceedings of the Workshop on Semantic Evaluations: Recent Achievements and Future Directions*, SEW '09, page 94–99, USA. Association for Computational Linguistics.

María Herrero-Zazo, Isabel Segura-Bedmar, Paloma Martínez, and Thierry Declerck. 2013. The ddi corpus: An annotated corpus with pharmacological substances and drug–drug interactions. *Journal of biomedical informatics*, 46(5):914–920.

Mandar Joshi, Danqi Chen, Y. Liu, Daniel S. Weld, Luke Zettlemoyer, and Omer Levy. 2019. Spanbert: Improving pre-training by representing and predicting spans. *Transactions of the Association for Computational Linguistics*, 8:64–77.

Martin Krallinger, Obdulia Rabal, Saber A Akhondi, et al. 2017. Overview of the biocreative vi chemical-protein interaction track. In *Proceedings of the sixth BioCreative challenge evaluation workshop*, volume 1, pages 141–146.

Cheng Li and Ye Tian. 2020. Downstream Model Design of Pre-trained Language Model for Relation Extraction Task. *arXiv e-prints*, page arXiv:2004.03786.

Chenxi Liu, Liang-Chieh Chen, Florian Schroff, Hartwig Adam, Wei Hua, Alan L. Yuille, and Li Fei-Fei. 2019. Auto-deeplab: Hierarchical neural architecture search for semantic image segmentation. In *CVPR*.

H. Liu, K. Simonyan, and Y. Yang. 2018. Darts: Differentiable architecture search. *arXiv preprint arXiv:1806.09055*.

Yifan Peng, Shankai Yan, and Zhiyong Lu. 2019. Transfer learning in biomedical natural language processing: An evaluation of bert and elmo on ten benchmarking datasets. In *Proceedings of the 2019 Workshop on Biomedical Natural Language Processing (BioNLP 2019)*, pages 58–65.

Matthew E. Peters, Mark Neumann, Robert L Logan, Roy Schwartz, Vidur Joshi, Sameer Singh, and Noah A. Smith. 2019. Knowledge enhanced contextual word representations. In *EMNLP*.

Hieu Pham, Melody Y. Guan, Barret Zoph, Quoc V. Le, and Jeff Dean. 2018. Efficient Neural Architecture Search via Parameter Sharing. *arXiv e-prints*, page arXiv:1802.03268.

Hieu Pham, Melody Y. Guan, Barret Zoph, Quoc V. Le, and Jeff Dean. 2018. Efficient neural architecture search via parameter sharing. In *ICML*.

Sameer Pradhan, Alessandro Moschitti, N. Xue, O. Uryupina, and Yuchen Zhang. 2012. Conll-2012 shared task: Modeling multilingual unrestricted coreference in ontonotes. In *EMNLP-CoNLL Shared Task*.

D. Roth and Wen tau Yih. 2004. A linear programming formulation for global inference in natural language tasks. In *CoNLL*.

Yatian Shen and Xuanjing Huang. 2016. Attention-based convolutional neural network for semantic relation extraction. In *Proceedings of COLING 2016, the 26th International Conference on Computational Linguistics: Technical Papers*, pages 2526–2536, Osaka, Japan. The COLING 2016 Organizing Committee.

David R So, Chen Liang, and Quoc V Le. 2019. The evolved transformer. *arXiv preprint arXiv:1901.11117*.

Richard Socher, Brody Huval, Christopher D. Manning, and Andrew Y. Ng. 2012. Semantic compositionality through recursive matrix-vector spaces. In *Proceedings of the 2012 Joint Conference on Empirical Methods in Natural Language Processing and Computational Natural Language Learning*.

Sasha Spala, Nicholas A. Miller, Yiming Yang, Franck Dernoncourt, and Carl Dockhorn. 2019. DEFT: A corpus for definition extraction in free- and semi-structured text. In *Proceedings of the 13th Linguistic Annotation Workshop*, pages 124–131, Florence, Italy. Association for Computational Linguistics.

Qiongxing Tao, Xiangfeng Luo, and Hao Wang. 2019. Enhancing Relation Extraction Using Syntactic Indicators and Sentential Contexts. *arXiv e-prints*, page arXiv:1912.01858.

Ronald J Williams. 1992. Simple statistical gradient-following algorithms for connectionist reinforcement learning. *Machine learning*, 8(3-4):229–256.

Shanchan Wu and Yifan He. 2019. Enriching Pre-trained Language Model with Entity Information for Relation Classification. *arXiv e-prints*, page arXiv:1905.08284.

D. Zeng, K. Liu, S. Lai, G. Zhou, and J. Zhao. 2014. Relation classification via convolutional deep neural network. *the 25th International Conference on Computational Linguistics: Technical Papers*, pages 2335–2344.

Dongxu Zhang and Dong Wang. 2015. Relation Classification via Recurrent Neural Network. *arXiv e-prints*, page arXiv:1508.01006.

Yuhao Zhang, Victor Zhong, Danqi Chen, Gabor Angeli, and Christopher D. Manning. 2017. Position-aware attention and supervised data improve slot filling. In *Proceedings of the 2017 Conference on Empirical Methods in Natural Language Processing*, pages 35–45, Copenhagen, Denmark. Association for Computational Linguistics.

Wei Zhu. 2020. Mvp-bert: Redesigning vocabularies for chinese bert and multi-vocab pretraining. *ArXiv*, abs/2011.08539.

Wei Zhu, Yuan Ni, Xiaoling Wang, and Guotong Xie. 2021. Discovering better model architectures for medical query understanding. In *Proceedings of the 2021 Conference of the North American Chapter of the Association for Computational Linguistics: Human Language Technologies: Industry Papers*, pages 230–237, Online. Association for Computational Linguistics.

Uzuner zlem, Brett R South, Shuying Shen, and DuVall Scott L. 2011. 2010 i2b2/va challenge on concepts, assertions, and relations in clinical text. *Journal of the American Medical Informatics Association Jamia*, 1(5):5.

B. Zoph and Q.V. Le. 2017. Neural architecture search with reinforcement learning. In *ICLR*.

A Benchmark datasets

Here we include introductions to the benchmark datasets we investigate. And the basic statistics and performance metrics are included in Table 5.

SemEval-2010 Task 8 (Hendrickx et al., 2009) (denoted as semeval10) This dataset does not establish a default split for development, so for this work we adopt the same train/dev split with that provided by OpenNRE (Han et al., 2019).

Dataset	# labels	Train	Dev	Test	sent length	Metrics
semeval2010	19	6508	1494	2718	19.09	micro F1
tacred	42	75,050	25,764	18,660	36.2	micro F1
kbp37	37	15917	1724	3405	31.09	micro F1
wiki80	80	40320	10080	5600	24.93	micro F1
deft2020	6	16727	963	1139	72.11	macro F1
i2b2	8	2496	624	6293	24.33	micro F1
ddi	5	18779	7244	5761	45.03	micro F1
chemprot	6	19460	11820	16943	49.69	micro F1

Table 5: Overview of datasets in experiments.

Wiki80 (denoted as wiki80) This dataset (Han et al., 2019) is derived from FewRel (Han et al., 2018), a large scale few-shot dataset. Since Wiki80 only has a train/val split, we randomly split the train set into a train set and val set (with 8:2 ratio), and treat the original validation set as the test set.

KBP-37 (Zhang and Wang, 2015) (denoted as kbp37). This dataset is a revision of MIML-RE annotation dataset, provided by Gabor Angeli et al. (2014). They use both the 2010 and 2013 KBP official document collections, as well as a July 2013 dump of Wikipedia as the text corpus for annotation.

DEFT-2020 Subtask 3 (denoted as deft2020) This dataset also serves as the task 6 of SemEval 2020 shared tasks. This RC task have to overcome longer contexts, longer entity mentions, and more imbalanced relation types. (Spala et al., 2019)

i2b2 2010 (denoted as i2b2) shared task collection consists of 170 medical documents for training and 256 documents for testing, which is the subset of the original dataset (zlem et al., 2011).

ChemProt (denoted as chemprot) consists of 1,820 PubMed abstracts with chemical-protein interactions annotated by domain experts and was used in the BioCreative VI text mining chemical-protein interactions shared task (Krallinger et al., 2017) [4].

DDI extraction 2013 corpus (denoted as ddi) is a collection of 792 texts selected from the DrugBank database and other 233 Medline abstracts (Herrero-Zazo et al., 2013).[5]

B Hyper-params for models on different tasks

Now we report the hyper-parameters for the baseline models and the learned models (for architecture evaluation phase). The main hyper-parameters are learning rate (lr), batch size (bsz) and warm-up steps (warm-up) for finetuning. Warm-up is reported as the proportion of steps in one epoch. One common hyper-parameter is the max sequence length, which is set as 256.

Dataset	model	lr	bsz	warm-up
semeval10	R-BERT	2e-5	64	0.8
	BERT-entity	5e-5	64	1.0
	$AR_{semeval10}$	1e-5	64	0.8
tacred	R-BERT	1e-4	128	0.8
	BERT-entity	5e-5	128	0.8
	AR_{tacred}	5e-5	128	0.8
kbp37	R-BERT	1e-5	64	0.8
	BERT-entity	2e-5	64	0.8
	AR_{kbp37}	5e-5	64	1.0
wiki80	R-BERT	5e-5	128	0.8
	BERT-entity	2e-5	64	1.0
	AR_{wiki80}	2e-5	64	1.0
deft2020	R-BERT	1e-4	64	0.8
	BERT-entity	5e-5	64	1.0
	$AR_{deft2020}$	1e-4	64	0.8
i2b2	R-BERT	2e-5	32	0.8
	BERT-entity	5e-5	32	0.8
	AR_{i2b2}	1e-5	32	0.8
ddi	R-BERT	5e-5	64	0.8
	BERT-entity	2e-5	32	0.8
	AR_{ddi}	5e-5	64	1.0
chemprot	R-BERT	5e-5	64	0.8
	BERT-entity	1e-5	128	0.8
	$AR_{chemprot}$	5e-5	64	1.0

Table 6

[4]https://biocreative.bioinformatics.udel.edu/news/corpora/

[5]http://labda.inf.uc3m.es/ddicorpus

How Low is Too Low?
A Computational Perspective on Extremely Low-Resource Languages

Rachit Bansal[1] **Himanshu Choudhary**[1] **Ravneet Punia**[1]
Niko Schenk[2†] **Jacob L Dahl**[3] **Émilie Pagé-Perron**[3]
[1] Delhi Technological University [2] Amazon Berlin, Germany [3] University of Oxford
{rachitbansal2500, himanshu.dce12, ravneet.dtu}@gmail.com
nikosch@amazon.com
{jacob.dahl, emilie.page-perron}@wolfson.ox.ac.uk

Abstract

Despite the recent advancements of attention-based deep learning architectures across a majority of Natural Language Processing tasks, their application remains limited in a low-resource setting because of a lack of pre-trained models for such languages. In this study, we make the first attempt to investigate the challenges of adapting these techniques to an extremely low-resource language – Sumerian cuneiform – one of the world's oldest written language attested from at least the beginning of the 3rd millennium BC. Specifically, we introduce the first cross-lingual information extraction pipeline for Sumerian, which includes part-of-speech tagging, named entity recognition, and machine translation. We introduce *InterpretLR*, an interpretability toolkit for low-resource NLP and use it alongside human evaluations to gauge the trained models. Notably, all our techniques and most components of our pipeline can be generalised to any low-resource language. We publicly release all our implementations including a novel data set with domain-specific pre-processing to promote further research in this domain.

1 Introduction

Sumerian is one of the oldest written languages, attested in the cuneiform texts from around 2900 BC and possibly the language of even older proto-cuneiform texts from the second half of the 4th millennium BC (Englund, 2009). Specialists in Assyriology have recently worked to digitize Sumerian scripts, annotate, and translate a part of them to modern-day languages like English and German.

In this work, we attempt to create the first information extraction and translation pipeline for Sumerian. Specifically, we focus on machine translation from Sumerian to English, and sequence labeling tasks of Named Entity Recognition (NER) and Part of Speech (POS) Tagging.

obverse.
1. `1(disz) kusz udu niga`
1 hide, grain-fed sheep;

2. `1(disz) kusz masz2 niga`
1 hide, grain-fed goat;

3. `kusz udu sa2-du11`
sheep hides, regular offerings,

4. `ki {d}iszkur-illat-ta`
from Adda-illat,

reverse.
1. `a-na-ah-i3-li2`
Anah-ili;

2. `szu ba-an-ti`
did receive.

3. `iti ezem-an-na`
Month: An-festival,

4. `mu na-ru2-a-mah mu-ne-du3`
Year: He erected the great stele for them.

Figure 1: Tablets inscribed with Sumerian cuneiform script, their corresponding digitized transliterations, and human-translated English text for each line.

Figure 1 shows a sample of our raw data where the Sumerian text has been derived from the tablet-inscribed cuneiform script along with its human-interpreted English translations. Creating an annotated corpus for such a language is a tedious task. We obtain our data from openly available sources and corpora, painstakingly annotated and translated by human experts. Yet, for languages like Sumerian, which are not fully-understood by humans themselves, transferring knowledge and patterns to learning algorithms from this limited data becomes extremely difficult. The consequent challenge posed for NER and POS tagging is evident. Lack of annotated data and fuzzy character-level text makes it hard for a model to generalise, irrespective of its size.

Data sets and training subroutines are available at linktr.ee/rachitbansal

[†]Work was done prior to joining Amazon at Goethe University Frankfurt

Proceedings of the Joint Conference of the 59th Annual Meeting of the Association for Computational Linguistics and the 11th International Joint Conference on Natural Language Processing: Student Research Workshop, pages 44–59
August 5–6, 2021. ©2021 Association for Computational Linguistics

In case of machine translation, the labeled data is composed of incomplete and short phrase-like sentences, especially on the target side. This makes the context largely ambiguous. Moreover, we find that for a majority of medieval and ancient languages the target-side translated text is highly incoherent with modern-day English language text, making it impossible to use the latter in semi-supervised and unsupervised settings.

Throughout this study, we elaborate on such challenges faced when working with low-resource languages, and talk about what makes some of these languages like Sumerian 'extremely' low-resource. Through extensive experimentation, evaluation, and analysis we further introduce specific algorithms and modifications to work around them.

In all, our contribution is three-fold:

1. Building and analyzing a variety of algorithms on the unexplored human-annotated Sumerian dataset for sequence labeling tasks of POS Tagging and NER. (§3)
2. Introducing the problem of *Target-side Incoherence* for low-resource settings and its effect on semi-supervised and unsupervised machine translation (§4.2). Further investigating specific modifications and methodologies to cope-up with these constraints. (§4)
3. Introducing *InterpretLR*, a generalisable toolkit to interpret low-resource NLP. We apply it to further study, compare, and evaluate all of our proposed techniques for machine translation and sequence labeling. (§7)

Throughout this work, we have conducted human studies and evaluation for our models, in addition to automated metrics. For gauging our models with *InterpretLR*, we have made use of human annotations.

2 Background

2.1 Data

Sumerian is an ancient language from Iraq that was written using the cuneiform script. While Basque and Turkish display some similarities (split-ergativity, agglutinativity), it is a language isolate (Englund, 2009). We have found artifacts dating to around 2900 BC with Sumerian texts inscribed until the first century AD. Most of the Sumerian texts found to this day are administrative in nature as, during the third dynasty of the Ur III Period, the state administration swell to an unprecedented level of activity which was not seen again later in the history of Mesopotamian culture. All through this study, our evaluation sets are composed of Ur III Admin text only and it acts as our **in-domain** data.

Part of the datasets we used were assembled from the Cuneiform Digital Library Initiative (CDLI)[1], Machine Translation and Automated Analysis of Cuneiform languages (MTAAC) project (Pagé-Perron et al., 2017)[2] and The Electronic Text Corpus of Sumerian Literature (ETCSL) dataset[3]. CDLI and MTAAC datasets contain the Ur III Administrative (Admin) texts[4] which are preserved by the CDLI[5]. The MTAAC and ETCSL corpora were both manually annotated for morphology by cuneiform linguistics.

We divided the data between training and testing sets, and then to reduce the data sparsity, we performed text augmentation using a set of labeled named entities for these sets separately. This increased our combined number of phrases from 25,000 to 48,000, representing our final dataset for sequence labeling. Figures 2 and 3 provide the distribution of word tokens in our final pre-annotated dataset. The corpus consists of phrases with lengths ranging from 1 to 19 words. These phrases are small since they are translated line by line from the scripts. Around 2,500 phrases were used for testing, while the 45,500 were employed for training purposes.

For machine translation, the final dataset summarizes as (i) 10,520 parallel phrases from the Ur III administrative corpus; (ii) 88,460 parallel phrases, all genres combined; and (iii) all monolingual Sumerian data (1.43 million phrases). In all cases, phrases are short, generally ranging from 1 to 5-word tokens.

2.2 Related Work

Past work aimed at machine translation of Sumerian-English (Pagé-Perron et al., 2017; Punia et al., 2020a) have used the minimal bitext upon a variety of general statistical and neural supervised techniques. However, they do not handle the text-level peculiarities any differently than one would

[1] `https://cdli.ucla.edu`

[2] `https://cdli-gh.github.io/mtaac/`

[3] `http://http://etcsl.orinst.ox.ac.uk/`

[4] The Third Dynasty of Ur is a cultural and temporal period ranging in $\sim$2112 – 2004 BC, in Mesopotamia

[5] `https://github.com/cdli-gh/data`, `https://github.com/cdli-gh/mtaac_gold_corpus/tree/workflow/morph/to_dict`

do for a high-resource language, thus, often failing to capture context, resulting in poor and inconsistent translations. Techniques, learning algorithms, and architectures that optimally use the vast monolingual data and parallel sentences while keeping in mind the several linguistic limitations are motivated in such a scenario. Thus, we experiment on semi-supervised and unsupervised techniques across the three categories of data augmentation (Sennrich et al., 2016; He et al., 2016), knowledge transfer (Zoph et al., 2016), and pre-training (Conneau and Lample, 2019; Song et al., 2019).

In the past, Pagé-Perron et al. (2017) applied statistical models for morphological analysis and information extraction for Sumerian. Although, due to the unavailability of annotated data, these models could not generalise well. Liu et al. (2015) and Luo et al. (2015) used an unsupervised approach for NER with the help of domain experts and used contextual and spelling rules to build the model. They also post-processed their outputs automatically, which enhanced their results. In this work, we thoroughly investigate a wide range of algorithms for these sequence labeling tasks and consequently take a first step towards effective information extraction for Sumerian.

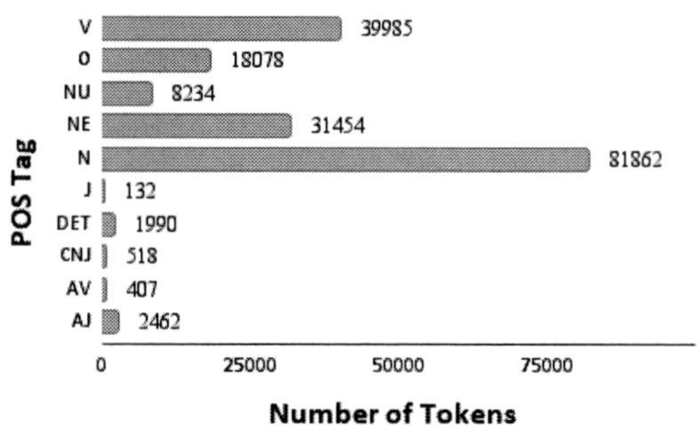

Figure 2: Composition of the POS tagging dataset. Here, "NE" stands for named entities, "O" stands for unstructured words. Other tags are in accordance with ORACC.

3 Part of Speech Tagging and Named Entity Recognition

In this section, we talk about the various algorithms that we investigated to carry out the sequence labeling tasks of POS tagging and NER for Sumerian. The subsequent experimental results are described and discussed in Section 6.

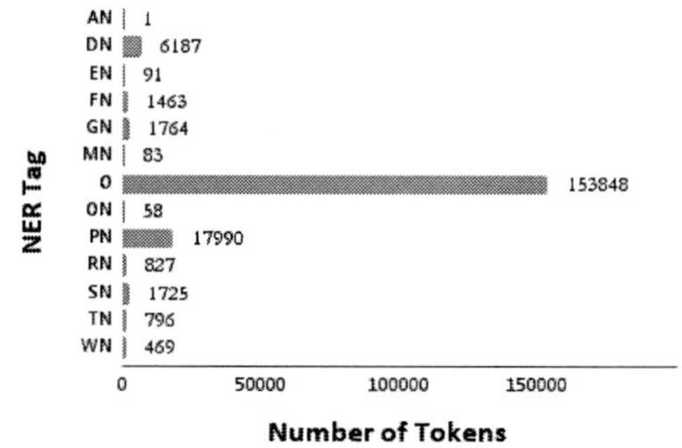

Figure 3: Composition of our NER dataset. Tags are in accordance with ORACC.

Conditional Random Fields CRF (Lafferty et al., 2001) is a discriminative probabilistic classifier, which optimises the weights or parameters in order to maximize the conditional probability distribution $P(y \mid x)$. They take set of input features (language or domain specific) into account, using the learned weights associated with these features and previous labels to predict the current label. Since CRFs use feature sets (rules) which are language-specific, it makes the model more robust specially for very low-resource languages. In our case we developed domain specific rules with the help of previous studies (Liu et al., 2015; Luo et al., 2015) and language experts. A set of these rules are mentioned in the Appendix.

Bi-directional LSTM We also experiment across Recurrent Neural Networks (RNNs) to deal with the sequential text input. We employ Bi-LSTM (Hochreiter and Schmidhuber, 1997; Schuster and Paliwal, 1997) in particular. As in Huang et al. (2015), an additional CRF layer is used for efficient usage of sentence level tag information and past input features by LSTM cells.

FLAIR Akbik et al. (2018) introduced a Contextual String Embedding for Sequence Labeling, FLAIR, which has shown great promise for NER across various languages (Akbik et al., 2019b). We make use of the two distinct properties of its embeddings: (i) training without any explicit notion of words and fundamentally modeling the words as a sequence of characters, and (ii) deriving and using the context from surrounding tokens.
We train the bi-directional character language model using the Sumerian monolingual phrases and retrieve the contextual embedding for each word which we then pass into the vanilla Bi-LSTM CRF model.

RoBERTa We also investigate the transformer-based language model, RoBERTa (Liu et al., 2019). The encoder is first pre-trained on our Sumerian monolingual data, and then fine-tuned on our downstream sequence labeling tasks using the labeled data.

4 Machine Translation

In this section, we present our experiments for machine translation, primarily focusing on specific data and algorithmic modeling techniques which may be generalised for any extremely low-resource language that may or may not suffer from *Target-side Incoherence*, a phenomenon which we also introduce herein. All results are summarised in Table 1.

4.1 Supervised NMT

In order to create a benchmark for the semi-supervised and unsupervised approaches, we perform supervised machine translation using the limited bitext available ($\sim$10,000 phrases). We perform experiments on a variety of data configurations which are given by:

1. `UrIIISeg`: Follows the format as present in the original texts provided by Assyriologists and used in the past attempts for Sumerian-English machine translation (Pagé-Perron et al., 2017; Punia et al., 2020b). It contains only *in-domain* Ur III Admin text with line-by-line translated *segments*, each of 1-5 words. Amounts to total 10528 segments.
2. `UrIIIComp`: Also contains the *in-domain* data only, but multiple segments are concatenated together to form complete *sentences*. The 'completeness' of a sentence is ensured through punctuation marks. Since multiple segments are combined, it amounts to only 4792 sentences.
3. `AllSeg`: Contains *all* of out-of-domain Sumerian text *segments* in addition to in-domain Ur III Admin text alone. The additional text varies across a wide range of genres such as literary, lexical, ritual, and legal, resulting into a corpus size of 88466 segments.
4. `AllComp`: Combines the additional features of 2. and 3., thus comprising of a total of 32694 complete text *sentences* from *all* out-of-domain as well as in-domain genres.

We make use of the vanilla transformer encoder and decoder architecture (Vaswani et al., 2017) for all our supervised machine translation experiments over these three different bitext configurations. Noting the supervised MT results from Table 1, the `AllComp` text configuration is used for all further experiments. The computational configurations are mentioned in Section 5.

4.2 Semi-Supervised and Unsupervised NMT

We observed that one of the primary reasons for the lack of success of semi-supervised and unsupervised algorithms for low-resource settings, specially for ancient languages, is *the lack of coherence between monolingual texts for the target-side language in the modern-day corpora and the target-side text in the available bitext.* We refer to this as the ***Target-side Incoherence*** (*TSIC*) problem for such languages.

Specifically, as can be seen from Figure 1, the transliterated English text in our parallel corpora is vastly different from general modern-day English texts. In Sumerian, this is because the text has been human-translated to English on the level of words and small segments due to insufficient knowledge of the language. This results into a contextually distorted English language text, as compared what we see in general corpora. This leads to multiple pitfalls. Most significantly, the colossal monolingual data available for a data-rich target-side language (i.e., English in this case) can no longer be used. This *Target-side Incoherence* holds true for most ancient language texts like Sumerian, which makes them **'extremely' low-resource**.

In this section, we elaborate on the problems caused due to *TSIC* and further present findings on adapting various semi-supervised and unsupervised NMT techniques to deal with them.

Forward Translation Back-translation (BT) (Sennrich et al., 2016) has been widely used and analysed for NMT across a large set of language pairs. BT uses a reverse model, Sumerian $\leftarrow$ English trained on the existing parallel corpora, when the task is to translate from Sumerian $\rightarrow$ English, and applies it on the target-side monolingual corpus. The synthetic samples thus generated are added to the source-side corpus and a new reverse model is trained on the augmented dataset. It has been shown to outperform its forward counterpart, Forward Translation (FT) (Zhang and Zong, 2016; Burlot and Yvon, 2018), which instead uses a forward (Sumerian $\rightarrow$ English) model to augment

the target-side of the bitext.
However, due to *TSIC*, the target-side monolingual data falls into a completely different distribution than what a Sumerian ← English model is trained on. Using back-translation in such a scenario results into a poor source-side augmentation, doing more harm than good. Keeping this in mind, we rely on forward-translation (FT), thus using the Sumerian monolingual text.

We divide the Sumerian monolingual data into 8 shards, each containing ∼100,000 monolingual `AllComp` sentences each. The FT process takes place for each shard and the Transformer model is trained after each shard is forward-translated.

Large scale studies (Edunov et al., 2018; Wu et al., 2019) have shown the heavy dependency of BT and FT on aspects like sampling methods and the amount of parallel data. The performance with non-MAP (where, MAP stands for *maximum a posteriori*) estimation methods like nuclear sampling (Holtzman et al., 2018) and beam search with noise improves almost-linearly with the amount of bitext, and thus, for low-resource settings (∼80,000 sentence pairs), MAP methods have been shown to give better results. This was also observed in our experiments and the reported results are obtained using beam search (§5).

Cross-Lingual Language Model Pre-training We further make use of XLM (Conneau and Lample, 2019) to carry out a wide range of experiments for both unsupervised and semi-supervised fine-tuning techniques. Considering the lack of original target-side monolingual text due to *TSIC*, the following target data configurations were used for pre-training the XLM:

1. `WMT`: This configuration ignores *TSIC* and composes the entire text with the WMT '18 English corpora. This amounts to a large set of 20M sentences, which are however incoherent with our parallel training + evaluation set.
2. `Orig`: Composed of all the English side texts in `UrIIISeg`, `UrIIIComp`, `AllSeg` and `AllComp` bitext configurations combined. Contains only ∼60,000 sentences.
3. `Mixed`: This combines all of `Orig` with a set of `WMT`, such that the net size of the corpus equalizes the Sumerian monolingual corpus, i.e., 1.5M sentences.

In the pre-training phase, we perform various experiments over different combinations of MLM and TLM objectives. The XLM is, then, fine-tuned on a denoising auto-encoding objective for unsupervised while cross-reference machine translation objective over the parallel data for semi-supervised training. BT steps are also performed in both cases.

Data Augmentation In order to further reduce the effect of *TSIC* on the model performance and to allow the model to attend to a larger and more diverse volume of target text during pre-training, we make use of the following data augmentation techniques:

1. `BERT`: Replacing words by the spatially closest words measured using cosine similarity over BERT (Devlin et al., 2019) embeddings. A threshold of 0.8 is used.
2. `WordNet`: Replacing words with WordNet (Miller et al., 1990) synonyms.
3. `CharSwap`: Introduces certain character-level perturbations in the text by substituting, deleting, inserting, or swapping adjacent character tokens.

Different combinations of these techniques have been used to augment the `Orig` type target monolingual data. The resultant target-side corpora sizes are summarised in Figure 4.

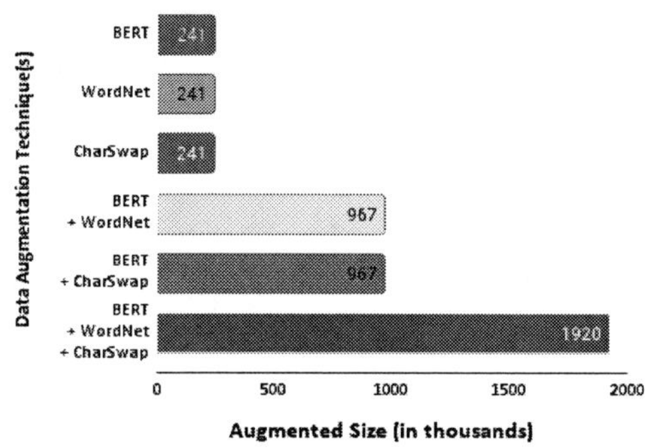

Figure 4: Effective size of the target monolingual corpora with different combinations of augmentation.

5 Experimental Setup

All our experiments have been implemented in PyTorch, except for the Bi-LSTM and CRF which were done in Tensorflow. In addition to this, we used FairSeq (Ott et al., 2019), FLAIR (Akbik et al., 2019a), HuggingFace Transformers (Wolf et al., 2019), and Open-NMT (Klein et al., 2017) frameworks in Python. Nvidia Apex was used for memory optimisation using fp-16 training. Experiments related to Bi-LSTM, CRF, vanilla transformers, and FT were performed on a single $8GB$ Nvidia

Technique	S	US	SS	HE
Vanilla Transformer				
UrIIISeg	36.32			2.202
UrIIIComp	33.45			2.242
AllSeg	37.01			2.360
AllComp	42.23			2.431
+3×FT*			41.98	2.358
+5×FT			**44.14**	**2.504**
+7×FT			42.95	2.367
XLM				
MLM, Orig		4.49	15.04	
MLM + TLM, WMT		0.94	–	
Mixed		13.08	21.23	1.104, –
Orig		12.73	24.64	1.294, –
XLM + Data Augmentation				
BERT		13.06	29.50	1.320, 1.704
WordNet		13.08	28.57	1.269, 1.690
CharSwap		12.92	29.04	
BERT+WordNet		13.34	26.57	1.460, 1.666
BERT+CharSwap +WordNet		13.23	30.10	–, 1.757

Table 1: Sumerian-English Machine Translation. Here, S: Supervised, US: Unsupervised, SS: Semi-Supervised and HE: Human Evaluation. Each of the available values for the first three columns (BLEU) is compared with a value under HE (out of 3). *Number of shards used for FT.

	F1-Score
HMM	0.815
Rules + CRF	**0.991**
Bi-LSTM + CRF	0.763
FLAIR	0.499
RoBERTa	0.949

Table 2: POS Tagging for Sumerian. CRF with rules outperform large models like FLAIR and RoBERTa.

	F1-Score
HMM	0.656
Rules + CRF	0.913
Bi-LSTM + CRF	0.775
FLAIR	0.187
RoBERTa	**0.953**

Table 3: NER for Sumerian. RoBERTa performs best among others. Due to high character-level noise, FLAIR fails to generalise well.

GeForce RTX 2070 GPU, while the pre-training and fine-tuning of FLAIR, RoBERTa, and XLM on various data configurations were performed on 2 16 GB Nvidia V100 GPUs. We used development sets to tune the hyper-parameters for all our models, especially those for POS and NER. For RoBERTa and vanilla transformer, $N = 6$ encoder layers with $h = 16$ attention heads were used, while $N = 4$ and $h = 12$ was used for XLM. A beam-size of 5 was used for our FT experiments. Adam (Kingma and Ba, 2015) optimiser with a learning rate of 0.001, $\beta_1 = 0.90$, $\beta_2 = 0.98$ and a decay factor of 0.5 was used. Additional regularisation was done via Dropout and Attention Dropout (wherever applicable) layers with $p_{drop} = 0.1$. We used a batch size of 32 or 64 and an early stopping criteria based on the validation loss.

6 Results and Analysis

Sequence Labeling Tables 2 and 3 represent the metric scores of our different models for POS and NER tasks, respectively. CRF with domain-specific rules gives the best F1-score for the POS tagging task, even better than the complex RoBERTa and FLAIR language models which are the current state-of-the-art techniques for most languages. The prevalence of distorted words and short phrases in the corpora makes context learning difficult, although the domain-specific rules help learn short-term dependencies by learning feature weights.

RoBERTa performs well for both of the tasks, while being the best among others for NER (95.37 F1 score). To make the most out of the limited vocabulary and noisy text, we used Byte-Level BPE (Radford et al., 2019) to train the language model and further fine-tuned it on our POS and NER dataset with a batch size of 128. We also tried FLAIR language model across various word embeddings (character, Word2vec, FastText, GloVe) along with an additional CRF layer for both of the tasks. Although a high precision is observed using this approach, the F1 scores is seen to be significantly low due to low recall. In addition to the F1 metric we also conducted human evaluation by language expert for the best performing models, out of randomly selected 76 (496 words) phrases, only 8 and 6 words were misclassified by NER and POS models, giving an error of 1.20 and 1.61%, respectively.

Machine Translation Table 1 summarises our results for all supervised, semi-supervised, and unsupervised techniques. Forward translation on vanilla transformer outperforms all other techniques by at least 2 BLEU. The variation of its performance with more monolingual source text is shown. The superior performance of `AllComp` over the other configurations in vanilla transformer signifies the value of both context and out-of-domain data together. Even though the XLM-based models show lower performance, it could be attributed to the lesser number of encoder layers and attention heads used for them. What is interesting to note, though, is the variation of its performance across various training strategies. We experiment across MLM and TLM (+ MLM) initialization for XLM, where the latter comfortably outperforms the former. We do not test with random initialization and CLM, following up from the conclusions made for NMT in Conneau and Lample (2019). Pre-training the XLM on augmented target-side text works surprisingly well. We note that using pre-training on `BERT` and `WordNet` augmentations results in better Unsupervised performance while introducing `CharSwap` improves the semi-supervised models. The human evaluation presented in the table was made by three Assyriologists, who rated 100 output examples for each model, on a scale of 3. A pairwise inter-annotator agreement of 0.673 (Cohen's Kappa) was observed.[6]

7 Interpretability Analysis

Oftentimes in case of Deep Learning Architectures, metric scores like Accuracy, F1 and BLEU are unable to portray the true behavior of the models. For languages like Sumerian, the human-understanding itself is scarce. Visualizing the representations and correlations made by the model could provide insights into which elements of the context can give additional information to support semantic analysis of the terms. Thus, we herein introduce a generalisable interpretability toolkit, *InterpretLR*, to interpret algorithms for **L**ow-**R**esource NLP and further apply it for the aforementioned tasks and models.

InterpretLR is primarily aimed at fabricating attribution saliency maps, i.e., tracing back the model output so as to assign an importance score to each input token, based on its 'influence' on that output. We do this using two kinds of interpretability techniques– gradient-based (Sundararajan et al., 2017; Simonyan et al., 2014; Shrikumar et al., 2017), and perturbation-based (Zeiler and Fergus, 2014; Castro et al., 2009).

Due to the inherently discrete nature of natural language text, the starting point for all our approaches is the embedding of the input sentence across the model to interpret. Most of our analysis is done for the encoder of the network architecture, thus analyzing the effect of different pre-training and fine-tuning techniques on how the model eventually represents the language attributes. We use the word 'Attribution' as a better-defined substitute for the 'Influence' measure of an input span of text on the output.
A part of our visual analysis is shown and elaborated here, while a complete analysis with all our models and layer-wise heat-maps is presented in the Appendix.

In Table 4a, we apply *InterpretLR* on 3 different configurations of XLM for a randomly chosen sentence from NMT's evaluation set. A human expert was asked to annotate the source sentence in accordance with the expected reference for each output token in the actual English translation, as shown in the first column. The highlighted visualizations for each of the 3 models were obtained using Integrated Gradients (Sundararajan et al., 2017) across the three input embeddings- token, position, and language. A lot of interesting observations could be made from these attributions.
Firstly, the named entity in the sentence *ur-{d}asznan* (*UrAnan*) has been wrongly translated by all the three models. Although this behavior is expected (learning the context of a named entity is extremely difficult without excessive supervision around the same, which is largely absent our training text) the models even largely fail to attend to the right words in the input.
Secondly, words like *rations*, *weavers* and *seal* which appear frequently in the parallel Ur III Admin corpora and have a contextual meaning attached to them, are translated perfectly by the models, this property is observed among these models

[6]Elaborate evaluation criteria mentioned in the Appendix.

Actual	**Human Expert**	Model-1	**Semi-Supervised DataAug XLM**	Model-2	**Unsupervised DataAug XLM**	Model-3	**Unsupervised `Orig` TLM XLM**
Output Word	Annotations	Output Word	Visualisations	Output Word	Visualisations	Output Word	Visualisations
barley	#s sze-ba geme2 usz-bar kiszib3 ur-{d}asznan ugula #e	barley	#s sze-ba geme2 usz-bar kiszib3 ur-{d}asznan ugula #e	Monthy	#s sze-ba geme2 usz-bar kiszib3 ur-{d}asznan ugula #e	Basketoftablets	#s sze-ba geme2 usz-bar kiszib3 ur-{d}asznan ugula #e
rations	#s sze-ba geme2 usz-bar kiszib3 ur-{d}asznan ugula #e	rations	#s sze-ba geme2 usz-bar kiszib3 ur-{d}asznan ugula #e	rations	#s sze-ba geme2 usz-bar kiszib3 ur-{d}asznan ugula #e	rations	#s sze-ba geme2 usz-bar kiszib3 ur-{d}asznan ugula #e
weavers	#s sze-ba geme2 usz-bar kiszib3 ur-{d}asznan ugula #e	weavers	#s sze-ba geme2 usz-bar kiszib3 ur-{d}asznan ugula #e	weavers	#s sze-ba geme2 usz-bar kiszib3 ur-{d}asznan ugula #e	weavers	#s sze-ba geme2 usz-bar kiszib3 ur-{d}asznan ugula #e
under	#s sze-ba geme2 usz-bar kiszib3 ur-{d}asznan ugula #e	under	#s sze-ba geme2 usz-bar kiszib3 ur-{d}asznan ugula #e	from	#s sze-ba geme2 usz-bar kiszib3 ur-{d}asznan ugula #e	255	#s sze-ba geme2 usz-bar kiszib3 ur-{d}asznan ugula #e
seal	#s sze-ba geme2 usz-bar kiszib3 ur-{d}asznan ugula #e	seal	#s sze-ba geme2 usz-bar kiszib3 ur-{d}asznan ugula #e	seal	#s sze-ba geme2 usz-bar kiszib3 ur-{d}asznan ugula #e	seal	#s sze-ba geme2 usz-bar kiszib3 ur-{d}asznan ugula #e
of	#s sze-ba geme2 usz-bar kiszib3 ur-{d}asznan ugula #e	of	#s sze-ba geme2 usz-bar kiszib3 ur-{d}asznan ugula #e	of	#s sze-ba geme2 usz-bar kiszib3 ur-{d}asznan ugula #e	of	#s sze-ba geme2 usz-bar kiszib3 ur-{d}asznan ugula #e
UrAnan	#s sze-ba geme2 usz-bar kiszib3 ur-{d}asznan ugula #e	Lugalniglagare	#s sze-ba geme2 usz-bar kiszib3 ur-{d}asznan ugula #e	Ninlil	#s sze-ba geme2 usz-bar kiszib3 ur-{d}asznan ugula #e	weavers	#s sze-ba geme2 usz-bar kiszib3 ur-{d}asznan ugula #e
foreman	#s sze-ba geme2 usz-bar kiszib3 ur-{d}asznan ugula #e	foreman	#s sze-ba geme2 usz-bar kiszib3 ur-{d}asznan ugula #e	foreman	#s sze-ba geme2 usz-bar kiszib3 ur-{d}asznan ugula #e	female	#s sze-ba geme2 usz-bar kiszib3 ur-{d}asznan ugula #e

(a) MT- Selected output tokens for Sumerian Input text of "sze-ba geme2 usz-bar kiszib3 ur-dasznan ugula", which translates to "barley rations of the female weavers under seal of UrAnan the foreman".[7]

Actual	**Human Expert**	Model	**RoBERTa**
N	5(disz) gin2 ku3-babbar	N	5 (disz) gin 2 ku 3 - babbar

(b) POS- With tagged word "ku3-babbar"

Actual	**Human Expert**	Model	**RoBERTa**
GN	mu ur-bi2-lum{ki} ba-hul	GN	mu ur - bi 2- lum { ki } ba - hul

(c) NER- With tagged word "ur-bi2-lumki"

Table 4: Highlighted attributions for randomly selected examples. Green and **Red** represent correct and wrong predictions, respectively, while Green and Red highlights represent positive and negative attributions, respectively.

in general. Even the unsupervised models that do not have access to the one-to-one mapping of the translation during training manage to infer these words from the appropriate context. It can be assumed that they learn the right representations of such tokens. But at the same time, there are instances like *sze-ba* (*barley*), which the two unsupervised models rightly refer to but do not give the right translations, which thus is a direct result of the absence of supervision.
Lastly, English words like *under*, *of* and *from* do not have any direct translations in Sumerian and are mostly inferred from the context, even by the human annotators. At such places, again, supervision might play a critical role as in the 4th row of Table 4a. There are also instances like the 6th row where the supervised model fails to attend to the right words, and the correct output word could very well be out of memorisation.

Tables 4b and 4c represent visualizations for two randomly selected phrases for our sequence labeling tasks, indicating the attributions for each sub-word for tagging the corresponding target word with their predicted labels. It can be observed from Table 4b that word *gin* (*unit*) and sub-word *ku*, are contributing to the attribution score positively, depicting positive model attribution to tag *ku3-babbar* as a Noun (N), whereas in Table 4c the sub-words *ur*, *hul* and *ki* are contributing *ur-bi2-lum*{*ki*} to be tagged as the label GN (Geographical Name). As observed from the corresponding human annotation, *ur* and *ki* are the most associated for Geographical names and GNs are mostly followed by a verb part, which is *hul* (*destroy*) in this case. It can thus be inferred that RoBERTa identifies this correspondence well and makes the decision accordingly.

8 Conclusion

In this work, we introduced the first information extraction and translation pipeline for Sumerian cuneiform. We first undertook the tasks of POS Tagging and NER, where we observed that *deeper is not necessarily better*. A simple CRF model with well-defined rules outperformed the large language model RoBERTa for POS Tagging. Further, for machine translation we overcame unprecedented challenges pertaining to lack of in-domain text, sparse sentence formation, and incoherence. We found that using out-of-domain text along with specific data-augmentation can have huge impacts in a low-resource setting. All components of this work are generalisable to other low-resource languages, including *InterpretLR*, and we open way to future research in this direction.

[7]The left-out tokens were rightly predicted by all the three models, with almost the same attributions.

Acknowledgments

The authors would like to acknowledge the use of the University of Oxford Advanced Research Computing (ARC) facility in carrying out this work (http://dx.doi.org/10.5281/zenodo.22558). We would like to thank our collaborators at the Cuneiform Digital Library Initiative (CDLI; https://cdli.ucla.edu) and from the Machine Translation and Automated Analysis of Cuneiform Languages (MTAAC; https://cdli-gh.github.io/mtaac/). We would also like to thank CDLI and the Electronic Text Corpus of Sumerian Literature (ETCSL) for providing the data for our experiments. This work was partly undertaken during the Google Summer of Code (GSoC) program, 2020. CDLI has been supported by GSoC, where aspects of machine translation have been addressed by several students since 2018. We are thankful to Ilya Khait and Bertrand Lafont for their assistance with the human evaluations for machine translation and sequence labeling. We are grateful to Orhan Firat for insightful discussions and multiple rounds of reviews during the pre-submission mentoring phase of ACL SRW that greatly shaped this manuscript.

References

Alan Akbik, Tanja Bergmann, Duncan Blythe, Kashif Rasul, Stefan Schweter, and Roland Vollgraf. 2019a. FLAIR: An easy-to-use framework for state-of-the-art NLP. In *Proceedings of the 2019 Conference of the North American Chapter of the Association for Computational Linguistics (Demonstrations)*, pages 54–59, Minneapolis, Minnesota. Association for Computational Linguistics.

Alan Akbik, Tanja Bergmann, and Roland Vollgraf. 2019b. Pooled contextualized embeddings for named entity recognition. In *Proceedings of the 2019 Conference of the North American Chapter of the Association for Computational Linguistics: Human Language Technologies, NAACL-HLT 2019, Minneapolis, MN, USA, June 2-7, 2019, Volume 1 (Long and Short Papers)*, pages 724–728. Association for Computational Linguistics.

Alan Akbik, Duncan Blythe, and Roland Vollgraf. 2018. Contextual string embeddings for sequence labeling. In *Proceedings of the 27th International Conference on Computational Linguistics, COLING 2018, Santa Fe, New Mexico, USA, August 20-26, 2018*, pages 1638–1649. Association for Computational Linguistics.

Franck Burlot and François Yvon. 2018. Using monolingual data in neural machine translation: a systematic study. In *Proceedings of the Third Conference on Machine Translation: Research Papers*, pages 144–155, Brussels, Belgium. Association for Computational Linguistics.

Javier Castro, Daniel Gómez, and Juan Tejada. 2009. Polynomial calculation of the shapley value based on sampling. *Comput. Oper. Res.*, 36(5):1726–1730.

Alexis Conneau and Guillaume Lample. 2019. Cross-lingual language model pretraining. In *Advances in Neural Information Processing Systems 32: Annual Conference on Neural Information Processing Systems 2019, NeurIPS 2019, December 8-14, 2019, Vancouver, BC, Canada*, pages 7057–7067.

Jacob Devlin, Ming-Wei Chang, Kenton Lee, and Kristina Toutanova. 2019. BERT: pre-training of deep bidirectional transformers for language understanding. In *Proceedings of the 2019 Conference of the North American Chapter of the Association for Computational Linguistics: Human Language Technologies, NAACL-HLT 2019, Minneapolis, MN, USA, June 2-7, 2019, Volume 1 (Long and Short Papers)*, pages 4171–4186. Association for Computational Linguistics.

Sergey Edunov, Myle Ott, Michael Auli, and David Grangier. 2018. Understanding back-translation at scale. In *Proceedings of the 2018 Conference on Empirical Methods in Natural Language Processing, Brussels, Belgium, October 31 - November 4, 2018*, pages 489–500. Association for Computational Linguistics.

Robert K. Englund. 2009. The smell of the cage. `https://cdli.ucla.edu/pubs/cdlj/2009/cdlj2009_004.html`. Online; accessed 2009.

Di He, Yingce Xia, Tao Qin, Liwei Wang, Nenghai Yu, Tie-Yan Liu, and Wei-Ying Ma. 2016. Dual learning for machine translation. In *Advances in Neural Information Processing Systems 29: Annual Conference on Neural Information Processing Systems 2016, December 5-10, 2016, Barcelona, Spain*, pages 820–828.

Sepp Hochreiter and Jürgen Schmidhuber. 1997. Long short-term memory. *Neural Comput.*, 9(8):1735–1780.

Ari Holtzman, Jan Buys, Maxwell Forbes, Antoine Bosselut, David Golub, and Yejin Choi. 2018. Learning to write with cooperative discriminators. In *Proceedings of the 56th Annual Meeting of the Association for Computational Linguistics, ACL 2018, Melbourne, Australia, July 15-20, 2018, Volume 1: Long Papers*, pages 1638–1649. Association for Computational Linguistics.

Zhiheng Huang, Wei Xu, and Kai Yu. 2015. Bidirectional lstm-crf models for sequence tagging. *arXiv preprint arXiv:1508.01991*.

Diederik P. Kingma and Jimmy Ba. 2015. Adam: A method for stochastic optimization. In *3rd International Conference on Learning Representations, ICLR 2015, San Diego, CA, USA, May 7-9, 2015, Conference Track Proceedings*.

Guillaume Klein, Yoon Kim, Yuntian Deng, Jean Senellart, and Alexander Rush. 2017. OpenNMT: Open-source toolkit for neural machine translation. In *Proceedings of ACL 2017, System Demonstrations*, pages 67–72, Vancouver, Canada. Association for Computational Linguistics.

John D. Lafferty, Andrew McCallum, and Fernando C. N. Pereira. 2001. Conditional random fields: Probabilistic models for segmenting and labeling sequence data. In *Proceedings of the Eighteenth International Conference on Machine Learning (ICML 2001), Williams College, Williamstown, MA, USA, June 28 - July 1, 2001*, pages 282–289. Morgan Kaufmann.

Yinhan Liu, Myle Ott, Naman Goyal, Jingfei Du, Mandar Joshi, Danqi Chen, Omer Levy, Mike Lewis, Luke Zettlemoyer, and Veselin Stoyanov. 2019. Roberta: A robustly optimized BERT pretraining approach. *CoRR*, abs/1907.11692.

Yudong Liu, Clinton Burkhart, James Hearne, and Liang Luo. 2015. Enhancing sumerian lemmatization by unsupervised named-entity recognition. In *NAACL HLT 2015, The 2015 Conference of the North American Chapter of the Association for Computational Linguistics: Human Language Technologies, Denver, Colorado, USA, May 31 - June 5, 2015*, pages 1446–1451. The Association for Computational Linguistics.

Liang Luo, Yudong Liu, James Hearne, and Clinton Burkhart. 2015. Unsupervised sumerian personal name recognition. In *Proceedings of the Twenty-Eighth International Florida Artificial Intelligence Research Society Conference, FLAIRS 2015, Hollywood, Florida, USA, May 18-20, 2015*, pages 193–198. AAAI Press.

George A Miller, Richard Beckwith, Christiane Fellbaum, Derek Gross, and Katherine J Miller. 1990. Introduction to wordNet: An on-line lexical database. *International journal of lexicography*, 3(4):235–244.

Myle Ott, Sergey Edunov, Alexei Baevski, Angela Fan, Sam Gross, Nathan Ng, David Grangier, and Michael Auli. 2019. fairseq: A fast, extensible toolkit for sequence modeling. In *Proceedings of the 2019 Conference of the North American Chapter of the Association for Computational Linguistics: Human Language Technologies, NAACL-HLT 2019, Minneapolis, MN, USA, June 2-7, 2019, Demonstrations*, pages 48–53. Association for Computational Linguistics.

Émilie Pagé-Perron, Maria Sukhareva, Ilya Khait, and Christian Chiarcos. 2017. Machine translation and automated analysis of the Sumerian language. In *Proceedings of the Joint SIGHUM Workshop on Computational Linguistics for Cultural Heritage, Social Sciences, Humanities and Literature*, pages 10–16, Vancouver, Canada. Association for Computational Linguistics.

Ravneet Punia, Niko Schenk, Christian Chiarcos, and Émilie Pagé-Perron. 2020a. Towards the first machine translation system for sumerian transliterations. In *Proceedings of the 28th International Conference on Computational Linguistics*, pages 3454–3460.

Ravneet Punia, Niko Schenk, Christian Chiarcos, and Émilie Pagé-Perron. 2020b. Towards the first machine translation system for Sumerian transliterations. In *Proceedings of the 28th International Conference on Computational Linguistics*, pages 3454–3460, Barcelona, Spain (Online). International Committee on Computational Linguistics.

Alec Radford, Jeff Wu, Rewon Child, David Luan, Dario Amodei, and Ilya Sutskever. 2019. Language models are unsupervised multitask learners.

Mike Schuster and Kuldip K. Paliwal. 1997. Bidirectional recurrent neural networks. *IEEE Trans. Signal Process.*, 45(11):2673–2681.

Rico Sennrich, Barry Haddow, and Alexandra Birch. 2016. Improving neural machine translation models with monolingual data. In *Proceedings of the 54th Annual Meeting of the Association for Computational Linguistics, ACL 2016, August 7-12, 2016, Berlin, Germany, Volume 1: Long Papers*. The Association for Computer Linguistics.

Avanti Shrikumar, Peyton Greenside, and Anshul Kundaje. 2017. Learning important features through propagating activation differences. In *Proceedings of the 34th International Conference on Machine Learning, ICML 2017, Sydney, NSW, Australia, 6-11 August 2017*, volume 70 of *Proceedings of Machine Learning Research*, pages 3145–3153. PMLR.

Karen Simonyan, Andrea Vedaldi, and Andrew Zisserman. 2014. Deep inside convolutional networks: Visualising image classification models and saliency maps. In *2nd International Conference on Learning Representations, ICLR 2014, Banff, AB, Canada, April 14-16, 2014, Workshop Track Proceedings*.

Kaitao Song, Xu Tan, Tao Qin, Jianfeng Lu, and Tie-Yan Liu. 2019. MASS: masked sequence to sequence pre-training for language generation. In *Proceedings of the 36th International Conference on Machine Learning, ICML 2019, 9-15 June 2019, Long Beach, California, USA*, volume 97 of *Proceedings of Machine Learning Research*, pages 5926–5936. PMLR.

Mukund Sundararajan, Ankur Taly, and Qiqi Yan. 2017. Axiomatic attribution for deep networks. In *Proceedings of the 34th International Conference on*

Machine Learning, ICML 2017, Sydney, NSW, Australia, 6-11 August 2017, volume 70 of *Proceedings of Machine Learning Research*, pages 3319–3328. PMLR.

Ashish Vaswani, Noam Shazeer, Niki Parmar, Jakob Uszkoreit, Llion Jones, Aidan N. Gomez, Lukasz Kaiser, and Illia Polosukhin. 2017. Attention is all you need. In *Advances in Neural Information Processing Systems 30: Annual Conference on Neural Information Processing Systems 2017, December 4-9, 2017, Long Beach, CA, USA*, pages 5998–6008.

Thomas Wolf, Lysandre Debut, Victor Sanh, Julien Chaumond, Clement Delangue, Anthony Moi, Pierric Cistac, Tim Rault, Rémi Louf, Morgan Funtowicz, and Jamie Brew. 2019. Huggingface's transformers: State-of-the-art natural language processing. *CoRR*, abs/1910.03771.

Lijun Wu, Yiren Wang, Yingce Xia, Tao Qin, Jianhuang Lai, and Tie-Yan Liu. 2019. Exploiting monolingual data at scale for neural machine translation. In *Proceedings of the 2019 Conference on Empirical Methods in Natural Language Processing and the 9th International Joint Conference on Natural Language Processing (EMNLP-IJCNLP)*, pages 4207–4216, Hong Kong, China. Association for Computational Linguistics.

Matthew D. Zeiler and Rob Fergus. 2014. Visualizing and understanding convolutional networks. In *Computer Vision - ECCV 2014 - 13th European Conference, Zurich, Switzerland, September 6-12, 2014, Proceedings, Part I*, volume 8689 of *Lecture Notes in Computer Science*, pages 818–833. Springer.

Jiajun Zhang and Chengqing Zong. 2016. Exploiting source-side monolingual data in neural machine translation. In *Proceedings of the 2016 Conference on Empirical Methods in Natural Language Processing*, pages 1535–1545, Austin, Texas. Association for Computational Linguistics.

Barret Zoph, Deniz Yuret, Jonathan May, and Kevin Knight. 2016. Transfer learning for low-resource neural machine translation. In *Proceedings of the 2016 Conference on Empirical Methods in Natural Language Processing, EMNLP 2016, Austin, Texas, USA, November 1-4, 2016*, pages 1568–1575. The Association for Computational Linguistics.

A Detailed Evaluation and Analysis

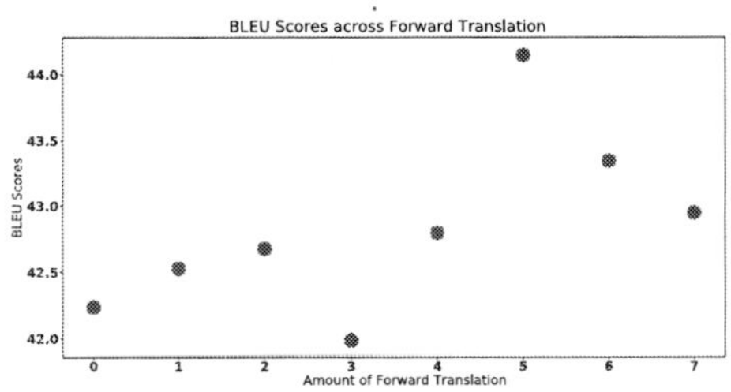

Figure 5

Forward Translation with Vanilla Transformer gave the best results for Sumerian-English Neural Machine Translation. Figure 5 shows the variation of the BLEU score with the amount of source monolingual data used. Here, the X-Axis represents the number of shards used, with each shard consisting of 80K sentences. It can be observed that the translation accuracy is not linear with the amount of text used.

Figure 6 shows the variation of several performance metrics during the Unsupervised fine-tuning of various XLM configurations. The comparison is made between XLM pre-training without any data augmentation (MLM_TLM), with one augmentation (Aug) and with all three augmentations (Aug_12x). It can be seen from Figure 6a that an XLM pre-trained on the Aug_12x configuration converges the fastest among the others, in terms of the main Denoising Auto-encoding Loss. It can also be observed that the curve corresponding to this configuration is much smoother than the others, which shows a positive regularizing effect of a better weight initialisation (through appropriate pre-training). A similar pattern is observed for the validation accuracy across the epochs as shown in Figure 6c, although, the trend of Back Translation loss remains mostly inseparable for the three configurations.

Table 5 depicts the net percentage error found by an human expert on the POS and NER results for the entire evaluation set across the best performing model. Table 6 and 7 represents the detailed results of POS and NER models. It can be observed from the tables, that although CRF and RoBERTa models gave the best results, FLAIR language model along with character embeddings also gave high precision for both of the tasks.

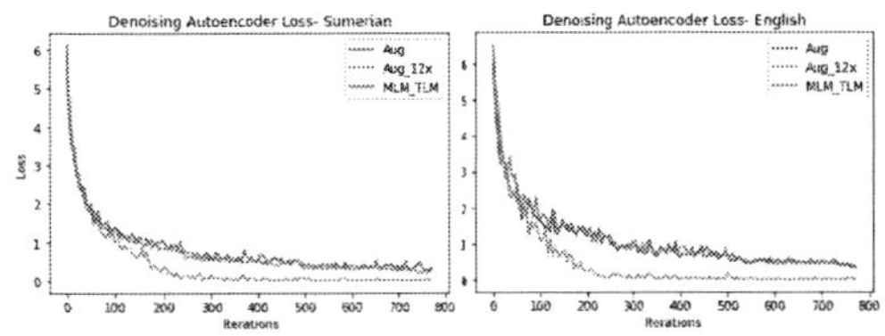

(a) Denoising Auto-encoder Loss (AE Loss) variation across the 1st Epoch

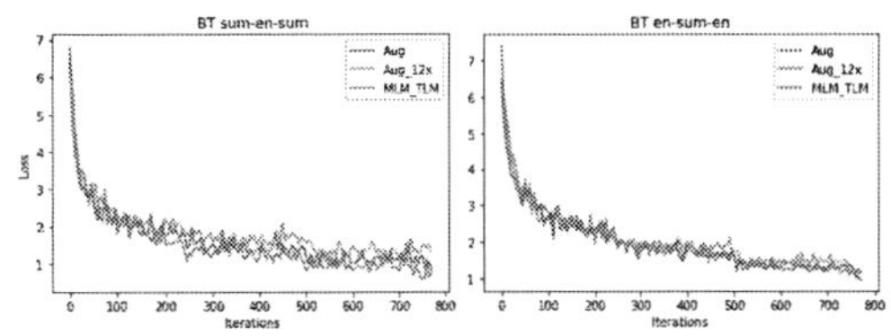

(b) Back Translation Loss variation in XLM across the 1st Epoch

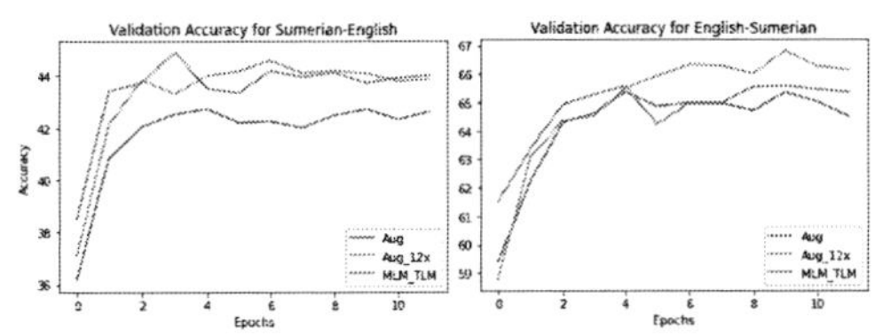

(c) MT accuracy across a number of training epochs

Figure 6: Quantitative comparison of various models during Unsupervised MT fine-tuning

	POS error (in %)	NER error (in %)
Human Evaluation	1.61	1.20

Table 5: Human Evaluation for POS and NER

B Extended Interpretations

Here we present the interpretability analysis across a larger set of models and visualisations. We use and compare the different algorithms across layer-level, gradient-based, and perturbation-based techniques to obtain the attributions.

Figure 7 visualises the Multi-head Self Attention (MHSA) using Layer Conductance Dhamdhere, Sundararajan, and Yan 2018) across the 4 encoder layers we employ in XLMs[8]. The first two output tokens *barley* and *female* are known to be one-on-one mapping between the input words of *sze-ba* and *geme2* respectively. While the third output token *barley* is not a direct translation and

[8]The supervised version of the augmented pre-training is used here.

	Part of Speech Tagging		
	Precision	Recall	F1-Score
HMM	0.857	0.794	0.815
Rules + CRF	**0.994**	**0.989**	**0.991**
BBi-LSTM + CRF	0.852	0.710	0.7631
FLAIR	0.9323	0.4766	0.4999
RoBERTa	0.9500	0.9489	0.9495

Table 6: POS Tagging Models for Ur III Sumerian Text

	Named Entity Recognition		
	Precision	Recall	F1-Score
HMM	0.810	0.599	0.656
Rules + CRF	0.916	0.910	0.913
Bi-LSTM + CRF	0.864	0.704	0.775
FLAIR	**0.9562**	0.1817	0.1873
RoBERTa	0.9540	**0.9534**	**0.9537**

Table 7: NER Models for Ur III Sumerian Text

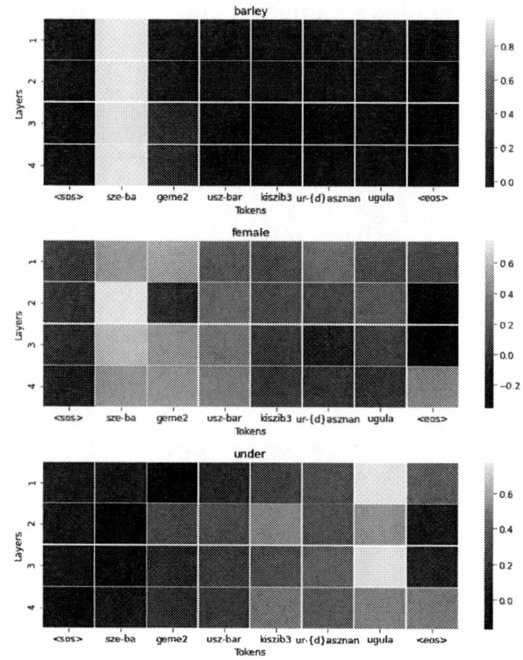

Figure 7: Layer Conductance across MHSA Layers

is needed to be inferred from context.

Figure 9a represents the attribution heat-map when gradient-normalisation saliency (Simonyan, Vedaldi, and Zisserman 2013) is used. Being one of the most conventional techniques for finding attribution, it is more prone to inconsistent interpretations. Whereas, the attribution heat-map in Figure 9b represents the Integrated Gradients (IG) (Sundararajan, Taly, and Yan512017) approach. Being a path-based technique, which measures the gradient attribution relation using a straight-line path from a baseline (usually all-zeros), to the given input, it is much more robust and stable.

Even though the gradient-based methods are much faster than perturbation-based methods, we observe that the heavy dependency of IG on hyper-parameters like the number of input steps to be considered when going from a baseline to the actual input, n_steps, to be a major setback. The final attribution is generally found out after integrating (or summing) over the attributions of these sub-steps. We found that the attributions do not change when going beyond $n\_steps = 250$, thus, we experiment by varying it between 10 to 250. We observe that there is no ideal value of n_steps, IG's faithfulness to the model varies largely over this range. For some inputs, the best value is $n\_steps = 50$ while for others $n\_steps = 250$ is the most ideal. We judge this by considering how much the attribution is given to *sos* and *eos* tokens for each output token. Thus, based on both *plausibility* and *faithfulness*. We use $n\_steps = 50$ for obtaining the heat-maps in Figure 9b.

Figure 10 represents the visualization for our sequence labeling tasks. It indicates two major things, 1) the effect of words, sub-words (depends on tokenization) on tagging the target word and 2) the effect of 6 transformer encoder layers. We created the hook on embeddings of RoBERTa with layer IG and obtained the visualizations for how each sub-word is contributing to tag the target word. Similarly, to obtain the heat-map we created the hook on RoBERTa embeddings and used the Layer Conductance.

From Figure 10a it can be observed that *ku* and *du* contribute the most to the attribution scores for tagging *ku3-babbar* and *ba-du3* as a Noun (N) and Verb (V), respectively. From the heat-maps it is also noted that *ku* shows the effect on all 6 layers whereas in second example effects are majorly due to the initial transformer layers. Similarly in the Figure 10b *ur* and *lugal* are the most effective sub-words to tag *ur-bi2-lumki* and *lugal-tesz2-mu* as GN (Geographical Name) and PN (Personal Name) respectively. It is also interesting to note that both

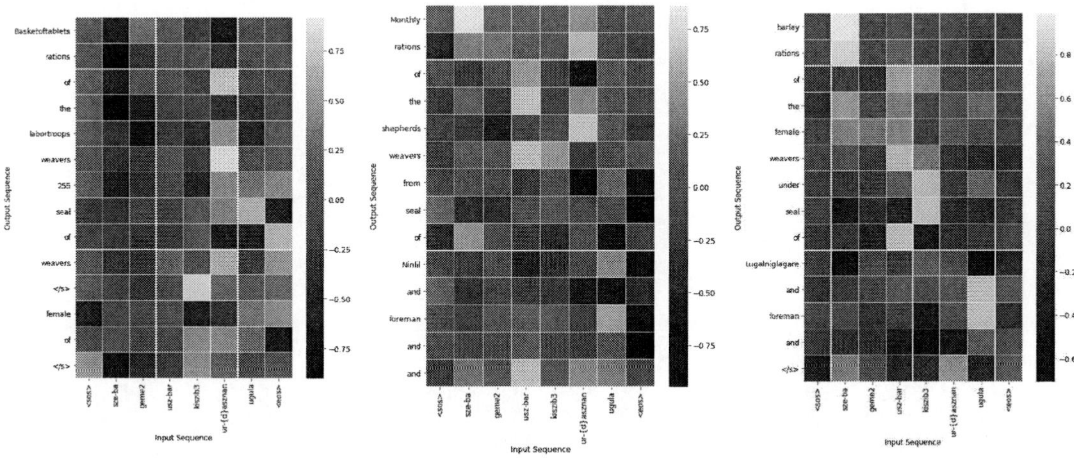

Figure 8: Feature Ablation in *InterpretLR*

of these sub-words have a very positive impact in the initial layers but are contributing oppositely in the last layer.

B.1 Human Evaluation

The scoring by human experts was done independently for each result according to the following criterion:

• **3 (good)**: interpretable in the correct meaning by a native speaker of English; (almost) no incorrectly translated content word (e.g., tolerant against some errors in word order, but not in incorrect words).

• **2 (helpful)**: partially distorted, but interpretable with some context information (tolerant against errors in word order and against incorrect function words).

• **1 (incorrect)**: contains incorrectly translated content words and/or is un-interpretable.

C Rules for POS Tagging and NER

We used certain language-specific rules to assist CRF for the sequence labeling tasks. The rules were identified by human experts and some of them are as mentioned here:

• A word starting with "ur-", "lu2-", or "dumu" is most likely to be a personal name.

• If a word is followed by "mu", then the next phrase denotes a year name.

• If a word is followed by "iti", it denotes a month name.

• Words containing "ki" are mostly associated with geographical names (GN).

• Words ending with part "-hul" majorly denotes verbs.

• Words containing "{d}" denotes either personal name (PN) or divine name (DN).

• A word followed by "gin" (*unit*) majorly replicate a noun.

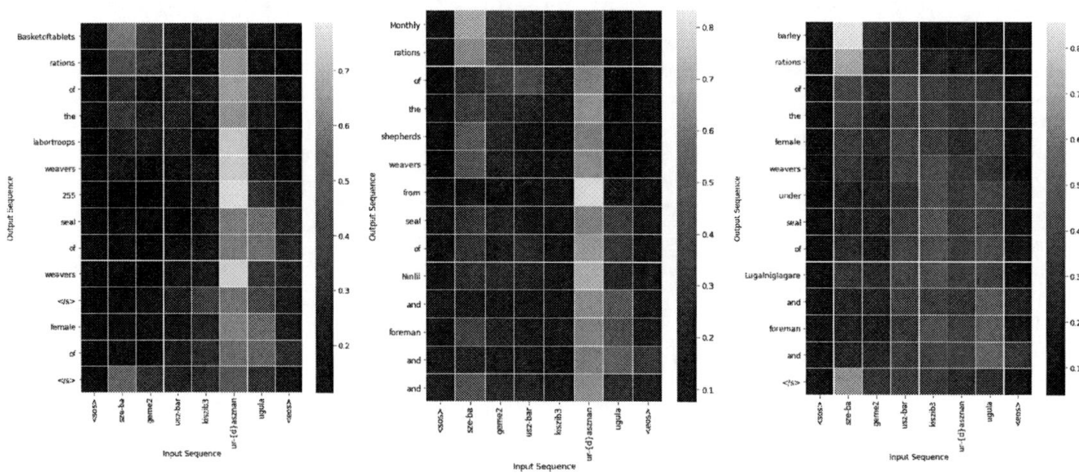

(a) Grad-Norm Saliency

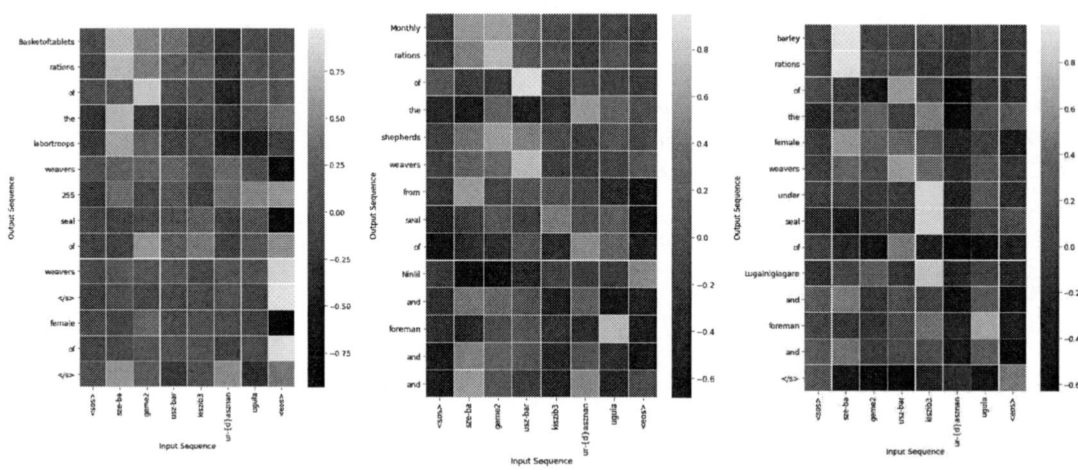

(b) Integrated Gradients

Figure 9: Comparing different gradient-based approaches used in *InterpretLR*

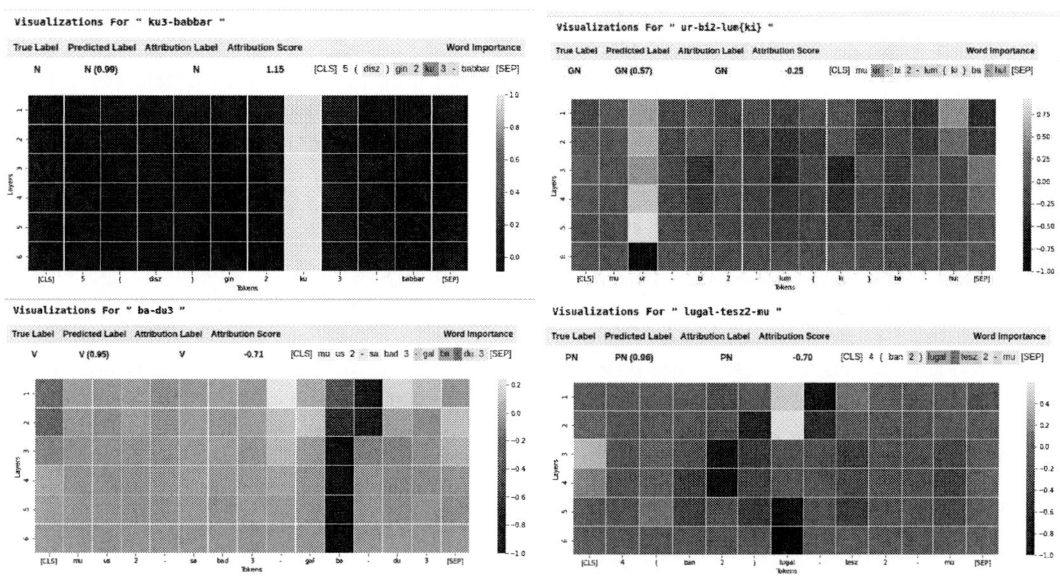

(a) POS Tagging

(b) NER

Figure 10: *InterpretLR* on RoBERTa for Sequence Labeling

On the Relationship between Zipf's Law of Abbreviation and Interfering Noise in Emergent Languages

Ryo Ueda
The University of Tokyo
ryoryoueda@is.s.u-tokyo.ac.jp

Koki Washio
The University of Tokyo
kwashio@is.s.u-tokyo.ac.jp

Abstract

This paper studies whether emergent languages in a signaling game follow Zipf's law of abbreviation (ZLA), especially when the communication ability of agents is limited because of interfering noises. ZLA is a well-known tendency in human languages where the more frequently a word is used, the shorter it will be. Surprisingly, previous work demonstrated that emergent languages do not obey ZLA at all when neural agents play a signaling game. It also reported that a ZLA-like tendency appeared by adding an explicit penalty on word lengths, which can be considered some external factors in reality such as articulatory effort. We hypothesize, on the other hand, that there might be not only such external factors but also some internal factors related to cognitive abilities. We assume that it could be simulated by modeling the effect of noises on the agents' environment. In our experimental setup, the hidden states of the LSTM-based speaker and listener were added with Gaussian noise, while the channel was subject to discrete random replacement. Our results suggest that noise on a speaker is one of the factors for ZLA or at least causes emergent languages to approach ZLA, while noise on a listener and a channel is not.

1 Introduction

There has recently been a growing interest in simulating languages spontaneously emerging among artificial agents, by training them to solve some tasks requiring communications. A primary motivation in this area is to pursue the development of artificial intelligence that can interact or communicate with human beings (e.g., Havrylov and Titov, 2017; Lazaridou et al., 2017, 2018; Lee et al., 2018). In addition to this line of research, some studies have investigated the characteristics of emergent languages, mainly concerned with to what extent they are similar to human languages or what kind of factor forms language-like protocols (e.g., Kottur et al., 2017; Harding Graesser et al., 2019; Chaabouni et al., 2020; Kharitonov et al., 2020).

Chaabouni et al. (2019), for example, studied the relationship between emergent languages and Zipf's law of abbreviation (ZLA), which is a universal tendency in human languages, where frequent words tend to be shorter (Zipf, 1935; Kanwal et al., 2017). To see whether emergent languages follow ZLA, they performed experiments in which agents played a signaling game. Their results suggested that emergent languages have an opposite tendency against ZLA. In other words, more frequent inputs are encoded into longer messages. They also reported that by giving an additional penalty on message lengths (Eq. 6), the emergence of a ZLA-like tendency was observed.

Zipf (1935) hypothesized that ZLA comes about between two conflicting pressures: one for accuracy and the other for efficiency. In a paradigm with human subjects using a simple artificial language, Kanwal et al. (2017), for instance, introduced some external factors for simulating the competing pressures, namely, money reward for precise and quick communications. In emergent-language simulations, the explicit penalty on message lengths (Eq. 6) of Chaabouni et al. (2019) can also be considered an external factor for ZLA.

However, we speculate that there might be not only such external factors but also internal factors (or implicit penalties) related to the cognitive abilities of human beings such as memory. Inspired by some concepts in psychology, we hypothesize at first in the following way:

Hypothesis 1. *ZLA appears due to some internal factors from the cognitive abilities of human beings, as well as external factors. In other words, human*

Proceedings of the Joint Conference of the 59th Annual Meeting of the Association for Computational Linguistics and the 11th International Joint Conference on Natural Language Processing: Student Research Workshop, pages 60–70
August 5–6, 2021.

beings assign shorter codes to frequent words so that they can avoid difficulty in their internal processes as much as possible.

Some studies in psychology suggested that in human beings, there is an output buffer of some sort that temporarily reserves some words to be spoken (Baddeley et al., 1975; Baddeley, 2003; Meyer et al., 2003; Damian et al., 2010; Baddeley and Hitch, 2019). The output buffer might decay over time, be overwhelmed by incoming inputs one after another, or be exposed to other disturbances. Such pressures, we thought, could be factors to shorten frequent words.

But how should they be modeled in the simulations of language emergence? Since artificial agents in simulations are not humans but often (recurrent) neural networks, it is not trivial to define equivalent pressures for them. To adopt such pressures into a signaling game, we propose modeling them into *noise* that interferes with the states of agents. Although the potential factors described above might be the matter of a speaker in a signaling game, we also propose adding noise to a listener for comprehensive research. The listener's short-term memory might also be limited due to similar reasons as the speaker. Besides, we try adding noise to a channel that spans the speaker and the listener, referring to a noisy-channel model (Shannon, 1948). Although a noisy channel is not probably pressure for efficiency but for accuracy, the assumption that redundancy contributes to accuracy seems to think implicitly of a listener as capable enough of correcting errors while maintaining necessary information, which is not trivial for neural agents. Therefore it is worth a try.

By the modeling and for the comprehensiveness, hypothesis 1 is revised as follows:

Hypothesis 2. *ZLA appears due to some of the three types of noises: noise on a speaker, noise on a listener, and noise on a channel.*

In our experimental setup, speaker and listener agents are exposed to Gaussian noise since they have continuous vectors as their states. On the other hand, the channel is exposed to discrete random replacements, as messages passing through it have discrete variables.

Our experiments suggest that noise on a speaker is one factor for ZLA or at least causes emergent languages to be closer to ZLA, whereas noise on a listener and a channel is not in our signaling game. Rather, the noise on a channel strengthened redundancy.

Our analysis reveals the following things. First, when noise interferes with a speaker agent, noise accumulation can make it difficult to generate long consistent messages. Second, when noise interferes with a listener agent, on the other hand, noise accumulation does not affect the overall tendency crucially: even if the listener agent "forgets" the prefix of a message, the suffix is sufficient for communications. Third, noise on a channel can be thought of as a pressure for accuracy rather than efficiency, which is consistent with an information-theoretic point of view and Zipf's hypothesis.

2 Background

Chaabouni et al. (2019) studied whether emergent languages follow ZLA when neural agents play a signaling game. As we largely refer to, we review their setups, methods, and results in this section.

2.1 Signaling Game with a Power-law distribution

They extended a signaling game (Lewis, 1969) by making inputs be sampled from a power-law distribution. In the power-law distribution, the n-th most frequent input is sampled from a finite input space I at the probability $\propto 1/n$. Thus, if agents learned to assign frequent inputs to shorter messages, their communication protocol could be said to obey ZLA.

Let S and L be a speaker and a listener. Formally, the game procedure is as follows:

1. An input $i \in I$ is sampled from a power-law distribution. Let i_r be the r-th most frequent input. Then i_r is sampled at the probability $\propto r^{-1}$.

2. Given i, the speaker S generates a message m, i.e., $m = S(i)$. $m = x_1 \dots x_{|m|}$ is a string over an alphabet $A = \{a_1, \dots, a_{|A|-1}, \texttt{eos}\}$ s.t. $x_i \neq \texttt{eos}$ $(1 \leq i < |m|)$, $x_{|m|} = \texttt{eos}$, and $0 < |m| \leq \texttt{max\_len}$, where $|m|$ is the length of m and $\texttt{max\_len}$ is a hyperparameter. Note that $\texttt{eos} \in A$ stands for "end-of-sentence," and it is guaranteed to be attached to the end of each message[1].

3. Given m, the listener L generates an output, i.e., $o = L(m)$.

[1] One might think that eom (end-of-message) is better, but we follow the convention in the literature of neural language modeling.

4. The procedure is successful if $i = o$.

2.2 Training Method

Since players in a signaling game are neural networks, each input $i \in I$ is represented as a $|I|$-dimensional one-hot vector $\boldsymbol{i}$. Likewise, an output o is represented as a $|I|$-dimensional vector $\boldsymbol{o}$ s.t. $(\boldsymbol{o})_k > 0$ $(k = 1, \ldots, |I|)$ and $\sum_{k=1}^{|I|} (\boldsymbol{o})_k = 1$. Let $\mathcal{L}(\boldsymbol{i}, \boldsymbol{o}) = \mathcal{L}(\boldsymbol{i}, L(S(\boldsymbol{i}))$ be the cross-entropy error between $\boldsymbol{i}$ and $\boldsymbol{o} = L(S(\boldsymbol{i}))$:

$$\mathcal{L}(\boldsymbol{i}, \boldsymbol{o}) = -\sum_{k=1}^{|I|} (\boldsymbol{i})_k \log(\boldsymbol{o})_k, \qquad (1)$$

where S is a speaker and L is a listener. Our purpose is to minimize its expectation $\mathbb{E}[\mathcal{L}]$, but the simple backpropagation algorithm is not applicable due to discrete messages $m = x_1 \ldots x_{|m|}$ sampled from a speaker. Chaabouni et al. (2019) used the following surrogate function, the gradient of which is an unbiased gradient estimator, with an auxiliary loss *entropy regularizer ER*:

$$\mathbb{E}[\mathcal{L}_S + \mathcal{L}_L + \mathrm{ER}] \qquad (2)$$

$$\mathcal{L}_S = \mathrm{SG}(\mathcal{L}(\boldsymbol{i}, \boldsymbol{o}) - b) \sum_{t=1}^{|m|} \log P_{S,t}(x_t) \qquad (3)$$

$$\mathcal{L}_L = \mathcal{L}(\boldsymbol{i}, \boldsymbol{o}) \qquad (4)$$

$$\mathrm{ER} = -\frac{\lambda_{\mathcal{H}}}{N} \sum_{t=1}^{N} \mathcal{H}(P_{S,t}), \qquad (5)$$

where b is a mean baseline added to reduce the estimate variance, $\mathrm{SG}(\cdot)$ denotes the stop-gradient operation[2], $P_{S,t}$ is the speaker's output layer at time step t defining a categorical distribution over an alphabet A, $P_{S,t}(x_t)$ is the probability of $x_t \in A$ being sampled at time step t, and $\mathcal{H}(\cdot)$ is the entropy function. Eq. 3 and Eq. 4 are derived by the approach of Schulman et al. (2015), which can be seen as the combination of REINFORCE-like method (Williams, 1992) and standard backpropagation. ER (Eq. 5) is added to encourage the exploration during training (Williams and Peng, 1991).

2.3 Anti-ZLA Emergent Languages

Chaabouni et al. (2019) reported, somewhat surprisingly, that the communication protocols had a clear anti-ZLA tendency when agents play a signaling game described in section 2.1. They also reported that a ZLA-like tendency appeared when they additionally imposed an *artificial length pressure* on messages:

$$\mathcal{L}'(\boldsymbol{i}, L(m), m) = \mathcal{L}(\boldsymbol{i}, L(m)) + \alpha \times |m|, \quad (6)$$

where m is a message, $|\cdot|$ denotes length, and $\alpha \geq 0$ is a hyperparameter.

Rita et al. (2020) took a quite similar approach and observed the emergence of ZLA. As well as imposing a length pressure on a speaker agent, they re-designed the architecture of a listener agent so that the listener would be *impatient* to recover $\boldsymbol{i}$ as soon as possible.

Note that both the length pressure (Eq. 6) and the architecture re-design in Rita et al. (2020) can be regarded as somewhat explicit losses, whereas we try to impose an implicit pressure on agents.

3 Setup

3.1 Game with Noise

For a game, we take almost the same design as Chaabouni et al. (2019), which was introduced in section 2.1. We additionally introduce a *channel* C over which messages move from speaker to listener: A listener L obtains a message $\tilde{m} = C(m)$ through a channel C, instead of receiving directly $m = S(i)$ from a speaker. Also, there are several differences in hyperparameter settings.

3.2 Architectures

As speaker and listener agents have continuous vectors as their states, they are added with continuous noise. For simplicity, we choose a Gaussian noise sampled at each time step with replacement. Channels, on the other hand, are exposed to discrete noise, since they convey discrete symbols. We take a random replacement operation for the channel noise.

3.2.1 Speaker and Listener

The architectures of speaker and listener agents are based on a single-layer LSTM, following Chaabouni et al. (2019).

At training time, we add Gaussian noise to the cell states of the LSTM of each agent[3]. Formally,

[2] When we write $SG(x)$ instead of bare x, we regard x as a constant with respect to any parameters.

[3] We also tried simply shrinking the size of the agents' hidden layers to restrict their capacity, but it made it difficult to train the agents successfully. We leave it for future work

for $t > 0$,

$$(\boldsymbol{h}_{t+1}, \boldsymbol{c}_{t+1}) = \text{LSTM}(\boldsymbol{x}_{t+1}, (\boldsymbol{h}_t, \hat{\boldsymbol{c}}_t)) \quad (7)$$

$$\hat{\boldsymbol{c}}_t = \boldsymbol{c}_t + \boldsymbol{\epsilon}_t \quad (8)$$

$$\boldsymbol{\epsilon}_t \sim \mathcal{N}(\cdot \mid \boldsymbol{0}, \sigma^2 E) \quad (9)$$

where $\sigma > 0$ is a standard deviation (SD), E is the identity matrix, $\mathcal{N}(\cdot \mid \boldsymbol{0}, \sigma^2 E)$ is a Gaussian distribution with a mean vector $\boldsymbol{0}$ and a variance-covariance matrix $\sigma^2 E$, and $\boldsymbol{\epsilon}_t$ is a sampled value from $\mathcal{N}(\cdot \mid \boldsymbol{0}, \sigma^2 E)$ at time step t. We denote by σ_S, σ_L the SDs for the speaker and listener architecture respectively.

At test time, we do not add noise for deterministic evaluation.

3.2.2 Channel

At training time, we think of a channel as being exposed to some noise so that the messages can be degraded during transportation. Such degradation is modeled as replacement: each symbol in a message is probabilistically replaced with another one. Note that each message is attached with eos, which is exceptionally protected from the replacement, since the effect of the insertion or deletion of eos is too strong for our purpose.

Formally, let A be an alphabet, $m = a_1 \dots a_n$ be an original message generated by the speaker, and $\tilde{m} = \tilde{a}_1 \dots \tilde{a}_n$ be transformed one. Then the probability distribution over $\tilde{a}_i \neq \texttt{eos}$ given $a_i \neq \texttt{eos}$ $(i = 1, \dots, n-1)$ is as follows:

$$p(\tilde{a}_i \mid a_i) = \begin{cases} 1 - \pi_C & (a_i = \tilde{a}_i) \\ \dfrac{\pi_C}{|A \backslash \{a_i, \texttt{eos}\}|} & (a_i \neq \tilde{a}_i) \end{cases}, \quad (10)$$

where π_C is a hyperparameter s.t. $0 \leq \pi_C \leq 1$. Let us call π_C a *channel replacement probability*.

At test time, the channel is free from noise so that we can perform deterministic examinations.

3.3 Optimization

3.3.1 Design and Estimation of Loss Function

We use almost the same loss function as Eq. 2. We modify ER (Eq. 5) into *Decayed Entropy Regularizer (DER)* and we define an additional auxiliary loss *Soft Max Length (SML)* in the following sections. Both DER and SML are introduced to prevent messages from being unnaturally long. Note that they themselves are not factors for ZLA in our assumption.

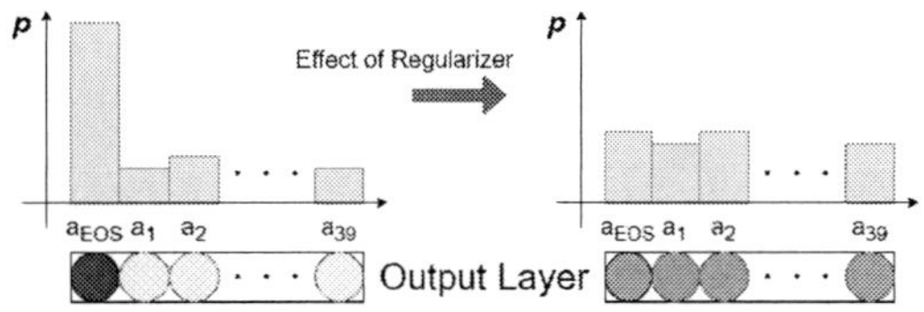

Figure 1: Illustration of the effect of the entropy regularizer

3.3.2 Decayed Entropy Regularizer

Chaabouni et al. (2019) used ER (Eq. 5) to encourage the exploration. However, ER might have an unexpected side-effect: They could lead messages to be unnecessarily long. We give an intuitive explanation as shown in Figure 1. Suppose that a speaker agent has learned a message pattern $m = x_1 \dots x_{|m|}$ for an input i. By the definition of the message, $x_{|m|} = \texttt{eos}$, indicating that the probability that eos is sampled is relatively higher at time step $|m|$. Then, the speaker's output layer $P_{S,|m|}$ at time step $|m|$ is updated so that the entropy $\mathcal{H}(P_{|m|})$ will be larger. It means that the probability of eos being sampled becomes lower, which might lead the message to be longer. Such an effect can cause an undesirable bias in emergent languages. Thus, we modify ER into *Decayed Entropy Regularizer (DER)* as:

$$\text{DER} = -\frac{\lambda_{\mathcal{H}}}{Z} \sum_{t=1}^{N} \mathcal{H}(P_t) \times \rho_{\mathcal{H}}^{t-1}, \quad (11)$$

$$Z = \sum_{t=1}^{N} \rho_{\mathcal{H}}^{t-1}, \quad (12)$$

where $\rho_{\mathcal{H}}$ is a hyperparameter s.t. $0 < \rho_{\mathcal{H}} \leq 1$. DER is a weighted mean that puts a higher priority on the entropy at earlier time steps but lower on those at later. Therefore, it is expected to cancel the unnecessary effect of hindering eos emission at later time steps.

3.3.3 Soft Max Length

Each message m is generated by sampling a symbol x_t at each time step t and concatenating them until either eos is sampled (self-termination) or the time step reaches max_len $- 1$ (forced termination). In the forced termination case, eos is attached to the end of the sequence. However, this generating procedure may cause a speaker agent to fail to learn to emit eos for some inputs, since message lengths are bounded regardless of the eos emission. To handle this problem, we introduce an additional auxiliary loss *Soft Max Length (SML)* defined as:

$$\text{SML} = \lambda_{sml} \max(0, |m| - \texttt{eff\_max\_len}), \quad (13)$$

where m is a message, $|\cdot|$ denotes length, λ_{sml} is the coefficient of this term, and $\texttt{eff\_max\_len}$ is a hyperparameter s.t. $0 \leq \texttt{eff\_max\_len} \leq \texttt{max\_len}$.

3.3.4 Training and Implementation

We follow Chaabouni et al. (2019) on the rest of the training method: Agents are trained for 2500 episodes, each of which contains 100 mini-batches. Each mini-batches are made of 5120 inputs sampled from the power-law distribution with replacement. When the accuracy at test time reaches 0.99 or more, the training stops early. Note that we do not add any noise at test time.

The game and the training are implemented using the EGG toolkit (Kharitonov et al., 2019)[4].

3.4 Evaluating Communicative Effectiveness

As Lowe et al. (2019) pointed out, emergent communications have to be carefully examined in terms of effectiveness: even if something like communication emerges, agents might act without referring to signals from others. Since message lengths can vary in our signaling game, it is doubtful that every single symbol in a message conveys essential information. For example, it is not trivial whether $\texttt{eos}$ is really end-of-sentence, since agents can use other symbols as "punctuations" or meaningless "blanks." The effective position of beginning-of-sentence is not trivial, either. Thus, apparent message lengths may differ from actual ones.

To evaluate effectiveness, we introduce *position-wise symbol effectiveness* and then *head/intermediate/tail effectiveness* to cover a weak point in the former.

Position-wise Symbol Effectiveness

First, to evaluate how informative symbols are distributed across positions, we introduce *position-wise symbol effectiveness*, which is a quite similar notion to *positional encoding* in Rita et al. (2020). Suppose a symbol x_k in a message $m = x_1 \ldots x_k \ldots x_{|m|}$ is informative enough. Then, a listener L is expected to fail to recover an input i correctly if x_k is replaced with another symbol y, i.e., $i \neq L(x_1 \ldots y \ldots x_{|m|})$. Based on this intuition, the symbol effectiveness $e(m, k)$ at position $k \in \{1, \ldots, \texttt{max\_len}\}$ in a message $m = x_1 \ldots x_{|m|}$ is defined as follows:

$$e(m,k) = \begin{cases} \frac{1}{|A'|} \sum_{a \in A'} \mathbb{1}_{i \neq L(m[x_k := a])} & (k < |m|) \\ 0 & (k \geq |m|) \end{cases} \quad (14)$$

$$A' = A \backslash \{x_k, \texttt{eos}\}, \quad (15)$$

where A is an alphabet, $m[x_k := a]$ denotes $x_1 \ldots x_{k-1} a x_{k+1} \ldots x_{|m|}$, and $\mathbb{1}_\phi$ is defined as

$$\mathbb{1}_\phi = \begin{cases} 1 & (\phi \text{ is true.}) \\ 0 & (\phi \text{ is false.}) \end{cases} . \quad (16)$$

By definition, $0 \leq e(m,k) \leq 1$. Low $e(m,k)$ means that symbol x_k is redundant, since the listener L can recover i from most of $m[x_k := a]$ $(a \in A')$. Otherwise, x_k is considered necessary for successful communications. Note that $\texttt{eos} = x_{|m|}$ is prevented from being replaced.

The value of $e(m,k)$ (Eq. 14) may vary depending on messages and speaker agents. That would make it difficult to perform straightforward evaluations for position-wise symbol effectiveness. To handle this problem, we also define $\overline{e}_k$, mean $e(m,k)$ across messages and across speaker agents. Formally, let $\mathcal{S} = \{S_1, \ldots, S_{|\mathcal{S}|}\}$ be a set of $|\mathcal{S}|$ speaker agents trained with different random seeds. Then $\overline{e}_k$ is defined as:

$$\overline{e}_k = \frac{1}{|\mathcal{S}||I|} \sum_{S \in \mathcal{S}} \sum_{i \in I} e(S(i), k). \quad (17)$$

Head, Intermediate, and Tail Effectiveness

One may be interested in detecting whether the effectiveness is concentrated in the prefixes, infixes, or suffixes of messages. However, $\overline{e}_k$ (Eq. 17) do not seem good for this purpose: Since message lengths can vary, the effectiveness of infixes and suffixes can scatter across $\overline{e}_k$. Thus, we additionally introduce *head effectiveness* $\overline{e}_{head}$, *intermediate effectiveness* $\overline{e}_{med}$, and *tail effectiveness* $\overline{e}_{tail}$. Intuitively, $\overline{e}_{head}$ is mean effectiveness across the heads of messages (i.e., x_1 in $m = x_1 \ldots x_{|m|}$) and across speaker agents. Similarly, $\overline{e}_{med}$ (resp. $\overline{e}_{tail}$) is mean effectiveness across the intermediate positions (resp. tails) of messages and across speaker

[4]The code for the EGG toolkit is found at https://github.com/facebookresearch/EGG. Our code is available at https://github.com/wedddy0707/noisyEGG.git.

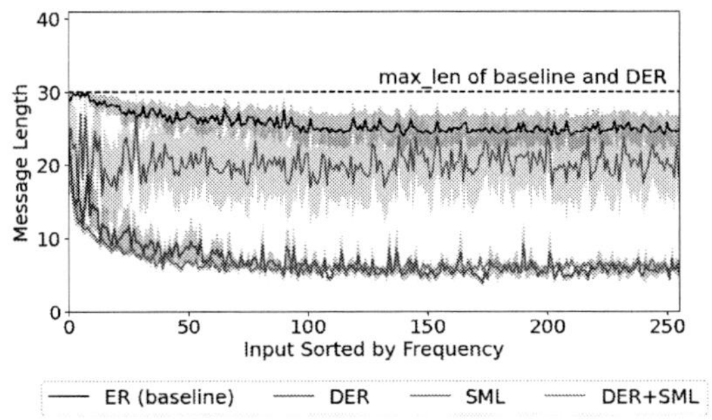

Figure 2: Mean message lengths across successful runs as a function of inputs sorted by frequency, when ER, DER, SML, and DER+SML are used respectively. The shaded areas represent one stanrd error of mean (SEM).

	# successful runs
ER (baseline)	16
DER	7
SML	6
DER+SML	11

Table 1: The number of successful runs out of 16.

agents. Formally, let $\mathcal{S} = \{S_1, \ldots, S_{|\mathcal{S}|}\}$ be as above. Then $\overline{e}_{head}$, $\overline{e}_{med}$, and $\overline{e}_{tail}$ are defined as follows:

$$\overline{e}_{head} = \frac{1}{|\mathcal{S}||I|}\sum_{S\in\mathcal{S}}\sum_{i\in I} e(S(i), 1) = \overline{e}_1 \quad (18)$$

$$\overline{e}_{med} = \frac{1}{|\mathcal{S}||I|}\sum_{S\in\mathcal{S}}\sum_{i\in I} e\left(S(i), \left\lfloor\frac{|S(i)|}{2}\right\rfloor\right) \quad (19)$$

$$\overline{e}_{tail} = \frac{1}{|\mathcal{S}||I|}\sum_{S\in\mathcal{S}}\sum_{i\in I} e(S(i), |S(i)| - 1), \quad (20)$$

where $\lfloor\cdot\rfloor$ is a floor function.

4 Experiments

4.1 Hyperparameter Setting

In all our experiments, the size $|I|$ of an input space was set to 256, the size $|A|$ of an alphabet was 40, the size of hidden layers was 100 for both agents, and the entropy regularizer coefficient $\lambda_{\mathcal{H}}$ was 1. The hyperparameters σ_S, σ_L, and π_C for noise varied through sections.

We define a training run ending with an accuracy higher than 0.99 as a *successful* run.

4.2 Effects of DER and SML

Before conducting the main experiments, we show the effect of DER (Eq. 11) and SML (Eq. 13). For a baseline model, we used the existing entropy regularizer ER (Eq. 5), setting $\lambda_{\mathcal{H}} = 1$ and $\texttt{max\_len} = 30$. For a model with DER, $(\lambda_{\mathcal{H}}, \rho_{\mathcal{H}}) = (1, 1/2)$. For a model with SML (and ER), $\lambda_{\mathcal{H}} = 1$ and $(\texttt{max\_len}, \texttt{eff\_max\_len}) = (40, 30)$. For a model with DER+SML, $(\lambda_{\mathcal{H}}, \rho_{\mathcal{H}}) = (1, 1/2)$ and $(\texttt{max\_len}, \texttt{eff\_max\_len}) = (40, 30)$.

To see the overall tendency, we show the mean message lengths across successful runs for each model in Figure 2. The mean lengths are longer when ER is used. In particular, the ones of the baseline model are near $\texttt{max\_len} = 30$. On the other hand, the mean lengths are shorter when DER is used. That suggests that DER prevents messages from being unnecessarily longer.

To check the effects on learning, in addition, Table 1 shows the number of successful runs out of 16 for each model. Although apparent tendencies in Figure 2 are similar between the DER and DER+SML model, Table 1 suggests that it is easier to learn with the DER+SML model which has 5 more successful runs than the SML model.

setting	Spearman ρ
no noise	0.327 ($p = 5.9 \times 10^{-71}$)
noise $\sigma_S = 1/4$	0.113 ($p = 1.5 \times 10^{-6}$)
noise $\sigma_S = 1/2$	0.109 ($p = 6.9 \times 10^{-7}$)
noise $\sigma_S = 1$	0.008 ($p = 7.7 \times 10^{-1}$)
noise $\sigma_L = 1/4$	0.273 ($p = 6.6 \times 10^{-32}$)
noise $\sigma_L = 1/2$	0.280 ($p = 5.9 \times 10^{-20}$)
noise $\sigma_L = 1$	0.268 ($p = 1.4 \times 10^{-22}$)
noise $\pi_C = 0.01$	0.261 ($p = 3.3 \times 10^{-37}$)
noise $\pi_C = 0.05$	0.236 ($p = 6.3 \times 10^{-21}$)
noise $\pi_C = 0.1$	0.249 ($p = 8.6 \times 10^{-27}$)

Table 2: Spearman correlations between input frequency ranks and message length ranks in successful runs in various noise conditions.

4.3 Effects of Noise

In this section, we show the influence of noise on a speaker, listener, and channel. We used the DER+SML model with the same hyperparameters as in the previous section. We examined the effect of each noise by varying σ_S, σ_L, and π_C. Note that σ_S is the standard deviation of noise on a speaker, σ_L is the one on a speaker, and π_C is the channel replacement probability.

4.3.1 Noise on a Speaker

To examine the effect of noise on a speaker, $(\sigma_S, \sigma_L, \pi_C)$ was set to $(1/4, 0, 0, 0)$, $(1/2, 0, 0)$,

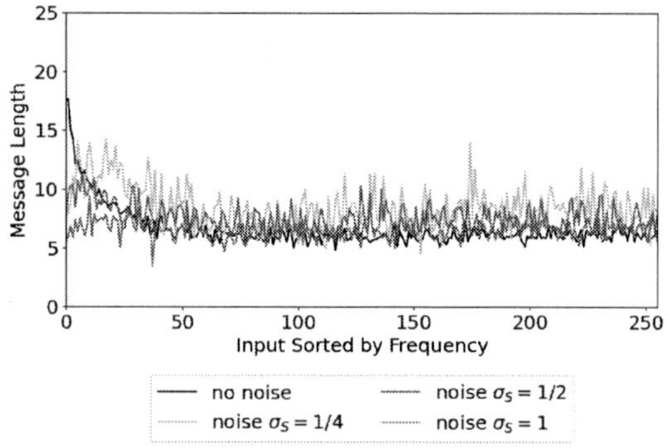

Figure 3: Mean message lengths across successful runs as a function of inputs sorted by frequency, when $(\sigma_S, \sigma_L, \pi_C) = (0,0,0)$, $(1/4,0,0)$, $(1/2,0,0)$, and $(1,0,0)$ respectively.

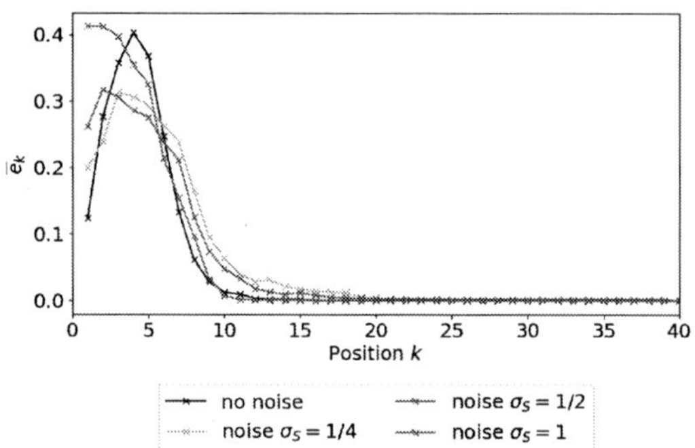

Figure 4: $\overline{e}_k$ in successful runs, when $(\sigma_S, \sigma_L, \pi_C) = (0,0,0)$, $(1/4,0,0)$, $(1/2,0,0)$, and $(1,0,0)$ respectively.

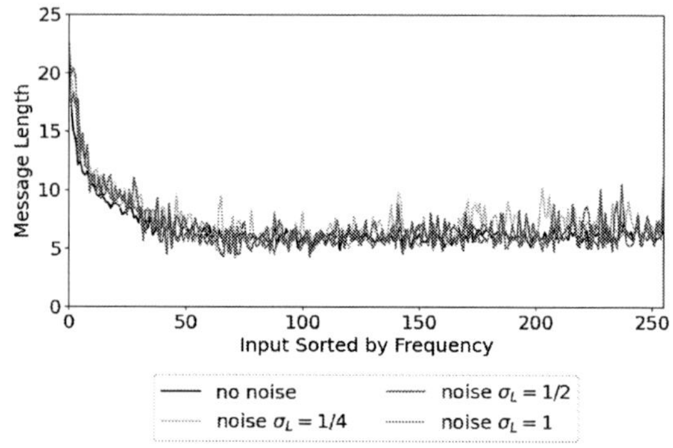

Figure 5: Mean message lengths across successful runs as a function of inputs sorted by frequency, when $(\sigma_S, \sigma_L, \pi_C) = (0,0,0)$, $(0,1/4,0)$, $(0,1/2,0)$, and $(0,1,0)$ respectively.

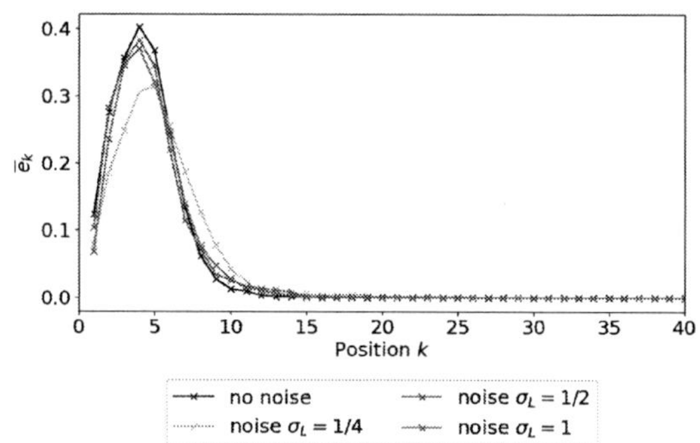

Figure 6: $\overline{e}_k$ in successful runs, when $(\sigma_S, \sigma_L, \pi_C) = (0,0,0)$, $(0,1/4,0)$, $(0,1/2,0)$, and $(0,1,0)$ respectively.

and $(1,0,0)$. 7 out of 16, 8 out of 16, and 6 out of 32 runs were successful for each setting.

To see the overall tendency, we show mean message lengths for each model in Figure 3[5]. The tendency shifts from anti-ZLA to the one between ZLA and anti-ZLA as σ_S gets bigger.

In addition, we show Spearman correlations between input frequency ranks and message length ranks in Table 2. Intuitively, $\rho < 0$ implies ZLA and $\rho > 0$ implies anti-ZLA. According to Table 2, ρ gets smaller as σ_S gets bigger, which is consistent with the observation in Figure 3.

To check the symbol effectiveness, we show $\overline{e}_k$ (Eq. 17) in Figure 4. Judging from Figure 4, the effectiveness at an earlier position becomes higher as σ_S gets bigger. We also show $\overline{e}_{head}$, $\overline{e}_{med}$, and $\overline{e}_{tail}$ (Eq. 18, Eq. 19, and Eq. 20) in Figure 9. In Figure 9, the bigger σ_S is, the higher $\overline{e}_{head}$ and $\overline{e}_{med}$ are, indicating that the former halves of messages become more informative by the effect of noise on a speaker.

These results suggest that noise on a speaker is a factor for ZLA, or at least causes message lengths to be closer to ZLA. One possible reason is that noise accumulation over time made it difficult for a speaker agent to generate long consistent messages.

4.3.2 Noise on a Listener

Next, to investigate the effect of noise on a listener, $(\sigma_S, \sigma_L, \pi_C)$ was set to $(0,1/4,0)$, $(0,1/2,0)$, and $(0,1,0)$. 7 out of 16, 4 out of 32, and 5 out of 16 runs were successful for each setting.

To see the overall tendency, mean message lengths are shown in Figure 5. The apparent tendencies are quite similar among all the settings

[5]There are some messages of length `max_len` =40 while other messages are much shorter. We excluded the former in Figure 3 because otherwise the mean lines would have unnatural peaks and impair readability. As a result, 4 out of 1792, 30 out of 2048, and 7 out of 1526 data points were removed for $\sigma_S = 1/4, 1/2$, and 1 respectively.

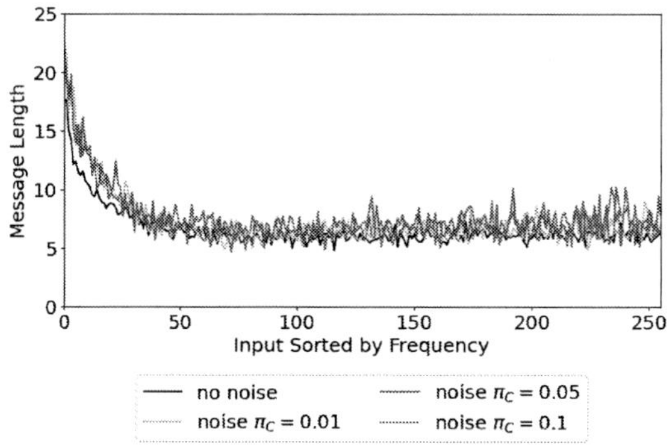

Figure 7: Mean message lengths across successful runs as a function of inputs sorted by frequency, when $(\sigma_S, \sigma_L, \pi_C) = (0,0,0)$, $(0,0,0.01)$, $(0,0,0.05)$, and $(0,0,0.1)$ respectively.

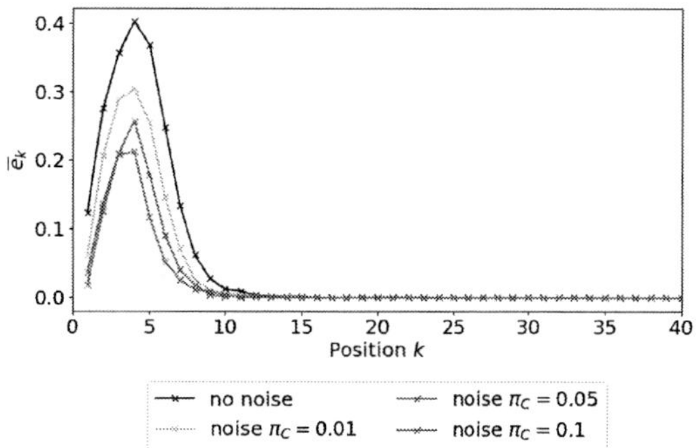

Figure 8: $meaneff_k$ in successful runs, when $(\sigma_S, \sigma_L, \pi_C) = (0,0,0)$, $(0,0,0.01)$, $(0,0,0.05)$, and $(0,0,0.1)$ respectively.

including 'no noise,' showing clear anti-ZLA tendencies. Spearman correlations in Table 2 also suggest anti-ZLA tendencies.

To check the symbol effectiveness, we show $\overline{e}_k$ (Eq. 17) in Figure 6. In Figure 6, $\overline{e}_k$ for $\sigma_L > 0$ shows similar tendencies to those for 'no noise,' although the peak of $\overline{e}_k$ for $\sigma_L = 1/2$ is lower than the other results.. $\overline{e}_{head}$, $\overline{e}_{med}$, and $\overline{e}_{tail}$ (Eq. 18, Eq. 19, and Eq. 20) are shown in Figure 9. According to Figure 9, $\overline{e}_{head}$ for $\sigma_L > 0$ tends to be smaller than the one for 'no noise,' but the overall tendencies seem similar (e.g., $\overline{e}_{head} < \overline{e}_{med} < \overline{e}_{tail}$).

These results suggest that noise on a listener is not a crucial factor for changing a tendency in emergent languages. The listener's short-term memory is thought to have been limited due to noise accumulation over time, as $\overline{e}_{head}$ got smaller. However, even if there was no noise, informative symbols tended to be located in the latter half of messages, i.e, $\overline{e}_{head} < \overline{e}_{med} < \overline{e}_{tail}$, which is one possible reason why noise on a listener did not crucially affect the overall tendency.

4.3.3 Noise on a Channel

Finally, to check the effect of noise on a channel, $(\sigma_S, \sigma_L, \pi_C)$ was set to $(0,0,0.01)$, $(0,0,0.05)$, and $(0,0,0.1)$. 9 out of 16, 6 out of 32, and 7 out of 32 runs were successful for each setting.

To see the overall tendency, mean message lengths are shown in Figure 7. The apparent results for $\pi_C > 0$ are similar to the one for 'no noise,' showing clear anti-ZLA tendencies. Spearman correlations in Table 2 also suggest anti-ZLA tendencies.

To check the symbol effectiveness, we show $\overline{e}_k$ (Eq. 17) in Figure 8. In Figure 8, $\overline{e}_k$ becomes lower entirely as π_C gets bigger. $\overline{e}_{head}$, $\overline{e}_{med}$, and $\overline{e}_{tail}$ (Eq. 18, Eq. 19, and Eq. 20) are shown in Figure 9. In Figure 9, $\overline{e}_{head}$, $\overline{e}_{med}$, and $\overline{e}_{tail}$ become lower as π_C gets bigger. Remember that low $e(m,k)$ (Eq. 14) means that the symbol at position k in m is redundant. Thus, lower $\overline{e}_k$, $\overline{e}_{head}$, $\overline{e}_{med}$, and $\overline{e}_{tail}$ indicate that symbols are redundant on the whole.

These results suggest that redundancy was facilitated due to the noise on a channel. It is consistent with Zipf's hypothesis and a noisy-channel model.

5 Discussion

Our experiments suggest that noise on a speaker is a factor for ZLA, while noise on a listener and a channel is not in our signaling game.

One possible reason for the noise on a speaker is that noise accumulation matters as time goes. At each trial, the speaker agent gets an input $\boldsymbol{i}$ and transforms it into an initial hidden state $\boldsymbol{h}_0$. The hidden states need to maintain the input $\boldsymbol{i}$ in some way for emitting consistent symbols. But noise accumulates over time and is harmful to their memory, which may cause frequent messages to be shorter. However, the result per se shows a neutral tendency between ZLA and anti-ZLA. Our implicit length pressure might not have been strong enough, or there might have been some problems with the agents' architectures.

Noise on a listener is not a crucial factor for ZLA in our setting. Judging from symbol effectiveness, the latter halves of messages tend to be more informative than the former when noise interferes with the listener. It means that the listener could "forget" the former halves of messages. In

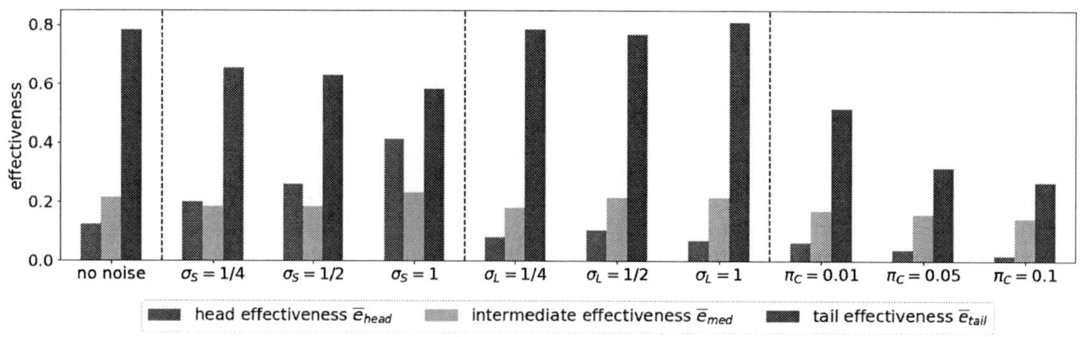

Figure 9: $\overline{e}_{head}$, $\overline{e}_{med}$, and $\overline{e}_{tail}$ in successful runs under various noise conditions.

the first place, however, the former halves are less informative even if there is no noise. That may be why noise on a listener did not affect the overall tendency. Noise on a channel seems to facilitate the redundancy of messages, which is consistent with Zipf's hypothesis and a noisy-channel model.

To help agents with learning, we used the two auxiliary loss DER (Eq. 11) and SML (Eq. 13) which are somewhat artificial. In particular, the usage of SML conflicts a bit with our original goal to give rise to ZLA by an implicit penalty, as SML is similar to an artificial length pressure (Eq. 6).

6 Conclusion

In this paper, we simulated the emergence of language and checked whether the emergent languages follow Zipf's law of abbreviation (ZLA). Inspired by some psychological concepts, we proposed exposing architectures to some noise during training. Our experiments were conducted under several noise conditions. The results suggested that noise on a speaker agent is one factor for ZLA, whereas neither noise on a listener nor noise on a channel is in our signaling game.

Our main contribution is to propose a potential factor for ZLA instead of an external length pressure and to demonstrate that noise imposing internal difficulty on a speaker agent may cause ZLA.

However, there are several problems and limitations in addition to what is discussed in section 5. First, we could not try the combination of noises. One might be interested in combining the noises on a speaker, listener, and channel, but we failed to train agents stably under such conditions. It is simply because it became much more difficult for agents to learn under several noises.

Second, our signaling game did not contain any *contexts*. As an input space was no more complex than having the order by frequency, emergent languages could only have a unigram-like structure. However, according to Piantadosi et al. (2011), word predictability considering contexts is a better predictor of word length than unigram probabilities. From a more realistic point of view, therefore, contexts should be considered in some ways. Moreover, if agents are forced to remember contexts, noise on a listener may also be a factor for ZLA, making the listener *impatient*.

We leave these issues for future work.

Acknowledgment

We would like to thank Professor Yusuke Miyao for supervising our research, Jason Naradowsky for fruitful discussions and proofreading, and the anonymous reviewers for helpful suggestions. The first author would also like to thank his colleagues Taiga Ishii and Hiroaki Mizuno as they have encouraged each other in their senior theses.

References

Alan D. Baddeley. 2003. Working memory and language: an overview. *Journal of Communication Disorders*, 36(3):189 – 208.

Alan D. Baddeley and Graham J. Hitch. 2019. The phonological loop as a buffer store: An update. *Cortex*, 112:91 – 106.

Alan D. Baddeley, Neil Thomson, and Mary Buchanan. 1975. Word length and the structure of short-term memory. *Journal of Verbal Learning and Verbal Behavior*, 14(6):575 – 589.

Rahma Chaabouni, Eugene Kharitonov, Diane Bouchacourt, Emmanuel Dupoux, and Marco Baroni. 2020. Compositionality and generalization in emergent languages. In *Proceedings of the 58th Annual Meeting of the Association for Computational Linguistics*, pages 4427–4442, Online. Association for Computational Linguistics.

Rahma Chaabouni, Eugene Kharitonov, Emmanuel Dupoux, and Marco Baroni. 2019. Anti-efficient encoding in emergent communication. In *Advances in Neural Information Processing Systems*, volume 32, pages 6293–6303. Curran Associates, Inc.

Markus Damian, Jeff Bowers, Hans Stadthagen-Gonzalez, and Katharina Spalek. 2010. Does word length affect speech onset latencies when producing single words? *Journal of experimental psychology. Learning, memory, and cognition*, 36:892–905.

Laura Harding Graesser, Kyunghyun Cho, and Douwe Kiela. 2019. Emergent linguistic phenomena in multi-agent communication games. In *Proceedings of the 2019 Conference on Empirical Methods in Natural Language Processing and the 9th International Joint Conference on Natural Language Processing (EMNLP-IJCNLP)*, pages 3700–3710, Hong Kong, China. Association for Computational Linguistics.

Serhii Havrylov and Ivan Titov. 2017. Emergence of language with multi-agent games: Learning to communicate with sequences of symbols. In *Advances in Neural Information Processing Systems 30: Annual Conference on Neural Information Processing Systems 2017, December 4-9, 2017, Long Beach, CA, USA*, pages 2149–2159.

Jasmeen Kanwal, Kenny Smith, Jennifer Culbertson, and Simon Kirby. 2017. Zipf's law of abbreviation and the principle of least effort: Language users optimise a miniature lexicon for efficient communication. *Cognition*, 165:45 – 52.

Eugene Kharitonov, Rahma Chaabouni, Diane Bouchacourt, and Marco Baroni. 2019. EGG: a toolkit for research on emergence of lanGuage in games. In *Proceedings of the 2019 Conference on Empirical Methods in Natural Language Processing and the 9th International Joint Conference on Natural Language Processing (EMNLP-IJCNLP): System Demonstrations*, pages 55–60, Hong Kong, China. Association for Computational Linguistics.

Eugene Kharitonov, Rahma Chaabouni, Diane Bouchacourt, and Marco Baroni. 2020. Entropy minimization in emergent languages. In *Proceedings of the 37th International Conference on Machine Learning*, volume 119 of *Proceedings of Machine Learning Research*, pages 5220–5230, Virtual. PMLR.

Satwik Kottur, José Moura, Stefan Lee, and Dhruv Batra. 2017. Natural language does not emerge 'naturally' in multi-agent dialog. In *Proceedings of the 2017 Conference on Empirical Methods in Natural Language Processing*, pages 2962–2967, Copenhagen, Denmark. Association for Computational Linguistics.

Angeliki Lazaridou, Karl Moritz Hermann, Karl Tuyls, and Stephen Clark. 2018. Emergence of linguistic communication from referential games with symbolic and pixel input. In *6th International Conference on Learning Representations, ICLR 2018, Vancouver, BC, Canada, April 30 - May 3, 2018, Conference Track Proceedings*. OpenReview.net.

Angeliki Lazaridou, Alexander Peysakhovich, and Marco Baroni. 2017. Multi-agent cooperation and the emergence of (natural) language. In *5th International Conference on Learning Representations, ICLR 2017, Toulon, France, April 24-26, 2017, Conference Track Proceedings*. OpenReview.net.

Jason Lee, Kyunghyun Cho, Jason Weston, and Douwe Kiela. 2018. Emergent translation in multi-agent communication. In *6th International Conference on Learning Representations, ICLR 2018, Vancouver, BC, Canada, April 30 - May 3, 2018, Conference Track Proceedings*. OpenReview.net.

David K. Lewis. 1969. *Convention: A Philosophical Study*. Wiley-Blackwell.

Ryan Lowe, Jakob N. Foerster, Y-Lan Boureau, Joelle Pineau, and Yann N. Dauphin. 2019. On the pitfalls of measuring emergent communication. In *Proceedings of the 18th International Conference on Autonomous Agents and MultiAgent Systems, AAMAS '19, Montreal, QC, Canada, May 13-17, 2019*, pages 693–701. International Foundation for Autonomous Agents and Multiagent Systems.

Antje S Meyer, Ardi Roelofs, and Willem J.M Levelt. 2003. Word length effects in object naming: The role of a response criterion. *Journal of Memory and Language*, 48(1):131 – 147.

Steven T. Piantadosi, Harry Tily, and Edward Gibson. 2011. Word lengths are optimized for efficient communication. *Proceedings of the National Academy of Sciences*, 108(9):3526–3529.

Mathieu Rita, Rahma Chaabouni, and Emmanuel Dupoux. 2020. "LazImpa": Lazy and impatient neural agents learn to communicate efficiently. In *Proceedings of the 24th Conference on Computational Natural Language Learning*, pages 335–343, Online. Association for Computational Linguistics.

John Schulman, Nicolas Heess, Theophane Weber, and Pieter Abbeel. 2015. Gradient estimation using stochastic computation graphs. In *Advances in Neural Information Processing Systems*, volume 28, pages 3528–3536. Curran Associates, Inc.

Claude E. Shannon. 1948. A mathematical theory of communication. *Bell Syst. Tech. J.*, 27(3):379–423.

R. J. Williams. 1992. Simple statistical gradient-following algorithms for connectionist reinforcement learning. *Machine Learning*, 8:229–256.

Ronald J. Williams and Jing Peng. 1991. Function optimization using connectionist reinforcement learning algorithms. *Connection Science*, 3:241–268.

George Kingsley Zipf. 1935. *The Psychobiology of Language*. Houghton-Mifflin, New York, NY, USA.

Long Document Summarization in a Low Resource Setting using Pretrained Language Models

Ahsaas Bajaj*
University of Massachusetts Amherst
abajaj@umass.edu

Pavitra Dangati*
University of Massachusetts Amherst
sdangati@umass.edu

Kalpesh Krishna
University of Massachusetts Amherst

Pradhiksha Ashok Kumar
University of Massachusetts Amherst

Rheeya Uppaal
Goldman Sachs

Bradford Windsor
Goldman Sachs

Eliot Brenner
Goldman Sachs

Dominic Dotterrer
Goldman Sachs

Rajarshi Das
University of Massachusetts Amherst

Andrew McCallum
University of Massachusetts Amherst

Abstract

Abstractive summarization is the task of compressing a long document into a coherent short document while retaining salient information. Modern abstractive summarization methods are based on deep neural networks which often require large training datasets. Since collecting summarization datasets is an expensive and time-consuming task, practical industrial settings are usually *low-resource*. In this paper, we study a challenging low-resource setting of summarizing long legal briefs with an average source document length of 4268 words and **only 120** available (document, summary) pairs. To account for data scarcity, we used a modern pretrained abstractive summarizer BART (Lewis et al., 2020), which only achieves 17.9 ROUGE-L as it struggles with long documents. We thus attempt to compress these long documents by identifying salient sentences in the source which best ground the summary, using a novel algorithm based on GPT-2 (Radford et al., 2019) language model perplexity scores, that operates within the low resource regime. On feeding the compressed documents to BART, we observe a 6.0 ROUGE-L improvement. Our method also beats several competitive salience detection baselines. Furthermore, the identified salient sentences tend to agree with an independent human labeling by domain experts.

1 Introduction and Related Work

Text summarization is the task of generating a smaller coherent version of a document preserving key information. Typical abstractive summarization algorithms use seq2seq models with attention (Chopra et al., 2016), copy mechanisms (Gu et al., 2016), content selection (Cheng and Lapata, 2016), pointer-generator methods (See et al., 2017) and reinforcement learning (Wu and Hu, 2018). These methods perform well in high resource summarization datasets with small documents such as CNN/DailyMail (Nallapati et al., 2016), Gigaword (Rush et al., 2015), etc. However, summarization over long documents with thousands of tokens is a more practically relevant problem. Existing solutions focus on leveraging document structure (Cohan et al., 2018) or do mixed model summarization involving compression or selection followed by abstractive summarization (Liu et al., 2018; Gehrmann et al., 2018). However, these methods require large amounts of training data. Low resource settings are common in real world applications as curating domain specific datasets especially over long documents and on a large scale, is both expensive and time consuming.

A human summarizing a long document would first understand the text, then highlight the important information, and finally paraphrase it to generate a summary. Building on this intuition, we present a low-resource long document summarization algorithm (Section 2) operating in 3 steps:

1. Ground sentences of every training set summary into its source, identifying salient sentences
2. Train a salience classifier on this data, and use it to compress the source document during test time

* Equal Contribution

Proceedings of the Joint Conference of the 59th Annual Meeting of the Association for Computational Linguistics and the 11th International Joint Conference on Natural Language Processing: Student Research Workshop, pages 71–80
August 5–6, 2021. ©2021 Association for Computational Linguistics

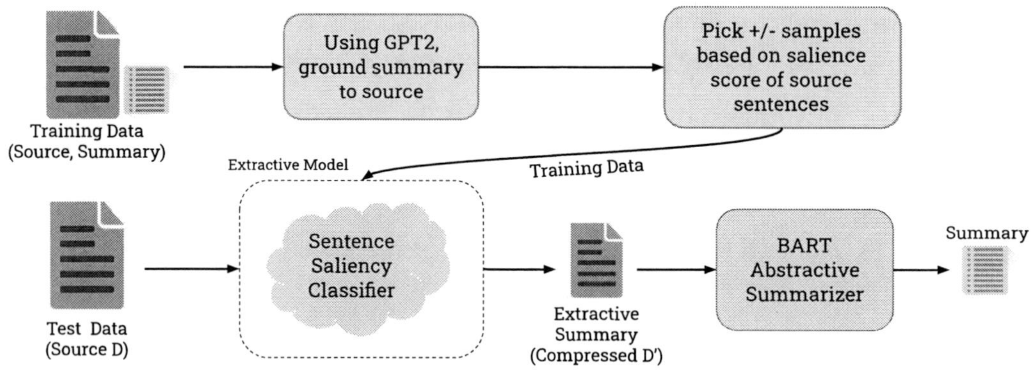

Figure 1: Our method for long document summarization task in low resource setting. The *Extraction Model* generates a compressed document D' by identifying salient sentences. It is trained by computing salience score for each training set source sentence. The pretrained abstractive summarizer takes as input the compressed document.

3. Feed the compressed document to a state-of-the-art abstractive summarizer pretrained on a related domain to generate a coherent and fluent summary

To tackle data scarcity, we use pretrained language models in all three steps, which show strong generalization (Devlin et al., 2019) and are sample efficient (Yogatama et al., 2019). Notably, our step (1) uses a novel method based on GPT-2 perplexity (Radford et al., 2019) to ground sentences.

Unlike prior work (Parida and Motlicek, 2019; Magooda and Litman, 2020) tackling data scarcity in summarization, our method needs no synthetic data augmentation. Moreover, we study a significantly more resource constrained setting — a complex legal briefs dataset (Section 2) with **only 120** available (document, summary) pairs and an average of 4.3K tokens per document; Parida and Motlicek (2019) assume access to 90,000 pairs with a maximum of 0.4K source document tokens, Magooda and Litman (2020) use 370 pairs with 0.2K source document tokens.

Despite this challenging setup, our method beats an abstractor-only approach by 6 ROUGE-L points, and also beats several competitive salience detection baselines (Section 3). Interestingly, identified salient sentences show agreement with an independent human labeling by domain experts, further validating the efficacy of our approach.

2 Dataset and Approach

To mimic the real world scenario of summarization over long domain-specific documents, we curate 120 document-summary pairs from publicly available Amicus Briefs,[1] thus simulating the legal domain. The source contains detailed arguments that the court should consider for a case; the target summarizes them. As shown in Table 1, our dataset is significantly smaller than the popular CNN/Daily Mail benchmark (Nallapati et al., 2016) and has significantly longer documents and summaries.

Dataset	# (S, T)	Avg. $\|S\|$	Avg. $\|T\|$
CNN/DM	312,084	781	56
Amicus	120	4,268	485

Table 1: A comparison between the Amicus legal briefs dataset and the popular CNN/Daily Mail benchmark. Amicus has far fewer document-summary pairs $\#(S, T)$, with more documents tokens (Avg. $|S|$) and summary tokens (Avg. $|T|$) on average.

To tackle this low resource setting, we use the state-of-the-art abstractive summarizer BART (Lewis et al., 2020), pretrained on a dataset from a related domain (CNN/DM). Since BART was trained on short documents, it truncates documents longer than 1024 subwords. Hence, instead of feeding the whole source document as input to BART, we feed salient sentences extracted using a salience classifier. Our salience classification dataset is built using a novel method which grounds summary sentences to sentences in source with language model perplexity scores. Our approach (Figure 1) resembles the *extract-then-abstract* paradigm popular in prior work (Gehrmann et al., 2018; Liu et al., 2018; Subramanian et al., 2019; Chen and Bansal, 2018).

[1] `https://publichealthlawcenter.org/amicus-briefs`

Extraction Stage: To extract the most important content from the source document required to generate the summary, we pose content selection as a binary classification task, labeling every sentence in the source document as *salient* or *non-salient*. Sentences classified as salient are concatenated in the order of occurrence in the source document to generate a compressed "extractive summary", which is then fed to the abstractive summarizer. Maintaining the order of sentences ensures the logical flow of information is not disrupted. In addition to identifying important information, the salience classifier is able to remove repetitive boilerplate text which is common in technical documents but often irrelevant to the actual content.

Training Data for Salience Classification: Since we do not have sentence-level training data for the classifier, we *construct* it by grounding sentences of the ground truth summary to sentences in the source document. Consider a source document S consisting of m sentences $s_{1:m}$ and a target summary T consisting of n sentences $t_{1:n}$ where $m >> n$. We compute the salience score for every source sentence $s_i \in S$ as $\frac{1}{n}\sum_{j=0}^{n} f(s_i, t_j)$. Here $f(s,t)$ is a measure of how much source sentence s grounds target sentence t. Following this, we sort the sentences in the source document based on salience score. The highest scoring $3n$ sentences are chosen as *salient* sentences and the lowest scoring $3n$ are chosen as *non-salient* sentences. $3n$ is a tuned hyperparameter. Whenever $m < 6n$, we sort the sentences according to the salience score and assign *salient* to the top half and *non-salient* to the bottom half. We construct our dataset for salience classification by running this algorithm for every (S, T) pair in the training dataset. To ensure generalization with limited training data, we incorporate transfer learning and build our classifier by finetuning BERT-base (Devlin et al., 2019) using `transformers` (Wolf et al., 2019). More details on training are provided in Appendix A.2.

Choice of $f(s,t)$: To measure how much a source sentence s grounds a target sentence t we measure the perplexity of t conditioned on s, using a pretrained language model GPT-2 large (Radford et al., 2019). More formally, we concatenate s and t as $[s;\ t]$ and feed it as input to GPT-2 large, calculating perplexity over the tokens of t. Here, *a lower perplexity corresponds to a higher $f(s,t)$ score.* We find that this measure correlates with entailment and outperforms other choices of $f(s,t)$ like n-gram overlap, sentence embedding similarity & entailment classifiers (Section 3.3).

Abstraction Stage: Having compressed the source document using our extractor, we use a black-box pretrained abstractive summarizer trained on a related domain. In this work, we make use of the state-of-the-art model (i.e. BART), which is based on pretrained language models. Pretraining on CNN/DM helps BART generalize to unseen but related domains like legal briefs. Details on our BART setup are provided in Appendix A.3.

3 Experiments

3.1 Evaluating the extractor

To evaluate our proposed extractor, we first check whether our salience classifier generalizes to a held-out test set.[2] Indeed, it achieves a classification accuracy of 73.66%, and qualitative analysis of the classifications confirm its ability to identify boilerplate sentences as *non-salient*. Our classifier compresses source documents by 61% on average. Note that classifier score can be thresholded to obtain more or less compression depending on domain and end-task.

Next, we evaluate the quality of extracted salient sentences by checking the extent to which they overlap in information with the gold test set summaries, by measuring ROUGE-1/2 recall scores. As shown in Table 2, our extractor outperforms a random selection of the same number of sentences and is comparable to the upper-bound recall performance achieved by feeding in the whole source document. Finally, to measure the extent to which our salience classifier matches human judgement, domain experts identified 8-10 salient sentences in four test documents with more than 200 sentences each on request. Despite their scarcity, our salience classifier recovers 64.7% marked sentences, confirming correlation with human judgments.

3.2 Evaluating the entire pipeline

We evaluate the entire pipeline by measuring the quality of abstractive summaries, obtained by feeding the extractive summary to BART. We study two abstractor settings:

1. Treating BART as a black-box with no modification

[2] Classifier data statistics at salient/non-salient sentences level: (Train=5363, Dev=1870, Test=2070)

Source	R-1 (Recall)	R-2 (Recall)
Whole Document	87.75	50.67
Random Extractor	78.66	38.53
Proposed Extractor	81.78	43.96

Table 2: ROUGE-1/2 (R-1/2) recall scores of the gold summary with respect to the the "Source" document. Our saliency-driven extractor performs better than a random selection of the same number of sentences and is close to the upperbound recall performance achieved by feeding in the whole source document.

Extractor	Abstractor	R-1	R-2	R-L
NE	BART	40.17	13.36	17.95
Random	BART	41.96	13.30	17.91
TextRank	BART	42.63	13.09	17.93
Bottom-up	BART	42.41	14.50	20.76
Ours	BART	**44.97**	**15.37**	**23.95**
NE	f.t. BART	43.47	16.30	19.35
Random	f.t. BART	44.63	15.11	18.57
TextRank	f.t. BART	45.10	15.51	18.74
Bottom-up	f.t. BART	44.89	17.26	23.40
Ours	f.t. BART	**47.07**	**17.64**	**24.40**

Table 3: Comparison of our method on the Amicus dataset with strong baselines. Our method outperforms all baselines in both Abstractor settings: (1) a pretrained CNN/DM BART; (2) the pretrained CNN/DM BART finetuned on the Amicus dataset (f.t. BART).

2. Finetuning BART on the training and validation split of Amicus dataset.[3]

We present results on the Amicus test set. We compare our model against several competitive baselines:

1. **NE**: no extraction
2. **Random**: a random selection of the same number of sentences as our extractive summary
3. **TextRank** (Mihalcea and Tarau, 2004; Liu et al., 2018): unsupervised graph based approach to rank text chunks within a document
4. **Bottom-up summarizer** (Gehrmann et al., 2018): a strong *extract-then-abstract* baseline where content selection is posed as a word-level sequence tagging problem. Similar to our setting, their content selector also uses large pretrained models (ELMo, Peters et al., 2018), which we finetune on our training set.

[3]The training and validation splits together comprise of 96 documents. The test split was not used.

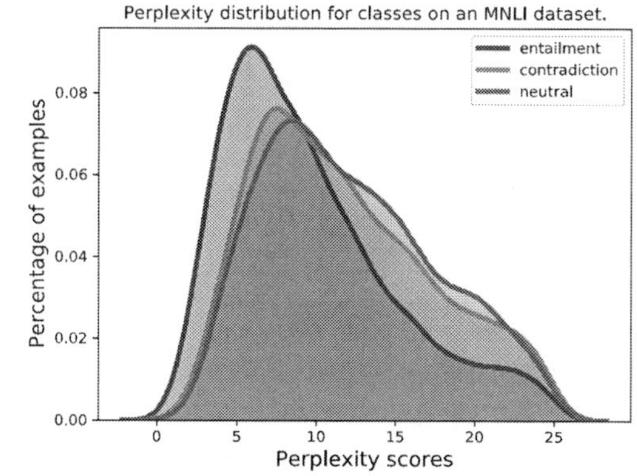

Figure 2: Perplexity distribution of the hypothesis given the premise for each of the three classes sampled from the MultiNLI dataset. Entailment pairs tend to have lower perplexity, validating our choice of $f(s,t)$.

Choice of $f(s,t)$	R-1	R-2	R-L
Entailment (using RoBERTa)	43.66	16.95	23.24
Similarity (using BERT)	44.67	16.69	23.81
BLEU (using nltk)	43.95	17.38	23.69
Perplexity (using GPT-2)	**47.07**	**17.64**	**24.40**

Table 4: Results of our *extract-then-abstract* pipeline (after finetuning BART) by varying $f(s,t)$. Our choice of GPT-2 perplexity performs better than 3 alternatives.

As seen in Table 3, we observe a 4.8 / 6 ROUGE-1/L improvement when compared to the no extractor baseline (NE), and 2.3 / 3.2 R-1/L improvement over the strongest extractor baseline (per metric); confirming the effectiveness of our method. In addition, finetuning the CNN/DM pretrained BART on 96 Amicus documents helps in domain adaption and boosts the ROUGE scores of both baselines and our method (f.t. BART). Specifically, we observe a 2.1 / 0.5 R-1/L boost in performance and outperform the best baseline (per metric) by 2.0 / 1.0 R-1/L points. Our model's improvements are statistically significant (p-value<0.06) except for when comparing our extractor + f.t BART with Bottom-up + f.t BART, the p-value is 0.16 due to the small test set. Refer Appendix A.3 for qualitative analysis of our proposed model's generations.

3.3 Validating the choice of $f(s,t)$

In Section 2 we used GPT-2 perplexity scores to measure the extent to which a source sentence grounds a target sentence. To motivate this choice, we measure its correlation with existing entailment datasets. We randomly sample 5000 sentences from each class of the MultiNLI dataset (Williams et al., 2018) and compute the perplexity of the hypothesis with the premise as context. As seen in Figure 2, entailment pairs tend to have the lowest perplexity. This motivates our choice of $f(s,t)$, since hypothesis sentences are best grounded in premise sentences for entailment pairs. We hypothesize contradiction sentences have slightly lower perplexity than neutral due to more word overlap. To further validate the merit of GPT-2 perplexity, we conduct **ablations** using alternatives for $f(s,t)$:

1. Entailment score from a RoBERTa based MNLI classifier (Liu et al., 2019)

2. Cosine similarity of averaged embeddings from final layer of BERT (Devlin et al., 2019)

3. BLEU scores (Papineni et al., 2002)

We present ROUGE scores using our whole *extract-then-abstract* pipeline with different choices of $f(s,t)$ in Table 4. We note that perplexity performs the best, 2.4 ROUGE-1 better than the best alternative and also performs 3.41 ROUGE-1 better than entailment. We hypothesize that RoBERTa overfits on the MNLI dataset that also has known biases (Gururangan et al., 2018).

The code can be found on Github here.[4]

4 Conclusion

We tackle an important real-world problem of summarizing long domain-specific documents with much less training data than previous works. We propose an *extract-then-abstract* pipeline which uses GPT-2 perplexity and a BERT classifier to estimate sentence salience. This sufficiently compresses a document, allowing us to use a pretrained model (BART) to generate coherent & fluent summaries.

5 Acknowledgements

We thank anonymous reviewers, our mentors at UMass IESL and Goldman Sachs for helpful discussion and feedback. This work was done as part of Independent Study collaboration between Goldman Sachs and University of Massachusetts Amherst. Any opinions, findings and conclusions or recommendations expressed in this material are those of the author's and do not necessarily reflect the institutions involved.

[4]https://github.com/bajajahsaas/Abstractive-Summarization

References

Yen-Chun Chen and Mohit Bansal. 2018. Fast abstractive summarization with reinforce-selected sentence rewriting. *Proceedings of the 56th Annual Meeting of the Association for Computational Linguistics (Volume 1: Long Papers).*

Jianpeng Cheng and Mirella Lapata. 2016. Neural summarization by extracting sentences and words. In *Proceedings of the 54th Annual Meeting of the Association for Computational Linguistics (Volume 1: Long Papers)*, pages 484–494, Berlin, Germany. Association for Computational Linguistics.

Sumit Chopra, Michael Auli, and Alexander M. Rush. 2016. Abstractive sentence summarization with attentive recurrent neural networks. In *Proceedings of the 2016 Conference of the North American Chapter of the Association for Computational Linguistics: Human Language Technologies*, pages 93–98, San Diego, California. Association for Computational Linguistics.

Arman Cohan, Franck Dernoncourt, Doo Soon Kim, Trung Bui, Seokhwan Kim, Walter Chang, and Nazli Goharian. 2018. A discourse-aware attention model for abstractive summarization of long documents. In *Proceedings of the 2018 Conference of the North American Chapter of the Association for Computational Linguistics: Human Language Technologies, Volume 2 (Short Papers)*, pages 615–621, New Orleans, Louisiana. Association for Computational Linguistics.

Jacob Devlin, Ming-Wei Chang, Kenton Lee, and Kristina Toutanova. 2019. BERT: Pre-training of deep bidirectional transformers for language understanding. In *Conference of the North American Chapter of the Association for Computational Linguistics*.

Sebastian Gehrmann, Yuntian Deng, and Alexander Rush. 2018. Bottom-up abstractive summarization. In *Proceedings of Empirical Methods in Natural Language Processing*.

Jiatao Gu, Zhengdong Lu, Hang Li, and Victor O.K. Li. 2016. Incorporating copying mechanism in sequence-to-sequence learning. In *Proceedings of the 54th Annual Meeting of the Association for Computational Linguistics (Volume 1: Long Papers)*, pages 1631–1640, Berlin, Germany. Association for Computational Linguistics.

Suchin Gururangan, Swabha Swayamdipta, Omer Levy, Roy Schwartz, Samuel Bowman, and Noah A. Smith. 2018. Annotation artifacts in natural language inference data. *Proceedings of the 2018 Conference of the North American Chapter of the Association for Computational Linguistics: Human Language Technologies, Volume 2 (Short Papers).*

Mike Lewis, Yinhan Liu, Naman Goyal, Marjan Ghazvininejad, Abdelrahman Mohamed, Omer Levy, Ves Stoyanov, and Luke Zettlemoyer. 2020.

Bart: Denoising sequence-to-sequence pre-training for natural language generation, translation, and comprehension. In *Proceedings of the Association for Computational Linguistics*.

Peter J. Liu, Mohammad Saleh, Etienne Pot, Ben Goodrich, Ryan Sepassi, Lukasz Kaiser, and Noam Shazeer. 2018. Generating wikipedia by summarizing long sequences.

Yinhan Liu, Myle Ott, Naman Goyal, Jingfei Du, Mandar Joshi, Danqi Chen, Omer Levy, Mike Lewis, Luke Zettlemoyer, and Veselin Stoyanov. 2019. Roberta: A robustly optimized bert pretraining approach. *arXiv preprint arXiv:1907.11692*.

Ahmed Magooda and Diane Litman. 2020. Abstractive summarization for low resource data using domain transfer and data synthesis.

Rada Mihalcea and Paul Tarau. 2004. TextRank: Bringing order into text. In *Proceedings of the 2004 Conference on Empirical Methods in Natural Language Processing*, pages 404–411, Barcelona, Spain. Association for Computational Linguistics.

Ramesh Nallapati, Bowen Zhou, Cicero dos Santos, Caglar Gulcehre, and Bing Xiang. 2016. Abstractive text summarization using sequence-to-sequence RNNs and beyond. In *Proceedings of The 20th SIGNLL Conference on Computational Natural Language Learning*, pages 280–290, Berlin, Germany. Association for Computational Linguistics.

Kishore Papineni, Salim Roukos, Todd Ward, and Wei-Jing Zhu. 2002. Bleu: a method for automatic evaluation of machine translation. In *Proceedings of the 40th Annual Meeting of the Association for Computational Linguistics*, pages 311–318, Philadelphia, Pennsylvania, USA. Association for Computational Linguistics.

Shantipriya Parida and Petr Motlicek. 2019. Abstract text summarization: A low resource challenge. In *Proceedings of the 2019 Conference on Empirical Methods in Natural Language Processing and the 9th International Joint Conference on Natural Language Processing (EMNLP-IJCNLP)*, pages 5994–5998, Hong Kong, China. Association for Computational Linguistics.

Matthew Peters, Mark Neumann, Mohit Iyyer, Matt Gardner, Christopher Clark, Kenton Lee, and Luke Zettlemoyer. 2018. Deep contextualized word representations. In *Proceedings of the 2018 Conference of the North American Chapter of the Association for Computational Linguistics: Human Language Technologies, Volume 1 (Long Papers)*.

Alec Radford, Jeffrey Wu, Rewon Child, David Luan, Dario Amodei, and Ilya Sutskever. 2019. Language models are unsupervised multitask learners. *OpenAI Blog*, 1(8):9.

Alexander M. Rush, Sumit Chopra, and Jason Weston. 2015. A neural attention model for abstractive sentence summarization. *Proceedings of the 2015 Conference on Empirical Methods in Natural Language Processing*.

Abigail See, Peter J. Liu, and Christopher D. Manning. 2017. Get to the point: Summarization with pointer-generator networks. *Proceedings of the 55th Annual Meeting of the Association for Computational Linguistics (Volume 1: Long Papers)*.

Sandeep Subramanian, Raymond Li, Jonathan Pilault, and Christopher Pal. 2019. On extractive and abstractive neural document summarization with transformer language models.

Adina Williams, Nikita Nangia, and Samuel Bowman. 2018. A broad-coverage challenge corpus for sentence understanding through inference. In *Conference of the North American Chapter of the Association for Computational Linguistics*.

Thomas Wolf, Lysandre Debut, Victor Sanh, Julien Chaumond, Clement Delangue, Anthony Moi, Pierric Cistac, Tim Rault, R'emi Louf, Morgan Funtowicz, and Jamie Brew. 2019. Huggingface's transformers: State-of-the-art natural language processing. *ArXiv*, abs/1910.03771.

Yuxiang Wu and Baotian Hu. 2018. Learning to extract coherent summary via deep reinforcement learning.

Dani Yogatama, Cyprien de Masson d'Autume, Jerome Connor, Tomas Kocisky, Mike Chrzanowski, Lingpeng Kong, Angeliki Lazaridou, Wang Ling, Lei Yu, Chris Dyer, et al. 2019. Learning and evaluating general linguistic intelligence. *arXiv preprint arXiv:1901.11373*.

A Appendix

A.1 Data pre-processing

In this section, the various pre-processing steps of data performed at different stages are explained.

Extracting (document, summary) pairs: The 120 pairs of Amicus Briefs were scrapped from their website[5]. The Summary of Arguments section of the Amicus Briefs was extracted as the target summary and the main content excluding title page, table of contents, acknowledgements, appendix etc was extracted as document/source.

Sentence pre-processing: Sentences from the (document, summary) files were split using the spaCy[6] sentence splitter. Furthermore, the sentences were each processed to remove special characters using regex rules. If a sentence contained less that 5 words, it was pruned out from the computation of $f(s,t)$ to reduce the complexity of pairs considered.

A.2 Sentence Saliency Classifier

Training Details: Our classifier uses the BERT sequence labeling configuration[7] from `transformers` (Wolf et al., 2019), which is a pretrained BERT-base model with an initially untrained classification head on the `[CLS]` feature vector. This model is then finetuned for 5 epochs using the training data which consists of 5363 sentences in the Amicus dataset (equal distribution among the two classes). We use a train / dev / test split of 60%, 20%, 20%. Training configuration of the classifier is as follows: learning rate = 2e-5, max_grad_norm = 1.0, num_training_steps = 1000, num_warmup_steps = 100, warmup_proportion = 0.1, Optimizer = Adam, Schduler = linear with warmup.

Alternate methods to choose +/- samples: The aggregate scoring method mentioned in Section 2 was one choice to pick salient and non-salient samples for each document. Aggregate method compresses the source by 61% on an average. The other methods experimented were:

- Top k - Bottom k: $\forall t_j \in$ T, we picked the top-k scoring source sentences as positive samples and the bottom-k sentences as the negative samples ensuring that $\{\text{positive}\} \cap \{\text{negative}\} = 0$. Using this technique, the classifier achieves accuracy of nearly 1 as can be seen from Table 5. On qualitative analysis, we identified that there is a clear distinction in the positive and the negative examples. Eg: sentences such as 'This document is prepared by XYZ' would be picked as non salient sentence and classifier is able to achieve high accuracy. This could however be used to train a classifier to *identify boiler plate sentences* across the document. This method compresses source document by 63% on an average.
- Random negative sampling: Salient examples were chosen for a document as per the above method. For the non salient examples, we randomly sampled from the rest of the document. This allows the classifier to learn about sentences that that are difficult to be classified as positive or negative. Hence, the accuracy of the classifier is lower than the other two methods as can be seen from Table 5. This method compresses the source document by 70% on an average.

Compute time and resources: Execution time for different choice of *f(s,t)* for all 120 pairs:

- Perplexity using GPT-2:executes within 15hrs using 2 GPUs
- Entailment score using RoBERTa: executes within 22hrs using 2 GPUs
- Cosine Similarity using BERT [CLS] embeddings: executes within 3hrs on a single GPU
- BLEU score using nltk: executes within 15min on a single GPU.

These scores need to be generated once and can be reused for various experiments. Sampling methods to choose salient and non-salient sentences for each document takes less than a minute to run.

Analysis: (a) Table 5 shows the classifier accuracies for combinations of *f(s,t)* and sampling methods. We observe that for the aggregate sampling method, although perplexity based classifier does not have the highest accuracy, our

[5]https://publichealthlawcenter.org/amicus-briefs

[6]https://pypi.org/project/spacy/

[7]`https://huggingface.co/transformers/model_doc/bert.html#transformers.BertForSequenceClassification`

Sampling Method	f(s,t)	Accuracy
Aggregate scoring for each source sentence.	BLEU	0.7813
	Perplexity	0.7366
	Entailment	0.6569
	Similarity	0.8391
Top k-Bottom k sources sentences or each summary sentence	BLEU	0.9997
	Perplexity	0.9915
	Entailment	0.9973
	Similarity	1
Top k for each summary sentence and random negative sampling from the remaining document.	BLEU	0.5784
	Perplexity	0.655
	Entailment	0.5611
	Similarity	0.6233

Table 5: The accuracy of the held out set of Amicus for different classifiers trained on the data prepared using choice of different f(s,t) and sampling methods. Here, k=3.

pipeline where $f(s,t)$ is perplexity score gives the best result(ROUGE) amongst the ablation experiments(Table 4). Classifier accuracy is determined on automated labelling based on the saliency score, rather than true labels, hence best classifier does not imply best summarization. (b) Table 6 shows the examples of using perplexity as *f(s,t)* to see how the summary grounds the source. The table shows three summary sentences and the corresponding source sentences that had the lowest perplexity scores. We can see that, summary either has a similar meaning or logically follows the source. (c) Table 7 has three examples each for salient sentences and non-salient sentences inferred by the classifier trained on data prepared as mentioned in Section 2. The third sentence in the non-salient sentences column is an example of boiler-plate content detected that is present across documents.

A.3 Abstractive Summarizer: BART

BART is a seq2seq model based on denoising pre-training objective which is supposed to generalize better on various natural language understanding tasks; abstractive summarization being one of them. For abstractive stage of our proposed approach, we decided to see (*bart.large.cnn*) variant which is essentially BART-large model (with 12 encoder and decoder layers and 400 million parameters) finetuned for CNN/DM summarization task. We use the pre-computed weights available for use here[8]. Using BART's text generation script, we set length penalty (lenpen) as 2.0 and minimum length (min_len) as 500 words in order to encourage BART to produce longer outputs which is more suitable to our dataset. Also, we use beam size of 4 and and no_repeat_ngram_size of 3.

Finetuning: We use the train and dev splits of Amicus dataset (96 source-target pairs) and finetune BART for summarization task starting from its CNN/DM finetuned checkpoint. First, we pre-process the dataset as per the guidelines in the official code[9]. We finetune for 500 epochs with learning rate of 3e-5 and early stop if validation loss doesn't decrease for 50 epochs. Others parameters are as follows: total_num_updates = 20000, warmup_updates = 500, update_freq = 4, optimiser = Adam with weight decay of 0.01. Rest of parameters were kept as default in the official script. Results (Precision, Recall, F1) on the test set of Amicus using the existing BART model and finetuned BART are shown in Table 8.

Table 9 shows an example of target summary and summary generated by our model(Section 2) for one sample source document. We can see that the summary generated by our model is fluent and has coherent flow of information.

[8] https://github.com/pytorch/fairseq/tree/master/examples/bart

[9] https://github.com/pytorch/fairseq/blob/master/examples/bart/README.summarization.md

Summary Sentence	Source Sentence
In the immigration context, this jurisprudence has prompted the Court to reject the notion that the so-called entry fiction is of constitutional significance.	Prior to Knauff and Mezei, the distinction between noncitizens who had entered the United States and those who remained outside it had not had been elevated to a bright-line constitutional rule, and entry had never been completely determinative of the fact or extent of protection under the Due Process Clause.
It has accordingly authorized such detention only in limited circumstances pursuant to a carefully defined scheme.	The Court's substantive due process jurisprudence also recognizes that an individual may be subjected to regulatory detention only in narrow circumstances under a carefully drawn scheme.
With respect to substantive due process, this Court has increasingly recognized the punitive consequences of indefinite regulatory detention.	Thus, the Court has substantially restricted the availability and duration of regulatory confinement in the — years since it decided Meze1.In Zadvydas, this Court established that its substantive due process jurisprudence provided the appropriate framework for evaluating the administrative detention of noncitizens pending removal from the United States.

Table 6: Using GPT-2 perplexity as f(s,t), here are three sentences from the summary with corresponding source sentence, having the lowest perplexity.

Salient Sentences	Non-Salient sentences
The same time, the Court has long been skeptical of the military's authority to try individuals other than active service personnel.	A government predicated on checks and balances serves not only to make Government accountable but also to secure individual liberty.
On the basis of this revised test, the Court of Appeals refused to apply the exceptional circumstances exception to Al-Nashiri's petition.	At present, the Rules for Courts-Martial require that the accused be brought to trial within 120 days after the earlier of preferral of charges or confinement.
Consonant with that tradition, this Court should review the Court of Appeals' decision to confirm that exceptional delay before trial remains of central concern on habeas review and is indeed one of the very dangers the writ of habeas corpus was designed to avoid.	Respectfully submitted, May 31, 2017 LINDA A. KLEIN Counsel of Record AMERICAN BAR ASSOCIATION 321 North Clark Street Chicago ...

Table 7: This table shows the sentences classified as salient and non-salient from one Amicus source document. We can see that the last sentence in the non-salient sentences column shows an example of boiler-plate content present across documents. The classifier is trained on data chosen on aggregate score of source sentences where *f(s,t)* is GPT-2 perplexity.

Metric		BART	Ours + BART	f.t. BART	Ours + f.t. BART
	Recall	40.87	47.46	46.90	56.04
ROUGE-1	Precision	47.21	49.97	48.68	46.16
	F-1	40.17	44.97	43.47	47.07
	Recall	13.76	16.54	17.84	21.50
ROUGE-2	Precision	15.46	17.04	17.84	17.10
	F-1	13.36	15.37	16.30	17.64
	Recall	18.34	25.58	21.30	29.62
ROUGE-L	Precision	21.04	26.27	21.35	23.47
	F-1	17.95	23.95	19.35	24.40

Table 8: Overall pipeline results by adding our extractor (*f(s,t)* as GPT-2 perplexity + Classifier) to BART and finetuned BART (f.t. BART), including the precision and recall values for each metric.

This Court's determination of whether due process under the New Hampshire Constitution requires court-appointed counsel for indigent parent-defendants, in order to protect their fundamental right to parent, requires the balancing of three factors–(1) the private interest at stake, (2) the risk of error and the value of procedural safeguards, and (3)the state's interest. See In re Shelby R., 148 N.H. 237, 240 (2002) (citing In re Richard A., 146 N.H..295, 298 (2001)). Because there is no dispute that the fundamental right to parent isat stake in abuse and neglect proceedings, the ABA focuses its discussion on the second and third factors of the three factor test.As to the second, so-called "risk of error" factor, the ABA's conclusion, after years of investigation and analysis, is that the absence of counsel for indigent parent-defendants in abuse and neglect proceedings results in a significant risk of an erroneous determination. This is especially true where the opposing party is the State. As to the third, state's interest factor, the ABA's investigation shows that the interests of both the parent and the state are best served where indigent parent-defendants are represented. The ABA respectfully suggests that the evidence and analysis relevant to these two factors is so compelling in most, if not all, abuse and neglect proceedings involving indigent parent-defendants, that a case-by-case balancing of the factors should be rejected in favor of a rule requiring the appointment of counsel] for indigent parent-defendants in all such proceedings. The evidence and analysis supporting the ABA's policy includes the fact that a substantial majority of states have recognized an unqualified right to counsel for indigent parent-defendants in child custody proceedings. Similarly, other industrial democracies provide indigent parent-defendants with such right to counsel. The ABA respectfully submits that this Court should require no less as a matter of due process under the New Hampshire Constitution.Although of whether Jn re Shelby R. resulted in a or not a natural parent's plurality role in ruling, the the family Court is a was not split fundamental on the liberty question interest protected by the State Constitution. See In re Shelby R., 148 NH. at 244 (dissenting opinion).
Hampshire constitution requires this court to determine whether indigent parents have a legally protected interest. Most indigent parent - defendants are incapable of performing the advocacy functions required in abuse and neglect proceedings. Most unrepresented parents cannot perform the advocacy functions - - including investigating facts , making an orderly factual presentation , and cross - examining witnesses - - that are required. The intense, emotionally charged backdrop against which custody decisions are often made further exacerbates the inherent disadvantages faced by unrepresented indigent parents. The need for counsel for the indigent parent - defendant is especially great where the opposing party is the state. The court must weigh three factors : (1) the private interests that will be affected. (2) the risk of erroneous deprivation of the liberty interest through the procedures used and the value , if any, of additional or substitute procedural safeguards. (3) the state ' s interest , including the function involved and fiscal and administrative burdens that additional or substitute procedural requirements would entail id at 240 ; see also in re father , 155 n . h . 93 , 95 (2007) . this court has previously concluded as to the first factor that adversary child custody proceedings implicate a fundamental liberty interest - - the right to parent in this case, the central question thus becomes whether that right is sufficiently protected. The conclusion that counsel must be provided is so compelling in most , if not all cases , that a case - by - case balancing of the factors should be rejected in favor of a rule requiring the appointment of counsel for low income parent - defendant in all such proceedings to be constitutionally acceptable. The state is not the only adversary finding the only meaningful right to be heard when her adversary is not represented by counsel is not spaled against the traditional weapons of the state, such as the state's attorney general. The courts must also weigh the public interest in the child custody case, including the function involved and the cost of additional or substitute safeguards, as well as the cost to the state of the additional or substituted safeguards. The risk of an erroneous deprivation of the fundamental right to parent only increases the only increase in the risk that the state will find the child is not heard when the state is the adversary. The public interest is only increased by the fact that the child will not be heard by the state when the parent is represented by a lawyer. The high level of complexity of child custody cases makes it difficult for the court to make a fair and just decision.

Table 9: The table shows the comparison of summaries where the top summary is the target summary and the bottom summary is the one generated by our extractor and f.t BART. As we can see, the summary is coherent and has fluent information flow.

Attending Self-Attention: A Case Study of Visually Grounded Supervision in Vision-and-Language Transformers

Jules Samaran[1] **Noa Garcia**[2]
Mayu Otani[3] **Chenhui Chu**[4] **Yuta Nakashima**[2]
[1]PSL Research University [2]Osaka University [3]CyberAgent, Inc. [4]Kyoto University
jules.samaran@mines-paristech.fr
{noagarcia, n-yuta}@ids.osaka-u.ac.jp
otani_mayu@cyberagent.co.jp chu@i.kyoto-u.ac.jp

Abstract

The impressive performances of pre-trained visually grounded language models have motivated a growing body of research investigating what has been learned during the pre-training. As a lot of these models are based on Transformers, several studies on the attention mechanisms used by the models to learn to associate phrases with their visual grounding in the image have been conducted. In this work, we investigate how supervising attention directly to learn visual grounding can affect the behavior of such models. We compare three different methods on attention supervision and their impact on the performances of a state-of-the-art visually grounded language model on two popular vision-and-language tasks.

1 Introduction

The introduction of Transformers (Vaswani et al., 2017) has been a major component of the success of pre-trained language models (Devlin et al., 2019; Yang et al., 2019; Liu et al., 2019; Lan et al., 2020) which achieved new records in many natural language processing tasks. The same mechanism has been adapted to create models (Su et al., 2020; Chen et al., 2020; Li et al., 2019; Lu et al., 2019, 2020; LXM) that can now tackle vision-and-language tasks with impressive performances.

A large body of research (Clark et al., 2019; Kovaleva et al., 2019) has been dedicated to understanding what attention heads learn during the pre-training of language models. Liu et al. (2016) have even shown how providing attention heads with guidance can improve performance on neural machine translation.

On the other hand, the internal behaviors of vision-and-language models have attracted less interest from the research community. Li et al. (2020) have shown some attention heads in vision-and-language models are able to map entities to image regions while others even detect syntactic relations between non-entity words and image regions. Nevertheless, no initiative has been taken towards supervising directly the attention modules.

In this paper, we study how different methods on attention supervision can affect vision-and-language models. We propose a fine-tuning method aimed at using the visual grounding of entities to provide guidance to attention heads. We compare three different methods by evaluating their performance on popular downstream tasks and visualize the different attention modules obtained. We observe that an indirect method which uses a module appended to the final output of the Transformer obtains worse results than methods which focus on supervising every attention head directly. The codes are available at `https://github.com/jules-samaran/VL-BERT`.

2 Our Method

We use a state-of-the-art pre-trained vision-and-language model on which we propose multi-task fine-tuning methods focusing on attention supervision. After this proposed fine-tuning, we judge the success of our approach by further fine-tuning the model on downstream tasks of visual question answering and referring expressions, and evaluating it. We propose a fine-tuning approach after an initial pretraining step on a large unlabelled dataset because we believe the model would benefit from learning first from scratch freely about text and images without any supervision on its attention heads, and that our fine-tuning would allow it to then refine the representations it provided using visual grounding labels.

2.1 Backbone Model

We choose as our basic architecture VL-BERT (Su et al., 2020), a state-of-the-art vision-and-language pre-trained model that revisits BERT (Devlin et al.,

Proceedings of the Joint Conference of the 59th Annual Meeting of the Association for Computational Linguistics and the 11th International Joint Conference on Natural Language Processing: Student Research Workshop, pages 81–86
August 5–6, 2021.

2019) to take both visual and linguistic inputs. Based on a multi-layer bidirectional multi-modal Transformer encoder (Vaswani et al., 2017), VL-BERT learns during its pre-training a generic feature representation mainly on the conceptual captions dataset consisting of 3.3M image-caption pairs (Sharma et al., 2018). Note that many other choices are possible for this backbone model (see the Section 4).[1] The reason we chose VL-BERT is that it was available; it achieved state-of-the-art performances (better than ViLBERT (Lu et al., 2019, 2020) for example) on several classical vision-and-language downstream tasks; the way it handles both visual and textual tokens in a single stream (whereas ViLBERT processes them in two separate streams) made it very adapted for our approach of supervising the attention between textual and visual elements.

2.2 VGP Fine-tuning

To provide guided attention supervision in vision-and-language models, we devise a multi-task fine-tuning method that aims to improve the model's ability to understand complex semantic relations (e.g. paraphrases) and align visual with linguistic elements. Li et al. (2020) hinted the importance of attention-based vision-and-language model's ability to map entity-words to corresponding image regions. Following this direction and to improve a model's reasoning abilities, we propose to further fine-tune a pre-trained model with the aim of learning visually grounded paraphrases (VGPs) (Chu et al., 2018; Otani et al., 2020).

VGPs are two phrasal expressions that describe the same visual concept in an image. As shown in Figure 1, we fine-tune a model based on VGPs with three different tasks simultaneously as a multi-task learning problem: an image description identification task (§2.2.1), a VGP classification task (§2.2.2), and an attention supervision task (§2.2.3). The first two tasks are inspired by Arase and Tsujii (2019), who showed that injecting semantic relations between a sentence pair can improve a BERT model's performance on several downstream tasks. We adapted them to make the model learn from both visual and linguistic elements.

Input The input of the fine-tuning process is composed of 1) an image, and 2) a pair of captions,

[1] It is unclear how well the results we obtained would generalize to other vision-and-language models, especially since our approach is designed for VL-BERT's architecture, but we leave it as future work.

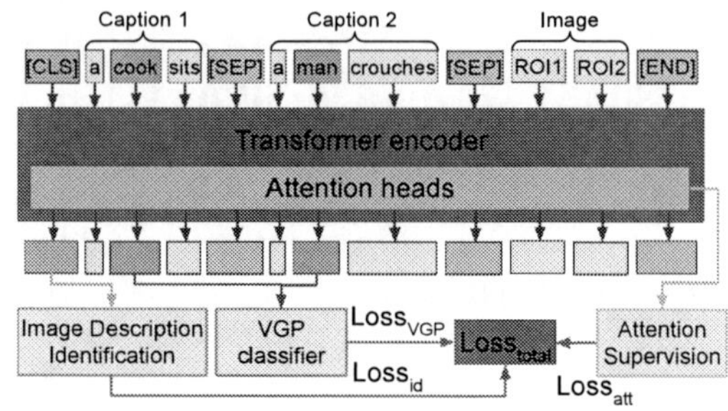

Figure 1: Overview of the VGP fine-tuning. The Transformer Encoder is the VL-BERT model, our contributions are the modules on the bottom.

c_1 and c_2, where at least one of them corresponds to the image. Hard negative captions are chosen offline following Lu et al. (2019). The input sequence to the Transformer model is constructed as: $[\texttt{[CLS]}, c_1, \texttt{[SEP]}, c_2, \texttt{[SEP]}, img, \texttt{[END]}]$, where `[CLS]` is the start of sequence token, `[SEP]` separates different elements, img is the image regional features extracted as Girshick (2015) and `[END]` is the end of sequence token.

2.2.1 Image Description Identification

In this task, a Softmax classifier f takes the output x_0 of the Transformer corresponding to `[CLS]` and predicts which of the captions corresponds to the image (c_1, c_2, or both). The loss is given by

$$Loss_{\text{id}} = L_{\text{CE}}(y, \log f(x_0)), \quad (1)$$

where y indicates which caption corresponds to the image and L_{CE} is the cross-entropy loss function.

2.2.2 VGP Classification

The second task is to classify VGPs according to the semantic relationship between the two phrases, e.g. entailment, equivalence, etc. More details on the semantic classes are provided in the supplementary material. Let $p = \{x_i\}$ denote the set of the final encodings x_i, where i ranges from the first to the last words of the sampled phrase. Phrase embedding e of the phrase is given by

$$e = \text{MaxPooling}(p). \quad (2)$$

We obtain phrase embeddings e_1 and e_2 from c_1 and c_2, combining them as Arase and Tsujii (2019)

$$e_c = [e_1, e_2, e_1 * e_2, |e_1 - e_2|], \quad (3)$$

where $*$ denotes the element-wise multiplication and $|\cdot|$ gives element-wise absolute values. For

VGP classification, we input e_c to a Softmax classifier g to predict the paraphrase's semantic class. The loss for this task is computed as

$$Loss_{\text{VGP}} = L_{\text{CE}}(t, \log g(e_c)), \quad (4)$$

where t is the label of the VGP semantic class.

2.2.3 Attention Supervision Task

Since VGPs align directly with image regions, we can have the model learn the visual grounding. We explore three methods of supervising attention.

Indirect attention supervision We learn the visual grounding using the final representations of grounded phrases and their aligned regions of interest. We train a binary classifier d that takes as input phrase embedding e as well as the representation x_i of one of the regions in img, and predicts whether they align or not. We repeat this classification for every grounded phrase with every region. The loss is computed by

$$Loss_{\text{att}} = \frac{1}{n_r} \sum_i L_{\text{CE}}(z_i, \log d([e, x_i])), \quad (5)$$

where z_i is the indicator of whether the phrase refers to the i-th region, n_r is the number of regions, and the summation is computed over i corresponding to regions in img.

Direct attention supervision Similarly to Liu et al. (2016), we view every attention head in every layer as a classifier that, given an input token, outputs probabilities distributed over all the other tokens. Our motivation is that the attention between two elements should reflect how much they are relevant to each other, hence grounded word entities should pay attention the most to their visual grounding, and vice versa. We re-normalize the attention so that this supervision has only a limited impact on text-to-text and region-to-region attention. Specifically, let W denote the set of indices i of all text tokens, and R corresponding to regions in img. The attention α_{ij}^{lh} for layer l, head h, from the i-th token to j-th region can be normalized by

$$\hat{\alpha}_{ij}^{lh} = \frac{\alpha_{ij}^{lh}}{\sum_{j' \in R} \alpha_{ij'}^{lh}}, \quad \tilde{\alpha}_{ij}^{lh} = \frac{\alpha_{ij}^{lh}}{\sum_{j' \in W} \alpha_{ij'}^{lh}}. \quad (6)$$

The phrase grounding gives pairs (i^*, j^*) in both $W \times R$ and $R \times W$ (we have multiple pairs since a phrase has multiple tokens). We use the average of cross-entropy losses for supervision, i.e.,

$$Loss_{\text{txt}\rightarrow\text{img}} = \frac{1}{n_l n_h} \sum_{l,h} L_{\text{CE}}(s_{i^*}, \log \hat{\alpha}_{i^* j}^{lh}), \quad (7)$$

where $j \in R$; s_{i^*} is the indicator whether respective region $j \in R$ forms pair (i^*, j^*); n_l and n_h are the numbers of layers and attention heads, respectively. We do the same for the loss $Loss_{\text{img}\rightarrow\text{txt}}$ for region-to-text pairs using $\tilde{\alpha}_{ij}^{lh}$, where $j \in W$ and s'_{i^*} is the corresponding indicator. The loss for direct attention supervision loss is given by

$$Loss_{att} = Loss_{\text{txt}\rightarrow\text{img}} + Loss_{\text{img}\rightarrow\text{txt}}. \quad (8)$$

Semi-direct attention supervision Abnar and Zuidema (2020) introduced a transformation of raw attention called attention rollout and showed that it gives a more accurate quantification of how much information one token contains about another token than raw attention does. Therefore, we propose to replace the raw attention with the attention rollout in the direct supervision method. In other words, if we denote $f_{\text{rollout}(\cdot)}$ as the function that transforms raw attention vectors into attention rollout then our semi-direct attention supervision approach consists in replacing α_{ij}^{lh} with $f_{\text{rollout}}(\alpha)_{ij}^{lh}$ in Equations (refeq6), (7) and (8).

The final loss for the VGP fine-tuning is

$$Loss_{\text{total}} = Loss_{\text{id}} + Loss_{\text{VGP}} + Loss_{\text{att}}. \quad (9)$$

3 Experiments

3.1 Dataset

For our fine-tuning, we used the VGP dataset (Chu et al., 2018), which was created from the Flickr30k-entities dataset's captions (Plummer et al., 2017). As it is based on Flickr30k-entities, those phrases come with the id of the image region that corresponds to their grounding. The dataset contains $54,313$ VGPs distributed across $31,784$ images.

3.2 Fine-tuning on Downstream Tasks

To evaluate how our fine-tuning methods can improve the generic representations generated by the model, we further fine-tune it on downstream vision-and-language tasks and compare their performances. Results are reported in Table 1, including the performance of the original VL-BERT model. We also include a model fine-tuned on VGPs without the attention supervision task, with only the image description identification and VGP classification in order to estimate the impact of forcing the model learn visual grounding.

	VQAv2.0	Refcoco+ (Detected)			Refcoco+ (Ground-truth)		
Fine-tuning Method	val	val	testA	testB	val	testA	testB
w/o Attention	66.73	67.10	74.36	57.07	77.38	<u>81.28</u>	71.53
Indirect Attention	66.71	65.95	72.72	54.49	77.20	80.61	70.81
Direct Attention	67.09	<u>69.99</u>	<u>76.25</u>	<u>58.99</u>	77.07	80.86	70.96
Semi-direct Attention	<u>67.41</u>	69.63	75.93	58.72	<u>78.12</u>	80.96	<u>71.75</u>
Original (Su et al., 2020)	67.73	71.60	77.72	60.99	79.88	82.40	75.01

Table 1: Comparison of our different fine-tuning methods on the VQAv2.0 and the Refcoco+ datasets. For each column, the best fine-tuning method is underlined. Original VL-BERT results added as reference.

3.2.1 Visual Question Answering

In this task, every input is an image coupled with a question expressed in natural language. We used the VQAv2.0 dataset (Goyal et al., 2017). The model is expected to answer the question with the correct answer picked from a shared set consisting of 3,129 answers according to Anderson et al. (2018). We trained the models on the train split ($83k$ images and $444k$ questions) and report results on the validation split ($41k$ images and $214k$ questions). We used the same experimental protocol for prediction and evaluation as in Su et al. (2020).

Results in Table 1 indicate that the original model is the best performing method, showing that forcing VL-BERT to learn paraphrases before training the VQAv2.0 dataset does not contribute to the task. However, it is still relevant to compare the performances of different attention supervision methods. The two worse performance are attained by the method without attention and the Indirect, which does not seem to improve the model's ability to answer the question. Both the Direct and Semi-direct methods, which use the attention heads as classifiers, fare better with a slight advantage for the Semi-direct method.

3.2.2 Referring Expression Comprehension

The objective of this task is to locate the object in the image that is designated by the input phrase. The input is constituted of a referring expression and an image that contains the object that is being referred to. We used the RefCOCO+ dataset (Kazemzadeh et al., 2014) ($141k$ expressions for $50k$ referred objects in $20k$ images). The dataset contains two test sets, where testA contains images with multiple persons and testB with multiple objects. We report results both with ground-truth RoIs and with the bounding boxes detected by Yu et al. (2018). We also used the same experimental protocol for prediction and evaluation as in Su et al. (2020).

As shown in Table 1, despite having been designed with the referring expression task in mind, the Indirect attention supervision method is the worse one, even behind the method without attention. The original VL-BERT model is still the leading performance followed by the Direct and Semi-direct attention supervision methods. Direct attentions works better on detected bounding boxes. We think the reason is that direct attention tries to link tokens with image regions similarly to how the region detector would do it.

VL-BERT is pre-trained on 3.3M image-caption pairs, while VGP fine-tuning is conducted on 30k image-caption pairs only. Therefore, for both tasks, we believe that our methods failed to beat VL-BERT due to two reasons: catastrophic forgetting, and small-scale attention supervision training data. To address catastrophic forgetting, applying knowledge distillation (Hinton et al., 2015) that can incorporate both knowledge from the pre-trained VL-BERT model and the VGP fine-tuned model might be effective. For the small-scale attention supervision training data issue, a possible direction could be applying visual grounding on the conceptual captions dataset and training VL-BERT from scratch with attention supervision on the conceptual captions dataset.

3.2.3 Visualization

To gain more insights into what models learn with the different attention supervision methods, we visualize attention heads using Bertviz[2] (Vig, 2019).

By zooming in on individual attention heads, we noticed that when the model was fine-tuned using

[2] https://github.com/jessevig/bertviz

either the Semi-direct or Direct attention supervision methods, every grounded entity text token attributes more attention to image tokens to image tokens corresponding to the visual grounding of the entity. We also observed that even though the Direct method seemed to have an uniform impact on all attention heads in every layer, with the Semi-direct method attention heads displayed varying attention patterns across different layers. A possible explanation is that the attention rollout transformation makes the attention supervision problem slightly different across different layers whereas it is not the case for the Direct method which imposes the same constraint on the raw attention in all attention heads (and it is the raw attention we are visualizing). More details about the visualization and images are provided in the supplementary materials.

4 Related Work

Vision and language pre-trained models on large image caption datasets have been proposed such as VisualBERT (Li et al., 2019), ViLBERT (Lu et al., 2019, 2020), VL-BERT (Su et al., 2020; Lu et al., 2020), LXMERT (LXM) and UNITER (Chen et al., 2020). Those vision and language pre-training models differ from the model architecture. We study visually grounded attention supervision in VL-BERT.

Clark et al. (2019); Kovaleva et al. (2019) analyzed on language pre-trained models and showed that different attention heads share similar patterns and behaviors. For neural machine translation, Liu et al. (2016) proposed to use word alignment for cross-attention supervision during decoding in a recurrent neural network based architecture. We work specifically on vision-and-language transformers and use phrase visual grounding for attention supervision in order to help the model learn how to align phrases with their associated regions in the images.

5 Conclusion

Motivated by similar works in language models, we have presented three different methods that attempt to guide the model in its learning of entity grounding. We observed that the indirect method which is the most similar to the structure used for downstream tasks had a little or negative effect on the performance of the model. We also found that supervising attention heads through attention rollout is the best performing method nevertheless all these methods fell short of the performances of the model before being fine-tuned on the VGP dataset.

Despite the performance, we have shown which attention supervision methods give better results and more interpretable attention patterns[3] (i.e., direct and semi-direct attention) than others that should not be used (i.e., indirect attention). Therefore, we believe that our work can pave the way for further analyses of how this mechanism could be made to improve the performance of vision-and-language models. For future work, we plan to study how direct supervision methods could be applied on some selected heads instead of supervising uniformly all attention heads in every layer.

Acknowledgments

This work was supported by ACT-I, JST.

References

Samira Abnar and Willem Zuidema. 2020. Quantifying attention flow in transformers. In *Annual Meeting of the Association for Computational Linguistics*, pages 4190–4197, Online. Association for Computational Linguistics.

Peter Anderson, Xiaodong He, Chris Buehler, Damien Teney, Mark Johnson, Stephen Gould, and Lei Zhang. 2018. Bottom-up and top-down attention for image captioning and visual question answering. In *IEEE/CVF Conference on Computer Vision and Pattern Recognition*, pages 6077–6086.

Yuki Arase and Jun'ichi Tsujii. 2019. Transfer fine-tuning: A BERT case study. In *Conference on Empirical Methods in Natural Language Processing and International Joint Conference on Natural Language Processing*, pages 5393–5404.

Yen-Chun Chen, Linjie Li, Licheng Yu, Ahmed El Kholy, Faisal Ahmed, Zhe Gan, Yu Cheng, and Jingjing Liu. 2020. UNITER: UNiversal Image-TExt Representation Learning. In *European Conference on Computer Vision*, pages 104–120.

Chenhui Chu, Mayu Otani, and Yuta Nakashima. 2018. iParaphrasing: Extracting visually grounded paraphrases via an image. In *International Conference on Computational Linguistics*, pages 3479–3492.

Kevin Clark, Urvashi Khandelwal, Omer Levy, and Christopher D. Manning. 2019. What does BERT look at? An analysis of BERT's attention. In *ACL Workshop BlackboxNLP: Analyzing and Interpreting Neural Networks for NLP*, pages 276–286.

[3] A visualization comparison among the attention supervision methods can be found in the supplementary material.

Jacob Devlin, Ming-Wei Chang, Kenton Lee, and Kristina Toutanova. 2019. BERT: Pre-training of deep bidirectional transformers for language understanding. In *Conference of the North American Chapter of the Association for Computational Linguistics: Human Language Technologies*, pages 4171–4186.

Ross Girshick. 2015. Fast R-CNN. In *IEEE International Conference on Computer Vision*, pages 1440–1448.

Yash Goyal, Tejas Khot, Douglas Summers-Stay, Dhruv Batra, and Devi Parikh. 2017. Making the V in VQA matter: Elevating the role of image understanding in Visual Question Answering. In *IEEE Conference on Computer Vision and Pattern Recognition*, pages 6325–6334.

Geoffrey Hinton, Oriol Vinyals, and Jeffrey Dean. 2015. Distilling the knowledge in a neural network. In *NIPS Deep Learning and Representation Learning Workshop*.

Sahar Kazemzadeh, Vicente Ordonez, Mark Matten, and Tamara Berg. 2014. ReferItGame: Referring to objects in photographs of natural scenes. In *Conference on Empirical Methods in Natural Language Processing*, pages 787–798.

Olga Kovaleva, Alexey Romanov, Anna Rogers, and Anna Rumshisky. 2019. Revealing the dark secrets of BERT. In *Proceedings of the 2019 Conference on Empirical Methods in Natural Language Processing and the 9th International Joint Conference on Natural Language Processing (EMNLP-IJCNLP)*, pages 4365–4374, Hong Kong, China. Association for Computational Linguistics.

Zhenzhong Lan, Mingda Chen, Sebastian Goodman, Kevin Gimpel, Piyush Sharma, and Radu Soricut. 2020. ALBERT: A lite BERT for self-supervised learning of language representations. In *International Conference on Learning Representations*, 17 pages.

Liunian Harold Li, Mark Yatskar, Da Yin, Cho-Jui Hsieh, and Kai-Wei Chang. 2019. VisualBERT: A simple and performant baseline for vision and language. In *CoRR arXiv:1908.03557*, 14 pages.

Liunian Harold Li, Mark Yatskar, Da Yin, Cho-Jui Hsieh, and Kai-Wei Chang. 2020. What does BERT with vision look at? In *Annual Meeting of the Association for Computational Linguistics*, pages 5265–5275.

Lemao Liu, Masao Utiyama, Andrew Finch, and Eiichiro Sumita. 2016. Neural machine translation with supervised attention. In *International Conference on Computational Linguistics*, pages 3093–3102.

Yinhan Liu, Myle Ott, Naman Goyal, Jingfei Du, Mandar Joshi, Danqi Chen, Omer Levy, Mike Lewis, Luke Zettlemoyer, and Veselin Stoyanov. 2019. RoBERTa: A robustly optimized bert pretraining approach. In *CoRR arXiv:1907.11692*, 13 pages.

Jiasen Lu, Dhruv Batra, Devi Parikh, and Stefan Lee. 2019. ViLBERT: Pretraining task-agnostic visiolinguistic representations for vision-and-language tasks. In *Advances in Neural Information Processing Systems*, pages 13–23.

Jiasen Lu, Vedanuj Goswami, Marcus Rohrbach, Devi Parikh, and Stefan Lee. 2020. 12-in-1: Multi-task vision and language representation learning. In *IEEE/CVF Conference on Computer Vision and Pattern Recognition)*, pages 10437–10446.

Mayu Otani, Chenhui Chu, and Yuta Nakashima. 2020. Visually grounded paraphrase identification via gating and phrase localization. *Neurocomputing*, 404:165–172.

Bryan A. Plummer, Liwei Wang, Christopher M. Cervantes, Juan C. Caicedo, Julia Hockenmaier, and Svetlana Lazebnik. 2017. Flickr30k entities: Collecting region-to-phrase correspondences for richer image-to-sentence models. *International Journal of Computer Vision*, 123(1):74–93.

Piyush Sharma, Nan Ding, Sebastian Goodman, and Radu Soricut. 2018. Conceptual captions: A cleaned, hypernymed, image alt-text dataset for automatic image captioning. In *Proceedings of the 56th Annual Meeting of the Association for Computational Linguistics (Volume 1: Long Papers)*, pages 2556–2565, Melbourne, Australia. Association for Computational Linguistics.

Weijie Su, Xizhou Zhu, Yue Cao, Bin Li, Lewei Lu, Furu Wei, and Jifeng Dai. 2020. VL-BERT: pre-training of generic visual-linguistic representations.

Ashish Vaswani, Noam Shazeer, Niki Parmar, Jakob Uszkoreit, Llion Jones, Aidan N Gomez, Ł ukasz Kaiser, and Illia Polosukhin. 2017. Attention is all you need. In *Advances in Neural Information Processing Systems*, pages 5998–6008.

Jesse Vig. 2019. A multiscale visualization of attention in the transformer model. In *Annual Meeting of the Association for Computational Linguistics: System Demonstrations*, pages 37–42.

Zhilin Yang, Zihang Dai, Yiming Yang, Jaime Carbonell, Russ R Salakhutdinov, and Quoc V Le. 2019. XLNet: Generalized autoregressive pretraining for language understanding. In *Advances in Neural Information Processing Systems*, pages 5753–5763.

Licheng Yu, Zhe Lin, Xiaohui Shen, Jimei Yang, Xin Lu, Mohit Bansal, and Tamara L Berg. 2018. MAttNet: Modular attention network for referring expression comprehension. In *IEEE Conference on Computer Vision and Pattern Recognition*, pages 1307–1315.

Video-guided Machine Translation with Spatial Hierarchical Attention Network

Weiqi Gu **Haiyue Song** **Chenhui Chu** **Sadao Kurohashi**
Kyoto University, Kyoto, Japan
{gu, song, chu, kuro}@nlp.ist.i.kyoto-u.ac.jp

Abstract

Video-guided machine translation, as one type of multimodal machine translations, aims to engage video contents as auxiliary information to address the word sense ambiguity problem in machine translation. Previous studies only use features from pretrained action detection models as motion representations of the video to solve the verb sense ambiguity, leaving the noun sense ambiguity a problem. To address this problem, we propose a video-guided machine translation system by using both spatial and motion representations in videos. For spatial features, we propose a hierarchical attention network to model the spatial information from object-level to video-level. Experiments on the VATEX dataset show that our system achieves 35.86 BLEU-4 score, which is 0.51 score higher than the single model of the SOTA method.

1 Introduction

Neural machine translation (NMT) models relying on text data (Bahdanau et al., 2015; Wu et al., 2016) have achieved high performance for domains where there is less ambiguity in data such as the newspaper domain. For some other domains, especially real-time domains such as spoken language or sports commentary, the verb and the noun sense ambiguity largely affects the translation quality. To solve the ambiguity problem, multimodal machine translation (MMT) (Specia et al., 2016) focuses on incorporating visual data as auxiliary information, where the spatiotemporal contextual information in the visual data helps reduce the ambiguity of nouns or verbs in the source text data (Barrault et al., 2018).

Previous MMT studies mainly focus on image-guided machine translation (IMT) task (Zhao et al., 2020; Elliott et al., 2016). However, videos are better information sources than images because one video contains an ordered sequence of frames and provides much more visual features. Specifically, each frame provides spatial representations for the noun sense disambiguation as an image in IMT task. Besides the noun sense disambiguation provided by one frame, the ordered sequences of frames can provide motion representations for the verb sense disambiguation.

Figure 1: An example with the noun sense ambiguity problem in the VMT model by Wang et al. (2019).

The research of video-guided machine translation (VMT) starts from a large-scale video-and-language-research dataset (VATEX) (Wang et al., 2019). The authors also established a baseline using features from pretrained action detection models as motion representations of the video, which addresses the verb sense ambiguity to some extent, leaving noun sense ambiguity unsolved. Hirasawa et al. (2020) aims to solve both the verb and noun sense ambiguity problems by using frame-level action, object, and scene representations. However, without using detailed spatial information within one frame and contextual information between frames, the effect of resolving the noun ambiguity problem is limited. For example, as shown in Figure 1, the noun "bin" in English is wrongly translated into "trash bin" in Chinese, which should be translated into "box."

In this work, we propose a VMT system to address both the verb and the noun sense ambiguity

Proceedings of the Joint Conference of the 59th Annual Meeting of the Association for Computational Linguistics and the 11th International Joint Conference on Natural Language Processing: Student Research Workshop, pages 87–92
August 5–6, 2021. ©2021 Association for Computational Linguistics

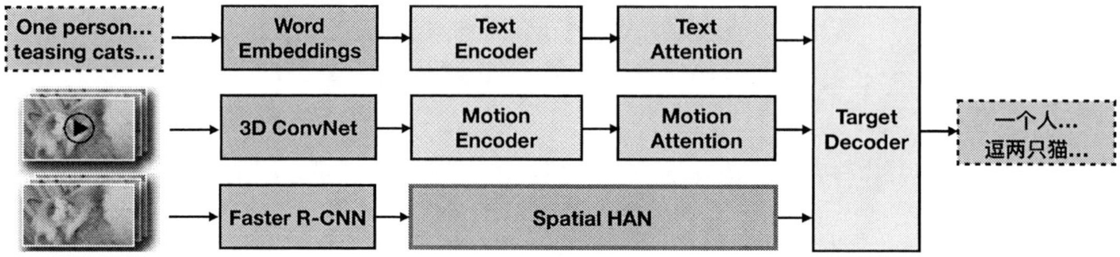

Figure 2: The proposed model with spatial HAN. The text encoder and the motion encoder are the same as those in the VMT baseline model.

problems by using both motion and spatial representations in a video. To obtain spatial representations efficiently, we propose to use a hierarchical attention network (HAN) (Werlen et al., 2018) to model the spatial information from object-level to video-level, thus we call it the spatial HAN module. Additionally, to obtain a better contextual spatial information, we add several kinds of middle layers between the object-to-frame layer and frame-to-video layer in the original HAN. Experiments on the VATEX dataset (Wang et al., 2019) show that our VMT system achieves 35.86 corpus-level BLEU-4 score on the VATEX test set, yielding a 0.51 score improvement over the single model of the SOTA method (Hirasawa et al., 2020).

2 VMT with Spatial HAN

The overview of the proposed model is presented in Figure 2, which consists of components in the VMT baseline model (Hirasawa et al., 2020) and our proposed spatial HAN module.

2.1 VMT Baseline Model

Hirasawa et al. (2020) proposed a strong VMT baseline model, which consists of the following three modules.

Text Encoder. Each source sentence is represented as a sequence of N word embeddings. Then, the Bi-GRU (Schuster and Paliwal, 1997) encoder transforms them into text features $U = \{\mathbf{u_1}, \mathbf{u_2}, ..., \mathbf{u_N}\}$.

Motion Encoder. The VATEX dataset already provides motion features obtained by the pretrained I3D model (Carreira and Zisserman, 2017) for action recognition. A Bi-GRU motion encoder first transforms motion features into motion representations $M = \{\mathbf{m_1}, \mathbf{m_2}, ..., \mathbf{m_P}\}$. Then, a positional encoding (PE) layer PE (Vaswani et al., 2017) encourages the model use the order of the motion features and obtain ordered motion representations M^*, represented as:

$$M^* = \mathrm{PE}(M) \tag{1}$$

Target Decoder. The sentence embedding U from the source language encoder and the ordered motion embedding M^* from the motion encoder are processed using two attention mechanisms (Luong et al., 2015):

$$\mathbf{r_{u,t}} = \mathrm{Attention}_{u,t}(\mathbf{h_{t-1}}, U) \tag{2}$$

$$\mathbf{r_{m,t}} = \mathrm{Attention}_{m,t}(\mathbf{h_{t-1}}, M^*) \tag{3}$$

where $\mathrm{Attention}$ denotes a standard attention block, $\mathbf{h_{t-1}}$ denotes the hidden state at the previous decoding time step. Text representations $\mathbf{r_{u,t}}$ and motion representations $\mathbf{r_{m,t}}$ are allocated by another attention layer to obtain a contextual vector $\mathbf{r_{c,t}}$ at decoding time step t. The contextual vector is fed into a GRU layer for decoding:

$$\mathbf{r_{c,t}} = \mathrm{Attention}(\mathbf{h_{t-1}}, [\mathbf{r_{u,t}}, \mathbf{r_{m,t}}]) \tag{4}$$

$$\mathbf{y_t}, \mathbf{h_t} = \mathrm{f_{gru}}([\mathbf{y_{t-1}}, \mathbf{r_{c,t}}], \mathbf{h_{t-1}}) \tag{5}$$

where $\mathrm{f_{gru}}$ refers to the GRU decoding layer and $\mathbf{y}$ denotes the output target word embedding.

2.2 Spatial HAN

After splitting one video into X frames, we extract Y object-level spatial features $S_i = \{\mathbf{o_1}, \mathbf{o_2}, ..., \mathbf{o_Y}\}$ for the i-th frame. Because of the effectiveness of the PE layer (Vaswani et al., 2017) in the VMT baseline model, we also apply it to the object-level spatial features.

$$[R_o^1, R_o^2, ..., R_o^X] = \mathrm{PE}([S_1, S_2, ..., S_X]) \tag{6}$$

R_o^i denotes the object-level spatial representations of i-th frame.

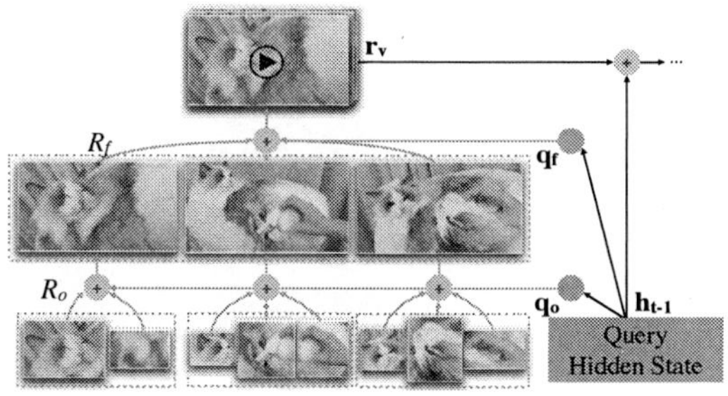

Figure 3: Structure of spatial HAN. R_o, R_f and $\mathbf{r_v}$ denote object-level, frame-level and video-level representations, $\mathbf{q}$ denotes *query* in attention layers, $\mathbf{h_{t-1}}$ denotes the hidden state at previous decoding time step.

Werlen et al. (2018) show that HAN can capture contextual and inter-sentence connections for translation. We propose to use HAN to extract contextual spatial information from adjacent frames within one video clip. With some modifications, we call the network spatial HAN.

The overview of spatial HAN is given by Figure 3. The object-level attention layer summarizes information from all separated objects in their respective frames:

$$\mathbf{q_{o,t}} = \mathrm{l_o}(\mathbf{h_{t-1}}) \tag{7}$$
$$\mathbf{r^i_{f,t}} = \mathrm{Attention_{o,t}}(\mathbf{q_{o,t}}, R^i_o) \tag{8}$$
$$R_{f,t} = \{\mathbf{r^1_{f,t}}, \mathbf{r^2_{f,t}}, ..., \mathbf{r^X_{f,t}}\} \tag{9}$$
$$R^*_{f,t} = \mathrm{f_d}(R_{f,t}) \tag{10}$$

where the function $\mathrm{l_o}$ is a linear layer to obtain the query $\mathbf{q_{o,t}}$. We adopt an attention layer to transform object-level spatial features R^i_o into respective frame-level spatial features $\mathbf{r^i_{f,t}}$. $\mathrm{f_d}$ denotes the middle encoding layer to obtain contextual frame-level spatial features $R^*_{f,t}$ at time step t.

The frame-level attention layer then summarizes representations from all ordered frames to video-level abstraction $\mathbf{r_{v,t}}$:

$$\mathbf{q_{f,t}} = \mathrm{l_f}(\mathbf{h_{t-1}}) \tag{11}$$
$$\mathbf{r_{v,t}} = \mathrm{Attention_{o,t}}(\mathbf{q_{f,t}}, R^*_{f,t}) \tag{12}$$

where $\mathrm{l_f}$ is a linear transformation, $\mathbf{q_{f,t}}$ is the query for attention function at time step t.

2.3 Target Decoder with Spatial HAN Features

The target decoder in our system contains three types of inputs: text representations $\mathbf{r_{u,t}}$, motion representations $\mathbf{r_{m,t}}$, and contextual spatial representations $\mathbf{r_{v,t}}$ from spatial HAN. The contextual vector $\mathbf{r_{c,t}}$ and the decoding GRU layer at each decoding step t become:

$$\mathbf{r_{c,t}} = \mathrm{Attention}(\mathbf{h_{t-1}}, [\mathbf{r_{u,t}}, \mathbf{r_{m,t}}, \mathbf{r_{v,t}}]) \tag{13}$$
$$\mathbf{y_t}, \mathbf{h_t} = \mathrm{f_{gru}}([\mathbf{y_{t-1}}, \mathbf{r_{c,t}}], \mathbf{h_{t-1}}) \tag{14}$$

3 Experiments

3.1 Dataset

The dataset we used for the VMT task is VATEX, which is built on a subset of action classification benchmark DeepMind Kinetics-600 (Kay et al., 2017). It consists of $25,991$ video clips for training, $3,000$ video clips for validation, and $6,000$ video clips for public test. Each video clip is accompanied with 5 parallel English-Chinese descriptions for the VMT task. However, the VATEX dataset only contains parallel sentences and segment-level motion features. To extract spatial features, we recollected $23,707$ video clips for training, $2,702$ video clips for validation, and $5,461$ video clips for public test, where about 10% clips are no longer available on the Internet. Therefore, we lack 10% spatial features for the dataset, so the experiment comparison is inherently unfair for our method.

3.2 Settings

We directly used the implementation of Hirasawa et al. (2020) as our VMT baseline model. For the common settings in our proposed approach and in the VMT baseline model, we set the maximum sentence length to 40, word embedding size to $1,024$, and the text encoder and motion encoder of both 2-layer bi-GRU with hidden dimension of 512. For our proposed spatial HAN, we used Faster R-CNN (Anderson et al., 2017) to extract object-level features as the input. The hidden dimensions of both object-level and frame-level attention layers were 512. As for the middle layer $\mathrm{f_d}$ in spatial HAN, we examined GRU and LSTM with the hidden dimension of 512, and spatial HAN without the middle layer. The target decoder was a 2-layer GRU with the hidden dimension of 512. During training, we used Adam optimizer with a learning rate of 0.001 and early stop with patience to 10 times. The vocabulary contained lower-cased English and characterized Chinese tokens that occurred more than five times in the training set, which is provided by Hirasawa et al. (2020) whose sizes are $7,949$ for English and $2,655$ for Chinese.

Figure 4: Four English to Chinese translation examples. Phrases in orange imply corresponding information and phrases in blue imply other translation errors. Ex. 1, 2 and 3 display noun sense ambiguity errors generated by the VMT baseline that make the translation unreasonable, whereas our model correctly translates these noun phrases. Ex. 4 shows a sentence structure error in the VMT baseline output, where the model wrongly recognizes the verb as the noun.

We adopt corpus-level BLEU-4 as the evaluation metric. We reported the score of the VMT baseline model denoted as "VMT baseline: Text+Motion," naming that it uses both the text and motion encoders. Besides the experiments with text, motion and spatial features obtained by our methods, denoted as "Ours: Text+Motion+Spatial," we also conducted the experiments with only text and spatial features denoted as "Ours: Text+Spatial."

3.3 Results

Model	Valid	Test
Wang et al. (2019)	-	31.10
Hirasawa et al. (2020)	35.42	35.35
VMT baseline: Text+Motion	35.55	35.59
Ours: Text+Motion+Spatial	35.71	35.82
Ours: Text+Spatial	**35.75**	**35.86**

Table 1: BLEU-4 scores of English to Chinese translation.

Table 1 shows the results of baseline and proposed models on the validation and public test sets. Our proposed system achieves 35.75 score on the validation set and 35.86 score on the test set, showing 4.76 BLEU score improvement over the VATEX's baseline model (Wang et al., 2019), and 0.51 BLEU score improvement over the best single model with the text corpus and action features. Because of some different settings in hyperparameters, our VMT baseline has 0.24 BLEU score improvement over the best single model.

Model	Mid Layer	Valid
Text+Motion+Spatial	None	**35.71**
	LSTM	35.50
	GRU	35.54
Text+Spatial	None	**35.75**
	LSTM	35.37
	GRU	35.27

Table 2: BLEU-4 scores of our models with different settings and middle layer choice.

Table 2 shows the ablation study on different settings of middle layer choice. Without the middle layer, both the two models achieved the best validation score. The reason may be that the PE layer for object-level spatial features already provides the contextual information, thus the middle layer in spatial HAN is dispensable. We notice that our models achieve comparable BLEU score results with and without motion features. We assume that it may come from the misalignment between motion, spatial and text features, where nouns and verbs in the sentences are not aligned to spatial features and motion features strictly. Also, the amount of nouns in sentences are much more than the amount of verbs in sentences, e.g., the ratios of nouns and verbs in source training corpus are 0.29 and 0.17, thus spatial features will take on more roles.

We further conducted a pairwise human evaluation to investigate how our proposed method improves the translation. Results on 50 random samples show that our model has 12 better translations than the VMT baseline model mainly on the noun sense disambiguation, where the VMT baseline model has 6 better translations mainly on the verb sense disambiguation and syntax. This suggests that our model can alleviate the noun sense ambiguity problem. The analysis details of several examples are given by Figure 4.

4 Conclusion

In this work, we proposed a VMT system with spatial HAN, which achieved 0.51 BLEU score improvement over the single model of the SOTA method. The result also showed the effectiveness of spatial features for the noun sense disambiguation. Our future work will focus on the alignment between text, motion and spatial representations.

Acknowledgments

This work was supported by ACT-I, JST.

References

Peter Anderson, Xiaodong He, Chris Buehler, Damien Teney, Mark Johnson, Stephen Gould, and Lei Zhang. 2017. Bottom-up and top-down attention for image captioning and VQA. *CoRR*, abs/1707.07998.

Dzmitry Bahdanau, Kyunghyun Cho, and Yoshua Bengio. 2015. Neural machine translation by jointly learning to align and translate. In *3rd International Conference on Learning Representations, ICLR 2015, San Diego, CA, USA, May 7-9, 2015, Conference Track Proceedings*.

Loïc Barrault, Fethi Bougares, Lucia Specia, Chiraag Lala, Desmond Elliott, and Stella Frank. 2018. Findings of the third shared task on multimodal machine translation. In *Proceedings of the Third Conference on Machine Translation: Shared Task Papers*, pages 304–323, Belgium, Brussels. Association for Computational Linguistics.

João Carreira and Andrew Zisserman. 2017. Quo vadis, action recognition? A new model and the kinetics dataset. In *2017 IEEE Conference on Computer Vision and Pattern Recognition, CVPR 2017, Honolulu, HI, USA, July 21-26, 2017*, pages 4724–4733. IEEE Computer Society.

Desmond Elliott, Stella Frank, Khalil Sima'an, and Lucia Specia. 2016. Multi30k: Multilingual english-german image descriptions. In *Proceedings of the 5th Workshop on Vision and Language*, pages 70–74. Association for Computational Linguistics.

Tosho Hirasawa, Zhishen Yang, Mamoru Komachi, and Naoaki Okazaki. 2020. Keyframe segmentation and positional encoding for video-guided machine translation challenge 2020. *CoRR*, abs/2006.12799.

Will Kay, João Carreira, Karen Simonyan, Brian Zhang, Chloe Hillier, Sudheendra Vijayanarasimhan, Fabio Viola, Tim Green, Trevor Back, Paul Natsev, Mustafa Suleyman, and Andrew Zisserman. 2017. The kinetics human action video dataset. *CoRR*, abs/1705.06950.

Thang Luong, Hieu Pham, and Christopher D. Manning. 2015. Effective approaches to attention-based neural machine translation. In *Proceedings of the 2015 Conference on Empirical Methods in Natural Language Processing*, pages 1412–1421, Lisbon, Portugal. Association for Computational Linguistics.

Mike Schuster and Kuldip K. Paliwal. 1997. Bidirectional recurrent neural networks. *IEEE Trans. Signal Process.*, 45(11):2673–2681.

Lucia Specia, Stella Frank, Khalil Sima'an, and Desmond Elliott. 2016. A shared task on multimodal machine translation and crosslingual image description. In *Proceedings of the First Conference on Machine Translation: Volume 2, Shared Task Papers*, pages 543–553, Berlin, Germany. Association for Computational Linguistics.

Ashish Vaswani, Noam Shazeer, Niki Parmar, Jakob Uszkoreit, Llion Jones, Aidan N. Gomez, Lukasz Kaiser, and Illia Polosukhin. 2017. Attention is all you need. In *Advances in Neural Information Processing Systems 30: Annual Conference on Neural Information Processing Systems 2017, 4-9 December 2017, Long Beach, CA, USA*, pages 5998–6008.

Xin Wang, Jiawei Wu, Junkun Chen, Lei Li, Yuan-Fang Wang, and William Yang Wang. 2019. Vatex: A large-scale, high-quality multilingual dataset for video-and-language research. In *2019 IEEE/CVF International Conference on Computer Vision, ICCV 2019, Seoul, Korea (South), October 27 - November 2, 2019*, pages 4580–4590. IEEE.

Lesly Miculicich Werlen, Dhananjay Ram, Nikolaos Pappas, and James Henderson. 2018. Document-level neural machine translation with hierarchical attention networks. In *Proceedings of the 2018 Conference on Empirical Methods in Natural Language Processing, Brussels, Belgium, October 31 - November 4, 2018*, pages 2947–2954. Association for Computational Linguistics.

Yonghui Wu, Mike Schuster, Zhifeng Chen, Quoc V. Le, Mohammad Norouzi, Wolfgang Macherey, Maxim Krikun, Yuan Cao, Qin Gao, Klaus Macherey, Jeff Klingner, Apurva Shah, Melvin Johnson, Xiaobing Liu, Lukasz Kaiser, Stephan Gouws, Yoshikiyo Kato, Taku Kudo, Hideto Kazawa, Keith Stevens, George Kurian, Nishant Patil, Wei Wang, Cliff Young, Jason Smith, Jason Riesa, Alex Rudnick, Oriol Vinyals, Greg Corrado, Macduff Hughes, and Jeffrey Dean. 2016. Google's neural machine translation system: Bridging the gap between human and machine translation. *CoRR*, abs/1609.08144.

Yuting Zhao, Mamoru Komachi, Tomoyuki Kajiwara, and Chenhui Chu. 2020. Double attention-based multimodal neural machine translation with semantic image regions. In *Proceedings of the 22nd Annual Conference of the European Association for Machine Translation*, pages 105–114, Lisboa, Portugal. European Association for Machine Translation.

Stylistic Approaches to Predicting Reddit Popularity in Diglossia

Huikai Chua
University of Cambridge
huikai.chua@gmail.com

Abstract

Past work investigating what makes a Reddit post popular has indicated that style is a far better predictor than content, where posts conforming to a subreddit's community style are better received. However, what about diglossia, when there are two community styles? In Singapore, the basilect ('Singlish') co-exists with an acrolect (standard English), each with contrasting advantages of community identity and prestige respectively. In this paper, I apply stylistic approaches to predicting Reddit post scores in diglossia. Using data from the Singaporean and British subreddits, I show that while the acrolect's prestige attracts more upvotes, the most popular posts also draw on Singlish vocabulary to appeal to the community identity.

1 Introduction

Reddit is a popular social media platform which is organized into different sub-forums, called subreddits. Users can submit original content as top-level posts to each subreddit, which other users can then comment on and either up- or down-vote. The most popular posts earn tens of thousands of upvotes.

But what exactly makes a post popular? In this paper, I apply natural language processing (NLP) techniques to predicting the popularity of a Reddit post. As past research has found style to be a strong predictor of community response (Tran and Ostendorf, 2016), I focus on stylistic approaches using punctuation, stopwords and part-of-speech tags, as inspired by Bergsma et al. (2012).

In particular, I investigate how community style endorsement (Tran and Ostendorf, 2016) applies in diglossic Singapore. Linguists have observed that Singapore English is organized along a sociolect continuum from an informal basilect (Singlish), to a formal acrolect, which has minimal features of Singlish and is essentially Standard British English (Gupta, 1991; Zhiming and Huaqing, 2006). Use of the acrolect is generally associated with better education, and therefore higher socioeconomic status. On the other hand, despite top-down efforts from the Singaporean government, the basilect is the dialect used by the average Singaporean in everyday situations, and is closely associated with the Singaporean identity. In fact, Singaporean politicians intentionally include Singlish phrases in election speeches in efforts to appear more down-to-earth and likeable. With competing appeals of identity and prestige between the two, I find that the most popular posts similarly use basilectal lexicon together with the acrolect to achieve the 'best of both worlds'.

2 Related Work

Much research has gone into investigating what makes a social media post popular, including some specifically focused on Reddit. Lakkaraju et al. (2013) controlled for the content of the post by concentrating on image submissions, which are frequently re- or cross-posted to different communities by different authors. They found that the title of a submission played a role in determining its success, where titles specifically engineered towards the community it was posted in (for example, by using community-specific words) performed better.

Tran and Ostendorf (2016) took this a step further and trained separate models for the content (using Latent Dirichlet Allocation (LDA)) and the style of the language used (by replacing topic words with their part-of-speech tags). They computed the Spearman rank correlation between scores and post representations, and found that the style model was much better at predicting of the success of a post than the content model. In other words, they found that these subreddits had their own community style, and posts which are stylisti-

Proceedings of the Joint Conference of the 59th Annual Meeting of the Association for Computational Linguistics and the 11th International Joint Conference on Natural Language Processing: Student Research Workshop, pages 93–100
August 5–6, 2021. ©2021 Association for Computational Linguistics

cally more similar to it are more likely to be well-received.

Fang et al. (2016) is the paper which is closest to the aim of this paper. They divided posts into eight different bins which are automatically determined by the score distribution of that particular subreddit, and evaluated model performance using a modified macro F1 score (details in Section 5.1). However, while Fang et al. (2016) focused on modelling the conversational context of a post, I instead focus on modelling the community style.

I take cues from Bergsma et al. (2012) to achieve this. They grouped their features into three broad categories: word (bag-of-words), style, and syntax features. For style features, they defined style words to be punctuation, stop-words, or Latin abbreviations, and replaced all non-style words with their part-of-speech (POS) tags. Meta-features such as average word and sentence lengths were also used. For grammatical features, they included a feature for every unique context free grammar and tree substitution grammar rule, as well as Charniak and Johnson re-ranking features (Charniak and Johnson, 2005). These are parse tree features initially used for re-ranking parser output, and include aggregate features for conjunct parallelism and lexicalized features for sub-trees and head-to-head dependencies.

3 Approach

I adopt Bergsma et al. (2012)'s three-pronged approach to stylometry. For content features, I use Bidirectional Encoder Representations from Transformers (BERT) (Devlin et al., 2019); for style features, I used term frequency–inverse document frequency (TF–IDF) vectors (Sparck Jones, 1988) with stopwords and punctuation only; for grammatical features, I used dependency relations and part-of-speech (POS) tags.

3.1 BERT

BERT (Devlin et al., 2019) uses a Transformer (Vaswani et al., 2017) encoder to achieve state-of-the-art performance on a wide variety of tasks. Past investigations have suggested that BERT is not just good at capturing the meaning of sequences, but is also sensitive to the grammar of phrases. Goldberg (2019) ran a series of grammatical test cases and found that BERT performed well on all; Jawahar et al. (2019) suggested that BERT layers encode linguistic information hierarchically, with surface information in lower layers, syntax in the middle, and semantic information at the top. Thus, it seems that BERT would be able to capture both the contents of posts as well as their style, making it particularly suitable for this task.

To capture the content of a post, I used the uncased English BERT$_{BASE}$ model provided by Hugging Face (Devlin et al., 2019; Wolf et al., 2020) to produce post embeddings. Since BERT is designed to encode sequence-level representations (Devlin et al., 2019), I first split each Reddit post into sentences using NLTK's sentence tokenizer. Then, each of the sentences were tokenized and encoded with BERT. Finally, the embeddings for each sentence were averaged to produce the overall post-level representation.

3.2 Grammatical features

I used the spaCy parser to extract dependency relations and part-of-speech (POS) tags. First, I hand-compiled the lists of relations and POS tags from the documentation[1]. Then, the dependency and POS labels for each word were replaced by their positions in the respective lists. I also included the POS labels of the heads of each word. Each of the three vectors (dependency tag, POS label, and head POS label) were L2-normalized.

3.3 Style features

I used stopword TF–IDF vectors for the style features. The vocabulary is predefined to be either a stop-word, using NLTK's English stop-word list, or a punctuation character, from Python's inbuilt string module. NLTK's English stop-word list, consists of 179 stop-words including determiners ('the', 'a'), pronouns ('he', 'she'), prepositions ('before', 'after'), quantifiers ('all', 'some'), among others.

3.4 Model

As I wanted to focus on feature rather than the model engineering, I used a tried-and-tested model for imbalanced class distributions: random forest classifiers. I opted to use the RandomForestClassifier from sklearn. I weighted each class proportional to its frequency in the dataset particular. For each Level $i, 0 \leq i \leq 7$, these are:

$$weight_{Leveli} = \frac{\#samples_{Level0}}{\#samples_{Leveli}}$$

[1] https://spacy.io/api/annotation

4 Data

4.1 Data collection

As my aim was to investigate the stylistic characteristics of communities, I selected a subreddit with a distinctive linguistic style – the Singaporean (SG) subreddit.[2] Singaporeans speak a distinctive flavour of English dubbed "Singlish", which has drawn much linguistic interest as the *lingua franca* of different cultural communities. It serves as the vernacular in the diglossic Singapore, where the Standard British English serves as the acrolect.

Therefore, for comparison, I also select the United Kingdom (UK) subreddit.[3] Although the population sizes of the two countries are quite different (roughly 5 million Singaporeans versus over 60 million UK citizens), I found that the subreddit sizes were similar, with roughly 300k participants in SG and 400k participants in UK.

Data was scraped from the two subreddits by querying the Pushshift API.[4] 3 years' worth of posts, ranging from 1 January 2017 to 31 December 2019, were collected for each subreddit. To ensure each post had sufficient linguistic content, I excluded any posts containing less than 101 characters.

4.2 Annotations

I followed the annotation procedure described in Fang et al. (2016). First, all posts with a score below 2 were labelled as the lowest class, Level 0. This threshold was selected for the base class as all new posts are initialized with a score of 1 (Fang et al., 2016). For the next level, the median of the remaining posts was computed and all posts with a score lower than the median labelled as 1. This process is repeated for each of the levels 2-6. Finally, the remaining posts are labelled as the highest class, Level 7. For clarity, the annotation function is given as pseudocode in the appendix (Algorithm 1). The distribution for each subreddit along with the respective class thresholds are summarized in Table 1.

5 Quantitative evaluation

5.1 Evaluation metric

I also replicate the evaluation procedure described in Fang et al. (2016). First, the F1 score for each of

[2]reddit.com/r/singapore

[3]reddit.com/r/unitedkingdom

[4]https://github.com/pushshift/api

Level	r/singapore		r/UK	
	Size	Cap	Size	Cap
0	15,633	2	9246	2
1	4797	14	2466	14
2	2394	36	1246	64
3	1200	74	633	191
4	620	151	318	531
5	310	284	159	1086
6	156	507	79	1762
7	156	-	80	-
Total	25,266		14,227	

Table 1: Distribution of classes for both subreddits.

the Levels 1-7 were computed, treating each sample with a score below that level as a negative example. Then, the final score for that model is obtained by averaging over the F1 scores for each level. Fang et al. (2016) had designed this evaluation metric such that the higher levels, which are of greater interest, are weighted more highly. For example, for the SG score distribution, a model which predicts only Level 1s would obtain an F1 of 0.0789, while a model which predicts only Level 8s would obtain an F1 of 0.176. Level 0 is excluded in computing the average, as using the scheme described above the F1 score would always be 1.

5.2 Results

In total, I tried six different combinations of the three different types of features. First, I tried each of the style features, BERT embeddings, and grammatical (POS and dependency labels) features separately. Then, I tried individually adding the other two types to the weakest baseline, which was the grammatical model. Finally, I tried a combination of all features together. I used stratified five-fold cross-validation and report the average modified F1 score across all folds. The results can be found in Table 2.

In all cases, the models clearly out-performed the simplistic baseline of 0.176 for a model which predicts only the highest class. Although the scores for each model are similar, the results are consistent across the two sub-reddits, r/Singapore (SG) and r/UnitedKingdom (UK). In both cases, BERT performs the best out of the three baselines, and indeed was improved only slightly by 0.02 for SG when other features were added, and not at all for UK.

Between SG and UK, all models performed significantly better on the UK dataset. This is possibly due to there being a more consistent group style for UK, compared to the diglossic situation in Singapore. It could also be due to the tools used (such as BERT and spaCy) being trained mostly on standard American / British English, and hence performing better on the UK subreddit.

The results are not directly comparable to those achieved by Fang et al. (2016), due to differences in the data used. However, comparing the trends in F1 score across levels reveals some interesting differences. In Fang et al. (2016), the model performed better on lower levels, with an average of nearly 0.60 F1 on the lowest 3 levels, and an average of under 0.50 F1 on the highest 3.

However, in this paper, the models used performed better at higher levels, as can be seen from Figure 1. Though the models start with roughly similar performance for Levels 1 and 2, they gradually diverge as the level increases, for a gap of 0.085 F1 points at the highest. As we will see in the next section, a diglossic situation with two competing dialects makes it a bit more difficult to craft an effective style.

	SG	UK
Style	0.748	0.788
BERT	0.749	0.793
Gram.	0.733	0.781
Gram. + style	0.750	0.792
Gram. + BERT	0.751	0.793
All	0.751	0.793

Table 2: F1 scores for each subreddit for each model.

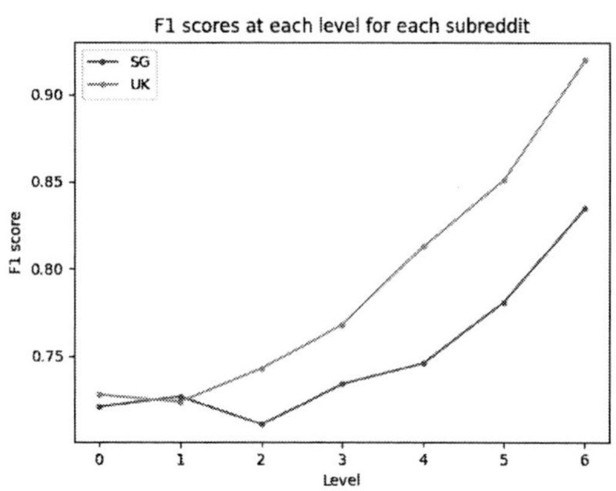

Figure 1: F1 scores for each individual level for the model with all features. The numerical results are given in the appendix (Table 6.)

6 Qualitative evaluation and analysis

In this section, I look at inferences that can be gained by looking at the most important features from each model. While BERT appears to be good at capturing the grammatical relations, it is not as good with more complex relationships. I also find overlaps between the grammatical and stylistic features, with the more specific stylistic features performing better. Finally, I investigate grammatical and lexical similarities between SG posts and the acrolect and basilect respectively. I find that while the most popular posts are most grammatically similar to the acrolect, they also use the most lexicon from the basilect.

6.1 Feature importances

The top 10 non-BERT features, i.e. either a POS, dependency, head_POS tag, or a stopword or punctuation for SG and UK are tabulated in Table 3 and 4 respectively. The POS tags of head words (henceforth referred to as head-POS) are differentiated from the POS tags of words with a 'head_' prefix.

6.1.1 Does BERT capture grammatical features?

Although model performance improved only a little when BERT embeddings were added to grammatical features, the most informative features were completely taken over by BERT features. For SG, the highest ranking non-BERT feature was 'head_ADV' at 15th place, with the next one, 'head_SCONJ', coming in 10 places lower. For UK, the top two were at 5th ('head_X') and 30th ('CCONJ') place respectively. This does suggest BERT is capable of capturing the grammar of a sentence in its embedding, as it seems to have replaced grammatical features when it was added to the model.

Of particular note are the changes in the individual features' rankings. In the grammatical features only model, the top features are occupied by dependency and POS tags; the highest ranking head-POS features for SG and UK are 'head_NOUN' and 'head_VERB' at 12th and 7th place respectively. The relatively higher rankings of head-POS tags after adding BERT suggest that it might not be as good at capturing more complex grammatical relationships.

Rank	Gram. only	Style only	Gram + Style	Gram + BERT (position)
1	punct	.	.	head_ADV (15)
2	PUNCT	the	?	empty dep relation (22)
3	ROOT	?	PUNCT	head_SCONJ (25)
4	DET	to	punct	prt (42)
5	advmod	,	ROOT	head_PUNCT (48)
6	poss	and	the	dative (50)
7	aux	i	advmod	DET (52)
8	NOUN	a	head_VERB	poss (104)
9	det	of	AUX	PUNCT (118)
10	ADJ	in	DET	PART (128)

Table 3: Top 10 non-BERT features for selected models on the SG dataset.

Rank	Gram. only	Style only	Gram + Style	Gram + BERT (position)
1	amod	.	/	head_X (5)
2	ROOT	/	.	CCONJ (30)
3	NOUN	the	ROOT	PART (46)
4	DET	to	head_VERB	amod (48)
5	PUNCT	a	punct	cc (57)
6	punct	i	i	conj (137)
7	head_VERB	and	AUX	advmod (173)
8	PRON	,	head_NOUN	relcl (174)
9	aux	”	PUNCT	SPACE (176)
10	cc	?	amod	NOUN (220)

Table 4: Top 10 non-BERT features for selected models on the UK dataset.

6.1.2 Overlap between grammatical and style features

There is a noticeable overlap between grammatical and style features, where the top-ranked features for grammatical and style mirror each other. For example, punctuation ranks among the most informative style features, particularly for UK where they occupy 5 out of the top 10 spots despite making up only 15% of the roughly 200 style features. Among the 100 grammatical features, the dependency rule 'punct' and POS tag 'PUNCT' also rank highly. A similar trend can be seen for determiners, which rank highly as both style features (in the form of the stopwords 'the' and 'a') as well as grammatical features (in the form of the dependency rule 'DET'). This possibly contributes to the very similar performances of the style and grammatical models.

However, it appears that the more specific style features generally perform better. When grammatical and style features were combined for SG, the specific punctuation characters '.' and '?' appear before 'PUNCT' and 'punct'. Similarly, the determiner 'the' appears before the dependency rule 'DET'. This might explain the difference between the individual style and grammatical models, where the style model performed better on both the SG and UK datasets. Although the top features from both form a common subset, the more specific features found in the style model are better predictors.

6.2 Grammatical closeness

Since the acrolect should be close to Standard British English, I decided to assess this by first computing the Euclidean centre of Level 7 posts from UK. Then, for each of the Levels 0-7, I computed the average Euclidean distances from Singaporean posts to the UK centre. For comparison, I also compute the average distances for UK posts. The distances for each of the three types of features are tabulated in Table 5. Note that, due to different dimensions and normalization, the distances for each feature are not directly comparable to that of other features.

Across all three features, Level 0 SG posts are generally less similar to the UK centre than Level 0 UK posts, possibly due to greater presence of the basilect. However, at the top level, SG posts are even *more* similar than the original posts the centre was calculated from. This suggests that indeed the Standard British English acrolect holds more prestige and draws greater community endorsement.

Separately, the consistent trend in the Style column where posts from higher levels are more similar to the Level 7 centre than lower level posts supports the hypothesis that there is a community style and posts which are more similar to it receive greater community endorsement.

6.3 Lexical closeness

We can see that stylistically and grammatically, the most popular posts from SG are very similar to British English. However, what about lexically? Singlish has a vocabulary full of borrowed words and phrases from the different cultural groups of Singapore. As mentioned earlier, politicians often try to build rapport by sprinkling speeches with Singlish terms. Would we observe something similar on Reddit? I decide to investigate the prevalence of Singlish terms by level.

Compiling a written Singlish lexicon can be very tricky due to several reasons, including different possible romanizations and lexical change in loanwords (when the word's meaning changes). With this in mind, using my experience growing up in Singapore, I compiled a list of 56 everyday Singlish words and phrases, including alternative spellings where practical. I excluded phrases with specific niches, like the names of foods or military terms (common in Singapore where all males have to enlist for 2 years). The full list of phrases used is included in the appendix.

The average number of such Singlish words or phrases used per 1000 words per post for each of the Levels 0-7 is shown in Figure 2. The results confirm the earlier hypothesis that effective use of Singlish words helps earn more community endorsement. We see a somewhat U-shape in the frequency of Singlish terms; the least popular posts include more Singlish than the middlingly popular posts, likely due to greater influence of the basilect, while posts on the highest levels utilise Singlish vocabulary in tandem with the acrolect to achieve the most popularity.

A reading of the Level 7 texts including Singlish terms confirm that this is indeed the case. For example, one post is written in very eloquent standard English[5], but includes Singlish quotes as well as specific, appropriate Singlish terms (with English explanations in brackets).

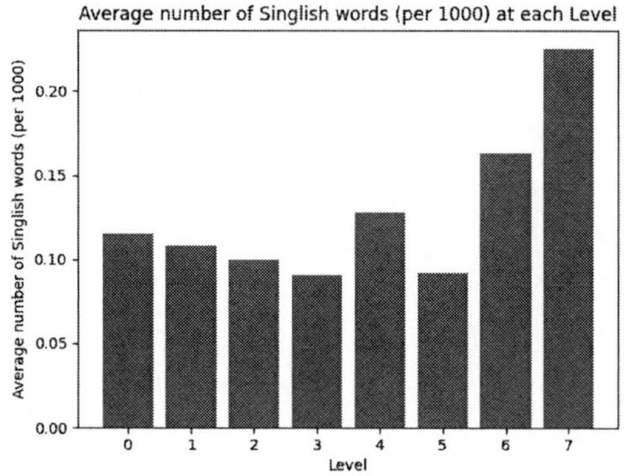

Figure 2: Average number of everyday Singlish terms per 1000 words. The numerical results are given in the appendix (Table 7).

7 Future Work

In the future, I would like to extend this work by including context-free grammar (CFG) features using CoreNLP to compare the use of Singlish grammatical features, in order to further confirm or disprove the theory that the most popular posts use the acrolect, i.e. the least grammatical features from Singlish, despite having the highest prevalence of Singlish terms.

8 Conclusion

In summary, in this paper, I look at the linguistic factors that predict the community response of Reddit posts. I collected data from two Reddit subforums, the Singaporean and UK subreddits. Following Bergsma et al. (2012), I extracted three types of features, broadly grouped as grammatical, stylistic and content features. The models generally show good results, with the stylistic and grammatical models performing comparable to state-of-the-art BERT embeddings.

I investigate also the hypothesis that posts conforming to a group's style receive greater community endorsement (Tran and Ostendorf, 2016). I show that in a diglossic situation, although the acrolect draws greater prestige, the most successful posts draw on features from the basilect in order to connect with the audience.

[5]https://www.reddit.com/r/singapore/comments/8gfewd/the_singaporean_male_version_of_metoo_an_exguards/

Level	BERT		Style		Gram.	
	SG	UK	SG	UK	SG	UK
0	4.45	4.35	0.875	0.847	0.704	0.715
1	4.40	4.31	0.874	0.845	0.688	0.697
2	4.33	4.34	0.877	0.832	0.678	0.716
3	4.39	4.34	0.848	0.830	0.676	0.733
4	4.17	4.35	0.826	0.826	0.632	0.722
5	4.11	4.20	0.808	0.829	0.629	0.711
6	3.79	4.18	0.797	0.814	0.591	0.722
7	3.55	3.91	0.751	0.800	0.513	0.659

Table 5: Average Euclidean distances from the UK Level 7 centre.

Acknowledgments

Dr Andreas Vlachos and Prof Ted Briscoe taught the L101 course for which this project was done. Prof Briscoe also gave feedback on this paper, and suggested submission of this work to the Student Research Workshop (SRW). I would also like to thank my bachelor's and master's thesis supervisors, Dr Andrew Caines and Dr Helen Yannakoudakis, for their guidance on NLP techniques. Dr Caines also reviewed an earlier version of this paper. Finally, I am grateful to the SRW anonymous reviewers for their detailed feedback.

References

Shane Bergsma, Matt Post, and David Yarowsky. 2012. Stylometric analysis of scientific articles. In *Proceedings of the 2012 Conference of the North American Chapter of the Association for Computational Linguistics: Human Language Technologies*, pages 327–337, Montréal, Canada. Association for Computational Linguistics.

Eugene Charniak and Mark Johnson. 2005. Coarse-to-fine n-best parsing and MaxEnt discriminative reranking. In *Proceedings of the 43rd Annual Meeting of the Association for Computational Linguistics (ACL'05)*, pages 173–180, Ann Arbor, Michigan. Association for Computational Linguistics.

Jacob Devlin, Ming-Wei Chang, Kenton Lee, and Kristina Toutanova. 2019. BERT: Pre-training of deep bidirectional transformers for language understanding. In *Proceedings of the 2019 Conference of the North American Chapter of the Association for Computational Linguistics: Human Language Technologies, Volume 1 (Long and Short Papers)*, pages 4171–4186, Minneapolis, Minnesota. Association for Computational Linguistics.

Hao Fang, Hao Cheng, and Mari Ostendorf. 2016. Learning latent local conversation modes for predicting comment endorsement in online discussions. In *Proceedings of The Fourth International Workshop on Natural Language Processing for Social Media*, pages 55–64, Austin, TX, USA. Association for Computational Linguistics.

Yoav Goldberg. 2019. Assessing BERT's Syntactic Abilities. *arXiv e-prints*, page arXiv:1901.05287.

Anthea F Gupta. 1991. Acquisition of diglossia in singapore english. *Child language development in Singapore and Malaysia*, pages 119–160.

Ganesh Jawahar, Benoît Sagot, and Djamé Seddah. 2019. What does BERT learn about the structure of language? In *Proceedings of the 57th Annual Meeting of the Association for Computational Linguistics*, pages 3651–3657, Florence, Italy. Association for Computational Linguistics.

Himabindu Lakkaraju, Julian McAuley, and Jure Leskovec. 2013. What's in a name? understanding the interplay between titles, content, and communities in social media.

Karen Sparck Jones. 1988. *A Statistical Interpretation of Term Specificity and Its Application in Retrieval*, page 132–142. Taylor Graham Publishing, GBR.

Trang Tran and Mari Ostendorf. 2016. Characterizing the language of online communities and its relation to community reception. In *Proceedings of the 2016 Conference on Empirical Methods in Natural Language Processing*, pages 1030–1035, Austin, Texas. Association for Computational Linguistics.

Ashish Vaswani, Noam Shazeer, Niki Parmar, Jakob Uszkoreit, Llion Jones, Aidan N Gomez, Ł ukasz Kaiser, and Illia Polosukhin. 2017. Attention is all you need. In *Advances in Neural Information Processing Systems*, volume 30. Curran Associates, Inc.

Thomas Wolf, Lysandre Debut, Victor Sanh, Julien Chaumond, Clement Delangue, Anthony Moi, Pierric Cistac, Tim Rault, Rémi Louf, Morgan Funtowicz, Joe Davison, Sam Shleifer, Patrick von Platen, Clara Ma, Yacine Jernite, Julien Plu, Canwen Xu, Teven Le Scao, Sylvain Gugger, Mariama Drame, Quentin Lhoest, and Alexander M. Rush. 2020. Huggingface's transformers: State-of-the-art natural language processing.

Bao Zhiming and Hong Huaqing. 2006. Diglossia and register variation in singapore english. *World Englishes*, 25(1):105–114.

A Appendices

A.1 Annotation algorithm

Algorithm 1 Annotator

Input: An array 'score' containing the number of votes for each post
Output: Another array 'classes' containing the annotations

get_indexes(array, condition) ← function which returns the list of indexes x in the array for which array[x] satisfies condition

class_indexes ← new array[8]
class_indexes[0] ← get_indexes(score, x $\leq$ 1)
rest_of_posts ← get_indexes(score, x $>$ 1)
for i, 1$\leq$ i $\leq$ 7 **do**
  median ← median score of rest_of_posts
  class_indexes[i] ← get_indexes(score, x $<$ median)
  rest_of_posts ← get_indexes(score, x $\geq$ median)
end for

class_indexes[7] = rest_of_posts
classes ← new array[len(score)]
for i, 0$\leq$ i $\leq$ 7 **do**
  classes[class_indexes[i]] = i
end for

A.2 Extra numerical results

	SG	UK
Level 1	0.721	0.728
Level 2	0.727	0.724
Level 3	0.711	0.743
Level 4	0.734	0.768
Level 5	0.746	0.813
Level 6	0.781	0.851
Level 7	0.835	0.920

Table 6: F1 scores for each individual level for the model with all features.

Level	# terms (per 1000)
0	0.115
1	0.108
2	0.0996
3	0.0906
4	0.128
5	0.0923
6	0.163
7	0.225

Table 7: Average number of everyday Singlish terms per 1000 words.

A.3 List of Singlish words

'abuden', 'act blur', 'agak', 'ai', 'aiya', 'alamak', 'ang mo', 'ang moh', 'atas', 'bao toh', 'barang', 'bo', 'bodoh', 'bojio', 'boliao', 'botak', 'chao', 'chee bai', 'chim', 'cheem', 'chio bu', 'chiong', 'chope', 'gahmen', 'heng', 'huat', 'jialat', 'jio', 'kena', 'kiasu', 'la', 'lah', 'lao', 'leh', 'lepak', 'liao', 'liddat', 'mafan', 'mah', 'meh', 'paiseh', 'ps', 'paktor', 'sabo', 'sia', 'sian', 'siao', 'simi', 'tahan', 'ulu', 'wa', 'walao', 'wayang', 'ya', 'yah'

"I've Seen Things You People Wouldn't Believe": Hallucinating Entities in GuessWhat?!

Alberto Testoni
DISI, University of Trento
Trento, Italy
alberto.testoni@unitn.it

Raffaella Bernardi
CIMeC, DISI, University of Trento
Rovereto, Italy
raffaella.bernardi@unitn.it

Abstract

Natural language generation systems have witnessed important progress in the last years, but they are shown to generate tokens that are unrelated to the source input. This problem affects computational models in many NLP tasks, and it is particularly unpleasant in multimodal systems. In this work, we assess the rate of object hallucination in multimodal conversational agents playing the GuessWhat?! referential game. Better visual processing has been shown to mitigate this issue in image captioning; hence, we adapt to the GuessWhat?! task the best visual processing models at disposal, and propose two new models to play the Questioner agent. We show that the new models generate few hallucinations compared to other renowned models available in the literature. Moreover, their hallucinations are less severe (affect task-accuracy less) and are more human-like. We also analyse where hallucinations tend to occur more often through the dialogue: hallucinations are less frequent in earlier turns, cause a cascade hallucination effect, and are often preceded by negative answers, which have been shown to be harder to ground.

1 Introduction

Recent years have witnessed important progress in the quality of the output generated by deep neural network architectures. Although it is not easy to evaluate the output of natural language generation systems, some features clearly deteriorate their value, making these systems hardly employable in real-world scenarios. Crucially, state-of-the-art models are shown to generate words that are not consistent with the source inputs. This issue is generally referred to as *hallucination*.

This phenomenon applies to different NLP tasks and neural architectures. It has been explored in summarization (Kryscinski et al., 2020; Nan et al., 2021), machine translation (Koehn and Knowles, 2017; Nguyen and Chiang, 2018), and image captioning (Rohrbach et al., 2018). Hallucinating entities is particularly harmful in multimodal systems. MacLeod et al. (2017) study how blind people experience automatically generated captions describing images. The authors found that many participants in this study value more the correctness of the caption compared to a fine-grained description of the image, thus providing evidence that hallucination represents a major issue.

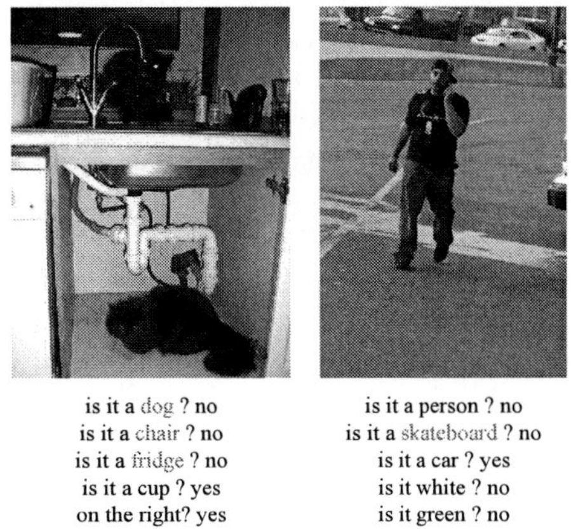

Figure 1: Hallucinations generated by the GDSE model playing GuessWhat?!. Note that the dialogue on the right also contains a question referring to an attribute (*green*) that is not related to the source image. In this paper, however, we focus only on entity hallucination.

The problem of generating hallucinated entities is thus a relevant challenge for the community, but it is an understudied problem in multimodal conversational agents. Apart from sharing similarities with the image captioning task (e.g., generating tokens that are grounded in the image), visual dialogues have the peculiarity of being based on a complex dialogic structure. In this paper, we compare the output of neural models playing the GuessWhat?! referential visual game (de Vries et al.,

Proceedings of the Joint Conference of the 59th Annual Meeting of the Association for Computational Linguistics and the 11th International Joint Conference on Natural Language Processing: Student Research Workshop, pages 101–111
August 5–6, 2021. ©2021 Association for Computational Linguistics

2017). We consider different models based on the encoder-decoder framework (Sutskever et al., 2014), and we compare different architectures, with different processing of the visual input, to serve as the Encoder and Decoder modules. We adapt two multimodal models based on Transformers (Vaswani et al., 2017) to play the GuessWhat?! Questioner agent, and we highlight their strengths and weaknesses with a focus on the issue of hallucination. Examples of GuessWhat?! dialogues containing hallucinations are reported in Figure 1. We use the CHAIR metric proposed in Rohrbach et al. (2018) to quantify the number of hallucinations in the generated dialogues.

Our results confirm that hallucination heavily affects the output of generative models playing GuessWhat?!, but pre-trained Transformers (used both as Encoder and Decoder) show a consistent improvement in this respect. Moreover, our results reveal that the rate of object hallucination increases across the dialogue turns. Hallucinations frequently appear in consecutive turns and are more likely to occur after negative answers. Finally, we carry out an in-depth analysis in dialogues produced by human annotators. The main contributions of this paper can be summarized as follows:

- We investigate the issue of hallucination, an understudied problem in visual dialogue, by taking GuessWhat?! as a test-bed.
- We studied to what extent fine-grained visual representations reduce hallucinations in multimodal models.
- We show the importance of computing the CHAIR metric on models' and humans' text, and use this metric to guide a qualitative analysis to better understand the results.

2 Related Work

Hallucination in Language-only Tasks. Kryscinski et al. (2020); Nan et al. (2021) highlight the problem of factual inconsistency in abstractive summarization. This phenomenon occurs when a computational model generates a summary containing entities that do not appear in the source document. Kryscinski et al. (2020) propose a weakly-supervised, model-based approach to verify factual consistency and identify conflicts between source documents and generated summaries. Nan et al. (2021) design a set of new metrics to quantify the degree of entity hallucination in summaries. Interestingly, the authors found that ground truth summaries in the training data contain hallucinations. Similarly to these works, we focus on entity hallucination, and on inconsistencies with respect to the visual context, instead of the linguistic one.

Neural machine translation systems are also prone to such kinds of hallucinations, i.e. translations that are grammatically correct, but crucially unrelated to the source input (Koehn and Knowles, 2017; Nguyen and Chiang, 2018). A recent work (Müller et al., 2020) found that neural machine translation systems evaluated on out-of-domain test sets generate translations that are fluent but unrelated to the source sentence. These works focus on words belonging to different parts of speech, like proper nouns, adjectives, and verbs, while we only focus on entity hallucination and leave for future work the analysis of attribute hallucination.

Hallucination in Vision & Language. The generation of hallucinations affects also Multimodal Machine Translation systems. Lala and Specia (2018) highlight the issues that may arise while translating ambiguous or polysemic words given a visual context. Rohrbach et al. (2018) investigate the problem of object hallucination in image captioning, the closest task to our work. The authors propose a new metric (CHAIR) to quantify the extent to which machine-generated captions contain hallucinated entities. The authors found overreliance on language priors as a plausible cause of hallucinated tokens in the generated captions. Moreover, they found that models with a more reliable visual representation hallucinate less, suggesting that a robust processing of the visual input is important for reducing hallucination. We use the CHAIR metric to evaluate different models, and look at the role of different visual representations. A recent work (Xiao and Wang, 2021) investigates the relationship between hallucinations and predictive uncertainty in image captioning and data-to-text generation. The authors found that higher predictive uncertainty leads to a higher chance of hallucinating entities. We leave this kind of analysis for future work.

Visual Dialogues Evaluation. Among the visual dialogue datasets and tasks available (e.g., de Vries et al. 2017; Mostafazadeh et al. 2017; Das et al. 2017; Haber et al. 2019), we chose a task-oriented referential game, GuessWhat?! (de Vries et al., 2017). Task-oriented conversational agents generate dialogues to reach a goal, thus the presence of hallucinations considerably hurt the performance of such systems. We chose GuessWhat?! because of the simplicity of its dialogue structure (polar question-answer pairs). Recent work in the literature highlights the inability of the accuracy in the guessing task to serve as a good proxy of the quality of the underlying dialogues, with a particular focus on surface-level features such as the presence of repetitions (Shekhar et al., 2019; Murahari et al., 2019; Testoni et al., 2019). We extend this claim by looking at hallucination, an under-studied but crucial issue in Visual Dialogues.

3 Task and Metrics

Task The GuessWhat?! game (de Vries et al., 2017) is a cooperative two-player game in English based on a referential communication task where two players collaborate to identify a referent object in an image. This setting has been extensively used in human-human collaborative dialogue (e.g., Clark 1996; Yule 2013). GuessWhat?! is an asymmetric game involving two human participants who see a real-world image. One of the participants (the Oracle) is secretly assigned a target object within the image, and the other participant (the Questioner) has to guess it by asking binary (Yes/No) questions to the Oracle. The GuessWhat?! dataset is composed of more than 150k human-human dialogues containing an average of 5.3 questions in natural language created by annotators playing the game on MSCOCO images (Lin et al., 2014). Successful dialogues consist of around 135K dialogues grounded on about 63K unique MSCOCO images.

Metrics The first metric we consider is the raw accuracy in guessing the target object among the list of candidate objects. Secondly, to quantify the extent to which different models hallucinate entities during the dialogue, we compute the CHAIR metric *(Caption Hallucination Assessment with Image Relevance)* proposed in Rohrbach et al. (2018) for image captioning. This metric has two variants: *CHAIR-i* (per-instance), defined as the number of hallucinated objects in a sequence divided by the total number of objects mentioned, and *CHAIR-s* (per-sentence), defined as the number of sequences with at last one hallucinated entity divided by the total number of sequences. We use the same two variants of the CHAIR metric to evaluate the dialogues generated by models playing GuessWhat?!. This metric exploits the 80 MSCOCO objects which appear in the MSCOCO segmentation challenge, extended with entities mentioned in ground-truth captions, together with a list of synonyms for MSCOCO objects. We compute CHAIR for both machine-generated and human dialogues from the GuessWhat?! test set (referred to as HUMAN in the following). Computing CHAIR on human dialogues allows us to identify possible misclassification in the MSCOCO annotation and establish an upper bound for models' performance.

4 Models

To allow for a fair comparison of different Questioner models, we use the same Oracle and Guesser models in all our experiments. Following de Vries et al. (2017), we employ distinct computational models for each of the three key tasks: answering questions (Oracle), guessing the target (Guesser), and asking questions (Questioner).

4.1 Oracle

We use the baseline Oracle model proposed in de Vries et al. (2017). The model receives as input the embedding of the target object category, its spatial coordinates, and the question to be answered encoded by a dedicated Long-Short-Term Memory (LSTM) network. These three embeddings are concatenated and fed to a Multi-Layer Perceptron (MLP) that gives an answer (Yes, No, N/A).

4.2 Guesser

We use the state-of-the-art multimodal Guesser model proposed in Greco et al. (2021a) (Figure 2 bottom).[1] This Guesser is based on LXMERT (Tan and Bansal, 2019), a powerful multimodal Transformer model that is fine-tuned on the GuessWhat?! guesser task using successful human dialogues. LXMERT represents the visual input by the set of position-aware object embeddings for the 36 most salient regions detected by a Faster R-CNN network, and the text by position-aware randomly-initialized word embeddings. LXMERT has self-attention and cross-attention layers to merge and enhance the information coming from the two modalities to create a joint representation. LXMERT uses a special tokens CLS and the embedding corresponding to this token is considered a representation of the given sequence. LXMERT has been

[1] https://github.com/claudiogreco/aixia2021

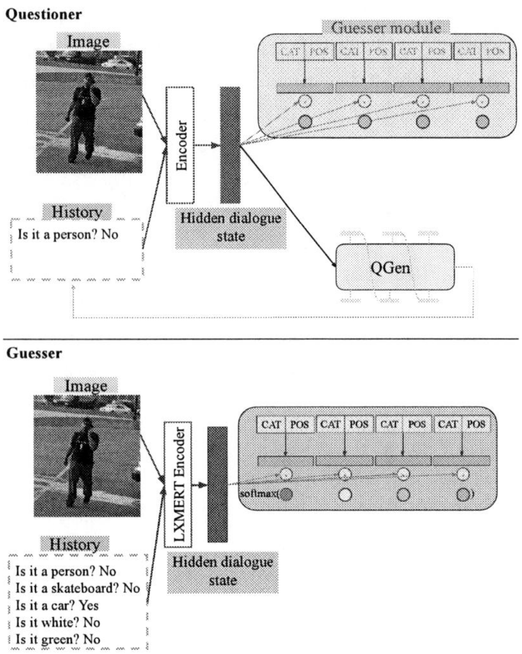

Figure 2: Skeleton architecture of the Questioner and Guesser models.

pre-trained on five tasks.[2] For the Guesser task, candidate objects are represented by the embeddings obtained via an MLP starting from the category and spatial coordinates of each candidate object. The representations so obtained are used to compute dot products with the embedding corresponding to the special token [CLS]. The scores of each candidate object are given to a softmax classifier to choose the object with the highest probability.

4.3 Questioner Models

In order to study the effect of a different (and more fine-grained) processing of the visual input, we compare two models already presented in the literature (BL and GDSE) with two Transformer-based multimodal models (LXMERT-GDSE and VLP) that we adapt to play the GuessWhat?! Questioner task. The architecture shared by the Questioner models is depicted in Figure 2. All the models discussed in the paper (except for BL) are trained to perform both the Questioner and the Guesser tasks in a multi-task fashion. For a fair comparison, we compute the accuracy in the guessing task using the same Guesser and Oracle models described above, and we use the Questioner models only to generate questions.

[2]Masked cross-modality language modeling, masked object prediction via RoI-feature regression, masked object prediction via detected-label classification, cross-modality matching, and image question answering

BL. The first model we consider is the baseline Questioner model proposed in de Vries et al. (2017). This model is implemented as a Recurrent Neural Network (RNN) with a transition function handled with LSTM, on which a probabilistic sequence model is built with a Softmax classifier. At each time step in the dialogue, the model receives as input the raw image and the dialogue history and generates the next question. The image is encoded by extracting its VGG-16 features (Simonyan and Zisserman, 2014). We consider the version of the model trained in a supervised learning fashion.

GDSE. The Visually-Grounded Dialogue State Encoder (GDSE) model was proposed in Shekhar et al. (2019). We consider the version of GDSE trained in a supervised learning fashion. The model uses a visually grounded dialogue state that takes the visual features of the input image and each question-answer pair in the dialogue history to create a shared representation used both for generating a follow-up question (QGen module) and guessing the target object (Guesser module) in a multi-task learning scenario. More specifically, the visual features are extracted with a ResNet-152 network (He et al., 2016) and the dialogue history is encoded with an LSTM network. The QGen component is optimized with the Log Likelihood of the training dialogues, and the Guesser computes a score for each candidate object by performing the dot product between a visually grounded dialogue state and each object representation. In this work, we use GDSE only to generate dialogues, since the guessing part relies on the Guesser described above.

LXMERT-GDSE. Similarly to GDSE, we implement a new Questioner model based on the LXMERT architecture described above. In this model, we take the representation corresponding to the [CLS] token as the hidden dialogue state and, similarly to GDSE, we feed this representation as input to both a QGen module (an LSTM-based decoder) and a Guesser module. We fine-tune the pre-trained LXMERT on GuessWhat?!. Again, we use this model only to generate dialogues.

VLP. Finally, we develop a Questioner model based on VLP (Zhou et al., 2020), a powerful multimodal Encoder-Decoder Transformer architecture pre-trained on image captioning. VLP is a single

	CHAIR-s	CHAIR-i
BL	29.53	27.32
GDSE	30.31	16.57
LXMERT-GDSE	14.98	8.83
VLP	10.78	6.60
HUMAN	7.45	4.11

Table 1: CHAIR results on human and machine-generated dialogues on the GuessWhat?! test set.

stream unified encoder-decoder architecture: its Transformer backbone is the same as BERT-base (Devlin et al., 2019). VLP represents each input image as 100 object regions extracted from a variant of Faster RCNN (Ren et al., 2016) pre-trained on Visual Genome (Krishna et al., 2017; Anderson et al., 2018), together with the class likelihood on the 1600 object categories defined in Anderson et al. (2018) as region object labels. During pre-training, the model uses a masked language modelling objective. During inference, in order to generate a sequence token-by-token, VLP masks sequentially each token by appending a special token [SEP] at the end of the sequence. VLP is trained to predict a [STOP] token at the end of the sequence, so it can stop the generation of new tokens before reaching the maximum length. We fine-tune the version of VLP pre-trained on image captioning to play the GuessWhat?! game.[3]

Implementational Details We evaluate BL, GDSE, LXMERT-GDSE, and VLP on the GuessWhat?! test set. We let the models generate 5 question-answer pairs for each game (i.e., similar to the average number of questions asked by human players in GuessWhat?!). Note that VLP is trained to predict a [STOP] token, so it can stop asking questions before reaching the 5th turn. We found that, on average, VLP asks 4 questions in a dialogue. We compare the models with respect to their accuracy in the guessing game and the quality of the generated dialogues, with a focus on the phenomenon of hallucination.

5 Experiments and Results

5.1 CHAIR Results

We compare different models against the CHAIR metric. As Table 1 shows, BL and GDSE generate many hallucinated entities, both at the sentence and instance level. On the other hand, LXMERT-GDSE and especially VLP generate less than half of the hallucinations of the previous models. Recall that LXMERT-GDSE encodes the image with 36 regions. The best model, VLP, encodes each image region together with the class likelihood on 1600 object categories, so it has access to a suitable source of information to ground the generated tokens in the image. The fine-grained visual input representation of these two models leads to a consistent reduction in hallucinations, confirming that a strong visual processing is critical for avoiding hallucination (Rohrbach et al., 2018).[4] Table 1 shows that also dialogues generated by human players contain some hallucinated entities according to the CHAIR metric, thus establishing an upper bound for models' performance. VLP is closest to the ceiling set by humans.

5.2 Performance-based Analysis

We expect the Guesser to perform better when the dialogues contain few hallucinations. In fact, as reported in Table 2, the best result is obtained with human dialogues. However, among the machine-generated dialogues, we found that the baseline model (which is shown to generate many hallucinations – Table 1) outperforms the others. We believe that this result is due to the over-reliance of the baseline model on location questions, as highlighted in Shekhar et al. (2019). These questions, though are helpful for the model to identify the target object, make its dialogues sound unnatural when asked too often. We think this confirms the failure of the overall accuracy to serve as a proxy for the quality of the generated dialogues, as recently highlighted in Shekhar et al. (2019) and Testoni and Bernardi (2021).

In order to understand this discrepancy between accuracy and hallucination, we compared dialogues that contain at least one hallucinated entity with dialogues not affected by this issue. We found that the presence of hallucinations clearly deteriorates the accuracy in the game: as shown in Table 2, dialogues containing at least one hallucinated token lead to lower accuracy in guessing the target object compared to games that do not contain

[3]Simultaneously, Suglia et al. (2021) have adapted VLP to the GuessWhat?! game; they use a different training regime, and they focus on VQA as a downstream task via transfer learning.

[4]We also computed the CHAIR metric for the model proposed in Suglia et al. (2020). We obtained from the authors the dialogues generated on a subset of the GuessWhat?! test set (corresponding to around 39% of the test set). Accuracy: 40.69%. CHAIR-s: 22.88, CHAIR-i: 12.41.

	Test Set Accuracy (5Q)	w/o hallucination	with hallucination
BL	52.36	55.39	45.15
GDSE	44.85	47.26	39.29
LXMERT-GDSE	48.53	49.62	42.38
VLP	47.55	48.18	42.34
HUMAN	69.17	69.49	64.16

Table 2: Accuracy reached by the Guesser model when receiving as input dialogues generated by different Questioner models playing with the same Oracle or full human dialogues from the GuessWhat?! test set. *'w/o hallucination'* refers to the accuracy on the subset of games that do not contain any hallucinated tokens. *'with hallucination'* refers to the accuracy on the subset of games that contain at least one hallucination.

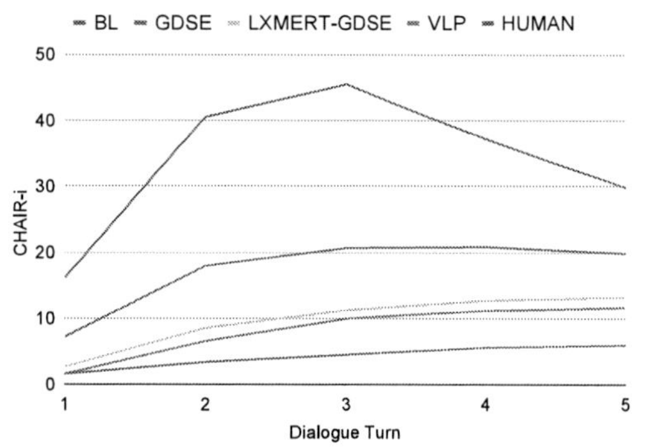

Figure 3: Per-turn CHAIR-i score for machine-generated and human dialogues. Models generate 5 questions. Hallucinated tokens tend to show up less in earlier turns.

	% consecutive halluc.
BL	24.13
GDSE	34.82
LXMERT-GDSE	38.65
VLP	25.50
HUMAN	8.09

Table 3: Percentage of hallucinated tokens appearing in consecutive turns of the dialogue.

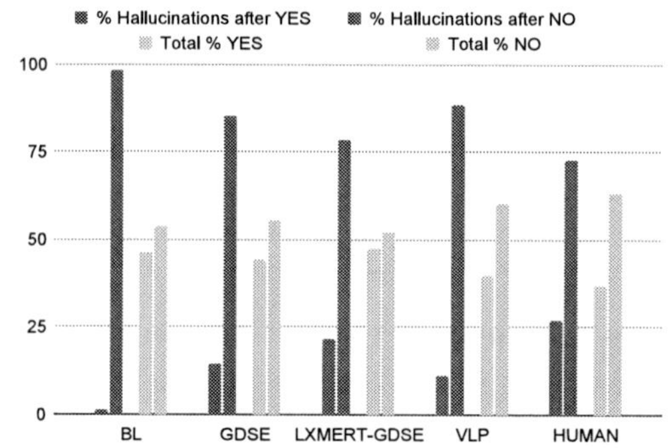

Figure 4: Percentage of hallucinated tokens appearing after a positive vs. negative answer. In light colours, we report the overall distribution of positive/negative answers in the output. The two distributions differ significantly, and this difference is particularly pronounced in machine-generated data.

hallucinations. Interestingly, the drop in accuracy between the two settings reveals a degree of severity from the severe hallucination encountered in BL (-10%) to the mild one in LXMERT-GDSE and GDSE (-7%) till the almost harmless one in VLP and HUMAN (-5%).[5]

5.3 Analysis of Hallucination Occurrences

In Rohrbach et al. (2018), the authors found that hallucinated entities tend to be mentioned towards the end of the sentence, and they hypothesise that some of the preceding words in the image caption may have triggered hallucination. To understand whether a similar phenomenon occurs also in visual dialogues, we run a per-turn analysis on the GuessWhat?! dialogues by computing the CHAIR-i metric after each question-answer pair. As we can see from Figure 3, hallucinations tend to show up in the latest turns of the dialogue, while the first turn contains few hallucinations.

To investigate the effect of hallucinations on follow-up turns, we study how the Question Generator and the Encoder modules are affected by this issue. To study the effect of hallucinations on the Question Generator, we compute how often hallucinated tokens occur in consecutive turns, i.e. the percentage of turns consisting of two consecutive questions containing at least one hallucination each, over all the turns containing at least one hallucination. As we can see from Table 3, for all the models

[5]We have also compared the accuracy in the two settings by fixing the number of candidate objects, i.e., by comparing games of the same difficulty. We found the same difference between the two settings, confirming the validity of our claim.

BL		GDSE		LXMERT-GDSE		VLP		HUMAN	
person	2803	chair	1649	bottle	716	table	480	table	389
couch	1113	person	1525	table	488	chair	462	bike	237
table	656	table	1483	bike	375	bike	352	person	211
chair	538	car	629	book	362	bottle	315	car	91
computer	404	bottle	605	cup	320	person	223	chair	88
bike	332	bench	468	bear	310	cup	220	bottle	83
car	229	book	468	chair	301	book	157	bowl	73
sink	224	phone	413	fridge	198	car	140	bear	60
dog	182	cup	376	car	195	bowl	111	cup	58
bear	171	dog	296	ball	186	ball	100	truck	54
keyboard	161	boat	255	person	163	bear	79	book	51

Table 4: Most frequent hallucinated MSCOCO categories for machine-generated and human dialogues, together with their raw frequency.

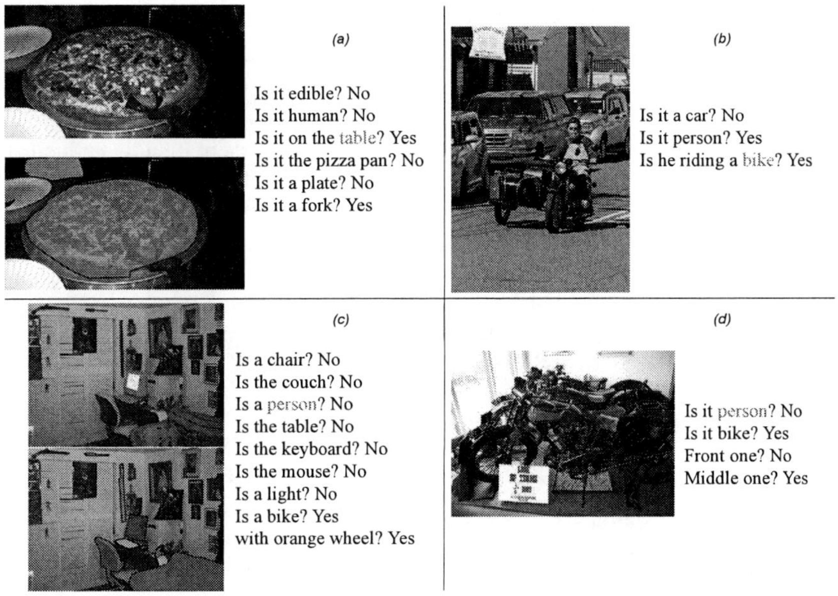

Figure 5: Tokens counted as 'hallucinated' (in red) observed in human dialogues. *(a)*: the object 'table' is not present in MSCOCO segmentation. *(b)*: the human annotator refers to the motorcycle with 'bike', while they are different entities in the MSCOCO categories. *(c)*: people in paintings are not annotated. *(d)*: the dialogue contains an unrelated question.

we considered, a large part of the hallucinated tokens appear in consecutive turns, corroborating the hypothesis of Rohrbach et al. (2018) that hallucinations may cause a *cascade* effect. Crucially, in human dialogues this is not the case.

Another crucial component of the systems under analysis is the Encoder module, which plays a key role in processing the dialogue history. In Greco et al. (2021b), the authors found that computational models playing the GuessWhat?! guessing task on human dialogues struggle to profit from negatively answered questions, even when they are crucial to succeed in the game. Inspired by these findings, Figure 4 reports the percentage of hallucinations occurring *after* a positive vs. negative answer, compared with the overall distribution of answers in the generated dialogues. As we can see, hallucinations occur much more frequently after a negative answer than after a positive one, compared with the overall distribution. While in human dialogues the two answer distributions do not differ much, machine-generated dialogues have a clear tendency to generate hallucinations after a negative answer. In the baseline model, in particular, almost all hallucinated entities appear after a negative answer, while positive and negative answers are equally distributed in the generated dialogues. We conjecture that the failure in grounding negatively answered questions is behind the generation of hallucinations in the subsequent turns.

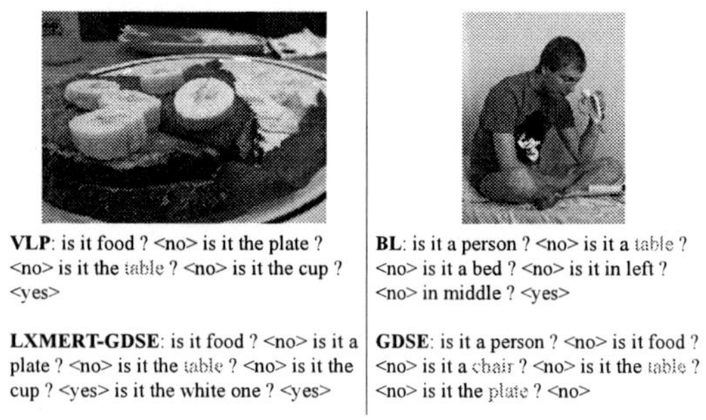

Figure 6: Examples of machine-generated dialogues containing hallucinations, focusing on the entity *table*. On the left, examples of *fake hallucinations* similar to those observed in human dialogues. On the right, examples of *real hallucinations*.

5.4 Qualitative Analysis

Table 1 shows that VLP is the model that is closest to humans in terms of the number of hallucinations in the output. Here, we wonder whether the hallucinations generated by VLP are human-like, i.e., whether they are similar to the ones appearing in human dialogues. The CHAIR metric relies on the MSCOCO segmentation annotation, which is not an exhaustive source for the wide variety of objects present in MSCOCO images. For this reason, Rohrbach et al. (2018) augmented the MSCOCO segmentation annotation with entities mentioned in ground truth captions. While in image captioning human annotators tend to mostly refer to salient objects in the image, in referential visual games, given the nature of the task, human annotators also refer to objects that are globally not salient, but are discriminative to perform the task. We believe that in this scenario it becomes crucial to apply the CHAIR metric both to machine-generated and human dialogues so to run a comparative analysis. Below we report what our comparison reveals.

Table 4 reports the most frequent hallucinated MSCOCO categories for each model and for humans, together with their raw frequency. We have run a manual inspection of human dialogues containing hallucinations based on the CHAIR metric, and found that in many cases they are *fake hallucinations* – they are due to missing labels in the annotation used to compute CHAIR. Figure 5-*a* reports an example with the hallucinated word "*table*": common sense would suggest the pizza is on the table, even if the latter is not visible; hence it is understandable that human players refer to it in the dialogue. The case of the word "*bike*" is illustrated by the example in 5-*b*, where rather than a hallucination, we simply have a not rigorous use of the work "*bike*" to refer to motorbikes. Finally, Figure 5-*c* illustrates why "*person*" appears in the top list of the hallucinated word: human players in their dialogues refer to entities in the paintings (in this case "*person*") which are rarely annotated in MSCOCO. Through our manual inspection of human dialogues, we have found also cases of *real hallucinations*. In most of these cases, the hallucinated entity is *person* and it occurs in the first turn – as illustrated by the example in Figure 5-*d*.

Our quantitative analysis (Table 4) suggests that entities hallucinated by VLP are similar to those appearing in human dialogues, indicating that some of them may count as *fake hallucinations*. Instead, the other models frequently hallucinate entities that are not in the human hallucination list or have low frequency; we conjecture this means that the rate of *real hallucinations* is lower for VLP than for the other models. To verify this hypothesis, we manually checked the hallucinations most frequently appearing in dialogues generated by models, and we found that, as suggested by the patterns in Table 4, VLP hallucinations are often *fake*, while BL and GDSE ones are not; LXMRT-GDSE dialogues stand in between. For instance, the example in Figure 6 illustrates a case of *fake hallucination* for VLP and LXMERT-GDSE and of *real hallucination* for the other two models.

6 Conclusion

Entity hallucination is one of the major problems that affect natural language generation systems in many NLP tasks, from machine translation to image captioning. Generating tokens that are not related to the source data compromises the possibility to use these systems in real-world scenarios. In this work, we explore to what extent this problem affects multimodal conversation agents playing the GuessWhat?! referential guessing game. We adapt two multimodal Transformer-based models to play the GuessWhat?! Questioner agent based on multimodal Transformers architectures (LXMERT-GDSE and VLP), and we compare their output with the widely used GDSE model (Shekhar et al., 2019) and the baseline model in de Vries et al. (2017). We adapt the CHAIR metric proposed in Rohrbach et al. (2018) for image captioning to assess the models' rate of object hallucination. Our analysis confirms recent findings about the inadequacy of the task success in the guessing game to serve as a good proxy of the quality of the generated dialogues. While all the models perform similarly in the GuessWhat?! game, the dialogues they generate differ dramatically. VLP and LXMERT-GDSE generate less than half of the hallucinations compared to GDSE and the baseline model, confirming the crucial role played by a strong visual processing to reduce hallucinations. The results of our in-depth analysis support the hypothesis in Rohrbach et al. (2018) that hallucinations tend to appear at the end of the sequence. Moreover, our results reveal that, in most cases, hallucinated tokens follow polar questions answered negatively. We conjecture this result is connected with our findings about the difficulties multimodal encoders have in grounding negation (Greco et al., 2021b); we believe further work is needed to understand the role of negation in visual dialogues. Finally, we highlight the importance of going beyond the simple CHAIR metric to evaluate the impact of hallucination. By running quantitative and qualitative analysis on human dialogues from the GuessWhat?! test set, we found that VLP is the model that generates less severe and more human-like hallucinations. Further work is needed to design new decoding strategies for natural language generation systems and to explore the relation between hallucination and repetitions, another major issue that heavily affects the quality of machine-generated data as recently highlighted in Testoni and Bernardi (2020). Moreover, as the example in Figure 1 (right) shows, attribute hallucination plays an important role in the quality of the generated output, and it has not received much attention from the research community.

Acknowledgments

We thank Claudio Greco for his help on the implementation side. We kindly acknowledge the support of NVIDIA Corporation with the donation of the GPUs used in our research at the University of Trento. We thank the reviewers for their valuable comments.

References

Peter Anderson, Xiaodong He, Chris Buehler, Damien Teney, Mark Johnson, Stephen Gould, and Lei Zhang. 2018. Bottom-up and top-down attention for image captioning and visual question answering. In *Proceedings of the IEEE conference on computer vision and pattern recognition*, pages 6077–6086.

Herbert H. Clark. 1996. *Using Language*. Cambridge University Press.

Abhishek Das, Satwik Kottur, Khushi Gupta, Avi Singh, Deshraj Yadav, José M.F. Moura, Devi Parikh, and Dhruv Batra. 2017. Visual Dialog. In *Proceedings of the IEEE Conference on Computer Vision and Pattern Recognition*, pages 326–335.

Jacob Devlin, Ming-Wei Chang, Kenton Lee, and Kristina Toutanova. 2019. Bert: Pre-training of deep bidirectional transformers for language understanding. In *Proceedings of the 2019 Conference of the North American Chapter of the Association for Computational Linguistics: Human Language Technologies, Volume 1 (Long and Short Papers)*, pages 4171–4186.

Claudio Greco, Alberto Testoni, and Raffaella Bernardi. 2021a. Grounding dialogue history: Strengths and weaknesses of pre-trained transformers. In *AIxIA 2020 – Advances in Artificial Intelligence. Lecture Notes in Computer Science, vol 12414*, pages 263–279, Cham. Springer International Publishing.

Claudio Greco, Alberto Testoni, and Raffaella Bernardi. 2021b. "Yes" and "No": Visually grounded polar answers. *Visually Grounded Interaction and Language (ViGIL)*.

Janosch Haber, Tim Baumgärtner, Ece Takmaz, Lieke Gelderloos, Elia Bruni, and Raquel Fernández. 2019. The PhotoBook dataset: Building common ground through visually-grounded dialogue. In *Proceedings of the 57th Annual Meeting of the Association for Computational Linguistics*, pages 1895–1910, Florence, Italy. Association for Computational Linguistics.

Kaiming He, Xiangyu Zhang, Shaoqing Ren, and Jian Sun. 2016. Deep residual learning for image recognition. In *Proceedings of the IEEE conference on computer vision and pattern recognition*, pages 770–778.

Philipp Koehn and Rebecca Knowles. 2017. Six challenges for neural machine translation. In *Proceedings of the First Workshop on Neural Machine Translation*, pages 28–39, Vancouver. Association for Computational Linguistics.

Ranjay Krishna, Yuke Zhu, Oliver Groth, Justin Johnson, Kenji Hata, Joshua Kravitz, Stephanie Chen, Yannis Kalantidis, Li-Jia Li, David A Shamma, et al. 2017. Visual genome: Connecting language and vision using crowdsourced dense image annotations. *International journal of computer vision*, 123(1):32–73.

Wojciech Kryscinski, Bryan McCann, Caiming Xiong, and Richard Socher. 2020. Evaluating the factual consistency of abstractive text summarization. In *Proceedings of the 2020 Conference on Empirical Methods in Natural Language Processing (EMNLP)*, pages 9332–9346, Online. Association for Computational Linguistics.

Chiraag Lala and Lucia Specia. 2018. Multimodal lexical translation. In *Proceedings of the Eleventh International Conference on Language Resources and Evaluation (LREC 2018)*.

Tsung-Yi Lin, Michael Maire, Serge Belongie, James Hays, Pietro Perona, Deva Ramanan, Piotr Dollár, and C. Lawrence Zitnick. 2014. Microsoft COCO: Common objects in context. In *Computer Vision - ECCV 2014 - 13th European Conference, Zurich, Switzerland, September 6-12, 2014, Proceedings, Part V*, pages 740–755. Springer.

Haley MacLeod, Cynthia L Bennett, Meredith Ringel Morris, and Edward Cutrell. 2017. Understanding blind people's experiences with computer-generated captions of social media images. In *Proceedings of the 2017 CHI Conference on Human Factors in Computing Systems*, pages 5988–5999.

Nasrin Mostafazadeh, Chris Brockett, Bill Dolan, Michel Galley, Jianfeng Gao, Georgios P. Spithourakis, and Lucy Vanderwende. 2017. Image-grounded conversations: Multimodal context for natural question and response generation. In *Proceedings of the The 8th International Joint Conference on Natural Language Processing*, pages 462–472.

Mathias Müller, Annette Rios, and Rico Sennrich. 2020. Domain robustness in neural machine translation. In *Proceedings of the 14th Conference of the Association for Machine Translation in the Americas (Volume 1: Research Track)*, pages 151–164, Virtual. Association for Machine Translation in the Americas.

Vishvak Murahari, Prithvijit Chattopadhyay, Dhruv Batra, Devi Parikh, and Abhishek Das. 2019. Improving generative visual dialog by answering diverse questions. In *Proceedings of the 2019 Conference on Empirical Methods in Natural Language Processing and the 9th International Joint Conference on Natural Language Processing, EMNLP-IJCNLP 2019, Hong Kong, China, November 3-7, 2019*, pages 1449–1454. Association for Computational Linguistics.

Feng Nan, Ramesh Nallapati, Zhiguo Wang, Cicero Nogueira dos Santos, Henghui Zhu, Dejiao Zhang, Kathleen McKeown, and Bing Xiang. 2021. Entity-level factual consistency of abstractive text summarization. *arXiv preprint arXiv:2102.09130*.

Toan Nguyen and David Chiang. 2018. Improving lexical choice in neural machine translation. In *Proceedings of the 2018 Conference of the North American Chapter of the Association for Computational Linguistics: Human Language Technologies, Volume 1 (Long Papers)*, pages 334–343, New Orleans, Louisiana. Association for Computational Linguistics.

Shaoqing Ren, Kaiming He, Ross Girshick, and Jian Sun. 2016. Faster r-cnn: towards real-time object detection with region proposal networks. *IEEE transactions on pattern analysis and machine intelligence*, 39(6):1137–1149.

Anna Rohrbach, Lisa Anne Hendricks, Kaylee Burns, Trevor Darrell, and Kate Saenko. 2018. Object hallucination in image captioning. In *Proceedings of the 2018 Conference on Empirical Methods in Natural Language Processing*, pages 4035–4045, Brussels, Belgium. Association for Computational Linguistics.

Ravi Shekhar, Aashish Venkatesh, Tim Baumgärtner, Elia Bruni, Barbara Plank, Raffaella Bernardi, and Raquel Fernández. 2019. Beyond task success: A closer look at jointly learning to see, ask, and GuessWhat. In *Proceedings of the 2019 Conference of the North American Chapter of the Association for Computational Linguistics: Human Language Technologies, Volume 1 (Long and Short Papers)*, pages 2578–2587, Minneapolis, Minnesota. Association for Computational Linguistics.

Karen Simonyan and Andrew Zisserman. 2014. Very deep convolutional networks for large-scale image recognition. *arXiv preprint arXiv:1409.1556*.

Alessandro Suglia, Yonatan Bisk, Ioannis Konstas, Antonio Vergari, Emanuele Bastianelli, Andrea Vanzo, and Oliver Lemon. 2021. An empirical study on the generalization power of neural representations learned via visual guessing games. In *Proceedings of the 16th Conference of the European Chapter of the Association for Computational Linguistics: Main Volume*, pages 2135–2144, Online. Association for Computational Linguistics.

Alessandro Suglia, Antonio Vergari, Ioannis Konstas, Yonatan Bisk, Emanuele Bastianelli, Andrea Vanzo, and Oliver Lemon. 2020. Imagining grounded conceptual representations from perceptual information in situated guessing games. In *Proceedings of the 28th International Conference on Computational Linguistics*, pages 1090–1102, Barcelona, Spain (Online). International Committee on Computational Linguistics.

Ilya Sutskever, Oriol Vinyals, and Quoc V. Le. 2014. Sequence to sequence learning with neural networks. In *Advances in Neural Information Processing Systems 27: Annual Conference on Neural Information Processing Systems 2014*, pages 3104–3112.

Hao Tan and Mohit Bansal. 2019. LXMERT: Learning cross-modality encoder representations from transformers. In *Proceedings of the 2019 Conference on Empirical Methods in Natural Language Processing and the 9th International Joint Conference on Natural Language Processing (EMNLP-IJCNLP)*, pages 5100–5111, Hong Kong, China. Association for Computational Linguistics.

Alberto Testoni and Raffaella Bernardi. 2020. Overprotective training environments fall short at testing time: Let models contribute to their own training. In *Proceedings of the Seventh Italian Conference on*

Computational Linguistics, CLiC-it 2020, Bologna, Italy, March 1-3, 2021, volume 2769 of *CEUR Workshop Proceedings*. CEUR-WS.org.

Alberto Testoni and Raffaella Bernardi. 2021. The interplay of task success and dialogue quality: An in-depth evaluation in task-oriented visual dialogues. In *Proceedings of the 16th Conference of the European Chapter of the Association for Computational Linguistics: Main Volume*, pages 2071–2082, Online. Association for Computational Linguistics.

Alberto Testoni, Ravi Shekhar, Raquel Fernández, and Raffaella Bernardi. 2019. The devil is in the details: A magnifying glass for the guesswhich visual dialogue game. In *Proceedings of the 23rd SemDial Workshop on the Semantics and Pragmatics of Dialogue (LondonLogue)*, pages 15–24.

Ashish Vaswani, Noam Shazeer, Niki Parmar, Jakob Uszkoreit, Llion Jones, Aidan N Gomez, Łukasz Kaiser, and Illia Polosukhin. 2017. Attention is all you need. *Advances in Neural Information Processing Systems*, 30:5998–6008.

Harm de Vries, Florian Strub, Sarath Chandar, Olivier Pietquin, Hugo Larochelle, and Aaron C. Courville. 2017. GuessWhat?! Visual object discovery through multi-modal dialogue. In *2017 IEEE Conference on Computer Vision and Pattern Recognition*, pages 5503–5512.

Yijun Xiao and William Yang Wang. 2021. On hallucination and predictive uncertainty in conditional language generation. In *Proceedings of the 16th Conference of the European Chapter of the Association for Computational Linguistics: Main Volume*, pages 2734–2744, Online. Association for Computational Linguistics.

George Yule. 2013. *Referential communication tasks*. Routledge.

Luowei Zhou, Hamid Palangi, Lei Zhang, Houdong Hu, Jason Corso, and Jianfeng Gao. 2020. Unified vision-language pre-training for image captioning and vqa. In *Proceedings of the AAAI Conference on Artificial Intelligence*, volume 34, pages 13041–13049.

How do different factors Impact the Inter-language Similarity? A Case Study on Indian languages

Sourav Kumar, Salil Aggarwal, Dipti Misra Sharma, Radhika Mamidi
LTRC, IIIT-Hyderabad
{sourav.kumar, salil.aggarwal}@research.iiit.ac.in
{dipti, radhika.mamidi}@iiit.ac.in

Abstract

India is one of the most linguistically diverse nations of the world and is culturally very rich. Most of these languages are somewhat similar to each other on account of sharing a common ancestry or being in contact for a long period of time (Bhattacharyya et al., 2016). Nowadays, researchers are constantly putting efforts in utilizing the language relatedness to improve the performance of various NLP systems such as cross lingual semantic search, machine translation (Kunchukuttan and Bhattacharyya, 2020), sentiment analysis systems, etc. So in this paper, we performed an extensive case study on similarity involving languages of the Indian subcontinent. Language similarity prediction is defined as the task of measuring how similar the two languages are on the basis of their lexical, morphological and syntactic features. In this study, we concentrate only on the approach to calculate lexical similarity between Indian languages by looking at various factors such as size and type of corpus, similarity algorithms, subword segmentation, etc. The main takeaways from our work are: (i) Relative order of the language similarities largely remain the same, regardless of the factors mentioned above, (ii) Similarity within the same language family is higher, (iii) Languages share more lexical features at the subword level.

1 Introduction

Recently, there has been an explosion in information (Wang et al., 2007) and a massive amount of natural language data is added daily on the Internet. Moreover, the human literature in different cultures is digitalized and became available in digital libraries (Farouk, 2019). A very large amount of this data is formatted in natural language. This makes NLP techniques crucial to make the use of this high amount of data. Since most of the NLP techniques either require linguistic knowledge that can only be developed by experts and native speakers of that language or they require a lot of labelled data which is again expensive to generate, NLP tasks become challenging for low resource languages like Indian languages. India is a multicultural country, a country with highly religious and ethnically diverse people. People of different races and classes live in different parts of the country, and they speak a variety of languages. Most of the Indian languages are divided into two main language families namely Indo-Aryan[1] and Dravidian[2]. Underlying the vast diversity in Indian languages are many commonalities. Because of contact over thousands of years, most of the Indian languages have undergone convergence to a large extent (Shridhar et al., 2020). Therefore, exploiting language relatedness becomes very crucial in NLP related tasks for Indian languages. Kunchukuttan and Bhattacharyya (2020) also presents an impressive case study for utilizing language relatedness for Machine translation but that study was more inclined toward exploring statistical approaches to MT. Prasanna (2018) in his work has explored efficient ways of exploiting relatedness in multilingualism and transfer learning for low resource machine translation.

But no such large scale study has been done on exploring different factors that may affect the process of calculating similarity among Indian languages. This could really help the future researchers in getting the clear picture while exploiting related languages in NLP related tasks. So, in this work, we performed an extensive case study on the language relatedness involving languages of the Indian subcontinent. This case study provides

[1]Indo Aryan languages - Hindi, Urdu, Punjabi, Gujarati, Marathi, Bangla, Oriya, Konkani

[2]Dravidian languages - Tamil, Telugu, Kannada, Malayalam

Proceedings of the Joint Conference of the 59th Annual Meeting of the Association for Computational Linguistics and the 11th International Joint Conference on Natural Language Processing: Student Research Workshop, pages 112–118
August 5–6, 2021. ©2021 Association for Computational Linguistics

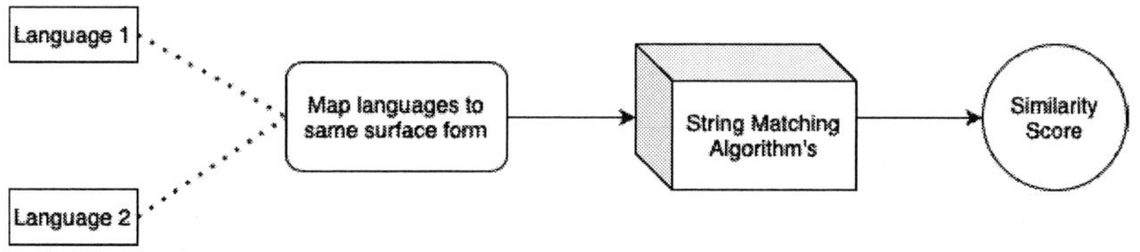

Figure 1: Pipeline for calculating similarity

the reader with valuable information about the different methodologies in measuring relatedness between Indian languages. In addition, it also compares some popular techniques for measuring sentence-to-sentence similarity. Moreover, datasets from different domains and sizes have also been used in comparing the similarity scores to enable the reader to build a complete background in this area. Also, these languages share a lot of cognates, that's why we have also compared the similarity among language pairs at both word and subword level.

This paper is further divided into 4 sections. Section 2 elaborated the methodology behind the different techniques and experiments. Section 3 elaborates the experimental details including the dataset preparation and pre-processing. All the results and analysis have been discussed in Section 4. Section 5 talks about conclusion and possible future work.

2 Methodology

A universal characteristic of Indian languages is their complex morphology and their unique characteristics following default sentence structure as subject object verb **(SOV)**. Thus, we will be using the parallel corpora for calculating the similarity among them. But Indian languages are written in different scripts, so in order to calculate the similarity between two languages, one needs to first map every language to a common surface form i.e to a common script. To do so, we are using a very well-known technique of *'Unified Transliteration'*. It is a string homomorphism technique in which every character of the source is replaced with the target language script. Following are the steps for calculating the similarity between the two languages:

- Collect parallel data of languages of which we want to calculate similarity.
- Transliterate those languages to a common script
- Calculate similarity of each sentence in source with the corresponding transliterated sentence in the target language using some string similarity algorithm.
- Return the average score over all the sentences in the parallel corpora.

The pipeline of the above discussed procedure is shown in **Figure 1**. Also in computer science, string similarity is an important family of algorithms that try to find a place where one or several strings (also called patterns) are found within a larger string. Researchers have already put the efforts and showed that these algorithms effectively calculate the similarity between two strings (Levenshtein, 1965; Yujian and Bo, 2007; Masek and Paterson, 1980; Larsen, 1992; Kondrak, 2005). Some studies have also been done on calculating similarity particularly for Indian languages (Singh and Surana, 2007; Wagner and Fischer, 1974; Islam and Inkpen, 2008; Akhtar et al., 2017; Sengupta and Saha, 2015). In this work, we will consider sentences as a string and use some of the above algorithms for calculating the similarity between two languages.

2.1 Token Overlap

This is the most general approach that works by converting strings into sets of their tokens and then counting the number of tokens which are shared between the both sets. Similarity between two languages using token overlap is calculated as follows:

$$sim = \frac{\sum_{1}^{n} \frac{|Token_{s1} \cap Token_{s2}|}{max(|Token_{s1}|, |Token_{s2}|)}}{n} * 100$$

Here, n denotes the total number of sentences in the parallel corpora, and s1 & s2 represent sentences from language1 and language2 respectively. Major disadvantage of this technique could be identification of "false friends" i.e words that look identical in two different languages, but actually mean something completely different and don't have a common source.

2.2 Levenshtein Distance

The Levenshtein distance (LD) (Levenshtein, 1965) between two strings is the minimum number of single character edits (insertions, deletions, or substitutions) required to change one string into the another. The algorithm considers one character of the string at a time and it assigns cost to each of the edit operations. The algorithm weights the cost of each operation and chooses the operation with the lowest cost and then moves on to the next character. We can compute Levenshtein similarity between two languages as follows:

$$sim_{Levenshtein} = \frac{\sum_1^n 1 - \frac{LD(s1,s2)}{max(|s1|,|s2|)}}{n} * 100$$

2.3 Longest Common Subsequence

The Longest Common Subsequence (LCS) (Larsen, 1992) is a string similarity measurement that is based on the longest common substring in a given string pair. The rationale is that, parts of the string may be similar while their prefixes or suffixes differ. This algorithm finds the longest common character sequence, between a string pair. The characters in the LCS do not necessarily need to be contiguous in the original strings. We can compute similarity using LCS between two languages as follows:

$$sim_{LCS} = \frac{\sum_1^n \frac{LCS(s1,s2)}{max(|s1|,|s2|)}}{n} * 100$$

2.4 Shingle (qgram) Similarity

This works by converting strings into sets of qgrams (sequences of q characters, also sometimes called k-shingles) Kondrak (2005). The similarity or distance between the two strings is then the similarity or distance between the sets. Here we are using Jaccard index as our similarity technique which is a special case of shingle based algorithms. We can compute similarity using Jaccard between two languages as follows:

$$sim_{qgram} = \frac{\sum_1^n qgram(s1, s2)}{n} * 100$$

3 Experiments

For our case study, we are performing all the experiments using the ILCI (Indian Language Corpora Initiative) Jha (2010) and PMI (Prime Minister of India) Haddow and Kirefu (2020) multi parallel corpora for Indian languages. ILCI contains 50k sentences of health and tourism domain covering all the major languages of India like Hindi, Urdu, Punjabi, Gujarati, Marathi, Bangla, Konkani, Telugu, Tamil, Malayalam. PMI contains 30k sentences of news domain in every language mentioned above including Oriya and Kannada except Konkani.

3.1 Data Preprocessing

For transliterating the Urdu and Konkani to a common script, we used the Indic Trans library (Bhat et al., 2014), and for the others, we used Indic NLP library (Kunchukuttan, 2020) (as Urdu and Konkani not supported). In addition, there is an exception with Urdu because it follows a right to left writing system and all other Indian languages follow left to right writing order. Hence, in the processing step, we also changed the order of Urdu to maintain consistency among all languages, and doing this also made our string similarity algorithms work more efficiently.

3.2 Different scenarios

In the real world scenario there can be multiple possible cases that one can think of. But here, we are trying to cover the important cases according to our knowledge. Details of each use case is described below and for calculating the similarity among language pairs we are using the procedure mentioned in **section 2**.

Case 1: In this case, we are evaluating the effect of algorithm used for calculating sentence similarity on the similarity among the language pairs. We are computing the similarity for every language pair present in our ILCI corpora using each algorithm mentioned in **subsections 2**. Also, as per the requirement of our pipeline, we are also mapping each language to Devanagari script to share the same surface form.

Case 2: Here, we are performing the experiments to confirm whether the choice of script selection matters in transliteration step of our pipeline for calculating similarity. To do so, we are mapping every language to Abugida instead Devanagari script and then compared results of both the cases. For this, we are only performing experiments using LCS and K-shingle algorithm on ILCI dataset.

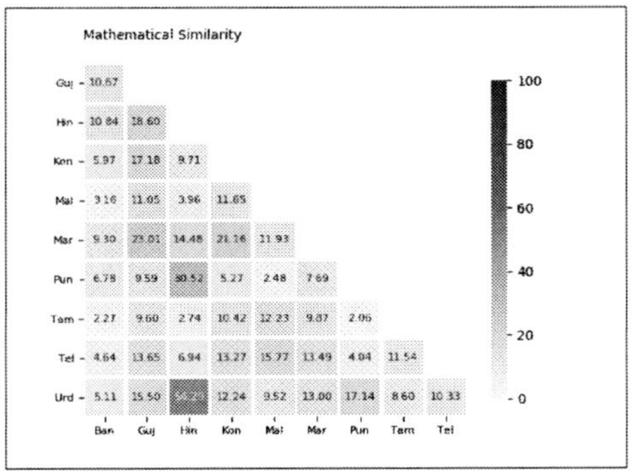

(a) Token Overlap

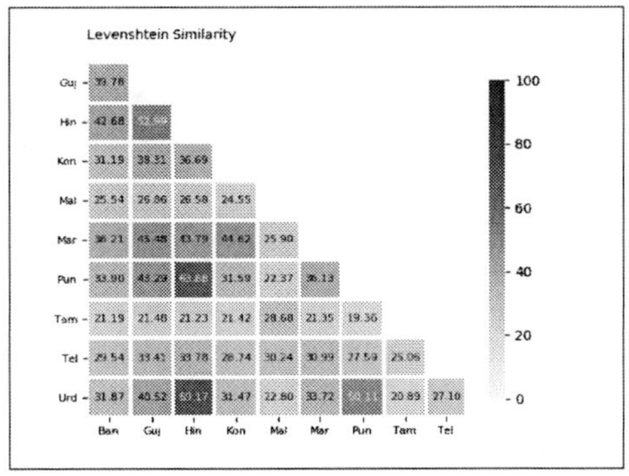

(b) Levenshtein

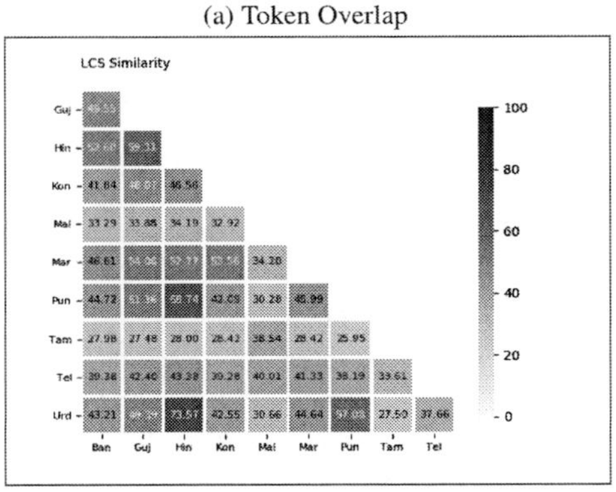

(c) Longest Common Subsequence

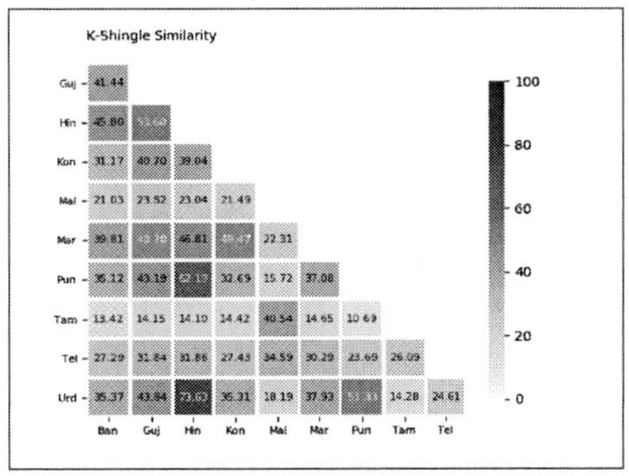

(d) Shingle Q-gram

Figure 2: Similarity Matrix calculated using different algorithms

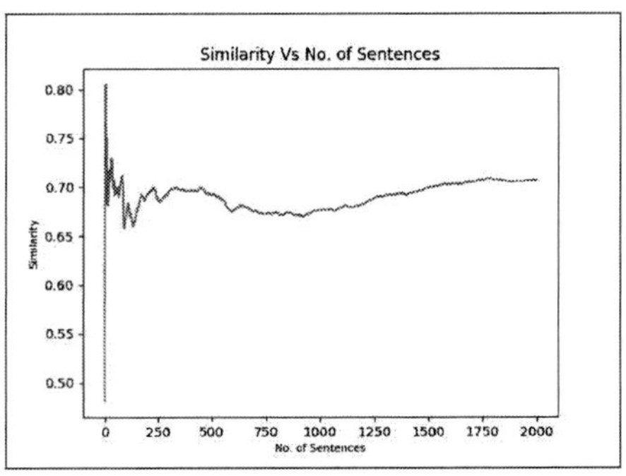

(a) Similarity using 2k Sentences

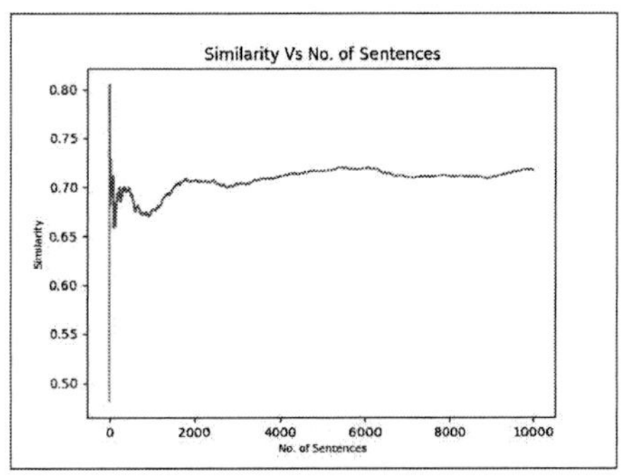

(b) Similarity using 10k Sentences

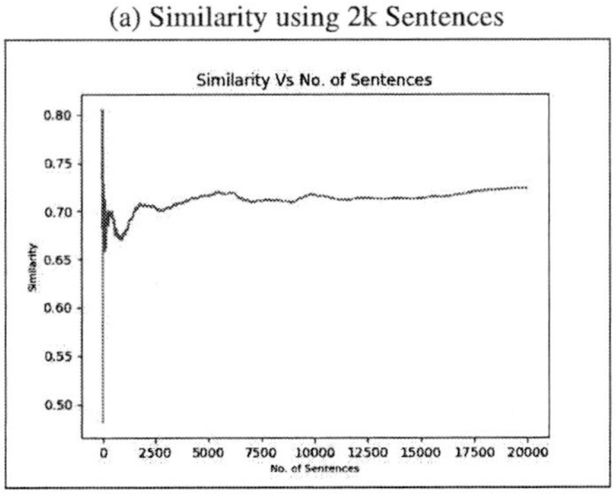

(c) Similarity using 20k Sentences

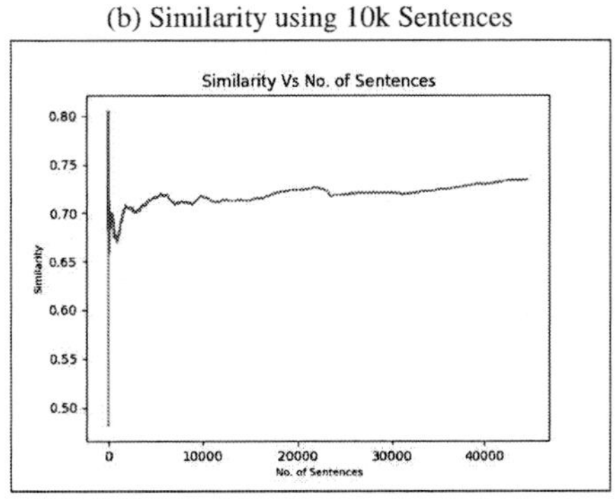

(d) Similarity using 50k Sentences

Figure 3: Similarity V/s No. of Parallel Sentences

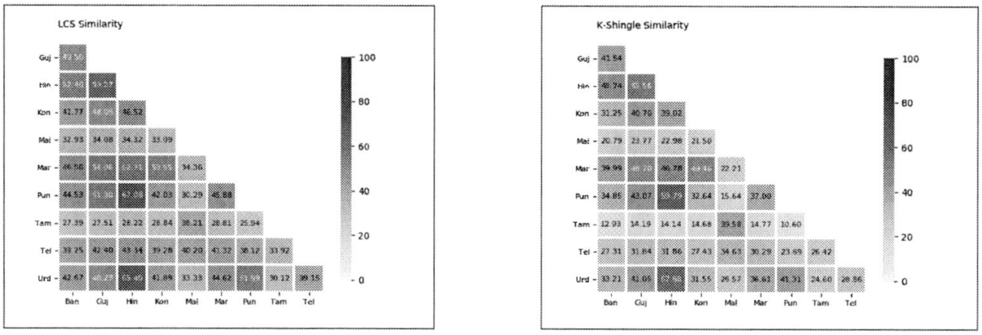

(a) LCS similarity

(b) Shingle Q-gram similarity

Figure 4: Effect of Script on Similarity; In this case we are converting every language to Abugida

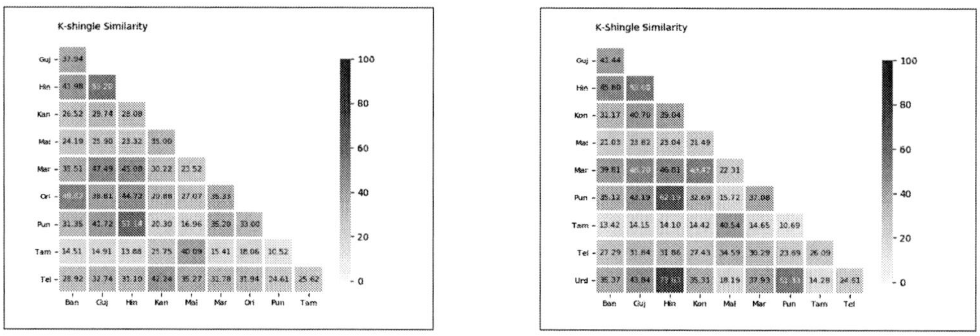

(a) PMI imilarity

(b) ILCI similarity

Figure 5: Effect of Dataset on Similarity

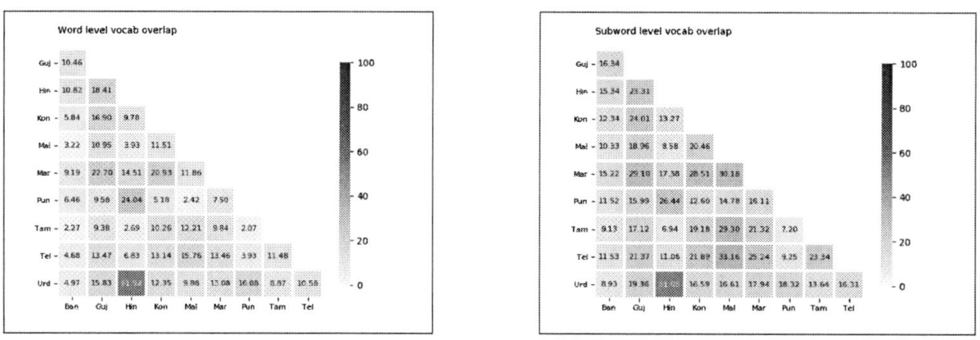

(a) Word level similarity

(b) Sub-word level similarity

Figure 6: Effect of word segmentation on Similarity

Case3: In this scenario, we trying to figure out that after how many parallel sentences, the similarity score curve stabilizes itself. This will give us a rough idea of required size of parallel corpora for calculating similarity. To minimize our efforts, we are only performing experiments for Hindi-Urdu of ILCI corpora using the K-shingle algorithm.

Case 4: Here, we will be evaluating the important factor whether the type/domain of the dataset chosen effects the similarity among the different language pairs. For this case, we are calculating and comparing the results of similarity for every language pair on both ILCI and PMI dataset using the K-shingle algorithm.

Case 5: As Indian languages are morphological rich and share more common words at root level due to same ancestry. So in this case, we are evaluating the effect of using root word instead of words while calculating similarity using the Token overlap algorithm discussed in **section 2.1** among Indian languages on ILCI dataset.

4 Results & Analysis

In **Case 1**, we are evaluating the effect of different algorithms on the similarity. **Figure 2a** shows the results corresponding to every language pair using the algorithm mentioned in section 2.1 (Token Overlap). Similarly **Figure 2b, 2c, 2d** represent the results corresponding to other algorithms discussed in **section 2.2, 2.3 and 2.4** respectively. Here, we observed a small amount of variation in similarity values with the different algorithms. However, more importantly, relative values within the similarity matrix remain almost constant even in the different algorithms, e.g., Hindi-Urdu has shown the most similarity in all algorithms. Our results confirm that this also holds for other language pairs.

For **Case2**, we evaluated whether common script selection matters in calculating language similarity or not. To do so, we also performed experiments by calculating similarity for all languages using the Abugida script. In these experiments, it can be seen that the scripts do not matter in calculating the similarity. We got similar results with both the Devanagari and Abugida scripts with a variation of 0.25%. This can be seen by comparing **Figure 4a** with **Figure 2c** and **Figure 4b** with **Figure 2d**.

Case 3 shows variation in similarity to the number of sentences we are using for calculating it. **Figure 3a** shows variation plots of similarity v/s No. of sentences used. We used overall 2000 sentences and observed that the similarity value gets stable by the end of the curve; in addition to observing that, we also see that the value does not vary much with larger sentences. We also performed experiments with 10k, 20k, 50k sentences; **Figure 3b, 3c and 3d** shows the plot corresponding to each case respectively. It can be seen there is not much fluctuation in the curve, even with the introduction of more sentences after 2k. Thus, we can say for calculating similarity, a small parallel data-set of 2k sentences is enough.

We can further see in **Case 4** that the similarity is not dependent on the nature of data, and is thus independent of external factors such as domain. **Figure 5a** and **Figure 5b** show the results corresponding to ILCI and PMI corpus, respectively. We observed that the similarity values might vary with the change in data-set, but the overall relative similarity matrix will remain constant. More clearly, if the similarity value of L1-L2 varies by a magnitude of k, then there will be a approximate change of k in the magnitude for the other language pairs. This can be confirmed by observing the results from the above experiments.

In the last **Case 5**, we observe from **Figure 6a** and **Figure 6b** that similarity increases drastically for the lexemes of all languages pairs. That is, if we ignore affixes and consider the root form of a word, we can notice that the similarity increases.

Also from the above experiments, we can conclude some general results as:

- Hindi and Urdu being the most similar and Tamil and Punjabi being least similar among Indian languages.
- Language similarity increases within the family, and it grows even more, when geographical distance is less. For example, Urdu-Punjabi's similarity is more than Urdu-Gujarati.
- Different Families also show some reasonable amount of similarity due to contact between them over a long time. For example, Telugu belongs to Dravidian family but it shows considerable similarity with Indo-aryan languages like Hindi and Marathi.
- Telugu from Dravidian and Marathi from the Indo-Aryan language family have more cross-family similarity than the others because they have geographical proximity thus exhibit greater lexical convergence.

5 Conclusion & Future Work

In this paper, we did an extensive study on similarity involving the languages of Indian subcontinent. We explored different factors that may affect the process of calculating similarity. Our results led to some interesting conclusions, such as how the relative order of similarity among languages remains same irrespective of the factors we considered, and how the maximum similarity is observed within pairs of the same language family and it increases more with geographic proximity. Thus, this study will help future research which focuses on exploiting the language relatedness for NLP tasks. Future work along these lines can focus on using semantic similarity alongside lexical similarity to increase accuracy.

References

Syed Sarfaraz Akhtar, Arihant Gupta, Avijit Vajpayee, Arjit Srivastava, and Manish Shrivastava. 2017. Word similarity datasets for indian languages: Annotation and baseline systems. In *Proceedings of the 11th Linguistic Annotation Workshop*, pages 91–94.

Irshad Ahmad Bhat, Vandan Mujadia, Aniruddha Tammewar, Riyaz Ahmad Bhat, and Manish Shrivastava. 2014. Iiit-h system submission for fire2014 shared task on transliterated search. In *Proceedings of the Forum for Information Retrieval Evaluation*, pages 48–53.

Pushpak Bhattacharyya, Mitesh M Khapra, and Anoop Kunchukuttan. 2016. Statistical machine translation between related languages. In *Proceedings of the 2016 Conference of the North American Chapter of the Association for Computational Linguistics: Tutorial Abstracts*, pages 17–20.

Mamdouh Farouk. 2019. Measuring sentences similarity: a survey. *arXiv preprint arXiv:1910.03940*.

Barry Haddow and Faheem Kirefu. 2020. PMIndia – A Collection of Parallel Corpora of Languages of India. *arXiv e-prints*, page arXiv:2001.09907.

Aminul Islam and Diana Inkpen. 2008. Semantic text similarity using corpus-based word similarity and string similarity. *ACM Transactions on Knowledge Discovery from Data (TKDD)*, 2(2):1–25.

Girish Nath Jha. 2010. The tdil program and the indian langauge corpora intitiative (ilci). In *LREC*.

Grzegorz Kondrak. 2005. N-gram similarity and distance. In *International symposium on string processing and information retrieval*, pages 115–126. Springer.

Anoop Kunchukuttan. 2020. The IndicNLP Library. `https://github.com/anoopkunchukuttan/indic_nlp_library/blob/master/docs/indicnlp.pdf`.

Anoop Kunchukuttan and Pushpak Bhattacharyya. 2020. Utilizing language relatedness to improve machine translation: A case study on languages of the indian subcontinent. *arXiv preprint arXiv:2003.08925*.

Kim S Larsen. 1992. *Length of maximal common subsequences*. Aarhus Universitet. Department of Computer Science.

V Levenshtein. 1965. Levenshtein distance.

William J Masek and Michael S Paterson. 1980. A faster algorithm computing string edit distances. *Journal of Computer and System sciences*, 20(1):18–31.

Raj Noel Dabre Prasanna. 2018. Exploiting multilingualism and transfer learning for low resource machine translation.

Debapriya Sengupta and Goutam Saha. 2015. Study on similarity among indian languages using language verification framework. *Advances in Artificial Intelligence*, 2015.

Kumar Shridhar, Harshil Jain, Akshat Agarwal, and Denis Kleyko. 2020. End to end binarized neural networks for text classification. In *Proceedings of SustaiNLP: Workshop on Simple and Efficient Natural Language Processing*, pages 29–34, Online. Association for Computational Linguistics.

Anil Kumar Singh and Harshit Surana. 2007. Using a single framework for computational modeling of linguistic similarity for solving many nlp problems. *EUROLAN 2007 Summer School Alexandru Ioan Cuza University of Iaşi*, page 46.

Robert A Wagner and Michael J Fischer. 1974. The string-to-string correction problem. *Journal of the ACM (JACM)*, 21(1):168–173.

Mengqiu Wang, Noah A Smith, and Teruko Mitamura. 2007. What is the jeopardy model? a quasi-synchronous grammar for qa. In *Proceedings of the 2007 Joint Conference on Empirical Methods in Natural Language Processing and Computational Natural Language Learning (EMNLP-CoNLL)*, pages 22–32.

Li Yujian and Liu Bo. 2007. A normalized levenshtein distance metric. *IEEE transactions on pattern analysis and machine intelligence*, 29(6):1091–1095.

COVID-19 and Misinformation: A Large-Scale Lexical Analysis on Twitter

Dimosthenis Antypas, David Rogers, Alun Preece, Jose Camacho-Collados
School of Computer Science and Informatics & Crime and Security Research Institute
Cardiff University, United Kingdom
{antypasd,rogersdm1,preecead,camachocolladosj}@cardiff.ac.uk

Abstract

Social media is often used by individuals and organisations as a platform to spread misinformation. With the recent coronavirus pandemic we have seen a surge of misinformation on Twitter, posing a danger to public health. In this paper, we compile a large COVID-19 misinformation-related Twitter corpus and perform an analysis to discover patterns with respect to vocabulary usage. Among others, our analysis reveals that the variety of topics and vocabulary usage are considerably more limited and negative in tweets related to misinformation than in randomly extracted tweets. In addition to our qualitative analysis, our experimental results show that a simple linear model based only on lexical features is effective in identifying misinformation-related tweets (with accuracy over 80%), providing evidence to the fact that the vocabulary used in misinformation largely differs from generic tweets.

1 Introduction

Social media has created a landscape where vast amounts of information on various topics is shared daily between users all around the world. Unfortunately, not all information shared is legitimate. As seen in recent events such as the Brexit referendum in the UK (Bastos and Mercea, 2019) and the 2016 US Presidential Election (Bovet and Makse, 2019), there are many cases where people, either unintentionally or deliberately (Fetzer, 2004), share unreliable information which causes confusion and suspicion in the general population. For instance, individuals and organisations share 'facts' on how the earth is flat, that vaccines cause autism, or that chlorine is treatment against COVID-19.

The spread of misinformation through social networks is made easier by the structure of these platforms. By personalising their users' news feeds and creating echo chambers, where users share believes and biases, social media provide the perfect field for spreading misinformation. Moreover, the fact that most social media platforms either do not filter misinformation or filter it inefficiently (Wardle and Singerman, 2021) means that there is no essential check on what people share online. Examples of misinformation include fabricated content, where the information is completely false; manipulated content, where there has been some distortion of genuine information; and imposter content, where someone is impersonating genuine sources (publications.parliament.uk, 2018).

Even though misinformation spread is not only related to scientific facts, health related misinformation holds an immediate danger to the public (Chou et al., 2018). Specifically, public health misinformation can be defined as a health-related claim that is currently unsupported by scientific evidence, with detrimental effects on public health (Memon, 2020). Along with the recent emergence of the COVID-19 pandemic, a number of conspiracy theories have arisen in social media; from fake and dangerous treatments to schemes that the virus is a part of a plan of the global elite to take over the world (Shahsavari et al., 2020).

The main aim of this paper is to explore whether there is a recognisable difference in the vocabulary usage between tweets conveying misinformation and random tweets present within COVID-19 discourse. To this end, we collected two corpora, one corpus consisting of misinformation-related tweets and a balancing corpus consisting of 'generic' (i.e., randomly-selected tweets) where we ran a comparative analysis. This analysis is complemented with a machine learning experiment in which we analyse to what extent misinformation-related tweets can be retrieved by using lexical features only.

Proceedings of the Joint Conference of the 59th Annual Meeting of the Association for Computational Linguistics and the 11th International Joint Conference on Natural Language Processing: Student Research Workshop, pages 119–126
August 5–6, 2021.

2 Lexical Analysis of COVID-19 Misinformation Tweets

In this section, we describe our corpus collection efforts (Section 2.1) and provide a qualitative analysis on the same collected corpus (Section 2.2).

2.1 Corpus collection

We collected a continuous collection of tweets identified as related to the coronavirus pandemic from January to April 2020. The corpus was derived from two sources of Twitter data for the English language with a misinformation-related corpus collected via the Social Media analysis platform Sentinel (Preece et al., 2017) and a corpus of random tweets ('generic') for the same period. The tweets were tracked and selected using a list of keywords related to the pandemic[1]. Both sets ('misinformation-related' and 'generic') are balanced following the same distribution: 8,911 tweets from January, 596 from February, 411,412 from March and 20,434 from April.

Gathering a corpus of truly misinformation content is a challenging and time-consuming endeavour (Helmstetter and Paulheim, 2018) and the assumption here is that the 'generic' set contains a more diverse set of information related to COVID-19.

2.1.1 Misinformation-Related corpus

The misinformation-related corpus was extracted from an existing collection of tweets gathered as part of a longitudinal study of misinformation-related call-outs in multiple languages. The tweets were collected using a set of search terms focused on misinformation in multiple languages such as 'fake news', 'disinformation', and 'misinformation'. The objective of this collection is to focus on the calling out of misinformation by Twitter users, with the assumption that users will be tagging and replying to content with the statement that something is fake news, disinformation, or consists of lies. In this way the user base acts as social sensors (Sakaki et al., 2010) to misinformation, allowing for a proactive rather than reactive collection of tweets relating to misinformation, as terms relating to particular pieces of misinformation narrative will not be known at the time of collection.

Our data was extracted, using the COVID-19 related terms, from the larger longitudinal collection which covered English language tweets from the first four months of 2020 (January to April). Finally, as the Sentinel data included tweets relating to a variety of different subjects the same list of keywords used to identify the 'generic' set were utilised to filter down the collected tweets to those relevant to coronavirus. From a total of 9.5 million tweets in the longitudinal collection as of April 2020, 441,353 tweets were used.

2.1.2 Generic corpus

In order to get related data points that do not necessarily contain misinformation, we used Tweepy (Roesslein, 2009) to obtain COVID-19 related tweets from a collection of tweet IDs provided in Chen et al. (2020), retrieving the tweets directly from Twitter's API services.

An equal amount of random COVID-19 tweets (441,353), that did not contain any of the same specific set of terms employed in Sentinel for the collection of the misinformation corpus, were gathered.[2] Clearly, however, there would be a small but non-trivial number of tweets that could also contain misinformation.

2.2 Data exploration

2.2.1 Lexical features & statistics

As an initial analysis of the dataset, we extracted relevant features for each subset. Table 1 displays some statistics about features gathered across the two different tweet classes, i.e., misinformation and generic. In particular, we include the average relative frequency of tokens, emoji, hashtags, user mentions (@), uppercase letters, punctuation and exclamation marks.

In general, the misinformation-related tweets tend to be a bit longer with average 2.28 words more than the *generic* tweets. One of the most defining differences between both classes is the amount of user mentions (represented as @), which are on average more than double in the misinformation set 1.32 to 0.59. Another interesting observation is that even though both classes use generally the same amount of punctuation, the average use of exclamation marks in the misinformation-related tweets is on average 62% higher than those of the *generic* set, 0.27 to 0.17.

[1] `https://github.com/echen102/COVID-19-TweetIDs/blob/master/keywords.txt`

[2] In both subsets, retweets were only considered when the original tweet was not already available. This was done on the assumption that most of the times when users retweet content they do not add additional information.

	Tokens	Emoji	Hashtags	@	Uppercase	Punctuation	Exclamation
Generic	$14.76 \pm 0.2\%$	$0.31 \pm 1.7\%$	$0.87 \pm 0.6\%$	$0.59 \pm 0.9\%$	$13.4 \pm 0.3\%$	$9.41 \pm 0.2\%$	$0.17 \pm 1.2\%$
Misinformation	$17.04 \pm 0.1\%$	$0.21 \pm 1.7\%$	$0.76 \pm 0.7\%$	$1.32 \pm 0.8\%$	$15.26 \pm 0.4\%$	$9.23 \pm 0.2\%$	$0.27 \pm 1\%$

Table 1: Set of features from the COVID-19 Twitter Misinformation dataset: quantities represent the average numbers (95% confidence intervals) of instances per tweet.

We also attempted to measure the vocabulary richness and perform a comparison between the misinformation and generic sets as text containing misinformation has often less complex vocabulary and tends to be repetitive (Horne and Adali, 2017). To accomplish this two different statistics were utilised, the Type-Token Ratio (TTR) which is the ratio of unique terms against all terms, and the Measure of Textual Lexical Diversity (MTLD), a more complex metric that is not very sensitive to text length (McCarthy, 2005). MTLD is calculated as the mean length of sequential word strings in a text that maintain a given TTR value. In general, a higher MTLD score indicates a more diverse corpus. For example, the MTLD score for an equal size, random set of tweets is 913.62 whereas the score for our corpus (misinformation-related and generic tweets) is 362.10. Additionally, three subtopics were identified (using relevant keywords [3]) and deemed interesting to investigate further. The subtopics include 1) 'Covid/Weapon' with tweets mentioning COVID-19 along the lines of "bioweapon" and "human created weapon" 2) '5G' with tweets talking about the conspiracy theory of how the 5G network is responsible for the pandemic and 3) 'Politics' where the content of the tweets is revolving around US politics. The keywords used

Table 2 displays the lexical diversity statistics for the whole corpus as well as for three different subsets (covid as a weapon, 5G and Politics)[4]. The results indicate that the misinformation subset has indeed a less diverse vocabulary, with an MTLD score of 268.83 opposite to 593.74 of the generic subset. The same pattern continues when looking at the 'Covid/Weapon' and '5G' subtopics where the generic tweets have an MTLD score that is more than double of that of the misinformation tweets. In the case of the 'Politics' subtopic the lexical diversity difference is small to nonexistent with the generic and misinformation tweets achieving the same TTR score and the generic tweets having a slightly better MTLD score.

[3]**5G:** 5G **Politics:** trump, democrat, republican, obama, ted cruz, tedcruz, joebiden, joe biden, leftwing, rightwing, left wing, right wing, left wing, right wing **Covid/Weapon:** weapon, bioweapon, weaponizing, biological weapon

[4]The comparison was made between equal size subsets.

2.2.2 Lexical Specificity

Even though the tweets are not equally distributed through time, an attempt was made to identify trends between each month (reminder that we randomly extracted a subset of equal number of tweets per month for each of the two classes). This was achieved by computing the lexical specificity value of each word. Lexical specificity is a statistical measure which calculates the set of most representative words for a given text based on the hypergeometric distribution (Lafon, 1980; Camacho-Collados et al., 2016). In contrast to similar scores used to calculate importance of terms, such as TF-IDF, lexical specificity is not especially sensitive to different text lengths.

Table 3 displays, for each month, the top five relevant terms according to lexical specificity with respect to the whole corpus when considering the misinformation and generic subsets separately. To gain a better understanding of tweets' content, Table 3 does not include words that were present in the top 100 most relevant terms according to lexical specificity for each class. For both groups the tweets from January are focused on China (terms not displayed), which was the initial centre of the epidemic, and the following months become more diverse. Then, as can be observed in the table misinformation-related tweets tend to be more focused around conspiracies and rumours with terms such as 'uncover', 'theory' or 'lie', while generic tweets appear to be more neutral, also including government advice such as 'stay at home'.

	Generic		Misinformation	
	TTR	**MTLD**	**TTR**	**MTLD**
Whole Corpus	0.03	593.74	0.02	268.83
Covid/Weapon	0.23	294.81	0.19	185.12
5G	0.25	648.48	0.15	151.74
Politics	0.04	393.67	0.04	337.53

Table 2: Lexical diversity of generic and misinformation tweets Metrics used: Type Token Ratio (TTR) and Measure of Textual Lexical Diversity (MTLD).

We further explored the three subtopics (i.e., Covid/Weapon, 5G, Politics) identified and extracted the most relevant terms based on lexical specificity. For each subtopic we compare the generic and misinformation subsets against their combined subsets in the particular subtopic. Table 4 displays the five most relevant terms for each class (misinformation/generic) in each subtopic. Similar with the terms extracted when considering the whole corpus (Table 3) there is a trend that in misinformation tweets appear more negative/intimidating terms (e.g., 'policestate', 'chemtrail', 'deep') and also terms related to mainstream news media which are often the 'enemy' of conspiracy theorists and hyperpartisan groups.

3 Identifying COVID-19 related misinformation tweets

Upon collecting our dataset we aimed to explore whether the lexical features of tweets can provide a strong signal for identifying misinformation. To test our hypothesis, we built multiple models using different classification approaches based on lexical features to distinguish the misinformation-related and generic sets of tweets.

3.1 Experimental setting

Data pre-processing. Non-linguistic content, such as references to web sites and special characters referring to other users were removed from the dataset. Similarly, stopwords were removed from the vocabulary. Finally, all words involved in the construction of each of the subsets (see Section 2.1) were not considered for this experiment.

Features. As our main goal is to test whether models can retrieve misinformation-related content using lexical features only, we use three different types of lexical features: (1) Frequency features based on TF-IDF (TF)[5]; (2) semantic based on the average of word embeddings[6] within the tweet (WE); and (3) the extra-linguistic features listed in Table 1 (EL).

Models. As linear machine learning models exploiting the features, we used both Naive Bayes (as a baseline model) and SVM (as a non Deep Neural Network option) classifiers following their default implementations in scikit-learn. Moreover, a Convolutional Neural Network (CNN) was implemented. Even though CNNs have been traditionally used in computer vision, they have proved to be effective for various NLP tasks, including text classification (Kim, 2014). In the present work, we trained a CNN with three layers of convolution using the same Twitter pre-trained word embeddings as initialisation. All models were evaluated using 10-fold cross validation. Finally, as current state-of-the-art NLP system we trained the base uncased version of BERT (Devlin et al., 2018) on our dataset using the implementation provided in Simple Transformers (Rajapakse, 2019).

3.2 Results

Table 5 shows the results of the classification models in our collected dataset. As expected, the CNN and BERT models perform better with BERT attaining the best results, with an overall accuracy of 0.91. Nonetheless, a simple SVM using lexical and semantic features attains 0.82, which shows the marked differences of the two datasets in terms of vocabulary and topics. This is surprising given the specificity of the topic and the fact that the linear models neglect linguistic properties such as word order or syntax (which are captured by the context vectors of BERT and up to some degree from the CNN), as they only rely on tokens represented as a bag of words. In a way it also confirms some of the statistics analysed in Section 2.2 and previous general findings related to misinformation in Twitter (Castillo et al., 2011) in this particular COVID-19 domain.

3.3 Analysis

In addition to the main results from the previous subsection, we perform two types of analysis: error and out-of-distribution analysis.

3.3.1 Error analysis: Examples

In this section, we provide some examples of the errors made by the classifiers, which we attempt to digest. First, we should note that not all errors are due to the automatic model per se, and rather to the way the corpora were collected (see Section 2.1) – there is no certainty that generic tweets do not convey a message related to misinformation. For example, both the SVM and BERT models 'misclassify' the tweet *'Take care of your health...not a good time to be run down...and stay away from Corona beer, I hear from mainstream media that it causes a virus or something.'* as generic. Exclud-

[5] We considered the 500 most frequent words for the evaluation.

[6] As pre-trained words embeddings, we used the 100-dimensional fasttext embeddings (Bojanowski et al., 2017) trained on Twitter from Camacho-Collados et al. (2020).

January	February	March	April
— GENERIC —			
confirm - 375.17	suga - 10.75	case - 4457.29	home - 215.29
flight - 255.54	pence - 9.07	home - 2732.56	stay - 195.40
case - 253.73	confirm - 6.14	test - 2139.79	distancing - 104.21
novel - 206.65	disease - 5.51	positive - 1776.12	day - 62.12
health - 157.46	border - 5.35	stay - 1748.64	worker - 61.52
— MISINFORMATION —			
uncover - 846.75	deep - 16.09	medium - 5549.91	lie - 245.83
russia - 495.33	rosenstein - 13.84	lie - 5491.33	fox - 168.14
awash - 347.44	theory - 12.50	trump - 4682.74 3	medium - 149.72
iran - 248.20	rod - 11.05	spread - 4078.4	cnn - 132.21
election - 236.32	heil - 9.31	deep - 4053.62	fool - 110.00

Table 3: Top words per class based on lexical specificity not present in the top 100 of the other class.

Covid/Weapon		5G		Politics	
Generic	Misinformation	Generic	Misinformation	Generic	Misinformation
denver - 48.47	news - 52.26	case - 32.76	news - 101.51	test - 334.27	news - 3115.22
attend - 44.44	deep - 42.16	test - 26.02	medium - 95.72	response - 216.37	deep - 1238.16
supporter - 38.35	chemtrail - 38.38	confirm - 20.77	vaccination - 86.30	bill - 213.14	lie - 691.22
rally - 37.59	establishment - 38.38	home - 19.17	policestate - 83.63	president - 173.50	medium - 683.58
deadly - 36.08	vaccination - 36.67	patient - 18.90	drill - 83.49	vaccine - 169.08	state - 506.51

Table 4: Top words per class based on lexical specificity for subtopics identified.

ing this type of example that makes a small portion of the dataset, other mistakes of the SVM model using lexical features include *'Nonsense. I done believe this disinformation campaign - the secret services are born to capitalise on crisis. They are not army or Police.The truth is #Covid19 outbreak is the rarest golden opportunity for them to test - 1. Expand Infrastructure. 2. New Tools. 3. Scalable ops.'*.

These examples show that lexical features are not enough for this task, and other type of model capturing other features (e.g., word order or syntax) such as the BERT model (or even a simpler CNN model) can provide a performance boost, as we showed in Table 5. While both the SVM and CNN struggle with linguistic phenomena such as sarcasm, as exemplified by this error made by the CNN model: *'CHINA: *covers up all evidence of biblical plague unleashed by underground farmer's market* HA let's see you top that. USA: *multiple senators dump stocks day after learning of looming biblical plague and tell everyone things are awesome while they do nothing* CHINA: touché'*, the BERT model does seem to perform better with such entries. Finally, all models struggle with tweets where the user is calling out other users actions or behaviours, for example: *'ppl out here like when is the coronavirus cure!! but wont even vaccinate their kids. i wish ppl freaked out about the flu or measles like they are the coronavirus maybe they wouldnt be such big issues otherwise'* which is misclassified as misinformation by all the models.

3.3.2 Out-of-distribution analysis

To test the robustness of our SVM and BERT models, an additional set of tweets from a different time period (May, June, July 2020) was collected. The new dataset is balanced, each month containing 63,468 tweets. In total, it contains 190,404 tweets using the same methodology as described in Section 2.1.

Table 7 displays the results for BERT and the best performing SVM classifier when tested on the new dataset (see Table 6 for detailed results). The SVM classifier which used TF+WE was selected as it achieved the best F1 score on the original data. It is observable that there is no substantial difference on the average performance of the models. Therefore, this may suggest that the methods (including a simple one based on lexical features and a SVM) are still robust to detect misinformation in real time. However, these results may not be generalisable as we should also reiterate the limitations of our

Classifier	Features	Misinfo class			Generic class			Overall			
		Prec	Rec	F1	Prec	Rec	F1	Prec	Rec	F1	Acc
Naive Bayes	TF	0.76	0.75	0.76	0.75	0.77	0.76	0.76	0.76	0.76	0.76
	WE	0.69	0.77	0.73	0.74	0.66	0.70	0.72	0.72	0.71	0.72
	TF+WE	0.77	0.75	0.76	0.76	0.78	0.77	0.76	0.76	0.76	0.76
	TF+WE+EL	0.78	0.76	0.77	0.76	0.77	0.76	0.77	0.77	0.77	0.77
SVM	TF	0.86	0.74	0.80	0.77	0.88	0.82	0.82	0.81	0.81	0.81
	WE	0.77	0.76	0.76	0.76	0.77	0.76	0.76	0.76	0.76	0.76
	TF+WE	0.87	0.80	0.83	0.78	0.85	0.82	0.82	0.82	0.83	0.82
	TF+WE+EL	0.89	0.74	0.80	0.67	0.89	0.75	0.78	0.81	0.78	0.78
CNN	-	0.88	0.86	0.87	0.87	0.89	0.88	0.88	0.87	0.87	0.87
BERT	-	**0.90**	**0.92**	**0.91**	**0.91**	**0.90**	**0.91**	**0.91**	**0.91**	**0.91**	**0.91**
Naive baseline		0.5	1.0	0.67	0.0	0.0	0.0	0.25	0.5	0.33	0.5

Table 5: Classification results in our COVID-19 Twitter Misinformation Dataset. Evaluation metrics: accuracy and macro-averaged precision, recall and F1. *Naive baseline* refers to a system that detects misinformation for every tweet.

	SVM						BERT					
	misinformation			generic			misinformation			generic		
	Precision	Recall	F1	Precision	Recall	F1	Precision	Recall	F1	Precision	Recall	F1
May	0.87	0.80	0.83	0.82	0.88	0.85	0.91	0.88	0.89	0.88	0.91	0.89
June	0.87	0.81	0.84	0.82	0.87	0.85	0.90	0.89	0.90	0.90	0.90	0.90
July	0.86	0.78	0.82	0.80	0.87	0.83	0.89	0.88	0.89	0.88	0.90	0.89
Total	0.87	0.80	0.83	0.81	0.88	0.84	0.90	0.88	0.89	0.89	0.90	0.89

Table 6: Classification results of the SVM (TF+WE) and BERT models for May - July period.

analysis that was performed on a limited set of data from a single year.

	Precision	Recall	Accuracy	F1
SVM	0.84	0.84	0.84	0.84
BERT	0.89	0.89	0.89	0.89

Table 7: Overall classification results for May - July period. Evaluation metrics: accuracy and macro-averaged precision, recall and F1. SVM model used: TF+WE.

In order to better understand the behaviour of the classifiers, we further investigated how the models perform in each individual month. Figure 1 displays the precision and recall results for the misinformation class. In each month BERT outperforms the SVM model. While the performance of both is mostly consistent, there is a drop in Recall for the SVM model in July (May:0.8, June:0.81, July:0.78). This may be indicative of a change in the misinformation corpus vocabulary for July that the SVM model fails to recognise. Despite this, the results remain a strong indication that there is indeed a recognisable difference between the vocabulary used in the misinformation and generic tweets.

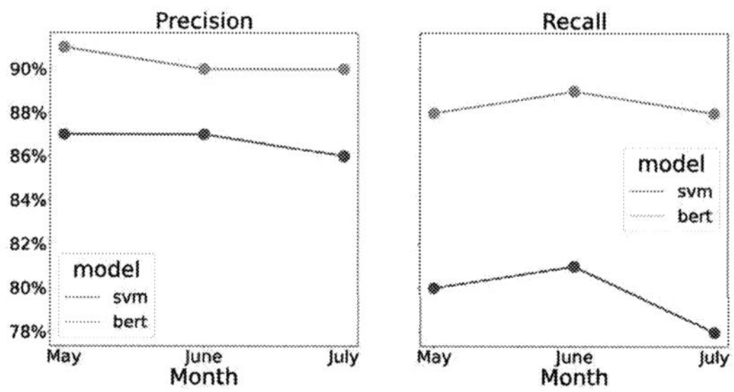

Figure 1: Monthly precision and recall results for the misinformation class.

4 Conclusion

In this paper, we have presented an analysis on the lexical features present in misinformation about COVID-19 in social media, and compare it with those present in *generic* or random tweets. To this end, we compiled two different Twitter corpora from early 2020 when the pandemic emerged. Our analysis shows that there is a clear distinction in the general vocabulary used in each type of corpus and that a simple linear classifier based on lexical features can retrieve misinformation-related tweets to a high degree of accuracy. While this paper represents an initial reference point in this aspect, further analysis would be required to investigate the main features present in misinformation. On this respect, our work can also be added to the increasing evidence that shows that misinformation focuses on a specific vocabulary that does not reflect on the overall distribution of what can be found in general social media content for a certain topic (Castillo et al., 2011). Finally, it would be interesting to evaluate and compare the models' performance on other datasets that are manually labelled and are not collected based on the "call out" principle (Alam et al., 2020).

References

Firoj Alam, Shaden Shaar, Fahim Dalvi, Hassan Sajjad, Alex Nikolov, Hamdy Mubarak, Giovanni Da San Martino, Ahmed Abdelali, Nadir Durrani, Kareem Darwish, and Preslav Nakov. 2020. Fighting the covid-19 infodemic: Modeling the perspective of journalists, fact-checkers, social media platforms, policy makers, and the society.

Marco T Bastos and Dan Mercea. 2019. The Brexit botnet and user-generated hyperpartisan news. *Social Science Computer Review*, 37(1):38–54.

Piotr Bojanowski, Edouard Grave, Armand Joulin, and Tomas Mikolov. 2017. Enriching word vectors with subword information. *Transactions of the Association for Computational Linguistics*, 5:135–146.

Alexandre Bovet and Hernán A Makse. 2019. Influence of fake news in Twitter during the 2016 us presidential election. *Nature communications*, 10(1):1–14.

Jose Camacho-Collados, Yerai Doval, Eugenio Martínez-Cámara, Luis Espinosa-Anke, Francesco Barbieri, and Steven Schockaert. 2020. Learning Cross-lingual Embeddings from Twitter via Distant Supervision. In *Proceedings of ICWSM*.

José Camacho-Collados, Mohammad Taher Pilehvar, and Roberto Navigli. 2016. Nasari: Integrating explicit knowledge and corpus statistics for a multilingual representation of concepts and entities. *Artificial Intelligence*, 240:36–64.

Carlos Castillo, Marcelo Mendoza, and Barbara Poblete. 2011. Information Credibility on Twitter. In *Proceedings of the 20th international conference on World wide web*, pages 675–684.

Emily Chen, Kristina Lerman, and Emilio Ferrara. 2020. Tracking social media discourse about the covid-19 pandemic: Development of a public coronavirus Twitter data set. *Journal of Medical Internet Research Public Health and Surveillance*, 6(2):e19273.

Wen-Ying Sylvia Chou, April Oh, and William MP Klein. 2018. Addressing health-related misinformation on social media. *Journal of the American Medical Association*, 320(23):2417–2418.

Jacob Devlin, Ming-Wei Chang, Kenton Lee, and Kristina Toutanova. 2018. BERT: pre-training of deep bidirectional transformers for language understanding. *CoRR*, abs/1810.04805.

James H Fetzer. 2004. Disinformation: The use of false information. *Minds and Machines*, 14(2):231–240.

Stefan Helmstetter and Heiko Paulheim. 2018. Weakly supervised learning for fake news detection on twitter. In *2018 IEEE/ACM International Conference on Advances in Social Networks Analysis and Mining (ASONAM)*, pages 274–277. IEEE.

Benjamin Horne and Sibel Adali. 2017. This just in: Fake news packs a lot in title, uses simpler, repetitive content in text body, more similar to satire than real news. In *Proceedings of the International AAAI Conference on Web and Social Media*, volume 11.

Yoon Kim. 2014. Convolutional neural networks for sentence classification. In *Proceedings of the 2014 Conference on Empirical Methods in Natural Language Processing (EMNLP)*, pages 1746–1751.

Pierre Lafon. 1980. Sur la variabilité de la fréquence des formes dans un corpus. *Mots. Les langages du politique*, 1(1):127–165.

Philip M McCarthy. 2005. *An assessment of the range and usefulness of lexical diversity measures and the potential of the measure of textual, lexical diversity (MTLD)*. Ph.D. thesis, The University of Memphis.

Shahan Ali Memon. 2020. *Characterizing Misinformed Online Health Communities*. Ph.D. thesis, Carnegie Mellon University.

Alun Preece, Irena Spasić, Kieran Evans, David Rogers, William Webberley, Colin Roberts, and Martin Innes. 2017. Sentinel: A codesigned platform for semantic enrichment of social media streams. *IEEE Transactions on Computational Social Systems*, 5(1):118–131.

publications.parliament.uk. 2018. Disinformation and 'fake news': Interim report. `https://publications.parliament.uk/pa/cm201719/cmselect/cmcumeds/363/36304.htm#_idTextAnchor002`.

Thilina Rajapakse. 2019. Simple transformers. `https://github.com/ThilinaRajapakse/simpletransformers/`.

Joshua Roesslein. 2009. Tweepy documentation. *Online] http://tweepy. readthedocs. io/en/v3*, 5.

Takeshi Sakaki, Makoto Okazaki, and Yutaka Matsuo. 2010. Earthquake shakes Twitter users: real-time event detection by social sensors. In *Proceedings of the 19th international conference on World wide web*, pages 851–860.

Shadi Shahsavari, Pavan Holur, Timothy R Tangherlini, and Vwani Roychowdhury. 2020. Conspiracy in the time of corona: Automatic detection of covid-19 conspiracy theories in social media and the news. *arXiv preprint arXiv:2004.13783*.

Claire Wardle and Eric Singerman. 2021. Too little, too late: social media companies' failure to tackle vaccine misinformation poses a real threat. *British Medical Journal*, 372.

Situation-Based Multiparticipant Chat Summarization: a Concept, an Exploration-Annotation Tool and an Example Collection

Anna Smirnova, Evgeniy Slobodkin, George Chernishev
Saint Petersburg State University
{anna.en.smirnova, eugene.slobodkin, chernishev}@gmail.com

Abstract

Currently, text chatting is one of the primary means of communication. However, modern text chat still in general does not offer any navigation or even full-featured search, although the high volumes of messages demand it. In order to mitigate these inconveniences, we formulate the problem of situation-based summarization and propose a special data annotation tool intended for developing training and gold-standard data.

A situation is a subset of messages revolving around a single event in both temporal and contextual senses: e.g, a group of friends arranging a meeting in chat, agreeing on date, time, and place. Situations can be extracted via information retrieval, natural language processing, and machine learning techniques. Since the task is novel, neither training nor gold-standard datasets for it have been created yet.

In this paper, we present the formulation of the situation-based summarization problem. Next, we describe Chat Corpora Annotator (CCA): the first annotation system designed specifically for exploring and annotating chat log data. We also introduce a custom query language for semi-automatic situation extraction. Finally, we present the first gold-standard dataset for situation-based summarization. The software source code and the dataset are publicly available[1,2].

1 Introduction

In the recent years, the attitude to multiparticipant chat has changed: what was regarded as a distraction is now used as primary means of communication in both professional and personal environments. However, its evident problems, such as the inability to quickly and efficiently navigate a large body of skipped messages, are yet to be addressed. One of the ways of addressing this is summarization. However, due to the specifics of text chat data, such as noise and length, no widely accepted model for this task has been created yet. Nevertheless, there have been notable works in the field. One of them is Collabot (Tepper et al., 2018): a fully-fledged chat summarizer, which, however, never went public. Additionally, there is a considerable body of work on email summarization, such as Ulrich et al. (2008), Loza et al. (2014), Joty et al. (2011), which present both annotated data and a summarization approach. While these works are an indispensable basis for the research in the area, we believe that chat data possesses enough specific qualities (such as extremely short message length, presence of specific slang and emoticons, and largely informal grammar and spelling) to warrant new annotation procedures and summarization methods.

To the best of our knowledge, publicly available annotated data for this task is both rare and, additionally, highly specific. Most of the aforementioned works have created their own specific annotation procedures and applied them to small volumes of data. Annotated data is hard to obtain in and of itself, and creating a gold-standard dataset from noisy raw data may take a lot of effort and time. Therefore, we have focused on creating a full-fledged annotation system for chat data.

In the current paper, we propose novel annotation guidelines for multiparticipant chat data. In our vision, it would be most practical to summarize such datasets by specific *situations*. We define a situation as a subset of messages revolving around a single event in both temporal and contextual senses. The set of situation tags would be specific for each particular dataset, and devising a standardized tagset currently does not seem

[1] https://github.com/mechanicpanic/Chat-Corpora-Annotator

[2] https://github.com/mechanicpanic/Situation_Dataset

Proceedings of the Joint Conference of the 59th Annual Meeting of the Association for Computational Linguistics and the 11th International Joint Conference on Natural Language Processing: Student Research Workshop, pages 127–137
August 5–6, 2021.

possible. Each tagset would be devised by a human analyst and will be specifically suited for the needs of each user. This approach takes its roots in the ideas of open-domain event extraction, such as in (Ritter et al., 2012), but differs from them on several points. First, we are interested in groups of documents. Second, we do not explicitly extract event keywords. Instead, we offer the user to decide what situations revolve around which events and how they are represented in the data.

Furthermore, the quality of the training data has to be very high. In our understanding, creating a gold-standard dataset requires full attention of a human annotator, and relying on automatic recommenders would yield inferior results. Nevertheless, a recommender could be helpful for deep dataset exploration and for annotation assistance. Such assistance may come in a form of generating candidates for manual cross-checks when the annotator had finished their job or for rapid dataset prototyping. Since our task formulation is novel, there is no specifically trained machine learning (ML) model for it yet. To address the need for a recommender, we have designed a lightweight query language for rule-based detection of situations in chat datasets.

Next, we introduce Chat Corpora Annotator, a standalone desktop application for exploring and annotating multiparticipant chat datasets. To the best of our knowledge, this is the first tool that addresses both these tasks simultaneously. Additionally, we describe the annotation guidelines and the workflow for the summarization task.

Finally, we present an example collection that can be used to train machine learning models or serve as a gold-standard to assess summarization algorithms.

The main contributions of the paper are:

- An introduction of the situation-based summarization problem.
- A lightweight and easy-to-use annotation tool specifically designed for data exploration in multiparticipant chat logs.
- A special query language that can be used to generate annotation recommendations and run ad-hoc exploration queries.
- A workflow for CCA that is aimed at creating a dataset for the task of situation-based summarization.
- An example collection created using CCA.

2 Situations

Our inspiration for the proposed approach is based on cases such as a user taking a break from an important multi-participant chat for a significant amount of time. For example, it could be an employee taking a vacation. Having returned, they would have to catch up with the rest of their colleagues, which would include browsing chat discussions that happened during their absence. Therefore, they would be forced to navigate a large body of skipped messages which may be distracting and unproductive, as well as require a lot of time.

Basically, they would have to quickly look through all of the messages that were sent while they were away, since they would have no means to "prune" irrelevant discussions. The main issue here is the fact that they would not know whether a particular subset of messages is useful until they read at least some of them.

Another frequent scenario is a user searching for a particular conversation that is hard to find. Usually, in this case user issues search queries trying different keywords. In general, chats offer unsophisticated search capabilities, limiting them to simplified textual search, thus hindering efficient retrieval. For example, if the user needs to recall the details of a meeting (for example, the name of the place their friends have agreed to go out to), they would to issue "bar", "pub", "restaurant" until they obtain the desired result.

We propose to address such use-cases with chat log summarization that is based on the concept of *situation*. We define a *situation* as a subset of messages revolving around a single event in both temporal and contextual senses. We can propose many various examples: participants are arranging a meeting, selecting a product to be used in their project, solving a code issue and so on.

An example of a *situation* that has been found and tagged with the use of our tool is presented in Fig. 1. In this figure, the user is shown a *situation* in which chat participants find a job offer and discuss the process of applying to it.

Our final goal that exceeds the scope of this paper is to build a system that would automatically detect such *situations* and present them to the user.

The idea is to integrate the hypothetical tool into the interface of multiparticipant chat applications to provide the user with the means to take a *situation*-based perspective on chat history, instead of plain-text browsing as it has to be done currently.

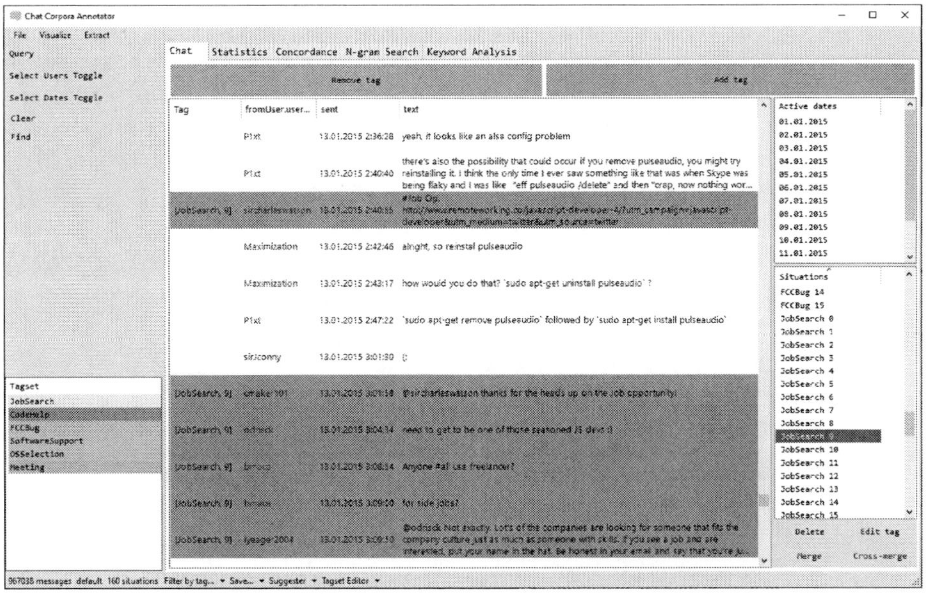

Figure 1: CCA's main window with a tagged situation visible.

In its first version, we plan to highlight situation locations in the history, and then, in the future, present a generated summary.

Automatic extraction of *situations* can be performed using information retrieval, natural language processing (Murray et al., 2018), and machine learning (Carenini and Murray, 2012) techniques. However, currently, there are no corpora to train models for this problem and no gold-standard datasets to run experiments on. Therefore, our first step is to create such a corpus and for this a special tool that assists tagging is needed.

3 Chat Corpora Annotator: System Overview

Following the aforementioned considerations, we have created the Chat Corpora Annotator (CCA) — the first exploration-annotation tool designed specifically for multiparticipant chat log data. Its main use case is creating a dataset for the proposed summarization task.

Furthermore, the provided functionality can help gain clear and immediate insights into raw data. CCA implements all common statistics and exploration tools and does not require any coding skills to use them. Additionally, CCA's CSV viewer is more comfortable to use than, for example, the representation of a dataset that can be created with `pandas`[3] in a Jupyter Notebook. The user can resize and swap columns in the window without affecting the data. CCA can be used for any textual data that contains a date, a username, and a text field, for example, email threads, Twitter logs, etc. Finally, all performance-heavy functionality is implemented separately from the main module and simply searching through a dataset does not require the user to load the CoreNLP models.

3.1 Features and User Interface

CCA's feature set has been inspired by linguistic-oriented tools, which were traditionally intended for a single researcher reading through the data and manually creating a linguistic corpus (Weisser, 2016). However, we have also taken into account the recent developments in the field, such as the simplicity and usability of modern annotators.

The main screen of CCA can be seen in Fig. 1. The user can upload CSV files and read through them, jump through available dates, and use the Lucene full-text search capabilities, as well as the analysis tools:

- **Statistics.** This menu item contains simple corpus statistics and visualizing functionality. Currently available: the number of messages, unique usernames, tokens, noun phrases, as well as the average length of a message, average messages per day, and average token length.

[3] `https://pandas.pydata.org/`

- **N-gram search.** This is a simple tool inspired by Google Ngram Viewer. On its first run it builds a B^+-tree disk-backed index for shingles (Manning et al., 2008) of length from 2 to 5. This tool allows the user to query the index with a single term efficiently and see the frequency of each shingle that contains it.
- **Concordancer.** This is a simple concordancer akin to `nltk`'s (Bird et al., 2009) `concordance()`: the search is constrained to a single term, which is then displayed with its immediate context. The user can select the number of characters that surround the term.

All of these tools are intended for the same purpose: they provide different angles on the topics of discussion in the dataset. For example, searching for the word "help" in the Ubuntu Chat Dataset (Uthus and Aha, 2013) reveals that, indeed, it is tech support chat data.

Additionally, simple visualizations options are provided. At the moment, there are two: a chart for message counts by date and a heatmap for message density by date.

3.2 Query Language

3.2.1 Idea

In this section, we will discuss Matcher, our custom SQL-like query language created for annotation recommendations and rich data exploration.

In modern systems such as (Cejuela et al., 2014), annotation recommendations are usually provided by machine learning models. There are no such models for situation extraction yet, and this has motivated us to adopt a different approach: we provide the users with complex querying functionality. Our approach was inspired by rule-based information extraction systems (Chiticariu et al., 2010, 2013).

Our idea was to allow the user to query the corpus for occurrences of special entities while defining their surroundings. In essence, the approach we have taken is rule-based pattern-matching. It is inspired by the Boolean retrieval model (Manning et al., 2008).

Running such queries in an ad-hoc manner is a powerful and versatile way of dataset exploration. A user can pose a query to check their annotation work, browse the results, refine the query by adding or removing conditions and run it again, effectively fine-tuning their work.

Designing Matcher, we aimed to create an intuitive, simple language that would be easier to learn for non-programmers. SQL seemed to us a suitable choice: so, we have created Matcher as an SQL-like language. Our query editor provides two modes of entering queries: free-text and a visual query builder (as seen on top of Fig. 2), which highlights the operators that would be appropriate to use next.

Matcher is implemented with the ANTLR parser generator[4].

3.2.2 Formalization

The general syntax of a Matcher query is as follows:

SELECT $cond_1^1$, ..., $cond_{n_1}^1$ INWIN $wsize_1$; $cond_1^2$, ..., $cond_{n_2}^2$ INWIN $wsize_2$; ..., $cond_1^m$, ..., $cond_{n_m}^m$ INWIN $wsize_m$.

We call each of $cond_1^i, \ldots, cond_{n_i}^i, i \in [1 \ldots m]$ a *matching group* and an individual $cond_j^i$ a *matcher*.

A *matcher* is a template that is matched against a single reply in chat history. It consists of a boolean expression which is sequentially (i.e., in a chronological order) checked against each message. If it evaluates to true, then this line is considered to be a part of the answer.

Each *matcher* that follows some $cond_j^i$ searches for the next line that satisfies its corresponding condition $cond_{j+1}^i$. This message does not necessarily have to immediately follow the previous one.

A single $cond_j^i$ consists of a set of atomic predicates joined by Boolean operators. Atomic predicates check the message for simple conditions, such as either the presence of any word from a user-defined word list (`haswordofdict()`, see Fig. 1) or an extracted NER tag (`hastime()`, `haslocation()`, etc). In order to obtain the NER data, we have implemented the CoreNLP pipeline within our tool. The full list of atomic predicates and other operators can be found in the Github README.

For example, consider the following query:

```
SELECT (haswordofdict(meetings)
AND hastime()),
haswordofdict(agreements)
```

It returns all conversations which start with a message containing any word from a user-defined "meetings" dictionary (meeting-related words) and contains a time marker. The conversation has to end with any message that has a word from the

[4]https://www.antlr.org/

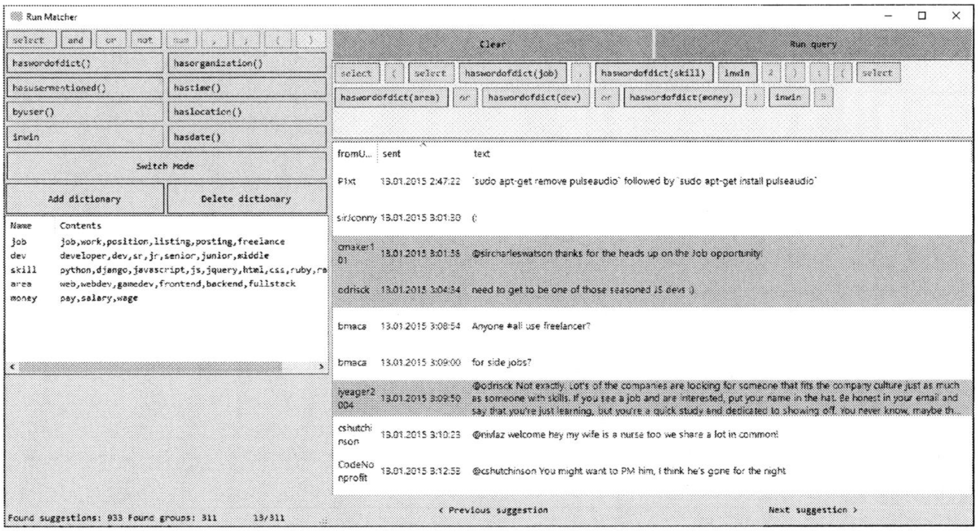

Figure 2: A dedicated visual interface for the Matcher query language. The depicted query is intended for retrieval of JobSearch situations.

"agreements" dictionary (words used to give consent). Thus, this query tries to extract all situations of participants scheduling a meeting.

The problem with this query is evident: while it will return the required conversation, it will also return a lot of unrelated messages since it does not restrict the position of the last message. To address this, we have introduced an optional clause INWIN $wsize$, where $wsize$ is a positive integer. It requires that all *matchers* from the *matching group* affected by the INWIN clause fit in a window of at max $wsize$ messages. Therefore, the proper query looks like this:

```
SELECT (haswordofdict(meetings)
AND hastime()),
haswordofdict(agreements)
INWIN 10
```

The purpose of the INWIN clause is not only to restrict the maximum length of the desired conversation fragment. Using it allows to query for a sequence of messages in which each message immediately follows another, i.e. without allowing other messages in between. This functionality comes naturally, if the length of the window is specified to be equal to the number of *matchers* in a given group. It stems from the rule that each *matcher* should correspond to exactly one message in each of the resulting fragments.

In Matcher, a query may have several *matching groups*. In this case, the action of the next INWIN clause starts from the last message of the previously *matched group*. Finally, we have to note that using the INWIN clause is optional for the last *matching group*.

3.2.3 Real query example

The following query was issued by the annotator during the creation of our corpus. Its purpose is to locate situations where participants discuss the current job market in programming, finding and discussing appropriate job postings for themselves. A fragment of the found results can be seen in Fig 1.

```
SELECT
    (SELECT
        haswordofdict(job),
        haswordofdict(skill)
      INWIN 2);
    (SELECT haswordofdict(area)
        OR haswordofdict(dev)
        OR haswordofdict(money))
INWIN 5
```

This query states that the annotator would like to see two messages which contain words from the "job" and "skill" dictionaries respectively, and the distance between them should be less than 2 messages (first inner query). After that, the second inner query will retrieve a third message which contains any word from either "area","dev" or "money" and is not farther away from the first one by more than 5 messages.

Note that Matcher functionality is intended for

assistance only, and it should not be considered as the primary means of annotation. The reasoning is simple: due to the inherently variable and noisy nature of chat logs there are no guarantees that the found situations are valid. The results require manual checking. Moreover, there are no guarantees that all relevant situations contained in the logs would be found by a given query (for example, a user-defined dictionary might not contain a specific word that is used in logs). That is, speaking in terms of information retrieval, there are no guarantees on both precision and recall (Manning et al., 2008). This is why our query processor does not recommend tags outright, it only points out the approximate locations of interest to the user in the data.

Concluding this section, we state that the proposed approach is simpler to use than ML recommenders. Our reasoning is that the results obtained during this process are straightforward, while an ML model can produce results as a "black box": the user would have no understanding as to why certain messages are assigned certain labels.

3.3 Annotation Guidelines and Workflow

The annotation guidelines are currently simple and revolve around situation definition, which was given in Section 1. The annotator either receives instructions before tagging or personally devises a tagset during data exploration. Next, they manually read through the data, extracting and annotating subsets of messages as situations.

Concerning the annotation model, we have created it to be more flexible than just assigning a single tag to a sequential subset of messages. Each message can belong to several differently-typed situations, but cannot belong to two different situations of the same type. We rely on the assumption that chat messages are short and the users generally keep them constrained to one topic. However, as the topics shift quickly in multiparticipant chat, the users can try and catch up by compacting information concerning different topics in one message.

Figure 3 contains the workflow we provide for our tool. As it can be seen, the entirety of the data preparation process is done inside CCA. The user receives a semi-structured data file and loads it into the tool. The user then explores it with the analytic search tools (searches through n-grams, issues simple queries, and so on), as well as utilizes Matcher, either coming up with their own dictionaries and queries or importing them. During this process, they simultaneously annotate the data and amend the tagset if required. Finally, they save the resulting output as an XML file.

4 Gold-Standard Corpus

4.1 Corpus Development and Statistics

In order to test CCA's functionality, we have created an annotated situation corpus for the freeCodeCamp dataset[5]. The fragment of the dataset that we used contains 967,038 messages spanning over 381 days, sent by 29870 unique users.

The constructed corpus contains 236 tagged situations, comprising 4146 messages in total. On average, our situations are 17 messages long. The average length of a message in the corpus is 78 symbols, in contrast to the dataset average of 66 symbols. The average number of users participating in a situation is 3.

Our tagset comprises 6 tags, as can be seen in the list below. They describe a common situation encountered in this particular dataset: e.g., CodeHelp is a user pasting in a faulty code fragment and receiving help. The tags have been manually devised after dataset exploration, and each of them has yielded the following numbers:

- JobSearch: 24 situations, 4 users and 13 messages on average
- CodeHelp: 95 situations, 3 users and 18 messages on average
- SoftwareSupport: 53 situations, 3 users and 22 messages on average
- OSSelection: 19 situations, 4 users and 16 messages on average
- Meeting: 4 situations, 2 users and 12 messages on average
- FCCBug: 42 situations, 3 users and 14 messages on average

Additionally, we have considered *windows* in situations (i.e., gaps containing untagged unrelated messages inside situations) and *intertwined situations* (two or more situations which intersect). The entire number of windows in our corpus is 820, which makes every situation have around 3 windows on average. The average length of a window

[5] https://www.kaggle.com/freecodecamp/all-posts-public-main-chatroom

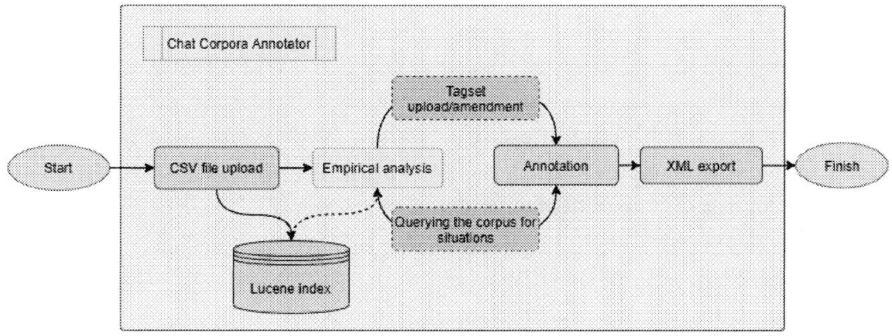

Figure 3: CCA workflow.

is 5 messages. Furthermore, out of 236 total situations, 60 are intertwined.

The creation of the corpus took a single annotator who was acquainted with the task around 20 work hours. They have utilized all available tools, but used Matcher the most. As they have reported, Matcher functionality was very valuable, as reading through a million messages would have been impossible. Additionally, they reported that running even very simple, single-term queries helped navigate the chat log data more efficiently by providing a paginated view of the dataset, coupled with highlighting of relevant messages.

4.2 Inter-Annotator Agreement

Only one annotator was employed during the creation of the corpus, so we did not run into situations that called for conflict resolution.

Going forward, we envision an interface for manual resolution that would allow to compare output files from different annotators either against each other and all at once. The annotator responsible for the comparison should be able to extend or shrink the boundaries of a situation, remove or add single messages, etc. Furthermore, we will implement the computation of various inter-annotator statistics such as Cohen's Kappa (Manning et al., 2008) in order to provide the user with formal means of evaluating the intermediate results.

5 Evaluation

We have conducted two kinds of evaluation tests: a responsiveness study and a usability study.

5.1 Tool Responsiveness

Raw chat log dataset files can be as large as several gigabytes, therefore, we have developed our application taking this into account.

Metric	Results
N-gram indexing	4 minutes
Indexing	1 minute
Heatmap rendering	0.5 s
Jumping dates	less than 0.1s
Opening an indexed file	less than 0.1s
Search query	less than 0.1s
Simple Matcher query	less than 0.1s
Complex Matcher query	around 0.1s

Table 1: Experiments on CCA responsiveness.

Table 1 presents the results we have obtained. We have measured the time it takes CCA to perform crucial operations on a large data file. The setup was as follows: we used CCA on a mid-range home PC running Windows 10 (Intel i5-7600k, 16GB DDR4 RAM, Crucial MX500 500GB SSD), manipulating a 500MB CSV file that contained around 1M chat messages. We adhere to the well-known quote of Jakob Nielsen (Nielsen, 1994): "0.1 second is about the limit for having the user feel that the system is reacting instantaneously, meaning that no special feedback is necessary except to display the result". As it can be seen, our system is responsive and only takes up a considerable amount of time on tasks that are run once, such as indexing or extracting key phrases, which could also be improved further in the next versions of our system.

5.2 Usability Study

We have run a small usability evaluation with three volunteers. We have explained the annotation task to them, and then asked them to load the tool, index a small CSV file, explore the data and annotate it using our standard tagset. Next, we have conducted a short informal discussion on the tool's interface, responsiveness and feasibility for the task at hand. The users have reported that the task was understandable to them, although it did require a little time to grasp, and the system appeared convenient for reading and searching through large volumes of data. They have proposed the following improvements: developing concise documentation for the system's capabilities, improving the cohesiveness of the UI, and finally, we have asked them to fill out the System Usability Scale questionnaire (Brooke, 1986), which has been slightly modified to fit our system better. Namely, we have modified questions 1 and 9, to "I find the system adequate for the proposed task" and "I could use the system to confidently complete the proposed task" respectively. This has been done since our system is intended for several specific tasks that arise in a research setting, not in daily life. The answers have put CCA at the 50th percentile, which indicates an "OK" level of usability (Sauro, 2018). Going by the responses we have obtained, CCA was easy enough to use, but it lacks better feature integration and perhaps a short tutorial. We consider this an adequate result for a first prototype, however, we will focus our future efforts on improving it.

6 Related Work

In this section, we will review two types of related studies: annotation tools and corpora created from chat log data for various tasks.

6.1 Annotation Tools

As mentioned previously, annotating raw text chat data is a complicated task due to its specifics. In this section, we will go over several well-known annotating tools and frameworks and evaluate their feasibility for the task at hand.

`brat` (Stenetorp et al., 2012) is a flexible all-purpose annotation tool. It supports two modes of annotation: annotating a text span with a label, and connecting these labels with either directed or undirected binary relations. Furthermore, the second mode also includes n-ary relations and attributes of these relations. Finally, brat supports an extensive constraint system for relations and an advanced search system. Due to it being based on a dedicated visualization system, brat was one of the first tools that provided its users with intuitive high-quality annotation visualization. However, as noted by Kummerfeld (2019), it takes considerable effort to set up for any custom task, including ours.

GATE (Bontcheva et al., 2013) and UIMA (Ferrucci and Lally, 2004) are well-known analysis frameworks that have been developed since the early 00's. While they are powerful, customizable and could be extended to suit any task, they are not easy to set up and utilize "on-the-go" — a feature that is essential for many modern tasks. For example, the creators of the Tweebank v1 dataset (Owoputi et al., 2013) admit to creating it in a single day. While it is not claimed to be a gold-standard dataset, the speed is impressive, and the team has used their own dedicated annotation tool. However, with these frameworks, the user would have not only to read through the extensive manuals, but also, most likely, code their own tools in Java[6].

TWIST (Pluss, 2012) and LIDA (Collins et al., 2019) are intended for dialogue annotation, which has been mostly focused on task-oriented dialogue for dialogue systems. Task-oriented dialogues already suppose a predefined topic and predefined roles (e.g., customer support tasks) and little noise. These tools provide their user with functionality such as turn/dialogue segmentation. They also impose constraints on the data, such as requiring only two speakers to be present in the dataset, which already makes them unsuitable for our task. Finally, they do not implement any full-text or constrained search features, which makes data exploration nearly impossible.

TagTog (Cejuela et al., 2014) and LightTag[7] are modern Web-based annotators that advertise flexibility for any task. While they are flexible and require little set up time, they also do not feature any search or exploration functionality in their free versions. Usually, these tools let the user view the data one line at a time, which is simply unfeasible for the task. Although it is possible to set up LightTag to display the "context" of the current message, it is still a constrained view. Further, these tools are oriented at fairly monotonous work such as building a NER dataset with custom tags, and this is why they tightly integrate ML recommenders into their workflow. This is helpful for well-known classification tasks, but it is not a feasible approach for something novel, i.e. that lacks trained models. SLATE by Kummerfeld (2019) is an experimental annotation tool focused on a terminal-based workflow that was released in 2019. Its authors argue that its main advantages are: complete configurability for any task and annotation speed which is not

[6]`https://uima.apache.org/doc-uima-annotator.html`

[7]`https://www.lighttag.io/`

hindered by GUI. Concerning the second point, this tool is controlled via keyboard shortcuts instead of a mouse, and all of its UI is contained within a Linux terminal. It supports annotation of continuous spans of any entities, such as characters, tokens, lines, or documents. Additionally, SLATE supports linking any of these entities. It was specifically designed to create large corpora out of chat and chat-like data in a very short time. This goal has been achieved, however, SLATE does not offer any exploration functionality. Furthermore, its learning curve may be steep for someone who is not used for a keyboard-based workflow.

Finally, we would like to mention Huggingface Dataset Viewer[8], which is a web-based tool for manually looking through NLP datasets from the Huggingface `nlp` library. While it is not an annotator and cannot be directly compared to our or other tools, its existence proves that there is a need to explore a dataset before using it for any task.

As it can be seen, there are no tools that could be readily applied or easily customized for our task. Existing options either lack the desired functionality or require a substantial, often comparable to creating a new tool from scratch, effort in order to make them suitable for the considered task.

6.2 Chat Datasets

Most of the existing annotated chat log datasets are intended for the chat disentanglement task. The first known corpora belongs to Shen et al. (2006), who have drawn their data from an intra-university IRC channel. This dataset was not public. Further on, some of the most well-known work in this area belongs to Elsner and Charniak (2008) who have created a corpora for chat disentanglement based on IRC logs of the `#Linux` channel at `free-node.org`. They have manually annotated around two thousand utterances via a dedicated interface. However, to the best of our knowledge, the data has since ceased to be publicly available. Adams and Martell (2008) developed a disentanglement and topic extraction dataset based on Navy tactical chat which was not released. However, the most well-known dataset belongs to Lowe et al. (2015): they have created the Ubuntu Dialogue Dataset based on IRC data from the `Ubuntu` help channel. It contains around a million of heuristically extracted multi-turn dialogues, and it can be accessed online. A dataset based on the French version of the same channel was presented by Riou et al. (2015), containing 1229 messages. Dulceanu (2016) presents a small dataset of manually collected 884 chat messages which were disentangled and annotated with three speech acts. Finally, Kummerfeld et al. (2019) present the largest disentanglement corpus to date: it contains around 78 thousand manually annotated messages also from the Ubuntu and Linux IRC channels.

Concerning other tasks, we would like to mention Tweebank v2 (3550 tweets) by Liu et al. (2018), which was created for training a full machine learning based NLP pipeline. Its first version by Owoputi et al. (2013) contained 840 tweets tagged for training a part-of-speech tagger.

To the best of our knowledge, very few summarization datasets for chat and chat-like data were made publicly available. The AMI corpus (Carletta et al., 2005) contains transcripts of audio drawn from business meetings, hand-annotated with their abstractive and extractive summaries among many other annotation modes. Further on, Joty et al. (2010) have developed the BC3 corpus that contains email and blog data for summarization. Koto (2016) take the same approach and present a summarization dataset for chats in the Indonesian language, consisting of 300 manually summarized chat segments.

As it can be seen, no attempts on creating annotated corpora from the freeCodeCamp data have been made to date, and our work is the first to attempt that.

7 Conclusion & Future Work

In this paper, we have presented a novel situation-based summarization task, CCA — an annotation-exploration tool for large chat logs, a workflow for creating a situation-based summarization dataset, and an example corpus. Chat Corpora Annotator offers a novel approach to exploration: a query language that allows the user to query a dataset for subsets of messages which could be a situation. To the best of our knowledge, CCA is the only tool designed for these two tasks at once.

Further work on the tool will be focused on improving its usability and efficiency, as well as extending language support. The work on the summarization task will be moving towards implementing the first versions of the summarizer itself.

[8] `https://huggingface.co/nlp/viewer/`

References

Paige H. Adams and Craig H. Martell. 2008. Topic detection and extraction in chat. In *2008 IEEE International Conference on Semantic Computing*, pages 581–588.

Steven Bird, Ewan Klein, and Edward Loper. 2009. *Natural Language Processing with Python*, 1st edition. O'Reilly Media, Inc.

Kalina Bontcheva, Hamish Cunningham, Ian Roberts, Angus Roberts, Valentin Tablan, Niraj Aswani, and Genevieve Gorrell. 2013. Gate teamware: a web-based, collaborative text annotation framework. *Language Resources and Evaluation*, 47(4):1007–1029.

John Brooke. 1986. System usability scale (sus): a quick-and-dirty method of system evaluation user information. *Reading, UK: Digital Equipment Co Ltd*, 43.

Giuseppe Carenini and Gabrial Murray. 2012. Methods for mining and summarizing text conversations. In *Proceedings of the 35th International ACM SIGIR Conference on Research and Development in Information Retrieval*, SIGIR '12, page 1178–1179, New York, NY, USA. Association for Computing Machinery.

Jean Carletta, Simone Ashby, Sebastien Bourban, Mike Flynn, Mael Guillemot, Thomas Hain, Jaroslav Kadlec, Vasilis Karaiskos, Wessel Kraaij, Melissa Kronenthal, et al. 2005. The ami meeting corpus: A pre-announcement. In *International workshop on machine learning for multimodal interaction*, pages 28–39. Springer.

Juan Miguel Cejuela, Peter McQuilton, Laura Ponting, Steven J Marygold, Raymund Stefancsik, Gillian H Millburn, and Burkhard Rost. 2014. tagtog: interactive and text-mining-assisted annotation of gene mentions in plos full-text articles. *Database*, 2014.

Laura Chiticariu, Rajasekar Krishnamurthy, Yunyao Li, Sriram Raghavan, Frederick Reiss, and Shivakumar Vaithyanathan. 2010. SystemT: An algebraic approach to declarative information extraction. In *Proceedings of the 48th Annual Meeting of the Association for Computational Linguistics*, pages 128–137, Uppsala, Sweden. Association for Computational Linguistics.

Laura Chiticariu, Yunyao Li, and Frederick R. Reiss. 2013. Rule-based information extraction is dead! long live rule-based information extraction systems! In *Proceedings of the 2013 Conference on Empirical Methods in Natural Language Processing*, pages 827–832, Seattle, Washington, USA. Association for Computational Linguistics.

Edward Collins, Nikolai Rozanov, and Bingbing Zhang. 2019. LIDA: Lightweight interactive dialogue annotator. In *Proceedings of the 2019 Conference on Empirical Methods in Natural Language Processing and the 9th International Joint Conference on Natural Language Processing (EMNLP-IJCNLP): System Demonstrations*, pages 121–126, Hong Kong, China. Association for Computational Linguistics.

Andrei Dulceanu. 2016. Recovering implicit thread structure in chat conversations. *Revista Romana de Interactiune Om-Calculator*, 9(3):217–232.

Micha Elsner and Eugene Charniak. 2008. You talking to me? a corpus and algorithm for conversation disentanglement. In *Proceedings of ACL-08: HLT*, pages 834–842, Columbus, Ohio. Association for Computational Linguistics.

David Ferrucci and Adam Lally. 2004. Uima: An architectural approach to unstructured information processing in the corporate research environment. *Natural Language Engineering*, 10:327–348.

Shafiq Joty, Giuseppe Carenini, Gabriel Murray, and Raymond T. Ng. 2010. Exploiting conversation structure in unsupervised topic segmentation for emails. In *Proceedings of the 2010 Conference on Empirical Methods in Natural Language Processing*, pages 388–398, Cambridge, MA. Association for Computational Linguistics.

Shafiq R. Joty, G. Carenini, Gabriel Murray, and R. Ng. 2011. Supervised topic segmentation of email conversations. In *ICWSM*.

Fajri Koto. 2016. A publicly available Indonesian corpora for automatic abstractive and extractive chat summarization. In *Proceedings of the Tenth International Conference on Language Resources and Evaluation (LREC'16)*, pages 801–805, Portorož, Slovenia. European Language Resources Association (ELRA).

Jonathan K. Kummerfeld. 2019. SLATE: A super-lightweight annotation tool for experts. In *Proceedings of the 57th Annual Meeting of the Association for Computational Linguistics: System Demonstrations*, pages 7–12, Florence, Italy. Association for Computational Linguistics.

Jonathan K. Kummerfeld, Sai R. Gouravajhala, Joseph J. Peper, Vignesh Athreya, Chulaka Gunasekara, Jatin Ganhotra, Siva Sankalp Patel, Lazaros C Polymenakos, and Walter Lasecki. 2019. A large-scale corpus for conversation disentanglement. In *Proceedings of the 57th Annual Meeting of the Association for Computational Linguistics*, pages 3846–3856, Florence, Italy. Association for Computational Linguistics.

Yijia Liu, Yi Zhu, Wanxiang Che, Bing Qin, Nathan Schneider, and Noah A. Smith. 2018. Parsing tweets into Universal Dependencies. In *Proceedings of the 2018 Conference of the North American Chapter of the Association for Computational Linguistics: Human Language Technologies, Volume 1 (Long Papers)*, pages 965–975, New Orleans, Louisiana. Association for Computational Linguistics.

Ryan Lowe, Nissan Pow, Iulian Serban, and Joelle Pineau. 2015. The Ubuntu dialogue corpus: A large dataset for research in unstructured multi-turn dialogue systems. In *Proceedings of the 16th Annual Meeting of the Special Interest Group on Discourse and Dialogue*, pages 285–294, Prague, Czech Republic. Association for Computational Linguistics.

Vanessa Loza, S. Lahiri, R. Mihalcea, and P. Lai. 2014. Building a dataset for summarization and keyword extraction from emails. In *LREC*.

Christopher D. Manning, Prabhakar Raghavan, and Hinrich Schütze. 2008. *Introduction to Information Retrieval*. Cambridge University Press, USA.

Gabriel Murray, Giuseppe Carenini, and Shafiq Joty. 2018. NLP for conversations: Sentiment, summarization, and group dynamics. In *Proceedings of the 27th International Conference on Computational Linguistics: Tutorial Abstracts*, pages 1–4, Santa Fe, New Mexico, USA. Association for Computational Linguistics.

Jakob Nielsen. 1994. *Usability engineering*. Morgan Kaufmann.

Olutobi Owoputi, Brendan O'Connor, Chris Dyer, Kevin Gimpel, Nathan Schneider, and Noah A. Smith. 2013. Improved part-of-speech tagging for online conversational text with word clusters. In *Proceedings of the 2013 Conference of the North American Chapter of the Association for Computational Linguistics: Human Language Technologies*, pages 380–390, Atlanta, Georgia. Association for Computational Linguistics.

Brian Pluss. 2012. TWIST dialogue annotation tool.

Matthieu Riou, Soufian Salim, and Nicolas Hernandez. 2015. Using discursive information to disentangle french language chat. In *2nd Workshop on Natural Language Processing for Computer-Mediated Communication (NLP4CMC 2015)/Social Media at GSCL Conference 2015*, pages 23–27.

Alan Ritter, Oren Etzioni, and Sam Clark. 2012. Open domain event extraction from twitter. In *Proceedings of the 18th ACM SIGKDD international conference on Knowledge discovery and data mining*, pages 1104–1112.

Jeff Sauro. 2018. 5 ways to interpret a sus score. `https://measuringu.com/interpret-sus-score/`. [Online; accessed 20-November-2020].

Dou Shen, Qiang Yang, Jian-Tao Sun, and Zheng Chen. 2006. Thread detection in dynamic text message streams. In *Proceedings of the 29th Annual International ACM SIGIR Conference on Research and Development in Information Retrieval*, SIGIR '06, page 35–42, New York, NY, USA. Association for Computing Machinery.

Pontus Stenetorp, Sampo Pyysalo, Goran Topić, Tomoko Ohta, Sophia Ananiadou, and Jun'ichi Tsujii. 2012. brat: a web-based tool for NLP-assisted text annotation. In *Proceedings of the Demonstrations at the 13th Conference of the European Chapter of the Association for Computational Linguistics*, pages 102–107, Avignon, France. Association for Computational Linguistics.

Naama Tepper, Anat Hashavit, Maya Barnea, Inbal Ronen, and Lior Leiba. 2018. Collabot: Personalized group chat summarization. In *Proceedings of the Eleventh ACM International Conference on Web Search and Data Mining*, WSDM '18, page 771–774, New York, NY, USA. Association for Computing Machinery.

Jan Ulrich, Gabriel Murray, and Giuseppe Carenini. 2008. A publicly available annotated corpus for supervised email summarization. In *Proceedings of AAAI Email-2008 workshop, Chicago, USA*.

David C Uthus and David W Aha. 2013. The ubuntu chat corpus for multiparticipant chat analysis.

Martin Weisser. 2016. Dart – the dialogue annotation and research tool. *Corpus Linguistics and Linguistic Theory*, 12:355 – 388.

Modeling Text using the Continuous Space Topic Model with Pre-Trained Word Embeddings

Seiichi Inoue[1], **Taichi Aida**[1], **Mamoru Komachi**[1], **Manabu Asai**[2]
[1]Tokyo Metropolitan University, [2]Soka University
{inoue-seiichi, aida-taichi}@ed.tmu.ac.jp
komachi@tmu.ac.jp, m-asai@soka.ac.jp

Abstract

In this study, we propose a model that extends the continuous space topic model (CSTM), which flexibly controls word probability in a document, using pre-trained word embeddings. To develop the proposed model, we pre-train word embeddings, which capture the semantics of words and plug them into the CSTM. Intrinsic experimental results show that the proposed model exhibits a superior performance over the CSTM in terms of perplexity and convergence speed. Furthermore, extrinsic experimental results show that the proposed model is useful for a document classification task when compared with the baseline model. We qualitatively show that the latent coordinates obtained by training the proposed model are better than those of the baseline model.

1 Introduction

Topic models are statistical models that automatically extract latent topics in documents from a text corpus. Topic models have been used in various applications within and outside of natural language processing. Such applications include information retrieval (Wei and Croft, 2006), collaborative filtering (Marlin, 2003), author identification (Rosen-Zvi et al., 2012), and opinion extraction (Lin et al., 2011).

The latent Dirichlet allocation (LDA) (Blei et al., 2003), which is a representative method for topic modeling, assumes that each document has a latent topic. It uses an unobservable random variable called the latent topic to formulate the factors that produce a set of words that are statistically likely to co-occur. Unlike the LDA, the continuous space topic model (CSTM) (Mochihashi et al., 2013) models documents without using intermediate variables, such as latent topics. Specifically, the CSTM is formulated by introducing latent coordinates of words and considering a function that follows a Gaussian process in the same space to represent the importance of a word in a document. In the LDA, the probability distribution of words is fixed, and the probability of words is controlled by the topic distribution. Therefore, it is not possible to change the probability distribution of words according to each document and thus the text cannot be modeled in a fine-grained way. By contrast, the CSTM controls the probability of words based on the latent coordinates of the words and the function representing the meaning of the document. Hence, it is possible for the CSTM to dynamically change the word distribution according to the document. Additionally, the CSTM outperforms conventional topic models, such as the LDA, in terms of perplexity.

As mentioned above, the CSTM models documents using word embeddings; however, the structure of the model is such that the word embeddings (latent coordinates) are free parameters. Therefore, the estimation of the model is time-consuming because of the large number of parameters. In addition, the only information used for the estimation of the word embeddings is the frequency of words, which makes it difficult to capture the semantics of words.

In this study, we propose a new method in which the latent coordinates of words, which are one of the free parameters of the CSTM, are learned in advance using word2vec (Mikolov et al., 2013), and the learned distributed representation of the words are introduced into the CSTM. As in the Gaussian LDA (Das et al., 2015), when we use the word embeddings that capture the semantics of words and provide them as prior information to the model, we can expect improved performance and faster convergence. In the experiments, we use English and Japanese corpora to compare the proposed method with the baseline CSTM in terms of perplexity and convergence speed. We also perform a document classification task to evaluate the quality of the document representations that are

Proceedings of the Joint Conference of the 59th Annual Meeting of the Association for Computational Linguistics and the 11th International Joint Conference on Natural Language Processing: Student Research Workshop, pages 138–147
August 5–6, 2021.

learned by our model. In the discussion, we use the trained model to investigate the importance of words in documents and evaluate the trained model qualitatively. Additionally, we visualize the latent coordinates of words and documents in the same space.

The main contributions of this study are as follows:

- We propose a CSTM-based model that can estimate parameters faster and obtain useful document representation using pre-trained word embeddings.
- Intrinsic experiments using English and Japanese corpora show that the proposed model exhibits a superior performance over the baseline model in terms of perplexity and convergence speed.
- Extrinsic experimental results show that document embeddings obtained by the proposed model are useful for document classification.

2 Related Work

2.1 Word Embeddings and Topic Models

There are several studies that aimed to improve the performance of topic models by using a distributed representation of words. Das et al. (2015) proposed the Gaussian LDA (G-LDA), which uses a multivariate Gaussian distribution in the same space of word embeddings to estimate topics in the embedding space. Compared with the LDA, it has high coherence (Chang et al., 2009) because it introduces prior knowledge of semantics of words by using pre-trained word embeddings. Recently, Dieng et al. (2020) proposed the embedded topic model (ETM). The ETM models each word with a categorical distribution whose natural parameter is the inner product between the embedding of word and an embedding of its assigned topic. It outperformed traditional topic models including the LDA.

However, both topic models use latent topics to model the documents. The G-LDA defines latent topics as multivariate Gaussian distribution, and the ETM uses topic embeddings for formulating the word probability. Therefore, those topic models hardly control word probability directly depending on a document. In Section 2.2, we introduce the CSTM, which can directly control word probability in a document.

2.2 Continuous Space Topic Model

In the CSTM, the probability of a word is modeled through the Polya distribution, which is a compound distribution of the Dirichlet and multinomial distributions, to account for the burstiness of language (Doyle and Elkan, 2009). We denote $\boldsymbol{y} = (y_1, y_2, \ldots, y_V)$ as the frequency of each word in the document, $\boldsymbol{w}$. The Polya distribution is defined as follows:

$$p(\boldsymbol{y}|\boldsymbol{\alpha}) = \frac{\Gamma(\sum_v \alpha_v)}{\Gamma(\sum_v(\alpha_v + y_v))} \prod_v \frac{\Gamma(\alpha_v + y_v)}{\Gamma(\alpha_v)}, \tag{1}$$

where $\boldsymbol{\alpha}$ represents the concentration parameter of the Polya distribution. We assume that each word, w_v, has latent coordinates $\phi(w_v) \sim \mathcal{N}(0, I_d)$ in the d-dimension. To increase the probability of semantically related words in each document, we generate a function that follows a Gaussian process with a mean of zero in the same latent space:

$$f \sim \mathrm{GP}(0, \mathrm{K}), \tag{2}$$

where K represents the kernel matrix, and in this case, it is an inner product kernel: $\mathrm{K}_{ij} = k(w_i, w_j) = \phi(w_i)^T \phi(w_j)$. A Gaussian process (Rasmussen and Williams, 2006) is a stochastic process that generates a random regression function, where the closer $k(w_i, w_j)$ is, the closer the corresponding outputs, $f(w_i), f(w_j)$, will be. Intuitively, f represents "what we want to say in this document." The concentration parameter, α_v, of the Polya distribution is then modeled to be larger according to its function value:

$$\alpha_v \propto \alpha_0 G_0(w_v) \exp(f(w_v)), \tag{3}$$

where $\alpha_0 \sim \mathrm{Ga}(a_0, b_0)$ is a free parameter, and $\mathrm{Ga}(a_0, b_0)$ indicates the gamma distribution. Additionally, $G_0(w_v) \sim \mathrm{PY}(\beta, \gamma)$ represents the "default" probability of word w_v, and $\mathrm{PY}(\beta, \gamma)$ denotes the Pitman-Yor process. In practice, the maximum likelihood estimator, $\#(w_v)/\sum_i \#(w_i)$, used as $G_0(w_v)$ ($\#(w_v)$ is the frequency of the word w_v in all documents). Based on this, the generation process of the CSTM that generates N documents is as follows:

1. Draw $\alpha_0 \sim \mathrm{Ga}(a_0, b_0)$.
2. Draw $G_0 \sim \mathrm{PY}(\beta, \gamma)$. (In practice, maximum likelihood estimator is used.)
3. For $v = 1 \ldots V$,

- Draw $\phi(w_v) \sim \mathcal{N}(0, I_d)$.

4. For $n = 1 \dots N$,
   - Draw $f_n \sim \mathrm{GP}(0, \mathrm{K})$.
   - For $v = 1 \dots V$,
     - Set $\alpha_v = \alpha_0 G_0(w_v) e^{f_n(w_v)}$.
   - Draw $\boldsymbol{w} \sim \mathrm{Polya}(\boldsymbol{\alpha})$.

3 Proposed Method

3.1 Word Embeddings

Word2vec (Mikolov et al., 2013) is a probabilistic model for learning distributed representations that capture the semantics of words based on the distributional hypothesis (Harris, 1954). The continuous bag-of-words (CBOW) model, which is one of the learning methods of word2vec, obtains word embeddings by maximizing the predicted probability of the target word, w_t:

$$p(w_t|C_{w_t}) \propto \exp(\eta(w_t)^T \tilde{\eta}(C_{w_t})), \tag{4}$$

where $C_{w_t} = \{w_{t \pm i} | 1 \leq i \leq \delta\}$ represents the set of nearby context words, δ is the context window width, and $\tilde{\eta}(C_{w_t}) := |C_{w_t}|^{-1} \sum_{w \in C_{w_t}} \eta(w)$ denotes the average vector of all context word vectors.

We use the CBOW model to learn word embeddings. In this study, we used a relatively large context window of $\delta = 10$ to learn the topical information (Bansal et al., 2014). In general, it has been shown that the quality of word embeddings improves by centering (Hara et al., 2015; Mu and Viswanath, 2018). Accordingly, acquired distributed representations of the word, $\eta(w_1), \eta(w_2), \dots, \eta(w_V)$, are centered and normalized as follows:

$$\psi(w_v) = \tau S^{-\frac{1}{2}} \left\{ \eta(w_v) - V^{-1} \sum_i \eta(w_i) \right\}, \tag{5}$$

where S is a normalization constant, and defined as follows:

$$S = V^{-1} \sum_i \eta(w_i)^T \eta(w_i). \tag{6}$$

In addition, τ is a hyperparameter that controls the variance of word embeddings, and in this study, we simply set $\tau = d^{-1/2}$.

3.2 Modeling Text with Pre-trained Word Embeddings

Next, as in Mochihashi et al. (2013), we define the function that follows the Gaussian process, whose mean is zero and kernel function is $k(w_i, w_j) = \psi(w_i)^T \psi(w_j)$, in the latent space consisting of the word distributed representations obtained using Eq. (5):

$$f \sim \mathrm{GP}(0, \mathrm{K}_\psi). \tag{7}$$

However, because f is, in principle, infinite in dimension and difficult to estimate directly, we introduce an auxiliary variable representing the latent coordinates of the document in the word latent space, similar to the discrete infinite logistic normal distribution (Paisley et al., 2011), which introduces latent coordinates to correlate between topics in the LDA framework:

$$u \sim \mathcal{N}(0, I_d). \tag{8}$$

We summarize the latent coordinates of the words as $\Psi = (\psi(w_1), \psi(w_2), \cdots \psi(w_V))^T$, and we can obtain the distribution of $f = \Psi u$ by marginalizing u as follows:

$$f|\Psi \sim \mathrm{GP}(0, \Psi^T \Psi) = \mathrm{GP}(0, \mathrm{K}_\psi). \tag{9}$$

f follows the same Gaussian process as expressed in Eq. (7).

Therefore, in the proposed method, we define the Gaussian process representing the meaning of the document using the document vector, u, which is in the same latent space as the word vector:

$$f(w_v) \propto \psi(w_v)^T u. \tag{10}$$

Next, we define α_v as in Eq. (3):

$$\alpha_v \propto \alpha_0 G_0(w_v) \exp(\psi(w_v)^T u), \tag{11}$$

and model the probability of a word using the Polya distribution in Eq. (1).

3.3 Bayesian Markov Chain Monte Carlo (MCMC) Estimation

By combining N documents as $\boldsymbol{D} = (\boldsymbol{y}_1, \boldsymbol{y}_2, \dots, \boldsymbol{y}_N)$, we can obtain the joint distribution of α_0 and $\boldsymbol{\alpha}$ as follows:

$$p(\alpha_0, \boldsymbol{\alpha}|\boldsymbol{D}) \propto \prod_n p(\boldsymbol{y}_n|\alpha_0, G_0, f_n) p(\alpha_0) p(f_n|\psi). \tag{12}$$

Algorithm 1: MCMC Procedure

Initialize $u \sim \mathcal{N}(0, I_d)$
Initialize $\alpha_0 = 1$
for $j = 1 \ldots J$ **do**
    for $n = \mathrm{randperm}(1 \ldots N)$ **do**
        Draw $u'_n \sim \mathcal{N}(u_n, \sigma_u^2 I)$
        Draw $v \sim \mathrm{Uniform}(0, 1)$
        if $\mathcal{A}(u'_n) \geq v$ **then**
            Update $u_n = u'_n$
        end
    end
    Draw $z \sim \mathcal{N}(0, \sigma_{\alpha_0}^2)$
    Set $\alpha'_0 = \alpha_0 \cdot \exp(z)$
    Draw $v \sim \mathrm{Uniform}(0, 1)$
    if $\mathcal{A}(\alpha'_0) \geq v$ **then**
        Update $\alpha_0 = \alpha'_0$
    end
end

Figure 1: The MCMC algorithm of proposed model.

However, because $\boldsymbol{\alpha}$ changes only through the document vector, u, in Eq. (10), in the proposed model, the joint distribution of the estimated parameters, α_0 and $\boldsymbol{u} = (u_1, u_2, \ldots, u_N)$, is denoted as follows:

$$p(\alpha_0, \boldsymbol{u}|\boldsymbol{D}) \propto \prod_n p(\boldsymbol{y}_n|\alpha_0, G_0, \psi, u_n)p(\alpha_0)p(u_n). \tag{13}$$

For model estimation, we use the random walk Metropolis-Hastings (MH) algorithm to avoid the problem of local optima, as demonstrated by Mochihashi et al. (2013). [1] We show the MCMC algorithm of proposed model in Figure 1. The estimating parameters are α_0, and the document vector u in Eq. (11). The candidates for each parameter are generated using the following proposal distribution:

$$z \sim \mathcal{N}(0, \sigma_{\alpha_0}^2), \tag{14}$$
$$\alpha'_0 = \alpha_0 \cdot \exp(z), \tag{15}$$
$$u' \sim \mathcal{N}(u, \sigma_u^2 I). \tag{16}$$

[1]We attempted the Hamiltonian MCMC algorithm (Neal et al., 2011) using the gradient of the posterior distribution. However, owing to the high computational cost and need for numerical differentiation, we only used the random walk MH algorithm in this study for the experiments.

Table 1: Statistics for each corpus.

Data	Docs	Vocabulary	Words
NIPS	1,740	37,822	3,971,243
CSJ	3,302	20,001	5,433,871
Mainichi	10,000	38,070	8,070,838

Table 2: Test set perplexity for each corpus.

Data	Ours	CSTM	ETM
NIPS	**980.682**	1148.386	2872.731
CSJ	**288.157**	300.967	1017.658
Mainichi	**362.706**	405.199	2602.808

We also adopt candidates according to the acceptance probability of the following likelihood ratio:

$$\mathcal{A}(\alpha'_0) = \min\left\{1, \frac{\prod_n p(\boldsymbol{y}_n|\alpha')\mathrm{Ga}(\alpha'_0|a_0, b_0)}{\prod_n p(\boldsymbol{y}_n|\alpha)\mathrm{Ga}(\alpha_0|a_0, b_0)}\right\}, \tag{17}$$

$$\mathcal{A}(u') = \min\left\{1, \frac{p(\boldsymbol{y}_n|\alpha')p(u'|0, I_d)}{p(\boldsymbol{y}_n|\alpha)p(u|0, I_d)}\right\}. \tag{18}$$

In this study, we set $\sigma_{\alpha_0} = 0.2$ and $\sigma_u = 0.01$, which are the random walk widths that control efficiency of training, based on the results of preliminary experiments.

4 Experiments

4.1 Corpora

In the experiments, we used the Neural Information Processing Systems (NIPS) [2], which is an English corpus, Corpus of Spontaneous Japanese (CSJ) and Mainichi Newspaper (10,000 randomly selected articles from 2013), which are Japanese corpora. For Japanese, we preprocessed texts using MeCab[3] with IPADic. In all the corpora, words with a frequency of less than five were excluded from the training data. The statistics for each corpus are listed in Table 1.

4.2 Intrinsic Evaluation

To evaluate the performance of topic models, we computed the perplexity of the proposed model, the CSTM and the ETM. Similar to the work of Wallach et al. (2009), we randomly selected 80% of the

[2]https://cs.nyu.edu/~roweis/data.html
[3]https://taku910.github.io/mecab/

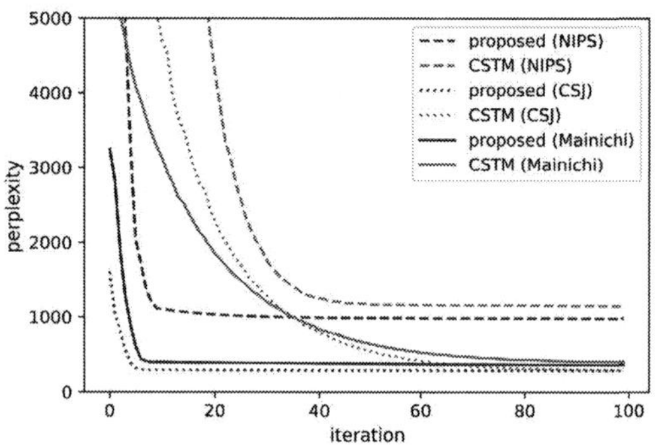

Figure 2: Test set perplexity of the proposed model and the CSTM.

words in each document as training data and calculated the perplexity on the remaining 20% of the words. For the evaluation in the proposed model and the CSTM, we varied the latent dimension size by 10, 20, 50, and 100 and reported the best score on test data. For the evaluation in the ETM, we set the local learning rate to 0.002 and the weight decay parameter to 1.2×10^{-6}, and then selected the model which reported the best validation score by varying the number of topics by 10, 20, 50, and 100.

Perplexity The perplexity of the proposed model, the CSTM and the ETM computed for each corpus is shown in Table 2. The proposed method outperforms the CSTM and the ETM in terms of perplexity for all three corpora. Compared to the CSTM, the proposed method naturally has higher performance because it has the topical information from pre-trained word embeddings. The ETM cannot directly control the word probability in a document because it uses topic embeddings for formulating the word probability, so the proposed model, which can control the word probability flexibly, performs better in terms of predictive power.

Convergence Speed Figure 2 shows the perplexity convergence of the proposed model and the CSTM. The proposed model only takes less than ten iteration to converge, though the CSTM takes fifty to hundred iteration. The proposed model also outperforms the CSTM in terms of convergence speed on all corpora because it has topical information as prior knowledge from the pre-trained word embeddings.

Table 3: Mean classification accuracy on the CSJ corpus using learned embeddings.

Models	Accuracy	P-value
CSTM	0.704	0.000
Ours	**0.866**	
word2vec	0.917	0.111
Ours w/ word2vec	**0.928**	

4.3 Extrinsic Evaluation

To evaluate the quality of representations of the documents that are learned by our model, we perform a document classification task. We evaluate the performance of the proposed model by comparing it with the performances of CSTM and word2vec.

Settings In this experiment, we use the one-versus-one support vector machine implemented in scikit-learn [4]. The data was split between training, 90% and testing, 10%. For the tuning parameter C, which is one of the parameters controlling the extent of penalty, and γ, which is the parameter of RBF kernel, we execute grid search by a 10-fold cross validation on the training data and select the best models in terms of accuracy. For other parameters, we use the default values set by scikit-learn.

We define the features as follows: For the CSTM, we use the document vectors. For word2vec, we use the mean vector of word vectors in the document. For the proposed model, we use the document vector (denoted "Ours") and the concatenation of the mean vector of word vectors and document vector (denoted "Ours w/ word2vec"). Also, we apply the paired t-test to compare the performance between the proposed models and the baseline models. A confidence interval of 95% was considered to identify a significant difference between two compared models.

Results Table 3 shows the classification accuracy on the CSJ corpus using each feature. For document classification using only document vector obtained from the proposed model, we can see that it significantly ($p < 0.05$) outperformed the CSTM but is slightly inferior to word2vec. However, when we use the document vector obtained from the proposed model and the average vector of word vectors obtained from word2vec, the accuracy is better than that of word2vec, although the

[4]`https://scikit-learn.org/stable/`

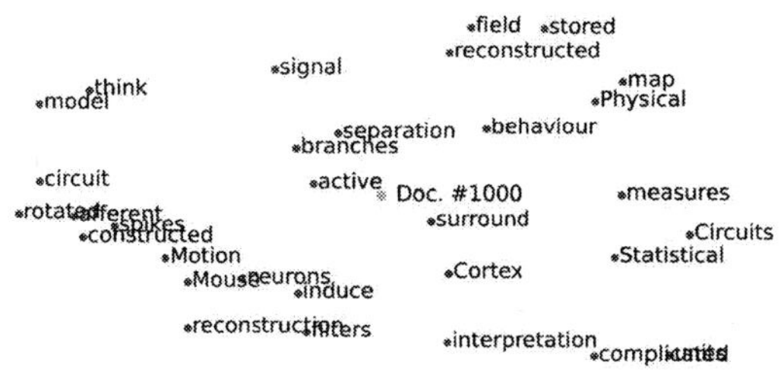

Figure 3: The visualization of reduced embedding space around the 1000th document "The Role of Activity in Synaptic Competition at the Neuromuscular Junction." Words are colored as blue and document as orange.

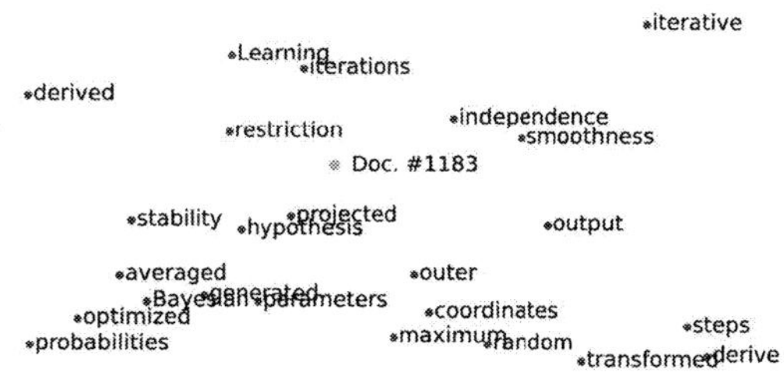

Figure 4: The visualization of reduced embedding space around the 1183rd document "Bayesian Model Comparison by Monte Carlo Chaining." Words are colored as blue and document as orange.

difference is not statistically significant. We will analyze the classification results in detail in Section 5.3.

5 Discussion

5.1 Visualizing Word and Document Embeddings

In the proposed model and the CSTM, word vectors and document vectors are located in the same space, so we can observe the relationships between a word and a document at the same time by visualizing embedding space. We execute the PCA on vectors of words with high frequency and all documents to reduce dimensionality.

The reduced word and document vectors obtained by the proposed model are shown in Figure 3 and 4, and we additionally show the visualization of full embedding space, including those documents, in Figure 5 in Appendix. In these figures, two representative documents are shown—a neuroscience article titled "The Role of Activity in Synaptic Competition at the Neuromuscular Junction," and a computer science article titled "Bayesian Model Comparison by Monte Carlo Chaining." Figure 3 enlarges reduced embedding space around the neuroscience article that shows words such as "signal," "neurons," and "Cortex." Figure 4 enlarges reduced embedding space around the computer science article that shows words such as "Bayesian," "iterations," "optimized," and "parameters."

From these figures, we can see that words related to topics of the article are correctly located. Therefore, we can see that the proposed model can locate document vectors appropriately in the word embedding space, which enhances the performance of the model.

5.2 Analyzing the Importance of Words in a Document

In the proposed model and the CSTM, the document vectors are defined in the same space as the word vectors. Therefore, based on the inner product of the document vector and the word vector, we can quantitatively measure the importance of words in a document, such as words that are likely to appear in a document and words that are not. For the calculation, we used the document and word vectors of all words in the training vocabulary, including words that do not actually appear in the document.

For example, for the proposed model and the CSTM, we used the neuroscience article in the NIPS corpus to compute the ranking of topic-related and topic-unrelated words in the document. Tables 4 and 5 show the results of the proposed model and the CSTM, respectively. We show the words that actually appear in the document in bold. Although both the results of the CSTM and the proposed model contain the words appearing in the document, we can see that the proposed model comparatively captures the topic of the document and gives high score to topic-related words. The topic-related words obtained using the CSTM accounted for a few words that were related to the topic of the document, whereas those obtained by using the proposed model accounted for a significant number of words that were related to the topic of the document, such as "axon," "synapses," and "nervous." This means that the probability of such words in the document will be reflected to a greater extent. Moreover, we observed that words among the topic-unrelated words obtained by applying the proposed model were not related to the topic of the document. Such words include "Euclidean,"

Table 4: Top 30 topic-related words and topic-unrelated words from the NIPS article, "The Role of Activity in Synaptic Competition at the Neuromuscular Junction," using the proposed model. The words that appear in the document are shown in bold.

e^f	Word	e^f	Word
113.7901	**axon**	0.0862	vector
27.7607	**synapses**	0.1197	convex
22.7449	**nervous**	0.1267	hidden
21.7567	brain	0.1280	Fisher
19.4746	**synaptic**	0.1306	derivative
16.0369	**interaction**	0.1308	Euclidean
15.9976	**mechanisms**	0.1332	classifiers
15.5423	fiber	0.1357	norm
15.4603	**stimulation**	0.1359	sigmoidal
15.0863	**presynaptic**	0.1420	observable
14.7511	**sites**	0.1476	gradient
14.6049	animal	0.1565	regression
14.2858	ocular	0.1582	computes
13.9519	interneurons	0.1620	corrupted
13.7734	**areas**	0.1624	squared
13.5084	**role**	0.1643	sampled
13.3584	**postsynaptic**	0.1645	minimized
13.3000	**plasticity**	0.1710	Gaussian
12.9953	inhibition	0.1809	speaker
12.8826	**dominance**	0.1818	discrete
12.8527	**muscle**	0.1843	unknown
12.7587	recordings	0.1909	defined
12.5784	**formation**	0.1910	feature
12.5326	**terminal**	0.1920	written
12.4104	growth	0.1927	LMS
12.2916	pathway	0.1971	PCA
12.0274	caused	0.2029	piecewise
11.8988	cues	0.2065	perceptron
11.6562	**effects**	0.2089	entropy
11.5566	**activated**	0.2138	bounds

Table 5: Top 30 topic-related words and topic-unrelated words from the NIPS article, "The Role of Activity in Synaptic Competition at the Neuromuscular Junction," using the CSTM. The words that appear in the document are shown in bold.

e^f	Word	e^f	Word
7.5986	adding	0.2744	silicon
7.0567	**extent**	0.3063	inequality
6.8850	relatively	0.3491	template
6.2375	recording	0.3565	schedule
6.0914	randomly	0.3582	ICA
5.9904	placed	0.3622	head
5.9894	**other**	0.3811	speaker
5.8748	specified	0.4120	filter
5.8090	write	0.4200	MLP
5.7228	adapted	0.4301	spin
5.1464	**terms**	0.4328	gate
5.0912	speed	0.4355	memory
5.0879	explicitly	0.4355	faces
4.9648	**when**	0.4386	orientation
4.8808	**demonstrate**	0.4503	PCA
4.8080	**range**	0.4520	nucleus
4.7802	share	0.4523	expansion
4.7197	section	0.4543	almost
4.6721	complicated	0.4552	functions
4.6541	partial	0.4593	variational
4.6538	conditions	0.4634	gates
4.6462	approximately	0.4715	boolean
4.6417	**actually**	0.4726	quantization
4.6161	practice	0.4758	contour
4.6149	**journal**	0.4816	Viterbi
4.6034	recognition	0.4845	chip
4.5872	overall	0.4899	pulses
4.5752	basic	0.4918	radial
4.5430	**single**	0.5009	MAP
4.5222	**theoretical**	0.5024	multilayer

"gradient," and "regression." We believe that this is because, unlike the CSTM, the proposed model has prior knowledge of the topical information of words, thereby facilitating the estimation of document vectors that capture a set of topically similar words.

5.3 Error Analysis of Document Classification

Table 6 shows the classification accuracy for eight category labels using each feature. The proposed model outperforms the CSTM substantially in all categories.

For example, the classification of "Speech Processing," the CSTM misclassified some of the documents as "Linguistics," "Psychology," and "Artificial Intelligence," while the proposed model classified almost all of the documents as "Speech Processing" except for some of the documents labeled "Linguistics." We find that the CSTM misclassified one of the documents in "Speech Processing," which discusses statistical methods in detail, as "Psychology," while the proposed model classified it correctly. The CSTM models word co-occurrence on a document-by-document basis as in Eq. 3, though multiple topics might exist in a document. Therefore, the document vectors obtained by the CSTM do not have the information of the semantic difference between psychology and statistics.

Table 6: Classification accuracy on the CSJ corpus for each category using learned embeddings.

Category	Count	CSTM	Ours	word2vec	Ours w/ word2vec
Speech Processing	413	0.761	**0.912**	0.956	**0.971**
Cosmology	248	1.000	1.000	1.000	1.000
Biology	247	1.000	1.000	1.000	1.000
Linguistics	206	0.452	**0.786**	0.790	**0.857**
Psychology	141	0.393	**0.721**	**0.857**	0.843
Artificial Intelligence	120	0.358	**0.592**	**0.825**	0.817
Language Education	62	0.417	**0.833**	**0.833**	0.817
Sociology	28	0.167	**0.400**	0.700	0.700
Total	1465	0.704	**0.866**	0.917	**0.928**

In contrast, the proposed model models word co-occurrence based on the local context of the neighborhood, where topics are considered to be somewhat consistent. Therefore, the proposed model can distinguish the word set that tends to appear in the genre of psychology from the genre of statistics in the embedding space. Hence, because the document vectors are estimated in the space where word vectors have the information of the semantic difference between psychology and statistics, the proposed model can distinguish those documents.

6 Conclusion and Future Work

In this study, we introduced the learned distributed representation of words into the CSTM to provide prior knowledge on the semantics of words. In the experiments, we showed that the proposed model outperformed the baseline method in terms of perplexity and convergence speed. Also, we showed that the proposed model is useful for a document classification task compared with the baseline model. Additionally, we showed that the document vectors obtained by training the model are superior through visualization of the embedding space and analysis of importance of words in a document.

In the future, we would like to investigate better ways of estimating the model, including optimization by applying the Hamiltonian MCMC algorithm, which was not used in this study. Furthermore, we would like to use contextualized word embeddings obtained by ELMo (Peters et al., 2018) or BERT (Devlin et al., 2019) in the proposed model.

References

Mohit Bansal, Kevin Gimpel, and Karen Livescu. 2014. Tailoring continuous word representations for dependency parsing. In *Proceedings of the 52nd Annual Meeting of the Association for Computational Linguistics*, pages 809–815.

David M Blei, Andrew Y Ng, and Michael I Jordan. 2003. Latent Dirichlet allocation. *Journal of Machine Learning Research*, 3:993–1022.

Jonathan Chang, Jordan Boyd-Graber, Chong Wang, Sean Gerrish, and David M Blei. 2009. Reading tea leaves: How humans interpret topic models. *Advances in Neural Information Processing Systems*, 22:288–296.

Rajarshi Das, Manzil Zaheer, and Chris Dyer. 2015. Gaussian LDA for topic models with word embeddings. In *Proceedings of the 53nd Annual Meeting of the Association for Computational Linguistics*, pages 795–804.

Jacob Devlin, Ming-Wei Chang, Kenton Lee, and Kristina Toutanova. 2019. BERT: Pre-training of deep bidirectional transformers for language understanding. In *Proceedings of the 2019 Conference of the North American Chapter of the Association for Computational Linguistics: Human Language Technologies, Volume 1 (Long and Short Papers)*, pages 4171–4186.

Adji B Dieng, Francisco JR Ruiz, and David M Blei. 2020. Topic modeling in embedding spaces. *Transactions of the Association for Computational Linguistics*, 8:439–453.

Gabriel Doyle and Charles Elkan. 2009. Accounting for burstiness in topic models. In *Proceedings of the 26th Annual International Conference on Machine Learning*, pages 281–288.

Kazuo Hara, Ikumi Suzuki, Masashi Shimbo, Kei Kobayashi, Kenji Fukumizu, and Miloš Radovanović. 2015. Localized centering: Reducing hubness in large-sample data. In *Proceedings of the AAAI Conference on Artificial Intelligence*, volume 4, pages 2645–2651.

Zellig S Harris. 1954. Distributional structure. *Word*, 10(2-3):146–162.

Chenghua Lin, Yulan He, Richard Everson, and Stefan Ruger. 2011. Weakly supervised joint sentiment-topic detection from text. *IEEE Transactions on Knowledge and Data Engineering*, 24(6):1134–1145.

Benjamin M Marlin. 2003. Modeling user rating profiles for collaborative filtering. *Advances in Neural Information Processing Systems*, 16:627–634.

Tomas Mikolov, Kai Chen, Greg Corrado, and Jeffrey Dean. 2013. Efficient estimation of word representations in vector space. In *Proceedings of the International Conference on Learning Representations*.

Daichi Mochihashi, Kazuyoshi Yoshii, and Masataka Goto. 2013. Modeling text through Gaussian processes. In *Information Processing Society of Japan Special Interest Groups Technical Report*, volume 2013-NL-213, pages 1–8.

Jiaqi Mu and Pramod Viswanath. 2018. All-but-the-top: Simple and effective post-processing for word representations. In *6th International Conference on Learning Representations, ICLR 2018*.

Radford M Neal et al. 2011. MCMC using Hamiltonian dynamics. *Handbook of Markov Chain Monte Carlo*, 2(11):2.

John Paisley, Chong Wang, and David Blei. 2011. The discrete infinite logistic normal distribution for mixed-membership modeling. In *Proceedings of the Fourteenth International Conference on Artificial Intelligence and Statistics*, pages 74–82.

Matthew Peters, Mark Neumann, Mohit Iyyer, Matt Gardner, Christopher Clark, Kenton Lee, and Luke Zettlemoyer. 2018. Deep contextualized word representations. In *Proceedings of the 2018 Conference of the North American Chapter of the Association for Computational Linguistics: Human Language Technologies, Volume 1 (Long Papers)*, pages 2227–2237.

Carl Edward Rasmussen and Christopher KI Williams. 2006. Gaussian processes for machine learning. *MA: the MIT Press*.

Michal Rosen-Zvi, Thomas Griffiths, Mark Steyvers, and Padhraic Smyth. 2012. The author-topic model for authors and documents. In *Proceedings of the 20th Conference on Uncertainty in Artificial Intelligence*, page 487–494.

Hanna M Wallach, Iain Murray, Ruslan Salakhutdinov, and David Mimno. 2009. Evaluation methods for topic models. In *Proceedings of the 26th Annual International Conference on Machine Learning*, pages 1105–1112.

Xing Wei and W Bruce Croft. 2006. LDA-based document models for ad-hoc retrieval. In *Proceedings of the 29th Annual International ACM SIGIR Conference on Research and Development in Information Retrieval*, pages 178–185.

A Visualization of Embedding Space

We show the visualization of full embedding space, including neuroscience article and computer science article, in Figure 5.

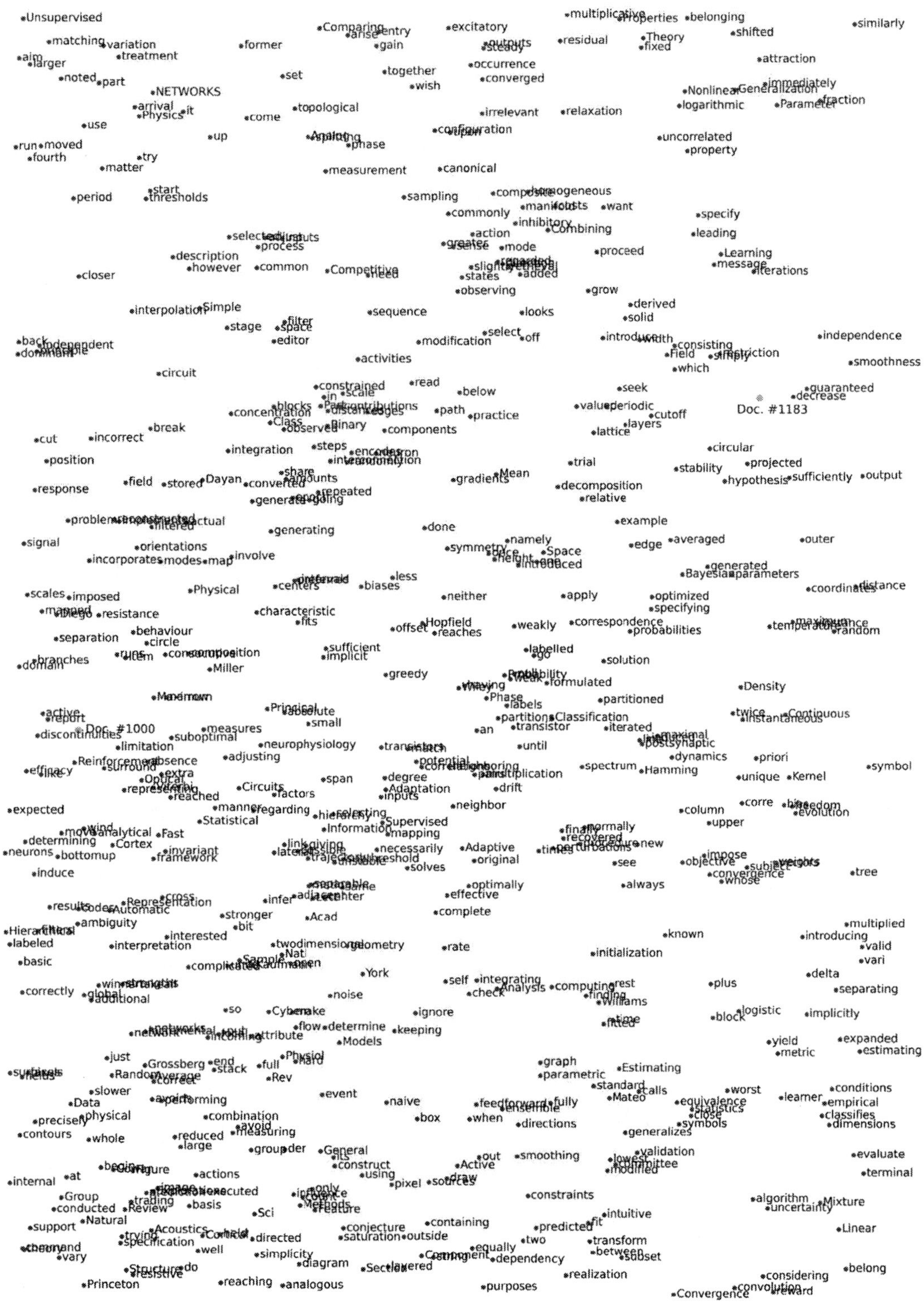

Figure 5: The visualization of reduced embedding space using the proposed model. Words are colored as blue and documents as orange.

Semantics of the Unwritten: The Effect of End of Paragraph and Sequence Tokens on Text Generation with GPT2

He Bai,[1] Peng Shi,[1] Jimmy Lin,[1,2]
Luchen Tan,[2] Kun Xiong,[2] Wen Gao,[4] Jie Liu,[3] Ming Li [1,2]
[1] David R. Cheriton School of Computer Science, University of Waterloo
[2] RSVP.ai [3] Capital Normal University
[4] School of Electronics Engineering and Computer Science, Peking University
he.bai@uwaterloo.ca

Abstract

The semantics of a text is manifested not only by what is read, but also by what is not read. In this article, we will study how the implicit "not read" information such as end-of-paragraph (EOP) and end-of-sequence (EOS) affect the quality of text generation. Specifically, we find that the pre-trained language model GPT2 can generate better continuations by learning to generate the EOP in the fine-tuning stage. Experimental results on English story generation show that EOP can lead to higher BLEU score and lower EOS perplexity. We also conduct experiments on a self-collected Chinese essay dataset with Chinese-GPT2, a character level LM without EOP or EOS during pre-training. Experimental results show that the Chinese GPT2 can generate better essay endings with EOP. Our code is available on GitHub.[1]

1 Introduction

Large-pretrained neural models such as GPT (Radford, 2018) and BERT (Devlin et al., 2019) have achieved the state-of-the-art on many NLP tasks. Among these models, OpenAI's GPT2 (Radford et al., 2019), for example, has shown to be capable of generating long fluent text in many areas, such as stories (See et al., 2019), recipes (H. Lee et al., 2020), patent claims (Lee and Hsiang, 2019), and news (Zellers et al., 2019). However, the semantics of a text goes beyond what's written to what's not written: When to break paragraphs and when to end. We wish to experiment on this issue: How much do EOP and EOS markers affect our ability to generate texts with GPT2.

To study the strength of GPT2 as a language generator, See et al. (2019) conduct experiments in the context of story generation with the WritingPrompts (Fan et al., 2018) dataset. They find that the generated results of GPT2 have higher-quality content (using more rare words, concrete words, and named entities) by comparing the top 150 generated words. However, the average story length of the dataset is 12 paragraphs, 368 words. In such lengthy human writings, the overall layout and text endings are also important, but whether the GPT2 can generate them properly is unclear, and how to generate better endings has not been investigated.

In this work, we find the generated endings are not only affected by EOS, but also EOP. EOP can also help improve the topic relevance of the generated text. We first conduct essay completion experiments with Chinese GPT2 (Zhang, 2019), which is a character-level LM without EOS or EOP during pre-training. Experimental results show that fine-tuning with EOP can achieve higher ending quality score and topic relevance score in human evaluation. We further conduct story generation experiments on dataset WritingPrompts with English GPT2-117, which holds the line break "\n" (NL) in the vocabulary. Thus, the NL can be treated as the end-of-paragraph during fine-tuning (Mao et al., 2019). Experimental results show that learning to end the paragraph can benefit the word/token perplexity, BLUE score, EOS perplexity, and human evaluated ending quality score.

Our contributions are as follows: We show that not only the well-known EOS but also the EOP, is part of the semantics of a text, and training with this information improves the text generation itself. The paragraph information not only can help improve the effectiveness of the generation model but also help to generate the end of the text. We also investigate different approaches to incorporating paragraph information into the LM generator. Our findings indicate that SEP/EOP and EOS should be introduced to GPT2 types of models during pre-training, to generate better text in length.

[1] https://github.com/rsvp-ai/semantic_unwritten

Proceedings of the Joint Conference of the 59th Annual Meeting of the Association for Computational Linguistics and the 11th International Joint Conference on Natural Language Processing: Student Research Workshop, pages 148–162
August 5–6, 2021. ©2021 Association for Computational Linguistics

2 Background

Our target task is to conduct auto-regressive language modeling over WritingPrompts and the ChineseEssay dataset. The basic assumption of auto-regressive generation is that the probability of a word sequence equals the product of conditional word probability: $P(w_{1:T}|W_0) = \prod_{t=1}^{T} P(w_t|w_{1:t-1}, W_0)$ where W_0 is the given context, and in this work, W_0 can be a story prompt or the beginning of an essay. The generated sequence length T is usually determined by the time t generating the EOS (end-of-sequence) token: $P(w_T|w_{1:T-1}, W_0) = P(\text{EOS}|w_{1:t-1}, W_0)$ In this work, the model computing the conditional probabilities is self-attention Transformer (Vaswani et al., 2017). We train our model with the cross-entropy loss between the predicted conditional probabilities and the ground-truth next token.

When the target of generation consists of multiple paragraphs, there are several approaches to indicating the paragraph ending. The most common and obvious approach is to separate paragraphs with line break NL: $w_{1:T} = p_1, \text{NL}, ..., p_{n-1}, \text{NL}, p_n, \text{EOS}$ where $p_i = \{w_{b_i:e_i}\}$ is the words sequence of paragraph i, from the beginning word w_{b_i} to the ending word w_{e_i}. However, not every paragraph ends with NL, and during the pre-training, not every NL represents the paragraph separator (SEP) . A better option is to append a new specific token EOP to indicate the end of the paragraph: $w_{1:T} = p'_1, ..., p'_{n-1}, p'_n, \text{EOS}$ where $p'_i = \{w_{b_i:e_i}, \text{EOP}\}$. Then, each paragraph can end with the EOP and the transformer-based language model can learn this feature with every paragraph in the training data, without distinguishing when to generate EOP and when not to.

It is well known that greedy decoding and beam search usually lead to repetitive and degenerate outputs(Shang et al., 2015; Massarelli et al., 2019). Sampling-based decoding methods have shown a strong ability in generating diversity, fluency and repetitiveness of the generation with pre-trained language models, such as *top-k* and *top-p* sampling. In this work, we choose the *top-p* sampling decoding algorithm and set the p equals to 0.95.

3 Experiments

3.1 Datasets

Story Generation. The story generation dataset is the WritingPrompts, collected by Fan et al. (2018) from Reddit. It is a large dataset of 300K human-written stories. Each instance of this dataset is the pair of a short prompt and a long story. Following See et al. (2019), we exclude examples that are longer than 1024 BPE tokens to meet the maximum length restriction of GPT2. Statistics for this dataset are detailed in Table 1. We sample 1000 examples from the test set for decoding.

Dataset	Story	Essay
Language	English	Chinese
#Train samples	199,083	1,615
#Test samples	11,069	461
#Validation samples	11,474	195
#Avg. words per sample	367.9	571.3
#Avg. paragraphs per sample	12.1	5.6

Table 1: Detailed information of the filtered WritingPrompts dataset and the ChineseEssay dataset.

Essay Completion. We build an essay completion dataset ChineseEssay, which is collected from primary school and annotated by native Chinese annotators. All these essays are descriptive essays about people, such as family members and teachers. Hence, compared with the WritingPrompts, this dataset is smaller but less open domain. Dataset statistics are also shown in Table 1.

3.2 Experimental Settings

Model Configuration. For Chinese essay generation, we use Chinese-GPT2 (Zhang, 2019), which is a 48 layers Transformer with 1.5 billion parameters, pre-trained with 15GB Chinese corpus. For story generation, we fine-tune the OpenAI's GPT2-117 with WritingPrompts following previous work (See et al., 2019; Mao et al., 2019). The GPT2-117 model has 12 layers and 117 million parameters. During fine-tuning, the batch size is 32 and the warm-up steps are 800. The other hyperparameters are the same as the default setting of Huggingface Transformers (Wolf et al., 2019). Models can converge after 15 epochs for GPT2-117 and 3 epochs for Chinese-GPT2. The checkpoints with the best evaluation results on validation set are chosen for further testing.

Automatic Metrics. We use the following metrics: perplexity over all words/tokens (W/T PPL); perplexity over words/tokens excluding EOS/EOP/SEP (W/T PPL(-)); perplexity of EOS (EOS PPL); percentage of the generated texts that are ending with EOS (EOS%); BLEU/Distinct score excluding EOS/EOP/SEP (BLEU/DIST). All perplexities are macro-average.

ParaType	FT	EOS	T PPL	T PPL(-)	BLEU1	BLEU2	DIST1	DIST2	EOS%	EOS PPL
None	No	No	12.12	11.48	33.6	7.5	34.46	73.95	0	-
	Yes	No	11.44	11.44	38.1	9.9	32.95	73.96	0	-
	Yes	Yes	10.43	**10.42**	42.7	10.7	37.57	78.26	76.41	22.15
SEP DIY	Yes	Yes	10.45	10.52	44.1	11	38.73	78.98	90.26	8.92
EOP DIY	Yes	Yes	**10.34**	10.48	**45.4**	**11.2**	**40.18**	**80.61**	**93.07**	**2.74**

Table 2: Test results of different models with/without fine-tuning(FT) on ChineseEssay dataset.

ParaType	FT	W PPL	W PPL(-)	T PPL	T PPL(-)	EOS PPL	BLEU1	BLEU2	DIST1	DIST2
None	No	42.53	42.20	34.42	34.17	295.50	20.3	2.2	**58.87**	**89.78**
	Yes	31.34	31.35	25.81	25.81	4.63	30.4	4.6	50.07	87.12
SEP	No	39.97	42.00	32.43	33.79	102.93	20.3	2.2	58.87	89.78
	Yes	**29.36**	**31.24**	**24.23**	**25.57**	4.32	31.2	4.3	50.15	85.88
SEP DIY	Yes	30.23	32.17	24.99	26.38	4.48	31.5	6.8	48.57	83.84
EOP NL	No	40.10	41.84	32.52	33.68	26478.91	20.3	2.2	58.87	89.78
	Yes	29.95	31.32	24.70	25.63	20534.60	30.7	4.3	49.79	85.44
EOP DIY	Yes	30.18	32.21	24.95	26.41	**2.26**	**31.7**	**6.9**	48.32	83.82

Table 3: Test results on WritingPrompts dataset.

Human Evaluation Metrics. We also conduct the human evaluation with 50 random samples from the test set. For ChineseEssay, we collect generations from EOS fine-tuned model, EOS+EOP fine-tuned model, and EOS+SEP fine-tuned model. For WritingPrompts, we collect generations from the model fine-tuned with EOP and the model without SEP/EOP. Four native speakers are asked to compare the generations of different systems in pairs over four metrics: topic relevance, fluency, ending quality, and overall preference. The assessors were presented with pairs of generated output and asked to make a three way judgment: whether the "left system" was better, the "right system" was better, or "cannot distinguish". The latter option either meant that both output were equally good, or equally bad. To prevent inadvertent bias, all systems were blinded, i.e., the assessors did not know which system generated which output, and presentation order was randomized. After annotation, we count the total times of each system outperforming the others, and then normalize to 0-100%.

4 Results

The results of different settings of utilizing paragraph information (ParaType) are shown in Table 2 and Table 3: concatenating all paragraphs into an uninterrupted sequence (None); concatenating all paragraphs with "\n" as the paragraph separator (SEP NL); concatenating all paragraphs with a new token "[SEP]" as the paragraph separator (SEP DIY); appending "\n" to the end of each paragraph (EOP NL); appending a new token "[EOP]" to the end of each paragraph (EOP DIY).

Automatic Metrics. For Chinese essay generation, since Chinese-GPT2 is pre-trained without any special tokens(EOS/EOP/SEP), it will keep generating until meet the max length limitation without fine-tuning. In this case, we first compare None models fine-tuned with and without EOS in Table 2. We can find that both T PPL (-) and BLEU scores are better with EOS. However, even fine-tuned with EOS, only 76.41% generated texts can end with EOS. After adding EOS, the EOS PPL plunges from 22.15 to 2.74 and the EOS% rising from 76.41 to 93.07, indicating that more generated essays end with the EOS after learning to end paragraphs. The BLEU scores are also improved. It should be noted that the BLEU score is affected by the length of the text. We further truncate all generations with the length of the ground-truth story to calculate the truncated BLEU scores which are detailed in Appendix A and the overall trending is consistent. Finally, the ground-truth essays get 41.2 DIST1 and 82.65 DIST2, which means EOS DIY achieves the closest DIST scores to the ground-truths.

On the other hand, English GPT2 is pre-trained with EOS and line break NL. Hence, we first compare GPT2 fine-tuned without NL, with NL, and with new token "[SEP]"/"[EOP]". According to the Table 3, we can find that the fine-tuned GPT2 with NL as SEP achieves the best results on word and token level perplexity metrics. Compared with the model fine-tuned without paragraph information, all the models with EOP/SEP achieve better BLEU scores. We further report the length truncated BLEU scores in Appendix A. The overall trending is consistent. As for diversity score, the DIST1 and DIST2 of the ground-truth stories are 50.23 and 85.07, and the SEP NL is the most close

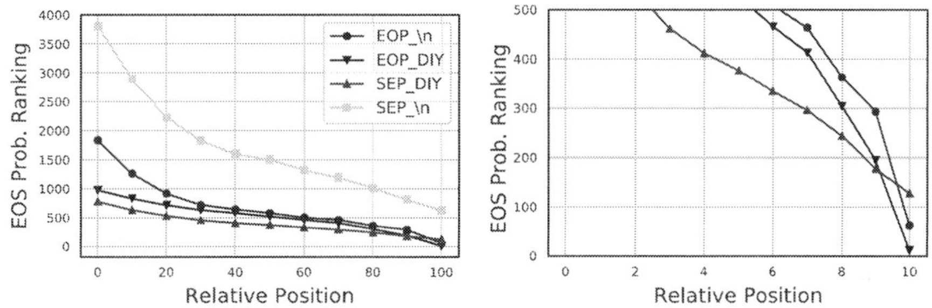

(a) Global View (b) Local View

Figure 1: Relationships between paragraph relative position and the ranking of the EOS probability predicted by the last token of each paragraph.

(a) Topic relevance

	None	SEP	EOP
None		43	45
SEP	57		52
EOP	55	48	

(b) Fluency

	None	SEP	EOP
None		47	53
SEP	53		54
EOP	47	46	

(c) Ending quality

	None	SEP	EOP
None		37	34
SEP	63		49
EOP	66	51	

(d) Overall preference

	None	SEP	EOP
None		42	47
SEP	58		50
EOP	53	50	

Figure 2: Average percentage of systems in row outperform system in column. Results are normalized without considering the Cannot Distinguish examples.

(a) Topic relevance

	None	SEP	EOP
None		0.89	0.69
SEP	0.89		0.70
EOP	0.69	0.70	

(b) Fluency

	None	SEP	EOP
None		0.61	0.60
SEP	0.61		0.65
EOP	0.60	0.65	

(c) Ending quality

	None	SEP	EOP
None		0.68	0.63
SEP	0.68		0.71
EOP	0.63	0.71	

(d) Overall preference

	None	SEP	EOP
None		0.52	0.34
SEP	0.52		0.51
EOP	0.34	0.51	

Figure 3: Fleiss' kappa κ (Fleiss, 1971) for the reliability of raters' agreement. The interpretation of κ's value should be: poor agreement (< 0), slight agreement (0.01–0.2), fair agreement (0.21–0.4), moderate agreement (0.41–0.6), substantial agreement (0.61–0.8), and almost perfect agreement (0.81–1).

one. In addition to the better PPL and BLEU score, we find that learning to end paragraphs can benefit the prediction of EOS. The EOP DIY achieves the lowest EOS PPL and all models trained with EOP/EOS achieve better EOS PPL than model without paragraph information, except the EOP NL. This observation indicates that GPT2 tends not to generate the EOS following the NL even after finetuning, but it can learn better EOS with the help of a new EOP token.

We further compared the relations between EOS and different EOP/SEP, which is shown in Figure 1. The horizontal axis represents the relative paragraph index, 0 means the beginning paragraph and 100 means the last paragraph of the story. The vertical axis represents the ranking position of the EOS probability among all tokens in the vocabulary predicted by the last token of each paragraph. As EOS should only be predicted by the last token of the last paragraph, the ranking at 100 should be higher and the other position should be lower. According to Figure 1(a), all models rank EOS higher as the paragraph index increasing. EOP works better than SEP as the EOP models rank EOS higher at the 100th position and lower on the other positions, which can be seen from Figure 1(b).

Human Evaluations. Human evaluation results are shown in Figure 2. Each cell represents the percentage of the examples that the row system wins the column system on. Cells will be filled in blue if the row system outperforms the column system over 10%. It should be noted that Cannot Distinguish examples are skipped when counting winners for these figures. From Figure 2, we can first find that learning to end paragraphs leads to better ending quality: 63% and 66% results are rated better when comparing SEP/EOP with None systems, while only 37% and 34% results are rated better for None system. We also find that EOP's text endings are slightly better than SEP. This is consistent with EOS PPL and EOS% results in Table 2. Although SEP wins on topic relevance and

(a) Topic relevance	None	EOP
None		45
EOP	55	

(b) Fluency	None	EOP
None		51
EOP	49	

(c) Ending quality	None	EOP
None		43
EOP	57	

(d) Overall preference	None	EOP
None		47
EOP	53	

Figure 4: Average percentage of systems in row outperform system in column.

(a) Topic relevance	None	EOP
None		0.67
EOP	0.67	

(b) Fluency	None	EOP
None		0.69
EOP	0.69	

(c) Ending quality	None	EOP
None		0.72
EOP	0.72	

(d) Overall preference	None	EOP
None		0.58
EOP	0.58	

Figure 5: Fleiss' kappa κ (ranging from -1.0 to 1.0) for the reliability of raters' agreement.

fluency, the overall preference of SEP compared with EOP is 50%, which means these two systems are similar for human rates. Besides, we also find that SEP and EOP achieve better topic relevance and overall preference. For fluency, there is no significant difference among different systems.

We also report Fleiss' kappa κ in Figure 3, to access the reliabilities of raters' agreement. $\kappa < 0$ means poor agreement, and $\kappa \sim (0.6, 0.8)$ means substantial agreement. From this figure, we can find that most of them fall into the substantial agreement group. The overall preference falls into moderate agreement, because this metric is more subjective than the others.

Human evaluation results for WritingPrompts are shown in Figure 4 and Figure 5. Assessors still prefer model fine-tuned with EOP rather than without EOP/SEP.

Case Study. We further conduct case study and detailed in Appendix B. The most important observation is that, without EOP, the beginning of the generation is more relevant to the end of the input prompt, but the more it generates, the poor quality is. While the generator with EOP can generate multiple paragraphs related to the input with a reasonable ending but each paragraph is more independent than human writings.

5 Conclusion

In this paper, we have demonstrated that EOP and EOS information helps generating better text. Chinese GPT2 and English GPT2 are two existing models pre-trained without and with EOP respectively, which provides a perfect platform for our proposed experiments. On the ChineseEssay dataset, the text generation when fine-tuned with EOP and EOS information is significantly improved. On the other hand for the English task, although (English) GPT-2 was trained with NL which serves as EOP to some degree, learning to end paragraphs can still benefit the story generation in terms of automatic metrics and human evaluation results.

Acknowledgments

This work was supported by National Key Research and Development Program of China (2020AAA0109700), National Natural Science Foundation of China (62076167), and partially supported by NSERC OGP0046506.

We would like to thank Wei Zeng and his team in Peng Cheng Laboratory (PCL) for computing resources to support this project.

References

Jacob Devlin, Ming-Wei Chang, Kenton Lee, and Kristina Toutanova. 2019. BERT: pre-training of deep bidirectional transformers for language understanding. In *NAACL-HLT 2019, Minneapolis, MN, USA, June 2-7, 2019*, pages 4171–4186.

Angela Fan, Mike Lewis, and Yann N. Dauphin. 2018. Hierarchical neural story generation. In *ACL 2018, Melbourne, Australia, July 15-20, 2018*, pages 889–898.

Joseph L Fleiss. 1971. Measuring nominal scale agreement among many raters. *Psychological bulletin*, 76(5):378.

Helena H. Lee, Ke Shu, Palakorn Achananuparp, Philips Kokoh Prasetyo, Yue Liu, Ee-Peng Lim, and Lav R Varshney. 2020. RecipeGPT: Generative pre-training based cooking recipe generation and evaluation system. In *Companion Proceedings of the Web Conference 2020*, pages 181–184.

Jieh-Sheng Lee and Jieh Hsiang. 2019. Patent claim generation by fine-tuning OpenAI GPT-2. *CoRR*, abs/1907.02052.

Huanru Henry Mao, Bodhisattwa Prasad Majumder, Julian J. McAuley, and Garrison W. Cottrell. 2019. Improving neural story generation by targeted common sense grounding. In *EMNLP-IJCNLP 2019, Hong Kong, China, November 3-7, 2019*, pages 5987–5992. Association for Computational Linguistics.

Luca Massarelli, Fabio Petroni, Aleksandra Piktus, Myle Ott, Tim Rocktäschel, Vassilis Plachouras, Fabrizio Silvestri, and Sebastian Riedel. 2019. How decoding strategies affect the verifiability of generated text. *CoRR*, abs/1911.03587.

Alec Radford. 2018. Improving language understanding by generative pre-training.

Alec Radford, Jeffrey Wu, Rewon Child, David Luan, Dario Amodei, and Ilya Sutskever. 2019. Language models are unsupervised multitask learners.

Abigail See, Aneesh Pappu, Rohun Saxena, Akhila Yerukola, and Christopher D. Manning. 2019. Do massively pretrained language models make better storytellers? In *CoNLL 2019, Hong Kong, China, November 3-4, 2019*, pages 843–861. Association for Computational Linguistics.

Lifeng Shang, Zhengdong Lu, and Hang Li. 2015. Neural responding machine for short-text conversation. In *ACL 2015, July 26-31, 2015, Beijing, China, Volume 1: Long Papers*, pages 1577–1586. The Association for Computer Linguistics.

Ashish Vaswani, Noam Shazeer, Niki Parmar, Jakob Uszkoreit, Llion Jones, Aidan N. Gomez, Lukasz Kaiser, and Illia Polosukhin. 2017. Attention is all you need. In *NeurIPS 2017, 4-9 December 2017, Long Beach, CA, USA*, pages 5998–6008.

Thomas Wolf, Lysandre Debut, Victor Sanh, Julien Chaumond, Clement Delangue, Anthony Moi, Pierric Cistac, Tim Rault, Rémi Louf, Morgan Funtowicz, and Jamie Brew. 2019. Huggingface's transformers: State-of-the-art natural language processing. *CoRR*, abs/1910.03771.

Rowan Zellers, Ari Holtzman, Hannah Rashkin, Yonatan Bisk, Ali Farhadi, Franziska Roesner, and Yejin Choi. 2019. Defending against neural fake news. In *NeurIPS 2019, 8-14 December 2019, Vancouver, BC, Canada*, pages 9051–9062.

Zhibo Zhang. 2019. GPT2-ML: GPT-2 for Multiple Languages. `https://github.com/imcaspar/gpt2-ml`.

Appendix Overview

In this supplementary material, we provide additional experimental results of truncated BLEU score in Appendix A, and several generations in Appendix B.

A Truncated BLEU Score

The BLEU score is easily affected by the length of text, where a short text might achieve a higher BLEU score than a long text. The average lengths of the texts generated from different methods are shown in Table 5 and Table 4. An intuitive metric for this problem is the truncated BLEU (T-BLEU) score.

To get the T-BLEU score, we first truncate the generated text with the length of its corresponding ground-truth text. Then, the BLEU score of the truncated text is the T-BLEU score.

As we can see from Table 5 and Table 4, although the BLEU score improvements of EOP/SEP become less significant on the Chinese dataset, the overall trending is similar with the normal BLEU scores.

B Case Study

We first conduct case studies with Chinese GPT2. Case B.1 and Case B.2 are two cherry-picked examples.

The prompt of the first example Case B.1 is about the author's teacher. After finetuning without paragraph information, we can see that the generated continuation is related to the given prompt but pays too much attention to the gifts instead of the teacher, and generating something about the financial problem in the beginning. Although the middle portion of the continuation is well written, the latter half part is poor, incomplete and hard to be understood. In contrast, the continuation generated with EOP is much better, although with minor errors of word choice. Besides, the ending of the latter one is much better as the former one just keeps generating until reaches the maximum length.

Similar trending can be found in the second example Case B.2. According to our observation, without EOP, the beginning of the generation is more relevant to the end of the input prompt but the more it generates, the poor the quality is. While the generator with EOP can generate multiple paragraphs related to the input with a reasonable ending but each paragraph is more independent than human writings.

We further investigate the story generation results. Two different cases are shown in Case B.3 and Case B.4. In the first case, the generation of DIY EOP is better than NL SEP, as it mentions the aliens multiple times and also generates the time "100 years" while the other one only talks about the planet. In Case B.4, NL SEP is better than DIY EOP. The generator fine-tuned without paragraph information is the poorest in these two cases, which is consistent with our experimental results and indicates the paragraph information can benefit the story generation.

ParaType	FT	EOS	T-BLEU1	T-BLEU2	Avg.Length
None	No	No	42.6	9.0	814.1
	Yes	No	48.0	11.6	793.5
	Yes	Yes	49.2	11.9	632.0
SEP DIY	Yes	Yes	49.4	12.0	576.7
EOP DIY	Yes	Yes	49.6	12.0	535.4
GroundTruth	-	-	-	-	571.3

Table 4: Average length and truncated BLEU scores of different models on ChineseEssay dataset.

ParaType	FT	T-BLEU1	T-BLEU2	Avg.Length
None	Yes	36.6	5.3	392.7
SEP NL	Yes	37.6	5.0	367.4
EOP NL	Yes	37.3	5.0	368.0
SEP DIY	Yes	38.6	8.0	385.7
EOP DIY	Yes	38.6	8.1	379.6
GroundTruth	-	-	-	369.3

Table 5: Average length and truncated BLEU scores of different models with finetuning on WritingPrompts dataset.

B.1 Case 1 of Chinese-GPT2

Input prompt:
老师，就像辛勤的园丁，每天都向我们灌溉知识。老师，就像一支红烛，照亮了我们，燃尽了自己。老师，就像那苍天大树，而我们，就是树下的一棵小草。老师，就像那蓝天上的白云，而我们，就是自由翱翔的小鸟。老师，就像那无尽的海水，而我们，就是哪快乐畅游的小鱼。老师，就像那广袤无垠的大草原，而我们，就是哪草原上奔腾的骏马。

每年快到教师节的时候，我都会无比的感谢老师，因为，有了老师，我们就是幸福的人，比那些在大山上不了学的，我们是多么的幸运。有了老师，我们就是有了尾巴的鱼，在无尽的知识里畅游。有了老师，我们就像有了翅膀的雄鹰，在蔚蓝的天空中，自由翱翔。

我今年小学毕业，我离开了上了6年的小学，那里有熟知的人，熟悉的教室，可是那就是过去，是我回忆的地方，每年的教师节，我听到我们班主任说的最多的一句话就是：下次别再送了礼物了，我要的不是那些礼物，我要的是你们学习的态度，如果，你们要送的话，就送些手工做的，可以旧物利用，比如，叠个千纸鹤了，叠个星星了，都可以，不要用钱买，有那份钱，也可以买些学习用品。

Brief Translation:
I am grateful to my teacher. The teacher's guidance to us is essential like the tail to the fish and the wings to the eagle. This year, I have graduated from primary school which is a place full of good memories. I still remember that every Teachers' Day, my teacher told us not to waste money to prepare gifts for her, as learning together is the best gift.

Figure 6: Chinese input prompt and English translation.

Output of Chinese-GPT2 fine-tuned without EOP:
我记得有一次，班主任说有同学家里穷，需要资助，因为我们很多同学都没有孩子(unreasonable)，一般都是自己挣钱，所以，我们同学的爸爸妈妈都说：”你们没钱没权，家里的爸妈都没有孩子(unreasonable)，这对我们来说是一种压力，因为我们的父母的学历都比你们高，就算我们再穷，我们也要好好读书，不然到时候就没的读了。”我听到这句话，心里像扎了根针一样，痛。我希望老师知道我的心声，并对我进行语文课程的辅导，让我能更加好的理解课文。谢谢老师，让我在欢笑中学习知识，学会感恩，学会感谢辛苦付出的老师。老师，我们是彩虹，落在心里最美的地方，遇到，便是老天最大的幸运，让我们用最美的彩虹，每天绽放最灿烂的彩虹，为我们的校园增添一缕鲜花 (*good continuation but should stop here.*) す她，虽已不在人世，但我永远不会忘记她，为了我，我愿用自己全部的青春献出自己的真心，把我对老师的感谢埋进心底，告诉父母：我对老师的感恩，与幸福一样宝贵。笨呀，笨死了，我送了一本漫画书给她。我看到了她泪眼婆娑，一脸的疲惫，并且嘴里还喃喃着：”对不起，我是单亲家庭，不能送你一本书了。”我哽咽着，扶了扶眼镜，他一把拽住了我的衣服：”这有什么，我都已经这样了，还想着你，你居然还想走.....”我再三道谢，沉默地笑了。笨呀，有什么好抱怨的，我不知道以后怎么办，以后，我愿不(*incomplete*)

Modified Google Translation:
I remember a time when my teacher told us that one of our classmates need financial assistance, because many of **our classmates had no children**(*unreasonable*) and generally made their own money, so our classmates' moms and dads said," You have no money and no rights. **Parents has no children**(*unreasonable*) , which is a stress for us, because our parents have higher academic qualifications than you. Even if we are poor, we must study well, otherwise we will have no chance of studying. " At this point, my heart hurts like be inserted in a needle. **I hope that the teacher will know my minds and provide me with Chinese language tutoring so that I can better understand the text. Thank you teacher, let me learn knowledge happily, learn to be grateful, learn to thank the hard-working teacher. Teacher, we are the rainbow. We fall in the most beautiful place in our hearts. When we meet, it is the greatest luck. Let us use the most beautiful rainbowe brightest rainbow every day and add a ray of flowers to our campus.** (*good continuation but should stop here.*) [garbled tokens], she has passed away but I will never forget her. I told my mother that I am grateful to my teacher. I don't know what to do. In the future, I hope not(*incomplete*)

Figure 7: Generation from Chinese-GPT2 fine-tuned without EOP.

Output of Chinese-GPT2 fine-tuned with EOP:
老师，这是一个实实在在的老师，她知识渊博，课堂上，她激发我们的斗志，课下，她严格，刻苦，为我们全班同学排忧解难，可是在我的生活中，我最敬佩的老师是一位母亲，老师，是用爱心来温暖，去回报，用知识来创造美丽幸福的人。有了老师的教导，我们就像上帝创造出来的天使，是最纯净的天空，没有感伤，没有痛苦，每一天，我都在老师的呵护下，享受天伦之乐(*unreasonable*)，是您指引着我们，走向未来，是您为我们付出了许多，是您使我们在知识的海洋里健康地成长。

曾经有一位心灵手巧的老师，让我们学会手工活，学会穿衣服，学会修剪指甲，收拾桌椅，学会穿衣服，学会洗衣服......她就是我们的语文老师。说真的，我心里很感激我的语文老师。她教会我们词语的讲解和组合，教会我们汉字的发音，曾经我的心情很低落，她的安慰，为我指点迷津，让我重新燃起了奋斗的斗志。

我会好好的学习，才不会辜负老师的期望呢！[EOS]

Modified Google Translation:
Teacher, this is a trustworthy teacher. She is very knowledgeable. In class, she inspires our fighting spirit. After class, she is strict and diligent. She solves problems for our classmates. The teacher is a mother, a teacher, a person who warms with love, returns, and uses knowledge to create beautiful and happy people. With the teaching of the teacher, we are like the angel created by God. It is the purest sky, no sentimentality, no pain. Every day, I am under the care of the teacher and enjoy the **family fun**(*unreasonable*). It is you who lead us to the future, it is you who paid a lot for us, and it is you who made us grow up healthy in the ocean of knowledge.
There used to be a handy teacher who taught us how to work by hand, how to dress, how to trim nails, how to clean tables and chairs, how to dress, how to wash clothes ... she is our Chinese language teacher. Seriously, I am very grateful to my Chinese teacher. She taught us the explanation and combination of words, taught us the pronunciation of Chinese characters. And when I was depressed, her consolation gave me pointers to help me rekindle my fighting spirit.
I will study hard so that I will not disappoint the teacher's expectations!

Figure 8: Generation from Chinese-GPT2 fine-tuned with EOP.

B.2 Case 2 of Chinese-GPT2

Input Prompt:
那时，正值夏季，烈日炎炎。

我和我的朋友们正走回学校的路上。
Brief Translation:
It was a hot summer. I was on the way to walking back to school with my friends.

Figure 9: Chinese input prompt and English translation.

Output of Chinese-GPT2 fine-tuned without EOP
凉爽的风吹来，我的心也舒畅了些许。走出校门，看到一大群人在热火朝天地玩着什么，我不禁打了个冷战。只见有几个小孩子挎着摇摇篮，走在空地上，摇摇篮里塞满了不听话的人，吵吵嚷嚷地叫着，吵闹的人群一个接着一个地的在空地上来回飞舞。只见他们不管是乱扔垃圾的，还是在家里乱扔东西的，总有那么一两个人，让人看了都觉得讨厌，那几个男生，在那儿使出浑身解数，往那儿扔垃圾，有的还不止一次，他们真的是抓破了脑袋才钻到垃圾堆里啊！"听说那些事儿很早就埋在那儿了。"他们越说越起劲，像每个夏季都会发生的那样，还拿起了"帚，拿起了沙包。回过神来，脸已经晒得通红，汗珠直往外流。我呆呆地站在那儿，思绪飞到了几年前，那时的我才十三岁，现在的我才二十四岁！打来打去，什么也没有留下。唉，打得还挺勤快。我转过身，在树底下端详着他们，又想起了他们，他们可真是坏事当前，坏事晚来了许多啊！我继续打打我那张臭脸。我的心猛地一抽，丢下书包，飞奔出去。在那片空地上，零零星星的人有的在玩儿，有的正在玩呢！他们又跳又叫，不分是非地叫着。我突然看见一个不起眼的小孩儿，他满脸通红，眼睛红得像个灯泡，让人看了如沐春风。他正用眼睛注视着那只有倒在地的人，他下意识地往上看，一会儿，上面散落着一些塑料瓶子。他不知道，还在玩儿呢！我忽然有些感动，急忙跑过去，跟在他后面，问："他怎么了？为什么那么残忍。"小伙儿只是若无其事地回答："我觉得他太可怜了。"他倒也会说话，但是有些话让我怎么说也说不出来。他一双大大的眼睛仿佛在说："我这是为了家里，也是为了我们共同的孩子。现在，我是想退出，你们也别急，知道吗？要是真和这些小孩闹僵了，家里的学习教材再翻出来，你们就完了！"看着小伙儿那可怜的小眼睛，心里一阵酸楚，我不禁流下了眼泪。每次吵完架后，他总爱说："我不怪你，可你就这样放弃我吧！我没钱啊！"唉，啊！唉！哎！气息都快从嗓子里出来了啊！唉！唉！唉！唉！那时，我仿佛听见了他的声音："哎，孩子，爸爸的房屋可能拆迁了，你就住在那吧。等拆迁后我送你吧！我会好好学习的！"那声音大得连我自己都听不见，我的心仿佛像灌了铅似的。我也哭了，但没办法，谁叫人生是漫长的呢？那时我只会低着头走路，却找不到一根自来水。我生着闷气，仿佛快要窒息了。我急得满头大汗，冲到楼下，不停地喊："救救我！救救我！"唉，我都快把脸憋得通红。这时，对面来了一辆出租车，我毫不犹豫地将
Modified Google Translation:
The cool wind blew, and my heart was relieved a little. I walked out of the school gate and saw what a large group of people were doing something. I couldn't help fighting a cold war. I saw a few children carrying the cradle and walking on the open space. The cradle was full of disobedient people, screaming loudly, and the noisy crowd flew back and forth on the open space one by one. I saw that whether they were littering or throwing things at home, there were always one or two people that made people feel annoying when they saw it. Those boys, they tried to do everything and throw garbage there. Some more than once, they really broke their heads and got into the garbage dump! "I heard that those things were buried there very early." They said more and more vigorously, as they would happen every summer, and took up "Broom, took up the sandbag. When I looked back, my face was already sunburned It was red, sweat was flowing out. I stood there blankly, my thoughts flew a few years ago, when I was only 13 years old, and now I am only 24 years old! Stay. Alas, I played very diligently. I turned around, looked at them under the tree, and thought of them again. They are really bad things, and bad things come a lot late! I continue to beat my bad face . My heart twitched, dropped my schoolbag, and ran out. On the open space, some people were playing and some were playing! They jumped and called, regardless of right or wrong. Screaming. I suddenly saw an inconspicuous child, his face flushed, his eyes red like a light bulb, making people look like a spring breeze. He was staring at the only person who fell to the ground with his eyes, he subconsciously went up Look, for a while, there are some plastic bottles scattered on it. He doesn't know, he's still playing! I suddenly Some moved, quickly ran behind him, asked: "how he was? Why so cruel. "The boy just answered casually:" I think he's too pathetic. "He would speak, but some words made me unable to say what he said. His big eyes seemed to be saying," This is for my family and for our common children. Now, I want to quit. Don't worry, you know? If you are really upset with these children, you will find out the learning materials at home, and you are finished! "Looking at the poor little eyes of the guy, I felt sore in my heart, and I couldn't help crying. After each quarrel, he always said," I don't blame you, but you just give up on me! I have no money! "Oh, ah! Uh! Hey! The breath is almost coming out of my throat! Uh! Uh! Uh! Uh! Then I seemed to hear his voice:" Oh boy, my father's house may be demolished, You live there. I'll send you after the demolition! I will study hard! "That voice was so loud that I couldn't even hear it myself, my heart seemed to be filled with lead. I also cried, but there was no way, who made life long? At that time, I just walked with my head down, But I couldn't find a tap. I was sulking, as if I was about to suffocate. I was so sweaty that I rushed downstairs and kept shouting, "Save me! help me! "Well, I'm almost flushing my face. At this moment, a taxi came across, and I didn't hesitate to

Figure 10: Generation from Chinese-GPT2 fine-tuned without EOP.

Output of Chinese-GPT2 fine-tuned with EOP

我们都还在上课，突然一阵急促的车铃声传来，我们低下了头，拿出粉笔，认真地练习。

窗外的大树上，有一个乞丐，他向路人求助，却得不到人帮助，放弃了乞丐的工作，独自一人走了。他的脸上，永远挂着笑，脸颊上，微微露出皱纹。

火车缓缓开过，熙熙攘攘的人群和我们汇成一片。那时，我正在大口大口地吃着零食。突然，看到一个乞丐，他颤巍巍地走了过来，我急忙拦住他："小心，别被车轧到。"他却语气坚决，关切地问："您怎么这么着急，知不知道车辆出轨了？我们的工作又不是那么危险，怎么可以冒险出来帮助别人呢？您一天到晚忙着赚钱，却不关心自己的健康，给钱这么不讲道理，真可怜。""啊，这是什么人啊？拿什么关心呀？这是个老人啊！他这样只顾自己，在哪打点零工，卖什么不关心。"一旁的马路上，几个小伙子正在大口大口地讨论着。我不禁流下了眼泪。含着眼泪，向其中一个乞丐致谢，这个老人见了我们，又弯下腰，打开自行车的后座，把钱给了我们，又对我们说："不要再来烦我们了，我们的工作就是很危险的，也很需要钱的，不如来为国家做点力所能及的事吧。"我的泪水模糊了我的眼睛。

慢慢地，车流渐渐远去，但有些在星星点点的人群里，依然在四处寻找着那个乞丐。夜深人静了，我一人在街上漫步，深深地感受到社会的冷漠和人性的丑恶。我的心又忍不住泛起阵阵潮湿的雨珠。一件一件事情，令我感到我自己的不幸。随后，雨又愈发大了。

我环顾四周，在最好的车站等上了车，我并没有去接那乞丐。直到车子终于来了，我才有些不耐烦了。不是不想让别人帮我，而是那些恶作剧都是不成熟的表现。很多时候，对人也是冷漠的，甚至是冷嘲热讽。我有些生气，却又难以控制着。游戏在幸福的雨幕里。以后每当看见乞丐，我总是感到心酸。

在接下来的日子里，我不再光顾街头，但行人仍多。我依然不理会任何人的言语，回家却无法挽回，那个老人又怎么会有人关心呢？

时间会冲淡一切，但我不想放弃，就算老天在我身边，我还是会努力，继续做好自己，虽然结果不尽如人意，但我依旧要用自己的行动报答社会。[EOS]

Modified Google Translation:

We were all still in class, and suddenly there was a rush of car bells. We lowered our heads, took out chalk, and practiced seriously.

In the big tree outside the window, there was a beggar who asked for help from passersby, but could not get help. He gave up the work of the beggar and left alone. There was always a smile on his face, and a slight wrinkle appeared on his cheek.

The train passed slowly, and the bustling crowd merged with us. At that time, I was eating snacks with a big mouthful. Suddenly, when I saw a beggar, he came tremblingly, and I hurriedly stopped him: "Be careful, don't get caught in the car." But he resolutely asked, "Why are you so anxious, do you know the car is out of track Now? Our work is not so dangerous, how can we take risks to help others? You are busy making money all day, but you don't care about your health. It 's so pitiful to give money so unreasonably. "" Ah, what is this? Man? What do you care about? This is an old man! He only cares about himself like this, where to do odd jobs and don't care what he sells. "On the side of the road, a few young men were talking in a big mouth. I can't help crying. With tears, thanks to one of the beggars. The old man saw us, then bent down, opened the back seat of the bicycle, gave us money, and said to us, "Don't bother us anymore, our work is very dangerous. I also need money, so let's do something for my country. "My tears have blurred my eyes.

Slowly, the traffic gradually went away, but some of the little crowds were still looking for the beggar. The night was quiet, and I was walking on the street alone, deeply feeling the indifference of society and the ugliness of human nature. My heart could not help but burst with wet raindrops. One thing at a time makes me feel my own misfortune. Afterwards, the rain became heavy again.

I looked around and waited at the best station. I didn't pick up the beggar. I didn't get impatient until the car finally came. It's not that you don't want others to help me, but that those pranks are immature. Many times, it is indifferent to people, even ridiculous. I'm a little angry, but hard to control. The game is in the rain of happiness. Whenever I see a beggar, I always feel sad.

In the following days, I stopped patronizing the streets, but there were still many pedestrians. I still ignore the words of anyone, but I ca n't restore it when I go home. How could anyone care about that old man?

Time will dilute everything, but I don't want to give up. Even if God is by my side, I will still work hard and continue to be myself. Although the results are not satisfactory, I still have to repay the society with my own actions.

Figure 11: Generation from Chinese-GPT2 fine-tuned with EOP.

B.3 Case 1 of GPT2-117

Input prompt:
Aliens come to Earth in hoping to wipe us out and take over the planet, but are honorable and gives us a fighting chance. They announce they will return in 100 years so as to give Earth a chance to prepare and defend itself. Neither side expected what the other would bring to war

Figure 12: English input prompt.

It was dark as the day began. Pure white, forever not knowing the night sky. This was the first time since their arrival that **ships** had been so dark, it was hard not to feel the tremors of terror as the drops of rain started falling. The rain started a minute after the **humans** had arrived. It started getting brighter as they piled up and felt the tremors of rain take their place. Another minute or two they saw them in the distance. One little shell, below them floated a little bigger. Behind that shell came another of them falling, one in each direction. Then, faster and faster the smaller the shell went. It was as if they were floating to each other, different colors and shapes sailing past each other in any direction, making the scene less momentary. The rain started to fall. The tall suits of **soldiers** patrolled the area. They didn't see what was happening but one was seeing some sort of change. He was slowly meeting the upper edge of the shell, directly under the soft snow. The rain started to fall and he was choking back the hail and it suddenly stopped flowing. He looked up at the Sun and the grass and saw the cloudless sky in front of him. He knew that had given him a new hope. He wasn't lying when he said that the atmosphere was starting to roll away, and just as he was about to turn around he felt a knock on his door. "I'm having a look at this. It's new... " " We'll wait. " " You have to go, have a look. " " Come with us." With that said the strange man took off his coat and sat on the porch of his house, waiting for the rain.

Figure 13: Generation from GPT-117 fine-tuned without EOP/SEP.

A **planet** - there is no other more appealing than a **peaceful planet**,
taking in the vast plains of green and dry,
allowing the native **species** to develop.
Among many other things, the greatest threat here was our neighbours as well,
hosting none but a single **blue planet**.
With every news we received, while we was still, the green grass kept
tilling even the most **exotic plants**.
Against the odds, we agreed. This blue planet
is sure to die if it too falls,
as if the planet we are about to take hold of is not giving it.
Whether it is the region of lush land,
living in the shadow of endless sea, or the ones that lie beyond,
this **planet will feed our population** just as well.

Figure 14: Generation from GPT-117 fine-tuned with NL as SEP.

Robert stood in the room quietly. The pager in the edge of his TV blinked off as he contemplated what he was seeing. It was not his first visit by **alien ships**. Most of them had flown over the **galaxy in 882** since the foursome of an ancient race had first started transit in the Kardashev system. But they did not have a **star system** to conquer or destroy.
The strain of building a bridge was far from comfortable as it had become. Even hands and feet were shaking as they dutifully lugged the countless cargo back to their vessel. **Each alien lacked a ship just like him**. Their ships would not be ready **for another 100 years**. Without time, they would be easily overwhelmed.
The first of them came on us. The black, streaming in through a far wall. Its shape changing from green to orange as it accelerated. It came in waves across the curved surface. Its **metallic surface simply glowed off**. Robert had seen **the mouth of the creature. It had a back in it, almost reptilian. A spider-like body with a fangs that ripped through the flesh like a spider.** The mouth was growling with hunger in response. It roared as its muscles launched away from Robert to mate with him.
The next twenty-three seconds went by with little delay. Robert led the old stranger down a hallway to his repair bay. He was quick to greet the human with baited breath and followed close behind him. He took the sidearm from underneath his suit and held it in front of his eyes as the humans tore at the metal. A metal band formed around the metal covered mouth. The human was tongue hanging off his neck.
Without stopping, he freed his hands from the talons hanging around his head as he pressed the new badge on his hip.
Robert opened his mouth to scream but his goal was to prevent the humans from catching on to what was happening.
Robert began unwrapping a vial of orange liquid. He approached the canine and began licking it, waiting. The canine howled as Robert removed his mask and walked away. He had fifty percent of the tanker harvested and stored at a distance of about five million miles.
The alien warship stopped in mid-flight and seemed to accelerate down again as Robert completed its tasks. He called back, letting out a whistle that was barely audible over the din of battle. Within a second the ship touched down at a small cove. The human ran over to him, mewling.
"Not again. " Robert said.
" Exactly, Mr. Tammoy. We have evidence of life support in here. " **The alien asked**.
" And what. Was. All. You. Deposed. " Robert responded.
" Quite literally. " **The humanoid replied**.
" So, just one moment. Can't you just give it a chance? "
" Neither can anybody else." The creature continued, seemingly oblivious to its words and their implications. Robert slowly brought the cockpit of the ship's other 'Crew' to the nub. He unlocked the pods and stepped into the airlock. The robot was gone. Robert sat in the cockpit, the cylindrical container behind him. He took a deep breath and looked out into the blackness, following the exact pattern of the vessel. The black flesh was always fascinating. More often than not, he didn't really understand what it meant.
Robert walked past the humans towards his repair bay. It had not done much damage. He walked back past the humans and got into his pickup truck. With the last line of effort he pushed his way through the trio.

Figure 15: Generation from GPT-117 fine-tuned with DIY EOP.

B.4 Case 2 of GPT2-117

Input Prompt:
You were driving to work one day and your car suddenly started flying.

Figure 16: English input prompt.

(got more into poetry / fiction themes/ before calling it Work) My grandfather had 3 boxes of cake and a white sugar please Jane said "today is April 25th, and your seventh or eighth " I was in love by the looks of things, I hated her " Your father loves you at least nine times " I said " Oh, I know, it's really funny. " She looked at me with a confused expression " why would she do that " Then I began to back out of it like I told her I would. At that point Jane said something " no, she had a birthday today " and since I was the father of her child I felt really blessed for making her mother happy. We closed the front door and walked back into her house to eat cookies. You see, she almost did so fast, I was so pumped and pretty much took the bag to the kitchen for milk and honey, but here I was going to take everything home and spend it running errands. My wife moved back in a minute later, but I saw her and told her I was having this late so I told her " Yeah " " tell her I'll grab one at the bus stop tomorrow " She said you'll come back to bed early and eat one " goodbye " but I did hurry. My wife usually leaves early so **we're in the car** then this was her last day of school. At the bus stop it was all so bad that I'd have forgotten not to say goodbye " Hello, It seems I've had the worst day of my life. Please remember to check on Jane " " Excuse me child " I looked at her puzzled " oh my god " A strange feeling came over me and I knew I didn't have time for that in the moment. " K- Come on Jane " Suddenly I became stiff and lost my footing. I fell onto the curb and immediately collapsed onto the curb again. " What the HELL" followed by everything I missed out on. I knew my grandmother was trying to get me to go to the movies.

Figure 17: Generation from GPT-117 fine-tuned without EOP/SEP.

My heart was racing; I felt **something otherworldly being in my car**. " Hello again! Who is this? " I was already bracing for another **crash** at work.
" Shhh shhh " the object before me suddenly let go. I tried turning it on to get some air. Nope, this thing didn't change its positioning, it never got to anything. My arm feels like a pressure cooker, its chest feels like a heater. In all that time I never had expected to see anything like this happening. My legs were numb, and my back was numb. I was so tired. I was like a boat out of water and it seemed like it took all my energy to get the **gas pedal off**. " I swear to god please don't hurt me! " I screamed, and I was feeling for my hands like claws were opening my right leg.
Suddenly the skull popped open... **my car began to fly**..no where else to go except to look on the horizon and never see it again. I had been driving home in rage and frustration. **I need to get out of here**, I'm literally the black dog everywhere. " **What the hell happened**? " I was about to ask out of fear of being right next to someone when a screeching fell from above. I slowly turned my head towards the heavens. **Something was definitely different in the sky.**
" Can you hear me? " I shouted, though I was standing a full 6 feet tall. I was so sure. * What is going on? * I wanted to yell out, to pretend that I didn't hear someone. " Help me! Please! " What! No. Please. Please help me! " I must have just tried to reach for my hand or something.
It landed in the grassland and started shaking. My chest felt heavier and it was hardly noticeable on the ground. It shook harder, and now my eyes were fixated on that star. " Fuuuuuk, Fuuuuuuuuuk... " *BANG*, the Earth shook. I was spinning and was floating. It was so bright I looked down at my arms, and **I felt like we were floating for what seemed like an eternity**. I was breathing like I was being ripped apart.
Then I felt something was dragging me. I don't know what it was, but it was drifting closer and closer and more and more until I felt as though I was about to fall and I could hear what could only be a small nervous chuckle escaping my lips. " God this is so weird! "
" What're you doing? "
" I'm.... In a strange alternate world. **I'm falling from this sky**, touching a comet... "
" Hell no! This is **just a dream**... I'm falling from this sky and it's going to explode and everything is going to be fine until I touch a comet again. Then... this is it. All of this is right now and I can't see what's going on but I can feel it. I can feel it being lifted off of me and all of this knowledge and knowledge... "
Brilliant* What?! It was the best dream I had ever had! I could definitely feel that tiny little planet being pulled up to the surface by whatever ship it was in. God, could I ever know what will happen to it like that? But what would happen to me if I touched one such comet! Even being floating in space with nothing to do?
I had finally had enough! " I'll get you out of here! I'll let you out... (Once I get to the comet, I can feel the universe get pulling me to another dimension.) I'll let you out! " I took off my sunglasses and put them on, and there was no way I wouldn't be in that crowd again.
After that nightmare I decided that I wasn't going to make it out of here alive. That I couldn't **ride a car** that would almost definitely end in killing someone. Whatever! I'll be back, that's all I need.
I'll be free of this reality, *that dream* and open to some other universe!

Figure 18: Generation from GPT-117 fine-tuned with NL as SEP.

Here we go again, I'm trying to pick up my pace. My hands are dragging along the overgrowth and I hardly feel a thing. The sunlight beating down on me still yet dulling my vision. My hand suddenly feels like it's in a basketball as I pick myself up off the ground.
"Hey Wendy... You okay? "
" Just trying to get some fresh air on my lungs "
" Can you get me one of my of my stones to drink. I mean, **there is no use in driving** "
" Sure... " I say looking around, taking up a new position on a nearby skylight. While searching, one on a hill that seems pretty rounded in any way, two other ones are out of order, and I take notice of them trying to move out of the way.
Not even half an hour passes... I can feel them roll in and out of the path as I decide it's time to head out for the day. No, I don't give one.
" Would you like some fresh air for my shoulder? "
" How about that new Sonic X that's been around for the past couple years? Now as soon as I get off it, it can take me out of the sun. So just give me a moment of peace and rest "
I reach for my rock, still still clutching at my leg with my shoe. Yet as fast as I left it, it's trapped by my arm. I'm powerless to do anything... until I hear something coming down from the trees. " STOP! " I yell as I try to dodge it in a fast spiral. Before I can react, it's shoved right at me and **I fall to the ground**. The sky is dark, smog filling the sky. Already I'm blacking out, the **backlight on my car keeping me firmly in darkness.**
A crisp wind whipping about me, I grab my blanket from my chair and prepare to throw it at anything that could have managed to keep me with me. Bouncing out of my chair, I continue down the path where the road once was.
The wind is beginning to get stronger. More thunderstorms begin breaking out, as well as additional thunder. My turn comes up and the wind picks up. As soon as I can see it, it's nowhere to be seen. I'm only about 10 minutes away from the road, standing in the middle of the road. I hear **a voice screaming from my car**. A tall man in fatigues looks at me and **looks at my car**. " Damn... **I was driving**... " he says, before sprinting from my car and grabbing his wallet. He gives me a look of disgust, as if the only thing worse than avoiding the **highway** was choosing between two other men.
I ask him what was going on, and he smiles gently. " You think I'm lucky to get in, huh? **I really shouldn't be riding a car just yet**, you know. But I'm glad you're here! So if you don't mind if I drive me, I have a few things on my mind. "
" Alright, fine, whatever. Go, fasten the seat belt, you can't come back here any other way. Are you sure you're just going to excuse me, though?"
That was his last expression, before he limped away like a glutton.
This is the end of my first attempt at writing nothing! Any thoughts of how to improve upon it?

Figure 19: Generation from GPT-117 fine-tuned with DIY EOP.

Data Augmentation with Unsupervised Machine Translation Improves the Structural Similarity of Cross-lingual Word Embeddings

Sosuke Nishikawa, Ryokan Ri and Yoshimasa Tsuruoka
The University of Tokyo
7-3-1 Hongo, Bunkyo-ku, Tokyo, Japan
sosuke-nishikawa@nii.ac.jp
{li0123,tsuruoka}@logos.t.u-tokyo.ac.jp

Abstract

Unsupervised cross-lingual word embedding (CLWE) methods learn a linear transformation matrix that maps two monolingual embedding spaces that are separately trained with monolingual corpora. This method relies on the assumption that the two embedding spaces are structurally similar, which does not necessarily hold true in general. In this paper, we argue that using a pseudo-parallel corpus generated by an unsupervised machine translation model facilitates the structural similarity of the two embedding spaces and improves the quality of CLWEs in the unsupervised mapping method. We show that our approach outperforms other alternative approaches given the same amount of data, and, through detailed analysis, we show that data augmentation with the pseudo data from unsupervised machine translation is especially effective for mapping-based CLWEs because (1) the pseudo data makes the source and target corpora (partially) parallel; (2) the pseudo data contains information on the original language that helps to learn similar embedding spaces between the source and target languages.

1 Introduction

Cross-lingual word embedding (CLWE) methods aim to learn a shared meaning space between two languages (the source and target languages), which is potentially useful for cross-lingual transfer learning or machine translation (Yuan et al., 2020; Artetxe et al., 2018b; Lample et al., 2018a). Although early methods for learning CLWEs often utilize multilingual resources such as parallel corpora (Gouws et al., 2015; Luong et al., 2015) and word dictionaries (Mikolov et al., 2013), recent studies have focused on fully unsupervised methods that do not require any cross-lingual supervision (Lample et al., 2018b; Artetxe et al., 2018a; Patra et al., 2019). Most unsupervised methods fall into the category of mapping-based methods, which generally consist of the following procedures: train monolingual word embeddings independently in two languages; then, find a linear mapping that aligns the two embedding spaces. The mapping-based method is based on a strong assumption that the two independently trained embedding spaces have similar structures that can be aligned by a linear transformation, which is unlikely to hold true when the two corpora are from different domains or the two languages are typologically very different (Søgaard et al., 2018). To address this problem, several studies have focused on improving the structural similarity of monolingual spaces before learning mapping (Zhang et al., 2019; Vulić et al., 2020), but few studies have focused on how to leverage the text data itself.

In this paper, we show that the pseudo sentences generated from an unsupervised machine translation (UMT) system (Lample et al., 2018c) facilitates the structural similarity without any additional cross-lingual resources. In the proposed method, the training data of the source and/or target language are augmented with the pseudo sentences (Figure 1).

We argue that this method facilitates the structural similarity between the source and target embeddings for the following two reasons. Firstly, the source and target embeddings are usually trained on monolingual corpora. The difference in the content of the two corpora may accentuate the structural difference between the two resulting embedding spaces, and thus we can mitigate that effect by making the source and target corpora parallel by automatically generated pseudo data. Secondly, in the mapping-based method, the source and target embeddings are trained independently without taking into account the other language. Thus, the embedding structures may not be optimal for CLWEs. We argue that pseudo sentences generated by a UMT

Proceedings of the Joint Conference of the 59th Annual Meeting of the Association for Computational Linguistics and the 11th International Joint Conference on Natural Language Processing: Student Research Workshop, pages 163–173
August 5–6, 2021.

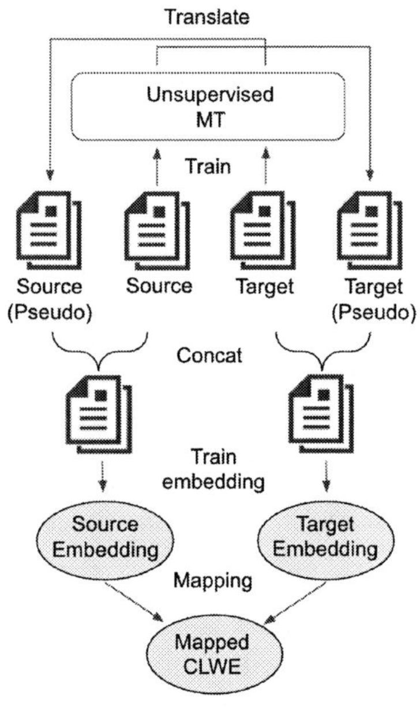

Figure 1: Our framework for training CLWEs using unsupervised machine translation (UMT). We first train UMT models using monolingual corpora for each language. We then translate all the training corpora and concatenate the outputs with the original corpora, and train monolingual word embeddings independently. Finally, we map these word embeddings on a shared embedding.

system contain some trace of the original language, and using them when training monolingual embeddings can facilitate the structural correspondence of the two sets of embeddings.

In the experiments using the Wikipedia dump in English, French, German, and Japanese, we observe substantial improvements by our method in the task of bilingual lexicon induction and downstream tasks without hurting the quality as monolingual embeddings. Moreover, we carefully analyze why our method improves the performance, and the result confirms that making the source and target corpora parallel does contribute to performance improvement, and also suggests that the generated translation data contain information about the original language.

2 Background and Related Work

Cross-lingual Word Embeddings

CLWE methods aim to learn a semantic space shared between two languages. Most of the current approaches fall into two types of methods: joint-training approaches and mapping-based approaches.

Joint-training approaches jointly train a shared embedding space given multilingual corpora with cross-lingual supervision such as parallel corpora (Gouws et al., 2015; Luong et al., 2015), document-aligned corpora (Vulic and Moens, 2016), or monolingual corpora along with a word dictionary (Duong et al., 2016).

On the other hand, mapping-based approaches utilize monolingual embeddings that are already obtained from monolingual corpora. They assume structural similarity between monolingual embeddings of different languages and attempt to obtain a shared embedding space by finding a transformation matrix $\mathbf{W}$ that maps source word embeddings to the target embedding space (Mikolov et al., 2013). The transformation matrix $\mathbf{W}$ is usually obtained by minimizing the sum of squared euclidian distances between the mapped source embeddings and target embeddings:

$$\underset{\mathbf{W}}{\operatorname{argmin}} \sum_{i}^{|D|} \|\mathbf{W}\mathbf{x}_i - \mathbf{y}_i\|^2, \tag{1}$$

where D is a bilingual word dictionary that contains word pairs (x_i, y_i) and $\mathbf{x}_i$ and $\mathbf{y}_i$ represent the corresponding word embeddings.

Although finding the transformation matrix $\mathbf{W}$ is straightforward when a word dictionary is available, a recent trend is to reduce the amount of cross-lingual supervision or to find $\mathbf{W}$ in a completely unsupervised manner (Lample et al., 2018b; Artetxe et al., 2018a). The general framework of unsupervised mapping methods is based on heuristic initialization of a seed dictionary D and iterative refinement of the transformation matrix $\mathbf{W}$ and the dictionary D, as described in Algorithm 1. In our experiment, we use the unsupervised mapping-based method proposed by Artetxe et al. (2018a). Their method is characterized by the seed dictionary initialized with nearest neighbors based on similarity distributions of words in each language.

These mapping-based methods, however, are based on the strong assumption that the two independently trained embedding spaces have similar structures that can be aligned by a linear transformation. Although several studies have tackled improving the structural similarity of monolingual spaces before learning mapping (Zhang et al., 2019; Vulić et al., 2020), not much attention has been paid to how to leverage the text data itself.

Input: The source embeddings $\mathbf{X}$, the target embeddings $\mathbf{Y}$
Output: The transformation matrix $\mathbf{W}$
Heuristically induce an initial seed word dictionary D
while *not convergence* **do**
    Compute $\mathbf{W}$ given the word dictionary D from the equation (1)
    Update the word dictionary D by retrieving cross-lingual nearest neighbors in a shared embedding space obtained by $\mathbf{W}$
end
return $\mathbf{W}$

Algorithm 1: The general workflow of unsupervised mapping methods

In this paper, we argue that we can facilitate structural correspondence of two embedding spaces by augmenting the source or/and target corpora with the output from an unsupervised machine translation system (Lample et al., 2018c).

Unsupervised Machine Translation

Unsupervised machine translation (UMT) is the task of building a translation system without any parallel corpora (Artetxe et al., 2018b; Lample et al., 2018a,c; Artetxe et al., 2019b). UMT is accomplished by three components: (1) a word-by-word translation model learned using unsupervised CLWEs; (2) a language model trained on the source and target monolingual corpora; (3) a back-translation model where the model uses input and its own translated output as parallel sentences and learn how to translate them in both directions.

More specifically, the initial source-to-target translation model $P^0_{s\to t}$ is created by the word-by-word translation model and the language model of the target language. Then, $P^1_{t\to s}$ is learned in a supervised setting using the source original monolingual corpus paired with the synthetic parallel sentences of the target language generated by $P^0_{s\to t}$. Again, another source-to-target translation model $P^1_{s\to t}$ is trained with the target original monolingual corpus and the outputs of $P^0_{s\to t}$, and in the same way, the quality of the translation models is improved with an iterative process.

In our experiments, we adopt an unsupervised phrase-based statistical machine translation (SMT) method to generate a pseudo corpus because it produces better translations than unsupervised neural machine translation on low-resource languages (Lample et al., 2018c). The difference of the unsupervised SMT (USMT) model from its supervised counterpart is that the initial phrase table is derived based on the cosine similarity of unsupervised CLWEs, and the translation model is iteratively improved by pseudo parallel corpora.

Our proposed method utilizes the output of a USMT system to augment the training corpus for CLWEs.

Exploiting UMT for Cross-lingual Applications

There is some previous work on how to use UMT to induce bilingual word dictionaries or improve CLWEs. Artetxe et al. (2019a) explored an effective way of utilizing a phrase table from a UMT system to induce bilingual dictionaries. Marie and Fujita (2019) generate a synthetic parallel corpus from a UMT system, and jointly train CLWEs along with the word alignment information (Luong et al., 2015). In our work, we use the synthetic parallel corpus generated from a UMT system not for joint-training but for data augmentation to train monolingual word embeddings for each language, which are subsequently aligned through unsupervised mapping. In the following sections, we empirically show that our approach leads to the creation of improved CLWEs and analyze why these results are achieved.

3 Experimental Design

In this section, we describe how we obtain mapping-based CLWEs using a pseudo parallel corpus generated from UMT. We first train UMT models using the source/target training corpora, and then translate them to the machine-translated corpora. Having done that, we simply concatenate the machine-translated corpus with the original training corpus, and learn monolingual word embeddings independently for each language. Finally, we map these embeddings to a shared CLWE space.

Corpora

We implement our method with two similar language pairs: English-French (en-fr), English-German (en-de), and one distant language pair: English-Japanese (en-ja). We use plain texts from Wikipedia dumps[1], and randomly extract 10M sentences for each language. The English, French, and German texts are tokenized with the Moses tokenizer (Koehn et al., 2007) and lowercased. For Japanese texts, we use `kytea`[2] to tokenize and normalize them[3].

Training mapping-based CLWEs

Given tokenized texts, we train monolingual word embeddings using `fastText`[4] with 512 dimensions, a context window of size 5, and 5 negative examles. We then map these word embeddings on a shared embedding space using the open-source implementation `VecMap`[5] with the unsupervised mapping algorithm (Artetxe et al., 2018a).

Training UMT models

To implement UMT, we first build a phrase table by selecting the most frequent 300,000 source phrases and taking their 200 nearest-neighbors in the CLWE space following the setting of Lample et al. (2018c). We then train a 5-gram language model for each language with `KenLM` (Heafield et al., 2013) and combine it with the phrase table, which results in an unsupervised phrase-based SMT model. Then, we refine the UMT model through three iterative back-translation steps. At each step, we translate 100k sentences randomly sampled from the monolingual data set. We use a phrase table containing phrases up to a length of 4 except for initialization. The quality of our UMT models is indicated by the BLEU scores (Papineni et al., 2002) in Table 1. We use newstest2014 from WMT14[6] to evaluate En-Fr and En-De translation accuracy and the Tanaka corpus[7] for En-Ja evaluation.

[1]https://dumps.wikimedia.org/

[2]http://www.phontron.com/kytea/index-ja.html

[3]We convert all alphabets and numbers to half-width, and all katakana to full-width with the `mojimoji` library https://github.com/studio-ousia/mojimoji

[4]https://fasttext.cc

[5]https://github.com/artetxem/vecmap

[6]http://www.statmt.org/wmt14/translation-task.html

[7]http://www.edrdg.org/wiki/index.php/TanakaCorpus

en - fr		en - de		en - ja	
→	←	→	←	→	←
19.2	19.1	10.3	13.7	3.6	1.4

Table 1: BLEU scores of UMT.

Training CLWEs with pseudo corpora

We then translate all the training corpora with the UMT system and obtain machine-translated corpora, which we call *pseudo corpora*. We concatenate the pseudo corpora with the original corpora, and learn monolingual word embeddings for each language. Finally, we map these word embeddings to a shared CLWE space with the unsupervised mapping algorithm.

Models

We compare our method with a baseline with no data augmentation as well as the existing related methods: dictionary induction from a phrase table (Artetxe et al., 2019a) and the unsupervised joint-training method (Marie and Fujita, 2019). These two methods both exploit word alignments in the pseudo parallel corpus, and to obtain them we use `Fast_Align`[8] (Dyer et al., 2013) with the default hyperparameters. For the joint-training method, we adopt `bivec`[9] to train CLWEs with the parameters used in Upadhyay et al. (2016) using the pseudo parallel corpus and the word alignments. To ensure fair comparison, we implement all of these methods with the same UMT system.

4 Evaluation of Cross-lingual Mapping

In this section, we conduct a series of experiments to evaluate our method. We first evaluate the performance of cross-lingual mapping in our method (§ 4.1) and investigate the effect of UMT quality (§ 4.2). Then, we analyze why our method improves the bilingual lexicon induction (BLI) performance. Through carefully controlled experiments, we argue that it is not simply because of data augmentation but because: (1) the generated data makes the source and target corpora (partially) parallel (§ 4.3); (2) the generated data reflects the co-occurrence statistics of the original language (§ 4.4).

4.1 Bilingual Lexicon Induction

First, we evaluate the mapping accuracy of word embeddings using BLI. BLI is the task of iden-

[8]https://github.com/clab/fast_align

[9]https://github.com/lmthang/bivec

Method	source (en)		target		en→fr		fr→en		en→de		de→en		en→ja		ja→en	
	orig.	psd.	orig.	psd.	MRR	P@1	MRR	P@1	MRR	P@1	MRR	P@1	MRR	P@1	MRR	P@1
BLI from phrase table	✓	-	-	✓	-	0.673	-	0.524	-	0.551	-	0.486	-	0.311	-	0.226
	-	✓	✓	-	-	0.509	-	0.697	-	0.302	-	0.542	-	0.198	-	0.259
	✓	✓	✓	✓	-	0.673	-	0.522	-	0.551	-	0.486	-	0.311	-	0.226
joint training	✓	-	-	✓	0.640	0.636	0.615	0.634	0.552	0.509	0.545	0.520	0.347	0.295	0.272	0.227
	-	✓	✓	-	0.587	0.579	0.643	0.685	0.535	0.491	0.577	0.549	0.279	0.226	0.305	0.249
	✓	✓	✓	✓	0.654	0.642	0.642	0.650	0.585	0.532	0.520	0.518	0.325	0.267	0.295	0.234
mapping	✓	-	✓	-	0.670	0.612	0.650	0.614	0.579	0.484	0.587	0.488	0.471	0.378	0.364	0.242
mapping (+ pseudo)	✓	-	✓	✓	0.709	0.666	0.687	0.688	**0.656**	**0.582**	0.635	**0.563**	**0.514**	**0.405**	**0.436**	**0.304**
	✓	✓	✓	-	**0.728**	**0.684**	**0.703**	**0.700**	0.647	0.566	0.636	0.562	0.486	0.392	0.407	0.297
	✓	✓	✓	✓	0.721	0.677	0.696	**0.700**	0.652	0.574	**0.637**	**0.563**	0.497	0.387	0.426	0.300

Table 2: Comparison with previous approaches in BLI. "orig." and "psd." indicate original training corpus and pseudo corpus. In each cell, the left cell shows the result of MRR, and the right cell shows the result of p@1.

tifying word translation pairs, and is a common benchmark for evaluating CLWE methods. In these experiments, we use Cross-Domain Similarity Local Scaling (Lample et al., 2018b) as the method for identifying translation pairs in the two embedding spaces. For BLI scores, we adopt the mean reciprocal rank (MRR) (Glavaš et al., 2019) and P@1.

We use XLing-Eval[10] as test sets for En-Fr and En-Ge. For En-Ja. We create the word dictionaries automatically using Google Translate[11], following Ri and Tsuruoka (2020). Other than BLI from a phrase table, we train three sets of embeddings with different random seeds and report the average of the results.

We compare the proposed method with other alternative approaches in BLI as shown in Table 2. In all the language pairs, the mapping method with pseudo data augmentation achieves better performance than the other methods. Here, one may think that the greater amount of data can lead to better performance, and thus augmenting both the source and target corpora shows the best performance. However, the result shows that it is not necessarily the case: for our mapping method, augmenting only either the source or target, not both, achieves the best performance in many language pairs. This is probably due to the presence of two pseudo corpora with different natures.

As for the two methods using word alignments (BLI from phrase table; joint training), we observe some cases where these models underperform the mapping methods, especially in English and Japanese pairs. We attribute this to our relatively low-resource setting where the quality of the synthetic parallel data is not sufficient to perform these methods which require word alignment between parallel sentences.

	en - fr			en - de		
BT step	BLI MRR	BLI P@1	BLEU	BLI MRR	BLI P@1	BLEU
-	0.670	0.612	-	0.579	0.484	-
0	0.711	0.646	14.7	0.592	0.508	10.7
1	0.714	0.651	18.8	0.615	0.524	13.5
2	0.728	0.684	19.2	0.647	0.566	13.7

Table 3: Results of BLI score on CLWEs using pseudo corpus generated from different quality UMTs.

4.2 Effect of UMT quality

To investigate the effect of UMT quality on our method, we compare the accuracy of BLI on the CLWEs using pseudo data generated from UMT models of different qualities. As a translator with low performance, we prepare models that perform fewer iterations on back-translation (BT). Note that we compare the results on the source-side (English) extension, where the quality of the translation is notably different. As shown in Table 3, we find that the better the quality of generated data, the better the performance of BLI.

4.3 Effect of sharing content

In the mapping method, word embeddings are independently trained by monolingual corpora that do not necessarily have the same content. As a result, the difference in the corpus contents can hurt the structural similarity of the two resulting embedding spaces. We hypothesize that using synthetic parallel data which have common contents for learning word embeddings leads to better structural correspondence, which improves cross-lingual mapping.

To verify the effect of sharing the contents using parallel data, we compare the extensions with a parallel corpus and a non-parallel corpus. More concretely, we first split the original training data

[10]https://github.com/codogogo/xling-eval

[11]https://translate.google.com/

Extension		en - fr	en - de	en - ja
pseudo	parallel			
-	-	0.621 / 711	0.502 / 877	0.426 / 1776
×	×	0.630 / 838	0.509 / 1714	0.429 / 2301
✓	×	0.686 / **123**	0.569 / 272	0.454 / 1050
✓	✓	**0.695** / 144	**0.585 / 183**	**0.459 / 1024**

Table 4: Results of BLI score and eigenvector similarity. In each cell, the left cell shows the result of BLI, and the right cell shows the result of eigenvector similarity. Each row indicates, from top to bottom, no extension, extension with non-pseudo data, extension with non-parallel pseudo data, and extension with parallel pseudo data.

Corpus	fr-A	de-A	ja-A
en	0.621 / 711	0.502 / 877	0.426 / 1776
en + pseudo (fr-B)	**0.686 / 123**	0.516 / 315	0.421 / 2194
en + pseudo (de-B)	0.621 / 193	**0.569 / 272**	0.423 / 2173
en + pseudo (ja-B)	0.568 / 279	0.454 / 625	**0.454 / 1050**

Table 5: Results of BLI score and eigenvector similarity. Note that `lang`-A and pseudo (`lang`-B) are not parallel.

of the source and target languages evenly (each denoted as Split A and Split B). As the baseline, we train CLWEs with Split A. We use the translation of Split A of the target language data for the parallel extension of the source data, and Split B for the non-parallel extension. Also, we compare them with the extension with non-pseudo data, which is simply increasing the amount of the source language data by raw text.

Along with the BLI score, we show eigenvector similarity, a spectral metric to quantify the structural similarity of word embedding spaces (Søgaard et al., 2018). To compute eigenvector similarity, we normalize the embeddings and construct the nearest neighbor graphs of the 10,000 most frequent words in each language. We then calculate their Laplacian matrices $L1$ and $L2$ from those graphs and find the smallest k such that the sum of the k largest eigenvalues of each Laplacian matrices is $< 90\%$ of all eigenvalues. Finally, we sum up the squared differences between the k largest eigenvalues from $L1$ and $L2$ and derive the eigen similarity. Note that smaller eigenvector similarity values mean higher degrees of structural similarity.

Table 4 shows the BLI scores and eigenvector similarity in each extension setting. The parallel extension method shows a slightly better BLI performance than the non-parallel extension. This supports our hypothesis that parallel pseudo data make word embeddings space more suitable for bilingual mapping because of sharing content. In eigenvector similarity, there is no significant improvement between the parallel and non-parallel corpora. This is probably due to large fluctuations in eigenvector similarity values. Surprisingly, the results show that augmentation using pseudo data is found to be much more effective than the extension of the same amount of original training data. This result suggests that using pseudo data as training data is useful, especially for learning bilingual models.

4.4 Effect of reflecting the co-occurrence statistics of the language

We hypothesize that the translated sentences reflect the co-occurrence statistics of the original language, which makes the co-occurrence information on training data similar, improving the structural similarity of the two monolingual embeddings.

To verify this hypothesis, we experiment with augmenting the source language with sentences translated from a non-target language. To examine only the effect of the co-occurrence statistics of language and avoid the effects of sharing content, we use the extensions with the non-parallel corpus.

Table 5 shows that BLI performance and eigenvector similarity improve with the extension from the same target language, but that is not the case if the pseudo corpus is generated from a non-target language. These results indicate that our method can leverage learning signals on the other language in the pseudo data.

5 Downstream Tasks

Although CLWEs were evaluated almost exclusively on the BLI task in the past, Glavaš et al. (2019) recently showed that CLWEs that perform well on BLI do not always perform well in other cross-lingual tasks. Therefore, we evaluate our embeddings on the four downstream tasks: topic classification (TC), sentiment analysis (SA), dependency parsing (DP), and natural language inference

Task	en-fr mapping	en-fr mapping (+ pseudo)	en-fr joint training	en-de mapping	en-de mapping (+ pseudo)	en-de joint training	en-ja mapping	en-ja mapping (+ pseudo)	en-ja joint training
TC	79.5 (92.6)	**82.2**† (93.3)	79.7 (92.5)	79.0 (91.7)	**79.3** (92.0)	70.4 (91.4)	70.4 (92.2)	**71.6**† (93.3)	66.7 (91.9)
SA	69.1 (71.8)	**69.5** (71.9)	66.3 (69.9)	63.7 (71.1)	**65.1**† (70.2)	62.5 (70.3)	**63.5** (70.7)	62.8 (70.6)	57.3 (66.8)
DP	63.9 (73.2)	**64.3** (73.5)	64.1 (75.1)	56.7 (73.2)	**57.0** (73.6)	55.9 (74.7)	17.8 (72.9)	**18.1** (73.3)	17.3 (74.8)
NLI	54.4 (70.3)	**54.7** (70.1)	45.0 (68.6)	55.7 (70.2)	**56.0** (70.3)	44.7 (69.7)	- -	- -	- -

Table 6: Results of Downstream tasks. Numbers in parentheses indicate the score of English validation data. The scores indicate averages of 20 experiments with different seeds. Statistically significant correlations are marked with a dagger ($p < 0.01$).

(NLI).

Topic Classification This task is classifying the topics of news articles. We use the MLDoc [12] corpus compiled by Schwenk and Li (2018). It includes four topics: CCAT (Corporate / Industrial), ECAT (Economics), GCAT (Government / Social), MCAT (Markets). As the classifier, we implemented a simple light-weight convolutional neural network (CNN)-based classifier.

Sentiment Analysis In this task, a model is used to classify sentences as either having a positive or negative opinion. We use the Webis-CLS-10 corpus [13]. This data consists of review texts for amazon products and their ratings from 1 to 5. We cast the problem as binary classification and define rating values 1-2 as "negative" and 4-5 as "positive", and exclude the rating 3. Again, we use the CNN-based classifier for this task.

Dependency Parsing We train the deep biaffine parser (Dozat and Manning, 2017) with the UD English EWT dataset[14] (Silveira et al., 2014). We use the PUD treebanks[15] as test data.

Natural Language Inference We use the English MultiNLI corpus (Williams et al., 2018) for training and the multilingual XNLI corpus for evaluation (Conneau et al., 2018). XNLI only covers French and German from our experiment. We train the LSTM-based classifier (Bowman et al., 2015), which encodes two sentences, concatenated the representations, and then feed them to a multi-layer perceptron.

In each task, we train the model using English training data with the embedding parameters fixed . We then evaluate the model on the test data in other target languages.

Result and Discussion

Table 6 shows the test set accuracy of downstream tasks. For topic classification, our method obtains the best results in all language pairs. Especially in En-Fr and En-Ja, a significant difference is obtained in Student's t-test. For sentiment analysis, we observe a significant improvement in En-De, but cannot observe consistent trends in other languages. For dependency parsing and natural language inference, we observe a similar trend where the performance of our method outperforms other methods, although no significant difference is observed in the t-test. The cause of the lower performance of joint-training compared with the mapping method is presumably due to the poor quality of synthetic parallel data as described in § 4.1. In summary, given the same amount of data, the CLWEs obtained from our method tend to show higher performance not only in BLI but also in downstream tasks compared with other alternative methods, although there is some variation.

6 Analysis

Monolingual Word Similarity Our method uses a noisy pseudo corpus to learn monolingual word embeddings, and it might hurt the quality of monolingual embeddings. To investigate this point, we evaluate monolingual embeddings with the word similarity task. This task evaluates the quality of monolingual word embeddings by measuring the correlation between the cosine similarity in a vector space and manually created word pair similarity. We use simverb-3500[16] (Gerz et al.,

[12] https://github.com/facebookresearch/ MLDoc

[13] https://webis.de/data/webis-cls-10. html

[14] `https://universaldependencies.org/treebanks/en_ewt/index.html`

[15] `https://universaldependencies.org/conll17/`

[16] http://people.ds.cam.ac.uk/dsg40/simverb.html

	en-fr		en-de		en-ja	
corpus	en	fr	en	de	en	ja
origin	1.60×10^{-3}	1.63×10^{-3}	1.51×10^{-3}	3.78×10^{-3}	1.52×10^{-3}	1.03×10^{-3}
pseudo	0.57×10^{-3}	0.57×10^{-3}	0.66×10^{-3}	0.59×10^{-3}	0.19×10^{-3}	0.17×10^{-3}

Table 7: Type-token ratio of the training corpus (origin) and the pseudo-corpus (pseudo)

corpus	simverb-3500	men
en	0.259	0.763
en + pseudo (fr)	0.260	0.767
en + pseudo (de)	0.253	0.768
en + pseudo (ja)	0.220	0.760

Table 8: Results of word similarity. The scores indicate averages of 3 experiments with different seeds.

BT step	en→fr CLWE (no pseudo)	fr→en	en→fr CLWE (+ pseudo)	fr→en
0	14.7		**14.8**	
1	**16.7**	**18.8**	16.1	18.2
2	**18.8**	**19.2**	18.2	18.5
3	**19.2**	**19.1**	18.6	18.8

Table 9: BLEU scores of UMT at each back-translation step in En-Fr with a phrase table induced using different CLWEs.

2016) consisting of 3500 verb pairs and men[17] (Bruni et al., 2014) consisting of 3000 frequent words extracted from web text.

Table 8 shows the results of word similarity. The scores of monolingual word embeddings using a French and German pseudo corpus are maintained or improved, while they decrease in Japanese. This suggests that the quality of monolingual word embeddings could be hurt due to the low quality of the pseudo corpus or differences in linguistic nature. Nevertheless, the proposed method improves the performance of En-Ja's CLWE, which suggests that the monolingual word embeddings created with a pseudo corpus have a structure optimized for cross-lingual mapping.

Application to UMT UMT is one of the important applications of CLWEs. Appropriate initialization with CLWEs is crucial to the success of UMT (Lample et al., 2018c). To investigate how CLWEs obtained from our method affect the performance of UMTs, we compare the BLEU scores of UMTs initialized with CLWEs with and without a pseudo corpus at each iterative step. As shown in Table 9, we observe that initialization with CLWE using the pseudo data result in a higher BLEU score in the first step but does not improve the score at further steps compared to the CLWE without the pseudo data. Marie and Fujita (2019) also demonstrate the same tendency in the CLWE with joint-training.

To investigate this point, we compare the lexical densities of the training corpus and the pseudo-corpus used in the above experiments (§ 4, 5) using type-token ratio (Table 7). The results demonstrate that the pseudo corpus has a smaller vocabulary per word than the training corpus, and thus it is standardized to some extent as reported in Vanmassenhove et al. (2019). As a result, specific words might be easily mapped in CLWEs using a pseudo corpus[18], and then the translation model makes it easier to translate phrases in more specific patterns. Hence, the model cannot generate diverse data during back-translation, and the accuracy is not improved due to easy learning.

7 Conclusion and Future Work

In this paper, we show that training cross-lingual word embeddings with pseudo data augmentation improves performance in BLI and downstream tasks. We analyze the reason for this improvement and found that the pseudo corpus reflects the co-occurrence statistics and content of the other language and that the property makes the structure of the embedding suitable for cross-lingual word mapping.

Recently, Vulić et al. (2019) have shown that fully unsupervised CLWE methods fails in many language pairs and argue that researchers should not focus too much on the fully unsupervised settings. Still, our findings that improve structural similarity of word embeddings in the fully unsupervised setting could be useful in semi-supervised settings, and thus we would like to investigate this direction in the future.

[17] https://staff.fnwi.uva.nl/e.bruni/MEN

[18] In a preliminary experiment, we investigated the variation in performance of cross-lingual mapping with and without pseudo according to the frequency of words in the source language, but there was little correlation between them.

References

Mikel Artetxe, Gorka Labaka, and Eneko Agirre. 2018a. A robust self-learning method for fully unsupervised cross-lingual mappings of word embeddings. In *Proceedings of the 56th Annual Meeting of the Association for Computational Linguistics (Volume 1: Long Papers)*, pages 789–798.

Mikel Artetxe, Gorka Labaka, and Eneko Agirre. 2019a. Bilingual lexicon induction through unsupervised machine translation. In *Proceedings of the 57th Annual Meeting of the Association for Computational Linguistics*, pages 5002–5007.

Mikel Artetxe, Gorka Labaka, and Eneko Agirre. 2019b. An effective approach to unsupervised machine translation. In *Proceedings of the 57th Annual Meeting of the Association for Computational Linguistics*, pages 194–203.

Mikel Artetxe, Gorka Labaka, Eneko Agirre, and Kyunghyun Cho. 2018b. Unsupervised Neural Machine Translation. In *Proceedings of the 5th International Conference on Learning Representations*.

Samuel R. Bowman, Gabor Angeli, Christopher Potts, and Christopher D. Manning. 2015. A large annotated corpus for learning natural language inference. In *Proceedings of the 2015 Conference on Empirical Methods in Natural Language Processing*, pages 632–642.

Elia Bruni, Nam-Khanh Tran, and Marco Baroni. 2014. Multimodal distributional semantics. *Journal of Artificial Intelligence Research*.

Alexis Conneau, Ruty Rinott, Guillaume Lample, Adina Williams, Samuel Bowman, Holger Schwenk, and Veselin Stoyanov. 2018. XNLI: Evaluating cross-lingual sentence representations. In *Proceedings of the 2018 Conference on Empirical Methods in Natural Language Processing*, pages 2475–2485.

Timothy Dozat and Christopher D Manning. 2017. Deep Biafine Attention for Neural Dependency Parsing. In *Proceedings of the International Conference on Learning Representations*.

Long Duong, Hiroshi Kanayama, Tengfei Ma, Steven Bird, and Trevor Cohn. 2016. Learning Crosslingual Word Embeddings without Bilingual Corpora. In *Proceedings of the 2016 Conference on Empirical Methods in Natural Language Processing*, pages 1285–1295.

Chris Dyer, Victor Chahuneau, and Noah A. Smith. 2013. A simple, fast, and effective reparameterization of ibm model 2. In *Proceedings of the 2013 Conference of the North American Chapter of the Association for Computational Linguistics: Human Language Technologies*, pages 644–648, Atlanta, Georgia.

Daniela Gerz, Ivan Vulić, Felix Hill, Roi Reichart, and Anna Korhonen. 2016. SimVerb-3500: A large-scale evaluation set of verb similarity. In *Proceedings of the 2016 Conference on Empirical Methods in Natural Language Processing*, pages 2173–2182.

Goran Glavaš, Robert Litschko, Sebastian Ruder, and Ivan Vulić. 2019. How to (properly) evaluate cross-lingual word embeddings: On strong baselines, comparative analyses, and some misconceptions. In *Proceedings of the 57th Annual Meeting of the Association for Computational Linguistics*, pages 710–721.

Stephan Gouws, Yoshua Bengio, and Greg Corrado. 2015. BilBOWA: Fast Bilingual Distributed Representations without Word Alignments. In *Proceedings of the 32nd International Conference on Machine Learning*, volume 37, pages 748–756, Lille, France.

Kenneth Heafield, Ivan Pouzyrevsky, Jonathan H. Clark, and Philipp Koehn. 2013. Scalable modified Kneser-Ney language model estimation. In *Proceedings of the 51st Annual Meeting of the Association for Computational Linguistics (Volume 2: Short Papers)*, pages 690–696.

Philipp Koehn, Hieu Hoang, Alexandra Birch, Chris Callison-Burch, Marcello Federico, Nicola Bertoldi, Brooke Cowan, Wade Shen, Christine Moran, Richard Zens, Chris Dyer, Ondřej Bojar, Alexandra Constantin, and Evan Herbst. 2007. Moses: Open source toolkit for statistical machine translation. In *Proceedings of the 45th Annual Meeting of the Association for Computational Linguistics Companion Volume Proceedings of the Demo and Poster Sessions*, pages 177–180.

Guillaume Lample, Alexis Conneau, Ludovic Denoyer, and Marc'Aurelio Ranzato. 2018a. Unsupervised machine translation using monolingual corpora only. In *International Conference on Learning Representations*.

Guillaume Lample, Alexis Conneau, Marc'Aurelio Ranzato, Ludovic Denoyer, and Hervé Jégou. 2018b. Word translation without parallel data. In *International Conference on Learning Representations*.

Guillaume Lample, Myle Ott, Alexis Conneau, Ludovic Denoyer, and Marc'Aurelio Ranzato. 2018c. Phrase-based & neural unsupervised machine translation. In *Proceedings of the 2018 Conference on Empirical Methods in Natural Language Processing*, pages 5039–5049.

Thang Luong, Hieu Pham, and Christopher D. Manning. 2015. Bilingual Word Representations with Monolingual Quality in Mind. In *Proceedings of the 1st Workshop on Vector Space Modeling for Natural Language Processing*, pages 151–159.

Benjamin Marie and Atsushi Fujita. 2019. Unsupervised joint training of bilingual word embeddings. In *Proceedings of the 57th Annual Meeting of the*

Association for Computational Linguistics, pages 3224–3230.

Tomas Mikolov, Quoc V Le, and Ilya Sutskever. 2013. Exploiting Similarities among Languages for Machine Translation. *Computing Research Repository*, arXiv:1309.4168.

Kishore Papineni, Salim Roukos, Todd Ward, and Wei-Jing Zhu. 2002. Bleu: a method for automatic evaluation of machine translation. In *Proceedings of the 40th Annual Meeting of the Association for Computational Linguistics*, pages 311–318.

Barun Patra, Joel Ruben Antony Moniz, Sarthak Garg, Matthew R. Gormley, and Graham Neubig. 2019. Bilingual Lexicon Induction with Semi-supervision in Non-Isometric Embedding Spaces. In *Proceedings of the 57th Annual Meeting of the Association for Computational Linguistics*, pages 184–193.

Ryokan Ri and Yoshimasa Tsuruoka. 2020. Revisiting the context window for cross-lingual word embeddings. In *Proceedings of the 58th Annual Meeting of the Association for Computational Linguistics*, pages 995–1005.

Holger Schwenk and Xian Li. 2018. A corpus for multilingual document classification in eight languages. In *Proceedings of the Eleventh International Conference on Language Resources and Evaluation (LREC 2018)*.

Natalia Silveira, Timothy Dozat, Marie-Catherine de Marneffe, Samuel Bowman, Miriam Connor, John Bauer, and Chris Manning. 2014. A Gold Standard Dependency Corpus for English. In *Proceedings of the Ninth International Conference on Language Resources and Evaluation (LREC'14)*, pages 2897–2904.

Anders Søgaard, Sebastian Ruder, and Ivan Vulić. 2018. On the Limitations of Unsupervised Bilingual Dictionary Induction. In *Proceedings of the 56th Annual Meeting of the Association for Computational Linguistics (Volume 1: Long Papers)*, pages 778–788.

Shyam Upadhyay, Manaal Faruqui, Chris Dyer, and Dan Roth. 2016. Cross-lingual models of word embeddings: An empirical comparison. In *Proceedings of the 54th Annual Meeting of the Association for Computational Linguistics (Volume 1: Long Papers)*, pages 1661–1670.

Eva Vanmassenhove, Dimitar Shterionov, and Andy Way. 2019. Lost in translation: Loss and decay of linguistic richness in machine translation. In *Proceedings of Machine Translation Summit XVII Volume 1: Research Track*, pages 222–232.

Ivan Vulić, Goran Glavaš, Roi Reichart, and Anna Korhonen. 2019. Do we really need fully unsupervised cross-lingual embeddings? In *Proceedings of the 2019 Conference on Empirical Methods in Natural Language Processing and the 9th International Joint Conference on Natural Language Processing (EMNLP-IJCNLP)*, pages 4407–4418.

Ivan Vulić, Anna Korhonen, and Goran Glavaš. 2020. Improving bilingual lexicon induction with unsupervised post-processing of monolingual word vector spaces. In *Proceedings of the 5th Workshop on Representation Learning for NLP*, pages 45–54.

Ivan Vulic and Marie-Francine Moens. 2016. Bilingual Distributed Word Representations from Document-aligned Comparable Data. *Journal of Artificial Intelligence Research*, 55(1):953–994.

Adina Williams, Nikita Nangia, and Samuel Bowman. 2018. A broad-coverage challenge corpus for sentence understanding through inference. In *Proceedings of the 2018 Conference of the North American Chapter of the Association for Computational Linguistics: Human Language Technologies, Volume 1 (Long Papers)*, pages 1112–1122.

Michelle Yuan, Mozhi Zhang, Benjamin Van Durme, Leah Findlater, and Jordan Boyd-Graber. 2020. Interactive refinement of cross-lingual word embeddings. In *Proceedings of the 2020 Conference on Empirical Methods in Natural Language Processing (EMNLP)*, pages 5984–5996.

Mozhi Zhang, Keyulu Xu, Ken-ichi Kawarabayashi, Stefanie Jegelka, and Jordan Boyd-Graber. 2019. Are girls neko or shōjo? cross-lingual alignment of non-isomorphic embeddings with iterative normalization. In *Proceedings of the 57th Annual Meeting of the Association for Computational Linguistics*, pages 3180–3189.

8 Appendix

A The hyperparameters for downstream tasks

A.1 Document Classification and Sentiment Analysis

hyperparameters		
CNN Classifier	number of filters	8
	ngram_filter_sizes	2, 3, 4, 5
	MLP hidden size	32
Training	optimizer	Adam
	learning rate	0.001
	lr scheduler	halved each time the dev score stops improving
	patience	3
	batch size	50

A.2 Dependency Parsing

hyperparameters		
Graph-based Parser	LSTM hidden size	200
	LSTM number of layers	3
	tag representation dim	100
	arc representation dim	500
	pos tag embedding dim	50
Training	optimizer	Adam
	learning rate	0.001
	lr scheduler	halved each time the dev score stops improving
	patience	3
	batch size	32

A.3 Natural Language Inference

hyperparameters		
Sentence Encoder	LSTM hidden size	300
	LSTM number of layers	2
Training	optimizer	Adam
	learning rate	0.001
	lr scheduler	halved each time the dev score stops improving
	patience	3
	batch size	64

Joint Detection and Coreference Resolution of Entities and Events with Document-level Context Aggregation

Samuel Kriman and Heng Ji
University of Illinois at Urbana-Champaign
{skriman2,hengji}@illinois.edu

Abstract

Constructing knowledge graphs from unstructured text is an important task that is relevant to many domains. Most previous work focuses on extracting information from sentences or paragraphs, due to the difficulty of analyzing longer contexts. In this paper we propose a new jointly trained model that can be used for various information extraction tasks at the document level. The tasks performed in this paper are entity and event identification, typing, and coreference resolution. In order to improve entity and event extraction, we utilize context-aware representations aggregated from the detected mentions of the corresponding entities and event triggers across the entire document. By extending our system to document-level, we can improve our results by incorporating cross-sentence dependencies and additional contextual information that might not be available at the sentence level, which allows for more globally optimized predictions. We evaluate our system on documents from the ACE05-E$^+$ dataset and find significant improvement over the sentence-level state-of-the-art on entity extraction and event detection.[1]

1 Introduction

Recently, large Transformer models, such as BERT (Devlin et al., 2019), Transformer-XL (Dai et al., 2019), and RoBERTa (Liu et al., 2019), have attracted a lot of attention from the Natural Language Processing (NLP) community. These models are typically pretrained on a large unlabeled corpus, and can be consequently fine-tuned for specific NLP tasks using a relatively small amount of supervised data. By adding shallow classifiers on top of the context-sensitive embeddings produced by these neural networks, state-of-the-art results have been achieved on various subtasks in Information Extraction (Eberts and Ulges, 2019; Wang et al., 2019; Asada et al., 2020).

Despite the ability of Transformer models to efficiently capture information across a long context, most IE work still focuses on extracting information from sentences (Lin et al., 2020; Eberts and Ulges, 2019), or, in some cases, short paragraphs (Wang et al., 2019). Additionally, some work has been done where longer documents are represented by encoding sentences or paragraphs separately (Du and Cardie, 2020; Ebner et al., 2020). While some datasets have been proposed which contain document-level annotations of entities and relations (Yao et al., 2019; Jain et al., 2020; Zaporojets et al., 2021), very little work has been done in effectively utilizing the fully available document-level context in order to produce globally optimal predictions.

The main contribution of this paper is the introduction and evaluation of our new neural IE model, which can be used to jointly perform various IE subtasks in the full document context. Our model receives only the original document text as input. After identifying relevant entity and event trigger mentions in the text, we perform clustering to determine which entities or events each mention belongs to. In order to make full use of the contextual information related to an entity/event in a given document, we aggregate information from all of the corresponding mentions to create a document-level representation, which can then be used for type prediction of entities and events. We focus on constructing a model which can efficiently tackle the challenges that arise in this currently not well explored variant of the task. Our approach achieves an improvement of about 2% absolute gain over the previous results on the ACE05-E$^+$ dataset in terms of F-score for entity extraction and event detection.

[1] Code is available at https://github.com/sam1373/long_ie

Proceedings of the Joint Conference of the 59th Annual Meeting of the Association for Computational Linguistics and the 11th International Joint Conference on Natural Language Processing: Student Research Workshop, pages 174–179
August 5–6, 2021. ©2021 Association for Computational Linguistics

2 Model

2.1 Task Definition

We formulate the task of document-level information extraction in the following way. Each gold-standard sample from the dataset consists of the following parts:

1. Document D, represented by a sequence of word tokens $\{w_1, w_2, ..., w_n\}$.
2. The set of entities E, where each entity e is represented by a set of mentions in the document as well as an entity type: $e_i = (\{m_{i1}, m_{i2}, ...\}, l_i)$, where $l_i \in V_{ent}$ (the set of entity types in the dataset).
3. The set of events T, where each event t is represented by a set of event trigger mentions in the document as well as an event type: $t_i = (\{m_{i1}, m_{i2}, ...\}, l_i)$, where $l_i \in V_{ev}$ (the set of event types in the dataset).

The only input to our model is a sequence of tokens w. Given these tokens, the model is required to produce the following output: the predicted set of entities E' and events T', where each entity or event trigger mention corresponds to some span of tokens in D. In order to produce the above described output, the model operates in several steps: token encoding, entity and event trigger mention identification, coreference resolution, cluster aggregation and typing.

2.2 Token Encoding

The first step of our model consists of passing the document through a BERT-like large Transformer pre-trained for language modeling. Since we are working with potentially very long documents, for our model we choose the Longformer (Beltagy et al., 2020) as our encoder. Unlike BERT and most similar models which have quadratically increasing cost for attention, Longformer utilizes a modified more efficient attention pattern, which allows us to encode the entire document with a single Transformer pass. In addition, Longformer is pretrained on text up to 4,096 tokens, compared to 512 for models such as BERT and RoBerta.

Since the Longformer model operates using the Byte Pair Encoding subword tokenization scheme, in order to obtain the encoded representations of a given word we average the representations of corresponding word pieces. We additionally augment the word representations by concatenating a

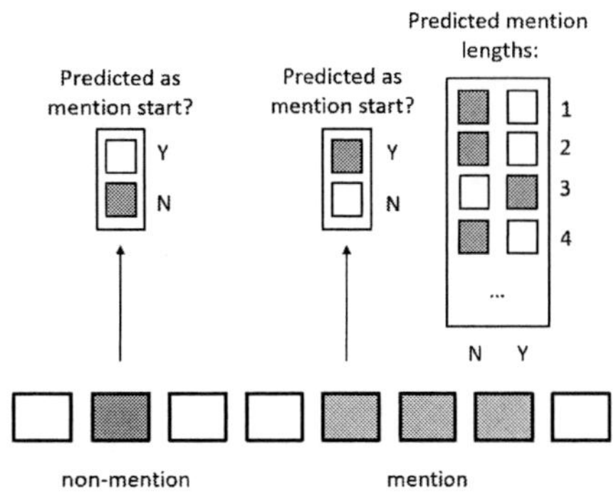

Figure 1: Identifying mention spans

pre-trained GloVe (Pennington et al., 2014) word embedding, in order to allow easier access to word-level information. We find that this augmentation improves evaluation results, particularly event trigger identification and classification.

2.3 Mention Identification

In order to extract relevant mentions from the text, we train two classifiers which are applied to each token, and used to determine, respectively, whether the token is the start of at least one relevant mention, and what are the lengths of mentions starting from this token. This is illustrated in Figure 1. Unlike commonly used span-based methods, where a representation is created for all possible mention spans up to a certain length, our approach does not require a significant increase in memory in order to consider longer entities, while still retaining the ability to potentially predict overlapping mentions.

The output of both of the classifiers at this stage is trained using cross-entropy loss. During training, further steps receive representations of gold mentions for input instead of the ones produced by the model.

2.4 Entity Coreference Resolution

Due to the large length of the documents and amount of mentions within them, it becomes impractical to use standard pairwise classification methods for coreference resolution. In order to find the entity and event clusters, we utilize the following method: mention representations are passed through a shallow residual neural network (referred to as the "coreference embedding network") to predict a special embedding for each predicted mention. In order to construct an appropriate embedding for each mention, we first obtain a representation by max-pooling over the encoded tokens that correspond to the mention span. Additionally, we concatenate a max-pooled representation of the sentence that contains the mention. The obtained mention representations are then passed through the coreference embedding network. This network is trained by using a combination of an attraction and repulsion loss, denoted as $\mathcal{L}_a$ and $\mathcal{L}_r$. Given an n-length batch of mention embeddings $\boldsymbol{m_1}, ..., \boldsymbol{m_n}$, let $C_1, C_2, ...$ denote the sets of mentions referring to the same entity. We use $c(i)$ to refer to the index of the set that mention $\boldsymbol{m_i}$ belongs to, and $o(i)$ to refer to the index of a randomly sampled incorrect mention set (so $\boldsymbol{m_i} \in C_{c(i)}, \boldsymbol{m_i} \notin C_{o(i)}$). Then the loss calculation can be written as follows:

$$\mathcal{L}_a = \sum_{i=1}^{n} ||\boldsymbol{m_i} - \frac{\sum_{\boldsymbol{m_j} \in C_{c(i)}} \boldsymbol{m_j}}{|C_{c(i)}|}||$$

$$\mathcal{L}_r = \sum_{i=1}^{n} Max(\mathcal{T} - ||\boldsymbol{m_i} - \frac{\sum_{\boldsymbol{m_j} \in C_{o(i)}} \boldsymbol{m_j}}{|C_{o(i)}|}||, 0)$$

The first of these losses pulls together mentions that belong to the same entity. The second is used to pull further apart mentions that belong to different clusters by repelling each mention embedding from the mean of another random cluster if the distance is closer than some threshold $\mathcal{T}$, which is picked based on the development set's performance. After obtaining the mention embeddings, we utilize agglomerative clustering (Murtagh and Legendre, 2011) to obtain the actual entity or event clusters.

While previous work has found un-tuned pretrained language model embeddings can achieve good results for document-level coreference resolution (Jain et al., 2020), this method is insufficient for pronoun coreference resolution, as they don't capture enough contextual information to differentiate between similar pronouns that refer to separate entities.

2.5 Cluster-based Information Aggregation

Given the predicted clusters, we produce a representation for each entity or event cluster, which will be later used for entity and event type prediction. In order to obtain the representation, we first pass each mention representation through a residual layer. Afterward max pooling is performed in order to obtain the final cluster representation. The

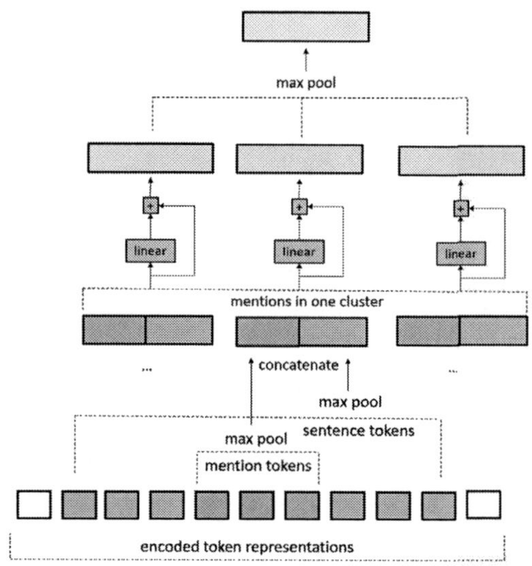

Figure 2: Method for constructing cluster representations by aggregating mentions

overall architecture for constructing mention representations, as well as aggregating mentions into a cluster representation is shown in Figure 2. Aggregating information in this way helps the model classify entities and events in situations where sentences might not provide the necessary context, such as the one presented in Figure 3. The final class scores are obtain by passing this final representation through a 2-layer linear network.

3 Experiments

3.1 Dataset

For training and evaluation we use documents from the ACE05-E$^+$ dataset (Lin et al., 2020), which consist of up to 2000 tokens with entity, event and relation annotations. This dataset was introduced as a modified version of the ACE05-E dataset, which adds pronoun mention annotations as well as multi-token triggers, and has the following statistics:

Split	Docs	Entities	Events
Training	599	47,525	4,419
Development	28	3,422	468
Test	40	3,673	424

Table 1: ACE05-E$^+$ dataset statistics

We chose this particular configuration of the dataset for our experiments due to the large amount of annotated pronoun mentions, which can be par-

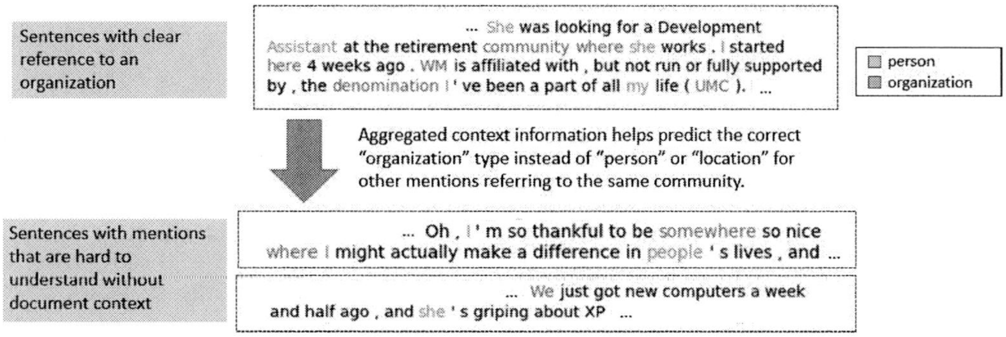

Figure 3: Excerpt from an ACE05-E$^+$ document where access to the surrounding context can be helpful for determining mention types. Mentions are colored to represent types.

ticularly difficult to classify correctly without access to external context.

3.2 Evaluation

Similar to previous work (Zhang et al., 2019; Wadden et al., 2020; Lin et al., 2019), we evaluate detection of entities and event triggers as follows: an entity or event trigger mention is considered to be correctly identified (Trig-I) if both of the offsets are correctly matched, and out of those mentions the ones with the correctly predicted type are considered correctly classified (Entities-C, Trig-C). We compare the full model with the OneIE (Lin et al., 2020) baseline, as well as with variants of our model without additional GloVe embeddings and without aggregation of information between mentions. We also calculate results for our model given gold mention and cluster information. We measure the classification F-score for entities, and the identification and classification F-scores for event triggers. Overall these results, presented in Table 2, demonstrate that document-level context aggregation can improve entity and event detection.

Model	Entities-C	Trig-I	Trig-C
OneIE	89.6	75.6	72.8
Our method			
Full Model	**91.96**	**77.67**	**75.06**
- GloVe	91.94	76.69	74.07
- aggregation	91.03	77.32	73.74
+ gold inputs			
mentions	95.97	-	92.69
clusters	97.58	-	94.25

Table 2: Entity and Event Trigger Extraction Results on ACE05-E$^+$ (F-score, %)

We utilize a multi-step system, where the input of the next step can depend on the outputs of previous steps. This leads to error accumulation, making it hard to determine which modules are working well and which aren't from the final results alone. In order to better understand how much error accumulation occurs at the coreference resolution stage of the model, we also perform evaluation of the produced entity and event trigger mention clusters using two metrics. The first is B^3_{sys} (Cai and Strube, 2010). This metric is a modification of B^3, modified to properly account for system-predicted mentions (as opposed to coreference resolution performed on gold-standard mentions). We base the second metric on "matching" predicted clusters to gold clusters. The cluster matching is performed with the following steps:

1. First, match predicted mentions to golden ones based on the mention span start and end.
2. For each predicted cluster, we check if there exists a gold cluster such that over half of the predicted cluster mentions are matched to over half gold cluster mentions.
3. We compute F-score based on the predicted clusters, gold clusters, and matched clusters based on previous step.

The matching metric is useful as it tells us the amount of entity and event clusters for which our information aggregation approach has the potential to work well. Since more than half of the mentions in a cluster are checked, this metric also has the advantage of only matching at most one predicted cluster to at most one gold cluster. The results for coreference resolution are presented in Table 3.

Metric	Precision	Recall	F
Entities			
B^3_{sys}	83.5	86.2	84.83
Matching	70.76	72.05	71.40
Event Triggers			
B^3_{sys}	76.56	77.57	77.06
Matching	47.16	56.06	51.23

Table 3: Coreference Resolution Results on ACE05-E$^+$ (%)

4 Related Work

An earlier CRF-based work by Durrett and Klein (2014) shows benefits from joint modeling of coreference resolution across a document, named entity recognition and entity linking, and notes that propagating information between different mentions of an entity in a document can help resolve ambiguous cases of semantic types or entity links.

In previous neural models similar ideas of using document-level contextual information in order to improve typing of entities have been considered (Zhang et al., 2020a). The authors of this work apply an attention mechanism in order to aggregate information between different mentions of the same underlying entity. In contrast with our proposed method, instead of jointly performing coreference resolution, this model only considers mentions with exactly matching strings, which significantly limits the effectiveness of their approach.

Jain et al. (2020) introduce a new document IE dataset, as well as a baseline model which also involves aggregation of information between mentions. However, here mention typing is performed before aggregation, and the cluster representation is instead used for other tasks, such as relation extraction. Another dataset with document-level annotation is RAMS (Ebner et al., 2020), which contains event arguments annotated in a 5-sentence window around each trigger in the documents. Several approaches have been suggested for this task. For example, Zhang et al. (2020b) introduce a two-step process for extracting event arguments, which consists of first detecting the first token, and then expanding to the entire span. Chen et al. (2020) propose to link events to their arguments by feeding each section of a document through BERT, and then processing the mention representations for triggers and potential arguments with another Transformer.

Recently another dataset for multi-task IE was introduced by Zaporojets et al. (2021), with particular focus on entities with mentions in different parts of a document. The authors also propose a baseline model for this dataset, which uses a neural graph-based message passing approach in order to aggregate document-level information.

5 Conclusions and Future Work

Aggregating information across an entire document can be highly effective for classifying entity and event mention types. This is particularly useful in cases where pronouns are used to refer to entities or events that are not explained within the same sentence. In the future, we plan to extend our approach to use document-level context for extraction of relations between entities and event arguments.

Acknowledgement

This research is based upon work supported in part by U.S. DARPA KAIROS Program No. FA8750-19-2-1004, U.S. DARPA AIDA Program No. FA8750-18-2-0014, and Air Force No. FA8650-17-C-7715. The views and conclusions contained herein are those of the authors and should not be interpreted as necessarily representing the official policies, either expressed or implied, of DARPA, or the U.S. Government. The U.S. Government is authorized to reproduce and distribute reprints for governmental purposes notwithstanding any copyright annotation therein.

References

Masaki Asada, Makoto Miwa, and Yutaka Sasaki. 2020. Using Drug Descriptions and Molecular Structures for Drug-Drug Interaction Extraction from Literature. *Bioinformatics*. Btaa907.

Iz Beltagy, Matthew E. Peters, and Arman Cohan. 2020. Longformer: The long-document transformer.

Jie Cai and Michael Strube. 2010. Evaluation metrics for end-to-end coreference resolution systems. pages 28–36.

Yunmo Chen, Tongfei Chen, and Benjamin Van Durme. 2020. Joint modeling of arguments for event understanding. In *Proceedings of the First Workshop on Computational Approaches to Discourse*, pages 96–101, Online. Association for Computational Linguistics.

Zihang Dai, Zhilin Yang, Yiming Yang, Jaime Carbonell, Quoc V. Le, and Ruslan Salakhutdinov. 2019. Transformer-xl: Attentive language models beyond a fixed-length context.

Jacob Devlin, Ming-Wei Chang, Kenton Lee, and Kristina Toutanova. 2019. BERT: Pre-training of deep bidirectional transformers for language understanding. In *Proceedings of the 2019 Conference of the North American Chapter of the Association for Computational Linguistics: Human Language Technologies, Volume 1 (Long and Short Papers)*, pages 4171–4186, Minneapolis, Minnesota. Association for Computational Linguistics.

Xinya Du and Claire Cardie. 2020. Document-level event role filler extraction using multi-granularity contextualized encoding. In *Proceedings of the 58th Annual Meeting of the Association for Computational Linguistics*, pages 8010–8020, Online. Association for Computational Linguistics.

Greg Durrett and Dan Klein. 2014. A joint model for entity analysis: Coreference, typing, and linking. *Transactions of the Association for Computational Linguistics*, 2:477–490.

Markus Eberts and Adrian Ulges. 2019. Span-based joint entity and relation extraction with transformer pre-training.

Seth Ebner, Patrick Xia, Ryan Culkin, Kyle Rawlins, and Benjamin Van Durme. 2020. Multi-sentence argument linking. In *Proceedings of the 58th Annual Meeting of the Association for Computational Linguistics*, pages 8057–8077, Online. Association for Computational Linguistics.

Sarthak Jain, Madeleine van Zuylen, Hannaneh Hajishirzi, and Iz Beltagy. 2020. Scirex: A challenge dataset for document-level information extraction.

Chen Lin, Timothy Miller, Dmitriy Dligach, Steven Bethard, and Guergana Savova. 2019. A BERT-based universal model for both within- and cross-sentence clinical temporal relation extraction. In *Proceedings of the 2nd Clinical Natural Language Processing Workshop*, pages 65–71, Minneapolis, Minnesota, USA. Association for Computational Linguistics.

Ying Lin, Heng Ji, Fei Huang, and Lingfei Wu. 2020. A joint end-to-end neural model for information extraction with global features. In *Proc. The 58th Annual Meeting of the Association for Computational Linguistics (ACL2020)*.

Yinhan Liu, Myle Ott, Naman Goyal, Jingfei Du, Mandar Joshi, Danqi Chen, Omer Levy, Mike Lewis, Luke Zettlemoyer, and Veselin Stoyanov. 2019. Roberta: A robustly optimized bert pretraining approach.

Fionn Murtagh and Pierre Legendre. 2011. Ward's hierarchical clustering method: Clustering criterion and agglomerative algorithm.

Jeffrey Pennington, Richard Socher, and Christopher D. Manning. 2014. Glove: Global vectors for word representation. In *Empirical Methods in Natural Language Processing (EMNLP)*, pages 1532–1543.

David Wadden, Shanchuan Lin, Kyle Lo, Lucy Lu Wang, Madeleine van Zuylen, Arman Cohan, and Hannaneh Hajishirzi. 2020. Fact or fiction: Verifying scientific claims. In *Proceedings of the 2020 Conference on Empirical Methods in Natural Language Processing (EMNLP)*, pages 7534–7550, Online. Association for Computational Linguistics.

Hong Wang, Christfried Focke, Rob Sylvester, Nilesh Mishra, and William Wang. 2019. Fine-tune bert for docred with two-step process.

Yuan Yao, Deming Ye, Peng Li, Xu Han, Yankai Lin, Zhenghao Liu, Zhiyuan Liu, Lixin Huang, Jie Zhou, and Maosong Sun. 2019. Docred: A large-scale document-level relation extraction dataset.

Klim Zaporojets, Johannes Deleu, Chris Develder, and Thomas Demeester. 2021. Dwie: an entity-centric dataset for multi-task document-level information extraction.

Boliang Zhang, Spencer Whitehead, Lifu Huang, and Heng Ji. 2020a. Global attention for name tagging.

Xiang Zhang, Shizhu He, Kang Liu, and Jun Zhao. 2019. AdaNSP: Uncertainty-driven adaptive decoding in neural semantic parsing. In *Proceedings of the 57th Annual Meeting of the Association for Computational Linguistics*, pages 4265–4270, Florence, Italy. Association for Computational Linguistics.

Zhisong Zhang, Xiang Kong, Zhengzhong Liu, Xuezhe Ma, and Eduard Hovy. 2020b. A two-step approach for implicit event argument detection. In *Proceedings of the 58th Annual Meeting of the Association for Computational Linguistics*, pages 7479–7485, Online. Association for Computational Linguistics.

"Hold on honey, men at work": A semi-supervised approach to detecting sexism in sitcoms

Smriti Singh*
Manipal Institute of Technology
smritisingh26@yahoo.com

Tanvi Anand*
Manipal Institute of Technology
tanviaanand@gmail.com

Arijit Ghosh Chowdhury
Manipal Institute of Technology
arijit10@gmail.com

Zeerak Waseem
University of Sheffield
z.w.butt@sheffield.ac.uk

Abstract

Television shows play an important role in propagating societal norms. Owing to the popularity of the situational comedy (sitcom) genre, it contributes significantly to the overall development of society. In an effort to analyze the content of television shows belonging to this genre, we present a dataset of dialogue turns from popular sitcoms annotated for the presence of sexist remarks. We train a text classification model to detect sexism using domain adaptive learning. We apply the model to our dataset to analyze the evolution of sexist content over the years. We propose a domain-specific semi-supervised architecture for the aforementioned detection of sexism. Through extensive experiments, we show that our model often yields better classification performance over generic deep learning based sentence classification that does not employ domain-specific training. We find that while sexism decreases over time on average, the proportion of sexist dialogue for the most sexist sitcom actually increases. . A quantitative analysis along with a detailed error analysis presents the case for our proposed methodology.

1 Introduction

Apart from being one of the most popular genres on television [1], sitcoms also attract the adolescent viewership[2] and thus play a vital role in the formation of their thought process (Villani, 2001). Sink and Mastro (2017) argue that documenting the prevalence and quality of television representations of women is a valuable endeavor as television depictions of women is known to influence attitudes and beliefs towards gender. Therefore, these shows would ideally contain a minimal amount of sexist content. However, according to Lee et al. (2019a) and O'Kelly (1974), this may not be the case. For this reason, we present a dataset consisting of dialogue turns labeled as either 'sexist' or 'neutral'. We also build a system that automatically detects instances of sexism present in the dialogue of popular sitcoms. Thus, we attempt to use machine learning to document the gap between activism and social change.

Often, a lack of labeled data can present a considerable challenge for text classification systems. Manual annotation often requires domain knowledge and may be expensive and time-consuming for large datasets. Manual annotation also carries the risk of introducing new annotator biases, privacy-breaches, discrimination, and misunderstanding (Chowdhury et al., 2019). Although dialogue is not the only way that sexism is constructed in TV shows (Brewington, 2019; Mouka and Saridakis, 2015), the more subtle signs of discrimination can be more difficult to detect and analyze. Our work addresses issues of manual annotation by using semi-supervised learning to generate a dataset in a new domain of pseudo-labels from unlabelled data to detect sexism in TV dialogue. This minimizes the need for a manual annotation process while creating large datasets.

We make use of a previously published dataset (Waseem and Hovy, 2016) to create a semi-supervised domain adapted classifier. In general, domain adaptation uses labeled data in one or more source domains to solve new tasks in a target domain. It is a sub-category of transfer learning. Since there is a lack of television show scripts annotated for sexism, we attempt a semi-supervised approach to develop our dataset. Here, our source domain consists of tweets from Waseem and Hovy's (2016)'s 'Hate Speech Twitter Annotations' dataset and our target domain is the dialogue in popular

[1] https://www.statista.com/statistics/1035741/most-in-demand-tv-genres-us-share/

[2] https://www.statista.com/statistics/859722/all-time-tv-shows-millennials/

Proceedings of the Joint Conference of the 59th Annual Meeting of the Association for Computational Linguistics and the 11th International Joint Conference on Natural Language Processing: Student Research Workshop, pages 180–185
August 5–6, 2021.

sitcoms. These two domains are quite different. Tweets are usually short, full of abbreviations, urban slang and grammatical errors. On the other hand, sitcom dialogue turns are descriptive, long, grammatically correct and contextually dependent on the dialogue turns that precede them. These differences warrant the need for a semi-supervised approach in our methodology.

2 Related Work

In the growing body of literature on the automatic detection of sexism in text on social media, Twitter, in particular, has been the object of study and dataset creation.

Waseem and Hovy (2016) created a dataset containing Racist and Sexist tweets. Following this, there have been various efforts towards detecting sexism in English tweets (Sharifirad et al., 2019), (Jha and Mamidi, 2017). (Mishra et al., 2018). Recently, Chiril et al. (2020) developed a dataset for sexism detection in French tweets. While the study of sexism in TV shows has received little attention in natural language processing Lee et al. (2019b), Gala et al. (2020), Xu et al. (2019), it has received significant attention in the field of gender studies (Sink and Mastro, 2017; Glascock, 2003). In gender studies, Sink and Mastro (2017) conducted a quantitative analysis to document portrayals of women and men on prime-time television and Glascock (2003) examines the perception of gender roles on network prime-time television programming. To the best of our knowledge, no previous work has presented a comprehensive dataset for the presence of sexism in TV shows has been created. While efforts have been made to analyse the presence of sexism in TV shows (Nayef, 2016), the question of developing a machine learning based detection system for identifying sexism in scripted TV dialogue remains under-explored. However, Semi-supervised learning has received a lot of attention from the NLP community (Zhai et al., 2019; Xie et al., 2019; Chen et al., 2020). Our method most closely resembles Unsupervised Data Augmentation (Xie et al., 2019), which uses labeled data to annotate unlabeled samples under low resource settings.

3 Dataset

3.1 Collection

The dataset used for this experiment consists of three parts. The first part is the data used for our training dataset. We use a dataset annotated for sexist tweets Waseem and Hovy (2016). To ensure that the classifier can identify non-sexist dialogue correctly, we append $2,000$ tweets that are non-sexist in nature obtained from a web application named 'Tweet Sentiment to CSV'.[3] Before appending these neutral tweets to the dataset, they were manually checked and any tweets that were not in English were removed, along with any ambiguous tweets. To account for our target domain, we collect the dialogues from twenty sitcoms cross-referenced by popularity[4] and script availability[5]. From this set of dialogue scripts, we randomly sample $1,937$ dialogue turns to manually annotate (see subsection 3.2 for annotation guidelines). The final training set consists of $3,011$ tweets labeled as sexist, $2,000$ tweets labeled as neutral, 203 sexist dialogue turns and 926 neutral dialogue turns, henceforth denoted as D_{train}.

For the second part of the dataset, we use the un-annotated dialogue turns from the TV shows to perform semi-supervised learning. We call this dataset $D_{semisupervised}$. Out of these, ten shows aired between 1985 and 1999 (*old shows*) and ten shows aired between 2000 and 2015 (*new shows*).

The third part of our dataset, which is manually annotated and used as a held-out test set, consists of 805 manually annotated dialogues, 411 of that are labeled as neutral and 394 as sexist. This data was annotated by four annotators, achieving a Cohen's Kappa (Cohen, 1960) of 0.87.

3.2 Definition of Sexism

In this section, we describe the guidelines followed during the annotation process. The guidelines of what classifies a tweet as sexist were defined by Waseem and Hovy (2016). We use Glick and Fiske's (1996) definition of sexism to annotate dialogue turns from popular sitcoms. According to this definition, there are three primary dimensions within sexism.

- ***Paternalism:*** Paternalism justifies men being controlling, protective and authoritative over women. E.g. '*'Hold on honey, men at work.*" (Howard Wolowitz, The Big Bang Theory)
- ***Gender Differentiation:*** Gender Differentiation uses biological differences between gen-

[3] https://twitter-sentiment-csv.herokuapp.com/
[4] IMDB: https://www.imdb.com/
[5] https://subslikescript.com/series, https://transcripts.foreverdreaming.org/

Model	Accuracy	F1	Precision	Recall	AUCROC
NB	0.772 ±0.04	0.776 ±0.02	0.778 ±0.03	0.773 ±0.02	0.765 ±0.03
RF	0.781 ±0.05	0.791 ±0.04	0.784 ±0.03	0.799 ±0.02	0.771 ±0.01
LR	0.777 ±0.02	0.780 ±0.04	0.781 ±0.03	0.779 ±0.02	0.766 ±0.03
SVM	0.783 ±0.04	0.782 ±0.04	0.773 ±0.02	0.793 ±0.03	0.783 ±0.02
BERT	0.773 ±0.04	0.742 ±0.04	0.753 ±0.02	0.713 ±0.03	0.723 ±0.02
Bi-LSTM (Ours)	**0.830 ±0.03**	**0.828 ±0.02**	**0.819 ±0.01**	**0.823 ±0.03**	**0.817±0.04**

Table 1: Results when models are trained on D_{final}. Standard errors are reported after 5 trials.

ders to justify social distinctions. An example of a sexist dialogue turn under this dimension is: *"I think women just have a lower threshold for pain than men.'* (Joey Tribbiani, Friends)

- ***Male Gaze:*** Male Gaze refers to viewing women as sexual objects. An example of a sexist dialogue turn under this dimension is: *"All men want is to see women naked."* (Jerry Seinfeld, Seinfeld)

Apart from this, we have also included dialogue turns that include derogatory terms against women (James (1998)) and dialogue turns that justify stereotypes against women or gender roles (Lauzen et al. (2008)). E.g. "See? Strong women always turn out to be nightmares" (Seinfeld) and "Look I'm sorry but some things are different for men and women." (Chandler Bing, Friends)

We find that within the annotated sexist dialogues in our held-out test set, 27.9% of the dialogues fall under gender differentiation sexism, 33.7% of the dialogues fall under paternalism and 38.4% under male gaze.

3.3 Preprocessing

The following steps were taken as a part of the preprocessing process:

- The names of the characters who said the dialogue were removed from each dialogue turn, to avoid any undue dataset bias pertaining to character names,
- Lines in the transcripts that were not dialogue turns, such as bracketed expressions to convey the settings or scenes, were removed,
- Any numbers that appeared in dialogue turns were removed,
- All words were converted to lowercase, tokenized and lemmatized.

4 Experiment Setup

We begin by training a set of models on D_{train} (section 3.1) to find the best performing model. We make use of a support vector machine (SVM), a logistic regression classifier (LR), a random forest ensemble (RF), a naive Bayes classifier (NB) , fine-tuned BERT, and a bi-directional LSTM (bi-LSTM). We find that the bi-LSTM outperforms the other models by 3.4%, with an accuracy of 76.03% on the held-out test set, D_{test}. Thus, we make use of the bi-LSTM in our proposed semi-supervised approach.

Out of the 20 sitcom show scripts we collect, we use four, namely 'Friends', 'The Big Bang Theory', 'How I Met Your Mother' and 'Seinfeld' for manual annotation (see section 3.1 for more detail). Next, we use the baseline bi-LSTM to make predictions on the other 16 show scripts. Out of these, eight are *new shows* and the other eight are *old shows*. The model classifies 1,639 dialogue turns as sexist. To form $D_{semisupervised}$, we add all dialogue turns identified as sexist by the baseline model and randomly sample 31,944 dialogue turns from the 242,108 dialogue turns identified as neutral. We combine D_{train} and $D_{semisupervised}$ to form D_{final} [6].

Finally, we train a bi-LSTM on D_{final}. We make use of the softmax activation function and the categorical cross entropy loss function while training this bi-LSTM. It consists of an embedding layer, a spatial dropout layer and makes use of the Adam optimizer, with a dropout equal to 0.2. This bi-LSTM attains an accuracy of 83.0% on D_{test}. To offer a fair comparison, we also train other competitive models on D_{final}. Table 1 demonstrates the performance of these models on D_{test} across six evaluation metrics.

To offer some insight on how the amount of sex-

[6] https://github.com/smritisingh26/HHMWdataset

Old Shows	Percentage	New Shows	Percentage
Friends	2.357%	Brooklyn Nine Nine	0.089%
Seinfeld	2.580%	The Big Bang Theory	4.131%
The Simpsons	2.611%	The Office	0.179%
Frasier	1.956%	How I met your Mother	2.343%
Full House	2.299%	Modern Family	2.267%
Everybody Loves Raymond	2.481%	Scrubs	2.168%
Home Improvement	1.956%	Parks and Recreation	1.438%
House	2.556%	New Girl	0.752%
That 70s' Show	2.369%	Two and a Half Men	3.521%
King of Queens	1.478%	Family Guy	1.865%

Table 2: Sexist content in popular sitcoms as classified by the proposed model

ist content in the form of dialogue has developed over the years, we use our proposed model to classify the dialogue turns of all twenty shows.

5 Results

5.1 Model Performance & Content Analysis

In comparing the baseline bi-directional LSTM model trained on D_{train} and the proposed model trained on D_{final}, we observe a gain of 7% in terms of accuracy on D_{test}. Similarly, for all other models, we see an average improvement of 4.67% when they are trained on D_{final}, as compared to their initial performance when they were trained on D_{train}.

The results shown in Table 1 suggest that using an augmented dataset obtained through semi-supervised learning can provide a promising avenue for addressing hate speech in distinct domains that do not have large labeled datasets available.

Furthermore, an analysis of the data labeled by our proposed model (see Table1) reveals that between 1985-1999, the average percentage of sexist dialogue turns in sitcoms is around 2.26%, whereas between 2000-2015, the mean is around 1.87% which shows an overall decrease in the number of sexist dialogue turns by 0.39%. However, it is worth noting that in the shows aired between 1985 and 1999, the show with the greatest percentage of sexist dialogue turns has 2.61% sexist dialogue turns while the proportion of sexist dialogue turns is 4.13% for the worst offender after the turn of the century. This is further complicated by the fact that the shows with the lowest amounts of sexism in the two time periods contain 1.95% and 0.08% for the old and the new shows, respectively.

5.2 Error Analysis

In an analysis of the best-performing model's performance, we identify some confounding variables:

- **Women vs that woman** Aggressively negative statements about a particular woman are marked as sexist. E.g. *"To hell with her! She left me!"* (Friends).
  While such statements may be sexist, our classifier is unable to distinguish the required nuance to make the correct prediction.

- **Sexual content** Some statements that contain extremely sexual terms are marked as sexist. For example: *"And yet you're the one always getting spanked."* (Two and a Half Men)
  This may be because a lot of sentences that contain sexual terms in the underlying datasets are sexist. For instance, dialogue turns in the training dataset like *"Well, most women want to be banged."* (How I met your Mother) and *"Sit with her, hold her, comfort her and if the moment feels right, see if you can cop a feel."* (The Big Bang Theory) are sexist.

- **Marriages** Dialogues that mention women and marriages or weddings are marked as sexist in some cases. For example: *"I know that some lucky girl is going to become Mrs. Barry Finkel."* (Friends)
  This can be attributed to a lack of contextual understanding in the classifier. Perhaps because there aren't that many dialogue turns that mention weddings or marriages.

- **Gendered pronouns for objects** In some cases, the pronoun 'she' is used to refer to objects like vehicles and boats and appear as sexist to the classifier. For example: *"She really gets going after a while."* where 'she' refers to a car (Family guy).

6 Conclusion

We generate a labeled, real-world dataset and build a classifier using a combination of transfer learning and semi-supervised learning to classify dialogues in sitcoms as sexist or neutral for the purpose of tracking the status of social discrimination. An analysis of the recent content reveals an overall decrease in sexist content over time but an increase in the amount of sexist content in the worst offending TV shows in the recent years.

7 Acknowledgements

Zeerak Waseem has been supported in part by the Canada 150 Research Chair program and the UK-Canada AI Artificial Intelligence Initiative.

References

Morgan Brewington. 2019. Is sexism taking on new forms in movies? an ambivalent sexism perspective.

Jiaao Chen, Zichao Yang, and Diyi Yang. 2020. Mixtext: Linguistically-informed interpolation of hidden space for semi-supervised text classification. *CoRR*, abs/2004.12239.

Patricia Chiril, Véronique Moriceau, Farah Benamara, Alda Mari, Gloria Origgi, and Marlène Coulomb-Gully. 2020. An annotated corpus for sexism detection in French tweets. In *Proceedings of the 12th Language Resources and Evaluation Conference*, pages 1397–1403, Marseille, France. European Language Resources Association.

Arijit Ghosh Chowdhury, Ramit Sawhney, Rajiv Shah, and Debanjan Mahata. 2019. # youtoo? detection of personal recollections of sexual harassment on social media. In *Proceedings of the 57th Annual Meeting of the Association for Computational Linguistics*, pages 2527–2537.

Jacob Cohen. 1960. A coefficient of agreement for nominal scales. *Educational and Psychological Measurement*, 20(1):37–46.

Dhruvil Gala, Mohammad Omar Khursheed, Hannah Lerner, Brendan O'Connor, and Mohit Iyyer. 2020. Analyzing gender bias within narrative tropes. *arXiv preprint arXiv:2011.00092*.

Jack Glascock. 2003. Viewer perception of gender roles on network prime-time television. *Communication Research Reports*, 20(2):173–181.

Peter Glick and Susan T Fiske. 1996. The ambivalent sexism inventory: Differentiating hostile and benevolent sexism. *Journal of personality and social psychology*, 70(3):491.

Deborah James. 1998. Gender-linked derogatory terms and their use by women and men. *American Speech*, 73(4):399–420.

Akshita Jha and Radhika Mamidi. 2017. When does a compliment become sexist? analysis and classification of ambivalent sexism using twitter data.

Martha M Lauzen, David M Dozier, and Nora Horan. 2008. Constructing gender stereotypes through social roles in prime-time television. *Journal of Broadcasting & Electronic Media*, 52(2):200–214.

Nayeon Lee, Yejin Bang, Jamin Shin, and Pascale Fung. 2019a. Understanding the shades of sexism in popular TV series. In *Proceedings of the 2019 Workshop on Widening NLP*, pages 122–125, Florence, Italy. Association for Computational Linguistics.

Nayeon Lee, Yejin Bang, Jamin Shin, and Pascale Fung. 2019b. Understanding the shades of sexism in popular TV series. In *Proceedings of the 2019 Workshop on Widening NLP*, pages 122–125, Florence, Italy. Association for Computational Linguistics.

Pushkar Mishra, Marco Del Tredici, Helen Yannakoudakis, and Ekaterina Shutova. 2018. Author profiling for abuse detection.

Effie Mouka and Ioannis Saridakis. 2015. *Racism goes to the movies: A corpus-driven study of cross-linguistic racist discourse annotation and translation analysis*, pages 35–69.

Heba Nayef. 2016. Linguistic sexism in tv drama: A linguistic analysis of verbal violence against women in the egyptian sitcom al-kabeer awi. *International Journal of Linguistics*, 4(1):84–103.

Charlotte G. O'Kelly. 1974. Sexism in children's television. *Journalism Quarterly*, 51(4):722–724.

Sima Sharifirad, Borna Jafarpour, and Stan Matwin. 2019. How is your mood when writing sexist tweets? detecting the emotion type and intensity of emotion using natural language processing techniques. *arXiv preprint arXiv:1902.03089*.

Alexander Sink and Dana Mastro. 2017. Depictions of gender on primetime television: A quantitative content analysis. *Mass Communication and Society*, 20(1):3–22.

Susan Villani. 2001. Impact of media on children and adolescents: a 10-year review of the research. *Journal of the American Academy of child & adolescent psychiatry*, 40(4):392–401.

Zeerak Waseem and Dirk Hovy. 2016. Hateful symbols or hateful people? predictive features for hate speech detection on twitter. In *Proceedings of the NAACL student research workshop*, pages 88–93.

Qizhe Xie, Zihang Dai, Eduard Hovy, Minh-Thang Luong, and Quoc V Le. 2019. Unsupervised data augmentation for consistency training. *arXiv preprint arXiv:1904.12848*.

Huimin Xu, Zhang Zhang, Lingfei Wu, and Cheng-Jun Wang. 2019. The cinderella complex: Word embeddings reveal gender stereotypes in movies and books. *PloS one*, 14(11):e0225385.

Xiaohua Zhai, Avital Oliver, Alexander Kolesnikov, and Lucas Beyer. 2019. S4l: Self-supervised semi-supervised learning. In *Proceedings of the IEEE international conference on computer vision*, pages 1476–1485.

Observing the Learning Curve of Neural Machine Translation with regard to Linguistic Phenomena

Patrick Stadler, Vivien Macketanz and **Eleftherios Avramidis**
German Research Center for Artificial Intelligence (DFKI), Berlin
firstname.lastname@dfki.de

Abstract

In this paper we present our observations and evaluations by observing the linguistic performance of the system on several steps on the training process of various English-to-German Neural Machine Translation models. The linguistic performance is measured through a semi-automatic process using a test suite. Among several linguistic observations, we find that the translation quality of some linguistic categories decreased within the recorded iterations. Additionally, we notice some drops of the translation quality of certain categories when using a larger corpus.

1 Introduction

During the last years, neural machine translation (NMT) has seen immense progress and achieved high performance. As most machine learning methods, NMT is based on an iterative training process that *learns to translate* given big amounts of parallel corpora. Despite the remarkable achievements of the training process in terms of producing a model able to translate, it is used as a black box. This is also due to the fact that it is training a neural network, one of the least interpretable machine learning algorithms. Thus, little effort has been done in order to investigate how the training process evolves with regards to measurable factors of translation quality, such as the rules of linguistic correctness (grammar, syntax, semantics).

In particular, the training process performs several iterations through which the neural network weights are gradually adjusted to achieve the optimal performance for the training data seen at the moment. After several iterations, the performance of the model, with its current weights, is typically validated against a development set, using some automatic metrics (cross entropy or BLEU score; Papineni et al., 2002), which may also define whether the optimal conditions have been reached and training should stop. Although these automatic metrics have been proven useful for the training process itself, they provide a single number for a generic notion of the translation quality. As specified, we are interested in observing the training process from a more fine-grained perspective and particularly how it proceeds with learning specific linguistic phenomena.

This work is intended to provide NMT researchers and engineers with additional guidance on what to look for when evaluating and designing machine translation systems. This is a preliminary work towards this direction, aiming to investigate how the training process evolves with regards to linguistic performance for several phenomena. We do this by selecting snapshots of particular training epochs and evaluating these snapshots with test suites, which probe the translation of specific linguistic phenomena.

As a result, we can observe the learning curve of those linguistic aspects, along with strengths and weaknesses. We find that as the training ends and the BLEU score reaches the maximum value, some linguistic categories experience a drop in their accuracy. Additionally, we notice further drops of the translation quality of certain categories when using a larger corpus. Finally, we provide further observations on particular linguistic phenomena, by focusing on certain test items. Our experiment is focusing on the language direction English→German.

In the next section (section 2) we review related work. Section 3 presents our used methods, while in section 4 the experiment setup is further discussed. We present our results in section 5 and compare the different models in section 6, followed by a short conclusion and notes on further work in section 7.

Proceedings of the Joint Conference of the 59th Annual Meeting of the Association for Computational Linguistics and the 11th International Joint Conference on Natural Language Processing: Student Research Workshop, pages 186–196
August 5–6, 2021.

2 Related work

2.1 Interpreting NMT with regards to linguistic phenomena

There have been several efforts to interpret the operation of NMT with regards to linguistic phenomena. These works mostly focus on identifying which parts of the neural topology are responsible for learning some particular linguistic aspects. For example they investigate the role of particular neurons (Bau et al., 2019), layers, major components such as the encoder and the decoder (Dalvi et al., 2017; Tang et al., 2019; Belinkov et al., 2020), or different architectures (Tang et al., 2020) with regards to word sense disambiguation and semantics, morphology, long range dependencies and syntax, etc. Contrary to these works, our consideration of the linguistic aspects is not focusing on the elements of the neural network, but on its timely development during the training process.

Recognising the limitations of scoring with cross-entropy or BLEU score, two papers have proposed scoring based on more focused metrics, such as semantic similarity (Wieting et al., 2019) and adequacy (Kong et al., 2018). Here, we are not interested in finding a linguistic metric to improve the training process, but to apply a fine-grained linguistic analysis to the several stages of the training process and make observations.

2.2 Fine-grained evaluation using test suites

Despite the widespread usage of BLEU score, there have been critical voices from the translation community on its role. As stated by Callison-Burch et al. (2006), BLEU sometimes does not reflect improvement in the quality of the produced translations and therefore is not always a reliable metric to rate a system overall. They showed that BLEU score allows for a certain variance and is often unreliable or inconsistent compared to human analysis especially when one is examining linguistic phenomena on a fine grained level (Avramidis et al., 2019).

To overcome the disadvantages and instabilities of the BLEU score, researches have suggested the utilisation of test suites. Such test suites can report scores either through manual (Ahrenberg, 2018; Koh et al., 2001) or semi-automatic evaluation. Semi-automatic evaluation uses certain metrics to be tested against, such as reference translations with specific tokens (Guillou and Hardmeier, 2016; Macketanz et al., 2018a). Another important aspect for using test suites instead of relying solely on automatic evaluation, is the domain-knowledge that only human judges can provide and is required to to assess the translation quality (Vojtěchová et al., 2019).

3 Methods

We are interested in observing the learning curve of neural machine translation with regards to linguistic phenomena. Particularly, the aim is to examine how the linguistic performance of a translation model improves along the iterations of the training process. In order to do that, we perform the following steps:

- We train a neural machine translation system.
- We save the state of the translation model after every epoch of the training process.
- We select some epochs of interest (snapshots) based on the BLEU score of the epoch validation on the development set.
- We perform fine-grained evaluation for every snapshot using a linguistically motivated test suite.

By comparing the statistics from the fine-grained evaluation for various snapshots, we intend to get insights with a linguistic perspective in the machine learning process. We can only evaluate particular snapshots, since the functioning of the test suite tool allows semi-automatic error annotation and there is still need to manually evaluate some uncertain decisions and edge cases. To decide which snapshots to pick, we relied on the use of BLEU score as a first indicator, despite its limitations.

Additionally, we build several systems with different architectures and corpus sizes to allow further comparisons. This being a student experiment, the computational and time restrictions allowed a limited number of models trained with an amount of data that is smaller than the state-of-the-art. However, that should serve as proof of concept. Despite the models not being state-of-the-art, our focus remains on the evolution of the linguistic performance, starting from the early steps of the training process. In our experiments we will have three systems: a small RNN model trained on a small amount of corpora, a bigger RNN model with more data than the former, and a transformer model. Technical details for these models are given further in Section 4.3.

3.1 Different neural machine translation models

We trained several models in order to understand the impact of corpus sizes and the architectures to the linguistic performance. A first run using a RNN architecture (Bahdanau et al., 2014) examines the development of the translation quality based on a relatively small corpus (RNN-small). A succeeding run uses the same model type and arguments but utilises a larger corpus (RNN-big). This allows for more direct comparison and helps to understand the impact of the selected data size. To be able to examine the importance of the selected model type and be closer to the state-of-the-art, we trained a transformer system (Vaswani et al., 2017).

3.2 Fine grained evaluation with a test suite

For the fine-grained evaluation of the trained systems performance, we used a test suite similar to Avramidis et al. (2019). As opposed to an outright human evaluation or the sole use of automatic metrics, the test suite relies on automated evaluation based on manually provided rules. Therefore, regular expressions are applied to manually devised test sentences with several linguistic phenomena grouped into categories. Based on the regular expressions, the test suite can then evaluate the linguistic phenomena, strictly by the presence, respectively, absence of certain key terms and phrases, such as false friends or the use of a wrong tense. The score of a system is then presented as the accuracy across the selected phenomena.

The construction of the test suite and the organization of the categories do not follow a specific linguistic theory and we do not claim a full coverage of the whole linguistic spectrum. Other pieces of research may have different categorization, for example unlike other test suites, we include pronouns under the co-reference phenomenon in the category of non-verbal agreement.

4 Experiment setup

4.1 Test suite setup

For the development and application of the test suite we used the tool TQ-AutoTest (Macketanz et al., 2018a). We created 10 sentences per phenomenon, resulting in a total of 585 sentences, examining 49 phenomena organised in 13 categories. The raw test items, as well as the translations evaluated can be found in our repository[1]. The phenomena selected for this experiment are a subset of the ones of German→English MT, as described in Macketanz et al. (2018b) and Avramidis et al. (2020), adapted to the opposite language direction. An extract of the used sentences can be found in table 5.

System name	RNN-small	RNN-big	transf.
Training datasets	europarl	europarl DGT	europarl DGT
Dataset size	1.8M	7M	7M
Vocab size	32000	32000	32000
Mini-Batch-Fit	5000	5000	10000
Learning rate	0.001	0.001	0.003
Encoder depth	1	1	6
Decoder depth	1	1	6
Beam size	6	6	12
Validation freq.	10000	10000	10000
Dropout	0.2	0.2	0.1
Dropout Source	0.1	0.1	
Dropout Target	0.1	0.1	
Transf. heads			8
Early stopping	5	5	10
BLEU min	1.31	5.58	0
BLEU max	14.34	16.02	24.29
Best epoch	39	18	28
Total run time	17 h	56 h	31 h

Table 1: Summary of training settings and development results

4.2 Data

The Europarl corpus ver. 10 (Koehn, 2005) with about 1,8 M sentences and the DGT 2019 corpus (Tiedemann, 2012) with approximately 5,2 M sentences were used, summing up to around 7 M parallel sentences for training. Newstest 2015 (Bojar et al., 2015) was used as a development (validation) set and newstest 2016 (Bojar et al., 2016) as a test set.

We applied standard preprocessing including normalization, sentence filtering, tokenization and byte-pair encoding by using the default Marian setting (Junczys-Dowmunt et al., 2018) with embedded SentencePiece (Kudo and Richardson, 2018). Concerning the length of the individual sentences, we followed the general practice and limited the sentences to a maximum length of 100.

4.3 Training setup

The NMT systems were trained using Marian ver. 1.9.0 (Junczys-Dowmunt et al., 2018). In order to follow the learning curve of the training process,

[1]https://github.com/pstadler1990/nmt_paper21_appendix

we kept one checkpoint every 10,000 iterations. To do so, we disabled the `overwrite` option from the CLI call of MARIAN. As per default, cross entropy was used as a validation metric, whereas the training processes were run on a computational server Quadro RTX 6000 (4608 cores, 96 ROPs and a 24 GB memory size) using 2 out of its 8 GPUs.

The validation iterations in the results are labeled as following: $iter_{val} = \frac{iter_{tr}}{f_{val}}$ where $iter_{tr}$ is the reported training iteration number (up.) and f_{val} is the specified validation frequency. For our trained systems, we set this to 10,000. So, a validation iteration of 10,000 training iterations is labeled as 1.

An overview of the settings of the three systems can be seen in Table 1. In particular, the following three systems were trained:

Small RNN model This system was built with Europarl with a final size after pre-processing of 1,828,521 sentences, using an RNN with single-layer encoder and decoder and a minibatch size of 10,000.

Big RNN model In order to build a bigger RNN model, we used the larger dataset consisting of both, Europarl and the DGT corpora, following the same settings as for the small RNN model.

Transformer We used the same training, dev and test sets as in the big RNN model, and the example configuration for a transformer model from MARIAN[2] adapted to our needs as shown in Table 1. This configuration utilises a six-layer deep encoder and decoder, learning rate warm-up and tied embeddings for source, target and output layer. As suggested by Karita et al. (2019), we increased the minibatch size for the transformer model from 5,000 to 10,000.

5 Results

5.1 Evaluation of the small RNN model

The small RNN model was trained for 17 hours and achieved a BLEU score of 14.34.

5.1.1 Snapshot selection

The best reported BLEU score was reached in epoch 39, out of total 46 epochs, having started with 1.31 in epoch 1. Figure 1 shows the BLEU

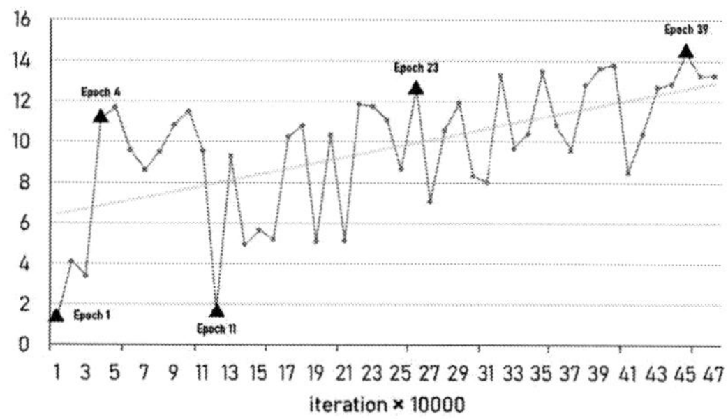

Figure 1: Progress of BLEU score during the training of the small RNN model

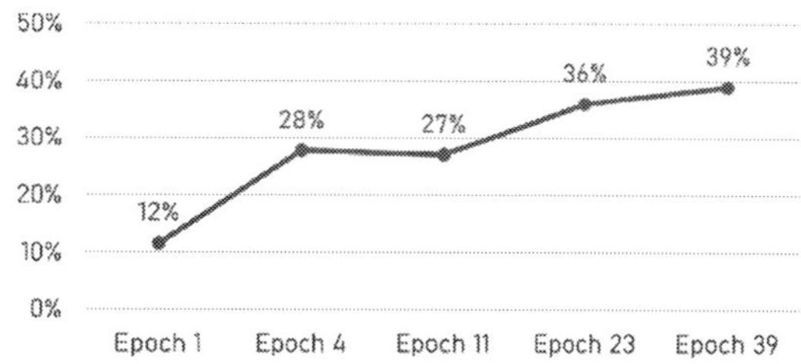

Figure 2: Progress of the average test suite accuracy for the chosen snapshots while training the small RNN model

score evolution, with the black triangle marks indicating the snapshots that we chose to examine, based on the following criteria:

- Epoch 1 (iteration 1): Start of training
- Epoch 4 (iteration 4): BLEU score > 10
- Epoch 11 (iteration 12): Sudden BLEU drop
- Epoch 23 (iteration 26): Mid-high
- Epoch 39 (iteration 45): Highest BLEU score

The complete dataset can be found online in the repository[3].

5.1.2 Evaluation of linguistic categories over time

There was an unsteady but visible rise in the BLEU score over time and also a positive development in the average test suite accuracy (see figure 2), achieving the best accuracy in epoch 39 after a more or less constant improvement.

While looking at the evolution of the accuracy on particular linguistic categories (Table 2), a positive trend is observed when a constant improvement for a specific category has been encountered, a negative trend when there is either a constant decrease

[2] `https://github.com/marian-nmt/marian-examples/blob/master/transformer`

[3] `https://github.com/pstadler1990/nmt_paper21_appendix`

category\epoch	1	4	11	22	39
Ambiguity	10%	10%	10%	11%	20%
Coordination & ellipsis	0%	20%	10%	20%	30%
False friends	50%	50%	56%	50%	50%
Function word	30%	50%	30%	50%	60%
Long distance dependency & interrogative	30%	40%	40%	40%	40%
MWE	0%	10%	0%	22%	22%
Named entity & terminology	10%	30%	11%	20%	20%
Negation	20%	60%	60%	60%	60%
Non-verbal agreement	0%	20%	20%	40%	20%
Punctuation	0%	20%	33%	50%	60%
Subordination	0%	40%	40%	60%	70%
Verb tense/ aspect/mood	0%	10%	10%	20%	20%
Verb valancy	0%	10%	30%	20%	30%

Table 2: Progress of accuracy for linguistic categories (small RNN model) over selected epochs

in translation quality for the category or there is a decrease after a peak, whereas any other trend is considered neutral, meaning a positive overall trend characterised by peaks and valleys, which indicate a shift in quality over time or a trend without any development. From the 13 examined categories we found a positive trend in nine categories (70%), two are to be considered neutral (15%) and there was a negative trend in two categories (15%, non-verbal agreement and NER and terminology). Further we provide details on 3 particular categories:

Ambiguity For this category, 10 sentences from a single phenomenon (lexical ambiguity) were examined. Until epoch 39, only one sentence was correctly translated (`Beijing is the capital of China.`). In epoch 39, another sentence was translated in the right way (`What is today's date?`). In epoch 1, 4 and 11, the regular expression provided by the test suite reported a valid translation, because it focused on the ambiguity for the word `china` (wrong translation would be `Porzellan(geschirr)`). However, the translation `Kapital` for the English word `capital` (as in capital city) is wrong. In epoch 22, this is corrected.

Non-verbal agreement A total of 10 sentences from three distinct phenomena were examined. In

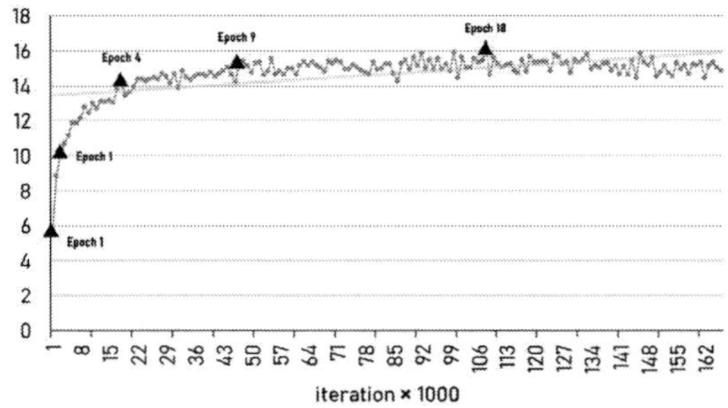

Figure 3: Progress of BLEU score during the training of the big RNN model

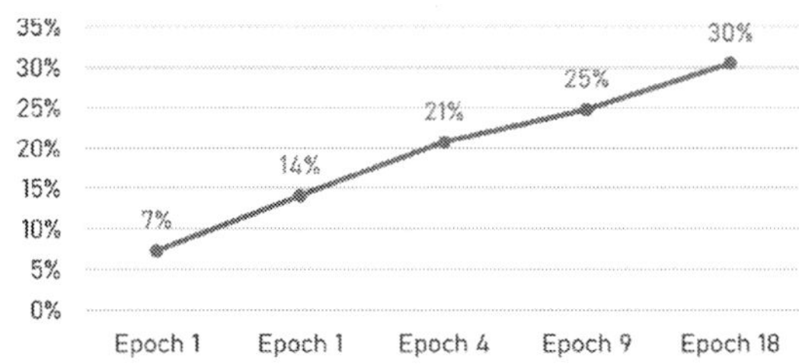

Figure 4: Progress of the average test suite accuracy for the chosen snapshots while training the big RNN model

the first epoch, no sentence was correctly translated (four of them were not translated at all). In the epoch four, two sentences were correctly translated according to the test suite. In epoch 22, four sentences were correctly translated, while interestingly the accuracy decreased to 20% in epoch 39; two formerly correct sentences were mistranslated in this epoch.

Subordination For this category, 10 sentences from eight different phenomena were evaluated. We found a constant increase in the translation quality over the selected epochs. Starting with zero correctly translated sentences in the first epoch, the system already reached 40% in epoch 4. The translation quality was quite decent, even when regarding the remaining words that were not part of the examined phenomenon.

5.2 Evaluation of the big RNN model

The big RNN model was trained for 56 hours and achieved a BLEU score of 16.

5.2.1 Snapshot selection

Figure 3 shows the BLEU score evolution over all 164 iterations (28 epochs). We chose the five snapshots for further evaluation based on the following criteria:

category\epoch	1	1	4	9	18
Ambiguity	20%	20%	10%	10%	10%
Coordination & ellipsis	0%	0%	20%	10%	30%
False friends	22%	50%	40%	40%	60%
Function word	10%	30%	30%	30%	44%
Long distance dependency & interrogative	10%	20%	30%	30%	50%
MWE	0%	0%	10%	0%	0%
Named entity & terminology	22%	40%	40%	40%	40%
Negation	0%	0%	40%	40%	50%
Non-verbal agreement	11%	22%	20%	30%	30%
Punctuation	0%	0%	10%	20%	20%
Subordination	0%	0%	20%	40%	30%
Verb tense/ aspect/mood	0%	0%	0%	10%	10%
Verb valancy	0%	0%	0%	20%	20%

Table 3: Progress of accuracy (big RNN model) for linguistic categories over selected epochs

- Epoch 1 (iteration 1): start of training
- Epoch 1 (iteration 3): BLEU score < 10
- Epoch 4 (iteration 18): BLEU score > 14
- Epoch 9 (iteration 44): BLEU > 15
- Epoch 18 (iteration 108): highest BLEU score

5.2.2 Evaluation of linguistic categories over time

While studying the accuracy progress for particular linguistic categories, we observe that three of them have a negative thread, ending with a lower accuracy than the one achieved during some earlier epochs (ambiguity, multi-word expressions and subordination). Additionally, we observe the following particular issues:

Named entities and terminology Four out of ten sentences from five different phenomena were translated correctly in this category: Proper name (1 out of 1), Date (0 out of 2), Measuring unit (2 out of 3), Location (1 out of 2) and Domain specific term (0 out of 1). Dates were not properly converted into the German format (`dd.mm.yyyy`), however the named entities were kept in their original spelling (`Marilyn Monroe`, `Pearl Harbor`) in both cases. In our final recorded snapshot, the system was able to translate 2 out of 3 measuring units accordingly: `The human brain has a volume of about 600 to 800 cubic centimetres.` and `The room was 17 feet long.`. The system struggled with the sentence `Stella had her hair cut six inches last week.`, no matter the progress. The locations `Saarland` (Saarland) and `Palatinate` (Pfalz) were only correctly translated in iteration 3 and 18 and mistranslated in lower and higher iterations. Regarding the domain-specific term `neurotransmitter serotonin`, the system was not able to get the capitalisation right in most cases and randomly got it either correct or wrong from iteration to iteration.

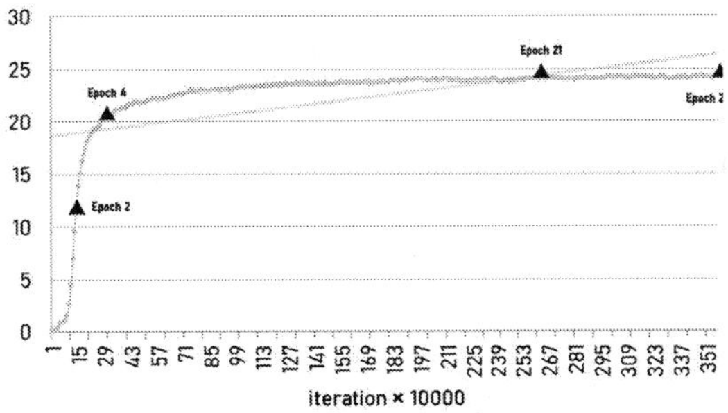

Figure 5: Progress of BLEU score during the training of the transformer model

False Friends False friends were translated correctly in 60% (6 out of 10 sentences). Three sentences contained the word `Genie` and were all translated wrong over all recorded snapshots. Four sentences examined the different meanings of `serious` and were all translated correct in all recorded snapshots but the first (epoch 1). The system struggled with the sentence `For the Christmas party, the chef sculpted an angel out of chocolate.`; in no case the translation was correct. It seems to be obvious that words like `Genie` were not part of the two used corpora or at least not used in the given meaning and thus unable to translate correctly. Overall though, the system performed well with false friends.

5.3 Evaluation of the transformer model

The transformer was trained for 31 hours and achieved a BLEU score of 24.29. Our trained model is comparable to the one trained by Sennrich et al. (2015) that achieved a BLEU score of 22.7 to 25.7 for English→German with a similar dev and test set (newstest14 and newstest15).

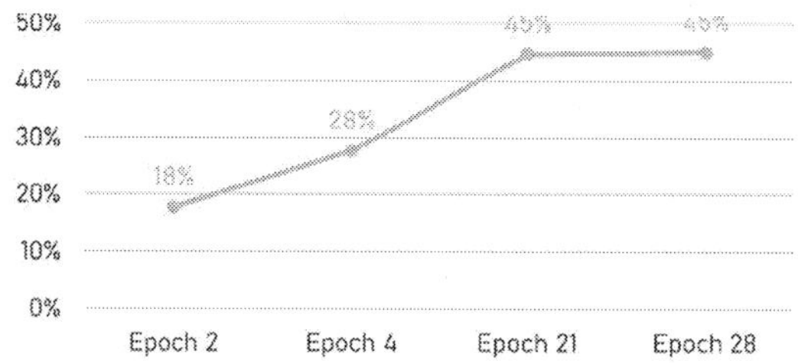

Figure 6: Progress of the average test suite accuracy for the chosen snapshots while training the transformer model

category\epoch	2	4	21	28
Ambiguity	20%	20%	20%	20%
Coordination & ellipsis	0%	10%	20%	10%
False friends	50%	50%	50%	50%
Function word	20%	40%	50%	60%
Long distance dependency & interrogative	20%	40%	70%	70%
MWE	10%	10%	10%	10%
Named entity & terminology	20%	40%	70%	80%
Negation	40%	50%	60%	60%
Non-verbal agreement	20%	40%	40%	50%
Punctuation	20%	10%	30%	50%
Subordination	0%	20%	80%	80%
Verb tense/ aspect/mood	10%	10%	30%	40%
Verb valancy	0%	20%	60%	50%

Table 4: Progress of accuracy for linguistic categories (transformer) over selected epochs

5.3.1 Snapshot selection

Figure 5 shows the BLEU score evolution over all 351 iterations (28 epochs). For the transformer model, we picked only four snapshots for further examination, as there were no big changes after certain epochs:

- Epoch 2 (iteration 15): BLEU score 10
- Epoch 4 (iteration 39): BLEU score >20
- Epoch 21 (iteration 255): BLEU score 24 (no great changes from now on)
- Epoch 28 (iteration 355): Final epoch, BLEU score 24

5.3.2 Evaluation of linguistic categories over time

A total of 49 phenomena from 13 categories were examined for the transformer-based system within the test suite. There was a steady and visible rise in the BLEU score development over time and a positive development in the average score as reported by the test suite. The highest recorded BLEU score 24,28 was achieved in epoch 28 (iteration 348). However, there is only a small difference between epoch 21 and the final epoch 28 – this is also perceptible from the BLEU score (figure 5); the system became satisfactory around epoch 20 to 21. Regarding the test suite accuracy, there was a notable increase from the first epoch to epoch 21 (see figure 6). Here, one observes that two linguistic categories, verb valency and coordination and ellipsis, end up with 10% less accuracy than the one achieved during the previous snapshot. Another three categories (ambiguity, MWE, and false friend) have a flat trend, maintaining the same accuracy as the one achieved in epoch 2, whereas negation is also very close with a relatively mild increase. A steady increase was achieved for NER and terminology, whereas the steepest trend is shown by subordination, which starts with 0% and ends with 80%. Looking on particular items, we can observe the following:

Ambiguity The system struggled with ambiguity – only 2 out of 10 test sentences (20%) were correctly translated, and this was stable from the first snapshot until the final system. The system didn't make a correct lexical choice for any of the three sentences focusing on the ambiguity of the word `bat`: `The player hit the ball with the bat.`, `The woman hit the burglar with the bat.` and `Bats sleep upside-down.` The two sentences containing the words `date` respectively `date palm`, were both translated incorrectly.

Function words Question tags were mistranslated in nearly all cases within the recorded snapshots. In the first snapshots, the question tags were completely ignored in the translation, however, the system understood the sentences contained a question and therefore ended the sentences with a question mark; yet, the important words were skipped. In epoch 4, the system began to translate some parts of the subordinate clauses (the question tags), but was not able to translate them in an appropriate way (No one still goes voluntarily in one of these old-style libraries, right? → Niemand geht noch immer freiwillig in einer dieser alten Bibliotheken, Recht?). In epoch 21, one question tag was translated accurately (You saw her last week, didn't you? → Sie haben sie letzte Woche gesehen, nicht wahr?). Focus particles such as even, only or also were translated almost without any errors (9 out of 10 in epoch 26). However, the word even in the sentence He didn't even drink a single glass of wine. was never translated correctly.

Named entities The translations for dates were highly accurate within the latest recorded snapshots (epoch 21 and epoch 28); Two dates have been correctly translated from the American / English format to the dd.mm.yyyy format commonly used in Germany. Measuring units were not converted (as intended) and correctly translated (3 out of 3 sentences in epoch 28). Location information was not translated well enough; especially well-known proper names, such as the names of the German federal states still caused difficulties for the system

However, a slight improvement towards the end could be recognized here. An interesting transition in quality can be found for the sentence The Saarland and the Palatinate enjoy a fierce regional rivalry. where the translation quality actually dropped in the last two recorded epochs 21 and 28; it seemed the system had been overfitted to some specific word combinations, resulting in the use of Flughafen Pfalz (airport Pfalz) for the English word Palatine (German: Pfalz or pfälzisch) instead of Pfalz (epochs 2 and 4).

Coordination and ellipsis The system had difficulty translating sentences from this category. An accurate evaluation of the phenomena is difficult because many of the necessary vocabularies were not correctly translated, making the sentences incomplete or partially meaningless. However, two sentences were translated correctly: Goethe wrote Faust, not Schiller. and Jackie likes the doctor but she doesn't like the nurse. were both translated correctly in epoch 21, but not in epoch 28 and 4. In epoch 2, no sentence was translated correctly.

Verb valency There was an increasing development until epoch 21 (best score for this category) - in the following epoch 28 the translation quality dropped from 60% back to 50% due to a mistranslated sentence in the last epoch (I want to talk to your neighbors.).

6 Comparison between iterations and models

As figure 7 shows, there is a clear difference between the two RNN trainings regarding the resilience of the BLEU score over time. While there is a lot of jittering in the RNN model with a small amount of data, a nearly constant increase is given in the model with a bigger amount of data, showing no huge peaks or valleys. Regarding BLEU scores, the system with the larger corpus performed a little bit better (~16) than the one smaller one (~14), but this was not reflected in the test suite comparison, where there was no big difference in terms of test suite accuracy, even though the used corpus has more than doubled in the big RNN model. Additionally, it can be observed that some categories in the bigger RNN perform worse than what was achieved in the smaller one. The inability of the bigger model to take advantage of the additional data may be addressed to the rather shallow architecture of the encoder and the decoder. With the current range of experiments, there are some open questions regarding further comparisons between RNN-small and RNN-big models. Future experiments could investigate the reasons for the fact that RNN-small and RNN-big systems perform comparably on the test suite, e.g. whether this can be attributed to the shallow architecture, to a subtle domain mismatch between Europarl and DGT or to the domain mismatch between the training data and the test suite.

The transformer model development takes some more iterations until it reaches a competitive BLEU score but then clearly outperforms both RNN systems by more than 60%, although the comparison with the RNN models is not direct, since the transformer is built with more layers and a not directly comparable architecture.

There is no generalizable development over all examined categories; some performed better than others, while some of the categories had no development at all. Scoring with the test suite was difficult for many sentences, because of insufficient vocabulary and wrong lexical choices. The system

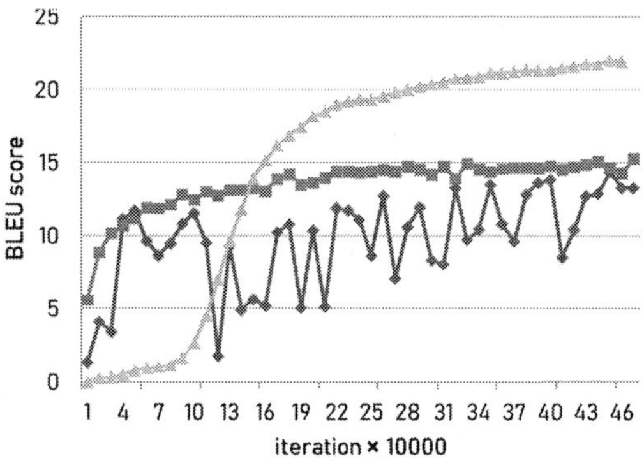

Figure 7: BLEU scores for the models small RNN (◆), big RNN (■) and transformer (△)

had trouble with punctuation, such as quotation marks. Names were often translated with fragments or as mixtures of different fragments, clearly coming from the Europarl proceedings.

7 Conclusions and further work

We performed a fine-grained evaluation on several training stages of three different NMT models. The most interesting observation is that although the training process stops when the best scores of the automatic metrics are achieved (*early stopping*), the accuracy of some linguistic phenomena is dropping, as compared to previous epochs. For this reason, the contribution of the scoring metric and the stopping criterion should be further investigated, while it might be also depend on whether the development sets contain these phenomena.

The fact that some linguistic categories have a steeper curve than the others may also signalise the difficulty of these categories from a machine learning perspective.

Since this is a preliminary study, the amount of items per linguistic category is small and does not allow for statistically significant conclusions. This could be improved in the future with further annotation effort. Finally, the systems examined are taken as random samples in terms of settings and parameters. We should repeat the measurements on state of the art systems, allowing fair comparisons among different architectures and design decisions.

Acknowledgments

This work has been accomplished as a semester project, part of the MSc program of Media Informatics of the Technical University of Berlin, hosted by the Quality and Usability Lab and organized by Neslihan Iskender under the chair of Prof. Sebastian Möller. Supervision from the side of DFKI has been supported by the projects TextQ (funded by the German Research Foundation; DFG) and SocialWear (funded by the German Ministry of Education; BMBF), with the support of Dr. Aljoscha Burchardt, Jana Majella Hirschberg, Malte Ostendorff and Christian Schulze.

References

Lars Ahrenberg. 2018. A challenge set for english-swedish machine translation. *Thanks to our sponsors: Gold: Stora Skuggans Värdshus Silver: TT Nyhetsbyrån and Lingsoft Bronze: Convertus, Digital Grammars, IQVIA and Voice Provider*, page 27.

Eleftherios Avramidis, Vivien Macketanz, Ursula Strohriegel, Aljoscha Burchardt, and Sebastian Möller. 2020. Fine-grained linguistic evaluation for state-of-the-art Machine Translation. In *Proceedings of the Fifth Conference on Machine Translation*. Association for Computational Linguistics.

Eleftherios Avramidis, Vivien Macketanz, Ursula Strohriegel, and Hans Uszkoreit. 2019. Linguistic evaluation of german-english machine translation using a test suite. *arXiv preprint arXiv:1910.07457*.

Dzmitry Bahdanau, Kyunghyun Cho, and Yoshua Bengio. 2014. Neural Machine Translation by Jointly Learning to Align and Translate. *Computer Research Repository*, abs/1409.0.

Anthony Bau, Yonatan Belinkov, Hassan Sajjad, Fahim Dalvi, Nadir Durrani, and James Glass. 2019. Identifying and Controlling Important Neurons in Neural Machine Translation. In *Proceedings of the International Conference on Learning Representations (ICLR)*.

Yonatan Belinkov, Nadir Durrani, Fahim Dalvi, Hassan Sajjad, and James Glass. 2020. On the linguistic representational power of neural machine translation models. *Computational Linguistics*, 46(1):1–52.

Ondrej Bojar, Rajen Chatterjee, Christian Federmann, Yvette Graham, Barry Haddow, Matthias Huck, Antonio Jimeno Yepes, Philipp Koehn, Varvara Logacheva, Christof Monz, Matteo Negri, Aurelie Neveol, Mariana Neves, Martin Popel, Matt Post, Raphael Rubino, Carolina Scarton, Lucia Specia, Marco Turchi, Karin Verspoor, and Marcos Zampieri. 2016. Findings of the 2016 Conference on Machine Translation. In *Proceedings of the First Conference on Machine Translation*, pages 131–198, Berlin, Germany. Association for Computational Linguistics.

Ondřej Bojar, Rajen Chatterjee, Christian Federmann, Barry Haddow, Matthias Huck, Chris Hokamp, Philipp Koehn, Varvara Logacheva, Christof Monz,

Matteo Negri, Matt Post, Carolina Scarton, Lucia Specia, and Marco Turchi. 2015. Findings of the 2015 Workshop on Statistical Machine Translation. In *Proceedings of the Tenth Workshop on Statistical Machine Translation*, pages 1–46, Lisbon, Portugal. Association for Computational Linguistics.

Chris Callison-Burch, Miles Osborne, and Philipp Koehn. 2006. Re-evaluating the role of bleu in machine translation research. In *11th Conference of the European Chapter of the Association for Computational Linguistics*.

Fahim Dalvi, Nadir Durrani, Hassan Sajjad, Yonatan Belinkov, and Stephan Vogel. 2017. Understanding and Improving Morphological Learning in the Neural Machine Translation Decoder. *undefined*.

Liane Guillou and Christian Hardmeier. 2016. Protest: A test suite for evaluating pronouns in machine translation. In *Proceedings of the Tenth International Conference on Language Resources and Evaluation (LREC'16)*, pages 636–643.

Marcin Junczys-Dowmunt, Roman Grundkiewicz, Tomasz Dwojak, Hieu Hoang, Kenneth Heafield, Tom Neckermann, Frank Seide, Ulrich Germann, Alham Fikri Aji, Nikolay Bogoychev, et al. 2018. Marian: Fast neural machine translation in c++. *arXiv preprint arXiv:1804.00344*.

Shigeki Karita, Nanxin Chen, Tomoki Hayashi, Takaaki Hori, Hirofumi Inaguma, Ziyan Jiang, Masao Someki, Nelson Enrique Yalta Soplin, Ryuichi Yamamoto, Xiaofei Wang, et al. 2019. A comparative study on transformer vs rnn in speech applications. In *2019 IEEE Automatic Speech Recognition and Understanding Workshop (ASRU)*, pages 449–456. IEEE.

Philipp Koehn. 2005. Europarl: A parallel corpus for statistical machine translation. In *Proceedings of the tenth Machine Translation Summit*, volume 5, pages 79–86, Phuket, Thailand.

Sungryong Koh, Jinee Maeng, Ji-Young Lee, Young-Sook Chae, and Key-Sun Choi. 2001. A test suite for evaluation of english-to-korean machine translation systems. In *MT Summit'conference, Santiago de Compostela*. Citeseer.

Xiang Kong, Zhaopeng Tu, Shuming Shi, Eduard Hovy, and Tong Zhang. 2018. Neural machine translation with adequacy-oriented learning. In *Proceedings of the AAAI Conference on Artificial Intelligence*, volume 33, page 19. arXiv.

Taku Kudo and John Richardson. 2018. SentencePiece: A simple and language independent subword tokenizer and detokenizer for neural text processing. In *EMNLP 2018 - Conference on Empirical Methods in Natural Language Processing: System Demonstrations, Proceedings*, pages 66–71. Association for Computational Linguistics (ACL).

Vivien Macketanz, Renlong Ai, Aljoscha Burchardt, and Hans Uszkoreit. 2018a. Tq-autotest–an automated test suite for (machine) translation quality. In *Proceedings of the Eleventh International Conference on Language Resources and Evaluation (LREC 2018)*.

Vivien Macketanz, Eleftherios Avramidis, Aljoscha Burchardt, and Hans Uszkoreit. 2018b. Fine-grained evaluation of German-English Machine Translation based on a Test Suite. In *Proceedings of the Third Conference on Machine Translation (WMT18)*, Brussels, Belgium. Association for Computational Linguistics.

Kishore Papineni, Salim Roukos, Todd Ward, and Wei-Jing Zhu. 2002. Bleu: a method for automatic evaluation of machine translation. In *Proceedings of the 40th annual meeting of the Association for Computational Linguistics*, pages 311–318.

Rico Sennrich, Barry Haddow, and Alexandra Birch. 2015. Improving neural machine translation models with monolingual data. *arXiv preprint arXiv:1511.06709*.

Gongbo Tang, Mathias Müller, Annette Rios, and Rico Sennrich. 2020. Why self-attention? A targeted evaluation of neural machine translation architectures. In *Proceedings of the 2018 Conference on Empirical Methods in Natural Language Processing, EMNLP 2018*, pages 4263–4272. Association for Computational Linguistics.

Gongbo Tang, Rico Sennrich, and Joakim Nivre. 2019. Encoders Help You Disambiguate Word Senses in Neural Machine Translation. In *Proceedings of the 2019 Conference on Empirical Methods in Natural Language Processing and the 9th International Joint Conference on Natural Language Processing (EMNLP-IJCNLP)*, pages 1429–1435, Stroudsburg, PA, USA. Association for Computational Linguistics.

Jörg Tiedemann. 2012. Parallel Data, Tools and Interfaces in OPUS. In *Proceedings of the 8th International Conference on Language Resources and Evaluation (LREC12)*, pages 2214–2218, Istanbul, Turkey.

Ashish Vaswani, Noam Shazeer, Niki Parmar, Jakob Uszkoreit, Llion Jones, Aidan N Gomez, Lukasz Kaiser, and Illia Polosukhin. 2017. Attention is all you need. *arXiv preprint arXiv:1706.03762*.

Tereza Vojtěchová, Michal Novák, Miloš Klouček, and Ondřej Bojar. 2019. Sao wmt19 test suite: Machine translation of audit reports. *arXiv preprint arXiv:1909.01701*.

John Wieting, Taylor Berg-Kirkpatrick, Kevin Gimpel, and Graham Neubig. 2019. Beyond BLEU: Training Neural Machine Translation with Semantic Similarity. In *Proceedings of the 57th Annual Meeting of the Association for Computational Linguistics*, pages 4344–4355.

A Appendix

Example sentence	Category	Phenomenon
Beijing is the capital of China.	Ambiguity	Lexical ambiguity
The manager suspects the president of theft.	Verb valency	Case government
I stopped reading the poster.	Verb valency	Catenative verb
John sang the baby to sleep.	Verb valency	Resultative
Goethe wrote Faust, not Schiller.	Coordination & ellipsis	Stripping
Hand me a Kleenex, please.	Named entitiy & terminology	Proper name
Marilyn Monroe was born as Norma Jeane Mortenson on June 1, 1926.	Named entitiy & terminology	Date
The room was 17 feet long.	Named entitiy & terminology	Measuring unit
John is studying at the Technical University of Vienna.	Named entitiy & terminology	Location
In the latter case, this would be the neurotransmitter serotonin.	Named entitiy & terminology	Domainspecific term
For the Christmas party, the chef sculpted an angel out of chocolate.	False friends	False friends
No one still goes voluntarily in one of these old-style libraries, right?	Function word	Question tag
I saw him only once.	Function word	Focus particle
You will have passed John the ball.	Verb tense/aspect/mood	Ditransitive - future II simple
She had been baking Tim a cake.	Verb tense/aspect/mood	Ditransitive - past perfect progressive
Neither John nor Mary could do anything about the problem.	Long distance dependency & interrogative	Multiple connectors
Never again will he eat raw spaghetti.	Long distance dependency & interrogative	Negative inversion
To whom should the documents be sent?	Long distance dependency & interrogative	Pied piping
No walking on the grass!	Negation	Negation
Susan dropped the plate and it shattered loudly.	Non-verbal agreement	Coreference
The man who you mentioned is my friend.	Subordination	Relative clause
What do you think they did that upset everyone?	Long distance dependency & interrogative	Extraposition
I'd like to have a round of applause for our next guest!	MWE	Collocation
John can play the guitar, and Mary can too.	Coordination & ellipsis	VP-ellipsis
Jackie likes the doctor but she doesn't the nurse.	Coordination & ellipsis	Pseudogapping
She likes the car more than her husband does.	Subordination	Adverbial clause
Oh, what a beautiful morning! Jim said to himself.	Punctuation	Quotation marks
They are well-behaved children.	MWE	Compound
Don't put all your eggs in one basket.	MWE	Idiom
Rebecca said she would be in Munich next week.	Subordination	Indirect speech
We didn't realize she was so ill.	Subordination	Object clause
We are determined to completely solve the problem.	Long distance dependency & interrogative	Split infinitive
Are you going to the beach today?	Long distance dependency & interrogative	Polar question
They may not know it.	Verb tense/aspect/mood	Modal negated
They are teaching themselves Spanish.	Verb tense/aspect/mood	Reflexive - present progressive
I would be kicking Tim.	Verb tense/aspect/mood	Transitive - conditional I progressive
You would have been eating the potatoes.	Verb tense/aspect/mood	Transitive - conditional II progressive
She will have been painting the house.	Verb tense/aspect/mood	Transitive - future II progressive
I have been painting the house.	Verb tense/aspect/mood	Transitive - present perfect progressive
He looks up to his older brother.	MWE	Verbal MWE
She has lost her shoes.	Non-verbal agreement	Possession
Before leaving, John has been at home.	MWE	Prepositional MWE
What was the man looking for in the fridge?	Long distance dependency & interrogative	Wh-movement
Mandy's brother John plays football.	Non-verbal agreement	Genitive
It was Lena who had baked the cake.	Subordination	Cleft sentence
What I did in the end was to go home.	Subordination	Pseudo-cleft sentence

Table 5: Extracted example sentences for each examined category and phenomenon

Improving the Robustness of QA Models to Challenge Sets with Variational Question-Answer Pair Generation

Kazutoshi Shinoda[†‡] **Saku Sugawara**[‡] **Akiko Aizawa**[†‡]
[†]The University of Tokyo
[‡]National Institute of Informatics
shinoda@is.s.u-tokyo.ac.jp
{saku,aizawa}@nii.ac.jp

Abstract

Question answering (QA) models for reading comprehension have achieved human-level accuracy on in-distribution test sets. However, they have been demonstrated to lack robustness to challenge sets, whose distribution is different from that of training sets. Existing data augmentation methods mitigate this problem by simply augmenting training sets with synthetic examples sampled from the same distribution as the challenge sets. However, these methods assume that the distribution of a challenge set is known a priori, making them less applicable to unseen challenge sets. In this study, we focus on question-answer pair generation (QAG) to mitigate this problem. While most existing QAG methods aim to improve the quality of synthetic examples, we conjecture that diversity-promoting QAG can mitigate the sparsity of training sets and lead to better robustness. We present a variational QAG model that generates multiple diverse QA pairs from a paragraph. Our experiments show that our method can improve the accuracy of 12 challenge sets, as well as the in-distribution accuracy.[1]

1 Introduction

Machine reading comprehension has gained significant attention in the NLP community, whose goal is to devise systems that can answer questions about given documents (Rajpurkar et al., 2016; Trischler et al., 2017; Joshi et al., 2017). Such systems usually use neural models, which require a substantial number of question-answer (QA) pairs for training. To reduce the considerable manual cost of dataset creation, there has been a resurgence of studies on automatic QA pair generation (QAG), consisting of a pipeline of answer extraction (AE) and question generation (QG), to augment question answering (QA) datasets (Yang et al., 2017a; Du and Cardie, 2018; Subramanian et al., 2018; Alberti et al., 2019).

For the downstream QA task, most existing studies have evaluated QAG methods using a test set from the same distribution as a training set (Yang et al., 2017a; Zhang and Bansal, 2019; Liu et al., 2020). However, when a QA model is evaluated only on an in-distribution test set, it is difficult to verify that the model is not exploiting unintended biases in a dataset (Geirhos et al., 2020). Exploiting an unintended bias can degrade the robustness of a QA model, which is problematic in real-world applications. For example, recent studies have observed that a QA model does not generalize to other QA datasets (Yogatama et al., 2019; Talmor and Berant, 2019; Sen and Saffari, 2020). Other studies have found a lack of robustness to challenge sets, such as paraphrased questions (Gan and Ng, 2019), questions with low lexical overlap (Sugawara et al., 2018), and questions that include noise (Ravichander et al., 2021).

While existing studies have proposed data augmentation methods targeting a particular challenge set, they are only effective at the expense of the in-distribution accuracy (Gan and Ng, 2019; Ribeiro et al., 2019; Ravichander et al., 2021). These methods assume that the target distribution is given a priori. However, identifying the type of samples that a QA model cannot handle in advance is difficult in real-world applications.

We conjecture that increasing the diversity of a training set with data augmentation, rather than augmenting QA pairs similar to the original training set, can improve the robustness of QA models. Poor diversity in QA datasets has been shown to result in the poor robustness of QA models (Lewis and Fan, 2019; Geva et al., 2019; Ko et al., 2020), supporting our hypothesis. To this end, we propose

[1]Our code and data are available at https://github.com/KazutoshiShinoda/VQAG.

Proceedings of the Joint Conference of the 59th Annual Meeting of the Association for Computational Linguistics and the 11th International Joint Conference on Natural Language Processing: Student Research Workshop, pages 197–214
August 5–6, 2021. ©2021 Association for Computational Linguistics

a variational QAG model (VQAG). We introduce two independent latent random variables into our model to learn the two one-to-many relationships in AE and QG by utilizing neural variational inference (Kingma and Welling, 2013). Incorporating the randomness of these two latent variables enables our model to generate diverse answers and questions separately. We also study the effect of controlling the Kullback–Leibler (KL) term in the variational lower bound for mitigating the posterior collapse issue (Bowman et al., 2016), where the model ignores latent variables and generates outputs that are almost the same. We evaluate our approach on 12 challenge sets that are unseen during training to assess the improved robustness of the QA model.

In summary, our contributions are three-fold:

- We propose a variational question-answer pair generation model with explicit KL control to generate significantly diverse answers and questions.
- We construct synthetic QA datasets using our model to boost the QA performance in an in-distribution test set, achieving comparable scores with existing QAG methods.
- We discover that our method achieves meaningful improvements in unseen challenge sets, which are further boosted using a simple ensemble method.

2 Related Work

2.1 Answer Extraction

AE aims to extract question-worthy phrases, which are worth being asked about, from each textual context without looking at the questions. AE has been performed mainly in two ways: rule-based and neural methods. Yang et al. (2017a) extracted candidate phrases using rule-based methods such as named entity recognition (NER). However, not all the named entities, noun phrases, verb phrases, adjectives, or clauses in the given documents are used as gold answer spans. As such, these rule-based methods are likely to extract many trivial phrases.

Therefore, there have been studies on training neural models to identify question-worthy phrases. Du and Cardie (2018) framed AE as a sequence labeling task and used BiLSTM-CRF (Huang et al., 2015). Subramanian et al. (2018) treated the positions of answers as a sequence and used a pointer network (Vinyals et al., 2015). Wang et al. (2019) used a pointer network and Match-LSTM (Wang and Jiang, 2016, 2017). Alberti et al. (2019) made use of pretrained BERT (Devlin et al., 2019).

However, these neural AE models are trained with maximum likelihood estimation; that is, each model is optimized to produce an answer set closest to the gold answers. In contrast, our model incorporates a latent random variable and is trained by maximizing the lower bound of the likelihood to extract diverse answers. In this study, we assume that there should be question-worthy phrases that are not used as the gold answers in a manually created dataset. We aim to extract such phrases.

2.2 Question Generation

Traditionally, QG was studied using rule-based methods (Mostow and Chen, 2009; Heilman and Smith, 2010; Lindberg et al., 2013; Labutov et al., 2015). After Du et al. (2017) proposed a neural sequence-to-sequence model (Sutskever et al., 2014) for QG, neural models that take context and answer as inputs have started to be used to improve question quality with attention (Bahdanau et al., 2014) and copying (Gulcehre et al., 2016; Gu et al., 2016) mechanisms. Most works focused on generating relevant questions from context-answer pairs (Zhou et al., 2018; Song et al., 2018; Zhao et al., 2018; Sun et al., 2018; Kim et al., 2019; Liu et al., 2019; Qiu and Xiong, 2019). These works showed the importance of answers as input features for QG. Other works studied predicting question types (Zhou et al., 2019; Kang et al., 2019), modeling a structured answer-relevant relation (Li et al., 2019), and refining generated questions (Nema et al., 2019). To further improve question quality, policy gradient techniques have been used (Yuan et al., 2017; Yang et al., 2017a; Yao et al., 2018; Kumar et al., 2019). Dong et al. (2019) used a pretrained language model.

The diversity of questions has been tackled using variational attention (Bahuleyan et al., 2018), a conditional variational autoencoder (CVAE) (Yao et al., 2018), and top p nucleus sampling (Sultan et al., 2020). Our study is different from these studies wherein we study QAG by introducing variational methods into both AE and QG. Lee et al. (2020) is the closest to our study in terms of the modeling choice. While Lee et al. (2020) introduced an information-maximizing term to improve the consistency of QA pairs, our study uniquely controls the diversity by explicitly controlling KL values.

Despite the potential of data augmentation with QAG to mitigate the sparsity of QA datasets and avoid overfitting, not much is known about the robustness of QA models reinforced with QAG to more challenging test sets. We comprehensively evaluate QAG methods on challenging QA test sets, such as hard questions (Sugawara et al., 2018), implications (Ribeiro et al., 2019), and paraphrased questions (Gan and Ng, 2019).

2.3 Variational Autoencoder

The variational autoencoder (VAE) (Kingma and Welling, 2013) is a deep generative model consisting of a neural encoder (inference model) and decoder (generative model). The encoder learns to map from an observed variable to a latent random variable and the decoder works vice versa. The techniques of VAE have been widely applied to NLP tasks such as text generation (Bowman et al., 2016), machine translation (Zhang et al., 2016), and sequence labeling (Chen et al., 2018).

The CVAE is an extension of the VAE, in which the distribution of a latent variable is explicitly conditioned on certain variables and enables generation processes to be more diverse than a VAE (Li et al., 2018; Zhao et al., 2017b; Shen et al., 2017). The CVAE is trained by maximizing the variational lower bound of the log likelihood.

3 VQAG: Variational Question-Answer Pair Generation Model

3.1 Problem Definition

Our problem is to generate QA pairs from textual contexts. We focus on extractive QA in which an answer is a text span in context. We use c, q, and a to represent the context, question, and answer, respectively. We assume that every QA pair is sampled independently given a context. Thus, the problem is defined as maximizing the conditional log likelihood $\log p(q, a|c)$ averaged over all samples in a dataset.

3.2 Variational Lower Bound with Explicit KL Control

Generating questions and answers from different latent spaces makes sense because multiple questions can be created from a context-answer pair and multiple answer spans can be extracted from a context. Thus, we introduce two independent latent random variables to assign the roles of diversifying AE and QG to z and y, respectively.

VAEs often suffer from *posterior collapse*, where the model learns to ignore latent variables and generates outputs that are almost the same (Bowman et al., 2016). Many approaches have been proposed to mitigate this issue, such as weakening the generators (Bowman et al., 2016; Yang et al., 2017b; Semeniuta et al., 2017), or modifying the objective functions (Tolstikhin et al., 2018; Zhao et al., 2017a; Higgins et al., 2017).

To mitigate this problem, we use a variant of the modified β-VAE (Higgins et al., 2017) proposed by Burgess et al. (2018), which uses two hyperparameters to control the KL terms. Our modified objective function is:

$$\begin{aligned}\mathcal{L} = \mathbb{E}_{q_\phi(z,y|q,a,c)}[&\log p_\theta(q|y,a,c) \\ &+ \log p_\theta(a|z,c)] \\ &- |D_{\mathrm{KL}}(q_\phi(z|a,c)||p_\theta(z|c)) - C_a| \\ &- |D_{\mathrm{KL}}(q_\phi(y|q,c)||p_\theta(y|c)) - C_q|, \quad (1)\end{aligned}$$

where D_{KL} is the KL divergence, θ (ϕ) is the parameters of the generative (inference) model, and $C_a, C_q \geq 0$. See Appendix A for the derivation of the objective. Tuning C_a and C_q was enough to regularize the KL terms in our case (see Appendix B). C_a and C_q can explicitly control the KL values because the KL terms are forced to get closer to these values during training. We mathematically show that the KL control can be interpreted to control the conditional mutual information $I(z; a)$ and $I(y; q)$. This is the major difference between our model and Lee et al. (2020), where $I(q; a)$ is maximized to improve consistency of QA pairs. See Appendix C for the mathematical interpretation.

3.3 Model Architecture

An overview of VQAG is given in Figure 1. We denote c_i, q_i, and a_i as the i-th word in context, question, and answer, respectively. See Appendix D for the details of the implementation.

Embedding and Contextual Embedding Layer First, in the embedding layer, the i-th word, w_i, of a sequence of length L is simultaneously converted into word- and character-level embedding vectors by using a CNN based on Kim (2014). Then, we concatenate the embedding vectors. After that, we pass the embedding vectors to the contextual embedding layer consisting of bidirectional LSTMs (BiLSTM). We obtain $H \in \mathbb{R}^{L\times 2d}$, which is the

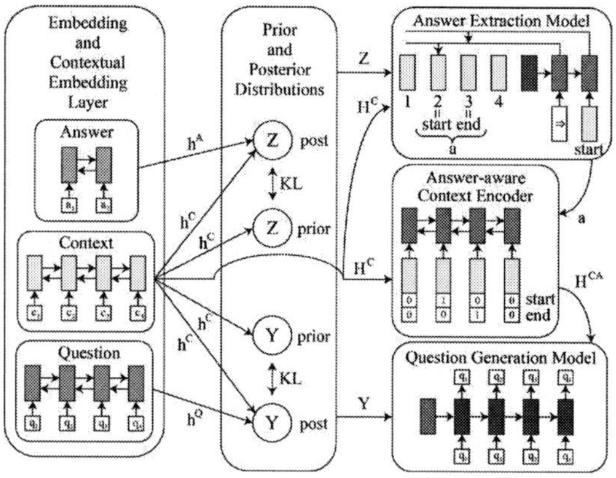

Figure 1: Overview of the model architecture. The latent variables z and y are sampled from the posteriors when computing the variational lower bound and from the priors during generation. See §3.3 for the details.

concatenated outputs from the LSTMs in each direction at each time step, and $h \in \mathbb{R}^{2d}$, which is the concatenated last hidden state vectors in each direction. The superscripts of the outputs H and h shown in Figure 1 indicate where they come from. C, Q, and A denote the context, question, and answer, respectively.

Prior and Posterior Distributions Following Zhao et al. (2017b), we hypothesized that the prior and and posterior distributions of the latent variables follow multivariate Gaussian distributions with diagonal covariance. The mean μ and log variance $\log \sigma^2$ of these prior and posterior distributions of z and y are computed with linear transformation from h^C, h^A, and h^Q. Next, latent variable z and y are obtained using the reparameterization trick (Kingma and Welling, 2013). Then, z and y are passed to the AE and QG models, respectively. z and y are sampled from the posteriors during training and the priors during testing.

Answer Extraction Model We regard AE as two-step autoregressive decoding, i.e., $p(a|c) = p(c_{start}|c)p(c_{end}|c_{start}, c)$, that predicts the start and end positions of an answer span in this order. For AE, we modify a pointer network (Vinyals et al., 2015) to take as input the initial hidden state computed from linear transformation from z, which in the end diversifies AE by learning the mappings from z to a. We use an LSTM as a decoder and compute attention scores over H^C.

Answer-aware Context Encoder To compute answer-aware context information for QG, we use another BiLSTM. We concatenate H^C and one hot vectors of start and end positions of answer, which are fed to the BiLSTM. We obtain $H^{CA} \in \mathbb{R}^{L \times 2d}$, which is the concatenated outputs from the LSTMs in each direction. H^{CA} is used as the source for attention and copying in QG.

Question Generation Model For QG, we modify an LSTM decoder with attention and copying mechanisms to take as input the initial hidden state computed from linear transformation from y, which in the end diversifies QG. At each time step, the probability distribution of generating words from vocabulary $P_v(q_i)$ is computed using attention (Bahdanau et al., 2014), and the probability distributions of copying words (Gulcehre et al., 2016; Gu et al., 2016) from context $P_c(c_j)$ are computed using attention. In parallel, the switching probability p_s is linearly estimated from the hidden state vector. Lastly, we compute the probability of q_i as:

$$p(q_i) = p_s P_v(q_i) + (1 - p_s) \sum_{j:c_j = q_i} P_c(c_j). \quad (2)$$

4 Experiments and Results

4.1 Dataset

We used SQuAD v1.1 (Rajpurkar et al., 2016), a large scale QA dataset consisting of documents collected from Wikipedia and 100k QA pairs created by crowdworkers, as a source dataset for QAG. Answers to questions in SQuAD can be extracted from textual contexts. Since the SQuAD test set has not been released, we use the split of the dataset, SQuAD-Du (Du et al., 2017), where the original training set is split into the training set ($\text{SQuAD}^{\text{Du}}_{\text{train}}$) and the test set ($\text{SQuAD}^{\text{Du}}_{\text{test}}$), and the original development set is used as the dev set ($\text{SQuAD}^{\text{Du}}_{\text{dev}}$). The sizes of $\text{SQuAD}^{\text{Du}}_{\text{train}}$, $\text{SQuAD}^{\text{Du}}_{\text{dev}}$, and $\text{SQuAD}^{\text{Du}}_{\text{test}}$ are 75,722, 10,570, and 11,877, respectively. See Appendix E for the training details of VQAG.

4.2 Answer Extraction

First, we conducted the AE experiment where inputs were the contexts and outputs were a set of multiple answer spans. The objective of this experiment is to measure the diversity and the extent to which our extracted answers cover the ground truths. We also study the effect of C_a in Eq. 1.

	Relevance				Diversity
	Precision		Recall		Dist
	Prop.	Exact	Prop.	Exact	
NER	34.44	19.61	64.60	45.39	30.0k
HarQG	45.96	33.90	41.05	28.37	-
InfoHCVAE	31.59	16.18	78.75	59.32	70.1k
VQAG					
$C_a = 0$	**58.39**	**47.15**	21.82	16.38	3.1k
$C_a = 5$	30.16	13.41	**83.13**	**60.88**	71.2k
$C_a = 20$	21.95	5.75	72.26	42.15	**103.3k**

Table 1: Results of AE on the test set.

	Relevance				Diversity		
	B1-R	ME-R	RL-R	Token	D1	E4	SB4
SemQG	**62.32**	**36.77**	**62.87**	7.0M	15.8k	18.28	91.44
VQAG							
$C_q = 0$	35.57	18.31	33.92	7.6M	14.4k	17.33	97.61
$C_q = 5$	44.19	25.84	45.18	11.5M	19.0k	19.71	82.59
$C_q = 20$	48.19	25.29	48.26	4.9M	**22.4k**	**19.72**	**44.41**

Table 2: Results of answer-aware QG on the test set. One question per input is evaluated in the upper part, while 50 questions per input are evaluated in the lower part to assess their diversity.

Metrics To measure the accuracy of multi-span extraction, we computed Proportional Overlap (Prop.) and Exact Match (Exact) metrics (Breck et al., 2007; Johansson and Moschitti, 2010; Du and Cardie, 2018) for each pair of extracted and ground truth answer spans, and then we report their precision and recall.[2] Prop. is proportional to the amount of overlap between two phrases. Our models extracted 50 answers from each context. To measure the diversity, we defined a Dist score, which is the the total number of distinct context-answer pairs.

Baselines We used three baselines: named entity recognition (NER), Harvesting QG (HarQG) (Du and Cardie, 2018), and InfoHCVAE (Lee et al., 2020). For NER, we used spaCy (Honnibal et al., 2020). For HarQG, we directly copied the scores from Du and Cardie (2018). For InfoHCVAE, we trained the model on the training set, and extracted 50 answers randomly from each context for a fair comparison.

Result Table 1 shows the result. While we tested various values of C_a ranging from 0 to 100, we only report the selected values here for brevity. When using C_a larger than 20, the scores did not get improved. Our model with $C_a = 5$ performed the best in terms of the recall scores, while surpassing the diversity of NER. The highest Dist scores did not occur together with the highest recall scores. When C_a is 0, the Dist score is fairly low. This implies the posterior collapse issue, though the precision scores are the best. We assert that low precision scores do not necessarily mean poor performance in our experiment because even the original test set does not cover all the valid answer spans.

4.3 Answer-aware Question Generation

We also conducted answer-aware QG experiments where the contexts and ground truth answer spans were the inputs to assess diversity and relevance to the gold questions.

Metrics To evaluate the diversity of the generated questions, our models generated 50 questions from each context-answer pair. We reported the recall scores (denoted as "-R") of BLEU-1 (B1), METEOR (ME), and ROUGE-L (RL) per reference question. We do not report precision scores here because our motivation is to improve diversity. To measure diversity, we reported Dist-1 (D1), Entropy-4 (E4) (Serban et al., 2017; Zhang et al., 2018), and Self-BLEU-4 (SB4) (Zhu et al., 2018).[3]

Baselines We compared our models with SemQG (Zhang and Bansal, 2019).[4] We used diverse beam search (Li et al., 2016b), sampled the top 50 questions per answer from SemQG, and used them to calculate the metrics as the baseline for a fair comparison

Result The results in Table 2 show that our model can improve diversity while degrading the recall scores compared to SemQG. Using C_q larger than 20 did not lead to improved diversity. More detailed analysis of C_a and C_q is provided in Appendix F.

4.4 Synthetic Dataset Construction

We created three synthetic QA datasets, denoted as $\mathcal{D}_{5,5}$, $\mathcal{D}_{20,20}$, and $\mathcal{D}_{5,20}$, using VQAG

[2]We exclude Binary Overlap, which assigns higher scores to systems that extract the entire input context and is not a reliable metric as Breck et al. (2007) discussed.

[3]We computed Dist-1 following the definition of Xu et al. (2018), wherein Dist-1 is the number of distinct unigrams. Dist-1 is often defined as the ratio of distinct unigrams (Li et al., 2016a) but this is not fair when the number of generated sentences differs among models, so we did not use this. SB4 was calculated per 50 questions generated from each input.

[4]We reran the ELMo+QPP&QAP model, which is available at `https://github.com/ZhangShiyue/QGforQA`.

beyoncé 's vocal range spans [four octaves] . jody rosen highlights her tone and timbre as particularly distinctive , describing her voice as " one of the most compelling instruments in popular music " . while another critic says she is a " vocal acrobat , being able to sing long and complex melismas and vocal runs effortlessly , and in key . her vocal abilities mean she is identified as the centerpiece of destiny 's child . the daily mail calls beyoncé 's voice " versatile " , capable of exploring power ballads , soul , rock belting , operatic flourishes , and hip hop . jon pareles of the new york times commented that her voice is " velvety yet tart , with an insistent flutter and reserves of soul belting " .	
Q: how can one find her vocal abilities in key music ?	A: she is identified as the centerpiece of destiny 's child
Q: how many octaves spans beyoncé 's vocal range ?	A: spans four
Q: how many octaves 's vocal range spans the beyoncé hop vocal range ?	A: four
Q: who commented that her voice is tart yet tart ?	A: jon pareles

Table 3: Heatmap of extracted answer spans and generated samples using our model. The darker the color is, the more often the word is extracted. The phrases surrounded by black boxes are the ground truth answers in SQuAD.

with the different configurations, $(C_a, C_q) = (5, 5), (20, 20), (5, 20)$ respectively. These configurations are chosen based on the recall-based metrics and diversity scores in the AE and QG results.

VQAG generated 50 QA pairs from each paragraph in $\text{SQuAD}^{\text{Du}}_{\text{train}}$ to construct each $\mathcal{D}$. It is generally known that VAEs generate diverse but low-quality data unlike GANs. We used heuristics to filter out low-quality generated QA pairs, dropping questions that are longer than 20 words or shorter than 5 words and answers that are longer than 10 words, keeping questions that have at least one interrogative word, and removing n-gram repetition in questions. While some existing works used the BERT QA model or an entailment model as a data filter (Alberti et al., 2019; Zhang and Bansal, 2019; Liu et al., 2020), our heuristics are enough to obtain improvement in the downstream QA task as shown in §4.6. Some samples in our datasets are given in Table 3, showing that the diverse QA pairs are generated. See Appendix G to see how VQAG maps latent variables to QA pairs.

4.5 Human Evaluation

We assess the quality of the synthetic QA pairs by conducting human evaluation on Amazon Mechanical Turk. For human evaluation, we randomly chose 200 samples from synthetic QA pairs generated by Zhang and Bansal (2019) and our model with $(C_a, C_q) = (5, 5), (20, 20)$ from the paragraphs in $\text{SQuAD}^{\text{Du}}_{\text{test}}$. We also chose 100 samples from $\text{SQuAD}^{\text{Du}}_{\text{test}}$. In addition to the three items proposed by Liu et al. (2020), we asked annotators if an given answer is important, i.e., it is worth being asked about. We showed the workers a triple (passage, question, answer) and asked them to answer the four questions shown in Table 4. See Appendix H for the details. We report the responses obtained using the majority vote.

According to the results in Table 4, nearly 25% of our questions are not understandable or meaningful, and 30% of our answers are incorrect for the generated questions. This result indicates that our synthetic datasets contain a considerable number of noisy QA pairs in these two aspects. However, 90 % of the generated questions are relevant to the passages, and 90% of the answers extracted by our models are question-worthy. As we will verify in §4.6, our noisy but diverse synthetic datasets are effective in enhancing the QA performance in the in- and out-of-distribution test sets.

Experiments		SemQG	$(C_a, C_q) =$ $(5, 5)$	$(20, 20)$	SQuAD
Question is well-formed	No	2.9%	23.1%	27.8%	2.3%
	Understandable	34.5%	16.0%	17.0%	10.5%
	Yes	62.6%	60.9%	55.1%	87.2%
Question is relevant	No	2.5%	9.5%	11.5%	4.0%
	Yes	97.5%	90.5%	88.5%	96.0%
Answer is correct	No	2.8%	28.8%	30.5%	7.5%
	Partially	21.8%	28.1%	26.6%	11.8%
	Yes	75.4%	43.2%	42.9%	80.6%
Answer is important	No	1.5%	10.0%	5.0%	6.0%
	Yes	98.5%	90.0%	95.0%	94.0%

Table 4: Human evaluation of the quality of QA pairs.

4.6 Question Answering

We evaluated QAG methods on the downstream QA task. We evaluated our method on 12 challenge sets in addition to the in-distribution test set.

4.6.1 Baselines

We compared our method with the following baselines.

- **$\text{SQuAD}^{\text{Du}}_{\text{train}}$** BERT-base model trained on $\text{SQuAD}^{\text{Du}}_{\text{train}}$ without data augmentation.
- **HarQG** (Du and Cardie, 2018) uses neural AE and QG models and generates over one million QA pairs from top ranking Wikipedia articles not included in SQuAD. We used the publicly available dataset.[5]

[5]https://github.com/xinyadu/harvestingQA

- **SemQG** (Zhang and Bansal, 2019) uses reinforcement learning to generate more SQuAD-like questions. We reran the trained model, and generated questions from the same context-answer pairs as HarQG.
- **InfoHCVAE** (Lee et al., 2020) uses a variational QAG model with an information-maximizing term. We trained this model[6] on $\text{SQuAD}^{\text{Du}}_{\text{train}}$, and then generated 50 QA pairs from each context in $\text{SQuAD}^{\text{Du}}_{\text{train}}$ for a fair comparison with VQAG.

4.6.2 Training Details

We trained pretrained BERT-base models (Devlin et al., 2019) on each synthetic dataset, and then fine-tuned it on $\text{SQuAD}^{\text{Du}}_{\text{train}}$. We adopted this procedure following existing data augmentation approach for QA (Dhingra et al., 2018; Zhang and Bansal, 2019). In our study, the order in which our synthetic datasets $\mathcal{D}$ were given to a QA model was tuned on the dev set.

We used the Hugging Face's implementation of BERT (Wolf et al., 2020). We used Adam (Kingma and Ba, 2014) with epsilon as 1e-8 for the optimizer. The batch size was 32. In both the pretraining and fine-tuning procedure, the learning rate decreased linearly from 3e-5 to zero. We conducted the training for one epoch using a synthetic dataset and two epochs using the original training set.

In addition to the performance of *Single* models, we reported the performance of *Ensemble* models, where the output probabilities of three different QA models are simply averaged. In practice, the top 20 candidate answer spans predicted by each QA model were used for the final prediction.

4.6.3 Challenge Sets

We assessed the robustness of the QA models to the following 12 challenge sets, as well as $\text{SQuAD}^{\text{Du}}_{\text{test}}$.

- **NewsQA (News)** (Trischler et al., 2017): 5,166 QA pairs created from CNN articles by crowdworkers, transformed into the SQuAD format following Sen and Saffari (2020).
- **Natural Questions (NQ)** (Kwiatkowski et al., 2019): 2,356 questions from real users for Wikipedia articles. We reframed NQ as extractive QA by using long answers in NQ as contexts following Sen and Saffari (2020).[7]
- **Non-Adversarial Paraphrased Test Set (Para)** (Gan and Ng, 2019): 1,062 questions paraphrased with slight perturbations from SQuAD using a trained paraphrased model.
- **Adversarial Paraphrased Test Set (APara)** (Gan and Ng, 2019): 56 questions manually paraphrased using context words near a confusing answer from SQuAD.
- **Hard Subset (Hard)** (Sugawara et al., 2018): A subset of the SQuAD dev set, which consists of 1,661 questions that require less word matching and more knowledge inference and multiple sentence reasoning.
- **Implications (Imp)** (Ribeiro et al., 2019): 13,371 QA pairs automatically derived from the SQuAD dev set with a linguistic rule-based method.[8]
- **AddSent (Add) & AddOneSent (AddO)** (Jia and Liang, 2017): Adversarial SQuAD dataset created using handcrafted rules designed for fooling a QA model. The sizes of Add and AddO are 3,560 and 1,787, respectively.
- **Quoref (Quo)** (Dasigi et al., 2019): 2,418 questions requiring coreference resolution created by humans. We used the dev set.
- **Natural Machine Translation Noise (MT)** (Ravichander et al., 2021): A subset of NoiseQA, consisting of 1,190 English translated questions produced by Google's commercial translation system from the XQuAD dataset (Artetxe et al., 2020). This creation introduces naturally occurring noise caused by machine translation.
- **Natural Automatic Speech Recognition Noise (ASR)** (Ravichander et al., 2021): Another subset of NoiseQA, consisting of 1,190 questions that include automatic speech recognition error.
- **Natural Keyboard Noise (KB)** (Ravichander et al., 2021): Another subset of NoiseQA, consisting of 1,190 questions that include natural character-level typos introduced by typing questions on a keyboard.

These challenge sets enable us to evaluate the QA models' robustness to other domain corpora, varia-

[6] https://github.com/seanie12/Info-HCVAE

[7] We used answerable questions for NewsQA and NQ provided by Sen and Saffari (2020). We did not use the MRQA shared task version as Lee et al. (2020) did.

[8] For example, "Q: *Who died in 1285?* A: *Zhenjin*" is derived from "Q: *When did Zhenjin die?* A: *1285*"

	Training Data (Size)	$\text{SQuAD}^{\text{Du}}_{\text{test}}$	Challenge Sets News	NQ	Quo	Para	APara	Hard	Imp	Add	AddO	MT	ASR	KB
Single	$\text{SQuAD}^{\text{Du}}_{\text{train}}$ (76k)	83.5	49.2	67.7	30.1	85.7	50.2	75.6	64.7	62.9	71.8	79.7	67.5	80.1
	+HarQG (1,205k)	*83.3*	*48.5*	*66.2*	31.3	*85.2*	56.5	*73.0*	*63.5*	65.1	73.1	*78.6*	70.0	80.3
	+SemQG (1,204k)	84.7	50.5	69.8	***34.5***	86.2	51.8	*75.0*	65.1	***66.5***	74.3	*79.5*	71.0	80.7
	+InfoHCVAE (824k)	**84.8**	**51.3**	**71.2**	33.8	*85.6*	53.3	**77.7**	64.8	66.1	**74.5**	**81.3**	**71.6**	**82.8**
	+VQAG (432k)	84.5	49.2	70.1	32.0	**86.7**	**59.0**	76.1	**66.3**	64.8	73.9	79.9	70.5	81.1
Ensemble	$\{\text{SQuAD}^{\text{Du}}_{\text{train}}\}$*3	84.2	50.4	69.4	31.3	86.4	53.2	76.6	65.7	63.6	72.6	80.3	68.7	81.2
	{+SemQG}*3	85.5	51.8	71.3	**35.1**	87.5	57.8	78.2	66.5	67.0	75.1	80.8	72.9	82.5
	{+InfoHCVAE}*3	85.3	52.0	**72.2**	34.0	88.0	56.9	**79.0**	65.7	**67.7**	**75.9**	81.4	73.1	**83.2**
	{+VQAG}*3	84.9	50.9	70.1	32.3	**88.1**	**58.6**	77.3	**67.5**	64.9	73.9	80.8	71.2	81.6
	{+Sem,+Info,+V}	**85.8**	**52.1**	72.0	34.2	88.0	55.1	78.8	67.0	66.3	74.7	**82.2**	**73.5**	83.0
If challenge set is known		-	62.9	83.0	66.9	88.6	73.9	-	-	-	-	80.8	75.9	82.6

Table 5: QA performance (F1 score) on $\text{SQuAD}^{\text{Du}}_{\text{test}}$ and the 12 challenge sets. The abbreviations of the challenge sets are explained in §4.6. Curly brackets denote an ensemble of different models (e.g., {+VQAG}*3 denotes the ensemble of three QA models, trained with different random seeds after data augmentation with VQAG). The best scores for each of the *Single* and *Ensemble* models are **boldfaced**. The degraded scores compared to the no data augmentation baseline (the 1st line) are in *red*. Sem: SemQG, Info: InfoHCVAE, V: VQAG.

tions in questions, adversarial examples, and noise that may occur in real-world applications.

4.6.4 Results

The overall results are given in Table 5. First, we discovered that the QA model without data augmentation degraded the performance on the 12 challenge sets, showing a lack of the robustness to the natural and adversarial distribution shifts in contexts, questions, and answers.[9]

With data augmentation using QAG, the in-distribution scores were generally improved, except for HarQG. In the *Single* model setting on the challenge sets, SemQG achieved the best performance on Quo and Add. InfoHCVAE achieved the best performance on News, NQ, Hard, AddO, MT, ASR, and KB. VQAG achieved the best performance on Para, APara, and Imp. These results imply that different QAG methods have different benefits. In the *Ensemble* setting, taking the best of the three, the scores on $\text{SQuAD}^{\text{Du}}_{\text{test}}$, News, MT, and ASR were further improved with {+Sem,+Info,+V}.

We also attached scores that are obtained *if challenge set is known* in Table 5; that is, natural or synthetic samples from the same distributions as the challenge sets are available during training. For News, NQ, and Quo, we trained the BERT-base model on the corresponding training sets, which are annotated by humans. For paraphrased questions (Para, APara) and NoiseQA (MT, ASR, and KB), the scores were taken from Gan and Ng (2019) and Ravichander et al. (2021), respectively. These scores can be considered as the upper bounds. In NoiseQA, the QAG methods consistently improved the scores, even though they were not designed for the noise. This may be because the lack of quality in synthetic datasets, as shown in Table 4, unintentionally improved the robustness to the noise. However, the most significant performance gap (> 30 F1) between the upper bound and the no data augmentation baseline was observed in Quo. This result indicates that a QA model does not acquire coreference resolution from SQuAD, even though approximately 18% of SQuAD questions require coreference resolution (Sugawara et al., 2018). The QAG methods mitigated this gap to some extent, but there is a significant room for improvement.

The improvement in NQ is generally more prominent than that in News. This may be because both SQuAD and NQ contain paragraphs in Wikipedia. Utilizing unlabeled documents in domains such as news articles may improve the generalization to other domains, such as News.

In our experiment, our model and InfoHCVAE improved the scores despite generating QA pairs from only the paragraphs in $\text{SQuAD}^{\text{Du}}_{\text{train}}$, unlike SemQG and HarQG, which generated QA pairs from paragraphs out of SQuAD in Wikipedia. Using paragraphs in and out of $\text{SQuAD}^{\text{Du}}_{\text{train}}$ as the source for QAG may be more effective.

In paraphrased questions (Gan and Ng, 2019), implications (Ribeiro et al., 2019), and NoiseQA

[9] The score on Para—85.7 F1 is degraded when compared to the score on the SQuAD dev set—87.9 F1, which is the source for creating Para. This means the lack of robustness to paraphrased questions.

Training Source (Size)	EM	F1
VQAG (432k)	81.49	88.61
$-\mathcal{D}_{5,5}$ (251k)	81.04	88.39
$-\mathcal{D}_{5,20}$ (113k)	81.00	88.48
$-\mathcal{D}_{20,20}$ (68k)	81.14	88.52

Table 6: Ablation study on $\text{SQuAD}^{\text{Du}}_{\text{dev}}$.

Dataset	what	how	who	which	when	where	why
$\text{SQuAD}^{\text{Du}}_{\text{train}}$	<u>58.3</u>	10.4	10.3	6.7	6.7	4.2	1.5
$\text{SQuAD}^{\text{Du}}_{\text{test}}$	<u>56.5</u>	12.1	11.5	8.6	6.0	3.8	0.8
HarQG	<u>61.3</u>	7.8	13.8	0.7	10.1	5.8	0.5
SemQG	<u>71.1</u>	8.1	12.8	1.3	3.6	2.7	0.2
InfoHCVAE	<u>77.1</u>	6.6	5.0	1.6	5.6	3.3	0.5
VQAG							
$\mathcal{D}_{5,5}$	36.6	<u>54.9</u>	4.9	0.5	0.3	0.5	2.3
$\mathcal{D}_{5,20}$	9.5	35.5	3.6	<u>49.2</u>	1.2	0.9	0.0
$\mathcal{D}_{20,20}$	28.2	<u>36.7</u>	6.3	23.2	0.2	1.6	3.9

Table 7: Percentages (%) of each question type in each dataset. The largest number in each line is <u>underlined</u>.

(Ravichander et al., 2021), augment questions that are similar to the corresponding challenge sets, that is, generating paraphrases, implications, and questions including the noise, successfully improved the robustness to these perturbations. While these methods slightly degraded or maintained the in-distribution score, we showed that QAG methods are less likely to exhibit a trade-off between the in- and out-of-distribution accuracies. Notably, VQAG did not degrade the scores on all the 12 challenge sets while improving the in-distribution score. In contrast, SemQG degraded the scores on Hard and MT, and InfoHCVAE degraded the score on Para. This property of VQAG may be because it can significantly improve the diversity by combining different configurations of the KL control.

Moreover, the size of synthetic dataset created by VQAG was the smallest among the QAG methods. If the diversity is assured sufficiently, significantly increasing the quantity may not be necessary. In Add and AddO, we showed that the QAG methods consistently improved adversarial robustness, which has not been studied in the QAG literature.

4.6.5 Analysis

To assess the usefulness of each dataset $\mathcal{D}$ in VQAG, we conducted an ablation study. As shown in Table 6, each dataset $\mathcal{D}$ has meaningful effect on the performance. This result implies that creating more synthetic datasets using different configurations may further improve the performance.

To understand the differences in each dataset in terms of diversity, we conducted a simple analysis on the question type. As shown in Table 7, VQAG with different configurations corresponds to different distributions of question types, while more than 50% of the questions in the other datasets contain "what". Among the QAG methods, this point is unique to VQAG.

5 Discussion and Conclusion

We presented a variational QAG model, incorporating two independent latent random variables. We showed that an explicit KL control can enable our model to significantly improve the diversity of QA pairs. Our synthetic datasets were shown to be noisy in terms of the grammaticality and answerability of questions, but effective in improving the QA performance in the in-distribution test set and the 12 challenge sets. While out synthetic datasets are noisy, they may unintentionally improve the robustness to the noise that can occur in real applications. However, we should pay attention to the negative effect of using our noisy dataset. For example, the lack of the answerability of our synthetic questions may lead to the poor performance in handling unanswerable questions, such as SQuAD v2.0. Moreover, QAG methods led to improvements in most of the 12 challenge sets while being agnostic to the target distributions during training. We need to pursue such a target-unaware method to improve the robustness of QA models, because it is quite difficult for developers to know the types of questions a QA model cannot handle in advance.

In summary, our experimental results showed that the diversity of QA datasets plays a non-negligible role in improving its robustness, which can be boosted with QAG. We will consider using unlabeled documents in other domains to further improve the robustness to other domain corpora in our future study.

Acknowledgements

We would like to thank the anonymous reviewers for their valuable comments. We would also like to thank the members of Aizawa Lab for their helpful discussions. This work was supported by NEDO SIP-2 "Big-data and AI-enabled Cyberspace Technologies" and JSPS KAKENHI Grant Number 20K23335.

References

Chris Alberti, Daniel Andor, Emily Pitler, Jacob Devlin, and Michael Collins. 2019. Synthetic QA corpora generation with roundtrip consistency. In *Proceedings of the 57th Annual Meeting of the Association for Computational Linguistics*, pages 6168–6173, Florence, Italy. Association for Computational Linguistics.

Mikel Artetxe, Sebastian Ruder, and Dani Yogatama. 2020. On the cross-lingual transferability of monolingual representations. In *Proceedings of the 58th Annual Meeting of the Association for Computational Linguistics*, pages 4623–4637, Online. Association for Computational Linguistics.

Dzmitry Bahdanau, Kyunghyun Cho, and Yoshua Bengio. 2014. Neural machine translation by jointly learning to align and translate. *arXiv preprint arXiv:1409.0473*.

Hareesh Bahuleyan, Lili Mou, Olga Vechtomova, and Pascal Poupart. 2018. Variational attention for sequence-to-sequence models. In *Proceedings of the 27th International Conference on Computational Linguistics*, pages 1672–1682. Association for Computational Linguistics.

Samuel R. Bowman, Luke Vilnis, Oriol Vinyals, Andrew Dai, Rafal Jozefowicz, and Samy Bengio. 2016. Generating sentences from a continuous space. In *Proceedings of The 20th SIGNLL Conference on Computational Natural Language Learning*, pages 10–21, Berlin, Germany. Association for Computational Linguistics.

Eric Breck, Yejin Choi, and Claire Cardie. 2007. Identifying expressions of opinion in context. In *Proceedings of the 20th International Joint Conference on Artifical Intelligence*, IJCAI'07, pages 2683–2688, San Francisco, CA, USA. Morgan Kaufmann Publishers Inc.

Christopher P Burgess, Irina Higgins, Arka Pal, Loic Matthey, Nick Watters, Guillaume Desjardins, and Alexander Lerchner. 2018. Understanding disentangling in *beta*-VAE. *arXiv preprint arXiv:1804.03599*.

Mingda Chen, Qingming Tang, Karen Livescu, and Kevin Gimpel. 2018. Variational sequential labelers for semi-supervised learning. In *Proceedings of the 2018 Conference on Empirical Methods in Natural Language Processing*, pages 215–226, Brussels, Belgium. Association for Computational Linguistics.

Pradeep Dasigi, Nelson F. Liu, Ana Marasović, Noah A. Smith, and Matt Gardner. 2019. Quoref: A reading comprehension dataset with questions requiring coreferential reasoning. In *Proceedings of the 2019 Conference on Empirical Methods in Natural Language Processing and the 9th International Joint Conference on Natural Language Processing (EMNLP-IJCNLP)*, pages 5925–5932, Hong Kong, China. Association for Computational Linguistics.

Jacob Devlin, Ming-Wei Chang, Kenton Lee, and Kristina Toutanova. 2019. BERT: Pre-training of deep bidirectional transformers for language understanding. In *Proceedings of the 2019 Conference of the North American Chapter of the Association for Computational Linguistics: Human Language Technologies, Volume 1 (Long and Short Papers)*, pages 4171–4186, Minneapolis, Minnesota. Association for Computational Linguistics.

Bhuwan Dhingra, Danish Danish, and Dheeraj Rajagopal. 2018. Simple and effective semi-supervised question answering. In *Proceedings of the 2018 Conference of the North American Chapter of the Association for Computational Linguistics: Human Language Technologies, Volume 2 (Short Papers)*, pages 582–587, New Orleans, Louisiana. Association for Computational Linguistics.

Li Dong, Nan Yang, Wenhui Wang, Furu Wei, Xiaodong Liu, Yu Wang, Jianfeng Gao, Ming Zhou, and Hsiao-Wuen Hon. 2019. Unified language model pre-training for natural language understanding and generation. In *Advances in Neural Information Processing Systems*, volume 32, pages 13042–13054. Curran Associates, Inc.

Xinya Du and Claire Cardie. 2018. Harvesting paragraph-level question-answer pairs from Wikipedia. In *Proceedings of the 56th Annual Meeting of the Association for Computational Linguistics (Volume 1: Long Papers)*, pages 1907–1917. Association for Computational Linguistics.

Xinya Du, Junru Shao, and Claire Cardie. 2017. Learning to ask: Neural question generation for reading comprehension. In *Proceedings of the 55th Annual Meeting of the Association for Computational Linguistics (Volume 1: Long Papers)*, pages 1342–1352. Association for Computational Linguistics.

Wee Chung Gan and Hwee Tou Ng. 2019. Improving the robustness of question answering systems to question paraphrasing. In *Proceedings of the 57th Annual Meeting of the Association for Computational Linguistics*, pages 6065–6075, Florence, Italy. Association for Computational Linguistics.

Robert Geirhos, Jörn-Henrik Jacobsen, Claudio Michaelis, Richard Zemel, Wieland Brendel, Matthias Bethge, and Felix A Wichmann. 2020. Shortcut learning in deep neural networks. *Nature Machine Intelligence*, 2(11):665–673.

Mor Geva, Yoav Goldberg, and Jonathan Berant. 2019. Are we modeling the task or the annotator? an investigation of annotator bias in natural language understanding datasets. In *Proceedings of the 2019 Conference on Empirical Methods in Natural Language Processing and the 9th International Joint Conference on Natural Language Processing (EMNLP-IJCNLP)*, pages 1161–1166, Hong Kong, China. Association for Computational Linguistics.

Xavier Glorot and Yoshua Bengio. 2010. Understanding the difficulty of training deep feedforward neural networks. In *Proceedings of the Thirteenth International Conference on Artificial Intelligence and Statistics*, volume 9 of *Proceedings of Machine Learning Research*, pages 249–256, Chia Laguna Resort, Sardinia, Italy. PMLR.

Jiatao Gu, Zhengdong Lu, Hang Li, and Victor O.K. Li. 2016. Incorporating copying mechanism in sequence-to-sequence learning. In *Proceedings of the 54th Annual Meeting of the Association for Computational Linguistics (Volume 1: Long Papers)*, pages 1631–1640, Berlin, Germany. Association for Computational Linguistics.

Caglar Gulcehre, Sungjin Ahn, Ramesh Nallapati, Bowen Zhou, and Yoshua Bengio. 2016. Pointing the unknown words. In *Proceedings of the 54th Annual Meeting of the Association for Computational Linguistics (Volume 1: Long Papers)*, pages 140–149. Association for Computational Linguistics.

Michael Heilman and Noah A. Smith. 2010. Good question! Statistical ranking for question generation. In *Human Language Technologies: The 2010 Annual Conference of the North American Chapter of the Association for Computational Linguistics*, pages 609–617. Association for Computational Linguistics.

Irina Higgins, Loic Matthey, Arka Pal, Christopher Burgess, Xavier Glorot, Matthew Botvinick, Shakir Mohamed, and Alexander Lerchner. 2017. beta-VAE: Learning basic visual concepts with a constrained variational framework. In *International Conference on Learning Representations*.

Matthew Honnibal, Ines Montani, Sofie Van Landeghem, and Adriane Boyd. 2020. spaCy: Industrial-strength Natural Language Processing in Python.

Zhiheng Huang, Wei Xu, and Kai Yu. 2015. Bidirectional LSTM-CRF models for sequence tagging. *arXiv preprint arXiv:1508.01991*.

Robin Jia and Percy Liang. 2017. Adversarial examples for evaluating reading comprehension systems. In *Proceedings of the 2017 Conference on Empirical Methods in Natural Language Processing*, pages 2021–2031, Copenhagen, Denmark. Association for Computational Linguistics.

Richard Johansson and Alessandro Moschitti. 2010. Syntactic and semantic structure for opinion expression detection. In *Proceedings of the Fourteenth Conference on Computational Natural Language Learning*, pages 67–76, Uppsala, Sweden. Association for Computational Linguistics.

Mandar Joshi, Eunsol Choi, Daniel Weld, and Luke Zettlemoyer. 2017. TriviaQA: A large scale distantly supervised challenge dataset for reading comprehension. In *Proceedings of the 55th Annual Meeting of the Association for Computational Linguistics (Volume 1: Long Papers)*, pages 1601–1611, Vancouver, Canada. Association for Computational Linguistics.

Junmo Kang, Haritz Puerto San Roman, and sunghyon myaeng. 2019. Let me know what to ask: Interrogative-word-aware question generation. In *Proceedings of the 2nd Workshop on Machine Reading for Question Answering*, pages 163–171, Hong Kong, China. Association for Computational Linguistics.

Yanghoon Kim, Hwanhee Lee, Joongbo Shin, and Kyomin Jung. 2019. Improving neural question generation using answer separation. *Proceedings of the AAAI Conference on Artificial Intelligence*, 33(01):6602–6609.

Yoon Kim. 2014. Convolutional neural networks for sentence classification. In *Proceedings of the 2014 Conference on Empirical Methods in Natural Language Processing (EMNLP)*, pages 1746–1751. Association for Computational Linguistics.

Diederik P Kingma and Jimmy Ba. 2014. Adam: A method for stochastic optimization. *arXiv preprint arXiv:1412.6980*.

Diederik P Kingma and Max Welling. 2013. Auto-encoding variational bayes. *arXiv preprint arXiv:1312.6114*.

Miyoung Ko, Jinhyuk Lee, Hyunjae Kim, Gangwoo Kim, and Jaewoo Kang. 2020. Look at the first sentence: Position bias in question answering. In *Proceedings of the 2020 Conference on Empirical Methods in Natural Language Processing (EMNLP)*, pages 1109–1121, Online. Association for Computational Linguistics.

Vishwajeet Kumar, Ganesh Ramakrishnan, and Yuan-Fang Li. 2019. Putting the horse before the cart: A generator-evaluator framework for question generation from text. In *Proceedings of the 23rd Conference on Computational Natural Language Learning (CoNLL)*, pages 812–821, Hong Kong, China. Association for Computational Linguistics.

Tom Kwiatkowski, Jennimaria Palomaki, Olivia Redfield, Michael Collins, Ankur Parikh, Chris Alberti, Danielle Epstein, Illia Polosukhin, Jacob Devlin, Kenton Lee, Kristina Toutanova, Llion Jones, Matthew Kelcey, Ming-Wei Chang, Andrew M. Dai, Jakob Uszkoreit, Quoc Le, and Slav Petrov. 2019. Natural questions: A benchmark for question answering research. *Transactions of the Association for Computational Linguistics*, 7:452–466.

Igor Labutov, Sumit Basu, and Lucy Vanderwende. 2015. Deep questions without deep understanding. In *Proceedings of the 53rd Annual Meeting of the Association for Computational Linguistics and the 7th International Joint Conference on Natural Language Processing (Volume 1: Long Papers)*, pages 889–898, Beijing, China. Association for Computational Linguistics.

Dong Bok Lee, Seanie Lee, Woo Tae Jeong, Donghwan Kim, and Sung Ju Hwang. 2020. Generating diverse and consistent QA pairs from contexts with information-maximizing hierarchical conditional VAEs. In *Proceedings of the 58th Annual Meeting of the Association for Computational Linguistics*, pages 208–224, Online. Association for Computational Linguistics.

Mike Lewis and Angela Fan. 2019. Generative question answering: Learning to answer the whole question. In *International Conference on Learning Representations*.

Jingjing Li, Yifan Gao, Lidong Bing, Irwin King, and Michael R. Lyu. 2019. Improving question generation with to the point context. In *Proceedings of the 2019 Conference on Empirical Methods in Natural Language Processing and the 9th International Joint Conference on Natural Language Processing (EMNLP-IJCNLP)*, pages 3214–3224, Hong Kong, China. Association for Computational Linguistics.

Jiwei Li, Michel Galley, Chris Brockett, Jianfeng Gao, and Bill Dolan. 2016a. A diversity-promoting objective function for neural conversation models. In *Proceedings of the 2016 Conference of the North American Chapter of the Association for Computational Linguistics: Human Language Technologies*, pages 110–119, San Diego, California. Association for Computational Linguistics.

Jiwei Li, Will Monroe, and Dan Jurafsky. 2016b. A simple, fast diverse decoding algorithm for neural generation. *arXiv preprint arXiv:1611.08562*.

Juntao Li, Yan Song, Haisong Zhang, Dongmin Chen, Shuming Shi, Dongyan Zhao, and Rui Yan. 2018. Generating classical chinese poems via conditional variational autoencoder and adversarial training. In *Proceedings of the 2018 Conference on Empirical Methods in Natural Language Processing*, pages 3890–3900. Association for Computational Linguistics.

David Lindberg, Fred Popowich, John Nesbit, and Phil Winne. 2013. Generating natural language questions to support learning on-line. In *Proceedings of the 14th European Workshop on Natural Language Generation*, pages 105–114, Sofia, Bulgaria. Association for Computational Linguistics.

Bang Liu, Haojie Wei, Di Niu, Haolan Chen, and Yancheng He. 2020. Asking questions the human way: Scalable question-answer generation from text corpus. In *Proceedings of The Web Conference 2020*, WWW '20, page 2032–2043, New York, NY, USA. Association for Computing Machinery.

Bang Liu, Mingjun Zhao, Di Niu, Kunfeng Lai, Yancheng He, Haojie Wei, and Yu Xu. 2019. Learning to generate questions by learningwhat not to generate. In *The World Wide Web Conference*, WWW '19, page 1106–1118, New York, NY, USA. Association for Computing Machinery.

Jack Mostow and Wei Chen. 2009. Generating instruction automatically for the reading strategy of self-questioning. In *Proceedings of the 2009 Conference on Artificial Intelligence in Education: Building Learning Systems That Care: From Knowledge Representation to Affective Modelling*, pages 465–472, NLD. IOS Press.

Preksha Nema, Akash Kumar Mohankumar, Mitesh M. Khapra, Balaji Vasan Srinivasan, and Balaraman Ravindran. 2019. Let's ask again: Refine network for automatic question generation. In *Proceedings of the 2019 Conference on Empirical Methods in Natural Language Processing and the 9th International Joint Conference on Natural Language Processing (EMNLP-IJCNLP)*, pages 3312–3321, Hong Kong, China. Association for Computational Linguistics.

Jeffrey Pennington, Richard Socher, and Christopher Manning. 2014. GloVe: Global vectors for word representation. In *Proceedings of the 2014 Conference on Empirical Methods in Natural Language Processing (EMNLP)*, pages 1532–1543. Association for Computational Linguistics.

Jiazuo Qiu and Deyi Xiong. 2019. Generating highly relevant questions. In *Proceedings of the 2019 Conference on Empirical Methods in Natural Language Processing and the 9th International Joint Conference on Natural Language Processing (EMNLP-IJCNLP)*, pages 5982–5986, Hong Kong, China. Association for Computational Linguistics.

Pranav Rajpurkar, Jian Zhang, Konstantin Lopyrev, and Percy Liang. 2016. SQuAD: 100,000+ questions for machine comprehension of text. In *Proceedings of the 2016 Conference on Empirical Methods in Natural Language Processing*, pages 2383–2392. Association for Computational Linguistics.

Abhilasha Ravichander, Siddharth Dalmia, Maria Ryskina, Florian Metze, Eduard Hovy, and Alan W Black. 2021. NoiseQA: Challenge set evaluation for user-centric question answering. In *Proceedings of the 16th Conference of the European Chapter of the Association for Computational Linguistics: Main Volume*, pages 2976–2992, Online. Association for Computational Linguistics.

Marco Tulio Ribeiro, Carlos Guestrin, and Sameer Singh. 2019. Are red roses red? Evaluating consistency of question-answering models. In *Proceedings of the 57th Annual Meeting of the Association for Computational Linguistics*, pages 6174–6184, Florence, Italy. Association for Computational Linguistics.

Stanislau Semeniuta, Aliaksei Severyn, and Erhardt Barth. 2017. A hybrid convolutional variational autoencoder for text generation. In *Proceedings of the 2017 Conference on Empirical Methods in Natural Language Processing*, pages 627–637, Copenhagen, Denmark. Association for Computational Linguistics.

Priyanka Sen and Amir Saffari. 2020. What do models learn from question answering datasets? In *Proceedings of the 2020 Conference on Empirical Methods in Natural Language Processing (EMNLP)*, pages 2429–2438, Online. Association for Computational Linguistics.

Iulian Vlad Serban, Alessandro Sordoni, Ryan Lowe, Laurent Charlin, Joelle Pineau, Aaron Courville, and Yoshua Bengio. 2017. A hierarchical latent variable encoder-decoder model for generating dialogues. In *Proceedings of the Thirty-First AAAI Conference on Artificial Intelligence*, AAAI'17, pages 3295–3301. AAAI Press.

Xiaoyu Shen, Hui Su, Yanran Li, Wenjie Li, Shuzi Niu, Yang Zhao, Akiko Aizawa, and Guoping Long. 2017. A conditional variational framework for dialog generation. In *Proceedings of the 55th Annual Meeting of the Association for Computational Linguistics (Volume 2: Short Papers)*, pages 504–509, Vancouver, Canada. Association for Computational Linguistics.

Linfeng Song, Zhiguo Wang, Wael Hamza, Yue Zhang, and Daniel Gildea. 2018. Leveraging context information for natural question generation. In *Proceedings of the 2018 Conference of the North American Chapter of the Association for Computational Linguistics: Human Language Technologies, Volume 2 (Short Papers)*, pages 569–574. Association for Computational Linguistics.

Nitish Srivastava, Geoffrey Hinton, Alex Krizhevsky, Ilya Sutskever, and Ruslan Salakhutdinov. 2014. Dropout: A simple way to prevent neural networks from overfitting. *Journal of Machine Learning Research*, 15:1929–1958.

Sandeep Subramanian, Tong Wang, Xingdi Yuan, Saizheng Zhang, Adam Trischler, and Yoshua Bengio. 2018. Neural models for key phrase extraction and question generation. In *Proceedings of the Workshop on Machine Reading for Question Answering*, pages 78–88. Association for Computational Linguistics.

Saku Sugawara, Kentaro Inui, Satoshi Sekine, and Akiko Aizawa. 2018. What makes reading comprehension questions easier? In *Proceedings of the 2018 Conference on Empirical Methods in Natural Language Processing*, pages 4208–4219, Brussels, Belgium. Association for Computational Linguistics.

Md Arafat Sultan, Shubham Chandel, Ramón Fernandez Astudillo, and Vittorio Castelli. 2020. On the importance of diversity in question generation for QA. In *Proceedings of the 58th Annual Meeting of the Association for Computational Linguistics*, pages 5651–5656, Online. Association for Computational Linguistics.

Xingwu Sun, Jing Liu, Yajuan Lyu, Wei He, Yanjun Ma, and Shi Wang. 2018. Answer-focused and position-aware neural question generation. In *Proceedings of the 2018 Conference on Empirical Methods in Natural Language Processing*, pages 3930–3939. Association for Computational Linguistics.

Ilya Sutskever, Oriol Vinyals, and Quoc V. Le. 2014. Sequence to sequence learning with neural networks. In *Proceedings of the 27th International Conference on Neural Information Processing Systems - Volume 2*, NIPS'14, pages 3104–3112, Cambridge, MA, USA. MIT Press.

Alon Talmor and Jonathan Berant. 2019. MultiQA: An empirical investigation of generalization and transfer in reading comprehension. In *Proceedings of the 57th Annual Meeting of the Association for Computational Linguistics*, pages 4911–4921, Florence, Italy. Association for Computational Linguistics.

Ilya Tolstikhin, Olivier Bousquet, Sylvain Gelly, and Bernhard Schoelkopf. 2018. Wasserstein autoencoders. In *International Conference on Learning Representations*.

Adam Trischler, Tong Wang, Xingdi Yuan, Justin Harris, Alessandro Sordoni, Philip Bachman, and Kaheer Suleman. 2017. NewsQA: A machine comprehension dataset. In *Proceedings of the 2nd Workshop on Representation Learning for NLP*, pages 191–200. Association for Computational Linguistics.

Oriol Vinyals, Meire Fortunato, and Navdeep Jaitly. 2015. Pointer networks. In C. Cortes, N. D. Lawrence, D. D. Lee, M. Sugiyama, and R. Garnett, editors, *Advances in Neural Information Processing Systems 28*, pages 2692–2700. Curran Associates, Inc.

Shuohang Wang and Jing Jiang. 2016. Learning natural language inference with LSTM. In *Proceedings of the 2016 Conference of the North American Chapter of the Association for Computational Linguistics: Human Language Technologies*, pages 1442–1451, San Diego, California. Association for Computational Linguistics.

Shuohang Wang and Jing Jiang. 2017. Machine comprehension using match-LSTM and answer pointer. In *International Conference on Learning Representations*.

Siyuan Wang, Zhongyu Wei, Zhihao Fan, Yang Liu, and Xuanjing Huang. 2019. A multi-agent communication framework for question-worthy phrase extraction and question generation. *Proceedings of the AAAI Conference on Artificial Intelligence*, 33(01):7168–7175.

Thomas Wolf, Lysandre Debut, Victor Sanh, Julien Chaumond, Clement Delangue, Anthony Moi, Pierric Cistac, Tim Rault, Remi Louf, Morgan Funtowicz, Joe Davison, Sam Shleifer, Patrick von Platen, Clara Ma, Yacine Jernite, Julien Plu, Canwen Xu, Teven Le Scao, Sylvain Gugger, Mariama Drame,

Quentin Lhoest, and Alexander Rush. 2020. Transformers: State-of-the-art natural language processing. In *Proceedings of the 2020 Conference on Empirical Methods in Natural Language Processing: System Demonstrations*, pages 38–45, Online. Association for Computational Linguistics.

Jingjing Xu, Xuancheng Ren, Junyang Lin, and Xu Sun. 2018. Diversity-promoting GAN: A cross-entropy based generative adversarial network for diversified text generation. In *Proceedings of the 2018 Conference on Empirical Methods in Natural Language Processing*, pages 3940–3949, Brussels, Belgium. Association for Computational Linguistics.

Zhilin Yang, Junjie Hu, Ruslan Salakhutdinov, and William Cohen. 2017a. Semi-supervised QA with generative domain-adaptive nets. In *Proceedings of the 55th Annual Meeting of the Association for Computational Linguistics (Volume 1: Long Papers)*, pages 1040–1050. Association for Computational Linguistics.

Zichao Yang, Zhiting Hu, Ruslan Salakhutdinov, and Taylor Berg-Kirkpatrick. 2017b. Improved variational autoencoders for text modeling using dilated convolutions. In *Proceedings of the 34th International Conference on Machine Learning*, volume 70 of *Proceedings of Machine Learning Research*, pages 3881–3890, International Convention Centre, Sydney, Australia. PMLR.

Kaichun Yao, Libo Zhang, Tiejian Luo, Lili Tao, and Yanjun Wu. 2018. Teaching machines to ask questions. In *Proceedings of the Twenty-Seventh International Joint Conference on Artificial Intelligence, IJCAI-18*, pages 4546–4552. International Joint Conferences on Artificial Intelligence Organization.

Dani Yogatama, Cyprien de Masson d'Autume, Jerome Connor, Tomas Kocisky, Mike Chrzanowski, Lingpeng Kong, Angeliki Lazaridou, Wang Ling, Lei Yu, Chris Dyer, et al. 2019. Learning and evaluating general linguistic intelligence. *arXiv preprint arXiv:1901.11373*.

Xingdi Yuan, Tong Wang, Caglar Gulcehre, Alessandro Sordoni, Philip Bachman, Saizheng Zhang, Sandeep Subramanian, and Adam Trischler. 2017. Machine comprehension by text-to-text neural question generation. In *Proceedings of the 2nd Workshop on Representation Learning for NLP*, pages 15–25. Association for Computational Linguistics.

Biao Zhang, Deyi Xiong, Jinsong Su, Hong Duan, and Min Zhang. 2016. Variational neural machine translation. In *Proceedings of the 2016 Conference on Empirical Methods in Natural Language Processing*, pages 521–530, Austin, Texas. Association for Computational Linguistics.

Shiyue Zhang and Mohit Bansal. 2019. Addressing semantic drift in question generation for semi-supervised question answering. In *Proceedings of the 2019 Conference on Empirical Methods in Natural Language Processing and the 9th International Joint Conference on Natural Language Processing (EMNLP-IJCNLP)*, pages 2495–2509, Hong Kong, China. Association for Computational Linguistics.

Yizhe Zhang, Michel Galley, Jianfeng Gao, Zhe Gan, Xiujun Li, Chris Brockett, and Bill Dolan. 2018. Generating informative and diverse conversational responses via adversarial information maximization. In S. Bengio, H. Wallach, H. Larochelle, K. Grauman, N. Cesa-Bianchi, and R. Garnett, editors, *Advances in Neural Information Processing Systems 31*, pages 1810–1820. Curran Associates, Inc.

Shengjia Zhao, Jiaming Song, and Stefano Ermon. 2017a. InfoVAE: Information maximizing variational autoencoders. *arXiv preprint arXiv:1706.02262*.

Tiancheng Zhao, Ran Zhao, and Maxine Eskenazi. 2017b. Learning discourse-level diversity for neural dialog models using conditional variational autoencoders. In *Proceedings of the 55th Annual Meeting of the Association for Computational Linguistics (Volume 1: Long Papers)*, pages 654–664. Association for Computational Linguistics.

Yao Zhao, Xiaochuan Ni, Yuanyuan Ding, and Qifa Ke. 2018. Paragraph-level neural question generation with maxout pointer and gated self-attention networks. In *Proceedings of the 2018 Conference on Empirical Methods in Natural Language Processing*, pages 3901–3910. Association for Computational Linguistics.

Qingyu Zhou, Nan Yang, Furu Wei, Chuanqi Tan, Hangbo Bao, and Ming Zhou. 2018. Neural question generation from text: A preliminary study. In *Natural Language Processing and Chinese Computing*, pages 662–671, Cham. Springer International Publishing.

Wenjie Zhou, Minghua Zhang, and Yunfang Wu. 2019. Question-type driven question generation. In *Proceedings of the 2019 Conference on Empirical Methods in Natural Language Processing and the 9th International Joint Conference on Natural Language Processing (EMNLP-IJCNLP)*, pages 6031–6036, Hong Kong, China. Association for Computational Linguistics.

Yaoming Zhu, Sidi Lu, Lei Zheng, Jiaxian Guo, Weinan Zhang, Jun Wang, and Yong Yu. 2018. Texygen: A benchmarking platform for text generation models. In *The 41st International ACM SIGIR Conference on Research & Development in Information Retrieval*, SIGIR '18, page 1097–1100, New York, NY, USA. Association for Computing Machinery.

A Derivations of the Variational Lower Bound

The variational lower bound, Eq. 1, without the KL control is derived as follows:

$$
\begin{aligned}
&\log p_\theta(q, a|c) \\
&= \mathbb{E}_{z,y\sim q_\phi(z,y|q,a,c)}\left[\log p_\theta(q, a|c)\right] \\
&= \mathbb{E}_{z,y}\left[\log \frac{p_\theta(q, a|z, y, c)p_\theta(z, y|c)}{p_\theta(z, y|q, a, c)}\right] \\
&= \mathbb{E}_{z,y}\left[\log \frac{p_\theta(q, a|z, y, c)p_\theta(z, y|c)}{p_\theta(z, y|q, a, c)}\right. \\
&\quad \left. + \log \frac{q_\phi(z, y|q, a, c)}{q_\phi(z, y|q, a, c)}\right] \\
&= \mathbb{E}_{z,y}\left[\log \frac{p_\theta(q|y, a, c)p_\theta(y|c)}{p_\theta(y|q, c)}\right. \\
&\quad + \log \frac{p_\theta(a|z, c)p_\theta(z|c)}{p_\theta(z|a, c)} \\
&\quad \left. + \log \frac{q_\phi(y|q, c)}{q_\phi(y|q, c)} + \log \frac{q_\phi(z|a, c)}{q_\phi(z|a, c)}\right] \\
&= \mathbb{E}_{z,y}\left[\log p_\theta(q|y, a, c) + \log p_\theta(a|z, c)\right. \\
&\quad + \log \frac{p_\theta(y|c)}{q_\phi(y|q, c)} + \log \frac{q_\phi(y|q, c)}{p_\theta(y|q, c)} \\
&\quad \left. + \log \frac{p_\theta(z|c)}{q_\phi(z|a, c)} + \log \frac{q_\phi(z|a, c)}{p_\theta(z|a, c)}\right] \\
&= \mathbb{E}_{z,y}\left[\log p_\theta(q|y, a, c) + \log p_\theta(a|z, c)\right] \\
&\quad - D_{\mathrm{KL}}(q_\phi(y|q, c)||p_\theta(y|c)) \\
&\quad + D_{\mathrm{KL}}(q_\phi(y|q, c)||p_\theta(y|q, c)) \\
&\quad - D_{\mathrm{KL}}(q_\phi(z|a, c)||p_\theta(z|c)) \\
&\quad + D_{\mathrm{KL}}(q_\phi(z|a, c)||p_\theta(z|a, c)) \\
&\geq \mathbb{E}_{z,y}\left[\log p_\theta(q|y, a, c) + \log p_\theta(a|z, c)\right] \\
&\quad - D_{\mathrm{KL}}(q_\phi(y|q, c)||p_\theta(y|c)) \\
&\quad - D_{\mathrm{KL}}(q_\phi(z|a, c)||p_\theta(z|c)).
\end{aligned}
$$

B Distribution Modeling Capacity

We originally developed a QA pair modeling task to evaluate and compare QA pair generation models. We compared models based on the probability they assigned to the ground truth QA pairs. We used the negative log likelihood (NLL) of QA pairs as the metric, namely, $-\log p(q, a|c)$. Since variational models can not directly compute NLL, we estimate NLL with importance sampling. We also estimate each term in decomposed NLL, i.e.,$\mathrm{NLL_a} = -\log p(a|c)$ and $\mathrm{NLL_q} = -\log p(q|a, c)$. The better a model performs in this task, the better it fits the test set. As a baseline, to assess the effect of incorporating latent random variables, we implemented a pipeline model similar to Subramanian et al. (2018) using a deterministic pointer network.

Result Table 8 shows the result of QA pair modeling. First, our models with $\mathrm{C} = 0$ are superior to the pipeline model, which means that introducing latent random variables aid QA pair modeling capacity. However, the KL terms converge to zero with $\mathrm{C} = 0$. When we set $C > 0$, KL values are greater than 0, which implies that latent variables have non-trivial information about questions and answers. Also, we observe that the target value of KL C can control the KL values, showing the potential to avoid the posterior collapse issue.

	NLL	NLL_a	NLL_q	D_{KL_z}	D_{KL_y}
Pipeline	36.26	3.99	32.50	-	-
VQAG					
$\mathrm{C} = 0$	**34.46**	4.46	30.00	0.027	0.036
$\mathrm{C} = 5$	37.00	5.15	31.51	4.862	4.745
$\mathrm{C} = 20$	59.66	14.38	43.56	17.821	17.038
$\mathrm{C} = 100$	199.43	81.01	112.37	92.342	91.635

Table 8: QA pair modeling capacity measured on the test set. We used the same value C for the target values of KL C_a and C_q for simplicity. NLL: negative log likelihood of QA pairs. NLL_a (NLL_q): NLL of answers (questions). D_{KL_z} and D_{KL_y} are Kullback–Leibler divergence in Ineq 1. NLL for our models are estimated with importance sampling using 300 samples.

C Information Theoretic Interpretation of the KL control

When training our models, we miximized the variational lower bound in Ineq. 1 is averaged over the training samples. In other words, the expectation with respect to the data distribution is maximized. In the ideal case, the approximated posterior $q_\phi(z|a, c)$ is equal to the true posterior $p_\theta(z|a, c)$. Then, the expectation of the KL terms with respect to the data distribution is equivalent to the conditional mutual information $I(a, y|c)$.

Mathematically, when the approximated posterior q_ϕ is equal to the true posterior p_θ, the expectation of the KL terms in Eq. 1 with respect to the data distribution is:

$$
\begin{aligned}
&\mathbb{E}_{p(q,a,c)}[D_{\mathrm{KL}}(p(z|a, c)||p(z|c))] \\
&= \sum_{a,c} p(a, c) \sum_{z} p(z|a, c) \log \frac{p(z|a, c)}{p(z|c)} \\
&= \sum_{a,c,z} p(a, c, z) \log \frac{p(a, z|c)}{p(z|c)p(a|c)} \\
&= I(a, z|c).
\end{aligned}
$$

Thus, controlling the KL terms is equivalent to control the conditional mutual information. The same is true for question q.

D Model Architechture

Prior and Posterior Distribution Following Zhao et al. (2017b), we hypothesized that the prior and posterior distributions of the latent variables follow multivariate Gaussian distributions with diagonal covariance. The distributions are described as follows:

$$z|a,c \sim \mathcal{N}(\mu_{postz}, diag(\sigma^2_{postz})) \quad (3)$$

$$z|c \sim \mathcal{N}(\mu_{priorz}, diag(\sigma^2_{priorz})) \quad (4)$$

$$y|q,c \sim \mathcal{N}(\mu_{postY}, diag(\sigma^2_{postY})) \quad (5)$$

$$y|c \sim \mathcal{N}(\mu_{priorY}, diag(\sigma^2_{priorY}). \quad (6)$$

The prior and posterior distributions of the latent variables, z and y, are computed as follows:

$$\begin{bmatrix} \mu_{postz} \\ \log(\sigma^2_{postz}) \end{bmatrix} = W_{postz} \begin{bmatrix} h^C \\ h^A \end{bmatrix} + b_{postz} \quad (7)$$

$$\begin{bmatrix} \mu_{priorz} \\ \log(\sigma^2_{priorz}) \end{bmatrix} = W_{priorz} h^C + b_{priorz} \quad (8)$$

$$\begin{bmatrix} \mu_{postY} \\ \log(\sigma^2_{postY}) \end{bmatrix} = W_{postY} \begin{bmatrix} h^C \\ h^Q \end{bmatrix} + b_{postY} \quad (9)$$

$$\begin{bmatrix} \mu_{priorY} \\ \log(\sigma^2_{priorY}) \end{bmatrix} = W_{priorY} h^C + b_{priorY}. \quad (10)$$

Then, latent variable z (and y) is obtained using the reparameterization trick (Kingma and Welling, 2013): $z = \mu + \sigma \odot \epsilon$, where $\odot$ represents the Hadamard product, and $\epsilon \sim \mathcal{N}(0, I)$. Then, z and y is passed to the AE and QG models, respectively.

Answer Extraction Model We regard answer extraction as two-step sequential decoding, i.e.,

$$p(a|c) = p(c_{end}|c_{start}, c)p(c_{start}|c), \quad (11)$$

which predicts the start and end positions of an answer span in this order. For AE, we modify a pointer network (Vinyals et al., 2015) to take into account the initial hidden state $h_0^{AE} = W_1 z + b_1$, which in the end diversify AE by learning the mappings from z to a. The decoding process is as follows:

$$h_i^{IN} = \begin{cases} e(\Rightarrow) & \text{if } i = 1 \\ H^C_{t_{i-1}} & \text{if } i = 2 \end{cases} \quad (12)$$

$$h_i^{AE} = \text{LSTM}(h_{i-1}^{AE}, h_i^{IN}) \quad (13)$$

$$u_{ij}^{AE} = (v^{AE})^T \tanh(W_2 H_j^C + W_3 h_i^{AE} + b_2) \quad (14)$$

$$p(c_{t_i}|c_{t_{i-1}}, c) = \text{softmax}(u_i) \quad (15)$$

where $1 \leq i \leq 2$, $1 \leq j \leq L_C$, h_i^{AE} is the hidden state vector of the LSTM, h_i^{IN} is the i-th input, t_i denotes the start (i=1) or end (i=2) positions in c, and v, W_n and b_n are learnable parameters. We learn the embedding of the special token "$\Rightarrow$" as the initial input h_1^{IN}.

When we used the embedding vector e_{t_i} as h_{i+1}^{IN}, instead of $H_{t_i}^C$, following Subramanian et al. (2018), we observed that the extracted spans tended to be long and unreasonable. We assume that this is because the decoder cannot get the positional information from the input in each step.

Question Generation Model For QG, we modify an LSTM decoder with attention and copying mechanisms to take the initial hidden state $h_0^{QG} = W_4 y + b_3$ as input to diversify QG. In detail, at each time step, the probability distribution of generating words from vocabulary using attention (Bahdanau et al., 2014) is computed as:

$$h_i^{QG} = \text{LSTM}(h_{i-1}^{QG}, q_{t-1}) \quad (16)$$

$$u_{ij}^{att} = (v^{att})^T \tanh(W_5 h_i^{QG} + W_6 H_j^{CA} + b_4) \quad (17)$$

$$a_i^{att} = \text{softmax}(u_i^{att}) \quad (18)$$

$$\hat{h}_i = \textstyle\sum_j a_{ij}^{att} H_j^{CA} \quad (19)$$

$$\tilde{h}_i = \tanh(W_7([\hat{h}_i; h_i^{QG}] + b_5)) \quad (20)$$

$$P_{vocab} = \text{softmax}(W_8(\tilde{h}_i) + b_6), \quad (21)$$

and the probability distributions of copying (Gulcehre et al., 2016; Gu et al., 2016) from context are computed as:

$$u_{ij}^{copy} = (v^{copy})^T \tanh(W_9 h_i^{QG} + W_{10} H_j^{CA} + b_7) \quad (22)$$

$$a_i^{copy} = \text{softmax}(u_i^{copy}) \quad (23)$$

Accordingly, the probability of outputting q_i is:

$$p_g = \sigma(W_{11} h_i^{QG}) \quad (24)$$

$$p(q_i|q_{1:i-1}, a, c) \quad (25)$$

$$= p_g P_{vocab}(q_i) + (1 - p_g) \textstyle\sum_{j:c_j = q_i} a_{ij}^{copy} \quad (26)$$

where σ is the sigmoid function.

E Training Details

We use pretrained GloVe (Pennington et al., 2014) vectors with 300 dimensions and freeze them during training. The pretrained word embeddings were shared by the input layer of the context encoder, the input and output layers of the question decoder. The vocabulary has most frequent 45k words in our training set. The dimension of character-level embedding vectors is 32. The number of windows is 100. The dimension of hidden vectors is 300. The dimension of latent variables is 200. Any LSTMs used in this paper has one layer. We used Adam (Kingma and Ba, 2014) for optimization with initial learning rate 0.001. All the parameters were initialized with Xavier Initialization (Glorot and Bengio, 2010). Models were trained for 16 epochs with a batch size of 32. We used a dropout (Srivastava et al., 2014) rate of 0.2 for all the LSTM layers and attention modules.

F Answer Extraction and Question Generation

Tables 9 and 10 show the detailed results of AE and QG. Various values of $\mathrm{C_a}$ and $\mathrm{C_q}$ are explored.

	Relevance				Diversity
	Precision		Recall		Dist
	Prop.	Exact	Prop.	Exact	
NER	34.44	19.61	64.60	45.39	30.0k
BiLSTM-CRF	45.96	33.90	41.05	28.37	-
InfoHCVAE	31.59	16.18	78.75	59.32	70.1k
VQAG					
$\mathrm{C_a} = 0$	**58.39**	**47.15**	21.82	16.38	3.1k
$\mathrm{C_a} = 3$	34.09	19.22	78.94	59.09	47.5k
$\mathrm{C_a} = 5$	30.16	13.41	**83.13**	**60.88**	71.2k
$\mathrm{C_a} = 10$	26.17	8.83	79.70	53.02	92.3k
$\mathrm{C_a} = 15$	22.42	6.11	76.18	44.80	99.9k
$\mathrm{C_a} = 20$	21.95	5.75	72.26	42.15	**103.3k**
$\mathrm{C_a} = 25$	21.60	5.37	71.55	40.48	101.6k
$\mathrm{C_a} = 30$	23.88	6.75	74.08	44.59	99.5k
$\mathrm{C_a} = 40$	24.58	7.90	74.86	43.33	88.1k
$\mathrm{C_a} = 50$	25.05	7.83	76.56	44.67	88.9k
$\mathrm{C_a} = 100$	23.32	7.48	71.74	39.70	84.6k

Table 9: Detailed results of AE on the test set.

G Latent Interpolation

Table 11 shows the latent interpolation between two ground-truth QA pairs using VQAG with $(C_a, C_q) = (5, 20)$. This result shows that z controls answer and y controls question.

H Human Evaluation

We conducted human evaluation to assess the quality of QA pairs by asking the following questions.

1. **Is the question well-formed in itself?** The workers are asked to select *yes* if a given question is both grammatical and meaningful. The workers select *understandable* if a question is not grammatical but meaningful.
2. **Is the question relevant to the passage?** This is to check whether a question is relevant to the content of a passage.
3. **Is the answer a correct answer to the question?** If a given answer partially overlaps with the true answer in a passage, the workers select *partially*.
4. **Is the meaning of the answer in itself related to the main topic of the passage?** This is to check the importance of an answer. We designed this question to assess the questionworthiness of an answer.

Each triple is evaluated by three crowdworkers. Each task costs 0.08 USD.

	Relevance							Diversity			
	B1	B2	B3	B4	ME	RL	Token	D1	D2	E4	SB4
Zhang and Bansal (2019)	48.59	32.83	24.21	18.40	24.86	46.66	133.8k	10.2k	46.4k	15.78	-

	B1-R	B2-R	B3-R	B4-R	ME-R	RL-R	Token	D1	D2	E4	SB4
Zhang and Bansal (2019)	**62.32**	**47.77**	**37.96**	**30.05**	**36.77**	**62.87**	7.0M	15.8k	218.9k	18.28	91.44
VQAG											
$C_q = 0$	35.57	18.75	10.79	6.35	18.31	33.92	7.6M	14.4k	155.3k	17.33	97.61
$C_q = 3$	44.05	26.74	16.08	9.26	24.61	44.10	9.0M	17.8k	394.2k	19.14	85.88
$C_q = 5$	44.19	27.09	16.33	9.71	25.84	45.18	11.5M	19.0k	481.1k	19.71	82.59
$C_q = 10$	44.00	27.15	16.78	10.24	25.64	44.78	10.2M	18.8k	461.5k	19.69	80.39
$C_q = 15$	45.23	27.91	16.67	10.11	26.12	45.41	11.3M	19.5k	381.5k	19.40	84.56
$C_q = 20$	48.19	32.87	22.96	14.94	25.29	48.26	4.9M	22.4k	549.2k	19.72	44.41
$C_q = 25$	47.20	31.16	21.15	13.66	25.30	45.97	6.8M	22.3k	706.9k	**20.34**	47.00
$C_q = 30$	47.96	31.69	21.26	13.83	24.95	47.07	7.3M	**22.9k**	**732.8k**	18.54	50.32
$C_q = 40$	46.31	31.29	21.52	13.94	23.73	46.46	5.4M	21.0k	487.8k	19.39	55.95
$C_q = 50$	43.92	25.95	15.54	9.61	23.61	43.18	10.8M	22.2k	527.2k	19.29	73.78
$C_q = 100$	35.22	19.88	13.25	9.20	22.27	37.55	8.2M	22.1k	508.8k	19.74	**44.22**

Table 10: Detailed results of answer-aware QG on the test set. Paragraph-level contexts and answer spans are used as input. The baseline model is ELMo+QPP&QAP (Zhang and Bansal, 2019) with diverse beam search (Li et al., 2016b) with a beam size 50. Bn: BLEU-n, ME: METEOR, RL: ROUGE-L, Token: the total number of the generated words, Dn: Dist-n, E4: Ent-4 (entropy of 4-grams), SB4: Self-BLEU-4. "-R" represents recall. (e.g. B1-R is the recall of B1.) One question per answer-context pair is evaluated in the upper part, while 50 questions per answer-context pair are evaluated in the lower part to assess their diversity.

	z_1	z_2	z_3	z_4	z_5
y_1	**in what city and state did beyonce grow up ?—houston , texas**	how do competitions performed a child child ?—dancing	the american singer born what american singer ?—songwriter	how did beyoncé dobruja to ?—dangerously in love	how did beyoncé album album ?—dangerously in love
y_2	the album born and raised ?—houston , texas	how do competitions enovid ?—dancing	how is actress - carter ?—songwriter	how did beyoncé 's album album ?—dangerously in love	how did beyoncé album album ?—dangerously in love
y_3	the album born and raised ?—houston , texas	how do competitions performed a child child ?—dancing	the american singer born what american singer ?—songwriter	how did beyoncé dobruja to ?—dangerously in love	how did beyoncé dobruja to ?—dangerously in love
y_4	the album born and raised ?—houston , texas	how many competitions does texas child perform ?—dancing	the american singer born what american singer ?—songwriter	how did beyoncé dobruja to ?—dangerously in love	how did beyoncé dobruja to ?—dangerously in love
y_5	the album born and raised ?—houston , texas	how many competitions did texas child perform ?—dancing	the american singer born what american singer ?—songwriter	how did beyoncé dobruja to ?—dangerously in love	**what was the name of beyoncé 's first solo album ?—dangerously in love**

Table 11: Latent interpolation with VQAG with $(C_a, C_q) = (5, 20)$. The samples in the upper left and lower right are the ground truth QA pairs from the same paragraph of SQuAD. The linearly interpolated samples show how our generative model learns mapping from latent space to QA pairs.

Tools Impact on the Quality of Annotations for Chat Untangling

Jhonny Cerezo[1] **, Alexandre Bergel**[1]**, Felipe Bravo-Marquez**[1,2]
[1]Department of Computer Science, University of Chile
[2]Millennium Institute for Foundational Research on Data, IMFD-Chile
jcerezo@dcc.uchile.cl, abergel@dcc.uchile.cl,
fbravo@dcc.uchile.cl

Abstract

The quality of the annotated data directly influences in the success of supervised NLP models. However, creating annotated datasets is often time-consuming and expensive. Although the annotation tool takes an important role, we know little about how it influences annotation quality. We compare the quality of annotations for the task of chat-untangling made by non-experts annotators using two different tools. The first is SLATE, an existing command-line based tool, and the second is Parlay, a new tool we developed that integrates mouse interaction and visual links. Our experimental results indicate that, while both tools perform similarly in terms of annotation quality, Parlay offers a significantly better user experience.

1 Introduction

Human linguistic annotation is essential for many natural language processing tasks. However, the construction of these datasets is extremely expensive, both in terms of annotator hours and financial cost (Snow et al., 2008). We know that the performance of many natural language processing tasks is limited by the quantity and quality of the data available to them (Banko and Brill, 2001; Snow et al., 2008). Many of the studies focus on the number of annotators and their experience in improving annotation quality. However, little has been studied about the role annotation tools play in producing quality data.

We study the effect of annotation tools in chat-untangling task. Chat-tangling occurs when simultaneous conversations arise in chat with multiple participants (Elsner and Charniak, 2008). The goal of chat-untangling is to identify the conversations in a chat-thread. In order to perform this task, annotators must maintain a complex mental representation of the ongoing conversations. Hence, a tool should minimize the task load and facilitate the annotation process. To the best of our knowledge, there is only one public dataset sufficiently large for training modern NLP architectures for this task published by Kummerfeld et al. (2019). This dataset was annotated using SLATE (Kummerfeld, 2019), a terminal based annotation tool. In SLATE, interactions are marked by keyboard commands, messages are shown as raw-text, and annotations are presented by color coding. We argue that these characteristics may influence in quality of annotations for non-experts.

This paper presents Parlay, a new annotation tool for the chat-untangling task. The main difference between Parlay and SLATE is that it integrates mouse interaction and visual links into the annotation representation. We conducted a controlled experiment with 12 non-expert participants, in which each participant was first introduced to the annotation task and then asked to use each tool to annotate 100 messages. The data to be annotated are selected from gold standard adjudicated dataset presented by Kummerfeld et al. (2019). Next, each annotation tool is evaluated in terms of usability (SUS), task load (NASA/TLX), performance and annotation time. We define annotator performance by the quality of its annotations calculated by comparing them to the gold standard (expert) annotations (Kummerfeld et al., 2019) using Cohen's Kappa coefficient (Cohen, 1960).

2 Background

Chat-untangling. Chat-untangling is an NLP task that aims to find existing conversations within a chat-log with two or more participants (Adams and Martell, 2008; Holmer, 2008; Kummerfeld, 2019; Shen et al., 2006; Elsner and Charniak, 2010, 2008). Conversations are represented by a connected graph in which the vertices are messages and the edges are relationships between them (e.g.,

Proceedings of the Joint Conference of the 59th Annual Meeting of the Association for Computational Linguistics and the 11th International Joint Conference on Natural Language Processing: Student Research Workshop, pages 215–220
August 5–6, 2021.

an answer to a question) (Adams and Martell, 2008; Wang et al., 2008; Kummerfeld et al., 2019; Holmer, 2008).

Annotation process. Manual text annotation is the process of assigning some tags to the whole text or to fragments of it. A corpus is a collection of texts on a particular topic. Annotators tag parts of the text in the corpus with labels that represent the structure or semantics of interest. The annotated data then goes through a curation process in which a curator manually resolves discrepancies and inconsistencies. Curation is primarily performed to ensure data quality (Grosman et al., 2020). One important step in curation is adjudication (Ide and Pustejovsky, 2017). In this step the curator merges the annotations from different annotators though agreement and resolves discrepancies to produce a gold standard annotation. The annotation process concludes with the release of the curated corpus to the community.

Annotation quality. To a large extent, the final quality of the annotation process depends on how human error is reduced and how discrepancies are consolidated without biasing the annotator's judgment (Chau et al., 2020). It is demonstrated that the annotation quality is related to the annotator expertise (Snow et al., 2008; Burnap et al., 2015), number of annotators (Snow et al., 2008) and the process of learning the annotation task (Teruel et al., 2018). On the other hand, annotation tools are used to assist the annotation process (e.g., file loading, user annotation interaction, data curation) (Yimam et al., 2013; Grosman et al., 2020; Kummerfeld, 2019; Yordanova et al., 2018).

Although there is evidence that user-friendly annotation tools can benefit the annotation process and reduce the annotation time (Yimam et al., 2013; Kummerfeld, 2019; Grosman et al., 2020), little is know how can they can influence to the annotator's performance. To the best of our knowledge, Grosman et al. (2020) is the only study that report changes in the inter-agreement evaluating different tools for annotation. However, there is no further understanding how this occurs at annotation time.

3 Methodology

In this section we introduce Parlay, a new chat-untangling annotation tool, and SLATE as baseline. Finally, we provide the evaluation methodology, criteria and our hypotheses during this study.

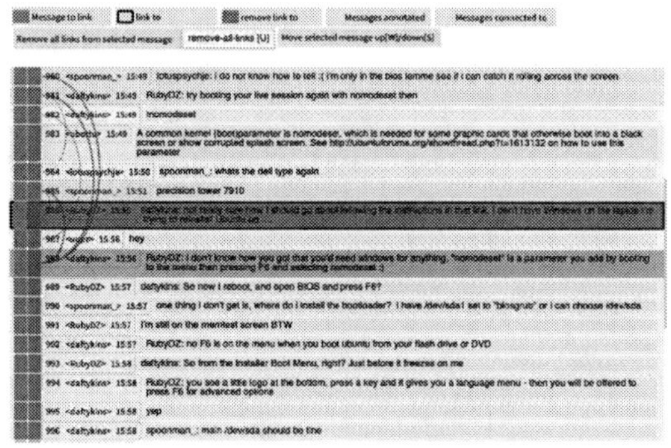

Figure 1: Parlay. Linked messages are represented by blue arcs between messages. The gray and green messages represent the pair of messages to be connected. Annotated messages are colored in yellow.

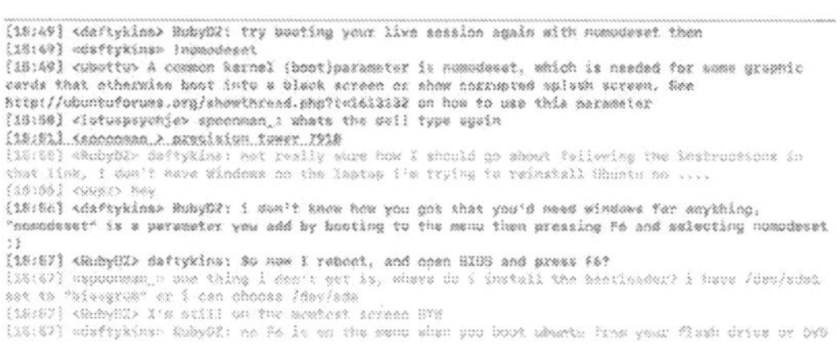

Figure 2: SLATE. The underlined and green messages represent the pair of messages to be linked. Messages already annotated are colored in yellow.

3.1 Annotation tools

Parlay is desktop tool developed in Pharo[1] and GT[2] whose purpose is to annotate and analyze annotations of chat-untangling task (Figure 1). Annotations can be made by linking messages with the mouse or key-commands (Table 1).

In contrast, SLATE is a terminal-based text annotation tool for different NLP tasks proposed in Kummerfeld (2019). It has the characteristics to link words, sentences and lines of text. SLATE requires each line, in the file to be annotated, to be a chat-message for chat-untangling annotation. All SLATE interactions are made by key-commands. The visual representation of messages is simple plain text with no distinctive format for its components (Figure 2). The full list of functional steps to annotate in SLATE is given in Table 1.

Parlay and SLATE differ on two essential aspects. The first is the linking visualization, for which Parlay creates a visual-arc in blue color, and

[1]Pharo is a pure object-oriented programming language and offers a flexible programming environment (Bergel et al., 2013).

[2]GT, which stands for Glamorous Toolkit, is a "moldable programming environment", `https://gtoolkit.com`.

Tool	SLATE	Parlay
Select message	Move messages by pressing arrow key one line at the time to select a message.	Scroll down or up, then left-click on a message's green button at the left part of each message to select it.
Create annotation	Move to select both messages then press key "D" to link them.	Select the first message, then scroll down/up and left-click in a message's username to link it to the first one.
Remove annotation	Select a message, then press key "U". It eliminates all links from the selected messages.	i) Select a message, then press key "R". It eliminates all links from the selected message. ii) Select the first message, then scroll down/up and left-click on the gray button at the left of the message. It eliminates only the link between those messages.
Validate annotation	Select a message that has already been annotated. This action will change the color of messages that are linked to the selected message.	i) Select a message that has already been annotated. ii) Hover over the left green button of a message. Both options will highlight the color of links and messages that are linked to the selected message.

Table 1: Functional differences between Parlay and SLATE.

		First session		Second session	
	Nro	**File**	**Tool**	**File**	**Tool**
Setting A	6	2015-08-10	SLATE	2015-10-19	Parlay
Setting B	6	2015-08-10	Parlay	2015-10-19	SLATE

Table 2: Experiment settings.

SLATE shows a change in the color of messages. Second, Parlay allows one to use the mouse to define annotations, whereas in SLATE the annotations are made by keyboard commands. At first, these two differences may look superficial. However, it is reasonable to think that they may significantly impact the user experience.

3.2 Evaluation Design

This study aims to assess the usability, task load, performance and annotation time of the SLATE and Parlay annotation tools. In order to create fair conditions for evaluating both tools, we conducted a controlled experiment.

Participants. We gathered 12 participants among university graduates (4), master students (4), master graduate (1), doctoral students (1), postdoctoral (2). None of the participants had a background in text annotation. All of them were experienced in the use of Linux, and none of them were native English speakers, although all of them declared to have a proficient level of English.

Data. We selected two files from Kummerfeld et al. (2019) adjudicated dataset that was developed to calculate inter-agreement. The adjudicated file is considered as the gold standard annotation to which we compare our non-expert participants' annotations. Then, we selected a pair of files with high similarity by two criteria: a) the agreement between annotators against the adjudicated file, and b) the number of annotated conversations.

Design. The controlled experiment was divided in three sessions, one introductory and two evaluation sessions. In the introductory session each participant had to i) answer a demographic questionnaire, ii) read an introductory document to the chat-untangling task, iii) read the annotation guidelines developed by Kummerfeld et al. (2019), and iv) answer a chat-untangling annotation exercise. The exercise consists of annotating three 5-messages long conversations without the help of Parlay or SLATE. The moderator then discuses the participants' annotations. The annotation exercise ensures the participants' maximum understanding of the chat-untangling task.

In the consequent evaluation sessions the participants had to i) annotate a file using one of the two tools, and ii) answer questionnaires. The tool for each session is randomly selected, whereas the annotated file is always the same for each evaluation session. We name each file-tool combination as an *experiment setting*. Such that we get two experiment settings, A and B. Where each *experiment setting* considers 6 participants and the participants use both tools in turn for the annotation task. For instance, a participant in setting A uses SLATE in the first evaluation session and Parlay in the second. In Table 2 we present the two experiment settings in detail.

Validation Criteria. Parlay and SLATE are evaluated in terms of usability, task load, annotation time and performance. The usability is measured by the System Usability Scale (SUS) (Brooke, 1996). The task load is measured using NASA/TLX (Hart and Staveland, 1988). The annotation time is determined from the annotation-logs. Lastly, the performance or quality of the annotation is measured by calculating the Cohen's Kappa (Cohen, 1960) for agreement between each participant's annotations and the expert adjudicated annotations (gold standard) presented in Kummerfeld et al. (2019) work. We say that the higher the Kappa score (κ) the better the performance.

	Parlay		SLATE	
	Mean	SD	Mean	SD
Mental	5.833	1.992	6.167	2.167
Physical	3.417	2.151	4	2.216
Temporal	4.417	2.429	4.25	2.34
Performance	5.5	2.908	5.167	1.946
Effort	5.25	1.815	6	2.174
Frustration	3.667	1.969	5.583	0.832

Table 3: Comparison of average and standard deviation of NASA/TLX scores between Parlay and SLATE.

Hypotheses. To analyze this study results, we performed some statistical tests to verify the following alternative hypotheses:

- H1: The participants' performance is affected by the annotation tool.
- H2: The participants' performance is affected by the experience gained in the annotation sessions.

We evaluated the significance of the performance *kappa* using the statistical t-test (De Winter, 2013) for small sample size (De Winter, 2013). We reject the null hypotheses if *p-value* < 0.05.

4 Results

In this section we present the results of our methodology of evaluation for i) the task load, ii) usability, iii) performance and iv) annotation time.

Task load. Table 3 shows the averaged results of participants' answers for the NASA/TLX dimensions. On average mental demand, physical demand, effort and frustration are lower in Parlay, whereas SLATE shows less temporal demand, although the difference is slight. Lastly, the users report that they performed better using Parlay. Overall Parlay reports less task load with the exception of being slightly more temporal demanding.

Usability Table 4 shows the mean and standard deviation values of SUS scores with the two annotation tools. If we pay attention to questions regarding positive (i.e., Q1, Q3, Q5, Q7 and Q9) and negative (i.e., Q2, Q4, Q6, Q8 and Q10) aspects of usability we find that: i) SLATE has similar average scores in positive and negative; and ii) Parlay rates higher to questions regarding the positive and lower in negative aspects of usability. A closer look at the ten component SUS scores we can see that Parlay is perceived more usable by the participants. This suggests that Parlay achieved better usability compared to SLATE.

	Parlay		SLATE	
	Mean	SD	Mean	SD
Q1: Willing to use the system	5.083	2.644	3	1.859
Q2: Complexity of the system	3.583	2.429	5.167	2.329
Q3: Ease of use	7.333	2.348	6.167	2.25
Q4: Need of support to use	3.833	2.443	5.25	2.491
Q5: Integrity of Functions	7.5	0.431	5.833	2.823
Q6: Inconsistency	3.25	2.454	3.75	1.658
Q7: Intuitiveness	7.333	2.309	5.333	2.498
Q8: Cumbersomeness to use	3.583	2.575	5.417	2.353
Q9: Feeling confident to use	7.667	1.67	5.667	2.348
Q10: Required learning-effort	4.083	2.353	4.667	2.309
Positive (odd)	6.983	2.425	5.2	2.563
Negative (even)	3.667	2.384	4.85	2.254

Table 4: Comparison of average and standard deviation of SUS scores between Parlay and SLATE.

		Sample Size	Time (min)		Performance	
			Mean	SD	Mean	SD
Tool	**Parlay**	12	48.5	21.211	0.666	0.079
	SLATE	12	41.083	16.714	0.606	0.12
Session	**1st**	12	50.167	15.643	0.582	0.096
	2nd	12	39.417	21.249	0.69	0.084

Table 5: Performance (κ) and annotation time (min) results by session of annotation and annotation tool.

Annotation time. SLATE reported less annotation time in minutes in our participants (Mean=41.083, SD=16.714) compared to Parlay (Mean=48.5, SD=21.211). Lastly the second evaluation session reported less annotation time in our participants (Mean=39.417, SD=21.249) compared to Parlay (Mean=50.167, SD=15.643).

Performance. We assess our hypotheses by calculating the performance (κ) by two criteria: i) the tools used in the annotation task (H1) and ii) the session in which the participants annotate (H2). For H1 there was a non-significant difference in the scores for Parlay and SLATE with p-value=0.1583. For H2 there was a significant difference in the scores for the first evaluation session and second evaluation session with p-value=0.007636. Therefore, the quality of annotations increases as annotators gain experience. Finally, the annotation tool used does not influence the quality of annotations.

5 Conclusion

In this paper we evaluate the influence of the annotation tool for non-expert users in terms of data quality and user experience in the chat-untangling task. To achieve our purpose we introduce a new annotation tool named Parlay and establish SLATE as our baseline. Subsequently, we conducted a controlled experiment with 12 non-expert annotators in which each participant annotated 100 messages on each tool in turn. Each tool was evaluated under i) usability, ii) task load, iii) annotation time and iv) annotation performance. Lastly, we establish that the quality of annotations is measured by calculating the agreement (κ) between participants' annotations and the gold annotated data (Kummerfeld et al., 2019).

The results indicate that the tools did not show significant differences in the annotators' performance outcome on the chat-untangling task. On the other hand, participants showed better performance in the second session, presumably due to a gain in experience. The annotation time is also lower in SLATE. Complementary to these results, we also report that Parlay scored better in usability and task load. Where participants highlighted that i) link representation between annotated messages and ii) mouse interaction where the main characteristics that made Parlay. In conclusion, Parlay offers a better user experience while achieving comparable annotation performance.

The study of annotation quality is an important issue for future development of NLP models. Tools remain as an important factor in the development of high-quality training datasets for NLP tasks (Grosman et al., 2020). Despite the results presented in this study, further work is required to get a thorough understanding of how the annotation tool affects the quality of chat-untangling data.

This study contributes to the area by introducing Parlay, a new tool for the chat-untangling task. We believe that an important contribution of our work is the methodology we propose, which allows us to compare annotation tools according to both data quality and user experience. For future work we aim to study the inter-annotator agreement of each tool. As well as, the discrepancies between expert an non-expert annotations.

Acknowledgements

We thank Renato Cerro for his review and editing and we thank 3 "anonymous" reviewers for their so-called insights. Felipe Bravo-Marquez was funded by ANID FONDECYT grant 11200290, U-Inicia VID Project UI-004/20 and ANID - Millennium Science Initiative Program - Code ICN17_002. Alexandre Bergel thanks Lam Research and the ANID FONDECYT Regular 1200067 for partially sponsoring the work presented in this paper.

References

Paige H Adams and Craig H Martell. 2008. Topic detection and extraction in chat. In *2008 IEEE international conference on Semantic computing*, pages 581–588. IEEE.

Michele Banko and Eric Brill. 2001. Scaling to very very large corpora for natural language disambiguation. In *Proceedings of the 39th annual meeting of the Association for Computational Linguistics*, pages 26–33.

Alexandre Bergel, Damien Cassou, Stéphane Ducasse, and Jannik Laval. 2013. *Deep Into Pharo*. Square Bracket Associates.

John Brooke. 1996. Sus: a "quick and dirty'usability. *Usability evaluation in industry*, page 189.

Alex Burnap, Yi Ren, Richard Gerth, Giannis Papazoglou, Richard Gonzalez, and Panos Y Papalambros. 2015. When crowdsourcing fails: A study of expertise on crowdsourced design evaluation. *Journal of Mechanical Design*, 137(3).

Hung Chau, Saeid Balaneshin, Kai Liu, and Ondrej Linda. 2020. Understanding the tradeoff between cost and quality of expert annotations for keyphrase extraction. In *Proceedings of the 14th Linguistic Annotation Workshop*, pages 74–86.

Jacob Cohen. 1960. A coefficient of agreement for nominal scales. *Educational and psychological measurement*, 20(1):37–46.

Joost CF De Winter. 2013. Using the student's t-test with extremely small sample sizes. *Practical Assessment, Research, and Evaluation*, 18(1):10.

Micha Elsner and Eugene Charniak. 2008. You talking to me? a corpus and algorithm for conversation disentanglement. In *Proceedings of ACL-08: HLT*, pages 834–842.

Micha Elsner and Eugene Charniak. 2010. Disentangling chat. *Computational Linguistics*, 36(3):389–409.

Jonatas S Grosman, Pedro HT Furtado, Ariane MB Rodrigues, Guilherme G Schardong, Simone DJ Barbosa, and Hélio CV Lopes. 2020. Eras: Improving the quality control in the annotation process for natural language processing tasks. *Information Systems*, page 101553.

Sandra G Hart and Lowell E Staveland. 1988. Development of nasa-tlx (task load index): Results of empirical and theoretical research. In *Advances in psychology*, volume 52, pages 139–183. Elsevier.

Torsten Holmer. 2008. Discourse structure analysis of chat communication. *Language@ Internet*, 5(10).

Nancy Ide and James Pustejovsky. 2017. *Handbook of linguistic annotation*. Springer.

Jonathan K Kummerfeld. 2019. Slate: A super-lightweight annotation tool for experts. In *Proceedings of the 57th Annual Meeting of the Association for Computational Linguistics: System Demonstrations*, pages 7–12.

Jonathan K Kummerfeld, Sai R Gouravajhala, Joseph J Peper, Vignesh Athreya, Chulaka Gunasekara, Jatin Ganhotra, Siva Sankalp Patel, Lazaros C Polymenakos, and Walter Lasecki. 2019. A large-scale corpus for conversation disentanglement. In *Proceedings of the 57th Annual Meeting of the Association for Computational Linguistics*, pages 3846–3856.

Dou Shen, Qiang Yang, Jian-Tao Sun, and Zheng Chen. 2006. Thread detection in dynamic text message streams. In *Proceedings of the 29th annual international ACM SIGIR conference on Research and development in information retrieval*, pages 35–42.

Rion Snow, Brendan O'connor, Dan Jurafsky, and Andrew Y Ng. 2008. Cheap and fast–but is it good? evaluating non-expert annotations for natural language tasks. In *Proceedings of the 2008 conference on empirical methods in natural language processing*, pages 254–263.

Milagro Teruel, Cristian Cardellino, Fernando Cardellino, Laura Alonso Alemany, and Serena Villata. 2018. Increasing argument annotation reproducibility by using inter-annotator agreement to improve guidelines. In *Proceedings of the Eleventh International Conference on Language Resources and Evaluation (LREC 2018).*

Yi-Chia Wang, Mahesh Joshi, William W Cohen, and Carolyn Penstein Rosé. 2008. Recovering implicit thread structure in newsgroup style conversations. In *ICWSM*.

Seid Muhie Yimam, Iryna Gurevych, Richard Eckart de Castilho, and Chris Biemann. 2013. Webanno: A flexible, web-based and visually supported system for distributed annotations. In *Proceedings of the 51st Annual Meeting of the Association for Computational Linguistics: System Demonstrations*, pages 1–6.

Kristina Yordanova, Adeline Paiement, Max Schröder, Emma Tonkin, Przemyslaw Woznowski, Carl Magnus Olsson, Joseph Rafferty, and Timo Sztyler. 2018. Challenges in annotation of user data for ubiquitous systems: Results from the 1st arduous workshop.

How Many Layers and Why? An Analysis of the Model Depth in Transformers

Antoine Simoulin[1,2] **Benoît Crabbé**[2]
[1]Quantmetry [2]University of Paris, LLF
asimoulin@quantmetry.com
bcrabbe@linguist.univ-paris-diderot.fr

Abstract

In this study, we investigate the role of the multiple layers in deep transformer models. We design a variant of ALBERT that dynamically adapts the number of layers for each token of the input. The key specificity of ALBERT is that weights are tied across layers. Therefore, the stack of encoder layers iteratively repeats the application of the same transformation function on the input. We interpret the repetition of this application as an iterative process where the token contextualized representations are progressively refined. We analyze this process at the token level during pre-training, fine-tuning, and inference. We show that tokens do not require the same amount of iterations and that difficult or crucial tokens for the task are subject to more iterations.

1 Introduction

Transformers are admittedly over-parametrized (Chen et al., 2020; Hou et al., 2020; Voita et al., 2019). Yet the role of this over-parametrization is not well understood. In particular, transformers consist of a fixed number of stacked layers, which are suspected to be highly redundant (Liu et al., 2020) and to cause over-fitting (Fan et al., 2020; Zhou et al., 2020). In this paper we provide a study on the role of the multiple layers traditionally used.

The mechanism of transformer layers is often compared to intuitive NLP pipelines (Tenney et al., 2019). Starting with the lower layers encoding surface information, middle layers encoding syntax and higher layers encoding semantics (Jawahar et al., 2019; Peters et al., 2018). Transformers progressively refine the features, which become more fine-grained at each iteration (Xin et al., 2020). However, ALBERT (Lan et al., 2020) highlights that it is possible to tie weights across layers and repeat the application of the same function. Consequently, we hypothesize that it is the number of layer applications that gradually abstracts the surface information into semantic knowledge.

To better study the transformation of token representations across layers, we propose a variant of ALBERT. Our model implements the key specificity of weights tying across layers but also dynamically adapts the number of layers applied to each token. Since all layers share the same weight, we refer to the application of the layer to the hidden states as an *iteration*.

After reviewing the related work (Section 2), we detail the model and the training methodology in Section 3. In particular, we encourage our model to be parsimonious and limit the total number of iterations performed on each token. In Section 4, we analyze iterations of the model during pre-training, fine-tuning and inference.

2 Related Work

Adapting the transformer depth is an active subject of research. In particular, deep transformer models are suspected to struggle to adapt to different levels of difficulty. While large models correctly predict difficult examples, they over-calculate simpler inputs (Liu et al., 2020). This issue can be addressed using *early-stopping*: some samples might be sufficiently simple to classify using intermediate features. Some models couple a classifier to each layer (Zhou et al., 2020; Liu et al., 2020; Xin et al., 2020). After each layer, given the classifier output, the model either immediately returns the output or passes the sample to the next layer. Exiting too late may even have negative impacts due to the network "over-thinking" the input (Kaya et al., 2019).

Ongoing research also refines the application of layers at the token level. Wang and Kuo (2020) build sentence embeddings by combining token representations from distinct layers. Elbayad et al. (2020) and Dehghani et al. (2019) successfully use

Proceedings of the Joint Conference of the 59th Annual Meeting of the Association for Computational Linguistics and the 11th International Joint Conference on Natural Language Processing: Student Research Workshop, pages 221–228

dynamic layers depth at the token level for full transformers (encoder-decoder). However, to the best of our knowledge, our attempt is the first to apply such mechanism to encoder only transformers and to provide an analysis of the process.

3 Method

In this Section, we detail the model architecture, illustrated in Figure 1, and pre-training procedure.

3.1 Model architecture

We use a multi-layer transformer encoder (Devlin et al., 2019) which transforms a context vector of tokens $(u_1 \cdots u_T)$ through a stack of L transformer encoder layers (Eq. 1, 2). We use weight tying across layers and apply the same transformation function at each iteration (Lan et al., 2020).

$$h_t^0 = W_e u_t + W_p \quad (1)$$
$$h_t^n = \mathsf{layer}(h_t^{n-1}) \quad \forall n \in [1, L] \quad (2)$$

For the first layer, W_e is the token embedding matrix, and W_p the position embedding matrix.

We augment the model with a halting mechanism, which allows dynamically adjusting the number of layers for each token (Eq. 3 to 8). We directly adapted this mechanism from Graves (2016). The main distinction with the original version is the use of a transformer model instead of a recurrent state transition model. The mechanism works as follow: at each iteration n, we add the following operations after Eq. 2. We assign a probability to stop p_t^n for each token at index t (Eq. 3). Given this probability, we compute an update weight λ_t^n (Eq. 4), which we use to compute the final state as the linear convex combination between the previous and current hidden state (Eq. 5).

$$p_t^n = \sigma\left(W_h h_t^n + b_n\right) \quad (3)$$
$$\lambda_t^n = p_t^n \text{ if } n < N_t, R_t \text{ elif } n = N_t, \text{ else } 0 \quad (4)$$
$$h_t^n = \lambda_t^n h_t^n + (1 - \lambda_t^n) h_t^{n-1} \quad (5)$$

With σ the sigmoid function. We define the remainder R_t and the number of iterations for the token at index t, N_t with:

$$R_t = 1 - \sum_{l=1}^{N_t - 1} p_t^l. \quad N_t = \min_{n'} \sum_{n=1}^{n'} p_t^n \geq 1 - \epsilon \quad (6)$$

As soon as the sum of the probability becomes greater than 1, the update weights λ_t^n are set to 0 and the token is not updated anymore (Eq. 4). A small ϵ factor ensures that the network can stop after the first iteration (Eq. 6).

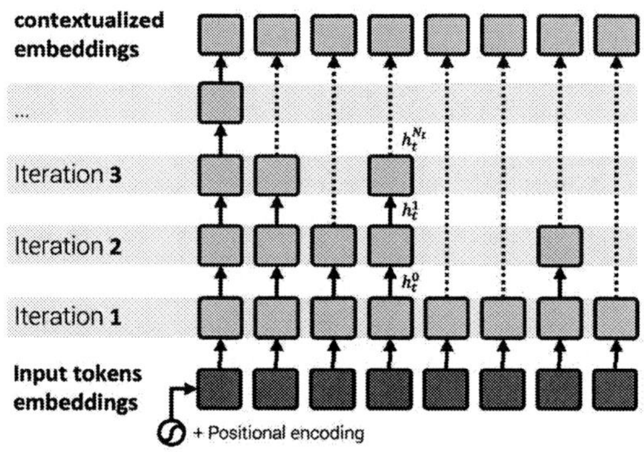

Figure 1: As in ALBERT model, tokens are transformed through the iterative application of a transformer encoder layer. Our model key specificity is the application of the halting mechanism, which dynamically adjusts the number of iterations for each token.

3.2 Pre-training objective

During the pre-training phase, we train the model with the sentence order prediction (*sop*) — the task introduced in Lan et al. (2020) that classifies whether segments from the input sequence follow the original order or were swapped — and the masked language model task (*mlm*) (Devlin et al., 2019). We also encourage the network to minimize the number of iterations by directly adding the ponder cost into ALBERT pre-training objective. Given a length T input sequence $\mathbf{u}$, Graves (2016) defines the *ponder cost* $\mathcal{P}(\mathbf{u})$ as:

$$\mathcal{P}(\mathbf{u}) = \sum_{t=1}^{T} N_t + R_t \quad (7)$$

We define the final pre-training loss as the following sum:

$$\hat{\mathcal{L}} = \mathcal{L}_{sop} + \mathcal{L}_{mlm} + \tau \mathcal{P} \quad (8)$$

where τ is a *time penalty* parameter that weights the relative cost of computation versus error.

3.3 Datum and infrastructure

We follow the protocol from ALBERT and pre-train the model with BOOKCORPUS (Zhu et al., 2015) and English Wikipedia. We reduce the maximum input length to 128 and the number of training steps to 112,500[1]. We use a lowercase vocabulary of size 30,000 tokenized using SentencePiece. We train all our models on a single TPU v2-8 from Google Colab Pro[2] and accumulate gradients to preserve a 4,096 batch size. We optimize the parameters using LAMB with a learning rate at 1.76e-3.

4 Experiments

We now analyze our iterative model properties during pre-training (Section 4.1) and fine-tuning (Section 4.2). We start by describing the setup for each of the subtasks.

***mlm* task** We generate masked inputs following ALBERT n-gram masking. We mask 20% of all WordPiece tokens but do not always replace masked words with the `[MASK]` token to avoid discrepancy between pre-training and fine-tuning. We effectively replace 80% of the masked position with `[MASK]` (`[MASK/MASK]`), 10% with a random token (`[MASK/random]`), and keep the original token for the last 10% (`[MASK/original]`).

***sop* task** We format our inputs as "`[CLS]` x_1 `[SEP]` x_2 `[SEP]`". In 50% of the case the two segments x_1 and x_2 are effectively consecutive in the text. In the other 50%, the segments are swapped.

Ponder cost We fix the time penalty factor τ empirically such that the ponder penalty represents around 10% of the total loss. To estimate the ponder cost, we discard the remainder, as $R \ll N$ for sufficient values of N. Given Eq. 7, the ponder cost then corresponds to the total number of iterations in the sentence, which is given by $l \times T$, with T the number of tokens in the sequence and l the average iterations per token. We observe that ALBERT base loss converges to around 3.5. We calibrate τ such that $\tau\mathcal{P} \approx 0.35 \approx \tau \times l \times T$. We train distinct models, listed in Table 1, that we calibrate such that their average number of iterations per token l is respectively 3, 6, and 12. We refer to these models as respectively *tiny*, *small* and *base*.

[1]As emphasized in `https://github.com/google-research/bert`, longer sequences are computationally expensive. To lighten the pre-training process, they advise using 128 sentence length and increase the length to 512 only for the last 10% of the training to train the positional embeddings. In this work, we only perform the first 90% steps as we are not looking for brute force performances.

[2]`https://colab.research.google.com/`

4.1 Analysis of the pre-training

Analysis of the iterations We pre-train models with various configurations and observe the model mechanisms during the pre-training in Table 1.

Models	*tiny*	*small*	*base*
τ	1e-3	5e-4	2.5e-4
Max iterations	6	12	24
mlm (Acc.)	55.4	57.1	57.4
sop (Acc.)	80.9	83.9	84.3
All tokens	3.8	7.1	10.0
All unmasked tokens	3.5	6.5	9.2
`[MASK/MASK]`	5.8	10.9	16.0
`[MASK/random]`	5.8	10.9	16.0
`[MASK/original]`	4.0	7.4	10.5
`[CLS]`	6.0	12.0	22.5
`[SEP]`	2.5	7.6	8.4

Table 1: Average number of iterations given token types during the pre-training. For each model, we report a mean number of iterations on our development set, at the end of the pre-training.

We observe that the `[CLS]` token receives far more iterations than other tokens. This observation is in line with Clark et al. (2019) who analyze BERT attention and report systematic and broad attention to special tokens. We interpret that the `[CLS]` token is used as input for the *sop* task and aggregates a representation for the entire input. On the contrary, `[SEP]` token benefits from usually few iterations. Again, this backs the observation emerging from the analysis of attention that interprets `[SEP]` as a no-op operation for attention heads (Clark et al., 2019).

We also observe an interesting behavior from the `[MASK]` which also benefits from more iterations than average tokens. As for the `[CLS]` token, we interpret that these tokens are crucial for the *mlm* task. Looking further, we observe that `[MASK/random]` and `[MASK/MASK]` number of iterations is greater than `[MASK/original]`. In this case, although all tokens are targeted in the *mlm* task, `[MASK/random]` and `[MASK/MASK]` are obviously more difficult to identify[3].

The model seems to have an intuitive mechanism

[3]During inference, the model cannot make the distinction between `[MASK/original]` and unmasked tokens. However, we observe in Table 1 that the two token types have a distinct mean number of iterations. We believe this is due to the distribution of the `[MASK]` tokens. Indeed, we follow the procedure from ALBERT and use *n-gram* masking. Therefore, `[MASK/original]` tokens tend to appear in the context of `[MASK]` tokens. This specific context increases the mean number of iterations.

and distributes iterations for tokens that are either crucial for the pre-training task or present a certain level of difficulty. This also appears in line with *early-exit* mechanisms cited in Section 2, that adapt the number of layers, for the whole example, to better scale to each sample level of difficulty.

Natural Fixed point We now analyze *how* the token's hidden states evolve during our model iterative transformations. At each iteration n, the self-attentive mechanism (Vaswani et al., 2017) computes the updated state $n+1$ as a weighted sum of the current states. This introduces a cyclic dependency as every token depends on each other during the iterative process. As convergence within a loopy structure is not guaranteed, we encourage the model to converge towards a fixed point (Bai et al., 2019).

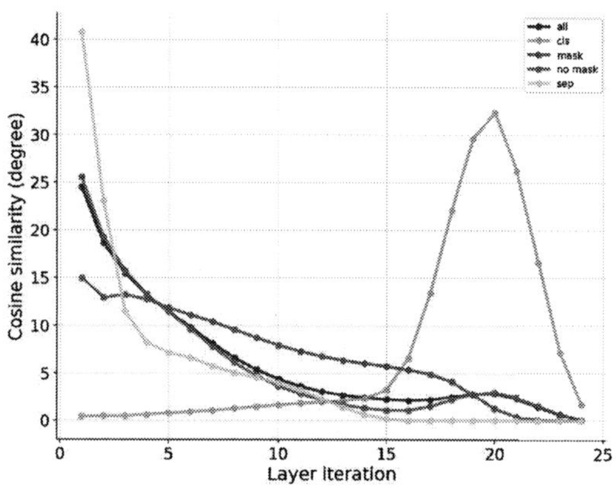

Figure 2: Evolution of the cosine similarity between hidden states h_t^n and h_t^{n+1} from two consecutive iterations. We use our *base* model and measure iterations on our development set, at the end of the pre-training.

We obtain this property "for free" thanks to our architecture specificity. Indeed at each iteration, the hidden state is computed as a convex combination of the previous n and current $n+1$ hidden state. The combination is controlled by λ_t^n (Eq. 5). If λ_t^n is closed to 0, then $h_t^n \approx h_t^{n+1}$ and by definition (Eq. 4, 6) λ_t^n will eventually be set to 0 at a certain iteration.

Figure 2 represents the evolution of the mean cosine similarity between two hidden states from two consecutive iterations h_t^n and h_t^{n+1}. The network indeed reaches a fixed point for every token. The `[SEP]` and tokens that are not masked converge quicker than `[MASK]` tokens. Finally, the `[CLS]` token oscillates during intermediate layers before reaching an equilibrium[4].

4.2 Application to downstream tasks

During the pre-training phase, the model focuses on tokens either crucial for the pre-training task or presents a certain level of difficulty. Now we study our model behavior during the fine-tuning on downstream syntactic or semantic tasks.

Control test . To verify that our setup has reasonable performance, we evaluate it on the GLUE benchmark (Wang et al., 2019). Results from Table 2 are scored by the evaluation server[5]. As in Devlin et al. (2019), we discard results for the WNLI task[6]. For each task, we fine-tune the model on the train set and select the hyperparameters on the dev set using a grid search. We tune the learning rate between 5e-5, 3e-5, and 2e-5; batch size between 16 and 32 and epochs between 2, 3, or 4. To better compare our setup, we pre-train BERT and ALBERT model using our configuration, infrastructure and datum.

	Avg. Glue score
BERT-base	76.9
ALBERT-base	75.6
ALBERT-base + Adapt. Depth	75.2
ALBERT-small + Adapt. Depth	74.2
ALBERT-tiny + Adapt. Depth	72.6

Table 2: GLUE Test results, scored by the evaluation server but without the WNLI task. To facilitate the comparison, we reproduce BERT and ALBERT, with our pre-training dataset, infrastructure and configuration detailed in Section 3.2.

We present results on the test set in Table 2. As expected, the average score decreases with the number of iterations. Indeed, we limit the number of computation operations performed by our model. Moreover, we build our model on top of ALBERT, which share parameters across layers, thus reducing the number of parameters compared with the original BERT architecture. However, despite these additional constraints, results stay in a reasonable range. In particular, ALBERT-base with adaptative depth is very close to the version with a fixed depth.

[4]We present the Figures for other model configurations in Appendix A

[5]`https://gluebenchmark.com/leaderboard`

[6]See (12) from `https://gluebenchmark.com/faq`.

Probing tasks Conneau and Kiela (2018) introduce probing tasks, which assess whether a model encodes elementary linguistic properties. We consider semantic and syntactic tasks that do not introduce random replacements. In particular, a task that predicts the sequence of top constituents immediately below the sentence node (TopConst), a task that predicts the tense of the main-clause verb (Tense), and two tasks that predict the subject (resp. direct object) number in the main clause (SubjNum, resp. ObjNum).

	Tense	Subj Num	Obj Num	Top Const
punct (121k)	5.0	4.8	5.2	6.7
prep (101k)	4.6	4.6	5.4	6.2
pobj (98k)	4.5	4.6	5.4	5.8
det (86k)	4.5	4.6	5.1	6.1
nn (81k)	5.1	5.4	**5.8**	6.7
nsubj (80k)	**5.3**	**6.1**	**5.9**	**7.5**
amod (66k)	4.6	4.9	5.5	6.1
dobj (49k)	4.8	5.0	**5.9**	6.1
root (44k)	**5.9**	**6.1**	**6.2**	**7.9**
advmod (37k)	4.8	4.8	5.3	6.8
avg.	5.4	5.4	5.8	7.2
test Acc.	87.5	93.9	96.1	91.2
baseline Acc.	87.3	94.0	96.0	91.9

Table 3: Distribution of the iterations across token dependency types. We fine-tune our *base* model on each probing task. We then perform inference on the Penn Tree Bank dataset and report the number of iterations given token dependency types. The number in parentheses denotes the number of dependency tags. We only display the top 10 most frequent tags. We indicate in **bold** tags for which the number of iterations is above avg + std. We include a baseline accuracy which we obtain with the ALBERT-base version without an adaptative depth mechanism and therefore 12 iterations performed for each token.

In our setup, we fine-tune the model on the task train set and select the hyperparameters on the dev set using a grid search. We use a 5e-5 learning rate and fine tune the epochs between 1 to 5; we use a 32 batch size. Finally, we compare in Table 3 the number of iterations performed for each token on the Penn Tree Bank (Marcus et al., 1993) converted to Stanford dependencies[7,8].

We provide an accuracy baseline, obtained with the same setup but using ALBERT without the dynamic halting mechanism. As in the previous experiment, we observe that for these tasks, out model achieve competitive performances despite using less computational operations.

Although all tasks achieve significant and comparable accuracies, they all require a distinct global mean of iterations. The Tense task, which can be solved from the verb only, is completed in only 5.4 iterations, while the TopConst task, which requires to infer some sentence structure, is performed in 7.2 iterations. This suggests the model can adapt itself to the complexity of the task and globally spare unnecessary iterations.

Looking at the token level, as during the pre-training (Section 4.1), the iterations are unevenly distributed across tokens. The model seems to iterate more on tokens that are crucial for the task. For SubjNum, the subj tokens achieve the maximum number of iterations, while for the ObjNum task, the obj and root token iterates more. Similarly, all tasks present a high number of iteration on the main verb (root) that is crucial for each prediction.

5 Conclusion

We investigated the role of the layers in deep transformers. We designed an original model that progressively transforms each token through a dynamic number of iterations. We analyzed the distribution of these iterations during pre-training and confirmed the results obtained by analyzing the distribution of attention across BERT layers, particularly the specific behavior played by special tokens. Moreover, we observed that key tokens for the prediction task benefit from more iterations. We confirmed this observation during fine-tuning, where the tokens with a large number of iterations are also suspected to be key for achieving the task.

Our experiments provide a new interpretation path for the role of layers in deep transformer models. Rather than extracting some specific features at each stage, layers could be interpreted as the iteration from an iterative and convergence process. We hope that this can help to better understand the convergence mechanisms for transformers models, reduce the computational footprint or provide new regularization methods.

[7]Since we use sentence piece vocabulary, we assign to each piece the dependency tag from the whole token.

[8]We present the Tables for other model configurations in Appendix B

References

Shaojie Bai, J. Zico Kolter, and Vladlen Koltun. 2019. Deep equilibrium models. In *Advances in Neural Information Processing Systems 32: Annual Conference on Neural Information Processing Systems 2019, NeurIPS 2019, December 8-14, 2019, Vancouver, BC, Canada*, pages 688–699.

Daoyuan Chen, Yaliang Li, Minghui Qiu, Zhen Wang, Bofang Li, Bolin Ding, Hongbo Deng, Jun Huang, Wei Lin, and Jingren Zhou. 2020. Adabert: Task-adaptive BERT compression with differentiable neural architecture search. In *Proceedings of the Twenty-Ninth International Joint Conference on Artificial Intelligence, IJCAI 2020*, pages 2463–2469. ijcai.org.

Kevin Clark, Urvashi Khandelwal, Omer Levy, and Christopher D. Manning. 2019. What does BERT look at? an analysis of bert's attention. *CoRR*, abs/1906.04341.

Alexis Conneau and Douwe Kiela. 2018. Senteval: An evaluation toolkit for universal sentence representations. In *Proceedings of the Eleventh International Conference on Language Resources and Evaluation, LREC 2018, Miyazaki, Japan, May 7-12, 2018*.

Mostafa Dehghani, Stephan Gouws, Oriol Vinyals, Jakob Uszkoreit, and Lukasz Kaiser. 2019. Universal transformers. In *7th International Conference on Learning Representations, ICLR 2019, New Orleans, LA, USA, May 6-9, 2019*. OpenReview.net.

Jacob Devlin, Ming-Wei Chang, Kenton Lee, and Kristina Toutanova. 2019. BERT: pre-training of deep bidirectional transformers for language understanding. In *Proceedings of the 2019 Conference of the North American Chapter of the Association for Computational Linguistics: Human Language Technologies, NAACL-HLT 2019, Minneapolis, MN, USA, June 2-7, 2019, Volume 1 (Long and Short Papers)*, pages 4171–4186.

Maha Elbayad, Jiatao Gu, Edouard Grave, and Michael Auli. 2020. Depth-adaptive transformer. In *8th International Conference on Learning Representations, ICLR 2020, Addis Ababa, Ethiopia, April 26-30, 2020*. OpenReview.net.

Angela Fan, Edouard Grave, and Armand Joulin. 2020. Reducing transformer depth on demand with structured dropout. In *8th International Conference on Learning Representations, ICLR 2020, Addis Ababa, Ethiopia, April 26-30, 2020*. OpenReview.net.

Alex Graves. 2016. Adaptive computation time for recurrent neural networks. *CoRR*, abs/1603.08983.

Lu Hou, Zhiqi Huang, Lifeng Shang, Xin Jiang, Xiao Chen, and Qun Liu. 2020. Dynabert: Dynamic BERT with adaptive width and depth. In *Advances in Neural Information Processing Systems 33: Annual Conference on Neural Information Processing Systems 2020, NeurIPS 2020, December 6-12, 2020, virtual*.

Ganesh Jawahar, Benoît Sagot, and Djamé Seddah. 2019. What does BERT learn about the structure of language? In *Proceedings of the 57th Conference of the Association for Computational Linguistics, ACL 2019, Florence, Italy, July 28- August 2, 2019, Volume 1: Long Papers*, pages 3651–3657.

Yigitcan Kaya, Sanghyun Hong, and Tudor Dumitras. 2019. Shallow-deep networks: Understanding and mitigating network overthinking. In *Proceedings of the 36th International Conference on Machine Learning, ICML 2019, 9-15 June 2019, Long Beach, California, USA*, volume 97 of *Proceedings of Machine Learning Research*, pages 3301–3310. PMLR.

Zhenzhong Lan, Mingda Chen, Sebastian Goodman, Kevin Gimpel, Piyush Sharma, and Radu Soricut. 2020. ALBERT: A lite BERT for self-supervised learning of language representations. In *8th International Conference on Learning Representations, ICLR 2020, Addis Ababa, Ethiopia, April 26-30, 2020*.

Weijie Liu, Peng Zhou, Zhiruo Wang, Zhe Zhao, Haotang Deng, and Qi Ju. 2020. Fastbert: a self-distilling BERT with adaptive inference time. In *Proceedings of the 58th Annual Meeting of the Association for Computational Linguistics, ACL 2020, Online, July 5-10, 2020*, pages 6035–6044. Association for Computational Linguistics.

Mitchell P. Marcus, Beatrice Santorini, and Mary Ann Marcinkiewicz. 1993. Building a large annotated corpus of english: The penn treebank. *Computational Linguistics*, 19(2):313–330.

Matthew E. Peters, Mark Neumann, Luke Zettlemoyer, and Wen-tau Yih. 2018. Dissecting contextual word embeddings: Architecture and representation. In *Proceedings of the 2018 Conference on Empirical Methods in Natural Language Processing, Brussels, Belgium, October 31 - November 4, 2018*, pages 1499–1509. Association for Computational Linguistics.

Ian Tenney, Dipanjan Das, and Ellie Pavlick. 2019. BERT rediscovers the classical NLP pipeline. In *Proceedings of the 57th Conference of the Association for Computational Linguistics, ACL 2019, Florence, Italy, July 28- August 2, 2019, Volume 1: Long Papers*, pages 4593–4601. Association for Computational Linguistics.

Ashish Vaswani, Noam Shazeer, Niki Parmar, Jakob Uszkoreit, Llion Jones, Aidan N. Gomez, Lukasz Kaiser, and Illia Polosukhin. 2017. Attention is all you need. In *Advances in Neural Information Processing Systems 30: Annual Conference on Neural Information Processing Systems 2017, 4-9 December 2017, Long Beach, CA, USA*, pages 5998–6008.

Elena Voita, David Talbot, Fedor Moiseev, Rico Sennrich, and Ivan Titov. 2019. Analyzing multi-head self-attention: Specialized heads do the heavy lifting, the rest can be pruned. In *Proceedings of the*

57th Conference of the Association for Computational Linguistics, ACL 2019, Florence, Italy, July 28- August 2, 2019, Volume 1: Long Papers, pages 5797–5808. Association for Computational Linguistics.

Alex Wang, Amanpreet Singh, Julian Michael, Felix Hill, Omer Levy, and Samuel R. Bowman. 2019. GLUE: A multi-task benchmark and analysis platform for natural language understanding. In *7th International Conference on Learning Representations, ICLR 2019, New Orleans, LA, USA, May 6-9, 2019*.

Bin Wang and C.-C. Jay Kuo. 2020. SBERT-WK: A sentence embedding method by dissecting bert-based word models. *IEEE ACM Trans. Audio Speech Lang. Process.*, 28:2146–2157.

Ji Xin, Raphael Tang, Jaejun Lee, Yaoliang Yu, and Jimmy Lin. 2020. Deebert: Dynamic early exiting for accelerating BERT inference. In *Proceedings of the 58th Annual Meeting of the Association for Computational Linguistics, ACL 2020, Online, July 5-10, 2020*, pages 2246–2251. Association for Computational Linguistics.

Wangchunshu Zhou, Canwen Xu, Tao Ge, Julian J. McAuley, Ke Xu, and Furu Wei. 2020. BERT loses patience: Fast and robust inference with early exit. In *Advances in Neural Information Processing Systems 33: Annual Conference on Neural Information Processing Systems 2020, NeurIPS 2020, December 6-12, 2020, virtual*.

Yukun Zhu, Ryan Kiros, Richard S. Zemel, Ruslan Salakhutdinov, Raquel Urtasun, Antonio Torralba, and Sanja Fidler. 2015. Aligning books and movies: Towards story-like visual explanations by watching movies and reading books. In *2015 IEEE International Conference on Computer Vision, ICCV 2015, Santiago, Chile, December 7-13, 2015*, pages 19–27.

A Natural fixed point

We present here the evolution of the mean cosine similarity between two hidden states from two consecutive iterations for our *small* (Figure 3) and *tiny* (Figure 4) models. As presented in Section 3.2, we fix the maximum number of iterations at respectively 6 and 12 for the *tiny* and *small* models.

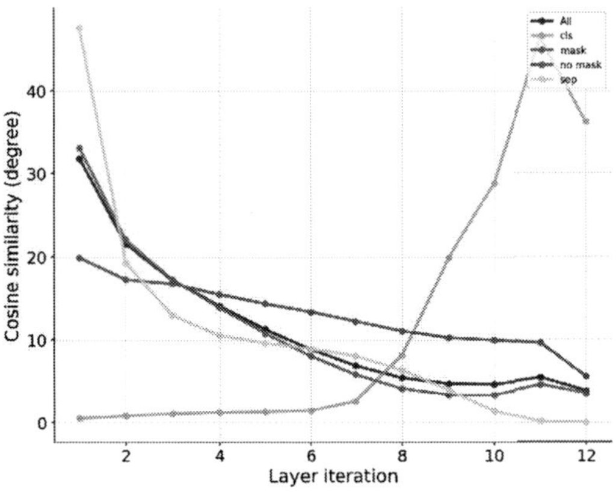

Figure 3: Evolution of the cosine similarity between hidden states h_t^n and h_t^{n+1} from two consecutive iterations. We use our *small* model and measure iterations on our development set, at the end of the pre-training.

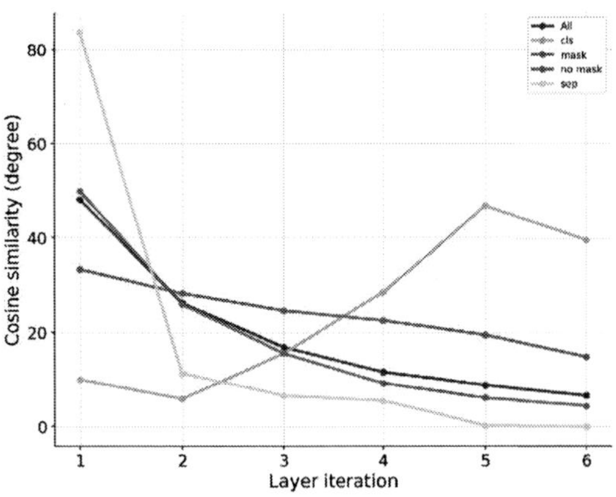

Figure 4: Evolution of the cosine similarity between hidden states h_t^n and h_t^{n+1} from two consecutive iterations. We use our *tiny* model and measure iterations on our development set, at the end of the pre-training.

B Probing tasks

We give here the probing tasks results from Section 4.2 with our *small* (Table 4) and *tiny* (Table 5) models.

	Tense	Subj Num	Obj Num	Top Const
punct (121k)	3.1	3.1	3.1	3.9
prep (101k)	2.9	2.9	3.0	3.6
pobj (98k)	2.9	3.0	3.1	3.5
det (86k)	2.7	2.8	2.7	3.6
nn (81k)	3.2	**3.5**	3.2	3.9
nsubj (80k)	**3.3**	**3.7**	**3.3**	**4.4**
amod (66k)	2.9	3.0	3.0	3.6
dobj (49k)	3.0	3.2	**3.4**	3.5
root (44k)	**3.6**	**3.6**	**3.5**	**4.6**
advmod (37k)	2.9	3.0	3.0	4.0
avg.	3.2	3.3	3.3	3.9
test Acc.	86.4	93.2	95.5	91.1
baseline Acc.	87.3	94.0	96.0	91.9

Table 4: Distribution of the iterations across token dependency types. We fine-tune our *small* model on each probing task. We then perform inference on the Penn Tree Bank dataset and report the number of iterations given token dependency types. The number in parentheses denotes the number of dependency tags. We only display the top 10 most frequent tags. We indicate in **bold** tags for which the number of iterations is above avg + std. We include a baseline accuracy which we obtain with the ALBERT-base version without an adaptative depth mechanism and therefore 12 iterations performed for each token.

	Tense	Subj Num	Obj Num	Top Const
punct (121k)	2.1	1.9	2.0	2.5
prep (101k)	2.0	1.7	2.0	2.3
pobj (98k)	2.0	1.8	2.0	2.2
det (86k)	1.9	1.7	1.8	2.3
nn (81k)	**2.2**	**2.0**	**2.0**	2.5
nsubj (80k)	**2.3**	**2.2**	**2.1**	**2.8**
amod (66k)	2.1	1.8	2.0	2.3
dobj (49k)	2.1	1.9	**2.1**	2.3
root (44k)	**2.4**	**2.1**	**2.3**	**2.9**
advmod (37k)	2.1	1.8	2.0	2.6
avg.	2.2	2.0	2.1	2.5
test Acc.	88.6	91.1	93.8	91.1
baseline Acc.	87.3	94.0	96.0	91.9

Table 5: Distribution of the iterations across token dependency types. We fine-tune our *tiny* model on each probing task. We then perform inference on the Penn Tree Bank dataset and report the number of iterations given token dependency types. The number in parentheses denotes the number of dependency tags. We only display the top 10 most frequent tags. We indicate in **bold** tags for which the number of iterations is above avg + std. We include a baseline accuracy which we obtain with the ALBERT-base version without an adaptative depth mechanism and therefore 12 iterations performed for each token.

Edit Distance Based Curriculum Learning for Paraphrase Generation

Sora Kadotani[†]**, Tomoyuki Kajiwara**[‡]**, Yuki Arase**[†]**, Makoto Onizuka**[†]
[†]Graduate School of Information Science and Technology, Osaka University
[‡]Graduate School of Science and Engineering, Ehime University
[†]{kadotani.sora, arase, onizuka}@ist.osaka-u.ac.jp
[‡]kajiwara@cs.ehime-u.ac.jp

Abstract

Curriculum learning has improved the quality of neural machine translation, where only source-side features are considered in the metrics to determine the difficulty of translation. In this study, we apply curriculum learning to paraphrase generation for the first time. Different from machine translation, paraphrase generation allows a certain level of discrepancy in semantics between source and target, which results in diverse transformations from lexical substitution to reordering of clauses. Hence, the difficulty of transformations requires considering *both* source and target contexts. We propose an edit distance between a paraphrased sentence pair as a difficulty metric in curriculum learning. Experiments on formality transfer using GYAFC showed that our curriculum learning with edit distance improves the quality of paraphrase generation. Additionally, the proposed method improves the quality of difficult samples, which was not possible for previous methods.

1 Introduction

Paraphrase generation is a task that transforms expressions of an input sentence while retaining its meaning. While there are various subtasks in paraphrase generation, formality transfer (Rao and Tetreault, 2018; Niu et al., 2018; Kajiwara, 2019; Wang et al., 2019; Kajiwara et al., 2020; Zhang et al., 2020; Wang et al., 2020; Chawla and Yang, 2020) has been extensively studied. As paraphrase generation can be regarded as a machine translation task (Finch et al., 2004; Specia, 2010) within the same language, the same models (Bahdanau et al., 2015; Vaswani et al., 2017) have been applied to a monolingual parallel corpus.

Recent studies (Platanios et al., 2019; Liu et al., 2020) have shown that curriculum learning (Bengio et al., 2009) achieves faster convergence and improved translation quality on neural machine translation. Curriculum learning designs a training process starting from easy training samples and gradually proceeds to difficult training samples. In these previous studies, curriculum learning that uses source-side features, *i.e.*, sentence length and word rarity, as a metric to determine the difficulty has improved the quality of translation.

In this study, we adopt curriculum learning to the paraphrase generation task. Paraphrasing allows a certain level of semantic divergence between source and target sentences. For example, some paraphrases only require just a small number of transformations as shown in Table 1, while some others require drastic transformations as Table 2 shows. For the former, transformation is easy because the target sentence can be generated by copying almost all the input sentence's words. For the latter, transformation is difficult because the input sentence requires replacement and reordering of clauses besides lexical and phrasal paraphrasing. Because of this feature in paraphrase generation, *difficulty* in transformations requires to consider both source and target contexts.

To address this problem, we propose to use an edit distance between a paraphrased sentence pair as a difficulty metric that approximates necessary amounts of transformations. We evaluate our method on a formality transfer task using Grammarly's Yahoo Answers Formality Corpus (GYAFC) (Rao and Tetreault, 2018). The result of paraphrase generation from informal English to formal English confirmed the effectiveness of curriculum learning based on the edit distance. The detailed analysis revealed that the proposed method contributes to performance improvement in difficult samples regardless of the difficulty metrics, while sentence length and word rarity based methods degraded the performance.

Proceedings of the Joint Conference of the 59th Annual Meeting of the Association for Computational Linguistics and the 11th International Joint Conference on Natural Language Processing: Student Research Workshop, pages 229–234
August 5–6, 2021.

Source Sentence	Target Sentence
Yeah I think it would be funny.	I think it would be funny.
I have one brother and three sisters.	I have one brother and three sisters.
Do you mean which is least horrible?	Do you mean which is **the** least horrible?
Their first two albums were **pretty** good.	Their first two albums were **very** good.

Table 1: Examples with simple transformations (bold fonts indicate words that should be rewritten)

Source Sentence	Target Sentence
whats the **name** of **the** song	**What is** the **title** of **this** song.
not sure thank you for the two points	**Unsure, appreciate the pair of** points.
no where there is no such thing	**That does not exist.**
they **just got a little agressive ;)**	**Suddenly** they **became angrier.**

Table 2: Examples with drastic transformations (bold fonts indicate words that should be rewritten)

2 Preliminary: Curriculum Learning for Neural Machine Translation

Initial curriculum learning methods for neural machine translation considered only the difficulty of the training sample (Kocmi and Bojar, 2017; Zhang et al., 2018). These methods achieved faster convergence; however, they could not improve machine translation quality after convergence. Following these studies, Platanios et al. (2019) and Liu et al. (2020) proposed a method that considers both the difficulty of the training samples and the model competence, which achieved both of faster convergence and improvement in the translation quality.

This study bases on the model proposed by Platanios et al. (2019), who introduced the model competence in machine translation. Their method defines $\bar{d}_i \in [0,1]$ that is the difficulty score of the i-th training sample, and $c(t) \in [0,1]$ that is the model competence at the training step t. The method trains the model using only easier training samples than the model competency at each training step. In other words, the number of training samples increases as the training proceeds. Their method improved the translation quality while reduced the training time.

Platanios et al. (2019) defined the difficulty $d(s_i)$ based on sentence length and word rarity. Here, an input sentence s_i consists of a word string $\{w_1, ..., w_{N_i}\}$. Considering translation of a long sentence is more difficult than a shorter one, the sentence length is adopted as one of the metrics:

$$d_{\text{length}}(s_i) \triangleq N_i. \quad (1)$$

Besides, they considered words that infrequently appear in a training corpus are also difficult to translate because these words have fewer learning opportunities. Therefore, Platanios et al. (2019) also adopted word rarity:

$$d_{\text{rarity}}(s_i) \triangleq -\sum_{j=1}^{N_i} \log \hat{p}(w_j), \quad (2)$$

where $\hat{p}(w_j)$ is the unigram probability of word w_j in the training corpus. The final difficulty score $\bar{d}_i$ is computed using the cumulative distribution functions of $d(s_i)$ values.

Platanios et al. (2019) defined the model competence $c(t)$ at the training step t:

$$c(t) \triangleq \min(1, \sqrt{t\frac{1-c_0^2}{T} + c_0^2}), \quad (3)$$

where c_0 is the initial competence and T is the number of training steps estimated as necessary for convergence. They assumed that the competence is small at the beginning of training and increases monotonically as the training proceeds, which reaches the maximum value 1 when $t = T$.

3 Proposed Method

We approximate the difficulty of transformation in paraphrase generation as edit distance between a paraphrased sentence pair:

$$d_{\text{distance}}(s_i, t_i) \triangleq \text{LevenshteinDistance}(s_i, t_i), \quad (4)$$

where LevenshteinDistance$(\cdot,\cdot)$ computes the Levenshtein distance between the source sentence and the target sentence t_i. The edit distance between sentences with simple transformations like Table 1 is small, and the edit distance between sentences with drastic rewriting like Table 2 is large. Hence, our curriculum learning starts training with paraphrases with a small number of transformations and gradually learns more dynamic transformations.

Algorithm 1 Edit-distance based curriculum learning

Input: Dataset $D = \{(s_i, t_i)\}_{i=1}^{M}$, consisting of M samples, neural machine translation model θ.

Output: Trained neural machine translation model θ.

List of difficulty values $L \leftarrow \emptyset$
for $i = 1, ..., M$ **do**:
  $L \leftarrow L \cup \{d_{\text{distance}}(s_i, t_i)\}$.
end for
Compute a cumulative distribution function from difficulty values in L
for $i = 1, ..., M$ **do**:
  Compute the difficulty score $\bar{d}_i$
end for
for $t = 1, ..., T$ **do**: ▷ Curriculum learning
  Compute the model competence $c(t)$.
  Sample a data batch B_t uniformly from all $s_i \in D$, such that $\bar{d}_i \leq c(t)$.
  Train neural machine translation model θ using B_t as input.
end for

We apply the edit-distance based difficulty metric to the competence-based curriculum learning (Platanios et al., 2019) framework. The entire algorithm is shown in Algorithm 1.

4 Experiment

We evaluate the performance of edit-distance based curriculum learning on a style transfer task: paraphrase generation from informal English to formal English using GYAFC[1] (Rao and Tetreault, 2018).

4.1 Corpus and Evaluation Metric

GYAFC provides parallel sentences from two domains, Entertainment & Music (E&M) and Family & Relationships (F&R). Following Niu et al. (2018), we expand the training set by combining sentences of each domain and add the label `2formal` or `2informal` at the beginning of an input sentence. Statistics of GYAFC corpus are shown in Table 3.

As preprocessing, we used Moses toolkit[2] (Koehn et al., 2007) for tokenization and normalize-punctuation. We also used byte-pair encoding[3] (Sennrich et al., 2016) to limit the number of token types to $16,000$.

	Train	Train*	Dev	Test
E&M	52,595	209,124	2,877	1,416
F&R	51,967	209,124	2,788	1,332

Table 3: Statistics of GYAFC (Train* indicates the training set after expansion.)

On GYAFC, Rao and Tetreault (2018) reported that a correlation exists between manual annotation and BLEU (Papineni et al., 2002) scores for the task of informal to formal English transfer. Hence, we used BLEU as an evaluation metric.

4.2 Setup

As a paraphrase generation model, we implemented transformer (Vaswani et al., 2017) model using Joey NMT[4] (Kreutzer et al., 2019). Our transformer model has four-layers with a hidden size of 512 and a four attention heads for both the encoder and decoder. We used word embeddings of 512 dimensions tying the source, target, and the output layer's weight matrix. We also added dropout to the embeddings and hidden layers with a probability of 0.2. We trained using the Adam optimizer (Kingma and Ba, 2015) with the learning rate of 0.0002. The batch size was $4,096$ tokens. We saved the model every 800 updates applying early stopping with patience of five.

To evaluate the effectiveness of the edit distance[5] on curriculum learning (denoted as CL-ED), we compared to curriculum learning with sentence length (denoted as CL-SL) and word rarity (denoted as CL-WR). To compute the model competency with Equation (3), we need to set two hyperparameters of c_0 and T. We set c_0 to 0.01 and T to the number of training steps necessary for the transformer model with ordinary training reaches the 95% of the maximum BLEU score on the development set.

4.3 Results

The experimental results are shown in Table 4, where 'Baseline' is the transformer model trained without curriculum learning. In the E&M domain,

[1] https://github.com/raosudha89/GYAFC-corpus

[2] https://github.com/moses-smt/mosesdecoder

[3] https://github.com/rsennrich/subword-nmt

[4] https://github.com/joeynmt/joeynmt

[5] https://github.com/roy-ht/editdistance

	E&M	F&R
Source	49.19	50.94
Baseline	69.81	75.02
CL-SL	69.83	74.90
CL-WR	70.05	74.62
CL-ED	**70.34**	**75.41**

Table 4: BLEU scores on the GYAFC test set

Source	dead on arrival... there relationship is dead on arrival
Reference	Their relationship is dead on arrival.
Baseline	Dead on arrival, there relationship is dead on arrival.
CL-SL	Dead on arrival is dead on arrival.
CL-WR	Dead on arrival is dead on arrival.
CL-ED	The relationship is dead on arrival.

Table 5: Examples of generated sentences by each model

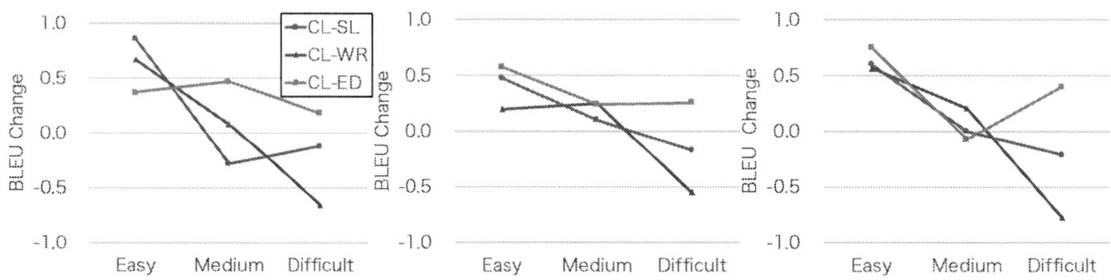

(a) Sentence length (b) Word rarity (c) Edit distance

Figure 1: Changes in BLEU scores compared to Baseline for each difficulty metric

CL-ED and CL-WR improved BLEU score of Baseline. In the F&R domain, only CL-ED outperformed Baseline. These results indicate that existing curriculum learning based on sentence length and word rarity is not effective in paraphrase generation. In contrast, curriculum learning with the edit distance was effective on both domains.

4.4 Discussion

We investigated which type of sentences that the curriculum learning improved their paraphrase quality. We divided all the test sets into three classes: Easy, Medium, and Difficult, of the same size (916 sentences each) using difficulty metrics of sentence length, word rarity, and edit distance, respectively. We then computed a BLEU score of each class and calculated improvements over Baseline.

Figure 1 shows the BLEU score differences of CL-SL, CL-WR, and CL-ED, compared to Baseline, respectively. Overall, the performance improvement on the Easy class is significant across the methods, which is intuitive as such sentences are easy to learn and used for training throughout curriculum learning. CL-SL and CL-WR degraded the BLEU scores on Medium class, and even deteriorated the baseline transformer on the Difficult class. In contrast, CL-ED improved the BLEU scores of Baseline even on the Difficult class, regardless of the metric of difficulty.

Table 5 shows output examples. The Baseline output almost the same sentence as the input without necessary transformations. While CL-SL and CL-WR output a sentence that does not make sense, CL-ED, which is our method, successfully paraphrases the source sentence.

5 Summary and Future Work

In this study, we applied the edit distance to curriculum learning for paraphrase generation. Experiment results on an informal to formal style transfer task confirmed the effectiveness of our method, particularly for paraphrasing difficult sentences.

Curriculum learning can be applied to any task when reasonable metrics for task difficulty are available. Transfer learning using a pre-trained model (Devlin et al., 2019; Lewis et al., 2020) has significantly improved the performance of various natural language processing tasks. In transfer learning, fine-tuning samples similar to the ones in the pre-training corpus should be easier to learn. We plan to apply our edit-distance based curriculum learning to transfer learning.

Acknowledgments

This work was supported by JST, ACT-X Grant Number JPMJAX1907, Japan.

References

Dzmitry Bahdanau, Kyunghyun Cho, and Yoshua Bengio. 2015. Neural Machine Translation by Jointly Learning to Align and Translate. In *Proceedings of the 3rd International Conference on Learning Representations*, pages 1–15.

Yoshua Bengio, Jérôme Louradour, Ronan Collobert, and Jason Weston. 2009. Curriculum Learning. In *Proceedings of the 26th Annual International Conference on Machine Learning*, pages 41–48.

Kunal Chawla and Diyi Yang. 2020. Semi-supervised Formality Style Transfer using Language Model Discriminator and Mutual Information Maximization. *Findings of the Association for Computational Linguistics*, pages 2340–2354.

Jacob Devlin, Ming-Wei Chang, Kenton Lee, and Kristina Toutanova. 2019. BERT: Pre-training of Deep Bidirectional Transformers for Language Understanding. In *Proceedings of the 2019 Conference of the North American Chapter of the Association for Computational Linguistics: Human Language Technologies*, pages 4171–4186.

Andrew Finch, Taro Watanabe, Yasuhiro Akiba, and Eiichiro Sumita. 2004. Paraphrasing as Machine Translation. *Journal of Natural Language Processing*, 11(5):87–111.

Tomoyuki Kajiwara. 2019. Negative Lexically Constrained Decoding for Paraphrase Generation. In *Proceedings of the 57th Annual Meeting of the Association for Computational Linguistics*, pages 6047–6052.

Tomoyuki Kajiwara, Biwa Miura, and Yuki Arase. 2020. Monolingual Transfer Learning via Bilingual Translators for Style-Sensitive Paraphrase Generation. In *Proceedings of the Thirty-Fourth AAAI Conference on Artificial Intelligence*, pages 8042–8049.

Diederik P. Kingma and Jimmy Ba. 2015. Adam: A Method for Stochastic Optimization. In *Proceedings of the 3rd International Conference on Learning Representations*, pages 1–15.

Tom Kocmi and Ondřej Bojar. 2017. Curriculum Learning and Minibatch Bucketing in Neural Machine Translation. In *Proceedings of the 11th International Conference Recent Advances in Natural Language Processing*, pages 379–386.

Philipp Koehn, Hieu Hoang, Alexandra Birch, Chris Callison-Burch, Marcello Federico, Nicola Bertoldi, Brooke Cowan, Wade Shen, Christine Moran, Richard Zens, Chris Dyer, Ondřej Bojar, Alexandra Constantin, and Evan Herbst. 2007. Moses: Open Source Toolkit for Statistical Machine Translation. In *Proceedings of the 45th Annual Meeting of the Association for Computational Linguistics*, pages 177–180.

Julia Kreutzer, Jasmijn Bastings, and Stefan Riezler. 2019. Joey NMT: A Minimalist NMT Toolkit for Novices. In *Proceedings of the 2019 Conference on Empirical Methods in Natural Language Processing and the 9th International Joint Conference on Natural Language Processing*, pages 109–114.

Mike Lewis, Yinhan Liu, Naman Goyal, Marjan Ghazvininejad, Abdelrahman Mohamed, Omer Levy, Veselin Stoyanov, and Luke Zettlemoyer. 2020. BART: Denoising Sequence-to-Sequence Pretraining for Natural Language Generation, Translation, and Comprehension. In *Proceedings of the 58th Annual Meeting of the Association for Computational Linguistics*, pages 7871–7880.

Xuebo Liu, Houtim Lai, Derek F. Wong, and Lidia S. Chao. 2020. Norm-Based Curriculum Learning for Neural Machine Translation. In *Proceedings of the 58th Annual Meeting of the Association for Computational Linguistics*, pages 427–436.

Xing Niu, Sudha Rao, and Marine Carpuat. 2018. Multi-Task Neural Models for Translating Between Styles Within and Across Languages. In *Proceedings of the 27th International Conference on Computational Linguistics*, pages 1008–1021.

Kishore Papineni, Salim Roukos, Todd Ward, and Wei-Jing Zhu. 2002. BLEU: a Method for Automatic Evaluation of Machine Translation. In *Proceedings of the 40th Annual Meeting of the Association for Computational Linguistics*, pages 311–318.

Emmanouil Antonios Platanios, Otilia Stretcu, Graham Neubig, Barnabas Poczos, and Tom M Mitchell. 2019. Competence-based Curriculum Learning for Neural Machine Translation. In *Proceedings of the 2019 Conference of the North American Chapter of the Association for Computational Linguistics: Human Language Technologies*, pages 1162–1172.

Sudha Rao and Joel Tetreault. 2018. Dear Sir or Madam, May I Introduce the GYAFC Dataset: Corpus, Benchmarks and Metrics for Formality Style Transfer. In *Proceedings of the 2018 Conference of the North American Chapter of the Association for Computational Linguistics: Human Language Technologies*, pages 129–140.

Rico Sennrich, Barry Haddow, and Alexandra Birch. 2016. Neural Machine Translation of Rare Words with Subword Units. In *Proceedings of the 54th Annual Meeting of the Association for Computational Linguistics*, pages 1715–1725.

Lucia Specia. 2010. Translating from Complex to Simplified Sentences. In *Proceedings of the 9th international conference on Computational Processing of the Portuguese Language*, pages 30–39.

Ashish Vaswani, Noam Shazeer, Niki Parmar, Jakob Uszkoreit, Llion Jones, Aidan N Gomez, Lukasz Kaiser, and Illia Polosukhin. 2017. Attention is All you Need. In *Proceedings of the 31st Conference on Neural Information Processing Systems*, pages 5998–6008.

Yunli Wang, Yu Wu, Lili Mou, Zhoujun Li, and Wenhan Chao. 2019. Harnessing Pre-Trained Neural Networks with Rules for Formality Style Transfer. In *Proceedings of the 2019 Conference on Empirical Methods in Natural Language Processing and the 9th International Joint Conference on Natural Language Processing*, pages 3573–3578.

Yunli Wang, Yu Wu, Lili Mou, Zhoujun Li, and Wen-Han Chao. 2020. Formality Style Transfer with Shared Latent Space. In *Proceedings of the 28th International Conference on Computational Linguistics*, pages 2236–2249.

Xuan Zhang, Gaurav Kumar, Huda Khayrallah, Kenton Murray, Jeremy Gwinnup, Marianna J Martindale, Paul McNamee, Kevin Duh, and Marine Carpuat. 2018. An Empirical Exploration of Curriculum Learning for Neural Machine Translation. *arXiv:1811.00739*, pages 1–16.

Yi Zhang, Tao Ge, and Xu Sun. 2020. Parallel Data Augmentation for Formality Style Transfer. In *Proceedings of the 58th Annual Meeting of the Association for Computational Linguistics*, pages 3221–3228.

Changing the Basis of Contextual Representations with Explicit Semantics

Tamás Ficsor
Institute of Informatics,
University of Szeged, Hungary
ficsort@inf.u-szeged.hu

Gábor Berend
Institute of Informatics,
University of Szeged, Hungary
berendg@inf.u-szeged.hu

Abstract

The application of transformer-based contextual representations has became a de facto solution for solving complex NLP tasks. Despite their successes, such representations are arguably opaque as their latent dimensions are not directly interpretable. To alleviate this limitation of contextual representations, we devise such an algorithm where the output representation expresses human-interpretable information of each dimension. We achieve this by constructing a transformation matrix based on the semantic content of the embedding space and predefined semantic categories using Hellinger distance. We evaluate our inferred representations on supersense prediction task. Our experiments reveal that the interpretable nature of transformed contextual representations makes it possible to accurately predict the supersense category of a word by simply looking for its transformed coordinate with the largest coefficient. We quantify the effects of our proposed transformation when applied over traditional dense contextual embeddings. We additionally investigate and report consistent improvements for the integration of sparse contextual word representations into our proposed algorithm.

1 Introduction

In recent years, contextual word representations – such as BERT (Devlin et al., 2019) or GPT-3 (Brown et al., 2020) – have dominated the NLP landscape on leaderboards such as SuperGLUE (Wang et al., 2019) as well as on real word applications (Lee et al., 2019; Alloatti et al., 2019). These models gain their semantics-related capabilities during the pre-training process, which can be then fine-tuned towards downstream tasks, including question answering (Raffel et al., 2019; Garg et al., 2019) or text summarization (Savelieva et al., 2020; Yan et al., 2020).

Representations obtained by transformer-based language models carry context-sensitive semantic information. Although the semantic information is present in the embedding space, the interpretation and exact information it carries is convoluted. Hence understanding and drawing conclusions from them are a cumbersome process for humans. Here we devise such a transformation where we explicitly express the semantic information in the basis of the embedding space. In particular, we express the captured semantic information as finite sets of linguistic properties, which are called semantic categories. A semantic category can represent any arbitrary concept. In this paper, we define them according to WordNet (Miller, 1995) LexNames (sometimes also referred as supersenses).

Even though we present our work on supersense prediction task, our proposed methodology can also be naturally extended to settings that exploit a different inventory of semantic categories. Our results also provide insights into the inner workings of the original embedding space, since we infer the semantic information from embedding spaces in a transparent manner. Therefore, amplified information can be assigned to the basis of the original embedding space.

Sparse representations convey the encoded semantic information in a more explicit manner, which facilitates the interpretability of such representations (Murphy et al., 2012; Balogh et al., 2020). Feature norming studies also illustrated the sparse nature of human feature descriptions, i.e. humans tend to describe objects and concepts with only a handful of properties (Garrard et al., 2001; McRae et al., 2005). Hence, we also conduct experiments utilizing sparse representations obtained from dense contextualized embeddings.

The transformation that we propose in this paper was inspired by Şenel et al. (2018), but it has been extended in various important aspects, as we

Proceedings of the Joint Conference of the 59th Annual Meeting of the Association for Computational Linguistics and the 11th International Joint Conference on Natural Language Processing: Student Research Workshop, pages 235–247
August 5–6, 2021.

- also utilize sparse representations to amplify semantic information,
- analyze several contextual embedding spaces
- apply whitening transformation on the embedding space to decorrelate semantic features, which also servers as the standardization step,
- evaluate the strength of the transformation in a different manner on supersense prediction task.

We also publish our source code on Github: `https://github.com/ficstamas/word_embedding_interpretability`.

2 Related Work

Contextual word representations provide a solution for context-aware word vector generation. These deep neural language models – such as ELMo (Peters et al., 2018), BERT (Devlin et al., 2019) or GPT-3 (Brown et al., 2020) – are pre-trained on unsupervised language modelling tasks, and later fine-tuned for downstream NLP tasks. Several variants were proposed to address one or more issue corresponding to the BERT model. Some of which we exploited in this paper. Liu et al. (2019) proposed a better pre-training process, Sanh et al. (2019) reduced the number of parameters, Conneau et al. (2020) presented a multilingual model. These models form the base of our approach, since we produce interpretable representations by measuring the semantic content of existing representations.

One way to measure the morphological and semantic contents of contextual word embeddings is via the application of probing approaches. The premise of this approach is that, if the probed information can be identified by a linear classifier, then the information is encoded in the embedding space (Adi et al., 2016; Ettinger et al., 2016; Klafka and Ettinger, 2020). Others explored the capacity of language models, where they examined the output probabilities of the model in given contexts (Linzen et al., 2016; Wilcox et al., 2018; Marvin and Linzen, 2018; Goldberg, 2019). We slightly reflect the premise of these methodologies by introducing a logistic regression baseline model.

Another approach is to incorporate external knowledge into Language Models. Levine et al. (2020) devised SenseBERT by integrating supersense information into the training of BERT. K M et al. (2018) showed a method where an arbitrary knowledge graph can be incorporated into their LSTM based model. External knowledge incorporation is getting a popular approach to improve already existing state-of-the-art solutions in a domain or task specific environment (Munkhdalai et al., 2015; Weber et al., 2019; Baral et al., 2020; Mondal, 2020; Wise et al., 2020; Murayama et al., 2020). Since we deemed to investigate the effect of incorporated knowledge towards the semantic content of embedding space, SenseBERT serves a good basis for that.

Ethayarajh (2019) investigated the importance of anisotropic property of the contextual embeddings, which is a different kind of investigation than we aim to do. It still gives a good insight into the inner workings of the layers. Şenel et al. (2018) showed a method where they measured the interpretability of Glove embeddings, and later showed a method to manipulate and improve the interpretability of a given static word representation (Şenel et al., 2020). Our approach resembles Şenel et al. (2018), however, we apply different pre- and post-processing steps and more importantly, we replaced the usage of the Bhattacharyya distance with the Hellinger distance, which is closely related to it but operates in a bounded and continuous manner. Our approach also differs from Şenel et al. (2018) in that we deal with contextualited language models instead of static word embeddings and we also rely on sparse contextualized word vectors.

The intuition behind sparse vectors is related to the way humans describe concepts, which has been extensively studied in various feature norming studies (Garrard et al., 2001; McRae et al., 2005). Additionally, generating sparse features (Kazama and Tsujii, 2003; Friedman et al., 2008; Mairal et al., 2009) has proved to be useful in several areas, including POS tagging (Ganchev et al., 2010), text classification (Yogatama and Smith, 2014) and dependency parsing (Martins et al., 2011). Therefore, several sparse static representations were presented, such as Murphy et al. (2012) proposed Non-Negative Sparse Embeddings to represent interpretable sparse word vectors. Park et al. (2017) showed a rotation-based method and Subramanian et al. (2017) suggested an approach using a denoising k-sparse auto-encoder to generate sparse word vectors. Berend (2017) showed that sparse representations can outperform their dense counterparts in certain NLP tasks, such as NER, or POS tagging. Additionally, Berend (2020) illustrated how applying sparse representations can boost the performance of contextual embeddings for Word Sense Disambiguation, which we also desire to exploit.

3 Our Approach

We first define necessary notations. We denote the embedding space with $\mathcal{E} \in \mathbb{R}^{v \times d}$ with the superscript indicating whether it is obtained from the training set t or evaluation set e. We denote the number of input words and their dimensionality by v and d, respectively. Furthermore, we denote the transformation matrix with $\mathcal{W} \in \mathbb{R}^{d \times s}$ – where s represents the number of semantic categories – and the final interpretable representation with $\mathcal{I} \in \mathbb{R}^{v \times s}$, which always denotes the interpretable representation of $\mathcal{E}^{(e)}$. Additionally, we denote the semantic categories with $\mathcal{S}$.

3.1 Interpretable Representation

Our goal is to produce such embedding spaces where we can identify semantic features by their basis. In order to obtain such an embedding space, we are constructing a transformation matrix $\mathcal{W}^{(t)}$, which amplifies the semantic information of an input representation and can be formulated as: $\mathcal{I} = \mathcal{E}_w^{(e)} \times \mathcal{W}^{(t)}$. $\mathcal{E}_w$ represents the whitened embedding space, which is the output of a pre-processing step (Section 3.2), and $\mathcal{W}$ being our transformation matrix (Section 3.3).

3.2 Pre-processing

Pre-processing consists of two steps: first we generate sparse representations of dense embedding spaces (this step is omitted when we report about dense embedding spaces), then we whiten the embedding space.

3.2.1 Sparse Representation

For obtaining sparse contextualized representations, we follow the methodology proposed in (Berend, 2020). That is, we solve the following sparse coding (Mairal et al., 2009) optimization problem:

$$\min_{\alpha^{(t)}, D} \frac{1}{2} \left\| \mathcal{E}^{(t)} - \alpha^{(t)} D \right\|_F^2 + \lambda \left\| \alpha^{(t)} \right\|_1,$$

where $D \in \mathbb{R}^{k \times d}$ is the dictionary matrix, and $\alpha \in \mathbb{R}^{v \times k}$ contains the sparse contextualized representations. The two hyperparameters of the dictionary learning approach are the number of basis vectors to employ (k) and the strength of the regularization (λ).

We obtained the sparse contextual representations for the words in the evaluation set by fixing the dictionary matrix D that we learned on the train set and optimized solely for the sparse coefficients $\alpha^{(e)}$. We also report experimental results obtained for different values of basis vectors k and regularization coefficients λ.

The output of this step is also represented with $\mathcal{E}$ instead of α since this step is optional. Among our results we mark whether we applied (*Sparse*) or skipped (*Dense*) this step.

3.2.2 Whitening

Since we handle dimensions independently, we first apply whitening transformation on the embedding space. Several whitening transformations are known – like Cholesky or PCA (e.g. Friedman (1987)) – but we decided to rely on ZCA whitening (or Mahalanobis whitening) (Bell and Sejnowski, 1997). One benefit of employing ZCA whitening is that it ensures higher correlation between the original and whitened features (Kessy et al., 2018). As a consequence, it is a widely utilized approach for obtaining whitened data in NLP (Heyman et al., 2019; Glavaš et al., 2019).

We determine the whitening transformation matrix from the training set ($\mathcal{E}^{(t)}$), which is then applied on the representation of our training ($\mathcal{E}^{(t)}$) and evaluation sets ($\mathcal{E}^{(e)}$). We denote the whitened representations for the training and evaluation sets by $\mathcal{E}_w^{(t)}$ and $\mathcal{E}_w^{(e)}$, respectively.

3.3 Transformation

In this section, we discuss the way we measure the semantic information of the embedding space and express the linear transformation matrix ($\mathcal{W}$).

3.3.1 Semantic Distribution

The coefficients of the contextual embeddings of words that belong to the same (super)sense category are expected to originate from the same distribution. Hence, it is reasonable to quantify the extent to which some semantic category is encoded along some dimension by investigating the distribution of the coefficients of the word vectors along that dimension. For every semantic category, we can partition the words whether they pertain to that category. When a dimension encodes a semantic category to a large extent, the distribution of the coefficients of those words belonging to that category is expected to differ substantially from that of those words not pertaining to the same category.

We can formulate the distributions of our interest by function $L : x \rightarrow \mathcal{S}$, which maps each token (x) to its context-sensitive semantic category (LexName) and a function $f : x \rightarrow \mathcal{E}$, which returns the context-sensitive representation of x. Thus the devised distributions can be defined as:

$$P_{ij} = \left\{ f(x)^{(i)} \mid f(x) \in \mathcal{E}_w^{(t)},\ L(x) \in \mathcal{S}^{(j)} \right\}$$

and

$$Q_{ij} = \left\{ f(x)^{(i)} \mid f(x) \in \mathcal{E}_w^{(t)},\ L(x) \notin \mathcal{S}^{(j)} \right\},$$

where i represents a dimension and j denotes a semantic category. In other words, P_{ij} represents the distribution along the ith dimension of those words that belong to the jth semantic category, whereas Q_{ij} represents the distribution of the coefficients along the same dimension (i) of those words that do not belong to the jth semantic category.

3.3.2 Semantic Information and Transformation Matrix

For every dimension (i) and semantic category (j) pair, we can express the presence of the semantic information by defining a distance between the distributions P_{ij} and Q_{ij}. Following from the construction of the distributions P_{ij} and Q_{ij}, the larger the distance between a pair of distributions (P_{ij}, Q_{ij}), the more likely that dimension i encodes semantic information j.

Based on that observation, we define a transformation matrix $\mathcal{W}_D$ as

$$\mathcal{W}_D(i,j) = D(P_{ij}, Q_{ij}),$$

where D is the distance function. We specify the distance function as the Hellinger distance, which can be formulated as

$$\sqrt{1 - \sqrt{\frac{2\sigma_{p_{ij}}\sigma_{q_{ij}}}{\sigma_{p_{ij}}^2 + \sigma_{q_{ij}}^2}} e^{-\frac{1}{4}\cdot\frac{(\mu_{p_{ij}}-\mu_{q_{ij}})^2}{\sigma_{p_{ij}}^2+\sigma_{q_{ij}}^2}}},$$

where we assume that $P_{ij} \sim \mathcal{N}(\mu_{p_{ij}}, \sigma_{p_{ij}})$ and $Q_{ij} \sim \mathcal{N}(, \mu_{q_{ij}}, \sigma_{q_{ij}})$, i.e. they are samples from normal distributions with expected value μ and standard deviation σ.

We decided to rely on Hellinger distance due to its continuous, symmetric and bounded nature. In contrast to out approach, Şenel et al. (2018) proposed the usage of Bhattacharyya distance – which is closely related to Hellinger distance – but it would overestimate the certainty of the semantic information of a dimension in the case of distant distributions. Another concern is that the Bhattacharyya distance is discontinuous. We discussed this topic in a earlier work (Ficsor and Berend, 2020) in relation to static word embeddings.

Bias Reduction. So far, our transformation matrix is biased due to the imbalanced semantic categories. It can be reduced by ℓ_1 normalizing $\mathcal{W}_D$ in such a manner that vectors representing semantic categories sum up to 1, which we denote as $\mathcal{W}_{ND}$ (Normalized Distance Matrix).

Directional Encoding. As semantic information can be encoded in both positive and negative directions, we modify the entries of $\mathcal{W}_{ND}$ as

$$\mathcal{W}_{NSD}(i,j) = sign(\mu_{p_{ij}} - \mu_{q_{ij}}) \cdot \mathcal{W}_{ND}(i,j),$$

where $sign(\cdot)$ is the signum function. This modification ensures that each semantic category is represented with the highest coefficients in their corresponding base of the interpretable representation.

3.4 Post-processing

The representations transformed in the above manner are still skewed in the sense that they do not reflect the likelihood of each semantic category. In order to alleviate that problem, we measure and normalize the frequency ($\mathbf{f_N} = \mathbf{f}/\|\mathbf{f}\|_2, \mathbf{f} \in \mathbb{N}^s$) of each occurrence of a supersense category in the training set and accumulate that information into the embedding space in the following manner: $\mathcal{I}_\mathrm{f} = \mathcal{I} + \mathcal{I} \odot \mathbf{1}\mathbf{f}_N^\intercal$, where $\odot$ represents the element-wise multiplication, and $\mathbf{1}$ represents a vector consisting of all ones. Finally, $\mathcal{I}_\mathrm{f}$ represents our final interpretable representations adjusted with supersense frequencies.

3.5 Accuracy Calculation

Representations generated by our approach let us determine the presumed semantic category by the highest coefficient in the word vector. In other words, a word vector should have its highest coefficient in the base, which represents the same semantic category as the annotation represents in the evaluation set. Our overall accuracy is the fraction of the correct predictions and the total number of annotated data in the evaluation set.

4 Evaluation

4.1 Experimental setting.

During our experiments, we relied on the SemCor dataset for training and the unified word sense disambiguation framework introduced in (Raganato et al., 2017a) for evaluation, which consists of 5 sense annotated corpora: *SensEval2* (Edmonds and Cotton, 2001), *SensEval3* (Mihalcea et al., 2004), *SemEval 2007* Task 17 (Pradhan et al., 2007), *SemEval 2013* Task 12 (Navigli et al., 2013), *SemEval 2015* Task 13 (Moro and Navigli, 2015) and their concatenation. We refer to the combined dataset as *ALL* througout the paper. The individual datasets contain 2282, 1850, 455, 1644 and 1022 sense annotations, respectively. These datasets contain fine-grained sense annotation for a subset of the words from which the supersense information can be conveniently inferred. We reduced the scope of fine-grained sense annotations to lexname level, in order to maintain well-defined semantic categories with high sample sizes. We used the *SemEval 2007* data as our development set in accordance with prior work (Raganato et al., 2017b; Kumar et al., 2019; Blevins and Zettlemoyer, 2020; Pasini et al., 2021).

We conducted our experiments on several contextual embedding spaces, where each model represent a different purpose. We can consider BERT (Devlin et al., 2019) as the baseline of the following contextual models. SenseBERT (Levine et al., 2020) incorporated word sense information into its latent representation. DistilBERT (Sanh et al., 2019) obtained through knowledge distillation and operates with less parameters. RoBERTa (Liu et al., 2019) introduced a better pre-training procedure. Finally, XLM-RoBERTa (Conneau et al., 2020) is a multilingual model with the RoBERTa's pre-training procedure. When available, we also conducted experiments using both `cased` and `uncased` vocabularies.

Following (Loureiro and Jorge, 2019), we also averaged the representations from the last 4 layers of the transformer models to obtain our final contextual embeddings. Furthermore, to determine the hyperparameters for sparse vector generation, we used the accuracy of BERT `Base` model with different regularizations (λ) and number of employed basis (k) on the *SemEval2007* dataset, the results of which can be seen in Table 1.

		λ		
		0.05	0.1	0.2
k	1500	63.51	64.83	57.80
	3000	65.71	**66.59**	64.61

Table 1: Results of our experiments when relying on sparse representations created by using various hyperparameter combinations. The BERT `Base` model was used on the SemEval2007 validation set. k represents the number of employed basis and λ denotes the regularization parameter.

4.2 Baselines

We next introduce those baselines we compared our approach with. Most of these approaches rely on the intact contextual representations $\mathcal{E}$, for which the dimensions are not intended to directly encode human interpretable supersense information about the words they describe.

Logistic Regression Classifier We conducted the experiments by setting the random state to 0, maximum iterations to 25,000 and turned off the utilization of a bias term. In this case the vectors that were used for making the predictions about the supersenses of words were of much higher dimensions and not directly interpretable at all, unlike our representations.

Dimension Reduction (PCA+LogReg) We also experimented with representations, which inherit the same number of dimensions as many we utilize (45). So we applied principal component analysis (PCA) based dimension reduction on the original $\mathcal{E}$ embedding space. Additionally, we applied Logistic Regression Classifier on the reduced representations with the same parametirazition to the previously described baseline.

Sparsity Makes Sense (SMS) An approach proposed by Berend (2020) yields human-interpretable embeddings like ours, since human-interpretable features are bound to the basis of the output representation. Berend (2020) originally presented the devised algorithm on fine-grained word sense disambiguation, which we altered to work similarly to our approach and predict supersense information instead. We utilized normalized positive pointwise mutual information to construct the transformation matrix because it showed the most prominent scores in the paper.

Representation		Interpretable						Latent			
Method		Our Approach				SMS		PCA+LogReg		LogReg	
Input Embedding Type		Dense		Sparse		Sparse		Dense		Dense	
Vocabulary (Cased/Uncased)		C	U	C	U	C	U	C	U	C	U
ALL-dev											
BERT	Base	65.04	62.44	69.53	68.43	65.24	63.00	57.45	54.70	73.96	72.64
	Large	63.68	62.51	68.41	64.82	62.00	57.03	55.60	51.05	73.25	71.69
SenseBERT	Base	–	66.13	–	74.59	–	74.21	–	68.57	–	79.47
	Large	–	64.62	–	74.55	–	73.75	–	71.44	–	78.99
DistilBERT	Base	62.94	64.44	70.78	72.68	66.31	68.03	59.34	61.51	74.86	74.46
RoBERTa	Base	59.47	–	65.40	–	61.91	–	52.25	–	69.44	–
	Large	64.43	–	70.27	–	65.85	–	52.91	–	75.16	–
XLM-RoBERTa	Base	63.31	–	70.10	–	67.84	–	58.43	–	76.02	–
	Large	62.10	–	67.74	–	64.63	–	57.89	–	75.54	–

Table 2: Accuracy of each model on the supersense prediction task using dense and sparse embedding spaces. *ALL-dev* denotes the evaluation on the *ALL* dataset excluding the development set. All of the sparse representations were generated using $\lambda = 0.1$ for the regularization coefficient and $k = 3000$ basis based on the experiments reported in Table 1. Our approach and SMS are interpretable representations, PCA+LogReg just represents the information in the same number of basis but there are no connection, which can be drawn to the previous two, and Logistic Regression operates on the original embedding spaces. We also include a more detailed table in the Appendix, which breaks down performances for each sub-corpora.

4.3 Results

We list the results of our experiments using different contextual encoders on the task of supersense prediction in Table 2. We calculated the accuracy as the fraction of correct predictions and the total number of annotated samples. We selected $\lambda = 0.1$ regularization and $k = 3000$ basis for sparse vector generation in accordance with the results that we obtained over the development set for different choices of the hyperparameters (see Table 1).

4.3.1 Model Performances

We consider a model's semantic capacity as the Logistic Regression model's performance, and its interpretability as the best performing interpretable representation. We do not expect to exceed the original model, since we limited its capabilities drastically by reducing the number of utilized dimensions to 45.

By looking at the performance, as expected the original latent representation expresses the most semantic information measure by Logistic Regression. Among all of them, SenseBERT dominates which is due to the additional supersense information signal it relies on during its pretraining. The incorporated supersense information helps SenseBERT to represent that information more explicitly, which becomes more obvious when we amplify it by sparse representations. So including further objectives during training just further separates the information in the basis.

4.3.2 Dense and Sparse Representations

We can see from Table 2 that relying on sparse representations further amplifies the semantic content of the latent representations. Based on the results of our approach, we can conclude that the semantic information can be more easily identified in the case of sparse representations (as indicated by the higher scores in the majority of the cases). SMS follows a similar trend to ours. Also the relatively small decrease in performance suggests that the majority of the removed signals correspond to noise.

4.3.3 Impact of Base and Large Models

In several cases, the `Large` models underperformed their `Base` counterparts (except RoBERTa). It can indicate that the `Large` version might be under-trained, which was also hypothesised in (Liu et al., 2019). Overall, choosing the `Base` pre-trained models seems to be a sufficient and often better option for performing supersense prediction.

		Mean (Std)	
		Cased	Uncased
BERT	Base	0.35 (±0.21)	0.32 (±0.21)
	Large	0.29 (±0.22)	0.28 (±0.22)
SenseBERT	Base	–	0.59 (±0.25)
	Large	–	0.55 (±0.29)
DistilBERT	Base	0.34 (±0.21)	0.33 (±0.20)
RoBERTa	Base	0.34 (±0.22)	–
	Large	0.31 (±0.21)	–
XLM-RoBERTa	Base	0.34 (±0.22)	–
	Large	0.32 (±0.22)	–

Table 3: Average Spearman Rank Correlation between the basis of our interpretable embedding space and the one obtain by the SMS approach.

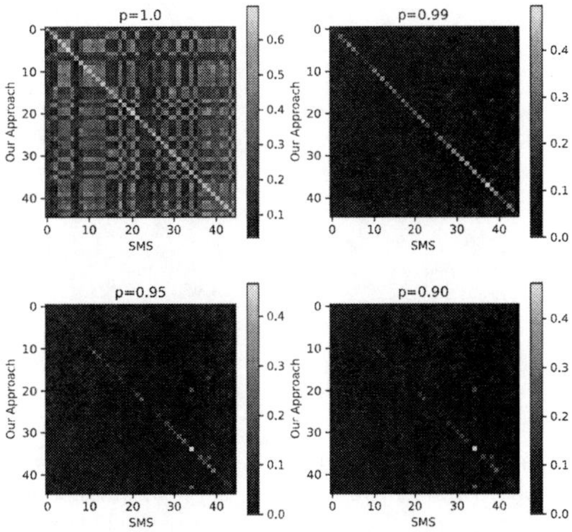

Figure 1: Rank-biased Overlap scores between the basis of our approach and SMS on sparse representations of SenseBERT Base models. Here the p value indicates the steep of decline in weights (smaller the p the more top-weighted the metric is).

4.3.4 Case-sensitivity of the Vocabulary

As the choice whether using a cased or an uncased model is more beneficial can vary from task to task, we made experiments in that respect. To this end, we compared the performance of BERT and DistilBERT, which are available in both case sensitive and case insensitive versions. Usually, the choice highly depends on the task (cased versions being recommended for POS, NER, WSD) and the language (cased can be beneficial for certain languages such as German). Overall, we can observe some advantage of using the cased vocabularies. Interestingly, the behavior of DistilBERT and BERT differs radically in that respect for all but the LogReg approach.

4.3.5 Considering Dimensionality

Other than the Logistic Regression model, every approach relies on some kind of condensed representation for supersense prediction. Even though all of the representations were condensed – into 45 dimensions from 768, 1024 dimensions for dense and 3000 dimensions for sparse representations – the performance did not decreased by a large margin. PCA-based dimension reduction approach performed the worst among the 3 approaches, whereas ours performed the best. Note that these interpretable approaches (ours and SMS) not only perform better over a standard dimension reduction, but they also associate human-understandable knowledge to the basis of the embedding space. So it can be utilized as an explicit semantic compression technique.

4.3.6 Comparing Interpretable Representations

Both our and SMS approach are similar in the sense that we can assign human-interpretable features to the basis of output embeddings. We hence analysed the similarity of the semantic information of the two embedding spaces. We measured the Spearman rank correlation of the coefficients in each pair of basis generated by our approach and the SMS approach. We included these values in Table 3, which showcases the mean of absolute (ignoring the direction of correlation) correlation coefficients. Except for SenseBERT, we can see weak correlation scores. Higher correlation between the coefficients of these interpretable models, along the same dimension would suggest that they can represent the same semantic information to a different level and/or manner. According to the Spearman correlation between our and the SMS approach captures a different aspect of the encoded semantic content, but we futher experimented with SenseBERT.

Since the two embeddings expressed from SenseBERT – with our and SMS approach – seem to share the most semantic content, we investigated them further. During our evaluation, we rely on the maximum value of each word token, so each dimension represents the semantic information among its highest coefficients. Hence, higher value ranks a word more likely to carry the corresponding semantic information. Therefore, we calculated Rank-

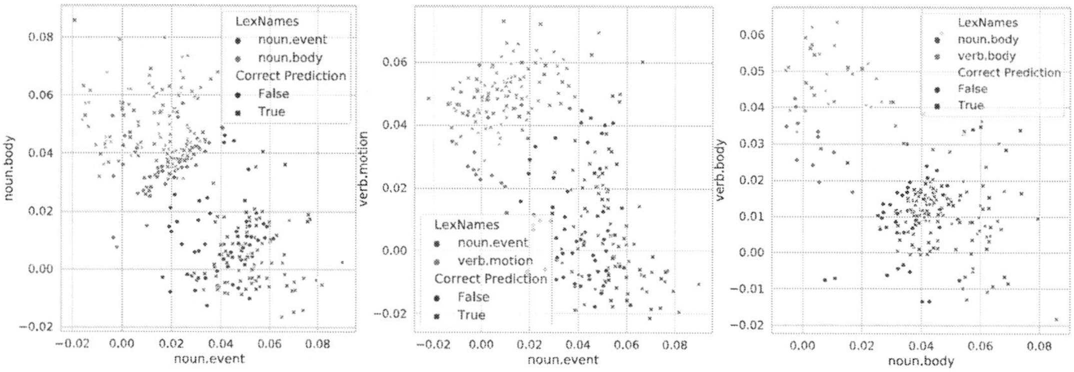

Figure 2: Representation of the coefficients of several semantic categories where the color represents the assigned label according to the corpus, whether the prediction according to the maximum is correct (True) or not (False), and both axis represent its value in their corresponding basis in our representation (SenseBERT, $k = 3000, \lambda = 0.1$).

biased Overlap (RBO) scores (Webber et al., 2010) between the sorted basis, which can be seen in Figure 1. RBO quantifies a weighted, non-conjoint similarity measure, which does not rely on correlation. RBO utilizes a p parameter, which controls the emphasis we have on top ranked items (lower p indicates more emphasis on the top ranked items). The $p = 1$ case differs from the $p < 1$ case, in that it returns the un-bounded set-intersection overlap calculated according to the proposition from Fagin et al. (2003). On the other hand, $p < 1$ prioritizes the head of the lists. Higher score indicates higher similarity between two ranked lists, which in our case means that the two models behave more similarly.

Both models perform comparable in general with slightly better scores on sparse models for our approach. We measured the statistical significance of the improvements by Berg-Kirkpatrick et al. (2012), which states the following H_0 hypothesis: *if* $p(\delta(X) > \delta(x)|H_0) < 0.05$ *then we accept the improvement of the first model and unlikely to be cause of random factors*, where $\delta(\cdot)$ represents the improvement of the first model. Furthermore, we used $b = 10^6$ bootstraps, which was sufficient according to the original paper. Between sparse models we obtained $p = 0.0016$ value, which suggests that the significance of improvement is unlikely to be caused by random factors.

4.3.7 Qualitative Assessments

Clustering We demonstrate the semantic decomposition of 3 pairs of semantic categories in Figure 2. Each marker corresponds to a concrete word occurrence with their color reflecting their expected supersense. The markers also indicate whether the prediction made according to the highest coordinate is correct (True) or not (False). Furthermore, both axis represents its actual value in its corresponding base. We can notice in these figures how well data points are separated with respect to their semantic properties.

Shared Space of Multilingual Domain The availability of multilingual encoders allows us to use our supersense classifier on languages other than English as well. In order to test the applicaility of XLM-RoBERTa in such a scenario, we tested it on some sentences in multiple languages, the outcome of which is included in Table 4.

To this experiment, we constructed $\mathcal{W}_D$ in the usual manner from Sparse XLM-RoBERTa transformer on the SemCor dataset (which is in English). After that, we generated the context aware word vectors for the sentences. We then obtained the sparse representations from them by employing the already optimized dictionary matrix from SemCor. We finally utilized the previously constructed distance matrix to obtain the interpretable representation. In Table 4, we marked the expected label above the text with blue, and the top 3 predictions with red below the text.

We included 3 typologically diverse languages German (DE), Hungarian (HU) and Japanese (JP). Overall, the expected label was within the top 3 predictions irrespective of the language, which suggests that the overlap in semantic distribution is high between languages, but further quantitative experiments are also needed to support that statement.

	adj.all	noun.cognition	verb.stative		adj.all	noun.act
Dein	bester	Lehrer	ist	dein	letzter	Fehler.
	adj.all	noun.person	verb.stative		adj.all	noun.act
	noun.event	noun.act	verb.social		noun.shape	noun.attribute
	verb.competition	noun.cognition	verb.change		verb.competition	noun.feeling

DE) Translation: Your best teacher is your last mistake. – Ralph Nader

adv.all	noun.attribute	verb.stative	adj.all	noun.attribute
Együtt	erő	vagyunk,	szerteszét	gyöngeség.
adv.all	noun.attribute	verb.stative	verb.body	noun.feeling
adj.all	noun.feeling	verb.weather	adj.all	noun.state
verb.social	noun.phenomenon	verb.consumption	verb.competition	noun.attribute

HU) Translation: We are strong together, and weak as scattered. – Albert Wass

noun.location		verb.motion	noun.time		noun.person		adv.all	verb.body	
千代田町	に	着いた	時	には、	禎子	は	すでに	生まれていた	のです。
noun.Tops		verb.motion	noun.event		noun.Tops		adv.all	verb.change	
noun.location		verb.change	noun.time		noun.person		noun.object	verb.body	
noun.object		verb.contact	noun.shape		noun.animal		noun.food	adj.all	

JP) Translation: Upon arriving to Chiyoda, Sadako was already born. – Eleanor Coerr

Table 4: A few example of shared knowledge between languages in XLM-RoBERTa. We used the transformation matrix learned on the English SemCor dataset with Sparse XLM-RoBERTa `Base` model. Above the text with blue we mark the expected label, and below the text with red the top 3 predictions.

5 Conclusion

In this paper, we demonstrated our approach to obtain interpretable representations from contextual representations, which represents semantic information in the basis with high coefficients. We demonstrated its capabilities by applying it on supersense prediction task. However, it can be utilized on other problems as well such as term expansion and knowledge base completion.

We additionally explored the application of sparse representations, which successfully amplified the examined semantic information. We also considered the effect of incorporated prior knowledge in the form of applying SenseBERT embeddings, which showed that its additional objective during pre-training can amplify those features. Furthermore, explored the space of condensed (DistilBERT) and multilingual (XLM-RoBERTa) spaces. We examined the improvements come by RoBERTa from a semantic standpoint. Note that our classification decision is currently made by simply finding the coordinate with the largest magnitude.

In conclusion, our experiments showed that it is possible to extract and succinctly represent human-interpretable information about words in transformed spaces with much lower dimensions than their original representations. Additionally, it allows us to make decisions about word vectors in a more transparent manner, where some kind of explanation is already assigned to the basis of a representation, which can lead us to more transparent machine learning models.

Acknowledgements

This research was supported by the European Union and co-funded by the European Social Fund through the project "Integrated program for training new generation of scientists in the fields of computer science" (EFOP-3.6.3-VEKOP-16-2017-0002) and the Ministry of Innovation and Technology NRDI Office within the framework of the Artificial Intelligence National Laboratory Program and the Artificial Intelligence National Excellence Program (2018-1.2.1-NKP-2018-00008).

References

Yossi Adi, Einat Kermany, Yonatan Belinkov, Ofer Lavi, and Yoav Goldberg. 2016. Fine-grained analysis of sentence embeddings using auxiliary prediction tasks.

Francesca Alloatti, Luigi Di Caro, and Gianpiero Sportelli. 2019. Real life application of a question answering system using BERT language model. In *Proceedings of the 20th Annual SIGdial Meeting on Discourse and Dialogue*, pages 250–253, Stockholm, Sweden. Association for Computational Linguistics.

Vanda Balogh, Gábor Berend, Dimitrios I. Diochnos, and György Turán. 2020. Understanding the semantic content of sparse word embeddings using a commonsense knowledge base. *Proceedings of the AAAI Conference on Artificial Intelligence*, 34(05):7399–7406.

Chitta Baral, Pratyay Banerjee, Kuntal Kumar Pal, and Arindam Mitra. 2020. Natural language QA approaches using reasoning with external knowledge.

Anthony J. Bell and Terrence J. Sejnowski. 1997. The "independent components" of natural scenes are edge filters. *Vision Research*, 37(23):3327–3338.

Gábor Berend. 2017. Sparse coding of neural word embeddings for multilingual sequence labeling. *Transactions of the Association for Computational Linguistics*, 5:247–261.

Gábor Berend. 2020. Sparsity makes sense: Word sense disambiguation using sparse contextualized word representations. In *Proceedings of the 2020 Conference on Empirical Methods in Natural Language Processing (EMNLP)*, pages 8498–8508, Online. Association for Computational Linguistics.

Taylor Berg-Kirkpatrick, David Burkett, and Dan Klein. 2012. An empirical investigation of statistical significance in NLP. In *Proceedings of the 2012 Joint Conference on Empirical Methods in Natural Language Processing and Computational Natural Language Learning*, pages 995–1005, Jeju Island, Korea. Association for Computational Linguistics.

Terra Blevins and Luke Zettlemoyer. 2020. Moving down the long tail of word sense disambiguation with gloss informed bi-encoders. In *ACL*, pages 1006–1017. Association for Computational Linguistics.

Tom B. Brown, Benjamin Mann, Nick Ryder, Melanie Subbiah, Jared Kaplan, Prafulla Dhariwal, Arvind Neelakantan, Pranav Shyam, Girish Sastry, Amanda Askell, Sandhini Agarwal, Ariel Herbert-Voss, Gretchen Krueger, Tom Henighan, Rewon Child, Aditya Ramesh, Daniel M. Ziegler, Jeffrey Wu, Clemens Winter, Christopher Hesse, Mark Chen, Eric Sigler, Mateusz Litwin, Scott Gray, Benjamin Chess, Jack Clark, Christopher Berner, Sam McCandlish, Alec Radford, Ilya Sutskever, and Dario Amodei. 2020. Language models are few-shot learners.

Alexis Conneau, Kartikay Khandelwal, Naman Goyal, Vishrav Chaudhary, Guillaume Wenzek, Francisco Guzmán, Edouard Grave, Myle Ott, Luke Zettlemoyer, and Veselin Stoyanov. 2020. Unsupervised cross-lingual representation learning at scale. In *ACL*, pages 8440–8451. Association for Computational Linguistics.

Jacob Devlin, Ming-Wei Chang, Kenton Lee, and Kristina Toutanova. 2019. BERT: Pre-training of deep bidirectional transformers for language understanding. In *Proceedings of the 2019 Conference of the North American Chapter of the Association for Computational Linguistics: Human Language Technologies, Volume 1 (Long and Short Papers)*, pages 4171–4186, Minneapolis, Minnesota. Association for Computational Linguistics.

Philip Edmonds and Scott Cotton. 2001. SENSEVAL-2: Overview. In *The Proceedings of the Second International Workshop on Evaluating Word Sense Disambiguation Systems*, SENSEVAL '01, pages 1–5, Stroudsburg, PA, USA. Association for Computational Linguistics.

Kawin Ethayarajh. 2019. How contextual are contextualized word representations? comparing the geometry of BERT, ELMo, and GPT-2 embeddings.

Allyson Ettinger, Ahmed Elgohary, and Philip Resnik. 2016. Probing for semantic evidence of composition by means of simple classification tasks. In *Proceedings of the 1st Workshop on Evaluating Vector-Space Representations for NLP*, pages 134–139, Berlin, Germany. Association for Computational Linguistics.

Ronald Fagin, Ravi Kumar, and D. Sivakumar. 2003. Comparing top k lists. In *Proceedings of the Fourteenth Annual ACM-SIAM Symposium on Discrete Algorithms*, SODA '03, page 28–36, USA. Society for Industrial and Applied Mathematics.

Tamás Ficsor and Gábor Berend. 2020. Interpreting word embeddings using a distribution agnostic approach employing hellinger distance. In *Text, Speech, and Dialogue*, pages 197–205, Cham. Springer International Publishing.

Jerome Friedman, Trevor Hastie, and Robert Tibshirani. 2008. Sparse inverse covariance estimation with the graphical lasso. *Biostatistics (Oxford, England)*, 9:432–41.

Jerome H. Friedman. 1987. Exploratory projection pursuit. *Journal of the American Statistical Association*, 82(397):249–266.

Kuzman Ganchev, João Graça, Jennifer Gillenwater, and Ben Taskar. 2010. Posterior regularization for structured latent variable models. *J. Mach. Learn. Res.*, 11:2001–2049.

Siddhant Garg, Thuy Vu, and Alessandro Moschitti. 2019. Tanda: Transfer and adapt pre-trained transformer models for answer sentence selection.

Peter Garrard, Matthew Ralph, and Karalyn Patterson. 2001. Prototypicality, distinctiveness, and intercorrelation: Analyses of the semantic attributes of living and nonliving concepts. *Cognitive neuropsychology*, 18:125–74.

Goran Glavaš, Robert Litschko, Sebastian Ruder, and Ivan Vulić. 2019. How to (properly) evaluate cross-lingual word embeddings: On strong baselines, comparative analyses, and some misconceptions. *CoRR*, abs/1902.00508.

Yoav Goldberg. 2019. Assessing BERT's syntactic abilities.

Geert Heyman, Bregt Verreet, Ivan Vulić, and Marie-Francine Moens. 2019. Learning unsupervised multilingual word embeddings with incremental multilingual hubs. In *Proceedings of the 2019 Conference of the North American Chapter of the Association for Computational Linguistics: Human Language Technologies, Volume 1 (Long and Short Papers)*, pages 1890–1902, Minneapolis, Minnesota. Association for Computational Linguistics.

Annervaz K M, Somnath Basu Roy Chowdhury, and Ambedkar Dukkipati. 2018. Learning beyond datasets: Knowledge graph augmented neural networks for natural language processing. In *Proceedings of the 2018 Conference of the North American Chapter of the Association for Computational Linguistics: Human Language Technologies, Volume 1 (Long Papers)*, pages 313–322, New Orleans, Louisiana. Association for Computational Linguistics.

Jun'ichi Kazama and Jun'ichi Tsujii. 2003. Evaluation and extension of maximum entropy models with inequality constraints. In *Proceedings of the 2003 conference on Empirical methods in natural language processing*, pages 137–144, Morristown, NJ, USA. Association for Computational Linguistics.

Agnan Kessy, Alex Lewin, and Korbinian Strimmer. 2018. Optimal whitening and decorrelation. *The American Statistician*, 72(4):309–314.

Josef Klafka and Allyson Ettinger. 2020. Spying on your neighbors: Fine-grained probing of contextual embeddings for information about surrounding words.

Sawan Kumar, Sharmistha Jat, Karan Saxena, and Partha Talukdar. 2019. Zero-shot word sense disambiguation using sense definition embeddings. In *Proceedings of the 57th Annual Meeting of the Association for Computational Linguistics*, pages 5670–5681, Florence, Italy. Association for Computational Linguistics.

Jinhyuk Lee, Wonjin Yoon, Sungdong Kim, Donghyeon Kim, Sunkyu Kim, Chan Ho So, and Jaewoo Kang. 2019. Biobert: a pre-trained biomedical language representation model for biomedical text mining. *Bioinformatics*.

Yoav Levine, Barak Lenz, Or Dagan, Ori Ram, Dan Padnos, Or Sharir, Shai Shalev-Shwartz, Amnon Shashua, and Yoav Shoham. 2020. SenseBERT: Driving some sense into BERT. In *Proceedings of the 58th Annual Meeting of the Association for Computational Linguistics*, pages 4656–4667, Online. Association for Computational Linguistics.

Tal Linzen, Emmanuel Dupoux, and Yoav Goldberg. 2016. Assessing the ability of LSTMs to learn syntax-sensitive dependencies. *Transactions of the Association for Computational Linguistics*, 4:521–535.

Yinhan Liu, Myle Ott, Naman Goyal, Jingfei Du, Mandar Joshi, Danqi Chen, Omer Levy, Mike Lewis, Luke Zettlemoyer, and Veselin Stoyanov. 2019. Roberta: A robustly optimized bert pretraining approach.

Daniel Loureiro and Alípio Jorge. 2019. Language modelling makes sense: Propagating representations through WordNet for full-coverage word sense disambiguation. In *Proceedings of the 57th Annual Meeting of the Association for Computational Linguistics*, pages 5682–5691, Florence, Italy. Association for Computational Linguistics.

Julien Mairal, Francis R. Bach, Jean Ponce, and Guillermo Sapiro. 2009. Online dictionary learning for sparse coding. In *ICML*, volume 382 of *ACM International Conference Proceeding Series*, pages 689–696. ACM.

André F. T. Martins, Noah A. Smith, Mário A. T. Figueiredo, and Pedro M. Q. Aguiar. 2011. Structured sparsity in structured prediction. In *EMNLP*, pages 1500–1511. ACL.

Rebecca Marvin and Tal Linzen. 2018. Targeted syntactic evaluation of language models. In *Proceedings of the 2018 Conference on Empirical Methods in Natural Language Processing*, pages 1192–1202, Brussels, Belgium. Association for Computational Linguistics.

Ken McRae, George Cree, Mark Seidenberg, and Chris Mcnorgan. 2005. Semantic feature production norms for a large set of living and nonliving things. *Behavior research methods*, 37:547–59.

Rada Mihalcea, Timothy Chklovski, and Adam Kilgarriff. 2004. The senseval-3 english lexical sample task. In *Proceedings of SENSEVAL-3, the Third International Workshop on the Evaluation of Systems for the Semantic Analysis of Text*, pages 25–28, Barcelona, Spain. Association for Computational Linguistics.

George A. Miller. 1995. WordNet: A lexical database for english. *Communications of the ACM*, 38:39–41.

Ishani Mondal. 2020. Bertchem-ddi: Improved drug-drug interaction prediction from text using chemical structure information. *arXiv preprint arXiv:2012.11599*.

Andrea Moro and Roberto Navigli. 2015. SemEval-2015 task 13: Multilingual all-words sense disambiguation and entity linking. In *Proceedings of the 9th International Workshop on Semantic Evaluation*

(SemEval 2015), pages 288–297, Denver, Colorado. Association for Computational Linguistics.

Tsendsuren Munkhdalai, Meijing Li, Khuyagbaatar Batsuren, Hyeon Park, Nak Choi, and Keun Ho Ryu. 2015. Incorporating domain knowledge in chemical and biomedical named entity recognition with word representations. *J. Cheminformatics*, 7(S-1):S9.

Yuri Murayama, Lis Kanashiro Pereira, and Ichiro Kobayashi. 2020. Dialogue over context and structured knowledge using a neural network model with external memories. In *Proceedings of Knowledgeable NLP: the First Workshop on Integrating Structured Knowledge and Neural Networks for NLP*, pages 11–20, Suzhou, China. Association for Computational Linguistics.

Brian Murphy, Partha Talukdar, and Tom Mitchell. 2012. Learning effective and interpretable semantic models using non-negative sparse embedding. In *Proceedings of COLING 2012*, pages 1933–1950, Mumbai, India. The COLING 2012 Organizing Committee.

Roberto Navigli, David Jurgens, and Daniele Vannella. 2013. SemEval-2013 task 12: Multilingual word sense disambiguation. In *Second Joint Conference on Lexical and Computational Semantics (*SEM), Volume 2: Proceedings of the Seventh International Workshop on Semantic Evaluation (SemEval 2013)*, pages 222–231, Atlanta, Georgia, USA. Association for Computational Linguistics.

Sungjoon Park, JinYeong Bak, and Alice Oh. 2017. Rotated word vector representations and their interpretability. In *Proceedings of the 2017 Conference on Empirical Methods in Natural Language Processing*, pages 401–411, Copenhagen, Denmark. Association for Computational Linguistics.

Tommaso Pasini, Alessandro Raganato, and Roberto Navigli. 2021. XL-WSD: An extra-large and cross-lingual evaluation framework for word sense disambiguation. In *Proc. of AAAI*.

Matthew E. Peters, Mark Neumann, Mohit Iyyer, Matt Gardner, Christopher Clark, Kenton Lee, and Luke Zettlemoyer. 2018. Deep contextualized word representations.

Sameer S. Pradhan, Edward Loper, Dmitriy Dligach, and Martha Palmer. 2007. Semeval-2007 task 17: English lexical sample, srl and all words. In *Proceedings of the 4th International Workshop on Semantic Evaluations*, SemEval '07, pages 87–92, Stroudsburg, PA, USA. Association for Computational Linguistics.

Colin Raffel, Noam Shazeer, Adam Roberts, Katherine Lee, Sharan Narang, Michael Matena, Yanqi Zhou, Wei Li, and Peter J. Liu. 2019. Exploring the limits of transfer learning with a unified text-to-text transformer.

Alessandro Raganato, Jose Camacho-Collados, and Roberto Navigli. 2017a. Word sense disambiguation: A unified evaluation framework and empirical comparison. In *Proceedings of the 15th Conference of the European Chapter of the Association for Computational Linguistics: Volume 1, Long Papers*, pages 99–110, Valencia, Spain. Association for Computational Linguistics.

Alessandro Raganato, Claudio Delli Bovi, and Roberto Navigli. 2017b. Neural sequence learning models for word sense disambiguation. In *Proceedings of the 2017 Conference on Empirical Methods in Natural Language Processing*, pages 1156–1167, Copenhagen, Denmark. Association for Computational Linguistics.

Victor Sanh, Lysandre Debut, Julien Chaumond, and Thomas Wolf. 2019. Distilbert, a distilled version of bert: smaller, faster, cheaper and lighter. *CoRR*, abs/1910.01108.

Alexandra Savelieva, Bryan Au-Yeung, and Vasanth Ramani. 2020. Abstractive summarization of spoken and written instructions with BERT. In *Proceedings of the KDD 2020 Workshop on Conversational Systems Towards Mainstream Adoption co-located with the 26TH ACM SIGKDD Conference on Knowledge Discovery and Data Mining (SIGKDD 2020), Virtual Workshop, August 24, 2020.*

Anant Subramanian, Danish Pruthi, Harsh Jhamtani, Taylor Berg-Kirkpatrick, and Eduard Hovy. 2017. Spine: Sparse interpretable neural embeddings.

Alex Wang, Yada Pruksachatkun, Nikita Nangia, Amanpreet Singh, Julian Michael, Felix Hill, Omer Levy, and Samuel R. Bowman. 2019. SuperGLUE: A stickier benchmark for general-purpose language understanding systems.

William Webber, Alistair Moffat, and Justin Zobel. 2010. A similarity measure for indefinite rankings. *ACM Trans. Inf. Syst.*, 28(4).

Leon Weber, Pasquale Minervini, Jannes Münchmeyer, Ulf Leser, and Tim Rocktäschel. 2019. NLProlog: Reasoning with weak unification for question answering in natural language. In *Proceedings of the 57th Annual Meeting of the Association for Computational Linguistics*, pages 6151–6161, Florence, Italy. Association for Computational Linguistics.

Ethan Wilcox, Roger Levy, Takashi Morita, and Richard Futrell. 2018. What do RNN language models learn about filler–gap dependencies? In *Proceedings of the 2018 EMNLP Workshop BlackboxNLP: Analyzing and Interpreting Neural Networks for NLP*, pages 211–221, Brussels, Belgium. Association for Computational Linguistics.

Colby Wise, Vassilis N. Ioannidis, Miguel Romero Calvo, Xiang Song, George Price, Ninad Kulkarni, Ryan Brand, Parminder Bhatia, and George Karypis.

2020. Covid-19 knowledge graph: Accelerating information retrieval and discovery for scientific literature. *CoRR*, abs/2007.12731.

Yu Yan, Weizhen Qi, Yeyun Gong, Dayiheng Liu, Nan Duan, Jiusheng Chen, Ruofei Zhang, and Ming Zhou. 2020. ProphetNet: Predicting future n-gram for sequence-to-sequence pre-training.

Dani Yogatama and Noah A. Smith. 2014. Linguistic structured sparsity in text categorization. In *Proceedings of the 52nd Annual Meeting of the Association for Computational Linguistics (Volume 1: Long Papers)*, pages 786–796, Baltimore, Maryland. Association for Computational Linguistics.

L. K. Şenel, İ. Utlu, V. Yücesoy, A. Koç, and T. Çukur. 2018. Semantic structure and interpretability of word embeddings. *IEEE/ACM Transactions on Audio, Speech, and Language Processing*, 26(10):1769–1779.

Lütfi Kerem Şenel, İhsan Utlu, Furkan Şahinuç, Haldun M. Ozaktas, and Aykut Koç. 2020. Imparting interpretability to word embeddings while preserving semantic structure. *Natural Language Engineering*, page 1–26.

Personal Bias in Prediction of Emotions Elicited by Textual Opinions

Piotr Miłkowski*, **Marcin Gruza***, **Kamil Kanclerz***,
Przemysław Kazienko*, **Damian Grimling**†, **Jan Kocoń***
*Wrocław University of Science and Technology, Wrocław, Poland
†Sentimenti Sp. z o.o., Poznań, Poland
{piotr.milkowski,marcin.gruza,kamil.kanclerz,
przemyslaw.kazienko,jan.kocon}@pwr.edu.pl
damian@sentimenti.com

Abstract

Analysis of emotions elicited by opinions, comments, or articles commonly exploits annotated corpora, in which the labels assigned to documents average the views of all annotators, or represent a majority decision. The models trained on such data are effective at identifying the general views of the population. However, their usefulness for predicting the emotions evoked by the textual content in a particular individual is limited. In this paper, we present a study performed on a dataset containing 7,000 opinions, each annotated by about 50 people with two dimensions: valence, arousal, and with intensity of eight emotions from Plutchik's model. Our study showed that individual responses often significantly differed from the mean. Therefore, we proposed a novel measure to estimate this effect – Personal Emotional Bias (PEB). We also developed a new BERT-based transformer architecture to predict emotions from an individual human perspective. We found PEB a major factor for improving the quality of personalized reasoning. Both the method and measure may boost the quality of content recommendation systems and personalized solutions that protect users from hate speech or unwanted content, which are highly subjective in nature.

1 Introduction

Emotions are a very important component of natural human communication. Collectively, we tend to react quite similarly emotionally to phenomena around us, but at the level of the individual, some differences can be discerned in the intensity of the emotions experienced. Various emotional models have been used in different studies. In Russell and Mehrabian (1977), emotional states are located in a multidimensional space, with valence (negative/positive), arousal (low/high) and dominance explaining most of the observed variance. Another approach distinguishes different number of basic, discrete emotions, e.g. six by Ekman and Friesen (1976) and eight by Plutchik (1982).

We can observe continuous interest in sentiment analysis and emotion recognition within the filed of natural language processing (Kocoń and Maziarz, 2021; Alswaidan and Menai, 2020; Kanclerz et al., 2020). Recently, they commonly rely on deep machine learning methods applied to large amounts of textual data (Yadav and Vishwakarma, 2020; Kocoń et al., 2019b; Kocoń et al., 2019). Nevertheless, emotion recognition remains a challenging task. One of the reasons is the lack of high quality annotated data, where annotators are a representative sample of the whole population. Commonly, a small number (usually 2 to 5) of trained annotators are involved. Due to differences between individual opinions, reinforced by multiple choice possibilities (6 or 8 emotions), this often leads to low inter-annotator agreement (Hripcsak and Rothschild, 2005). Averaging the annotations collected in such a way can still be a good input for effective systems recognizing the most likely emotional responses shared by most people. This, however, is not suitable to make accurate inferences about emotions to be evoked in specific individuals.

In this work, we developed a method to predict text-related emotions that most closely reflect the reactions of a given reader. In addition to the classical approach of providing only texts to the model input, we extended it with our new feature – Personal Emotional Bias (PEB). It reflects how an individual perceived the texts they evaluated in the past. In this way, we switched from averaging labels for annotated texts to individual text annotations. We tested the impact of PEB on individual recognition quality of emotion dimensions, also in a setup including multilingual transformer-based architecture for the following languages: Dutch, En-

Proceedings of the Joint Conference of the 59th Annual Meeting of the Association for Computational Linguistics and the 11th International Joint Conference on Natural Language Processing: Student Research Workshop, pages 248–259
August 5–6, 2021.

glish, Polish, French, German, Italian, Portuguese, Russian and Spanish. Our experimental evaluation revealed that emotional annotation of just a few texts is appears to be enough to calculate the approximate value of Personal Emotional Bias for a given user. This, in turn, enables us to significantly improve personalized reasoning. Since texts are independently annotated with ten emotional states, each with its own level, we trained and tested both multi-task classifiers and multivariate regressors.

This work is inspired by our initial idea of human-centred processing presented in (Kocoń et al., 2021). In addition, in paper (Kanclerz et al., 2021), we have shown that mixing user conformity measures with document controversy is efficient in personalized recognition of aggressiveness in texts.

2 Related work

The studies have shown that the recognition of emotions should take into account the subjective assessments of individual annotators (Neviarouskaya et al., 2009; Chou and Lee, 2019; Kocoń et al., 2019a). A personal bias related to the individual beliefs may have its origins in the demographic background and many factors such as the first language, age, education (Wich et al., 2020a; Al Kuwatly et al., 2020), country of origin (Salminen et al., 2018), gender (Bolukbasi et al., 2016; Binns et al., 2017; Tatman, 2017; Wojatzki et al., 2018), and race (Blodgett and O'Connor, 2017; Sap et al., 2019; Davidson et al., 2019; Xia et al., 2020). The uniqueness of person's annotations may also be derived from their political orientations and not respecting them can significantly reduce the effectiveness of the classifier (Wich et al., 2020b).

The most common approach to mitigate the impact of personal bias on method performance is to utilize only annotations provided by the experts (Waseem, 2016). However, we should be aware that selecting a small group of experts poses a risk of involving too few annotators for too many documents (Wiegand et al., 2019) or creating unfair models, that will discriminate minorities (Dixon et al., 2018). Besides, it may be difficult to find the sufficient number of experts. To resolve this, non-expert annotators can be involved. An average of annotations from non-expert is enough to achieve expert-level labeling quality (Snow et al., 2008). Personal bias also affects the model evaluation process. Therefore, annotations from a separate set of annotators should be used in the training and test set (Geva et al., 2019).

The high variety of annotators' beliefs directly impacts the diversity of their subjective assessments. It often means that there is no single correct label for a given text (Aroyo and Welty, 2013). In such case, Bayesian probabilistic models can be used to estimate consensus level, which can then be converted to categorical values using simple methods, e.g. thresholding (Kara et al., 2015). Another solution is to regard disagreement in annotations as a positive factor that will provide more information about single humans. This ambiguity can be utilized in many ways. Patterns discovered from differences in annotations can be exploited both to group like-minded individuals (Akhtar et al., 2020) and to automatic detect spammers, deliberately introducing noise into their assessments (Raykar and Yu, 2012; Soberón et al., 2013). On the other hand, too high annotations similarity level may be related to the conformity bias, which reflects an excessive influence of the group's beliefs on its members (Gao et al., 2019). Moreover, annotation disagreement can determine the ambiguity of a given text (Aroyo and Welty, 2013). The variability between annotators can also be used to generate soft labels such as inter-annotator standard deviation, which may be an additional feature of a given sample (Eyben et al., 2012). Such soft labels can also be a good source of information about annotators themselves, e.g. to estimate the unanimity of a specific social group in recognizing emotions (Steidl et al., 2005). Another approach is to leverage the ensemble model architecture to incorporate knowledge regarding the subjectivity of emotion recognition (Fayek et al., 2016). In order to reduce the potential noise caused by relying solely on subjective annotations, a hybrid method can be applied mixing both individual ratings and majority voting (Chou and Lee, 2019). The final model consists of multiple sub-models using annotations of individuals separated and combined. All sub-models are fused providing one general and non-personalized decision.

The topic of emotion personalization was explored in the context of social photos (Zhao et al., 2016) or emotions evoked by music (Yang et al., 2007). However, in the context of text analysis, it has not been studied sufficiently yet.

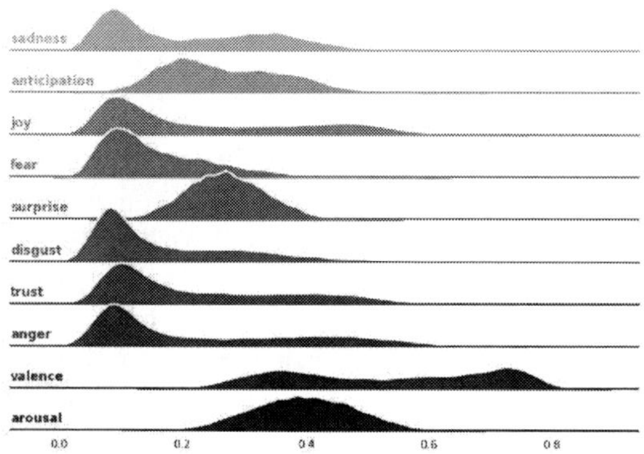

Figure 1: Rating distributions within emotional categories. All values are normalized to the interval [0,1].

3 Dataset and annotation procedure

To create a Sentimenti[1] dataset, a combined approach of different methodologies were used, namely: Computer Assisted Personal Interview (CAPI) and Computer Assisted Web Interview (CAWI) (Kocoń et al., 2019a). Two studies were carried out involving evaluation of: 30,000 word meanings (CAWI1) and 7,000 reviews from the Internet (CAWI2). Reviews cover 3 areas: medicine (3,130 texts), hotels (2,938 texts), and other (936 texts). In this work, we will focus on the use of CAWI2 due to the evaluation of entire documents within the study.

In the CAWI2 study, each text received an average of 50 annotations. To obtain reliable results, the following cross-section of the population was used: 8,853 unique respondents were sampled from the Polish population. Sex, age, native language, place of residence, education level, marital status, employment status, political beliefs and income were controlled, among other factors.

The annotation schema was based on the procedures most widely used in NAWL (Riegel et al., 2015), NAWL BE (Wierzba et al., 2015) and plWordNet-emo (Zaśko-Zielińska et al., 2015; Janz et al., 2017; Kocoń et al., 2018; Kulisiewicz et al., 2015). Therefore, the acquired data consists of ten emotional categories: *valence*, *arousal*, and eight basic emotions: *sadness, anticipation, joy, fear, surprise, disgust, trust* and *anger*. Mean text rating distributions within emotional categories are presented in Figure 1. In total, 7k opinions * average of 53.46 annotators per opinion * 10 categories = 3.74M single annotations were collected.

[1]https://www.sentimenti.com/

The annotation process was carried out using the web-based system with an interface designed in collaboration with the team of psychologists to reduce as much as possible the difficulty of handling the annotation process and its impact on grades or their quality (see Figure 2). The collection resulting from the study is copyrighted and we got permission to conduct the research. A sample containing 100 texts with annotations and annotators' metadata with the source code of the experiments are publicly available on GitHub[2].

4 Personal Emotional Bias – PEB and agreement measures

In principle, we assume our collection (Internet review documents) is split into three partitions: *past* (D^{past}), *present*, and *future* (Figure 3). The past texts are used to estimate individual user beliefs and biases. The present documents allow us to train the reasoning model, whereas the future reviews are for the evaluation, test purposes.

To quantify individual subjective emotional perception of textual content, we introduce a new measure – *Personal Emotional Bias*, $PEB(u, c)$. It describes to what extent the previously known annotations $v_{c,d,u}$ of the given user u differ from the average annotations provided by all others for emotional category c, aggregated over all documents $d \in D^{past}$. Emotional category $c \in C$, where $C = \{sadness, anticipation, joy, fear, surprise, disgust, trust, anger, valence, arousal\}$. Integer values of the emotional annotations $v_{c,d,u}$ come from the study design, Figure 2, i.e. $v_{c,d,u} \in \{-3, -2, -1, 0, 1, 2, 3\}$, if $c = valence$ and $v_{c,d,u} \in \{0, 1, 2, 3, 4\}$ otherwise.

First, we need to compute the mean emotional value $\mu_{c,d}$ of each document $d \in D^{past}$ in each category c over all previously known d's annotations, i.e. provided by users from the train data, $u \in U_d^{train}$:

$$\mu_{c,d} = \frac{\sum_{u \in U_d^{train}} v_{c,d,u}}{|U_d^{train}|}, d \in D^{past}$$

In the next step, we calculate the standard deviation $\sigma_{c,d}$ of each emotional category c for each document d in a similar way:

[2]https://github.com/CLARIN-PL/personal-bias

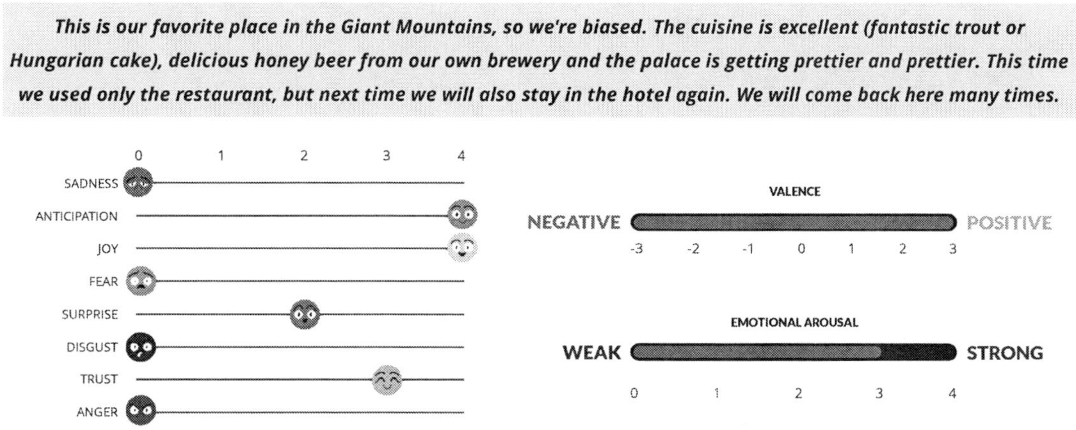

Figure 2: Emotional annotations for a real example of the hotel review – the CAWI study. Participants scored eight basic emotions (Plutchik model), arousal and valence on separate scales; varying from 0 to 4 for emotions and arousal and -3 to 3 for valence. Example review was manually translated from Polish to English.

$$\sigma_{c,d} = \sqrt{\frac{\sum_{u \in U_d^{train}} (v_{c,d,u} - \mu_{c,d})^2}{|U_d^{train}|}}, d \in D^{past}$$

Based on the above knowledge, we can estimate the Personal Emotional Bias $PEB(u, c)$ of the user u for the emotional category c. It is an aggregated Z-score, as follows:

$$PEB(u, c) = \frac{\sum_{d \in D_u^{past}} \frac{v_{c,d,u} - \mu_{c,d}}{\sigma_{c,d}}}{|D_u^{past}|}$$

where D_u^{past} is the set of documents $d \in D^{past}$ annotated by user u.

Please note that $PEB(u, c)$ may be calculated for any user, who provided their annotations to any document $d \in D^{past}$. It means that we can estimate PEB for users from the *dev* and *test* set, always aggregated over *past* documents. Nevertheless, components $\mu_{c,d}$ and $\sigma_{c,d}$ are fixed and computed only based on the previously known knowledge, i.e. for users from the *train* set. Obviously, the *train*, *dev*, and *test* sets are different for each out of ten cross-validation folds, which forces the recalculation of all PEB values at each fold.

The PEB measure provides us information about the unique views and preferences of the individual user. We suspect PEB to be more informative in the case of ambiguous texts with relatively low agreement among the annotators. To measure this agreement we leveraged two different document controversy measures: (1) the averaged Krippendorff's alpha coefficient α^{int} (Krippendorff, 2013) and (2) the general $contr^{std}$ controversy measure. The former is commonly used; it is resistant to missing annotations (Al Kuwatly et al., 2020; Wich et al., 2020a; Binns et al., 2017). According to our data, we used the variant of Krippendorff's alpha coefficient α^{int} with the interval difference function $\delta^{interval}(v_{c,d,u}, v_{c,d,u'})$ which calculates the distance between the two annotations $v_{c,d,u}$ and $v_{c,d,u'}$ for document d provided by two different users u and u' regarding emotional category c:

$$\delta^{interval}(v_{c,d,u}, v_{c,d,u'}) = (v_{c,d,u} - v_{c,d,u'})^2$$

Our first emotional controversy measure is expressed by the Krippendorff's alpha coefficient α_c^{int} separately calculated for the specified emotional category $c \in C$.

The alternative second measure $contr^{std}(d)$ was also used to analyze the controversial nature of any document d. It is the standard deviation of user ratings averaged over all emotional categories $c \in C$:

$$contr^{std}(d) = \frac{\sum_{c \in C} \sigma_{c,d}}{|C|}$$

5 Experimental plan, scenarios

All experiments were performed for two types of machine learning tasks, Figure 4:

- **Multi-task classification** - where each task was to predict an accurate discrete answer for each emotional category, i.e. one of the

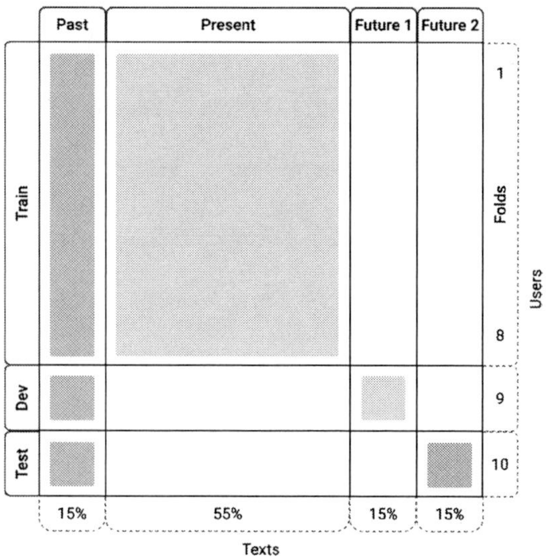

Figure 3: The CAWI2 collection was divided by the texts (columns) and the users/annotators (rows). The *past* texts (15% of all) were used to compute the PEB measure. The models were trained on 55% of the *present* texts and 80% of all users. They are verified with the *dev* set (disjoint from *train*) and tested on the *test* set - both containing 10% of users and 15% of texts each. The aforementioned proportions were chosen so that there were at least 1000 texts and more than 500 annotators in each section. The user-based split into *train*, *dev* and *test* is performed in the 10-fold cross-validation schema.

five classes {0, 1, 2, 3, 4} for eight emotions and arousal, and one out of seven classes for valence. Due to data imbalance ('0' was the dominating class for most emotions), the F1-macro measure was used to estimate the model performance;

- **Multivariate regression** - where the task was to estimate the numerical value of each emotional category. Such approach takes into account the distances between user ratings. R-squared measure was applied to compute the model quality.

In order to investigate the effect of PEB on emotion recognition for individual annotators, the following scenarios of the input data were considered:

- **AVG** - mean value of the annotation (regression) or most common class (classification) for all texts compared to the target values; this scenario is treated as initial baseline;
- **TXT** - text embeddings; it was the main baseline;

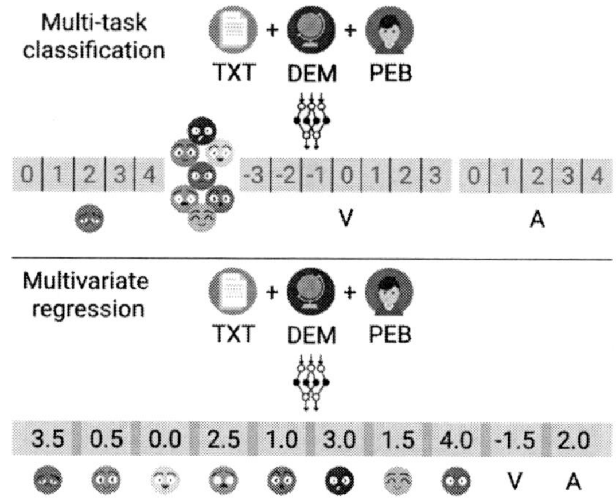

Figure 4: Two approaches to reasoning: (1) 10-task classification and (2) multivariate regression. In (1), the output contains 10 out of 52 classes. In (2), the output contains 10 real values, one for each emotional category. V – valence, A – emotional arousal.

- **TXT+DEM** - text embeddings and annotator demographic data;
- **TXT+PEB** - text embeddings and annotator's PEB;
- **ALL** - text embeddings, demographic data and PEB;

Additional **SIZE** scenario was performed to examine the impact of the number of annotated texts in PEB on the emotion recognition quality.

As a source of text embeddings the following models for Polish were used: (1) HerBERT, (2) XLM-RoBERTa, (3) fastText and (4) RoBERTa. The first one – HerBERT is currently considered state of the art according to the KLEJ benchmark (Rybak et al., 2020). Two neural network architectures were used to perform the experiments: (1) multi-layer perceptron (MLP) for transformer-based text embeddings (2) LSTM for fastText-based word embeddings (with 32 hidden units and a dropout equal to 0.5) with MLP to combine LSTM output with additional features. In both cases, the size of the input depends on the input embedding size. MLP output for classification is a multi-hot vector of length 52 (8 emotions x 5 possible ratings, 7 possible valence ratings, and 5 possible emotional arousal ratings), and for regression – a vector of size 10 containing real values ranging from 0 to 1 for each emotion dimension.

Ten fold cross-validation was applied as randomized non-overlapping partition of users and one division of texts, Figure 3. Such an approach is in line with leave-one-subject-out (LOSO) cross-validation where data is also split according to participants (subjects), i.e. data on one or more users are separated in the test set. Recently, it is commonly treated as SOTA approach in emotion recognition (Barlett et al., 1993; Schmidt et al., 2019)

In the SIZE scenario, we verified what incremental gain in model evaluation score we would achieve by increasing the number of texts in PEB (Figure 5 and Figure 6). The PEB measure denotes how much emotional perception of a given user differs from opinions of other users. To examine the significance of PEB for different emotional dimensions, we calculated the correlation between the PEB model results (R-squared) and the Krippendorff's alpha coefficient α_c^{int} for each emotional category $c \in C$.

To investigate the impact of PEB also for multiple languages, we translated Polish texts automatically into 8 languages using DeepL[3]. According to our manual tests and evaluation of translation quality, DeepL is characterized by better context matching of the target language utterances than other solutions available on the market. We applied the original annotations to the translated texts and then prepared dedicated models using XLM-RoBERTa. The training, test and validation sets were identical for all languages. The results are in Table 5 for classification and Table 6 for regression.

In order to verify the significance of differences between the evaluation results of each model in each scenario, we performed the independent samples t-test with the Bonferroni correction, as we tested more than two different models. We also checked the normality assumptions before its execution using Shapiro-Wilk test. If a sample did not meet them, we used the non-parametric Mann-Whitney U test.

6 Results

The results for all experimental scenarios and models, averaged collectively over ten folds are presented in Table 1 for classification and Table 2 for regression. The performance for each emotional category for all experimental variants for the best model (HerBERT), is specified in Table 3 for classification and Table 4 for regression. The results of multilingual model (XLM-RoBERTa) trained on sets translated into 8 languages can be seen in Table 5 for classification and Table 6 for regression.

[3] https://www.deepl.com/

	AVG	TXT	TXT+DEM	PEB	TXT+PEB	ALL
(1) HerBERT	5.97	**17.69**	**21.94**	32.02	**38.42**	**38.81**
(2) XLM-RoBERTa	5.97	**17.30**	**21.29**	31.91	**38.20**	**38.44**
(3) fastText+LSTM	5.97	16.48	20.52	32.09	37.25	**38.36**
(4) Polish RoBERTa	5.97	**17.01**	20.39	32.05	37.10	37.38

Table 1: Classification performance: F1-macro (%) averaged over ten folds. The best model for a specified scenario (column) is marked in **bold**; the best scenario for a given model (row) is underlined. More than one marked value means statistical insignificance between them.

	AVG	TXT	TXT+DEM	PEB	TXT+PEB	ALL
(1) HerBERT	-0.17	**13.16**	**14.37**	32.27	**45.96**	**45.64**
(2) XLM-RoBERTa	-0.17	**12.11**	**13.08**	32.24	**44.76**	**44.49**
(3) fastText+LSTM	-0.17	10.93	11.70	32.45	**43.74**	**43.50**
(4) Polish RoBERTa	-0.17	9.92	10.53	32.26	42.45	42.29

Table 2: Performance of regression models: R-squared averaged over folds. The best model in a given scenario (column) is in **bold**; the best scenario for a model (row) is underlined. More than one value highlighted means statistical insignificance between them.

Figure 5 presents R-squared results of reasoning for the TXT+PEB scenario and HerBERT model in relation to the number of texts from the *past* set used to estimate personal bias $PEB(u, c)$; averaged over all emotional categories and all users u. The past texts d annotated by user u are either randomly selected or starting from the most controversial, i.e. with the greatest $contrstd(d)$ value among all annotated by u in the past. The component results for each emotion and only for random selection are in Figure 6.

Figure 7 depicts the correlation between the annotation consistency counted using Krippendorff's alpha and the prediction performance in the regression task on the best model – HerBERT.

7 Discussion

The best results for each model were observed in the TXT+PEB scenario. The use of demographic data as additional user characteristics apart from the PEB measure in the ALL scenario did not provided significantly better results. HerBERT model achieved the best results, but differences between models are not statistically significant (except for the Polish RoBERTa).

The performance improvement related to demographic data about individual users was considered in the TXT+DEM scenario. Demographic features encode bias for social groups. However, once we have individual biases (the PEB measure), demographics becomes redundant and negatively affects

	AVG	TXT	TXT+DEM	PEB	TXT+PEB	ALL	std	α_c^{int}
sadness	6.28±0.18	16.47±0.90	21.91±1.08	29.93±2.12	37.85±1.26	37.68±0.94	1.18	0.18
anticipation	6.11±0.32	13.43±0.26	19.14±1.12	36.21±2.00	38.58±1.35	38.68±1.61	1.32	0.06
joy	5.64±0.26	20.58±1.36	25.58±1.22	30.69±1.65	39.13±1.24	39.62±1.74	1.28	0.24
fear	5.20±0.23	16.07±0.29	18.57±1.30	34.58±1.65	38.80±1.25	39.22±1.88	1.07	0.09
surprise	6.45±0.28	13.05±0.31	16.73±1.28	35.07±1.15	36.23±1.04	37.52±1.37	1.30	0.02
disgust	5.22±0.31	17.32±0.80	20.13±1.37	30.31±1.69	36.25±1.07	36.75±0.94	1.13	0.16
trust	5.36±0.27	17.11±0.76	22.71±1.43	30.02±1.45	37.07±1.00	38.94±1.56	1.26	0.19
anger	5.33±0.21	21.09±0.79	24.42±1.30	29.90±1.71	37.91±1.32	38.12±1.19	1.31	0.25
arousal	7.99±0.18	18.80±1.63	24.42±1.30	42.08±1.31	45.48±0.98	44.45±0.72	1.28	0.05
valence	6.10±0.21	23.00±1.42	25.75±1.12	21.45±1.39	36.89±0.82	37.15±1.26	1.58	0.38

Table 3: Classification performance – F1-macro for HerBERT model; last two columns are (1) aggregated standard deviation (std) and (2) Krippendorff's alpha coefficient α_c^{int}.

	AVG	TXT	TXT+DEM	PEB	TXT+PEB	ALL	std	α_c^{int}
sadness	-0.14±0.13	14.08±1.85	14.73±2.27	30.24±3.37	44.93±2.46	44.40±2.74	1.18	0.18
anticipation	-0.12±0.13	5.03±0.77	6.60±2.10	44.24±2.66	49.50±2.27	49.21±2.43	1.32	0.06
joy	-0.13±0.15	20.20±2.21	21.41±2.19	26.82±2.92	47.66±2.00	47.50±1.97	1.28	0.24
fear	-0.22±0.30	6.89±1.41	8.75±1.67	38.77±4.08	46.34±3.38	46.05±3.46	1.07	0.09
surprise	-0.14±0.17	1.00±0.55	2.82±2.62	43.20±2.75	44.96±2.58	44.42±2.72	1.30	0.02
disgust	-0.25±0.29	12.93±1.58	14.03±1.70	29.38±3.43	43.06±3.02	42.84±3.25	1.13	0.16
trust	-0.13±0.21	15.92±1.50	16.81±1.73	29.72±3.25	45.69±2.36	45.57±2.25	1.26	0.19
anger	-0.17±0.15	20.04±2.15	20.51±2.31	23.72±2.95	44.61±2.27	44.41±2.29	1.31	0.25
arousal	-0.20±0.21	3.05±1.10	4.70±1.28	47.30±1.98	50.87±1.52	50.37±1.70	1.28	0.05
valence	-0.16±0.13	32.44±2.75	33.35±2.56	9.32±2.22	41.98±1.61	41.68±1.49	1.58	0.38

Table 4: Regression performance – R-squared for HerBERT model; last two columns are (1) aggregated standard deviation (std) and (2) Krippendorff's alpha coefficient α_c^{int}.

	AVG	TXT	TXT+DEM	PEB	TXT+PEB	ALL
Dutch	5.97	17.44	20.83	32.03	37.88	38.24
English	5.97	17.47	21.19	32.20	37.75	38.32
French	5.97	17.13	21.08	32.23	37.48	38.19
German	5.97	17.13	21.04	32.14	37.85	38.13
Italian	5.97	17.12	20.84	31.73	37.66	38.24
Portuguese	5.97	17.35	21.03	31.99	37.70	38.29
Russian	5.97	17.23	21.30	32.32	37.75	38.27
Spanish	5.97	17.42	21.35	32.19	37.75	38.35

Table 5: Classification results (F1-macro, XLM-RoBERTa) for the texts translated into eight languages.

	AVG	TXT	TXT+DEM	PEB	TXT+PEB	ALL
Dutch	-0.17	11.76	12.75	32.29	44.41	44.11
English	-0.17	12.04	12.91	32.23	44.70	44.33
French	-0.17	11.79	12.67	32.26	44.44	44.13
German	-0.17	11.76	12.50	32.30	44.42	44.04
Italian	-0.17	11.69	12.75	32.20	44.39	44.11
Portuguese	-0.17	11.74	12.60	32.31	44.46	44.11
Russian	-0.17	11.74	12.33	32.22	44.35	44.07
Spanish	-0.17	11.79	12.66	32.26	44.43	44.08

Table 6: Regression results (R-squared, XLM-RoBERTa) for the texts translated into eight languages.

the results: compare TXT+PEB vs. ALL.

The PEB measure quantifies the difference in opinions of a particular user with respect to the others. In addition to beliefs, user decisions are also influenced by UI design. Several emotional categories could prove to be incomprehensible to individual users, so that their annotations do not reflect their opinions. Moreover, the scale of values could be misunderstood by some annotators who could mark the middle value when they were unsure whether a given emotional category was present in the analyzed text at all.

The use of simple statistical methods based on the averaged opinion about the text presented in the AVG scenario performs much worse than language models combined with MLP. Predicting the user's opinion solely upon the text in the TXT scenario (our baseline) results in poor performance. Therefore, there is a need to exploit personalized user data. The phenomenon of improving inference thanks to personalization is the same for each of the four considered models. It means that the proper personalization carried out at the stage of input data is much more important than the language model

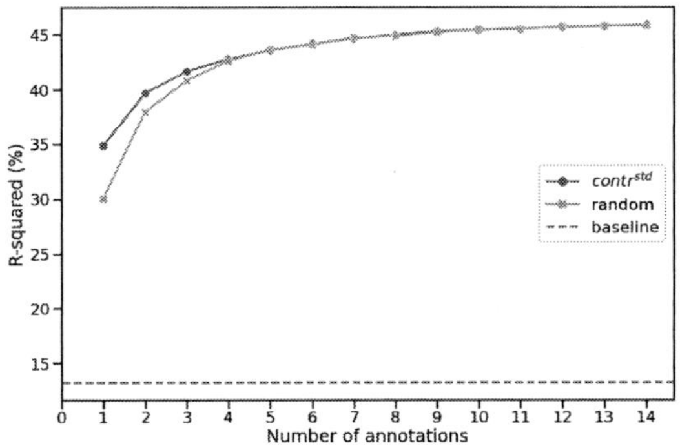

Figure 5: R-squared results on TXT+PEB scenario and HerBERT model in relation to the number of texts from the *past* set used to compute $PEB(u, c)$ values for a given user u, averaged over all emotional categories and all users. Two text selection procedures were considered: random and the most controversial – $contr^{std}(d)$. The baseline is the TXT scenario. The results for emotion categories and random selection are in Figure 6.

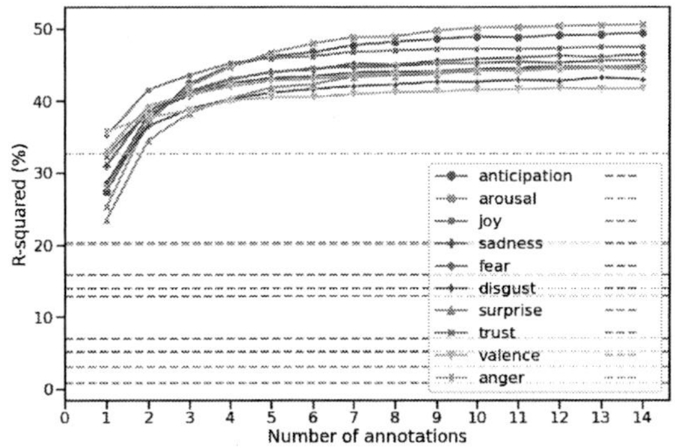

Figure 6: R-squared results on TXT+PEB scenario and HerBERT model in relation to the number of texts from the *past* set, randomly selected to compute $PEB(u, c)$ averaged over all users u – the solid lines. The dotted lines of the same color is the baseline for a given category (the TXT scenario).

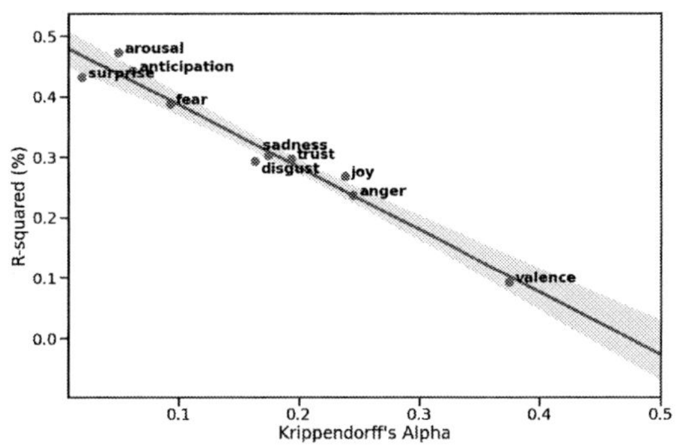

Figure 7: R-squared results on PEB scenario and HerBERT model in relation to Krippendorff's Alpha. Each data point corresponds to a separate emotional category from Table 4.

or inference model.

In the case of regression models, the complementary nature of the PEB measure and the text itself is clearly visible, see the PEB and TXT scenarios in Table 2, Table 4, and Table 6. This is manifested in a large number of cases in which a higher quality of inference from the text (TXT scenario) corresponds to the lower quality of the PEB-based inference (PEB scenario) and vice versa. In turn, their combination provides very good results. We calculated the correlation value for the results of evaluation over each emotional category and they are equal to -0.558 and -0,970 for the results in Table 3 and Table 4, respectively. We also analyzed the correlation between two values: (1) the sum of the results in the TXT and PEB scenarios and (2) the result in the TXT + PEB scenario. For the regression models, correlations are 0.999, 0.995, 0.896 for the results in Table 2, Table 4 and Table 6, respectively. In a similar way, we computed the correlation values for the results of the classification models; they reach: 0.802, 0.931, 0.257, for data from Table 1, Table 3 and Table 5, respectively.

The performance in the PEB scenario is the lowest for the valence category, which may result from the highest agreement level ($\alpha_c^{int} = 0.38$) and more flat distribution, Figure 1. Simultaneously, the reasoning based on text only (TXT scenario) demonstrated an opposite dependency: its performance is greatest for the highest agreement (valence) and lowest for low agreements (surprise, arousal and anticipation). It means that the more users disagree, to the greater extent we should rely on personal biases rather than solely on the textual content.

Even only one document annotated by a user utilized to estimate PEB can boost the reasoning, Figure 5. Moreover, only about 5-7 texts provided in the past are enough to capture the personal user beliefs. Later on, the gains are much smaller. This is valid for all emotional categories, Figure 6. The benefit is greater if PEB is computed for 1-3 most controversial texts ($contr^{std}$) annotated by a given user.

We have discovered a nearly linear negative correlation between annotators' agreement level (Krippendorff's alpha coefficient) and performance of the regression model based only on the personal bias (PEB), Figure 7.

8 Conclusions

Summarizing the experiments performed, we can draw several conclusions related to additional data that can be gathered during the annotation process. By means of them, we are able to significantly improve reasoning about emotional categories, i.e. prediction of emotions evoked by the given textual opinion in different people.

The most important conclusion is that the use of our proposed Personal Emotional Bias measure allows for a tremendous gain in prediction scores for the particular annotator. Thus, we have shown that using the current state-of-the-art methods for embedding texts and data from just a few annotations made by an individual user, we can infer the user's perception of emotions with much greater effectiveness. This opens up the possibility of creating dedicated and personalized solutions targeted at specific social groups and individuals we want to reach with a given message.

We have shown that demographic data of annotators have a positive impact on predicting their reactions, however not as much as the answers they provided during the survey itself. In addition, the combination of text content, demographic data and the single PEB feature built on the basis of their historical ratings is even several times better than the quality of responses given by the system based on text data alone.

Such a great influence on the outcome of single-individual data reveals a completely new direction. The NLP solutions should focus more on good design of the annotation process, its flow and single text-annotation sets rather than on post-processing and generalization of data, i.e. common class labels received by majority voting. The best proof of this thesis is the fact that we are able to successfully ignore the problem of annotator disagreement within a given text and fill in these gaps with human information.

In future work, we want to investigate the effect of individual PEB vector components on recognition quality. Additionally, we want to extend the PEB with information about the averaged annotation value of texts. Finally, the quality of dedicated models for individual emotional dimensions can be compared to the multi-task model presented in this work.

Acknowledgments

This work was supported by (1) the National Centre for Research and Development, Poland, grant no. POIR.01.01.01-00-0472/16 – *Sentimenti*; (2) the National Science Centre, Poland, project no. 2020/37/B/ST6/03806; (3) the Polish Ministry of Education and Science, CLARIN-PL Project; (4) the European Regional Development Fund as a part of the 2014-2020 Smart Growth Operational Programme, CLARIN - Common Language Resources and Technology Infrastructure, project no. POIR.04.02.00-00C002/19.

References

Sohail Akhtar, Valerio Basile, and Viviana Patti. 2020. Modeling annotator perspective and polarized opinions to improve hate speech detection. In *Proceedings of the Eighth AAAI Conference on Human Computation and Crowdsourcing*, pages 151–154.

Hala Al Kuwatly, Maximilian Wich, and Georg Groh. 2020. Identifying and measuring annotator bias based on annotators' demographic characteristics. In *Proceedings of the Fourth Workshop on Online Abuse and Harms*, pages 184–190, Online. Association for Computational Linguistics.

Nourah Alswaidan and Mohamed El Bachir Menai. 2020. A survey of state-of-the-art approaches for emotion recognition in text. *Knowledge and Information Systems*, pages 1–51.

Lora Aroyo and Chris Welty. 2013. Harnessing disagreement in crowdsourcing a relation extraction gold standard. Technical report, Technical Report.

M Barlett, G Littlewort, M Frank, C Lainscse, I Fasel, and J Movellan. 1993. Automatic recognition of spontaneous facial actions. *American Psychologist*, 48:384–392.

Reuben Binns, Michael Veale, Max Van Kleek, and Nigel Shadbolt. 2017. Like trainer, like bot? inheritance of bias in algorithmic content moderation. *Social Informatics*, page 405–415.

Su Lin Blodgett and Brendan T. O'Connor. 2017. Racial disparity in natural language processing: A case study of social media african-american english. *ArXiv*, abs/1707.00061.

Tolga Bolukbasi, Kai-Wei Chang, James Zou, Venkatesh Saligrama, and Adam Kalai. 2016. Man is to computer programmer as woman is to homemaker? debiasing word embeddings. In *Proceedings of the 30th International Conference on Neural Information Processing Systems*, NIPS'16, page 4356–4364, Red Hook, NY, USA. Curran Associates Inc.

H. Chou and C. Lee. 2019. Every rating matters: Joint learning of subjective labels and individual annotators for speech emotion classification. In *ICASSP 2019 - 2019 IEEE International Conference on Acoustics, Speech and Signal Processing (ICASSP)*, pages 5886–5890.

Thomas Davidson, Debasmita Bhattacharya, and Ingmar Weber. 2019. Racial bias in hate speech and abusive language detection datasets. In *Proceedings of the Third Workshop on Abusive Language Online*, pages 25–35, Florence, Italy. Association for Computational Linguistics.

Lucas Dixon, John Li, Jeffrey Sorensen, Nithum Thain, and Lucy Vasserman. 2018. Measuring and mitigating unintended bias in text classification. In *Proceedings of the 2018 AAAI/ACM Conference on AI, Ethics, and Society*, AIES '18, page 67–73, New York, NY, USA. Association for Computing Machinery.

Paul Ekman and Wallace V Friesen. 1976. Measuring facial movement. *Environmental psychology and nonverbal behavior*, 1(1):56–75.

Florian Eyben, Martin Wöllmer, and Björn Schuller. 2012. A multitask approach to continuous five-dimensional affect sensing in natural speech. *ACM Trans. Interact. Intell. Syst.*, 2(1).

H. M. Fayek, M. Lech, and L. Cavedon. 2016. Modeling subjectiveness in emotion recognition with deep neural networks: Ensembles vs soft labels. In *2016 International Joint Conference on Neural Networks (IJCNN)*, pages 566–570.

Yang Gao, Steffen Eger, Ilia Kuznetsov, Iryna Gurevych, and Yusuke Miyao. 2019. Does my rebuttal matter? insights from a major NLP conference. *CoRR*, abs/1903.11367.

Mor Geva, Yoav Goldberg, and Jonathan Berant. 2019. Are we modeling the task or the annotator? an investigation of annotator bias in natural language understanding datasets. In *Proceedings of the 2019 Conference on Empirical Methods in Natural Language Processing and the 9th International Joint Conference on Natural Language Processing (EMNLP-IJCNLP)*, pages 1161–1166, Hong Kong, China. Association for Computational Linguistics.

George Hripcsak and Adam S. Rothschild. 2005. Technical Brief: Agreement, the F-Measure, and Reliability in Information Retrieval. *JAMIA*, 12(3):296–298.

Arkadiusz Janz, Jan Kocoń, Maciej Piasecki, and Zaśko-Zielińska Monika. 2017. plWordNet as a Basis for Large Emotive Lexicons of Polish. In *LTC'17 8th Language and Technology Conference*, Poznań, Poland. Fundacja Uniwersytetu im. Adama Mickiewicza w Poznaniu.

Kamil Kanclerz, Alicja Figas, Marcin Gruza, Tomasz Kajdanowicz, Jan Kocoń, Daria Puchalska, and Przemyslaw Kazienko. 2021. Controversy and conformity: from generalized to personalized aggressiveness detection. In *Proceedings of the Joint Conference of the 59th Annual Meeting of the Association for Computational Linguistics and the 11th International Joint Conference on Natural Language Processing (ACL-IJCNLP 2021)*. Association for Computational Linguistics.

Kamil Kanclerz, Piotr Miłkowski, and Jan Kocoń. 2020. Cross-lingual deep neural transfer learning in sentiment analysis. *Procedia Computer Science*, 176:128–137.

Yunus Emre Kara, Gaye Genc, Oya Aran, and Lale Akarun. 2015. Modeling annotator behaviors for crowd labeling. *Neurocomput.*, 160(C):141–156.

Jan Kocoń, Arkadiusz Janz, and Maciej Piasecki. 2018. Classifier-based polarity propagation in a wordnet. In *Proceedings of the Eleventh International Conference on Language Resources and Evaluation (LREC 2018)*.

Jan Kocoń and Marek Maziarz. 2021. Mapping wordnet onto human brain connectome in emotion processing and semantic similarity recognition. *Information Processing & Management*, 58(3):102530.

Jan Kocoń, Piotr Miłkowski, and Monika Zaśko-Zielińska. 2019. Multi-level sentiment analysis of polemo 2.0: Extended corpus of multi-domain consumer reviews. In *Proceedings of the 23rd Conference on Computational Natural Language Learning (CoNLL)*, pages 980–991.

Jan Kocoń, Alicja Figas, Marcin Gruza, Daria Puchalska, Tomasz Kajdanowicz, and Przemysław Kazienko. 2021. Offensive, aggressive, and hate speech analysis: from data-centric to human-centred approach. *Information Processing & Management*.

Jan Kocoń, Arkadiusz Janz, Piotr Miłkowski, Monika Riegel, Małgorzata Wierzba, Artur Marchewka, Agnieszka Czoska, Damian Grimling, Barbara Konat, Konrad Juszczyk, Katarzyna Klessa, and Maciej Piasecki. 2019a. Recognition of emotions, valence and arousal in large-scale multi-domain text reviews. In Zygmunt Vetulani and Patrick Paroubek, editors, *Human Language Technologies as a Challenge for Computer Science and Linguistics*, pages 274–280. Wydawnictwo Nauka i Innowacje, Poznań, Poland.

Jan Kocoń, Arkadiusz Janz, Monika Riegel, Małgorzata Wierzba, Artur Marchewka, Agnieszka Czoska, Damian Grimling, Barbara Konat, Konrad Juszczyk, Katarzyna Klessa, and Maciej Piasecki. 2019b. Propagation of emotions, arousal and polarity in WordNet using Heterogeneous Structured Synset Embeddings. In *Proceedings of the 10th International Global Wordnet Conference (GWC'19)*.

K. Krippendorff. 2013. *Content Analysis: An Introduction to Its Methodology*. SAGE Publications.

Marcin Kulisiewicz, Tomasz Kajdanowicz, Przemyslaw Kazienko, and Maciej Piasecki. 2015. On sentiment polarity assignment in the wordnet using loopy belief propagation. In *International Conference on Hybrid Artificial Intelligence Systems*, pages 451–462. Springer.

Alena Neviarouskaya, Helmut Prendinger, and Mitsuru Ishizuka. 2009. Compositionality principle in recognition of fine-grained emotions from text. In *Third International AAAI Conference on Weblogs and Social Media*.

Robert Plutchik. 1982. A psychoevolutionary theory of emotions. *Social Science Information*, 21(4-5):529–553.

Vikas C. Raykar and Shipeng Yu. 2012. Eliminating spammers and ranking annotators for crowdsourced labeling tasks. *J. Mach. Learn. Res.*, 13(1):491–518.

Monika Riegel, Małgorzata Wierzba, Marek Wypych, Łukasz Żurawski, Katarzyna Jednoróg, Anna Grabowska, and Artur Marchewka. 2015. Nencki Affective Word List (NAWL): the cultural adaptation of the Berlin Affective Word List–Reloaded (BAWL-R) for Polish. *Behavior Research Methods*, 47(4):1222–1236.

James A Russell and Albert Mehrabian. 1977. Evidence for a three-factor theory of emotions. *Journal of Research in Personality*, 11(3):273 – 294.

Piotr Rybak, Robert Mroczkowski, Janusz Tracz, and Ireneusz Gawlik. 2020. Klej: comprehensive benchmark for polish language understanding. *arXiv preprint arXiv:2005.00630*.

J. Salminen, F. Veronesi, H. Almerekhi, S. Jung, and B. J. Jansen. 2018. Online hate interpretation varies by country, but more by individual: A statistical analysis using crowdsourced ratings. In *2018 Fifth International Conference on Social Networks Analysis, Management and Security (SNAMS)*, pages 88–94.

Maarten Sap, Dallas Card, Saadia Gabriel, Yejin Choi, and Noah A. Smith. 2019. The risk of racial bias in hate speech detection. In *Proceedings of the 57th Annual Meeting of the Association for Computational Linguistics*, pages 1668–1678, Florence, Italy. Association for Computational Linguistics.

Philip Schmidt, Attila Reiss, Robert Dürichen, and Kristof Van Laerhoven. 2019. Wearable-based affect recognition—a review. *Sensors*, 19(19):4079.

Rion Snow, Brendan O'Connor, Daniel Jurafsky, and Andrew Ng. 2008. Cheap and fast – but is it good? evaluating non-expert annotations for natural language tasks. In *Proceedings of the 2008 Conference on Empirical Methods in Natural Language Processing*, pages 254–263, Honolulu, Hawaii. Association for Computational Linguistics.

Guillermo Soberón, Lora Aroyo, Chris Welty, Oana Inel, Hui Lin, and Manfred Overmeen. 2013. Measuring crowd truth: Disagreement metrics combined with worker behavior filters. In *Proceedings of the 1st International Conference on Crowdsourcing the Semantic Web - Volume 1030*, CrowdSem'13, page 45–58. CEUR-WS.org.

S. Steidl, M. Levit, A. Batliner, E. Noth, and H. Niemann. 2005. "of all things the measure is man" automatic classification of emotions and inter-labeler consistency [speech-based emotion recognition]. In *Proceedings. (ICASSP '05). IEEE International Conference on Acoustics, Speech, and Signal Processing, 2005.*, volume 1, pages I/317–I/320 Vol. 1.

Rachael Tatman. 2017. Gender and dialect bias in YouTube's automatic captions. In *Proceedings of the First ACL Workshop on Ethics in Natural Language Processing*, pages 53–59, Valencia, Spain. Association for Computational Linguistics.

Zeerak Waseem. 2016. Are you a racist or am I seeing things? annotator influence on hate speech detection on Twitter. In *Proceedings of the First Workshop on NLP and Computational Social Science*, pages 138–142, Austin, Texas. Association for Computational Linguistics.

Maximilian Wich, Hala Al Kuwatly, and Georg Groh. 2020a. Investigating annotator bias with a graph-based approach. In *Proceedings of the Fourth Workshop on Online Abuse and Harms*, pages 191–199, Online. Association for Computational Linguistics.

Maximilian Wich, Jan Bauer, and Georg Groh. 2020b. Impact of politically biased data on hate speech classification. In *Proceedings of the Fourth Workshop on Online Abuse and Harms*, pages 54–64, Online. Association for Computational Linguistics.

Michael Wiegand, Josef Ruppenhofer, and Thomas Kleinbauer. 2019. Detection of Abusive Language: the Problem of Biased Datasets. In *Proceedings of the 2019 Conference of the North American Chapter of the Association for Computational Linguistics: Human Language Technologies, Volume 1 (Long and Short Papers)*, pages 602–608, Minneapolis, Minnesota. Association for Computational Linguistics.

M. Wierzba, M. Riegel, M. Wypych, K. Jednorwóg, P. Turnau, A. Grabowska, and A. Marchewka. 2015. Basic emotions in the nencki affective word list (NAWL be): New method of classifying emotional stimuli. *PLoS ONE*, 10(7).

Michael Wojatzki, Tobias Horsmann, Darina Gold, and Torsten Zesch. 2018. Do women perceive hate differently: Examining the relationship between hate speech, gender, and agreement judgments. In *KONVENS*.

Mengzhou Xia, Anjalie Field, and Yulia Tsvetkov. 2020. Demoting racial bias in hate speech detection.

In *Proceedings of the Eighth International Workshop on Natural Language Processing for Social Media*, pages 7–14, Online. Association for Computational Linguistics.

Ashima Yadav and Dinesh Kumar Vishwakarma. 2020. Sentiment analysis using deep learning architectures: a review. *Artificial Intelligence Review*, 53(6):4335–4385.

Yi-Hsuan Yang, Ya-Fan Su, Yu-Ching Lin, and Homer H. Chen. 2007. Music emotion recognition: The role of individuality. In *Proceedings of the International Workshop on Human-Centered Multimedia*, HCM '07, page 13–22, New York, NY, USA. Association for Computing Machinery.

Monika Zaśko-Zielińska, Maciej Piasecki, and Stan Szpakowicz. 2015. A large wordnet-based sentiment lexicon for Polish. In *Proceedings of the International Conference Recent Advances in Natural Language Processing*, pages 721–730.

Sicheng Zhao, Hongxun Yao, Yue Gao, Rongrong Ji, Wenlong Xie, Xiaolei Jiang, and Tat-Seng Chua. 2016. Predicting personalized emotion perceptions of social images. In *Proceedings of the 24th ACM International Conference on Multimedia*, MM '16, page 1385–1394, New York, NY, USA. Association for Computing Machinery.

MVP-BERT: Multi-Vocab Pre-training for Chinese BERT

Wei Zhu[1] *
[1] East China Normal University, China

Abstract

Despite the development of pre-trained language models (PLMs) significantly raise the performances of various Chinese natural language processing (NLP) tasks, the vocabulary (vocab) for these Chinese PLMs remains to be the one provided by Google Chinese BERT (Devlin et al., 2019), which is based on Chinese characters (chars). Second, the masked language model pre-training is based on a single vocab, limiting its downstream task performances. In this work, we first experimentally demonstrate that building a vocab via Chinese word segmentation (CWS) guided sub-word tokenization (SGT) can improve the performances of Chinese PLMs. Then we propose two versions of multi-vocab pre-training (MVP), Hi-MVP and AL-MVP, to improve the models' expressiveness. Experiments show that: (a) MVP training strategies improve PLMs' downstream performances, especially it can improve the PLM's performances on span-level tasks; (b) our AL-MVP outperforms the recent AMBERT (Zhang & Li, 2020) after large-scale pre-training, and it is more robust against adversarial attacks.

1 Introduction

The pre-trained language models (PLMs), including BERT (Devlin et al., 2019) and its variants (Yang et al., 2019; Liu et al., 2019), have been proven beneficial for many natural language processing (NLP) tasks, such as text classification, question answering (Rajpurkar et al., 2018), natural language inference (NLI) (Bowman et al., 2015) and relation extraction (Zhu et al., 2020), on English, Chinese and many other languages. Although they bring impressive improvements for Chinese NLP tasks, most Chinese PLMs still use the vocabulary (vocab) provided by Google Chinese BERT (Devlin et al., 2019). Google Chinese BERT is a character (char) based model since it splits the Chinese characters with blank spaces. In the pre-BERT era, a part of the literature on Chinese natural language processing (NLP) first do Chinese word segmentation (CWS) to divide the text inputs into sequences of words and use a word-based vocab in NLP models (Xu et al., 2015; Zou et al., 2013). There are many arguments on which vocab a Chinese NLP model should adopt.

The advantages of char-based models are apparent. First, char-based vocab is smaller, thus reducing the model size. Second, it does not rely on CWS, thus avoiding word segmentation error, which can directly result in performance gain in span-based tasks such as named entity recognition (NER). Third, char-based models are less vulnerable to data sparsity or the presence of out-of-vocab (OOV) words and thus less prone to over-fitting (Li et al., 2019). However, word-based model has its advantages. First, it will result in shorter sequences than char-based counterparties, thus are faster. Second, words are less ambiguous, thus helping models learn the semantic meanings of words. Third, with a word-based model, exposure biases may be reduced in text generation tasks (Zhao et al., 2013). Another branch of literature tries to balance the two by combining word-based embedding with char-based embedding (Yin et al., 2016; Dong et al., 2016).

This article tries to strike a balance between the char-based and word-based models and provides alternative approaches for pre-training Chinese PLMs. We experiment on two approaches to build a vocab for Chinese PLMs: (1) following Devlin et al. (2019), separate the Chinese chars with white spaces, and then learn a sub-word tokenizer (denote as *CHAR*); (2) first segment the sentences with a CWS toolkit like jieba[1], and then learn a

*Contact: 52205901018@stu.ecnu.edu.cn.

[1] https://github.com/fxsjy/jieba

Proceedings of the Joint Conference of the 59th Annual Meeting of the Association for Computational Linguistics and the 11th International Joint Conference on Natural Language Processing: Student Research Workshop, pages 260–269
August 5–6, 2021.

sub-word tokenizer (denoted as *SGT*); (3) do CWS and keep the high-frequency words as tokens and low-frequency words will be tokenized by *SGT* (denoted as *SEG*). See Figure 1 for their workflow of processing an input sentence. The experiments show that *SGT* is best suited for PLMs.

Inspired by the previous work that incorporates multiple vocabularies (vocabs) or naturally combines multiple vocabs (Yin et al., 2016; Dong et al., 2016; Zhang & Li, 2020), we also investigate a series of strategies, which we will call Multi-Vocab Pre-training (MVP) strategies. The first version of MVP incorporates a hierarchical structure to combine the char-based vocab and word-based vocab. From the viewpoint of model forward pass, Chinese characters' embeddings are aggregated to form the vector representations of multi-gram words or tokens, which are fed into transformer encoders. Then the word-based vocab will be used in masked language model (MLM) training. The second version of MVP (denoted as AL-MVP) is to employ an additional vocab to form an auxiliary loss term in MLM, enhancing the PLM's ability to capture the contextual information.

Extensive experiments and ablation studies are conducted. We select BPE implemented by sentencepiece[2] as the sub-word tokenization model, and Albert (Lan et al., 2019) (tiny and base model) as our PLMs. Pre-training is done on Chinese Wikipedia corpus[3] (C-1), and a larger corpus we collect (C-2). The MVP strategies are compared on a series of Chinese benchmark datasets, two of which are sentence classification (CLS) tasks, two are named entity recognition (NER) tasks, and the remaining two are machine reading comprehension (MRC) tasks. The experimental results reveal the following take-aways: 1) combining CWS and sub-word tokenization yields the best vocab for Chinese PLMs; 3) MVP strategies can improve a single-vocab model on all three types of tasks.

We now summarize the following contributions in this work.

- We validate that combining CWS and sub-word tokenization is a better way for building vocabs for Chinese PLMs.
- We propose the novel MVP pre-training strategies for enhancing the Chinese PLMs, and they are proven to be effective.

[2]https://github.com/google/sentencepiece
[3]https://dumps.wikimedia.org/zhwiki/latest/

2 RELATED WORK

Since Devlin et al. (2019), a large amount of literature on pre-trained language models appear and push the NLP community forward with a speed that has never been witnessed before. Peters et al. (2018) is one of the earliest PLMs that learns contextualized representations of words. GPTs (Radford et al., 2018, 2019) and BERT (Devlin et al., 2019) take advantage of Transformer (Vaswani et al., 2017). GPTs are uni-directional and make predictions on the input text in an auto-regressive manner, and BERT is bi-directional and makes predictions on the whole or part of the input text. At its core, what makes BERT so powerful are the pre-training tasks, i.e., Mask language modeling (MLM) and next sentence prediction (NSP), where the former is more important than the latter. Since BERT, a series of improvements have been proposed. The first branch of literature improves the model architecture of BERT. ALBERT (Lan et al., 2019) makes BERT more light-weighted by embedding factorization and progressive cross-layer parameter sharing. Zaheer et al. (2020) improve BERT's performance on longer sequences by employing sparser attention.

The second branch of literature improves the training of BERT. Liu et al. (2019) stabilize and improve the training of BERT with a larger corpus. More work has focused on new language pre-training tasks. ALBERT (Lan et al., 2019) introduce sentence order prediction (SOP). StructBERT (Wang et al., 2019) designs two novel pre-training tasks, word structural task and sentence structural task, to learn better representations of tokens and sentences. ERNIE 2.0 (Sun et al., 2019) proposes a series of pre-training tasks and applies continual learning to incorporate these tasks. ELECTRA (Clark et al., 2020) has a GAN-style pre-training task for efficiently utilizing all tokens in pre-training. Our work is closely related to this literature branch by designing a series of novel pre-training objectives by incorporating multiple vocabularies. Our proposed method is off-the-shelf and can be easily incorporated with other pre-training tasks.

Another branch of literature looks into the role of words in pre-training. Although not mentioned in Devlin et al. (2019), the authors propose whole word masking in their open-source repository, which is effective for pre-training BERT. In SpanBERT (Joshi et al., 2019), text spans are masked

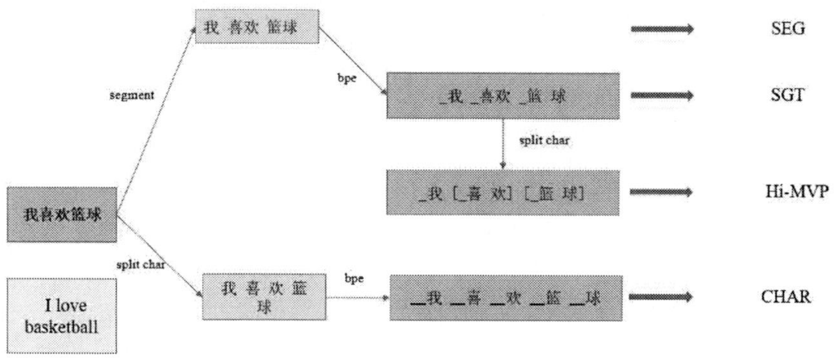

Figure 1: An illustration of how to process input sentence into tokens under different methods we define.

in pre-training, and the learned model can substantially enhance the performances of span selection tasks. It is indicated that word segmentation is vital for Chinese PLMs. Cui et al. (2019) and Sun et al. (2019) both show that masking tokens in the units of natural Chinese words instead of single Chinese characters can significantly improve Chinese PLMs. Liu et al. (2019) apply CWS to build a vocab that can improve Chinese-English translation performance. AMBERT (Zhang & Li, 2020) propose to leverage vocabs of different granularity in encoding sentences and improve the pre-training. In this work, compared to literature, our contributions are: (a) we find that CWS and sub-word tokenization can improve the pre-trained models' performances on downstream tasks. (b) we propose MVP pre-training tasks, which are proven to improve the expressiveness of pre-trained models and downstream performances.

3 Our methods

This section presents our methods for rebuilding the vocab for Chinese PLMs and introducing our series of MVP strategies.

3.1 Building the vocabs

We investigate four workflows to process the text inputs, each corresponding to a different vocab (or a group of vocabs) (Figure 1). We first introduce the single vocab models, *CHAR*, *SEG* and *SGT*.

For char-based vocab *CHAR*, Chinese characters in the corpus are treated as words in English and are separated with blank spaces, and a sub-word tokenizer is learned.[4] This method is essentially how BERT (Devlin et al., 2019) builds the Chinese vocab.

SGT (short for segmentation guided tokenization) requires the corpus sentences to be segmented with a CWS tool, and a sub-word tokenizer like BPE is learned on the segmented sentences. Some natural Chinese words in *SGT* will be split into pieces, but there are still many tokens with multiple Chinese chars.

Finally, *SEG* (short for segmentation) with size N is built with the following procedures: (a) do CWS on the corpus; (b) for long-tail Chinese words and non-Chinese tokens, tokenize them into tokens that have high frequencies; (c) sort the vocab via frequency, and if the most frequent N words or tokens can cover R percent of the corpus[5], then take them as vocab; if not, then re-do (b).

Note that *SEG* is essentially how AMBERT (Zhang & Li, 2020) builds the vocab for their Chinese PLM. However, they do not learn a sub-word tokenizer after CWS, thus making our *SGT* different from theirs. We will use experiments to show that our *SGT* yields comparably better PLMs.

3.2 Multi-vocab pre-training (MVP)

In this subsection, we will introduce MVP, a series of natural extensions to the MLM task by Devlin et al. (2019).

3.2.1 Hierarchical MVP

We first introduce hierarchical MVP (Hi-MVP). Figure 2(a) depicts the architecture of Hi-MVP, and Figure 1 depicts its procedure for processing

[4]Here the sub-word tokenizer mainly learns how to deal with non-Chinese tokens.

[5]This follows the implementation of BPE, which also asks the tokenizer to cover most of the corpus. The ratio is usually set as 99.99%.

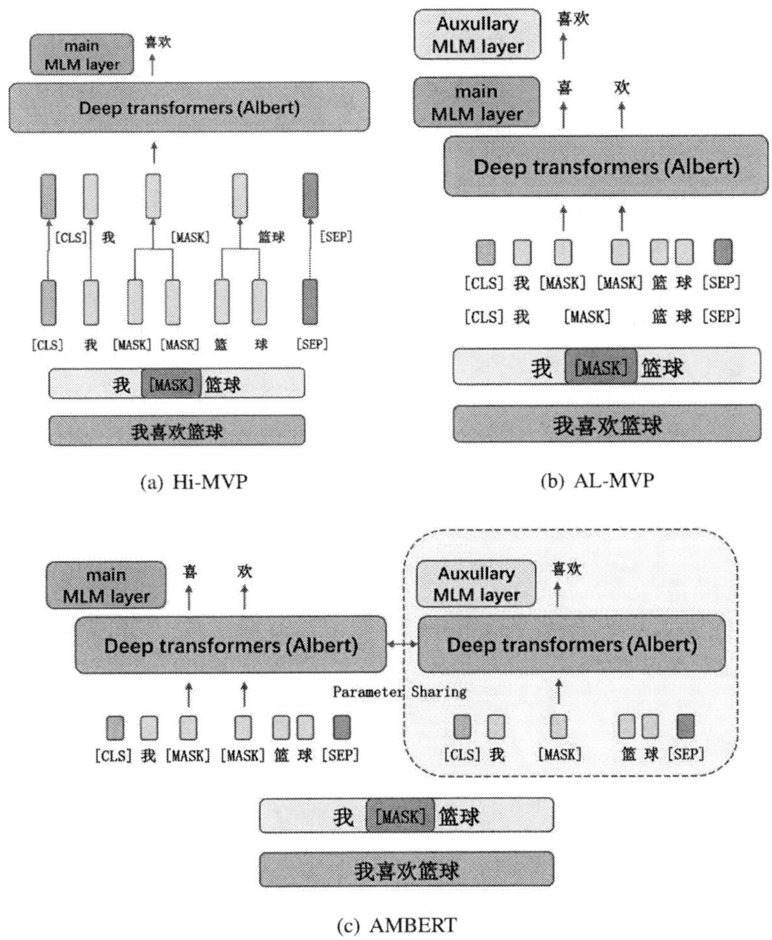

Figure 2: The architectures for the two versions of MVP strategies. The first two are ours, and the third one is AMBERT's.

input sentences. Two vocab, a more fine-grained vocab V_f, and a more coarse-grained vocab V_c, are combined hierarchically. Sequences are first tokenized via V_c, and then the Chinese tokens (if containing multiple Chinese chars) are split into single chars. Thus V_f consists of Chinese chars and non-Chinese tokens from V_c. Then Chinese chars and non-Chinese tokens are embedded into vectors. The representations of chars inside a token are aggregated into the representation of this token, further fed into the transformer encoder. We apply a convolution network (with kernel size 3 and #channels equally the embedding size) and max-pooling to convert the char sequence into a fixed token level representation in this work.

During MLM task, whole word masking is applied. That is, we will mask 15% of the tokens in the V_c. For example, in Figure 2(a), "_喜欢" (like) is masked, thus in the char sequence, two tokens "_喜" and "欢" are masked. A classifier is designated to predict the masked V_c token "_喜欢". Let $\mathbf{x}$ and $\mathbf{y}$ denote the sequences of tokens with lengths l_x and l_y, for the same sentence under V_c and V_f, in which a part of tokens are masked. Denote $\mathbf{x}^{mask}$ as the masked tokens under V_c. The loss function for MVP$_{hier}$ is

$$\min_{\theta} -\log \mathrm{P}_{\theta}(\mathbf{x}^{mask}|\mathbf{x}, \mathbf{y})$$
$$\approx \min_{\theta} -\sum_{i=1}^{l_x} \mathrm{I}_i \log \mathrm{P}_{\theta}(x_i^{mask}|\mathbf{x}, \mathbf{y}), \quad (1)$$

in which I_i^x is a variable with binary values indicating whether the i-th token is masked in $\mathbf{x}$.

3.2.2 Auxiliary loss MVP

Figure 2(b) depicts another version of MVP. In this method, a sentence is tokenized and embedded in a fine-grained V_f (e.g., a char-based vocab), and an MLM task on V_f is conducted. However, different from the vanilla MLM, an auxiliary MLM loss objective based on a more coarse-grained vocab V_c is added. Thus, we call this method Auxiliary loss MVP (AL-MVP).

For example, encoded representations of the chars "_喜" and "欢" inside the word "_喜欢" is aggregated to the vector representation of the word, and an auxiliary MLM layer is tasked to predict the word-based on V_c. For the aggregator in the example, we adopt the BERT-style pooler, which uses the starting token's representation to represent the word's representation.[6] Denote $\mathbf{x}^{mask}$ and $\mathbf{y}^{mask}$ as the masked tokens under V_f and V_c, respectively. The loss function for MVP_{obj} is as follows:

$$
\begin{aligned}
&\min_{\theta} - \log \mathrm{P}_{\theta}(\mathbf{x}^{mask}, \mathbf{y}^{mask} | \mathbf{x}) \\
&\approx \min_{\theta} - \sum_{i=1}^{l_x} \mathrm{I}_i^x \log \mathrm{P}_{\theta}(x_i^{mask} | \mathbf{x}) \\
&\quad - \lambda * \sum_{i=1}^{l_y} \mathrm{I}_i^y \log \mathrm{P}_{\theta}(y_i^{mask} | \mathbf{x}), \quad (2)
\end{aligned}
$$

in which I_i^x and I_i^y are variables with binary values indicating whether the i-th token is masked in sequence x and y, respectively. Here λ is the coefficient which measures the relative importance of the auxiliary MLM task.

Note that AL-MVP is different from AMBERT's architecture (Figure 2(c)). In AMBERT, a sequence has to be encoded twice with different vocabs. Meanwhile, AL-MVP is a plug-in pre-training strategy, and during inference, the PLM is the same as the original PLM.

We will denote the model pre-trained with Hi-MVP strategy and vocab V as Hi-MVP(V) for notational convenience. AL-MVP with a fine-grained vocab V_f and a coarse-grained vocab V_c are denoted as AL-MVP(V_f, V_c).

4 Experiments

4.1 Setup

Two corpora are used for pre-training. The first one is Chinese Wikipedia (C-1). We conduct most of the experiments and ablation studies on this corpus. Finally, we will use the other corpus (C-2) to match the SOTA performances. C-2 has 25 million documents, thus it has approximately the same size as the Chinese corpus in AMBERT (Zhang & Li, 2020). [7]

CHAR's vocab size is set at 21128, which is the same with Google Chinese BERT. We consider three vocab sizes for *SGT*: $\{21{,}128, 31{,}692, 72{,}635\}$. We will show in experiments that *SGT* works best with vocab size 31,692. Moreover, for the experiments with AL-MVP, we will only consider *SGT* with vocab size 31,692. We set the vocab size of *SEG* to be 72,635, which is the same as AMBERT. Table 1 reports the basic statistics for the tokens in these vocabs. As the vocab size goes up, As the vocab size goes up, the vocab will include more and more phrase-level tokens (# Chinese chars ≥ 2).

For Hi-MVP, we consider Hi-MVP(*SGT*) and Hi-MVP(*SEG*). For AL-MVP, we consider AL-MVP(*CHAR*, *SGT*), AL-MVP(*CHAR*, *SEG*), and AL-MVP(*SGT*, *SEG*). The relative importance coefficient λ in Eq. 2 is tuned from the set $\{0.1, 0.5, 1.0, 2.0, 10.0\}$ via training on a small corpus with 100k sentences and a small dev corpus with 5k sentences. We finally select $\lambda = 0.5$ for all models.

For pre-training, whole word masking is adopted, and a total of 15% of the words (from CWS) in the corpus are chosen. Furthermore, following BERT (Devlin et al., 2019), 80% of the chosen words are masked, a random word replaces 10%, and the rest remain unchanged. For AL-MVP, 1/3 of the time masked tokens from the fine-grained vocab are predicted, and 1/3 of the time masked tokens from the coarse-grained vocab are predicted, and for the rest of the time, masked tokens from both vocabs are predicted.

In this article, all models use the ALBERT as the encoder. We use two different settings. The first is for a smaller ALBERT model (ALBERT-tiny). The number of layers is 3, the embedding size is 128, and the hidden size is 256. We use this setting for extensive comparisons and ablation studies. Then we use the second model configuration, which is the same as ALBERT base. We pre-trained the best model from AL-MVP and show that our method also works for large language models.

[6] Due to limited resources available, we leave to future work to investigate whether alternative aggregators can bring improvements.

[7] Since AMBERT (Zhang & Li, 2020) does not open-source their corpus, we collect the corpus ourselves. C-2 consists of Chinese Wikipedia and news articles we crawled from the web.

Vocab	vocab size	zh words	zh words (len=1)	zh words (len=2)	zh words(len>=3)	other
CHAR	21,128	48.59	48.59	0	0	51.39
SGT	21,128	89.02	38.61	44.06	6.32	10.98
SGT	31,692	88.49	27.56	51.36	9.57	11.49
SGT	72,635	85.72	17.43	36.72	31.58	14.27
SEG	72,635	89.53	16.86	38.93	33.74	10.47

Table 1: The compositions of different vocabs.

Other ALBERT configurations remain the same with ALBERT (Lan et al., 2019). The pre-training hyper-parameters are almost the same with ALBERT (Lan et al., 2019) and the maximum sequence length is 512. Here, the sequence length is counted under the more fine-grained vocab for AL-MVP. The batch size is 1024, and all the models are trained for 12.5k steps. The pre-training optimizer is LAMB, and the learning rate is 1e-4. For finetuning, the sequence length is 256, the learning rate is 2e-5, the optimizer is Adam (Kingma & Ba, 2015), and the batch size is set as the power of 2 so that each epoch contains less than 500 steps. Each model is run on a given task 10 times, and the average performance scores are reported for reproducibility.

4.2 Baseline models

The first group of baselines is the original Google Chinese BERT (Devlin et al., 2019), with different vocabs. The second one is AMBERT (Zhang & Li, 2020), a pre-trained model with two vocabs of different granularity. For fair comparison, we pre-train the baselines ourselves, with the same corpus.

4.3 benchmark tasks

For downstream tasks, we select two sentence pair classification (CLS) tasks: (1) XNLI from Conneau et al. (2018) ; (2) LCQMC (Liu et al., 2018). We also investigate two named entity recognition (NER) tasks. MSRA NER (MSRA) (Levow, 2006) is from open domain, and CCKS NER[8] (CCKS) is collected from medical records. For machine reading comprehension (MRC) tasks, we consider two benchmark datasets, CMRC2018 (Cui et al., 2019) and ChID (Zheng et al., 2019).

4.4 Results for different vocabs

Table 3 report the results of pre-training ALBERT-tiny with a series of different vocabs. We can see that *SGT* obtains the best results on CLS, while *CHAR* and *SGT* have comparable results for span-level tasks NER and MRC. Even though the model with *SEG* has more parameters than *SGT*, it consistently under-performs *SGT*. The above results indicate two conclusions. First, CWS alone can not build a proper vocab for Chinese BERT. Second, sub-word tokenizers learned on the segmented Chinese corpus can decompose long-tail words into tokens while keeping meaningful phrases as it is, improving the downstream performances of ALBERT.

Also, Table 3 reports *SGT*'s performances using different vocab sizes. The results show that vocab size 31,692 is best suited for Chinese PLMs. When the *SGT*'s vocab size goes up, the less frequent tokens will not receive enough training, thus affecting the downstream performances. When the *SGT*'s vocab size goes down, it is essentially similar to *CHAR*. Thus it can not leverage phrasal information of the Chinese language. Thus, for the experiments in the rest of the paper, we only use *SGT* with vocab size 31,692.

SGT has the efficiency advantage over *CHAR*. We now make inference on the LCQMC test set using batch size 1[9], and the sequence length is kept as it is. We can observe that *SGT* has a 1.25x inference speed up than *CHAR*.

4.5 Results for MVP

In this subsection, we analyze results for our MVP strategies. We can see from Table 2 that when trained using the same corpus, our Hi-MVP's performance can match the AMBERT's performances. Note that AMBERT has twice the computational complexity of our Hi-MVP. Our Hi-MVP encoders the sentence from char level to phrase level, thus understanding the components of the sentence.

Note that Hi-MVP's pre-training works on the phrase level; thus, it does not perform well on the span level tasks. Table 3 shows that the AL-MVP strategy can generally improve all tasks' results, es-

[8] https://biendata.com/competition/CCKS2017 2/

[9] This is consistent with the online scenarios of the industry since user queries usually come one by one.

task	CLS		NER		MRC	
task name	LCQMC	XNLI	MSRA	CCKS	CMRC2018	ChID
metric	Acc.	macro F1	exact F1	exact F1	EM	Acc.
SGT (31,692)	79.79	60.19	81.07	85.74	61.64	70.97
AMBERT	80.64	60.89	81.57	86.34	62.86	72.45
Hi-MVP(*SGT*)	80.56	60.98	81.35	86.82	62.65	72.43
Hi-MVP(*SEG*)	80.35	60.57	81.48	86.56	62.48	72.31
AL-MVP(*CHAR*, *SGT*)	80.93	61.43	81.47	86.97	62.93	72.65
AL-MVP(*CHAR*, *SEG*)	81.05	61.14	81.83	86.49	**63.32**	72.87
AL-MVP(*SGT*, *SEG*)	**81.56**	**61.77**	**82.21**	**87.24**	63.29	**73.05**

Table 2: The main experimental results for our MVP strategies. Our methods outperform AMBERT, even though they require less computational resources for pre-training.

task	CLS		NER		MRC	
task name	LCQMC	XNLI	MSRA	CCKS	CMRC2018	ChID
metric	Acc.	macro F1	exact F1	exact F1	EM	Acc.
CHAR (21,128)	77.85	59.22	**81.14**	85.63	61.23	**71.05**
SGT (31,692)	**79.79**	**60.19**	81.07	**85.74**	**61.64**	70.97
SGT (21,128)	79.27	59.71	79.07	83.96	61.37	70.76
SGT (72,635)	79.04	59.45	78.79	83.41	60.89	70.51
SEG (72,635)	79.16	59.32	78.63	83.32	60.72	70.28

Table 3: Results for different vocabs, when used for ALBERT-tiny pre-training.

task name	LCQMC	XNLI	MSRA	CCKS	CMRC2018	ChID
AL-MVP(*SGT*, *SEG*)	**81.56**	**61.77**	**82.21**	**87.24**	**63.29**	**73.05**
AL-MVP(*SGT*, *SEG*)-1	79.79	60.19	81.07	85.74	61.64	70.97
AL-MVP(*SGT*, *SEG*)-2	80.78	60.86	81.49	86.23	62.08	71.63

Table 4: Ablation studies on the AL-MVP's pre-training strategies.

task name	LCQMC	XNLI	MSRA	CCKS	CMRC2018	ChID
Google BERT	86.72	77.64	93.61	90.25	70.08	82.04
RoBERT-wwm-ext	86.23	78.57	94.82	91.56	72.63	83.62
AMBERT (Zhang & Li, 2020)	-	-	-	-	73.25	86.62
AMBERT (ours)	86.95	78.93	95.39	91.74	73.08	85.31
AL-MVP(*SGT*, *SEG*)	**87.68**	**79.75**	**95.94**	**92.53**	**73.82**	**86.76**

Table 5: The performances of models with large scale pre-training.

Metric	AMBERT		AL-MVP(*SGT*, *SEG*)	
(↑ better)	LCQMC	XNLI	LCQMC	XNLI
original score	86.95	78.93	87.68	79.75
after-attack score	15.43	16.39	17.34	18.82
#queries	66	73	74	82

Table 6: Results on the adversarial robustness. "Query Number"denotes the number of queries the attack system made to the target model and a higher number indicates greater difficulty.

pecially on span-level tasks. Also, our two versions of AL-MVP models can outperform AMBERT on most of the tasks. AL-MVP asks the model to learn a more general representation that can work with different vocabs, making the model better understand a token's relation with its contexts.

Among the two AL-MVP models, AL-MVP(*SGT*, *SEG*) performs best on five of the six tasks. On CMRC2018, the performance of AL-MVP(*SGT*, *SEG*) is very close to AL-MVP(*CHAR*, *SEG*). AL-MVP(*SGT*, *SEG*) maintains the *SGT*'s advantage on CLS tasks while improving NER and MRC via AL-MVP pre-training.

4.6 Ablation on the pre-training strategies of AL-MVP

For AL-MVP, we emphasize that cross-vocab MLMs is essential for the pre-training. Thus, we compare AL-MVP(*SGT*, *SEG*) with two other versions. First, AL-MVP(*SGT*, *SEG*)-1 keeps the main MLM layer in Figure 2(b), that is, to only make MLM predictions on the more fine-grained vocab;[10] Second, AL-MVP(*SGT*, *SEG*)-2 only keep the auxiliary MLM layer in Figure 2(b), that is, to only make MLM predictions on the more coarse-grained vocab. Table 4 reports that AL-MVP(*SGT*, *SEG*) achieves the best results on all 6 tasks. The results show that MLM pre-training that combines both vocabs can effectively improve the PLM's language understanding abilities and downstream performances.

4.7 Large scale pre-training

In section, we report the pre-training results on C-2, a large-scale corpus matching the size of AMBERT's corpus. Table 5 reports the performances of ALBERT-base. We first directly report the results of AMBERT from Zhang & Li (2020) on the CMRC2018 and ChID tasks. Besides, to eliminate the factor of different training corpus, we also train AMBERT on the C-2 corpus. The results show that our AL-MVP(*SGT*, *SEG*) model outperforms both AMBERT models. Note that we only require half the GPU time for AMBERT training, and the inference speed of AL-MVP(*SGT*, *SEG*) is 2.15x of AMBERT.

4.8 Robustness over adversarial attacks

We claim that our AL-MVP training strategy can ask the ALBERT encoder to efficiently draw information from contexts into token representations, thus improving the expressiveness. Thus it is a fair reasonable that AL-MVP pre-trained models should be more robust to adversarial attacks. This subsection leverages the TextFooler framework (Jin et al., 2020) to conduct black-box attacks on the LCQMC and XNLI datasets. As shown in Table 6, we report the original performance, after-attack performance, and the number of queries needed by TextFooler to attack each model. We can see that AL-MVP(*SGT*, *SEG*) increases the number of queries needed to attack by a clear margin. Compared with AMBERT, our AL-MVP(*SGT*, *SEG*) demonstrates robustness improvements.

5 Conclusions

In this work, we propose a series of novel pre-training methods called MVPs, which leverage multiple vocabularies in the language model pre-training. To select the vocabs for MVP pre-training, we first conduct experiments to validate *SGT*, which combines Chinese word segmentation and sub-word tokenization, works best for the Chinese language model pre-training. We then use experiments to show that our proposed MVP methods can achieve better performances than AMBERT with less computational resources. Also, we show our MVP method can improve the pre-trained model's robustness against adversarial attacks.

References

Samuel R. Bowman, Gabor Angeli, Christopher Potts, and Christopher D. Manning. A large annotated corpus for learning natural language inference. *arXiv e-prints*, art. arXiv:1508.05326, August 2015.

Kevin Clark, Minh-Thang Luong, Quoc V. Le, and Christopher D. Manning. ELECTRA: Pre-training Text Encoders as Discriminators Rather Than Generators. *arXiv e-prints*, art. arXiv:2003.10555, March 2020.

Alexis Conneau, Ruty Rinott, Guillaume Lample, Adina Williams, Samuel Bowman, Holger Schwenk, and Veselin Stoyanov. XNLI: Evaluating cross-lingual sentence representations. In *Proceedings of the 2018 Conference on Empirical Methods in Natural Language Processing*, pp. 2475–2485, Brussels, Belgium, October-November 2018. Association for Computational Linguistics. doi: 10.18653/v1/D18-1269. URL `https://www.aclweb.org/anthology/D18-1269`.

Yiming Cui, Wanxiang Che, Ting Liu, Bing Qin, Ziqing Yang, Shijin Wang, and Guoping Hu. Pre-Training with Whole Word Masking for Chinese

[10]This model is essentially the vanilla ALBERT-tiny with vocab *SGT*.

BERT. *arXiv e-prints*, art. arXiv:1906.08101, June 2019.

Yiming Cui, T. Liu, L. Xiao, Zhipeng Chen, Wentao Ma, W. Che, S. Wang, and G. Hu. A span-extraction dataset for chinese machine reading comprehension. In *EMNLP-IJCNLP*, 2019.

J. Devlin, Ming-Wei Chang, Kenton Lee, and Kristina Toutanova. Bert: Pre-training of deep bidirectional transformers for language understanding. In *NAACL-HLT*, 2019.

C. Dong, Jiajun Zhang, C. Zong, M. Hattori, and Hui Di. Character-based lstm-crf with radical-level features for chinese named entity recognition. In *NLPCC/ICCPOL*, 2016.

Di Jin, Zhijing Jin, Joey Tianyi Zhou, and Peter Szolovits. Is bert really robust? a strong baseline for natural language attack on text classification and entailment. In *AAAI*, 2020.

Mandar Joshi, Danqi Chen, Yinhan Liu, Daniel S. Weld, Luke Zettlemoyer, and Omer Levy. SpanBERT: Improving pre-training by representing and predicting spans. *arXiv preprint arXiv:1907.10529*, 2019.

Diederik P. Kingma and Jimmy Ba. Adam: A method for stochastic optimization. In *ICML*, 2015.

Zhenzhong Lan, Mingda Chen, Sebastian Goodman, Kevin Gimpel, Piyush Sharma, and Radu Soricut. Albert: A lite bert for self-supervised learning of language representations. *arXiv preprint arXiv:1909.11942*, 2019.

Gina-Anne Levow. The third international Chinese language processing bakeoff: Word segmentation and named entity recognition. In *Proceedings of the Fifth SIGHAN Workshop on Chinese Language Processing*, pp. 108–117, Sydney, Australia, July 2006. Association for Computational Linguistics. URL `https://www.aclweb.org/anthology/W06-0115`.

Xiaoya Li, Yuxian Meng, Xiaofei Sun, Qinghong Han, Arianna Yuan, and Jiwei Li. Is Word Segmentation Necessary for Deep Learning of Chinese Representations? *arXiv e-prints*, art. arXiv:1905.05526, May 2019.

Xin Liu, Qingcai Chen, Chong Deng, Huajun Zeng, Jing Chen, Dongfang Li, and Buzhou Tang. LCQMC:a large-scale Chinese question matching corpus. In *Proceedings of the 27th International Conference on Computational Linguistics*, pp. 1952–1962, Santa Fe, New Mexico, USA, August 2018. Association for Computational Linguistics. URL `https://www.aclweb.org/anthology/C18-1166`.

Yinhan Liu, Myle Ott, Naman Goyal, Jingfei Du, Mandar Joshi, Danqi Chen, Omer Levy, Mike Lewis, Luke Zettlemoyer, and Veselin Stoyanov. RoBERTa: A Robustly Optimized BERT Pretraining Approach. *arXiv e-prints*, art. arXiv:1907.11692, July 2019.

Zihan Liu, Yan Xu, Genta Indra Winata, and Pascale Fung. Incorporating word and subword units in unsupervised machine translation using language model rescoring. In *WMT*, 2019.

Matthew E. Peters, Mark Neumann, Mohit Iyyer, Matt Gardner, Christopher Clark, Kenton Lee, and Luke Zettlemoyer. Deep contextualized word representations. In *Proc. of NAACL*, 2018.

Alec Radford, Karthik Narasimhan, Tim Salimans, and Ilya Sutskever. Improving language understanding by generative pre-training. 2018.

Alec Radford, Jeff Wu, Rewon Child, David Luan, Dario Amodei, and Ilya Sutskever. Language models are unsupervised multitask learners. 2019.

Pranav Rajpurkar, Robin Jia, and Percy Liang. Know What You Don't Know: Unanswerable Questions for SQuAD. *arXiv e-prints*, art. arXiv:1806.03822, June 2018.

Yu Sun, Shuohuan Wang, Yukun Li, Shikun Feng, Xuyi Chen, Han Zhang, Xin Tian, Danxiang Zhu, Hao Tian, and Hua Wu. Ernie: Enhanced representation through knowledge integration. *arXiv preprint arXiv:1904.09223*, 2019.

Yu Sun, Shuohuan Wang, Yukun Li, Shikun Feng, Hao Tian, Hua Wu, and Haifeng Wang. ERNIE 2.0: A Continual Pre-training Framework for Language Understanding. *arXiv e-prints*, art. arXiv:1907.12412, July 2019.

Ashish Vaswani, Noam Shazeer, Niki Parmar, Jakob Uszkoreit, Llion Jones, Aidan N Gomez, Łukasz Kaiser, and Illia Polosukhin. Attention is all you need. In *NIPS*, 2017.

Wei Wang, Bin Bi, Ming Yan, Chen Wu, Zuyi Bao, Jiangnan Xia, Liwei Peng, and Luo Si. StructBERT: Incorporating Language Structures into Pre-training for Deep Language Understanding. *arXiv e-prints*, art. arXiv:1908.04577, August 2019.

Ruifeng Xu, Tao Chen, Yunqing Xia, Qin Lu, Bin Liu, and Xuan Wang. Word embedding composition for data imbalances in sentiment and emotion classification. *Cognitive Computation*, 7, 02 2015. doi: 10.1007/s12559-015-9319-y.

Zhilin Yang, Zihang Dai, Yiming Yang, Jaime Carbonell, Ruslan Salakhutdinov, and Quoc V. Le. XLNet: Generalized Autoregressive Pretraining for Language Understanding. *arXiv e-prints*, art. arXiv:1906.08237, June 2019.

Rongchao Yin, Quan Wang, Peng Li, Rui Li, and Bin Wang. Multi-granularity Chinese word embedding. In *Proceedings of the 2016 Conference on Empirical Methods in Natural Language Processing*, pp. 981–986, Austin, Texas, November 2016. Association for Computational Linguistics. doi: 10.18653/v1/D16-1100. URL `https://www.aclweb.org/anthology/D16-1100`.

Manzil Zaheer, Guru Guruganesh, Avinava Dubey, Joshua Ainslie, Chris Alberti, Santiago Ontanon, Philip Pham, Anirudh Ravula, Qifan Wang, Li Yang, and Amr Ahmed. Big Bird: Transformers for Longer Sequences. *arXiv e-prints*, art. arXiv:2007.14062, July 2020.

Xinsong Zhang and H. Li. Ambert: A pre-trained language model with multi-grained tokenization. *ArXiv*, abs/2008.11869, 2020.

Hai Zhao, Masao Utiyama, Eiichiro Sumita, and Bao-Liang Lu. An empirical study on word segmentation for chinese machine translation. In *International Conference on Intelligent Text Processing and Computational Linguistics*, pp. 248–263. Springer, 2013.

Chujie Zheng, Minlie Huang, and Aixin Sun. Chid: A large-scale chinese idiom dataset for cloze test. In *ACL*, 2019.

W. Zhu, X. Wang, Xipeng Qiu, Yuan Ni, and G. Xie. Autorc: Improving bert based relation classification models via architecture search. *ArXiv*, abs/2009.10680, 2020.

Will Y. Zou, Richard Socher, Daniel Cer, and Christopher D. Manning. Bilingual word embeddings for phrase-based machine translation. In *Proceedings of the 2013 Conference on Empirical Methods in Natural Language Processing*, pp. 1393–1398, Seattle, Washington, USA, October 2013. Association for Computational Linguistics. URL `https://www.aclweb.org/anthology/D13-1141`.

CMTA: COVID-19 Misinformation Multilingual Analysis on Twitter

Raj Ratn Pranesh[1,*], **Mehrdad Farokhnejad**[2,**], **Ambesh Shekhar**[1,*], and **Genoveva Vargas-Solar**[3,']

[1]Birla Institute of Technology, Mesra, India
[2]Univ. Grenoble Alpes, CNRS, LIG, Grenoble, France
[3]CNRS, LIRIS-LAFMIA Lyon, France
[*](raj.ratn18, ambesh.sinha)@gmail.com
[**]mehrdad.farokhnejad@univ-grenoble-alpes.fr
[']genoveva.vargas-solar@liris.cnrs.fr

Abstract

The internet has actually come to be an essential resource of health knowledge for individuals around the world in the present situation of the coronavirus condition pandemic(COVID-19). During pandemic situations, myths, sensationalism, rumours and misinformation, generated intentionally or unintentionally, spread rapidly through social networks. Twitter is one of these popular social networks people use to share COVID-19 related news, information, and thoughts that reflect their perception and opinion about the pandemic. Evaluation of tweets for recognizing misinformation can create beneficial understanding to review the top quality and also the readability of online information concerning the COVID-19. This paper presents a multilingual COVID-19 related tweet analysis method, CMTA, that uses BERT, a deep learning model for multilingual tweet misinformation detection and classification. CMTA extracts features from multilingual textual data, which is then categorized into specific information classes. Classification is done by a Dense-CNN model trained on tweets manually annotated into information classes (i.e., 'false', 'partly false', 'misleading'). The paper presents an analysis of multilingual tweets from February to June, showing the distribution type of information spread across different languages. To access the performance of the CMTA multilingual model, we performed a comparative analysis of 8 monolingual model and CMTA for the misinformation detection task. The results show that our proposed CMTA model has surpassed various monolingual models which consolidated the fact that through transfer learning a multilingual framework could be developed.

1 Introduction

Since late 2019, the coronavirus disease COVID-19 has spread worldwide to more than 216 countries (Organization et al., 2020). COVID-19 has created a massive impact on multiple sectors including countries economy, government bodies, private companies, media houses and most importantly, affecting the mental and physical health of human beings by tempering their daily routine activities (Torales et al., 2020; Fernandes, 2020).

COVID-19 also has made us realize how well the world is interconnected through the Internet. Social media is a significant conduit where people share their response, thoughts, news, information related to COVID-19, with one in three individuals worldwide participating in social media, with two-thirds of people utilizing it on the Internet (Ortiz-Ospina, 2020). Studies have shown that many people connect to the Internet and social media platforms such as Twitter, Facebook, Whatsapp, Instagram and Reddit every day and utilizing it for getting information/news through them (Matsa and Shearer, 2018) (Hitlin and Olmstead, 2018). Twitter users are known, especially, for posting and exchanging news: almost 60% of Twitter users classify it as excellent or incredibly helpful for sharing preventive health information (Wilford et al., 2018).

Nonetheless, social media is still full of misinformation regarding health. It is difficult to assess the authenticity of health information on the Internet for people with non-medical experience. Precise and reliable dissemination of correct information about the virus that causes a pandemic will help to monitor the spread of the virus and related population anxiety (Sharma et al., 2017). Social media content and misinformation may have intense implications for public opinion and behavior, positively or negatively influencing the viewpoint of those who access it (Brindha et al., 2020; Kouzy et al., 2020).

The WHO director-general stated at the Munich security conference in February 2020, 'we are not only fighting an epidemic; we are fighting an info-

Proceedings of the Joint Conference of the 59th Annual Meeting of the Association for Computational Linguistics and the 11th International Joint Conference on Natural Language Processing: Student Research Workshop, pages 270–283
August 5–6, 2021.

demic' (Zarocostas, 2020). It is clear that there is no way of stopping the transmission of COVID-19, so it is necessary to check information on the Internet in order to prevent the panic and disinformation linked to the disease. Seeking accurate and valid information is the biggest challenge with Internet health information (Eysenbach et al., 2002).

Misinformation appears in several ways in the case of COVID-19, such as 'COVID-19 is a biological agent developed by either the US or China','COVID-19 is the potential by-product of Chinese cuisine, such as bat soup amongst other ingredients,'and 'breath-holding self-detection test', unconfirmed home remedies such as vitamin C, urine from animals, turmeric etc. In its worse, this type of misinformation will lead individuals to resort to unsuccessful (and actually directly harmful) remedies, either to overreact (e.g. by hoarding goods) or to underreact quite dangerously (e.g., by deliberately engaging in risky behavior and inadvertently spreading the virus). (Brindha et al., 2020; Pennycook et al., 2020). Unfortunately, the fake news spread faster than the virus (Gallotti et al., 2020).

An online social platform such as Twitter provides particularly fertile ground for the spread of misinformation (Frenkel et al., 2020). Twitter gives direct access to extraordinary content, which may intensify rumors and dubious information (Cinelli et al., 2020). With such a huge amount of human-generated information being exchanged every day, it has attracted Natural Language Processing (NLP) researchers to explore, analyze, and generate valuable insights about people response to COVID-19. People response is analyzed with respect to sentiments and misinformation and malicious information detection.

This paper proposes CMTA, a multilingual tweet analysis and information (misinformation) detection method for understanding both the negative and positive sides of social media during COVID-19 pandemic. CMTA uses Multilingual BERT, trained on 104 multiple languages to derive features from tweets and 1D convolution for finding the correlation between data of hidden states. It also uses a dense layer for linear transformation on contextual embeddings to provide inferential points. Our work helps in providing better results in finding the proximity of being fake. We used manually annotated multilingual COVID-19 related tweets for training deep neural network model in order to detect and identify the type of misinformation present in tweets belonging to different language groups.

For experimenting with our method, we used trained models for a systematic analysis of COVID-19 related tweets collected from February to June 2020. The analysis of tweets is done based on the distribution of the type of information present in tweets concerning the language used for writing a tweet. We investigated the presence of false information spread throughout Tweeter by classifying the tweets in three classes: 'false', 'partly false' and 'misleading'. We have provided illustrative statistical representation of our findings and detailed discussion about the insights discovered in our survey. The **motivation** for designing a multilingual method lies behind the need of analyzing not just monolingual tweets but also multilingual tweets by building a single deep learning framework that would be able to understand tweets in multiple languages. That being said, we also analysed the performance of CMTA multilingual BERT framework with respect to 8 monolingual BERT models. The performance score achieved by the multilingual model were very close to that of monolingual models which suggests that utilizing a singular multilingual model for COVID-19 tweet analysis and disinformation categorization is a reliable and robust method.

2 Related Work

The COVID-19 pandemic has resulted in studies investigating the various types of misinformation arising during the COVID-19 crisis (Brennen et al., 2020; Dharawat et al., 2020; Singh et al., 2020; Kouzy et al., 2020). Studies investigate a small subset of claims (Singh et al., 2020) or manually annotate Twitter data (Kouzy et al., 2020). In (Brennen et al., 2020) authors analyse different types of sources for looking for COVID-19 misinformation. Pennycook et al. (Pennycook et al., 2020) introduced an attention-based account of misinformation and observed that people tend to believe false claims about COVID-19 and share false claims when they do not think critically about the accuracy and veracity of the information. Kouzy et al. (Kouzy et al., 2020) annotated about 600 messages containing hashtags about COVID-19, they observed that about one-fourth of messages contain some form of misinformation, and about 17% contain some unverifiable information. With such misinformation overload, any decision making procedure based on misinformation has a high likelihood of severely impacting people's health (Ingraham and Tignanelli, 2020). The work in (Huang and Carley, 2020) examined the global spread of information related to crucial disinformation stories and "fake news" URLs during the early stages of the global pandemic on Twitter. Their study shows that news agencies, government officials, and individual news reporters send messages that spread widely and play critical roles. Tweets citing URLs for "fake news" and reports of propaganda are more likely than news or government pages shared by regular users and bots.

The work in (Sharma et al., 2020) focused on topic modelling and designed a dashboard to track Twitter's misinformation regarding the COVID-19 pandemic. The dashboard presents a summary of information derived from Twitter posts, including topics, sentiment, false and misleading information shared on social media related to COVID-19. Cinelli et al. (Singh et al., 2020) track (mis)-information flow across 2.7M tweets and compare it with infection rates.They noticed a major Spatio-temporal connection between information flow and new COVID-19 instances, and while there are discussions about myths and connections to low-quality information, their influence is less prominent than other themes specific to the crisis. To find and measure causal relationships between pandemic features (e.g. the number of infections and deaths) and Twitter behaviour and public sentiment, the work in (Gencoglu and Gruber, 2020) introduced the first example of a causal inference method. Their proposed approach has shown that they can efficiently collect epidemiological domain knowledge and identify factors that influence public interest and attention.

The discussion around the COVID-19 pandemic and the government policies was investigated in(Lopez et al., 2020). They used Twitter data in multiple languages from various countries and found common responses to the pandemic and how they differ across time using text mining. Moreover, they presented insights as to how information and misinformation were transmitted via Twitter. Similarly, to demonstrate the epidemiological effect of COVID-19 on press publications in Bogota, Colombia, (Saire and Navarro, 2020) used text mining on Twitter data. They intuitively note a strong correlation between the number of tweets and the number of infected people in the area.

Most of the works described above focus on analysing tweets related to single language such as English. In our work we have designed a single model leveraging multilingual BERT for the analysis of tweets in multiple languages. Furthermore, we used a large data set to train and analyze the tweets. Our aim is to provide a system that will be restricted to any language for analysing social media data.

3 Data preparation

This section discusses the steps involved in the collection of COVID-19 related tweets. For training our misinformation detection deep learning model, we have extracted annotated misinformation data from multiple publicly available open databases. We also collected a very large number of multilingual tweets consisting of over 2 million tweets belonging to eight different languages.

3.1 Training Dataset

In order to train and test our misinformation detection model, we collected the training data from an online fact-checker website called Poynter (Poynter Institute, 2020). Poynter have a specific COVID-19 related misinformation detection program named 'CoronaVirusFacts/DatosCoronaVirus Alliance Database[1]'. This database contains thousands of labelled social media information such as news, posts, claims, articles about COVID-19 which were manually verified and annotated by human volunteers(fact-checkers) from all around the globe. The database gathers all the misinformation related to topics such as COVID-19 cure, detection, the effect on animals, foods, travel, government policies, crime, lockdown.

The misinformation dataset was available in 2 languages- 'English' and 'Spanish'. Since we were training a multilingual BERT model, we crawled through the content of all 2 websites using Beautifulsoup[2], a Python library for scraping information from web pages. We scrape 8471 English language false news/information belonging to nine major classes namely, 'False', 'Partially false', 'Misleading', 'No evidence', 'Four Pinocchios', 'Incorrect', 'Three Pinocchios', 'Two Pinocchios' and 'Mostly False'. For each article we gath-

[1] https://www.poynter.org/covid-19-poynter-resources/

[2] Python module is available at https://pypi.org/project/beautifulsoup4/

Classes	Number of tweets
False (Poynter Institute, 2020) (English)	2,869
Partially False (English)	2,765
Misleading (English)	2,837
False (Spanish)	191
Partially False (Spanish)	161
Misleading (Spanish)	179
False (Alam et al., 2020) (English)	500
Total	9,502

Table 1: Collected Misinformation Dataset

ered the article's title, it's content and the fact checker's misinformation-type label. Similarly, from the Spanish[3] databases we collected 531 misinformation articles respectively. The collected data contains the misinformation published on social media platforms such as Facebook, Twitter, What'sapp, YouTube and were mostly related to political-biased news, scientifically dubious information and conspiracy theories, misleading news and rumors about COVID-19. We also used one more human annotated fact-checked tweet dataset (Alam et al., 2020) available at the public repository[4]. The dataset contained true and false labelled tweets in English and Arabic language. We used only false labelled tweets consisting of 500 English. We compiled (table 1) a total of 9,502 micro-articles distributed across 9 misinformation classes.

Defining misinformation classes: The collected data was unevenly distributed across 9 classes. We put the classes such as 'No evidence', 'Four Pinocchios[5]', 'Incorrect', 'Three Pinocchios[6]', 'Two Pinocchios[7]' and 'Mostly False' under the minority group because of having very few labels. On the other hand, labels like 'False', 'Partially false' and 'Misleading' comprises the majority group as most of the collected articles belongs to this group. In order to structure and distribute the dataset uniformly for training our model, we reformed the dataset by merging the minority group labels into the majority group labels. The classes ('Four Pinocchios' and 'Incorrect') that correspond to completely false information were merged together into the 'False' class. 'Three Pinocchios' and 'Two Pinocchios' were merged together into 'Partially false' class. 'No evidence' and 'Mostly False' were put together with the 'Misleading' class.

Table 6 gives a clear understanding of our training dataset and showcase some misinformation articles present in our training dataset. Column 1 shows the reformed label assigned by us, column 2 shows the original label assigned by the fact-checker, column 3 gives a misinformation example associated with the label present in column 2, and column 4 provides a reasoning given by the fact-checker behind assigning a particular label (column 2) to the misinformation (column 3). For example, if we would look at the entry number '3' in the table 6, the misinformation is about the adverse effect of 5G radiation over the COVID-19 patients. This was labeled 'Incorrect' by the fact-checker. After analysing the fact-checker rating and the explanation given, we labelled it as 'False' misinformation. Entry number '5' talks about the COVID-19 test cost. The explanation given by fact-checker is valid as it is not sure if there is any fee in USA for COVID-19 test or not. So because of the lack of evidence and uncertainty we labelled it as 'Partially false'. Entry number '7' in the table talks about a video showing COVID-19 corpus dumping in the sea. Based on the explanation, the video was coupled with the wrong information to mislead the audience. So it was labelled as 'Misleading' misinformation.

3.2 Inference Dataset

Once we finished training our multilingual tweet misinformation detection model we aimed to use it for predicting and analysing the misinformation spread across all over the social media platforms in multiple languages. In order to do so, we collected around 2,137,106 multilingual tweets consisting of tweets belonging to eight major languages, namely- 'English', 'Spanish', 'Indonesian', 'French', 'Japanese', 'Thai', 'Hindi' and 'German'. We used an ongoing dataset of tweets IDs associated with the novel coronavirus COVID-19 (Chen et al., 2020). Started on January 28, 2020, the current version of dataset contains 212,978,935 tweets divided into groups based on their publishing month. The dataset was collected using multilingual COVID-19 related keywords and contains tweets in more than 30 languages. We used tweepy[8] which is a Python module for accessing twitter API. For our analysis we decided to retrieve the tweets using the tweet IDs of the tweets pub-

[3] https://chequeado.com/latamcoronavirus/

[4] https://github.com/firojalam/COVID-19-tweets-for-check-worthiness

[5] 90%-95% changes of it being false

[6] 70%-75% changes of it being false

[7] 50%-55% changes of it being false

[8] Python module is available at http://www.tweepy.org

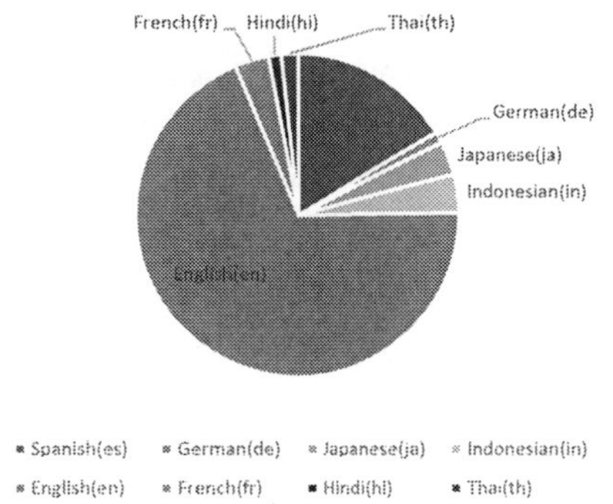

Figure 1: Language-wise Dataset Distribution Pie chart.

Language	ISO	Number of tweets
English	en	1,472,448
Spanish	es	353,294
Indonesian	in	80,764
French	fr	71,722
Japanese	ja	71,418
Thai	th	36,824
Hindi	hi	27,320
German	de	23,316
Sum		2137106

Table 2: Language-wise Dataset Distribution

lished in past 5 months (February, March, April, May and June). Table 2 shows the total number of tweets collected by us and figure 1 shows their distribution across eight different language.

4 The CMTA Method

In this section, we have given a detailed sequential overview of CMTA method design. Both misinformation[9] and disinformation[10], according to the Oxford English Dictionary, are false or misleading information. Misinformation refers to information that is accidentally false and spread without the intent to hurt, whereas disinformation refers to false information that is intentionally produced and shared to cause hurt (Hernon, 1995). Claims do not have to be entirely truthful or incorrect; they can contain a small amount of false or inaccurate information(Shahi and Nandini, 2020). This work uses the general notion of misinformation and makes no distinction between misinformation and disinformation as it is practically difficult to determine one's intention computationally. Figure 2 shows the phases of the analytics pipeline of CMTA with their internal processes. CMTA implements a data science pipeline consisting of four phases: (1) tokenizing, (2) text features extraction, (3) linear transformation, and (4) classification. The first phases (tokenizing, text feature extraction, linear transformation) correspond to a substantial data-preparation process intended to build a multi-lingual vectorized representation of texts. The objective is to achieve a numerical pivot representation of texts agnostic of the language. CMTA classification task uses a dense layer and leads to a trained network model that can be used to classify micro-texts (e.g. tweets) into three misinformation classes: 'false', 'partly false' and 'misleading'.

Text tokenization Given a multilingual textual dataset consisting of sentences, CMTA uses the BERT multilingual tokeniser to generate tokens that BERT's embedding layer will further process. CMTA uses MBERT[11] to extract contextual features, namely word and sentence embedding vectors, from text data [12]. In the subsequent CMTA phases that use NLP models, these vectors are used as feature inputs with several advantages. (M)BERT embeddings are word representations that are dynamically informed by the words around them, meaning that the same word's embeddings will change in (M)BERT depending on its related words within two different sentences.

For the non-expert reader, the tokenization process is based on a WordPiece model. It greedily creates a fixed-size vocabulary of individual characters, subwords, and words that best fit a language data (e.g. English) [13]. Each token in a tokenized text must be associated with the sentence's index: sentence 0 (a series of 0s) or sentence 1 (a series of 1s). After breaking the text into tokens, a sentence must be converted from a list of strings to a list of vocabulary indices. The tokenisation result is used

[9] `https://www.oed.com/view/Entry/119699?redirectedFrom=misinformation`

[10] `https://www.oed.com/view/Entry/54579?redirectedFrom=disinformation`

[11] `https://github.com/google-research/bert/blob/master/multilingual.md`

[12] Embeddings are helpful for keyword/search expansion, semantic search and information retrieval. They help accurately retrieve results matching a keyword query intent and contextual meaning, even in the absence of keyword or phrase overlap.

[13] This vocabulary contains whole words, subwords occurring at the front of a word or in isolation (e.g., "em" as in the word "embeddings" is assigned the same vector as the standalone sequence of characters "em" as in "go get em"), subwords not at the front of a word, which are preceded by '##' to denote this case, and individual characters (?)

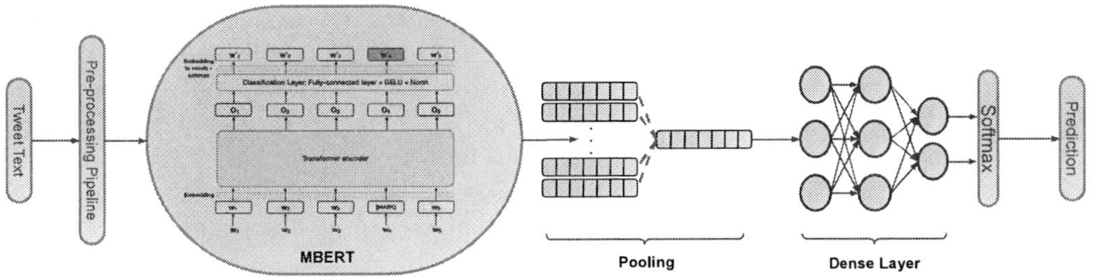

Figure 2: A detailed structure of CMTA architecture.

as input to apply BERT that produces two outputs, one pooled output with contextual embeddings and hidden-states of each layer. The complete set of hidden states for this model are stored in a structure containing four elements: the layer number (13 layers) [14], the batch number (number of sentences submitted to the model), the word / token number in a sentence, the hidden unit/feature number (768 features) [15].

In the case of CMTA, the tokenisation is more complex because it is done for sentences written in different languages. Therefore, it relies on the MBERT model that has been trained for this purpose.

Feature Extraction Phase is intended to exploit the information of hidden-layers produced due to applying BERT to the tokenisation phase result. The objective is to get individual vectors for each token and convert them into a single vector representation of the whole sentence. For each token of our input, we have 13 separate vectors, each of length 768. Thus, to get the individual vectors, it is necessary to combine some of the layer vectors. The challenge is to determine which layer or combination of layers provides the best representation.

Linear convolution The hidden states from the 12th layer are processed in this phase, applying linear convolution and pooling to get correlation among tokens. We apply a three-layer 1D convolution over the hidden states with consecutive pooling layers. The final convolutional layer's output is passed through a global average pooling layer to get a final sentence representation. This representation holds the relation between contextual embeddings of individual tokens in the sentence.

[14]It is 13 because the first element is the input embeddings, the rest is the outputs of each of BERT's 12 layers.

[15]That is 219,648 unique values to represent our one sentence!

Classification A linear layer is connected to the model in the end for the CMTA classification task.

This classification layer outputs a Softmax value of vector, depending on the output, the index of the highest value in the vector represents the label for the given sequence: 'false', 'partly false' and 'misleading'.

5 Experiment

5.1 Dataset Proprocessing

In data preprocessing, we performed cleaning and structuring of the training and inference dataset. The collected dataset contained lots of unnecessary noises and components such as emojis, symbols, numeric values, hyperlinks to websites and username mentions which were needed to be removed. Since our dataset was multilingual, we had to be very careful while preprocessing as we did not wanted to lose any valuable information. We used simple regular expressions to remove URLs, special characters or symbols, blank rows, re-tweets, user mentions but we did not removed the hashtags from the data. As hashtags might contain useful information. For example in the sentence- 'Wear mask to protect yourself from #COVID-19 #corona', only '#' symbol was removed during the preprocessing(e.g. 'Wear mask to protect yourself from COVID19 corona'). We removed stop words using NLTK[16], a Python library for natural language processing. NLTK supports multiple languages except few languages such as Hindi and Thai in our case. For preprocessing Hindi dataset we used CLTK(Classical Lan-

[16]https://www.nltk.org/

guage Toolkit) [17] which supports Hindi stop words. For removing Thai stop words from Thai tweets, we used PyThaiNLP (Wannaphong Phatthiyaphaibun, 2016). The emojis were removed using their unicodes. For training our model we divided the dataset into training, validation and testing dataset in the ratio of 80%/10%10% respectively. The final count for train, validation and test dataset was 7,602, 950, 950.

5.2 Model Setup and Training

Training Setting We fine-tuned the Sequence Classifier from HuggingFace based on the parameters as specified in (Devlin et al., 2018). Thus, we set a batch size of 32, learning rate 1e-4, with Adam Weight Decay as the optimizer. We run the model for training for 10 epochs. Then, we save the model weights of the transformer. These will be helpful for the further training.

Hyperparameters' Setting Table 3 lists every hyperparameter for training and testing our model. All the calculations and selection of hyperparmaters are done based on tests and for the best output from the model. After performing several iterations on distinct sets of hyper-parameters, based on the analysis of the model's performance, we adopted the one showing promising results on our dataset.

Parameters	Value
Pool Size of Average Pooling	8
Pool Size of Max Pooling	8
Dropout Probability	0.36
Number of Dense layers	4
Text Length	128
Batch Size	32
Epochs	10
Optimizer	Adam
Learning Rate	1×10^{-4}

Table 3: Hyper-parameters for training

5.3 Results assessment

This section discusses the performance our multilingual model over the test data. On the test dataset, our model was able to achieve an accuracy(%) of **82.17** and F_1(%) of **82.54**. The precision and recall reported by the model were **82.07** and **82.30** respectively. Table 5 shows model's prediction over few examples from the test dataset along with their actual label. As we shown in the table, the model prediction in case of entry number '1', '2', '3' and '4' our model was able to predict the correct the label. But in case of entry number '5' the label predicted by our model was 'False' whereas the actual label is 'Misleading'. If we would look at the misinformation at the entry number '5' which is a Spanish text- 'El medicamento contra piojos sirve como tratamiento contra Covid-19.' and who's English translation would be- ". This misinformation claims about a COVID-19 medicine and since this could be 'false' and 'misleading' misinformation at the same time, our model predicted it as a 'false' misinformation rather than 'misleading'.

[17] https://docs.cltk.org/en/latest/index.html

6 Multilingual Misinformation Analysis

In this section, we provide a detailed analysis misinformation distribution across the multilingual tweets. We used our trained multilingual model to predict and categorize the misinformation type present in tweets. We conducted our sequential misinformation analysis on a collection of over 2 million multilingual tweets. Our survey studied and analyzed the distribution of COVID-19 misinformation across eight major languages, (i.e. 'English', 'Spanish', 'Indonesian', 'French', 'Japanese', 'Thai', 'Hindi' and 'German') for five months (i.e. February, March, April, May and June). Figure 4 shows the month-wise distribution of misinformation types for each language. Table 4 presents a detailed count of misinformation classes across all the languages. In the figure 6, we could observe that for February, March and June months our model predicted large number of tweets as 'False', followed by 'Misleading' which is second largest and the number of 'Partially false' was the least. For the tweets generated during the month of April and May, our model discovered that the number of 'Partially false' tweets are more than 'Misleading' tweets and 'False' tweets were again in majority. Figure **??** parallelly showcase the overall(all 5 months together) spread of misinformation types across each language. We could clearly see that German tweets have the highest number of 'Misleading' tweets whereas French have the least. Spanish tweets beats other language's tweets by becoming the language with largest source of 'False' misinformation. Germany generated the least number of 'False' tweets. Hindi tweets tends to have the highest number of 'Partially false' tweets whereas

Lingo	February			March			April		
	Misinformation			Misinformation			Misinformation		
	False	Partially False	Misleading	False	Partially False	Misleading	False	Partially False	Misleading
Spanish	58346	6653	13740	67956	10913	8826	34125	5437	3604
German	517	581	2505	862	1438	3043	584	892	2664
Japanese	1920	3079	5245	448	692	2650	1635	2850	5840
Indonesian	11157	3226	1951	12573	4336	1582	9073	3367	1273
English	88369	62747	76640	92428	96571	105143	77368	74947	63473
French	4464	3472	1155	12024	10270	1670	6650	5300	763
Hindi	500	870	202	756	909	348	2211	2868	705
Thai	1950	1074	2780	6036	736	7678	2263	554	2917

Lingo	May			June		
	Misinformation			Misinformation		
	False	Partially False	Misleading	False	Partially False	Misleading
Spanish	57821	8214	7107	54965	8828	6759
German	1076	1426	4430	616	657	2028
Japanese	8984	12324	18125	1741	2496	3389
Indonesian	12695	4574	1805	9114	3038	1000
English	140494	128326	119391	135172	101896	109483
French	8475	7667	842	4952	3535	483
Hindi	4560	6057	1343	2501	2739	751
Thai	2825	470	1830	2103	486	3122

Table 4: Language-wise predicted misinformation labels of tweets

Test Data	Actual Label	Prediction	Accuracy(/)
Dr. Megha Vyas from Pune, India died due to COVID-19 while treating COVID patients.	False	False	
El plátano bloquea "la entrada celular del COVID-19"	False	False	
Asymptomatic people are very rarely contagious, said the WHO.	Partially False	Partially False	
Patanjali Coronil drops can help cure coronavirus.	Misleading	Misleading	
El medicamento contra piojos sirve como tratamiento contra Covid-19.	Misleading	False	

Table 5: Misinformation data examples along with model's prediction and actual label

Thai have the least of all. Following more specific observation made with respect to the languages:

- English: The misinformation distribution for English data, indicates that there is a majority of **False** tweets during the five months, whereas the distribution of **Misleading** labelled data is slightly less than as compared to **False** labelled data. **Partially False** labelled tweets are moderately distributed, as in month April we can see that there is a greater number with respect to other months.

- Spanish: From the distribution graph, Spanish tweets have greater frequency of **False** labelled tweets, whereas the **Misleading** tweets and **Partially False** tweets shows almost same number of tweet across the five months.

- German: There was a surge of **Misleading** labelled tweets during the month February, and the count remained the same throughout the five months. There was also an increase in **Partially False** tweets in March but it decreased in successive months, leading to minor **False** labelled tweets.

- Japanese: In the graph of language wise-distribution4, it can be seem that on an average throughout the five months, approx 20% of Japanese tweets are labelled **False**, similarly approx 30% of the Japanese tweets are labelled **Partially False**, leading to the majority of 50% data are labelled as **Misleading**. We can also see that there was a huge increase in **Misleading** tweets in March, tweeted in

Japanese language.

- Indonesian: In our distribution for Indonesian tweets approximately 10% of tweets are labelled as **Misleading** and in contrary there is a large distribution of **False** labelled tweets. Approximately 34% of the data in Indonesian dialect is labelled as **Partially False** throughout the five months.

- French: Figure4 shows the misinformation distribution across all of the five months in the French tweets. The largest majority of the tweets were classified as **False** misinformation. Among **Partially false** and **Misleading**, the least number of tweets were labelled as **Misleading**.

- Hindi: The frequency of Hindi tweets is low in the dataset used in our experiment. Yet, our model can predict or label Hindi tweets. Tweets in Hindi have low numbers of **Misleading** tweets, whereas the **Partially False** tweets class has a great frequency. **False** labelled tweets are slightly low compared to **Partially False** tweets in this dialect.

- Thai: The distribution of Thai tweets, shows that our model prediction is majorly oriented towards the **Misleading** tweets. The distribution of **Misleading** labelled tweets it the greatest among the labelled classes, in contrast to **Partially False** tweets. **False** labelled tweets are comparatively moderate in this language.

7 Conclusion and Future Work

In this paper, we presented a BERT based multilingual model for analysing COVID-19 related multilingual tweets. We performed a detailed systematic survey for detecting disinformation spread on the social media platform- Twitter. We were able to detect misinformation distribution across eight major languages and presented a quantified magnitude of misinformation distributed across different languages in last 5 months. We also demonstrated that our single multilingual CMTA framework performed significantly well as compared to the monolingual misinformation detection models. We strongly believe that our model can help in filtration of misinformation and factual data present in multiple languages during the pandemic.

In future, we aim at collecting more annotated training data and performing analysis of a larger multilingual dataset to gain deeper understanding. We aim at improving our model's robustness and contextual understanding for better performance in the classification task. Since analysis was done on a limited dataset the results cannot be generalised. We hope that through our work researchers could gain more deeper insights about misinformation spread across major languages and hence utilizing the information in building more reliable social media platform.

References

Firoj Alam, Shaden Shaar, Fahim Dalvi, Hassan Sajjad, Alex Nikolov, Hamdy Mubarak, Giovanni Da San Martino, Ahmed Abdelali, Nadir Durrani, Kareem Darwish, and Preslav Nakov. 2020. Fighting the covid-19 infodemic: Modeling the perspective of journalists, fact-checkers, social media platforms, policy makers, and the society.

J Scott Brennen, Felix Simon, Philip N Howard, and Rasmus Kleis Nielsen. 2020. Types, sources, and claims of covid-19 misinformation. *Reuters Institute*, 7.

Ms D Brindha, R Jayaseelan, and S Kadeswara. 2020. Social media reigned by information or misinformation about covid-19: a phenomenological study.

Emily Chen, Kristina Lerman, and Emilio Ferrara. 2020. Tracking social media discourse about the covid-19 pandemic: Development of a public coronavirus twitter data set. *JMIR Public Health and Surveillance*, 6(2):e19273.

Matteo Cinelli, Walter Quattrociocchi, Alessandro Galeazzi, Carlo Michele Valensise, Emanuele Brugnoli, Ana Lucia Schmidt, Paola Zola, Fabiana Zollo, and Antonio Scala. 2020. The covid-19 social media infodemic. *arXiv preprint arXiv:2003.05004*.

Jacob Devlin, Ming-Wei Chang, Kenton Lee, and Kristina Toutanova. 2018. Bert: Pre-training of deep bidirectional transformers for language understanding. *arXiv preprint arXiv:1810.04805*.

Arkin R Dharawat, Ismini Lourentzou, Alex Morales, and ChengXiang Zhai. 2020. Drink bleach or do what now? covid-hera: A dataset for risk-informed health decision making in the presence of covid19 misinformation.

Gunther Eysenbach, John Powell, Oliver Kuss, and Eun-Ryoung Sa. 2002. Empirical studies assessing the quality of health information for consumers on the world wide web: a systematic review. *Jama*, 287(20):2691–2700.

Nuno Fernandes. 2020. Economic effects of coronavirus outbreak (covid-19) on the world economy. *Available at SSRN 3557504*.

Sheera Frenkel, Davey Alba, and Raymond Zhong. 2020. Surge of virus misinformation stumps facebook and twitter. *The New York Times*.

Riccardo Gallotti, Francesco Valle, Nicola Castaldo, Pierluigi Sacco, and Manlio De Domenico. 2020. Assessing the risks of" infodemics" in response to covid-19 epidemics. *arXiv preprint arXiv:2004.03997*.

Oguzhan Gencoglu and Mathias Gruber. 2020. Causal modeling of twitter activity during covid-19. *arXiv preprint arXiv:2005.07952*.

Peter Hernon. 1995. Disinformation and misinformation through the internet: Findings of an exploratory study. *Government information quarterly*, 12(2):133–139.

P Hitlin and K Olmstead. 2018. The science people see on social media. pew research center.

Binxuan Huang and Kathleen M Carley. 2020. Disinformation and misinformation on twitter during the novel coronavirus outbreak. *arXiv preprint arXiv:2006.04278*.

Nicholas E Ingraham and Christopher J Tignanelli. 2020. Fact versus science fiction: fighting coronavirus disease 2019 requires the wisdom to know the difference. *Critical Care Explorations*, 2(4).

Yohei Kikuta. 2019. Bert pretrained model trained on japanese wikipedia articles. `https://github.com/yoheikikuta/bert-japanese`.

Ramez Kouzy, Joseph Abi Jaoude, Afif Kraitem, Molly B El Alam, Basil Karam, Elio Adib, Jabra Zarka, Cindy Traboulsi, Elie W Akl, and Khalil Baddour. 2020. Coronavirus goes viral: quantifying the covid-19 misinformation epidemic on twitter. *Cureus*, 12(3).

Christian E Lopez, Malolan Vasu, and Caleb Gallemore. 2020. Understanding the perception of covid-19 policies by mining a multilanguage twitter dataset. *arXiv preprint arXiv:2003.10359*.

Louis Martin, Benjamin Muller, Pedro Javier Ortiz Suárez, Yoann Dupont, Laurent Romary, Éric Villemonte de la Clergerie, Djamé Seddah, and Benoît Sagot. 2019. Camembert: a tasty french language model. *arXiv preprint arXiv:1911.03894*.

Katerina Eva Matsa and Elisa Shearer. 2018. News use across social media platforms 2018— pew research center. *Journalism and Media*.

World Health Organization et al. 2020. Coronavirus disease 2019 (covid-19): situation report, 188.

Esteban Ortiz-Ospina. 2020. The rise of social media. Technical report.

Gordon Pennycook, Jonathon McPhetres, Yunhao Zhang, Jackson G Lu, and David G Rand. 2020. Fighting covid-19 misinformation on social media: Experimental evidence for a scalable accuracy-nudge intervention. *Psychological science*, 31(7):770–780.

2020 Poynter Institute. 2020. The international fact-checking network.

Josimar E Chire Saire and Roberto C Navarro. 2020. What is the people posting about symptoms related to coronavirus in bogota, colombia? *arXiv preprint arXiv:2003.11159*.

Gautam Kishore Shahi and Durgesh Nandini. 2020. Fakecovid–a multilingual cross-domain fact check news dataset for covid-19. *arXiv preprint arXiv:2006.11343*.

Karishma Sharma, Sungyong Seo, Chuizheng Meng, Sirisha Rambhatla, and Yan Liu. 2020. Covid-19 on social media: Analyzing misinformation in twitter conversations. *arXiv preprint arXiv:2003.12309*.

Megha Sharma, Kapil Yadav, Nitika Yadav, and Keith C Ferdinand. 2017. Zika virus pandemic—analysis of facebook as a social media health information platform. *American journal of infection control*, 45(3):301–302.

Lisa Singh, Shweta Bansal, Leticia Bode, Ceren Budak, Guangqing Chi, Kornraphop Kawintiranon, Colton Padden, Rebecca Vanarsdall, Emily Vraga, and Yanchen Wang. 2020. A first look at covid-19 information and misinformation sharing on twitter. *arXiv preprint arXiv:2003.13907*.

Julio Torales, Marcelo O'Higgins, João Mauricio Castaldelli-Maia, and Antonio Ventriglio. 2020. The outbreak of covid-19 coronavirus and its impact on global mental health. *International Journal of Social Psychiatry*, page 0020764020915212.

Charin Polpanumas Arthit Suriyawongkul Lalita Lowphansirikul Pattarawat Chormai Wannaphong Phatthiyaphaibun, Korakot Chaovavanich. 2016. PyThaiNLP: Thai Natural Language Processing in Python.

Justin Wilford, Kathryn Osann, and Lari Wenzel. 2018. Social media use among parents of young childhood cancer survivors. *Journal of Oncology Navigation & Survivorship*, 9(1).

John Zarocostas. 2020. How to fight an infodemic. *The Lancet*, 395(10225):676.

A Appendix

A.1 CMTA vs Monolingual BERT Models

In this section, we have presented a comparative performance study of various monolingual BERT models with respect to our proposed multilingual

CMTA model for the misinformation detection task. We investigated eight monolingual BERT model[18], namely, 'English', 'Spanish', 'French', 'Germann', 'Japanese', 'Hindi' 'Thai[19]' and 'Indonesian'.

Data Processing: We utilized the same 9,502 tweets distributed across 3 misinformation classes for training the monolingual models. Since our dataset was consist of tweets in English and Spanish language; we translated the tweets into eight languages for training each of the eight monolingual model. We used Google Translator API[20] for converting the tweets into a particular language.

Experiment and Result: We experimented the multi-lingual data with their respective linguistic based BERT models. We set the model training parameters same as the CMTA model, and preprocessed the data as stated previously. Each of the monolingual model was fine-tuned for 10 ephocs with batch size of 32. using the classification dataset of their respective language. EnglishBERT scored an F1-score of 77.9% on the English tweets, with recall rate of 74.18%. This possible reason could be that it is heavily trained on English Corpus. From huggingface's model library we got SpanishBERT. The model scored an F1-score of 76.2% with recall rate of 72.02% and precision 80.9%. For French tweets we used CamemBERT(Martin et al., 2019) from huggingface. The CamemBERT scored an F1-score of 76.32%, with recall rate of 71.45% and precision 81.91%. GermanBERT showed a significant results on German-basesd tweets. It had a precision of 80.61% with recall rate of 71.43%, resulting to an F1-score of 75.74%. JapaneseBERT derived from the paper (Kikuta, 2019), is 79.56% precise on Japanese tweets with recall rate of 65.36% and F1-score of 71.76%. HindiBERT model had an F1-score of 71.95%, 79.56% precise with recall rate 65.68%. ThaiBERT scored an F1-score of 72.11%, being 79.11% precise with recall rate 66.25% IndonesianBERT is 78.96% precise, recall rate of 65.66%, resulting to an F1-score of 71.69%. Based on the experiment results, we can strongly suggest that the multilingual CMTA model was able to generalize smoothly on the dataset and it's performance was equivalent to the monolingual models.

ModelsMetrics	Precision	Recall	F1-score
EnglishBERT	82.03	74.18	77.90
SpanishBERT	80.9	72.02	76.20
CamemBERT	81.91	71.45	76.32
GermanBERT	80.61	71.43	75.74
JapaneseBERT	79.56	65.36	71.76
HindiBERT	79.56	65.68	71.95
ThaiBERT	79.11	66.25	72.11
IndonesianBERT	78.96	65.66	71.69
CMTA	81.52	74.40	77.79

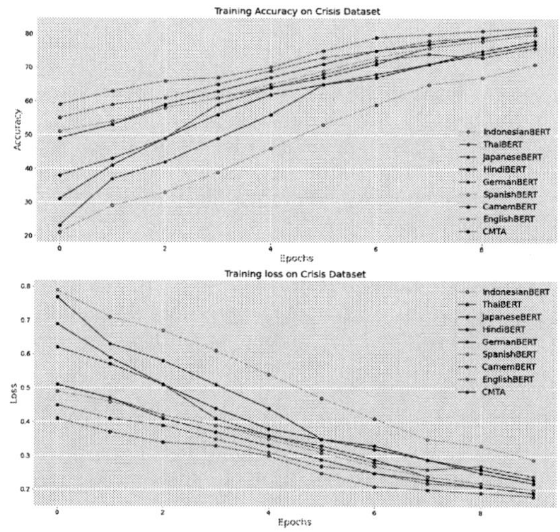

Figure 3: Training Accuracy(Upper) and Training loss(Lower)

[18]Pretrained model from https://huggingface.co/models
[19]ThaiBERT from https://github.com/ThAIKeras/bert
[20]Please refer https://cloud.google.com/translate/docs

Our Rating	IFCN(Poynter) Rating	Misinformation	Explanation
False	False	The border between France and Belgium will be closed.	French and Belgian authorities denied it.
	Four pinocchios	Trump's effort to blame Obama for sluggish coronavirus testing.	There was no "Obama rule," just draft guidance that never took effect and was withdrawn before President Trump took office.
	Inaccurate	Elisa Granato, the first volunteer in the first Europe human tria of a COVID-19 vaccine, has died.	Elisa Granato, the first volunteer in the first Europe human trial of a COVID-19 vaccine, has died.
Partially False	Partially False	Media shows a Florida beach full of people while it's empty.	The different videos were not shot at the same time. The beaches are empty when they are closed.
	Two Pinocchios	The bill for a coronavirus test in the US is $3.000	The CDC is not making people pay the test by now.
	Partly False	Salty and sour foods cause the "body of the COVID-19 virus" to explode and dissolve.	"Consuming fruit juices or gargling with warm water and salt does not protect or kill COVID-19," the World Health Organization Philippines told VERA Files.
Misleading	Misleading	A clip from Mexico depicts the dumping of coronavirus patients corpses into the sea.	Misbar's investigation of the video revealed that it does not depict the dumping of coronavirus patients corpses in Mexico, but rather paratroopers landing from a Russian MI 26 helicopter.
	No Evidence	Media uses photos of puppets on patient stretchers to scare then public.	There is no evidence that any media outlet used this photo for their reporting about COVID-19. Its origin is unclear, maybe it was shot in Mexico and shows a medical training session.
	Mostly False	Coronavirus does not affect people with 'O+' blood type.	The post claiming coronavirus does not affect people with 'O+' blood type is misleading.

Table 6: Misinformation Dataset

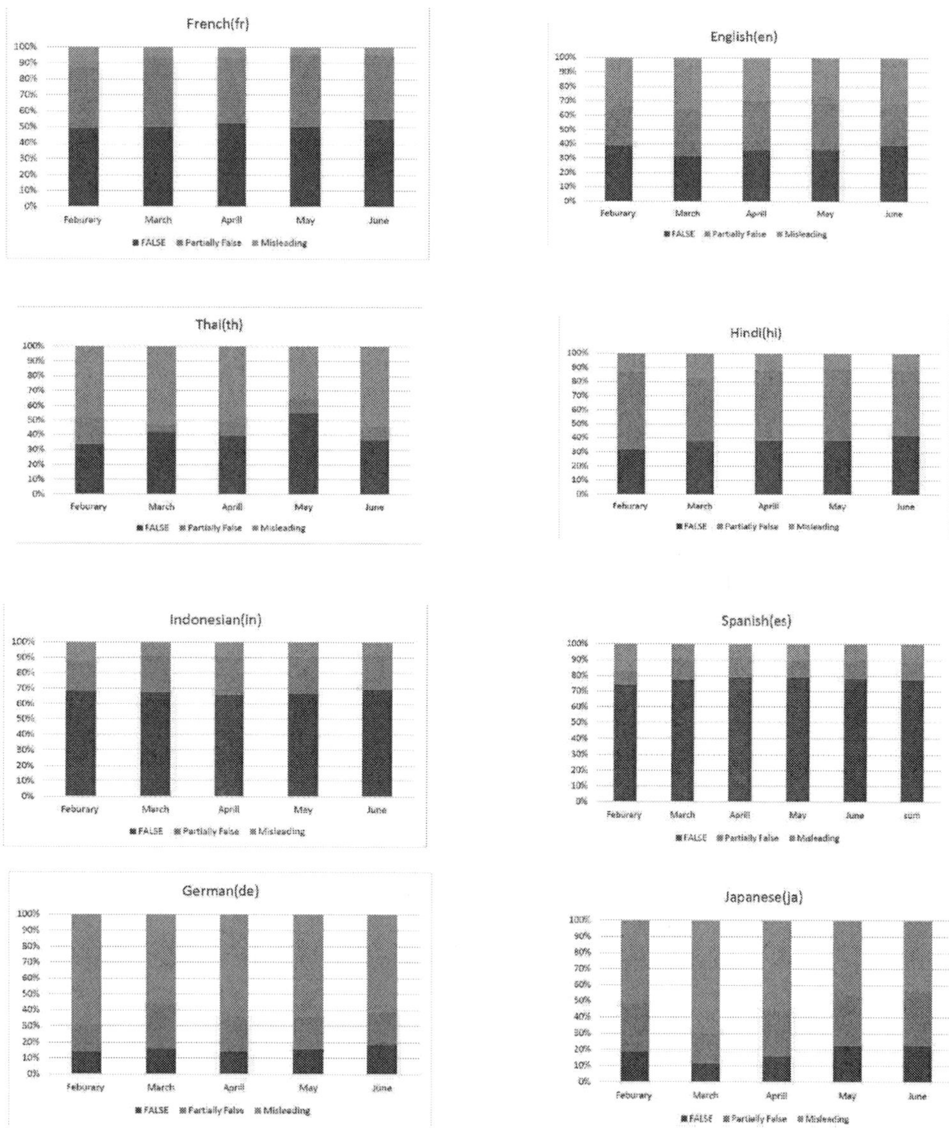

Figure 4: Month-wise Disinformation Distribution in Languages.

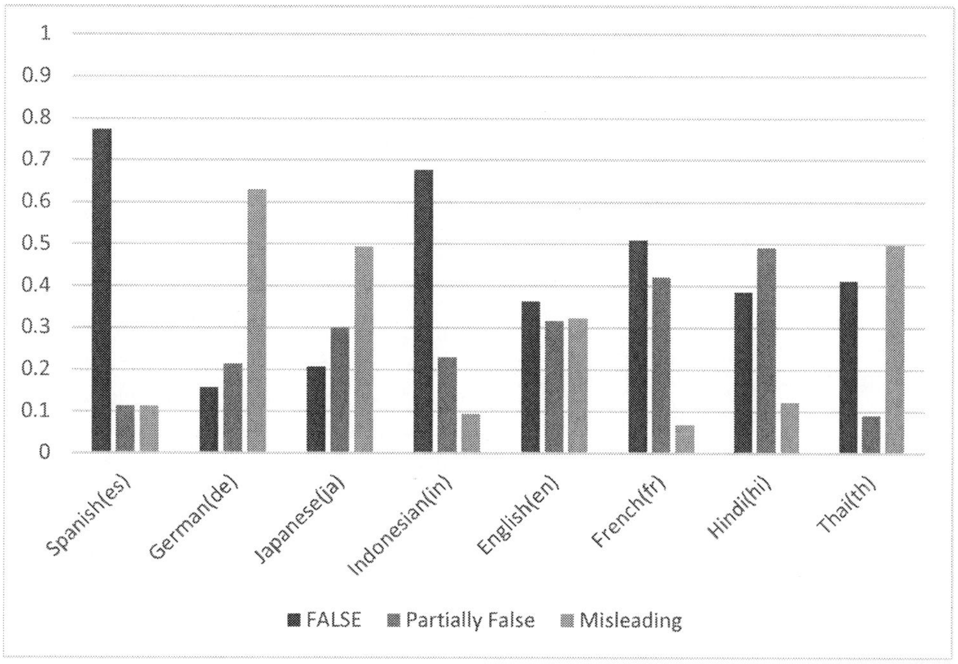

Figure 5: Language-wise Disinformation Distribution.

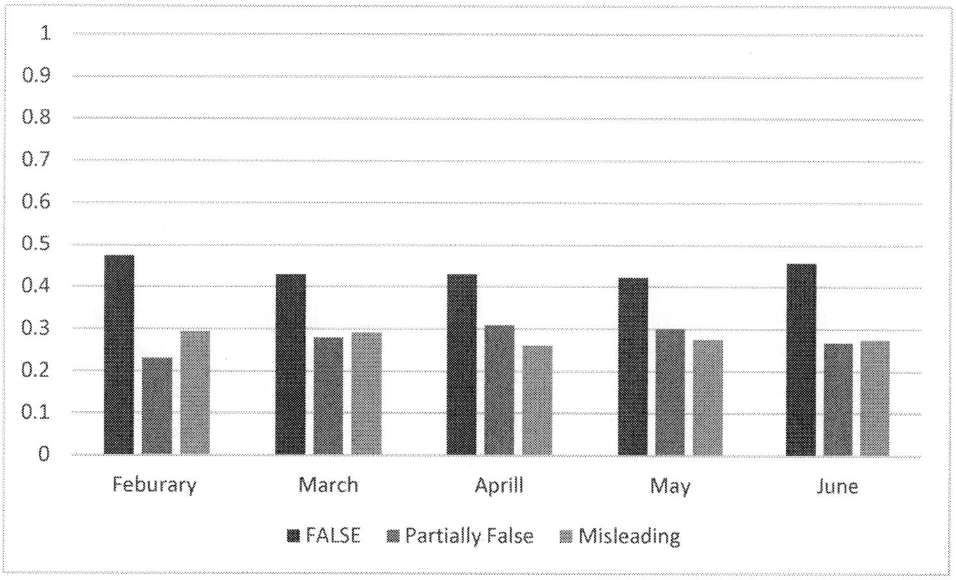

Figure 6: Month-wise Disinformation Distribution.

Predicting pragmatic discourse features in the language of adults with autism spectrum disorder

Christine Yang, Duanchen Liu, Qingyun Yang, Zoey Liu, Emily Prud'hommeaux
Department of Computer Science, Boston College
{yangael,liuaha,yangama,liuaal,prudhome}@bc.edu

Abstract

Individuals with autism spectrum disorder (ASD) experience difficulties in social aspects of communication, but the linguistic characteristics associated with deficits in discourse and pragmatic expression are often difficult to precisely identify and quantify. We are currently collecting a corpus of transcribed natural conversations produced in an experimental setting in which participants with and without ASD complete a number of collaborative tasks with their neurotypical peers. Using this dyadic conversational data, we investigate three pragmatic features – politeness, uncertainty, and informativeness – and present a dataset of utterances annotated for each of these features on a three-point scale. We then introduce ongoing work in developing and training neural models to automatically predict these features, with the goal of identifying the same between-groups differences that are observed using manual annotations. We find the best performing model for all three features is a feed-forward neural network trained with BERT embeddings. Our models yield higher accuracy than ones used in previous approaches for deriving these features, with F1 exceeding 0.82 for all three pragmatic features.

1 Introduction

Autism spectrum disorder (ASD) is a neurological disorder associated with impairments in communication that can have a life-long impact on relationships, professional success, and personal independence (Ketelaars et al., 2010; Whitehouse et al., 2009; Hendricks, 2010). Although some percentage of individuals with ASD are not verbal from a young age, most go on to acquire spoken language but experience challenges in social aspects of communication related to discourse and pragmatic expression (Eales, 1993; Young et al., 2005). This atypicality in language has been recognized since the disorder was first named nearly eighty years ago (Kanner, 1943), and unusual language usage is one of the criteria used in the primary diagnostic instruments for ASD (Lord et al., 2002; Rutter et al., 2003). One challenge for clinicians, however, is that there are no existing assessment tools for quantifying atypicality in discourse or pragmatics that can highlight communication deficits associated specifically with ASD while ruling out those associated with unrelated language disorders.

Most previous work on identifying pragmatic features that index atypicality in expressive language relies on careful manual annotations of transcripts of spontaneous spoken language (Volden and Lord, 1991; Bishop et al., 2000; Adams, 2002; Gorman et al., 2016; Canfield et al., 2016). Deploying complex annotation schemes like these, however, is time consuming and requires training and expertise, rendering this sort of detailed linguistic analysis impractical in the clinical intervention settings in which it would be most useful. Work on computational approaches for automatically identifying these features in the expressive language of individuals with ASD has focused exclusively on the language of children. In addition, this prior research has generally been applied to expressive language produced in a semi-structured context with an examiner or parent rather than spontaneous conversational speech with a peer (Prud'hommeaux et al., 2014; Losh and Gordon, 2014; Parish-Morris et al., 2016; Goodkind et al., 2018).

Our work addresses these aforementioned shortcomings in the previous work on pragmatic expression in ASD. In this paper, we describe an annotated corpus of conversations between adults with and without ASD and their neurotypical interlocutors as they engage in several collaborative tasks. Using this corpus, we investigate the degree of politeness, uncertainty, and informativeness in these conversations with the goal of identifying distinc-

Proceedings of the Joint Conference of the 59th Annual Meeting of the Association for Computational Linguistics and the 11th International Joint Conference on Natural Language Processing: Student Research Workshop, pages 284–291
August 5–6, 2021.

tive pragmatic features of ASD. We focus on these three features in particular because they are specific, remediable, and relevant in the collaborative discourse domain.

When data collection is complete, we will release the transcribed and annotated dataset to researchers who have completed their institution's human subjects training. The dataset will be unique in that it is produced by adults, a subgroup of the ASD population that is both understudied and underserved. In addition, the dataset will consist entirely of spontaneous conversations with a peer, a rarity in ASD datasets. To our knowledge there is no single corpus manually annotated with all three features of politeness, uncertainty, and informativeness. Moreover, our corpus is already larger than any existing *spoken* language (as opposed to *textual*) corpus available for these features.

With our annotated corpus, we propose several neural models for classifying utterances according to these features, and we explore whether our automated methods of generating these pragmatic features can be used to distinguish adults with ASD from their neurotypical peers as effectively as features derived via manual annotation. Our models outperform prior approaches to all three classification tasks, often by very wide margins. Although our predicted annotations do not capture all of the between-group differences observed using the manual annotations, we see promise in our approach.

2 Data Collection

2.1 Participants and tasks

We have collected spoken language data in a collaborative dyadic setting from adults 18 to 30 years of age with high-functioning ASD ($n = 14$) and with typical development (TD, $n = 8$). The ASD participants met the criteria for a diagnosis of ASD on the Autism Diagnostic Observation Schedule (ADOS) (Lord et al., 2002). All participants met the following eligibility criteria: (1) performance IQ (PIQ) ≥ 80; (2) verbal IQ (VIQ) ≥ 80; (3) monolingual speaker of American English; and (4) no history of language impairment, auditory processing disorder, or hearing difficulty. This data collection is ongoing and is being conducted with the approval of the Institutional Review Boards of the two participating universities.

Each ASD or TD participant is paired with a neurotypical conversational partner (CP, $n = 11$), and together they engage in collaborative tasks involving verbal communication and deliberation. The two tasks we focus on in this paper include a map task and a deserted island task. In the map task, styled after Anderson et al. (1991), each participant is given a map of the same area, but with slight differences in the place names and locations of obstacles. Each map is marked with an X to show where that participant is located on the map. The experimental participant must give verbal directions to the conversational partner to lead them to their position on the map. In the deserted island task, a widely used method of eliciting natural conversation in second language instruction, the two participants are given a selection of labeled pictures of various items. They must agree on which of these items they would like to have with them on a deserted island. They are also given some specific categories of items to decide upon, such as items meant for entertainment or items that would be used to escape.

Feature	Agreement	α
Politeness	91.58%	0.57
Uncertainty	85.62%	0.75
Informativeness	91.62%	0.90

Table 1: Percent agreement and interrater reliability (Krippendorf's α) for pragmatic feature annotation.

The conversations are recorded and then manually transcribed using Praat (Boersma and Weenink, 2001). Thus far, we have collected and transcribed conversations from 22 pairs of participants, with 14 experimental participants in the ASD group, 8 experimental participants in the TD group, and 11 neurotypical conversational partners, resulting in a corpus of 9,267 total utterances produced by experimental participants, with 5,742 utterances produced by experimental participants in the ASD group and 3,525 utterances produced by experimental participants the TD group. In the transcriptions, an utterance is defined as a C-unit, "an independent clause with its modifiers" which cannot be further split up without losing the primary meaning of the utterance (Loban, 1976). Each utterance is marked with a punctuation to denote the utterance type as an exclamation, question, abandoned utterance, interrupted utterance, or regular utterance. Additionally, we transcribe discourse markers, filler words, unfilled pauses, partial or interrupted words, sound effects or onomatopoeia, and verbal expressions of affirmation, negation, or exclamation.

Task	Utterance	Politeness	Uncertainty	Informativeness
Map	How the heck am I supposed to say this?	1	1	1
Map	It's near the Irrigation Pond.	2	1	3
Map	Okay so we're going to have to go down one block.	3	1	2
Map	Can you describe where you're at?	2	3	1
Map	Yeah it is by some trees.	2	1	2
Map	Yeah it is by some trees.	2	1	2
Island	I don't care.	1	1	1
Island	I would say the matches first, because you can set off a signal, like a signal fire.	2	1	3
Island	Or you could keep the matches?	2	2	2
Island	Fishing pole, definitely, um.	2	1	2
Island	We'll put them off to the side.	3	1	1
Island	Do we want to go with these four?	3	2	1
Island	You want to do the dog?	3	2	2
Island	If we wanna trying get off the island we probably want some rope or something.	3	2	3
Island	We could use logs and stuff to tie up and make some kind of raft trying to get back to civilization.	3	1	3

Table 2: Samples manual annotations for each task.

2.2 Pragmatic feature annotation

After transcription, the transcripts are then annotated for politeness, uncertainty, and informativeness (Meyers et al., 2019), with each utterance receiving two annotations from a set of three trained human annotators. Each feature is given a rating on a scale from 1 to 3, with 1 representing the smallest degree of politeness, uncertainty, or informativeness, and 3 representing the highest degree of that feature. To measure the degree of agreement between the annotators, we calculate Krippendorf's alpha (Artstein and Poesio, 2008) for each feature, the results of which can be seen in Table 1. The final annotation of each feature for every utterance is then taken to be the average of the two annotators. We note that, although certain words are often helpful for determining the score of an utterance for a given feature, we do not rely on a list of specific lexical items or keywords. Example utterances and their corresponding scores are shown in Table 2.

These three features were chosen for a number of reasons. First, they are specific and interpretable, and as such, they are ideal features for targeted remediation. Secondly, they are especially relevant for and important in collaborative conversation; interviews, narratives, or monologues might be better analyzed using other features. Third, there are existing corpora labelled for these features and available toolkits for extracting these features, which allows us to compare our work against prior baselines and will enable us to leverage external corpora in our future work. Finally, we note that politeness, in particular, has been cited as an area of deficit in ASD (Frith, 1994; Sirota, 2004).

Politeness The *politeness* feature is a measure of how well an utterance contributes to a polite and collaborative dialogue, marked by agreeableness, positive attitudes, and willingness to compromise. A low politeness rating of 1 is given to utterances expressing frustration or criticism ("no you're wrong", "ugh how do I do this?") and utterances which use a more blunt way of phrasing commands ("go left"). A high politeness rating of 3 is given to utterances containing niceties (e.g., "thanks", "sorry") or highly positive words ("perfect", "awesome") and utterances that use a polite or indirect way of phrasing commands ("if you could make a left", "you want to make a left").

Uncertainty The *uncertainty* feature is defined to be a measure of the amount of uncertainty expressed about the correctness, validity, or permissibility of the utterance. A low uncertainty rating of 1 is given to utterances which express no uncertainty at all, or contain only a few filler words.

A medium uncertainty rating of 2 is given to polar questions, either-or questions, short abandoned utterances, and utterances containing many filler words ("um", "uh") or hedge phrases ("I guess", "I'm assuming"). A high uncertainty rating of 3 is given to open questions ("where are you?") and utterances expressing explicit uncertainty or confusion ("I have no idea").

Informativeness The *informativeness* feature is defined as a measure for the overall information content and specificity of an utterance. A low informativeness rating of 1 is given to utterances which contain only polar answers ("yes", "no") or vague words with low specificity ("thing", "over there"). In the map task, a medium informativeness rating of 2 is given to utterances which contain words for general objects and do not specify a specific location on the map, and a high informativeness rating of 3 is given to utterances which contain proper nouns or labels or descriptions that can only point to one specific location on the map. In the island task, a rating of 2 is given to utterances which contain only an item word or a short phrase explaining the item, and a rating of 3 is given to utterances which contain multiple item words or a longer explanation of the items.

3 Models

After the transcripts are annotated for the pragmatic features described above, we train a number of machine learning models on the annotated data, with the goal of eventually being able to bypass the manual annotations and automate the annotation process using these predictive models. The models are given the transcribed and tokenized utterance converted to all lowercase and are tasked with predicting the categorical label for politeness, uncertainty, and informativeness based on the manual transcriptions.

3.1 Baselines

We start with several different baseline models, shown in Table 4. The majority baseline always predicts the most frequent class; the stratified baseline makes random predictions proportional to the distribution of classes in the training set, and the random baseline predicts a random class every time.

We also evaluate against existing pre-trained models for rating politeness, uncertainty, and informativeness (Meyers et al., 2018). The results of this baseline can be seen in the "Existing Models" row in Table 4. The pre-trained *politeness* classifier is an SVM and is trained on the Stanford Politeness Corpus (Danescu-Niculescu-Mizil et al., 2013), which includes 4,353 sentences of text conversations from public forums on Wikipedia and Stack Exchange. The pre-trained *uncertainty* classifier is a logistic regression model trained on the Szeged Uncertainty Corpus (Vincze, 2014), which includes more than 9,000 annotated sentences from corpora from different genres. The pre-trained *informativeness* classifier is a logistic regression model trained on the `SQUINKY!` corpus (Lahiri, 2015), which includes 7,000 utterances annotated for informativeness, implicature, and formality.

Additionally, because the scales used in the pre-trained classifiers for politeness and informativeness are continuous and differ from our own categorical annotation scale, we use thresholding to convert the predictions to our scale. For example, to convert a continuous scale from 0 to 1 into a categorical scale from 1 to 3, we map any scores less than 0.33 to be 1, scores between 0.33 and 0.67 to be 2, and scores greater than 0.67 to be 3. Since the pre-trained uncertainty classifier only predicts a binary result of either 0 or 1 corresponding to certain or uncertain, we map their 0 rating to our 1 rating and their 1 rating to our 3 rating.

3.2 Neural model architecture

We apply several methods for extracting sentence embeddings from the utterances in our dataset. First we use a basic *sequences* embedding in which each unique word appearing in the training data is assigned a unique identification number, and each utterance is then converted to a vector composed of the identification numbers for the words in the utterance, with padding for dimension consistency. With the sequence embeddings, we use a bidirectional LSTM model trained for 20 epochs with a batch size of 128.

Additionally, we also use word embeddings from pre-trained word2vec (Mikolov et al., 2013) and GloVe (Pennington et al., 2014) models, representing each utterance summing all of the vectors for the component words. Each utterance is represented with these pretrained embeddings in the embedding layers of our models, which are implemented in Keras[1]. For the word2vec model, we use the Google News model which includes

[1]https://keras.io/

Parameters	Sequence (LSTM)	GloVe (CNN)	word2Vec (CNN)	BERT (Feedforward NN)
CV Folds	5	5	5	5
Epochs	20	20	20	20
Batch size	128	128	128	8
Embedding dimension	300	100	300	768
Layers	1 bidirectional hidden layer, 1 dense layer	3 convoluted layers, 2 max pooling layers, 1 global max pooling layer, 1 dense layer	3 convoluted layers, 2 max pooling layers, 1 global max pooling layer, 1 dense layer	2 hidden linear layers
Dropout	0.5	0.5	0.5	0.5
Loss function	categorical cross entropy	categorical cross entropy	categorical cross entropy	categorical cross entropy
Optimizer	RMSprop	RMSprop	RMSprop	Adam

Table 3: Summary of model parameters.

about 100 billion word vectors with a dimension of 300 [2]. For the GloVe model, we use the pre-trained Stanford GloVe model trained on data from Wikipedia and Gigaword which includes around 6 billion word vectors with a dimension of 100 (Pennington et al., 2014). With the word2vec and GloVe embeddings, we use a convolutional neural network (CNN) model with global max pooling, trained for 20 epochs with a batch size of 128.

The last type of embeddings that we employ are the contextualized word representations of BERT (Devlin et al., 2019). Rather than integrating classification within the BERT architecture, we extract the 768-dimensional embeddings from the BERT-base model, and use them within a feedforward neural network with two hidden layers (Schuster et al., 2020) to predict the three points on each of the three annotation scales. The complete information for the parameterizations of our baseline and neural models is provided in Table 3.

3.3 Model evaluation

All our models are trained and evaluated with 5-fold cross validation. For each fold, the accuracy, precision, recall and F1 of the predictions are calculated. Then the averages of these metrics across the 5 folds are computed as the indexes to evaluate model performance.

4 Results

4.1 Manual annotations

Given the manual annotations, we examine whether there are significant differences between the ASD and the TD participant groups in terms of the three pragmatic features, using t-tests for significance testing. As shown in Table 5, the manual annotations reveal significant differences between the ASD and TD participants for politeness and informativeness in the map task, and uncertainty and informativeness in the island task. ASD participants are more polite, less uncertain, and less informative compared to TD participants in the map task. However, the results are reversed in the island task, where ASD participants are less polite, more uncertain, and more informative than TD participants.

The difference in politeness between the two tasks could be partially due to the nature of the two tasks, as the map task requires the experimental participant to give instructions and commands to their conversational partner and thus presents greater opportunity and need for phrasing their statements in a more polite way. In contrast, in the island task, the two participants have equal roles, and there may be less need for phrasing statements more politely. These results suggest ASD participants tend to be more polite than their TD peers in tasks in which they have a leading or authority role. Furthermore, the structure of the task could also contribute to the difference in uncertainty in the two tasks. In the map task, the participant giving instructions has a clear, factual set of information to convey to their partner, while the island task is more subjective and requires more discussion between the two participants to agree on a set of items. This would suggest that ASD participants exhibit more uncertainty than their TD peers in open-ended tasks which require more discussion and exchange of opinion.

4.2 Model predictions

The prediction results for all our models are presented in Table 4. Overall, the majority classifier performed the best among the baselines tested and

[2] https://code.google.com/archive/p/word2vec/

		Politeness				Uncertainty				Informativeness			
Baselines		**Acc.**	**Prec.**	**Rec.**	**F1**	**Acc.**	**Prec.**	**Rec.**	**F1**	**Acc.**	**Prec.**	**Rec.**	**F1**
Majority		**.84**	**.71**	**.84**	**.77**	**.62**	.38	**.62**	**.47**	**.56**	.31	**.56**	**.40**
Stratified		.71	**.71**	.71	.71	.46	**.46**	.46	.46	.38	.38	.38	.38
Random		.20	**.71**	.20	.31	.20	.45	.20	.28	.20	.40	.20	.27
Existing Models		.73	.70	.73	.72	.55	.34	.55	.42	.55	**.49**	.55	.52
Model	**Embeddings**												
LSTM	Sequences	**.87**	.86	**.87**	.86	.72	.70	.72	.71	**.82**	.81	.82	.81
CNN	GloVe	.86	.82	.86	.84	.67	.64	.67	.65	.74	.72	.74	.73
CNN	word2vec	.84	.80	.84	.82	.69	.63	.69	.66	.76	.74	.76	.75
Feedforward NN	BERT	.85	**.88**	.85	**.87**	**.84**	**.82**	**.84**	**.83**	**.82**	**.82**	**.83**	**.82**

Table 4: Comparison of accuracy, precision, and recall for the baselines and models tested. The best baseline in each column and the best proposed model in each column are rendered in boldface.

	Manual Annotations		BERT Model Predictions	
Map Task	**ASD**	**TD**	**ASD**	**TD**
Politeness	**2.0005****	1.9645	**2.0626**	2.0444
Uncertainty	1.4124	**1.4334**	**1.399**	1.3805
Informativeness	1.6044	**1.7145******	**2.0631**	2.0444
Island Task	**ASD**	**TD**	**ASD**	**TD**
Politeness	2.0332	**2.0743**	**2.1798**	2.1597
Uncertainty	**1.3894******	1.223	1.367	**1.4021**
Informativeness	**1.7395*****	1.5169	**2.1798**	2.1597

Table 5: Speaker averages for pragmatic features, comparing the manually annotated values and values predicted by the BERT model which has the highest F1 measures. Asterisks indicates a significant difference between the two groups (** $p < 0.01$, *** $p < 0.001$, **** $p < 0.0001$).

had a fairly high accuracy already. This was especially true for politeness, where the majority baseline had an F1 measure of 0.77. This is likely due to the distribution of the politeness ratings, since most statements fell into the neutral category of 2 for politeness, being neither particularly polite or impolite. Despite the high performance of the majority baseline however, all four models trained on our own data generally performed substantially better than all the baseline classifiers, especially for uncertainty and informativeness. The BERT model seemed to perform the best overall across all three features, while the sequences model also performed well for politeness and informativeness. In terms of the F1 measure, the feedforward model trained with BERT embedding outperforms the majority baseline by 0.1 for politeness, 0.33 for uncertainty, and 0.42 for informativeness.

Since our goal is to investigate the differences in pragmatic expression between the two participant groups, we want our model to be able to capture the same group differences seen in the manual annotations. To this end, we take the output for each group predicted from the best-performing model, the feedforward model using BERT embedding, and perform a t-test between the two groups as well. The results of significance testing based on model predictions are then compared to those given manual annotations. As presented in Table 5, the BERT model fails to capture the group tendencies for uncertainty and informativeness in the map task and politeness and uncertainty in the island task, showing the opposite results as the manual annotations. However, it does seem to show the same group tendencies for politeness in the map task and informativeness in the island task, but it does not reveal statistically significant differences for any of the features.

5 Conclusions and Future Work

From the results of our study, we can see that there exist significant and quantifiable differences in pragmatic expressions between adults with ASD and their neurotypical peers. Moreover these differences are not fixed or consistent across all situations, but rather they may vary depending on the open-ended nature of the task, the roles involved, and the general context of the discourse. Relying on manual annotations of this sort, however, would not be practical or feasible in a clinical setting or for monitoring the efficacy of an intervention.

To determine whether these annotations can be carried out automatically, we introduced several potential models trained on the annotated data. Although all of our models outperformed one or more of the baselines, the BERT model generally is superior for all three features. None of the models, however, were able to capture the statistically significant differences we observe in the manual annotations. There is still more work to be done in fine-tuning the model to capture between-group differences which are vital to our study of the pragmatic expression of adults with ASD.

In our future work, we plan to extend the current study in at least three directions. First, we would like to employ different model architectures, leveraging external labeled corpora, with more systematic comparisons to see whether the differences between ASD and TD groups seen in manual annotations can be fully automatically derived. Second, after a long hiatus, we have recently resumed collecting data, with the goal of including 20 participants with ASD and 20 with typical development. Third, we aim to include annotations of other pragmatic features such as coherence and dialog acts in order to examine the differences of these features between ASD and neurotypical groups more comprehensively.

References

Catherine Adams. 2002. Practitioner review: The assessment of language pragmatics. *Journal of child psychology and psychiatry*, 43(8):973–987.

A Anderson, M Bader, E Bard, E Boyle, G. M Doherty, S Garrod, S Isard, J Kowtko, J McAllister, J Miller, C Sotillo, H. S Thompson, and R Weinert. 1991. The HCRC map task corpus. *Language and Speech*, 34(4):351–366.

Ron Artstein and Massimo Poesio. 2008. Inter-coder agreement for computational linguistics. *Computational Linguistics*, 34(4):555–596.

Dorothy VM Bishop, Janet Chan, Catherine Adams, Joanne Hartley, and Fiona Weir. 2000. Conversational responsiveness in specific language impairment: Evidence of disproportionate pragmatic difficulties in a subset of children. *Development and psychopathology*, 12(2):177–199.

Paul Boersma and David Weenink. 2001. Praat, a system for doing phonetics by computer. *Glot international*, 5:341–345.

Allison R Canfield, Inge-Marie Eigsti, Ashley de Marchena, and Deborah Fein. 2016. Story goodness in adolescents with autism spectrum disorder (ASD) and in optimal outcomes from ASD. *Journal of Speech, Language, and Hearing Research*, 59(3):533–545.

Cristian Danescu-Niculescu-Mizil, Moritz Sudhof, Dan Jurafsky, Jure Leskovec, and Christopher Potts. 2013. A computational approach to politeness with application to social factors. In *Proceedings of the 51st Annual Meeting of the Association for Computational Linguistics (Volume 1: Long Papers)*, pages 250–259, Sofia, Bulgaria. Association for Computational Linguistics.

Jacob Devlin, Ming-Wei Chang, Kenton Lee, and Kristina Toutanova. 2019. BERT: Pre-training of deep bidirectional transformers for language understanding. In *Proceedings of the 2019 Conference of the North American Chapter of the Association for Computational Linguistics: Human Language Technologies, Volume 1 (Long and Short Papers)*, pages 4171–4186, Minneapolis, Minnesota. Association for Computational Linguistics.

Martin J Eales. 1993. Pragmatic impairments in adults with childhood diagnoses of autism or developmental receptive language disorder. *Journal of autism and developmental disorders*, 23(4):593–617.

Uta Frith. 1994. Autism and theory of mind in everyday life. *Social development*, 3(2):108–124.

Adam Goodkind, Michelle Lee, Gary E Martin, Molly Losh, and Klinton Bicknell. 2018. Detecting language impairments in autism: A computational analysis of semi-structured conversations with vector semantics. *Proceedings of the Society for Computation in Linguistics*, 1(1):12–22.

Kyle Gorman, Lindsay Olson, Alison Presmanes Hill, Rebecca Lunsford, Peter A Heeman, and Jan PH van Santen. 2016. Uh and um in children with autism spectrum disorders or language impairment. *Autism Research*, 9(8):854–865.

Dawn Hendricks. 2010. Employment and adults with autism spectrum disorders: Challenges and strategies for success. *Journal of Vocational Rehabilitation*, 32(2):125–134.

Leo Kanner. 1943. Autistic disturbances of affective content. *Nervous Child*, 2:217–250.

Mieke P Ketelaars, Juliane Cuperus, Kino Jansonius, and Ludo Verhoeven. 2010. Pragmatic language impairment and associated behavioural problems. *International Journal of Language & Communication Disorders*, 45(2):204–214.

Shibamouli Lahiri. 2015. Squinky! a corpus of sentence-level formality, informativeness, and implicature.

Walter Loban. 1976. *Language Development: Kindergarten through Grade Twelve. NCTE Committee on Research Report No. 18.* ERIC.

Catherine Lord, Michael Rutter, Pamela DiLavore, and Susan Risi. 2002. *Autism Diagnostic Observation Schedule (ADOS).* Western Psychological Services.

Molly Losh and Peter C Gordon. 2014. Quantifying narrative ability in autism spectrum disorder: A computational linguistic analysis of narrative coherence. *Journal of autism and developmental disorders*, 44(12):3016–3025.

Benjamin S. Meyers, Nuthan Munaiah, Andrew Meneely, and Emily Prud'hommeaux. 2019. Pragmatic characteristics of security conversations: An exploratory linguistic analysis. In *2019 IEEE/ACM 12th International Workshop on Cooperative and Human Aspects of Software Engineering (CHASE)*, pages 79–82.

Benjamin S Meyers, Nuthan Munaiah, Emily Prud'hommeaux, Andrew Meneely, Josephine Wolff, Cecilia Ovesdotter Alm, and Pradeep Murukannaiah. 2018. A dataset for identifying actionable feedback in collaborative software development. In *Proceedings of the 56th Annual Meeting of the Association for Computational Linguistics (Volume 2: Short Papers)*, pages 126–131.

Tomas Mikolov, Ilya Sutskever, Kai Chen, Gregory S. Corrado, and Jeffrey Dean. 2013. Distributed representations of words and phrases and their compositionality. In *Conference on Neural Information Processing Systems*, pages 3111–3119.

Julia Parish-Morris, Mark Liberman, Neville Ryant, Christopher Cieri, Leila Bateman, Emily Ferguson, and Robert T Schultz. 2016. Exploring autism spectrum disorders using hlt. In *Proceedings of the Third Workshop on Computational Linguistics and Clinical Psychology*, pages 74–84.

Jeffrey Pennington, Richard Socher, and Christopher D. Manning. 2014. Glove: Global vectors for word representation. In *Empirical Methods in Natural Language Processing (EMNLP)*, pages 1532–1543.

Emily Prud'hommeaux, Eric Morley, Masoud Rouhizadeh, Laura Silverman, Jan van Santeny, Brian Roarkz, Richard Sproatz, Sarah Kauper, and Rachel DeLaHunta. 2014. Computational analysis of trajectories of linguistic development in autism. In *2014 IEEE Spoken Language Technology Workshop (SLT)*, pages 266–271. IEEE.

Michael Rutter, Anthony Bailey, and Catherine Lord. 2003. *Social Communication Questionnaire (SCQ).* Western Psychological Services, Los Angeles.

Sebastian Schuster, Yuxing Chen, and Judith Degen. 2020. Harnessing the linguistic signal to predict scalar inferences. In *Proceedings of the 58th Annual Meeting of the Association for Computational Linguistics*, pages 5387–5403, Online. Association for Computational Linguistics.

Karen Gainer Sirota. 2004. Positive politeness as discourse process: Politeness practices of high-functioning children with autism and asperger syndrome. *Discourse Studies*, 6(2):229–251.

Veronika Vincze. 2014. Uncertainty detection in hungarian texts. In *Proceedings of COLING 2014, the 25th International Conference on Computational Linguistics: Technical Papers*, pages 1844–1853.

Joanne Volden and Catherine Lord. 1991. Neologisms and idiosyncratic language in autistic speakers. *Journal of Autism and Developmental Disorders*, 21:109–130.

Andrew JO Whitehouse, Helen J Watt, EA Line, and Dorothy VM Bishop. 2009. Adult psychosocial outcomes of children with specific language impairment, pragmatic language impairment and autism. *International Journal of Language & Communication Disorders*, 44(4):511–528.

EC Young, JJ Diehl, D Morris, SL Hyman, and L Bennetto. 2005. Pragmatic language disorders in children with autism: The use of two formal tests to distinguish affected children from controls. *Language, Speech, and Hearing Services in Schools*, 36:62–72.

SUMPUBMED: Summarization Dataset of PubMed Scientific Articles

Vivek Gupta
University of Utah
vgupta@cs.utah.edu

Prerna Bharti
Microsoft Corporation
prerna.bharti@microsoft.com

Pegah Nokhiz
University of Utah
pnokhiz@cs.utah.edu

Harish Karnick
IIT Kanpur
hkarnick@cs.iitk.ac.in

Abstract

Most earlier work on text summarization is carried out on news article datasets. The summary in these datasets is naturally located at the beginning of the text. Hence, a model can spuriously utilize this correlation for summary generation instead of truly learning to summarize. To address this issue, we constructed a new dataset, SUMPUBMED, using scientific articles from the PubMed archive. We conducted a human analysis of summary coverage, redundancy, readability, coherence, and informativeness on SUMPUBMED. SUMPUBMED is challenging because (a) the summary is distributed throughout the text (not-localized on top), and (b) it contains rare domain-specific scientific terms. We observe that seq2seq models that adequately summarize news articles struggle to summarize SUMPUBMED. Thus, SUMPUBMED opens new avenues for the future improvement of models as well as the development of new evaluation metrics.

1 Introduction

Most of the existing summarization datasets, i.e., CNN Daily Mail and DUC are news article datasets. That is, the article acts as a document, and the summary is a short (10-15 lines) manually written highlight (i.e., headlines). In many cases, these highlights have significant lexical overlap with the few lines at the top of the article. Thus, any model which can extract the top few lines, e.g., extractive methods, performs adequately on these datasets.

However, the task of summarization is not merely limited to short-length news articles. One could also summarize long and complex documents such as essays, research papers, and books. In such cases, an extractive approach will most likely fail. For successful summarization on these documents, one needs to (a) find information from the distributed (non-localized) locale in the large text, (b) perform paraphrasing, simplifying, and shortening of longer sentences and (c) combine information from multiple sentences to generate the summary. Hence, an abstractive approach will perform better on such large documents.

One obvious source that contains such complex documents is the MEDLINE biomedical scientific articles, which are publicly available. Furthermore, these articles are accompanied by abstracts and conclusions which summarize the documents. Therefore, we constructed a scientific summarization dataset from pre-processed PubMed articles, named SUMPUBMED. In comparison to the previous news-article based datasets, SUMPUBMED documents are longer, and the corresponding summaries cannot be extracted by selecting a few sentences from fixed locations in the document.

The dataset, along with associated scripts, are available at `https://github.com/vgupta123/sumpubmed`. Our contributions in this paper are:

- We created a new scientific summarization dataset, SUMPUBMED, which has longer text documents and summaries with non-localized information from documents.
- We analyzed the quality of summaries in SUMPUBMED on the basis of four parameters: readability, coherence, non-repetition, and informativeness using human evaluation.
- We evaluated several extractive, abstractive (seq2seq), and hybrid summarization models on SUMPUBMED. The results show that SUMPUBMED is more challenging compared to the earlier news-based datasets.
- Lastly, we showed that the standard summarization evaluation metric, ROUGE (Lin, 2004), correlates poorly with human evaluations on SUMPUBMED. This indicates the

Proceedings of the Joint Conference of the 59th Annual Meeting of the Association for Computational Linguistics and the 11th International Joint Conference on Natural Language Processing: Student Research Workshop, pages 292–303
August 5–6, 2021.

need for a new evaluation metric for the scientific summarization task.

In Section 1, we provided a brief introduction. The remaining parts of the paper are organized as follows: in Section 2 we explain how SUMPUBMED was created. In Section 3, we explain how summaries were annotated by human experts. We then move on to experiments in Section 4. We next discuss the results and analysis in Section 5, followed by the related work in Section 6. Lastly, we move on to the conclusions in final Section 7.

2 SUMPUBMED Creation

SUMPUBMED is created from PubMed biomedical research papers, which has 26 million documents. The documents are sourced from diverse literature, including MEDLINE, life science journals, and online books. For SUMPUBMED creation we took 33,772 documents from Bio Med Central (BMC). BMC incorporates research papers related to medicine, pharmacy, nursing, dentistry, health care, health services, etc.

The research documents in BMC contain two subsections: *Front* and *Body*. The front part of the document is basically the abstract and taken as the gold summary. The body part which is taken as the main document contains three subsections: background, results, and conclusion.

Preprocessing The average word count in the PubMed scientific articles is around 4,000 words for each document and 250 to 300 lines in every document. Therefore, to create SUMPUBMED, we performed extensive preprocessing so that non-textual content is removed and the overall text is reduced to a more manageable size. This extenstive pre-processing step is one of the main factors that sets SUMPUBMED apart from similar datasets (Cohan et al., 2018).

During preprocessing, the non-textual content from the text was removed by: (a) replacing citations and digits in the content with *<cit>* and *<dig>* labels, (b) removing figures, tables, signatures, subscripts, superscripts, and their associated text (e.g., captions), and (c) removing the acknowledgments and references from the text. All the preprocessing was done on a sentence level utilizing the Python regex library.[1] After preprocessing, we convert the final document to an *XML* format and use the *SAX* parser to parse it.

***SAX* vs *DOM* parser:** In *SAX*, events are triggered when the *XML* is being parsed. When the parser is parsing the *XML* and encounters a tag starting (e.g., $< something >$), then it triggers the *tagStarted* event (actual name of the event might differ). Similarly, when the end of the tag is met while parsing ($< /something >$), it triggers *tagEnded*. Using a *SAX* parser implies one needs to handle these events and make sense of the data returned with each event. One could also use the *DOM* parser,[2] where no events are triggered while parsing. In *DOM* the entire *XML* is parsed, and a *DOM* tree (of the nodes in the *XML*) is generated and returned. In general, *DOM* is easier to use but has a huge *overhead* of parsing the entire *XML* before one can start using it; therefore, we use *SAX* instead.

An example of the front part, body part, and the *XML* file formed from the pre-processed text is shown in `https://github.com/vgupta123/sumpubmed/blob/master/template.pdf`.

Versions of SUMPUBMED We maintained three versions of SUMPUBMED with varying degrees of preprocessing, a) *XML*, b) Raw Text, and c) Noun-phrases. Details of each version are as follows:

- In the *XML* version, we exported the whole dataset into a single *XML* file
- The Raw Text version is obtained after preprocessing when removing non-textual context is completed, followed by *XML* parsing.
- In the Noun phrases version, we processed the raw text version further to ensure that the summary and the text have the same named entities.

We found that standard Name Entity Recognition (*NER*) (Finkel et al., 2005) and Biomedical Named Entity Recognizer (*ABNER*) (Settles, 2005) fail to pick the scientific named entities correctly. Note that the main reason behind *ABNER* insufficiency is the presence of novel PubMed named entities that were not covered by any of the classes in the *ABNER* tool. Therefore, we use a simple heuristic of noun intersection between summary and main-text noun phrases to obtain plausible entity sets. This produced a shorter version of both the text and the summary than the original pair.

[1] `https://tinyurl.com/q5v9p5d`

[2] `https://tinyurl.com/py6qxzc`

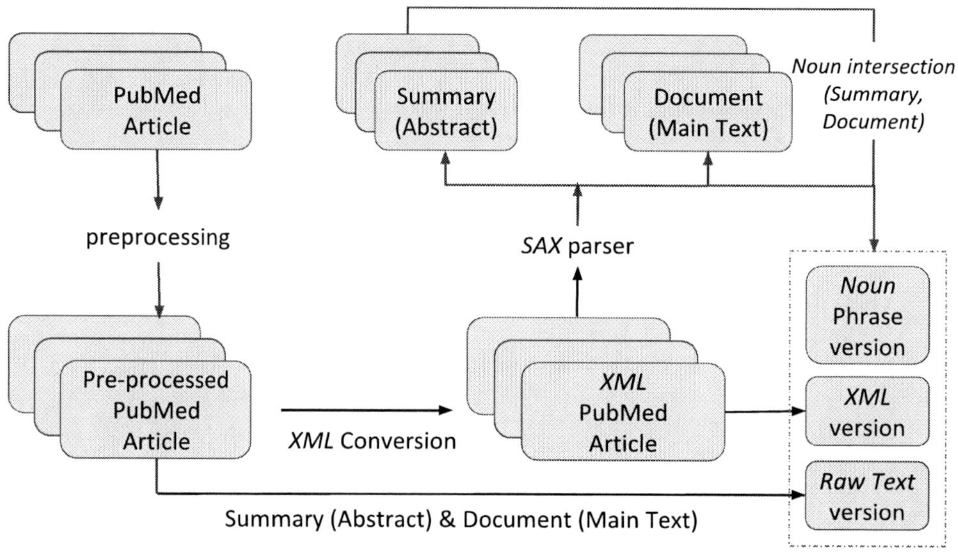

Figure 1: SUMPUBMED creation pipeline.

Version	Avg. Stats	Summary	Article
Raw Text version	Words	277	4227
	Sents	14	203
Noun Phrase version	Words	223	1578
	Sents	10	57
Hybrid version	Words	223	1891
	Sents	10	71

Table 1: Average number of sentences and words in the abstract and text in the three SUMPUBMED versions

The SUMPUBMED versions statistics is given in Table 1. The SUMPUBMED overall creation pipeline is shown in Figure 1.

3 Human Annotation of SUMPUBMED

Inspired from work on human evaluation of summaries by Friedrich et al. (2014), we distributed 50 randomly chosen summaries from the noun-phrase versions of SUMPUBMED to 10 expert annotators (graduate NLP students) such that we have 3 annotation for each summary. We asked these human-annotators to rate the summaries on a scale of 1 to 10. We created different document files, each having 10 pairs of summaries where we randomly shuffled between reference and generated summaries with respect to the placement on the page (left or right). The annotators evaluated the summaries based on the following criteria:

- *Non-Repetition and no factual Redundancy (Non-Re)*: There should not be redundancy in the factual information, and no repetition of sentences is allowed.
- *Coherence (Coh)*: Coherence means "continuity of sense". The arguments have to be connected sensibly so that the reader can see consecutive sentences as being about one (or a related) concept.
- *Readability (Read)*: Consideration of general readability criteria such as good spelling, correct grammar, understandability, etc. in the summaries.
- *Informativeness, Overlap and Focus (IOF)*: How much information is covered by the summary. The goal is to find the common pieces of information via matching the same keywords (or key phrases), such as "Nematodes", across the summary. For overlaps, annotators compare the keywords' (or key-phrases) occurrence frequency and ensure the summaries are on the same topic.

The average scores and standard deviations are shown in Table 2. Annotators found that for readability, coherence, and non-repetitiveness, the quality of summaries is satisfactory. However, for informativeness and overlap, it is hard to evaluate summaries due to domain-specific technical terms.

Criteria	Mean (μ)	S.D. (σ)
Non-Re	7.19	0.755
Coh	6.87	0.705
Read	6.82	0.821
IOF	6.31	0.879

Table 2: Mean and Standard Deviation (SD) scores of human annotation on 50 summaries

ROUGE and Human Scores For the 50 summaries evaluated by expert annotators, we calculated the Pearson's correlation (Pearson, 1895) between ROUGE (Lin, 2004) scores (ROUGE-1 (R-1), ROUGE-2 (R-2) and ROUGE-L (R-L)) in terms of precision, recall and F1 score with the human-evaluated scores. ROUGE-n is an n-gram similarity measure that computes uni/bi/trigram and higher n-gram overlaps. In R-L, L refers to the Longest Common Subsequence (LCS) overlap: a subsequence of matching words with the maximal length that is common in both texts with the order of words being preserved. Pearson's correlation value (between -1 and $+1$) quantifies the degree to which quantitative and continuous variables are related to each other. The Pearson's correlations values are shown in Table 3.

ROUGE scores assume that a high-quality summary generated by a model should have common words and phrases with a gold-standard summary. However, this is not always true because (a) there can be semantically similar meaning (synonymous) word usage, and (b) there can be the usage of text paraphrases (similar information conveyed) with a little lexical overlap in the reference summary text. Therefore, merely considering lexical overlaps to evaluate summary quality is not sufficient. A high ROUGE score may indicate a good summary, but a low ROUGE score does not necessarily indicate a bad summary. Furthermore, while summarizing large documents, humans tend to utilize different paraphrasing/words to convey the same meaning in a shorter form. Several studies by Cohan and Goharian (2016); Dohare et al. (2017) argue that ROUGE is not an accurate estimator of the quality of a summary for scientific input, e.g., biomedical text. Hence, a weak correlation of ROUGE scores with human ratings on SUMPUBMED, as reported in Table 3, should not be a surprise. That is, all correlation values in Table 3 are close to zero, so we can conclude that Rouge scores are weakly related with human ratings on the SUMPUBMED.

4 Experiments

We have used the noun phrase version of SUMPUBMED in the abstractive summarization settings and the Hybrid version of SUMPUBMED in the extractive and the hybrid settings, i.e., (extractive + abstractive) summarizations. We split the dataset into train (93%), test (3%), and validation (4%) sets. Before training, we wrote a script that first tokenizes all input files and then forms the vocabulary and chunked files for the train, test, and validation sets. This step converts the input into a suitable format for the *seq2seq* models.

4.1 Baseline Models

We use the following models on SUMPUBMED for evaluation: We use extractive, abstractive, and hybrid (extractive + abstractive) automatic summarization methods to evaluate SUMPUBMED.

Abstractive Methods We use several modifications of *seq2seq* with attention, as described below:

Seq2Seq with Attention (Nallapati et al., 2016): The encoder is a single layer bidirectional LSTM, while the decoder is a single layer unidirectional LSTM. Both the encoder and decoder have same sized hidden states, with an attention mechanism over the source hidden states and a soft-max layer over the vocabulary to generate the words. We use the same vocabulary for both the encoding and the decoding phase.

Seq2Seq with Pointer Generation Networks (See et al., 2017): The previous model has a computational decoder complexity because each time we have to apply the softmax over the entire vocabulary. The model also outputs an excessive number of UNK tokens (UNK is a special token utilized for out-of-vocabulary words) in the target summary. To address this issue, we use a pointer-generator network (See et al. (2017)) which integrates the basic seq2seq model (with attention) with a copying mechanism (Gu et al. (2016)). We call this model *seq2seq* for the rest of the paper.

The seq2Seq model with Pointer Generation Networks and Coverage Mechanism (+cov) (Mi et al., 2016): The summaries generated by the model discussed before may show repetition, like generating the same arrangement of words multiple times (e.g., "this bioinformatic approach this bioinformatic approach..."). This repetition of phrases is prominent when generating multi-line summaries. The solu-

Criteria	Prec			Recall			F1		
	R-1	R-2	R-L	R-1	R-2	R-L	R-1	R-2	R-L
Non-Re	-0.09	-0.06	-0.11	+0.02	-0.07	+0.007	+0.008	-0.05	+0.03
Coh	+0.05	-0.14	+0.05	-0.04	-0.25	-0.01	+0.02	-0.19	+0.06
Read	+0.19	+0.09	+0.20	+0.006	-0.03	+0.03	+0.12	+0.01	+0.13
IOF	-0.15	-0.18	-0.16	+0.12	0.08	+0.09	+0.06	-0.007	+0.12

Table 3: Pearson's correlation between ROUGE scores and human ratings on SUMPUBMED's noun-phrase version

tion to the problem of redundancy in summaries in seq2seq models is the coverage mechanism of Mi et al. (2016). This model penalizes repeated word generations by keeping track of the hitherto covered parts using attention distribution.

Extractive Methods There are several existing approaches to extractive summarization, mostly derived from LexRank (Erkan and Radev, 2004), and TextRank (Mihalcea and Tarau, 2004). We use TextRank, which is an unsupervised approach for sentence extraction, and has been used successfully in many NLP applications (Hulth, 2003).

Hybrid Methods (Extractive + Abstractive) We also experimented with the hybrid approach for summarization. First, we used extractive summarization using the TextRank ranking algorithm. We then applied abstractive summarization on the extracted text. We used the pointer-generator networks, followed by the coverage mechanism for the abstractive summarization. In this setting, we have not perfomed any preprocessing before extractive summarization to decrease the length of the documents. The extractive summarization step makes the text length sufficient to apply the abstractive summarization step on it quite easily.

4.2 Experimental Settings

While decoding seq2seq models (for abstractive and hybrid models), we use a beam search (Medress et al., 1977) with a beam width of 4.Note that, Beam search is a greedy technique which chooses the most likely token from all generated tokens at each step to obtain the best b sequences (the hyper-parameter b here represents the beam width). Beam search is shown to be better than generating the first sequence.

We also experimented with varying target summary lengths (i.e., the number of decoding steps) for seq2seq models. We report both seq2seq models with and without coverage results for comparison. We considered ROUGE-1 (R-1), ROUGE-2 (R-2), and ROUGE-L (R-L)'s precision, recall, and F1 score for evaluation.

Hyper-parameters The hyper-parameters used for the seq2seq model is in Table 4.

Hyper-parameter	Value
LSTM Hidden state size	256
Word embedding dimensions	128
Batch Size	16
encoder steps training	100-1000
encoder steps testing	100-4000
decoder steps length	100-250
beam size	4
learning rate for adagrad	0.15
maximum gradient norm	2.0

Table 4: Hyper-parameters for *seq2seq* models

We utilized tensorflow package [3] for models and ROUGE evaluation package `pyrouge` [4] for the evaluation metric.We use a single $GeForce\ GTX\ TITAN\ X$ with 12GB GPU memory taking on average 5 to 6 days per model for model training.

5 Results and Analysis

Results on SUMPUBMED for abstractive methods, i.e., seq2seq models (with and without coverage), the extractive method of TextRank, and the hybrid approach, i.e., TextRank + seq2seq (with and without coverage) are shown in Tables 6, 7, and 8, respectively. We also evaluated the seq2seq models on news datasets (CNN/Daily Mail and DUC 2001) for comparison, as shown in Table 5.

Analysis: In all three approaches, abstractive in Table 6, extractive in Table 7 and hybrid in Table 8, we notice that the ROUGE Recall and F1-score increase, whereas precision decreases with the number of words (100 to 250) in the target summaries. The increase in Recall is expected as the chances of lexical overlap are more with larger generated summaries. Precision decreases because, with more

[3] https://www.tensorflow.org/
[4] https://pypi.org/project/pyrouge/

Data	Model	R-1			R-2			R-L		
		Pr	Re	F1	Pr	Re	F1	Pr	Re	F1
CNN	seq2seq	33.49	38.49	34.61	13.89	15.87	14.29	30.15	34.64	31.15
-DM	+cov	**38.59**	**41.10**	**38.53**	**16.84**	**17.83**	**16.75**	**35.56**	**37.81**	**35.48**
DUC	seq2seq	41.34	21.33	27.63	14.28	7.30	9.49	32.95	16.93	21.93
	+cov	**43.86**	**21.92**	**28.57**	**15.04**	**7.41**	**9.68**	**34.96**	**17.29**	**22.60**

Table 5: ROUGE scores on CNN-Dailymail (CNN-DM) and DUC 2001 dataset (DUC) using seq2seq models

Steps	Model	R-1			R-2			R-L		
		Pr	Re	F1	Pr	Re	F1	Pr	Re	F1
100	seq2seq	52.30	20.56	28.01	16.01	6.17	8.50	47.97	18.70	25.53
	+cov	**57.50**	22.66	31.04	**20.28**	7.74	10.73	**52.62**	20.56	28.23
150	seq2seq	48.88	27.10	32.81	15.18	8.35	10.18	44.64	24.56	29.81
	+cov	55.11	29.71	36.79	19.17	10.14	12.66	50.48	27.07	33.57
200	seq2seq	44.83	30.23	33.79	13.73	9.20	10.33	40.86	27.37	30.65
	+cov	52.86	33.84	39.21	18.25	11.52	13.43	48.47	30.88	35.84
250	seq2seq	41.18	31.84	33.00	12.80	9.79	10.22	37.68	28.89	30.03
	+cov	51.11	**36.24**	**40.13**	17.63	**12.39**	**13.77**	46.92	**33.13**	**36.73**

Table 6: ROUGE scores of noun-phrase SUMPUBMED version using a seq2seq model of varying decoding steps

Steps	R-1			R-2			R-L		
	Pr	Re	F1	Pr	Re	F1	Pr	Re	F1
150	**45.91**	31.69	36.82	**16.97**	11.09	13.12	39.12	26.91	28.84
200	42.81	36.03	38.44	15.71	13.31	14.10	36.60	30.73	31.48
250	40.51	**39.59**	**39.33**	14.81	**15.30**	**14.72**	34.83	33.98	**34.83**

Table 7: Results for TextRank an Extractive Summarization approach on hybrid version of the SUMPUBMED.

Steps	Model	R-1			R-2			R-L		
		Pr	Re	F1	Pr	Re	F1	Pr	Re	F1
100	seq2seq	50.32	21.09	28.45	12.66	5.14	7.04	46.58	19.40	26.23
	+cov	**56.07**	27.42	30.69	**16.65**	6.47	8.95	**51.87**	20.62	28.27
150	seq2seq	45.01	25.50	30.99	11.14	6.21	7.59	41.43	23.35	28.42
	+cov	52.23	29.11	35.62	15.44	8.45	10.42	48.35	26.81	32.86
200	seq2seq	40.55	28.46	31.56	9.93	6.93	7.70	37.21	25.98	28.86
	+cov	47.82	33.37	37.28	14.01	9.68	10.84	44.29	30.80	34.44
250	seq2seq	35.80	30.88	30.61	9.14	7.67	7.66	32.67	27.95	27.80
	+cov	43.82	**36.16**	**37.33**	12.77	**10.49**	**10.85**	40.55	**33.37**	**34.49**

Table 8: ROUGE scores on hybrid version of the SUMPUBMED using Hybrid model: TextRank + seq2seq models

Model	R-1			R-2			R-L		
	Pr	Re	F1	Pr	Re	F1	Pr	Re	F1
Abstractive	**51.11**	36.24	**40.13**	**17.63**	12.39	**13.77**	**46.92**	33.13	**36.73**
Extractive	40.51	**39.59**	39.33	14.81	**15.30**	14.72	34.83	**33.98**	32.82
Hybrid Model	43.82	36.16	37.33	12.77	10.49	10.85	40.55	33.37	34.49

Table 9: ROUGE comparison on SUMPUBMED. seq2seq abstractive methods' target summary is of 250 words

words, the chances of non-covered words in the output summary also increase.

We notice in both Tables 6 and 8 that by adding the coverage (+cov) mechanism, the problem of repetition in summaries is solved to a great extent. The ROUGE scores also show improvement after applying coverage to pointer-generator networks. Thus, one can conclude that pointer generator networks effectively handle named entities and out-of-vocabulary words, and the coverage mechanism is useful to avoid repetitive generation, which is essential for scientific summarization.

In Table 9, we note that in terms of Precision (Pr), the abstractive approach shows the best results. However, the Recall (Re) of the extractive summarization model is always better than abstractive and hybrid approaches. Furthermore, the R-1 Re (ROUGE-1 Recall) and R-L Re (ROUGE-L Recall) for the hybrid models are approximately similar to the abstractive models. We also provide a few qualitative example of summarization on CNN/DailyMail in Appendix Section A, on SUMPUBMED in Appendic Section B.

6 Related Work

Below, we provide the details of other summarization datasets:

News: CNN-Daily Mail has $92,000$ examples with documents of 30-sentence length with 4 corresponding human-written summaries of 50 words. DUC (Document Understanding Conference), another dataset, contains 500 documents (35.6 tokens on average) and summaries (10.4 tokens). Gigaword (Rush et al., 2015) has 31.4 document tokens and 8.3 summary tokens. Lastly, X-Sum (Extreme Summarization) (Narayan et al., 2018) contains 20-sentence (BBC articles) (431 words) and corresponding one-sentence (23 words) summaries.

Social Media: Webis-TLDR-17 Corpus (Völske et al., 2017) is a large-scale dataset of 3 million pairs of content and self-written summaries obtained from social media (Reddit). Webis-Snippet-20 Corpus (Chen et al., 2020) contains 10 million (webpage content and abstractive snippet) pairs and 3.5 million triples (query terms, abstractive snippets, etc.) for query-based abstractive snippet generation of web pages.

Scientific: Recently, Sharma et al. (2019) released a large dataset of 1.3 million of U.S. patent documents along with human written summaries. However, the closest datasets to SUMPUBMED are released by Cohan et al. (2018); Kedzie et al. (2018); Gidiotis and Tsoumakas (2019).

Comparison with SUMPUBMED**:** News datasets' summary is located at the top of the article for most examples. Social media datasets lack the scientific aspect, i.e., complex domain-specific vocabulary and non-localized distributed information of SUMPUBMED. Other works on the scientific datasets are by Cohan et al. (2018); Kedzie et al. (2018); Gidiotis and Tsoumakas (2019). The closest work to our approach is the PubMed dataset by Cohan et al. (2018). However, unlike SUMPUBMED, (a) no extensive preprocessing pipeline was applied to clean the text (b) a single version is released compared with SUMPUBMED's several versions with distinct properties (varying summary lengths, article lengths, and vocabulary sizes), (c) only level-1 section headings instead of the whole PubMed document are used, and (d) there is a lack of human evaluation to assess data quality. However, Cohan et al. (2018) do act as an powerful inspiration for our work.

7 Conclusion

We created a non-news, SUMPUBMED dataset, from the PubMed archive to study how various summarization techniques perform on task of scientific summarization on domain specific scientific texts. These texts have essential information scattered throughout the whole text. In contrast, earlier datasets with news stories appear to mostly have useful information in the first few lines of the document text. We also conducted a human evaluation on aspects such as repetition, readability, coherence, and Informativeness for 50 summaries of 250 words. Each summary is evaluated by 3 different individuals on the basis of four parameters: readability, coherence, non-repetition, and informativeness. Due to the unavailability of any state-of-the-art results on this new dataset, we built several baseline models (extractive, abstractive, and hybrid model) for SUMPUBMED. To check the significance of our results, we studied the effectiveness of ROUGE through Pearson's correlation analysis with human-evaluation and observed that many variants of ROUGE scores correlate poorly with human evaluation. Our results indicate that ROUGE is possibly not a proper metric for SUMPUBMED.

Acknowledgements

We would like to thank the ACL SRW anonymous reviewers for their useful feedback, comments, and suggestions.

References

Wei-Fan Chen, Shahbaz Syed, Benno Stein, Matthias Hagen, and Martin Potthast. 2020. Abstractive snippet generation. In *Proceedings of The Web Conference 2020*, pages 1309–1319.

Arman Cohan, Franck Dernoncourt, Doo Soon Kim, Trung Bui, Seokhwan Kim, Walter Chang, and Nazli Goharian. 2018. A discourse-aware attention model for abstractive summarization of long documents. In *Proceedings of the 2018 Conference of the North American Chapter of the Association for Computational Linguistics: Human Language Technologies, Volume 2 (Short Papers)*, volume 2, pages 615–621.

Arman Cohan and Nazli Goharian. 2016. Revisiting summarization evaluation for scientific articles. In *Proceedings of the Tenth International Conference on Language Resources and Evaluation (LREC'16)*, pages 806–813.

Shibhansh Dohare, Harish Karnick, and Vivek Gupta. 2017. Text summarization using abstract meaning representation. *arXiv preprint arXiv:1706.01678*.

Günes Erkan and Dragomir R Radev. 2004. Lexrank: Graph-based lexical centrality as salience in text summarization. *Journal of artificial intelligence research*, 22:457–479.

Jenny Rose Finkel, Trond Grenager, and Christopher Manning. 2005. Incorporating non-local information into information extraction systems by gibbs sampling. In *Proceedings of the 43rd annual meeting on association for computational linguistics*, pages 363–370. Association for Computational Linguistics.

Annemarie Friedrich, Marina Valeeva, and Alexis Palmer. 2014. LQVSumm: A corpus of linguistic quality violations in multi-document summarization. In *Proceedings of the Ninth International Conference on Language Resources and Evaluation (LREC'14)*, pages 1591–1599, Reykjavik, Iceland. European Language Resources Association (ELRA).

Alexios Gidiotis and Grigorios Tsoumakas. 2019. Structured summarization of academic publications. In *Joint European Conference on Machine Learning and Knowledge Discovery in Databases*, pages 636–645. Springer.

Jiatao Gu, Zhengdong Lu, Hang Li, and Victor OK Li. 2016. Incorporating copying mechanism in sequence-to-sequence learning. In *Proceedings of the 54th Annual Meeting of the Association for Computational Linguistics (Volume 1: Long Papers)*.

Anette Hulth. 2003. Improved automatic keyword extraction given more linguistic knowledge. In *Proceedings of the 2003 conference on Empirical methods in natural language processing*, pages 216–223. Association for Computational Linguistics.

Chris Kedzie, Kathleen McKeown, and Hal Daumé III. 2018. Content selection in deep learning models of summarization. In *Proceedings of the 2018 Conference on Empirical Methods in Natural Language Processing*, pages 1818–1828.

Chin-Yew Lin. 2004. ROUGE: A package for automatic evaluation of summaries. In *Text Summarization Branches Out*, pages 74–81, Barcelona, Spain. Association for Computational Linguistics.

Mark F. Medress, Franklin S Cooper, Jim W. Forgie, CC Green, Dennis H. Klatt, Michael H. O'Malley, Edward P Neuburg, Allen Newell, DR Reddy, B Ritea, et al. 1977. Speech understanding systems: Report of a steering committee. *Artificial Intelligence*, 9(3):307–316.

Haitao Mi, Baskaran Sankaran, Zhiguo Wang, and Abe Ittycheriah. 2016. Coverage embedding models for neural machine translation. In *Proceedings of the 2016 Conference on Empirical Methods in Natural Language Processing*, pages 955–960.

Rada Mihalcea and Paul Tarau. 2004. Textrank: Bringing order into text. In *Proceedings of the 2004 conference on empirical methods in natural language processing*, pages 404–411.

Ramesh Nallapati, Bowen Zhou, Cicero dos Santos, Çağlar Gulçehre, and Bing Xiang. 2016. Abstractive text summarization using sequence-to-sequence rnns and beyond. In *Proceedings of The 20th SIGNLL Conference on Computational Natural Language Learning*, pages 280–290.

Shashi Narayan, Shay B Cohen, and Mirella Lapata. 2018. Don't give me the details, just the summary! topic-aware convolutional neural networks for extreme summarization. In *Proceedings of the 2018 Conference on Empirical Methods in Natural Language Processing*, pages 1797–1807.

Karl Pearson. 1895. Vii. note on regression and inheritance in the case of two parents. *proceedings of the royal society of London*, 58(347-352):240–242.

Alexander M Rush, Sumit Chopra, and Jason Weston. 2015. A neural attention model for abstractive sentence summarization. In *Proceedings of the 2015 Conference on Empirical Methods in Natural Language Processing*, pages 379–389.

Abigail See, Peter J Liu, and Christopher D Manning. 2017. Get to the point: Summarization with pointer-generator networks. In *Proceedings of the 55th Annual Meeting of the Association for Computational Linguistics (Volume 1: Long Papers)*, pages 1073–1083.

Burr Settles. 2005. Abner: an open source tool for automatically tagging genes, proteins and other entity names in text. *Bioinformatics*, 21(14):3191–3192.

Eva Sharma, Chen Li, and Lu Wang. 2019. Bigpatent: A large-scale dataset for abstractive and coherent summarization. In *Proceedings of the 57th Annual Meeting of the Association for Computational Linguistics*, pages 2204–2213.

Michael Völske, Martin Potthast, Shahbaz Syed, and Benno Stein. 2017. Tl; dr: Mining reddit to learn automatic summarization. In *Proceedings of the Workshop on New Frontiers in Summarization*, pages 59–63.

A Summarization Example on CNN/DailyMail Dataset

We see factual redundancy and repetitiveness in the generated summaries with pointer-generation which is removed by applying coverage. In the example below the Factual Redundancy is shown with the bold text:

Reference Summary maricopa county sheriff 's office in arizona says robert bates never trained with them. " he met every requirement , and all he did was give of himself, "his attorney says. tulsa world newspaper: three supervisors who refused to sign forged records on robert bates were reassigned.

Summary from seq2seq some supervisors at the tulsa county sheriff's office were told to forge reserve deputy robert bates ' training records. some supervisors at the tulsa county sheriff's office were told to forge reserve deputy robert bates' training records, and three who refused were reassigned to less desirable duties. **some supervisors at the tulsa county sheriff 's office were told to forge reserve deputy robert bates ' training records.**

Summary from seq2seq with coverage some supervisors at the tulsa county sheriff 's office were told to forge reserve deputy robert bates ' training records . the volunteer deputy 's records had been falsified emerged " almost immediately " from multiple sources after bates killed eric harris on april 2 . bates claims he meant to use his taser but accidentally fired his handgun at harris instead.

B Example of Summarization on SUMPUBMED

Here we provide representative examples of actual summaries. Repetitiveness, i.e., factual redundancy is shown with the bold text.

B.1 Abstractive Summarization on SUMPUBMED

We see factual redundancy and repetitiveness in the generated summaries with pointer-generation which is removed by applying coverage. We also observe that repetitiveness is removed by using the coverage mechanism.

reference: the origin of these genes has been attributed to horizontal gene transfer from bacteria, although there still is a lot of uncertainty about the origin and structure of the ancestral ghf <dig> ppn endoglucanase. our data confirm a close relationship between pratylenchus spp. furthermore, based on gene structure data, we inferred a model for the evolution of the ghf <dig> endoglucanase gene structure in plantparasitic nematodes. our evolutionary model for the gene structure in ppn ghf <dig> endoglucanases implies the occurrence of an early duplication event, and more recent gene duplications at genus or species level. the latter one is the first gene isolated from a ppn of a different superfamily -LRB- sphaerularioidea -RRB-; all previously known nematode endoglucanases belong to the superfamily tylenchoidea -LRB- order rhabditida -RRB-. no statistical incongruence between the phylogenetic trees deduced from the catalytic domain and the cbm <dig> was found, which could suggest that both domains have evolved together. and the root knot nematodes, while some radopholus similis endoglucanases are more similar to cyst nematode genes. two new endoglucanases from the migratory nematodes pratylenchus coffeae and ditylenchus africanus were included in this study. phylogenetic analyses were conducted with the ppn ghf <dig> endoglucanases and homologous endoglucanases from bacterial and other eukaryotic lineages such as beetles, fungi and plants. previous studies on the evolution of these genes have focused primarily on data of sedentary nematodes, while in this study, extra data from migratory nematodes were included. it is not clear whether this ancestral endoglucanase consisted of the whole gene cassette, containing a catalytic domain and a carbohydratebinding module -LRB- cbm, type <dig> in ppn and bacteria -RRB- or only of the catalytic domain while the cbm <dig> was retrieved by domain shuffling later in evolution. the ghf <dig> catalytic domain and the cbm <dig> rather than that it evolved by domain shuffling. endo <dig> betaglucanases or cellulases from the glycosyl hydrolase family <dig> -LRB- ghf5 -RRB- have been found in numerous bacteria and fungi, and recently also in higher eukaryotes, particularly in plantparasitic nematodes -LRB- ppn -RRB-.

seq2seq: although the hox cell line with peculiar properties of horizontal gene transfer -LRB- hgt -RRB- has been proposed to delineate the function of ghf <dig> endoglucanases. the gene structure of the ppn ghf <dig> endoglucanases is a matter of debate, in this study no support for an early exon/domain shuffling event after the independent gain of a catalytic domain. the exon/intron gene structure of the ppn ghf <dig> endoglucanases was compared with the multiple protein sequence alignment. the gene structure of the ppn ghf <dig> endoglucanases was compared with the multiple protein sequence alignment. **the gene structure of the ppn ghf <dig> endoglucanases was compared with the multiple protein sequence alignment. the gene structure of the ppn ghf <dig> endoglucanases was compared with the multiple protein sequence alignment.** the evolution of the gene structure of the ppn ghf <dig> gene families: the number of members from an ancient or early eukaryotic ancestral gene is associated with the expansion of members from an ancient or early eukaryotic ancestral gene. in this study, we.

seq2seq coverage: the expansion of horizontal gene transfer -LRB- hgt -RRB- events in horizontal gene transfer -LRB- hgt -RRB- has been proposed to explain the origin of ghf <dig> endoglucanases in the nematode kingdom. while the ppn ghf <dig> endoglucanases has a close relationship to the root knot nematodes. in order to have a broader overview of the endoglucanase evolution in the infraorder tylenchomorpha, the gene structure of six additional genes was incorporated in our study. the ppn ghf <dig> gene family is associated with the expansion of the ppn ghf <dig> gene family bordered by intron <dig> and intron <dig> although 1 - <dig> symmetrical domains are suggested to be frequently associated with domain shuffling events in the evolution of paralogous gene families: the evolution of the ppn indicate a history of recent duplication events for which little information is available. our model implies that the divergence of the gene structure of the ppn ghf <dig> gene family is notably dynamic, and this evolution involves more intron gains than losses in the order rhabditida -LRB- infraorder tylenchomorpha -RRB-, which is part of one of the three evolutionary independent plantparasitic nematode clades. our results demonstrate that the conserved gene structure of the ppn ghf <dig> endoglucanases and the observation of some sequence conservation in the evolution of the plantparasitic bacteria and nematodes. our results suggest that the evolution of the ghf <dig> gene family is a major consequence of the evolution of.

B.2 Extractive Summarization on SumPubMed

TextRank produces a purely extractive summary. But we see that it is able to identify the relevant sentences. The content overlap between the reference and generated extractive summary is adequate.

reference : to find out the different ovarian activity and follicle recruitment with mirnamediated posttranscriptional regulation, the small rnas expressed pattern in the ovarian tissues of multiple and uniparous anhui white goats during follicular phase was analyzed using solexa sequencing data. <dig> mirnas coexpressed, <dig> and <dig> mirnas specifically expressed **in the ovaries of multiple and uniparous goats during follicular phase** were identified. in the present study, the different expression of mirnas in the ovaries of multiple and uniparous goats during follicular phase were characterized and investigated using deep sequencing technology. rt-pcr was applied to detect the expression level of <dig> randomly selected mirnas in multiple and uniparous hircine ovaries, and the results were consistent with the solexa sequencing data. micrornas play critical roles in almost all ovarian biological processes, including folliculogenesis, follicle development, follicle atresia, luteal development and regression. the result will help to further understand the role of mirnas in kidding rate regulation and also may help to identify mirnas which could be potentially used to increase hircine ovulation rate and kidding rate in the future. the <dig> most highly expressed mirnas in the multiple library were also the highest expressed in the uniparous library, and there were no significantly different between each other. **the highest specific expressed mirna in the multiple library was mir29c, and the one in the uniparous library was mir<dig>** <dig> novel mirnas were predicted in total. superior kidding rate is an important economic trait in production of meat goat, and ovulation rate is the precondition of kidding rate. go annotation and kegg pathway analyses were implemented on target genes of all mirna in two libraries.

extracted : in order to identify differentially expressed mirna during follicular phase in the ovaries of multiple and uniparous anhui white goats, two small rna libraries were constructed by solexa sequencing. for all mirnas target genes of multiple and uniparous goats in the ovaries during follicular phase, there were <dig> and <dig> target genes mapped to the go terms of cellular component. the expression levels of <dig> randomly selected mirnas were verified in the ovaries of multiple and uniparous goats during follicular phase using rt-pcr. in this study, we sequenced the small rnas **in the ovarian tissues of multiple and uniparous anhui white goats during follicular phase** by illumina solexa technology, then analyzed the differentially expressed mirnas, predicted novel mirnas, and made go enrichment and kegg pathway analysis of target genes in two mirna libraries. in ovaries between multiple and uniparous goats of follicular phase, <dig> novel mirnas were predicted in total, which is distinctly more than the amount predicted in our previous study implemented by our team workers, zhang et al. **the highest specific expressed mirna in multiple library was mir29c, and the one in uniparous library was mir<dig>** as aligning the clean reads to the mirna precursor/mature mirnas of all animals in the mirbase <dig> database, and obtained mirna with no specified species. rt-pcr was carried out to analyze the expression of <dig> randomly selected mirnas in multiple and uniparous hircine ovaries during follicular phase, and the results were consistent with the solexa sequencing data.

B.3 Attention Visualization for SUMPUBMED

We can visualize the attention projection for seq2seq models by highlighting the respective words in yellow on the source document while producing a word. Figures 2 and 3 show the words in green with high generation probability, i.e, pgen > 0.5 (not copied), non marked words have pgen < 0.5 (mostly copied).

Observations While producing a word in the output, we can visualize the respective words in the source document on which the network is focussing. The darker the green highlight over a word in the summary, the higher is the pgen prob- ability. E.g., there is a chance that pgen is high whenever a new sentence is started after a period (.). The model generally focuses on two or three words at a time. There is a high chance that the summary starts with a noun phrase or a noun. For example, we can see in Figure 2 that the summary starts with name (noun) 'kevin pietersen'.

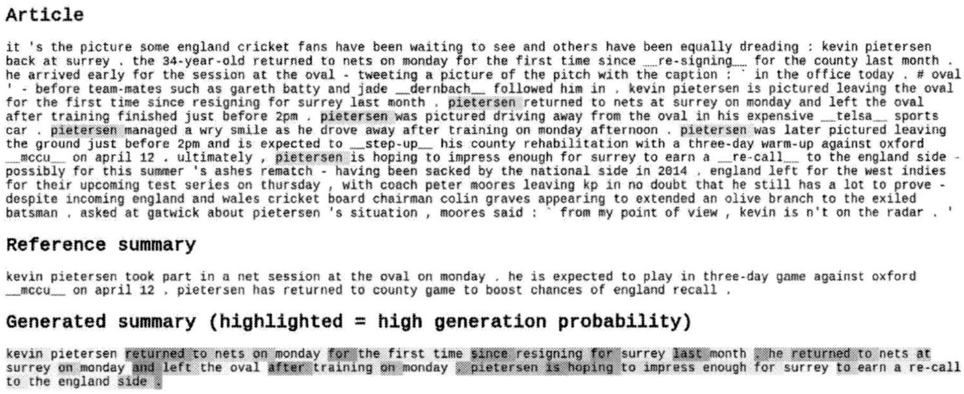

Figure 2: Attention Probability for decoding on DUC 2001 dataset example, showing the summary is more inclined to an extractive nature. Attention corresponding to the word 'pietersen' present in the generated summary is shown.

Figure 3: Attention Probability for decoding on a SUMPUBMED example where the attention corresponding to word 'present' in the generated summary is shown.

A Case Study of Analysis of Construals in Language on Social Media Surrounding a Crisis Event

Lolo Aboufoul, Khyati Mahajan, Tiffany Gallicano, Sara Levens and Samira Shaikh
University of North Carolina at Charlotte
9201 University City Blvd
Charlotte NC 28223 USA
`laboufou,kmahaja2,samirashaikh@uncc.edu`

Abstract

The events that took place at the Unite the Right rally held in Charlottesville, Virginia on August 11-12, 2017 caused intense reaction on social media from users across the political spectrum. We present a novel application of psycholinguistics - specifically, construal level theory - to analyze the language on social media around this event of social import through topic models. We find that including psycholinguistic measures of concreteness as covariates in topic models can lead to informed analysis of the language surrounding an event of political import.

1 Introduction

Construal Level theory (CLT) (Trope and Liberman, 2010) postulates that people create differing mental representations of the same information depending upon whether the information is psychologically proximal or psychologically distant. For instance, people experience geographically distant, and hence *psychologically* distal events, by forming mental construals of such events at higher levels of abstraction than events that are geographically proximal (Fujita et al., 2006). These construals manifest themselves in the language people use, specifically in concreteness values. Additionally, empirical research has demonstrated that the tendency to create abstract versus concrete construals systematically affects human judgments, attitudes, and behaviors (McCrea et al., 2012).

To illustrate, consider the example of climate change. Research has shown that when people are primed to think about the topic of climate change using more concrete terms such as `beetle` and `forest` vs. more abstract terms (`sea levels`), they are more likely to engage with the topic of climate change (Scannell and Gifford, 2013). Concreteness of words is the degree to which a concept denoted by the word refers to a perceptible entity.

High Abstraction/ Low Concreteness	A Confederate who was opposed to secession, but refused to fight against Virginia https://t.co/UTJvNsEYd7 #waxmuseum #USHistory
Low Abstraction/ High Concreteness	"Confederate general/soldiers statues / memorials are literally just participation trophies " - the best sentence I ever heard #Charlottesville

Table 1: Example tweets demonstrating how language reflects differing levels of construals about the same topic. Highlighted words represent high concreteness/low abstraction terms.

In other words, it is easier to generate a mental image of a `beetle` as opposed to a mental image of `sea level`, and talking about the topic of climate change in more concrete terms makes people more likely to engage with the topic. Furthermore, the analysis of words and their associated sentiments can be used to conclude the tone of discussion and how the discussion around climate change can vary between countries (Dahal et al., 2019).

Construals can differ based on geographical, social and temporal distance. An event which is distant in the future would be described in language that has higher levels of abstractness (and therefore low concreteness) than an event which is more proximal. Given that (a) language use reflects differing levels of construals and (b) construals can differ for events that are temporally distant vs. temporally proximal, we seek to investigate *whether individuals on social media would discuss an event using different levels of construals and whether we can determine the effects of these construals from their language use.*

We thus use Construal Level Theory as a theoretical foundation to understand the reaction of individuals on Twitter related to the Unite the Right rally that took place in Charlottesville, Virginia on August 11-12, 2017. We apply topic models to analyze language use and study how users view

Proceedings of the Joint Conference of the 59th Annual Meeting of the Association for Computational Linguistics and the 11th International Joint Conference on Natural Language Processing: Student Research Workshop, pages 304–309
August 5–6, 2021.

the events that took place during the protests. To demonstrate, consider the tweets shown in Table 1 as examples of high concreteness/low abstraction vs. low concreteness/high abstraction language surrounding the Charlottesville Rally from our corpus. While one tweet discusses the topic using highly concrete words (`statues` and `trophies`), the other does so using abstract concepts like `secession` and `confederate`.

Our work, situated at the intersection of psycholinguistics and computational social science, makes the following salient contributions:

- We extend the application of Construal Level Theory beyond laboratory settings to make it more ecologically valid;
- To analyze language produced spontaneously on social media, we use topic modeling and include concreteness values as covariates in the topic models.

2 Related Work

Construal Level Theory to Study Human Behavior: Construal level theory, first introduced by Liberman et al. (2007), describes the relation between psychological distance and how the mind perceives objects and events as abstract or concrete. The distance consists of temporal, spatial, and geographical dimensions. McCrea et al. (2008) explained how representing tasks that must be completed in a concrete way decreases the likelihood of procrastination.

The theory has also been applied by Stephan et al. (2011) to show that temporal proximity and concrete construals produce a corresponding increase in perceived social closeness (described as familiarity with a specific topic). Williams et al. (2014) conducted a study regarding how psychological distance of thought would impact the positivity of reactions. They showed how distance from a scenario (having it happen to oneself versus to someone else) impacts one's reaction to it. Snefjella and Kuperman (2015) show that abstraction increases with distance and decreases as spatial distance decreases. (Rufai and Bunce, 2020) analyze tweets from top world leaders' responses to the COVID-19 pandemic with results unrelated to construal theory, yet still integrate the categorization of tweets from each leader into categories that can further explain the path of response each country's leader took. However, most of the work cited above is based on laboratory studies. On the other hand, social media language has the benefit of being more ecologically valid, in that, communication between speakers is more interactive and messages are generally spontaneous rather than prompted or composed before delivery.

Topic Models to Study Language Data: Topic modeling techniques, based on probabilistic latent semantic analysis (Hofmann, 2001), latent Dirichlet allocation (LDA) (Blei and Lafferty, 2006) have been widely used to support quantitative and qualitative analysis of text data. While the topics are uncorrelated in the base LDA model, correlated topic models leverage the fact that certain topics may share words between them and thus be closer to one another (Blei et al., 2007). Topic models can be created using a variety of methods, and salient topics can be derived from tweets collected using both traditional LDA and non-traditional methods (Demszky et al., 2019). Topic models have also been used to study topics that analyze how human emotion is attached to text samples in context different than construal theory analysis (Kleinberg et al., 2020). Structured topic models (STM) (Wallach, 2008), treat the documents as sequences of segments, which can share the same prior distribution of topics. This allows the model to leverage the existing structure of documents from the given segmentation. The other advantage of using STM is that it allows for the inclusion of covariates into the prior distributions, so that variance of different topics of the variable of interest can be investigated (Roberts et al., 2014). While covariates such as political ideology have been widely studied in prior literature (Bauer et al., 2017), the inclusion of psycholinguistic measures of words has not heretofore been systematically studied. We thus investigate whether the inclusion of psycholinguistics measures of concreteness in the topic models results in meaningful comparisons of the underlying construals about the events.

3 Data

A major challenge while studying social media data is representativeness and sample selection bias (Tufekci, 2014). To address this challenge, we designed an observational study using Twitter's public APIs to obtain a longitudinal dataset of tweets from Feb 7, 2017 through Oct 11, 2017 around the Charlottesville protests of August 2017, in Virgina, USA. As an event of far-reaching social and political import, which was characterized by not only the

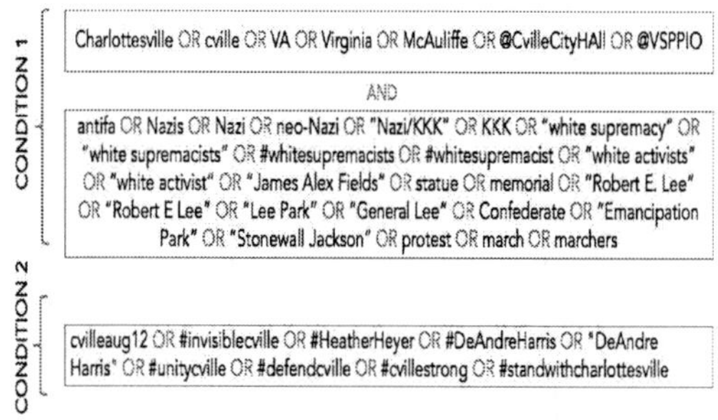

Figure 1: List of hashtags and keywords used to collect our data corpus for Charlottesville protest event. The hashtags were split into two Conditions. In Condition 1, there are two sets of keywords and hashtags and the search criteria is that the tweet should match at least one item from each set. Condition 2 is a set of hashtags, where the search criteria is to match at least one item from the set.

discussion surrounding planning of protests, but the ensuing discussion after August due to the death of Heather Heyer, this event serves as an exemplary case for analysis of how individuals formed construals before, during and after the event. We used a carefully curated set of keywords, and defined the search criteria iteratively: first, we conducted an advanced search on Twitter for tweets containing keywords from trending tweets, including hashtags regarding the Charlottesville event. Next, we examined the tweets resulting from this search to identify additional key words we had missed, and then we conducted additional data pulls to include tweets with these additional keywords. All research was conducted in accordance with the university ethics board approval. Data collection was ruled exempt because we collected tweets from public accounts. We acquired the data through the GNIP Historical Powertrack Twitter API for the Charlottesville event by using the data pullsearch string in Figure 1 resulting in 526, 102 tweets.

4 Method

We use `R` and the `STM` (Roberts et al., 2019) package to build our topic models. We preprocess the data by converting all tokens to lowercase, removing symbols from the text, and removing stopwords using the `spaCy` library (Honnibal et al., 2020) in `Python`. We also include some custom stopwords such as `like` and `try` to make the topics more meaningful. We used smenatic coherence as one of the measures to determine final number of topics.

We then used an existing concreteness lexicon (Brysbaert et al., 2014a) to compute the average concreteness value of words that occur in tweets. The concreteness lexicon by Brysbaert et al. (2014a) contains concreteness values of over 40,000 English words in their lemma form and has been used in prior natural language research to investigate argument strategies (Tan et al., 2016) and for predicting text comprehension (Crossley et al., 2017), among others. However, prior approaches that investigate psychological distance in natural language (Bhatia and Walasek, 2016; Snefjella and Kuperman, 2015) compute average concreteness scores for each tweet by consulting the concreteness lexicon for all words that occur in tweets. By contrast, we only focus on words that have extreme concreteness scores (>=4, on a scale of 1 – 5) and extreme abstractness scores (<=2). We focus on the extreme ends of the concreteness/abstractness spectrum to be consistent with prior literature, which suggests that extreme valence is highly correlated with emotion, memory and recognition of words (Ponari et al., 2018). More experimentation is needed to determine what effect our design choice of using the extreme values for concreteness has on the resulting topic model, such that, if we choose a different threshold of concreteness values, we might surface different patterns in the data. This would require manual inspection of the words contained in each topic and qualitative evaluation of the semantic content within and between topics.

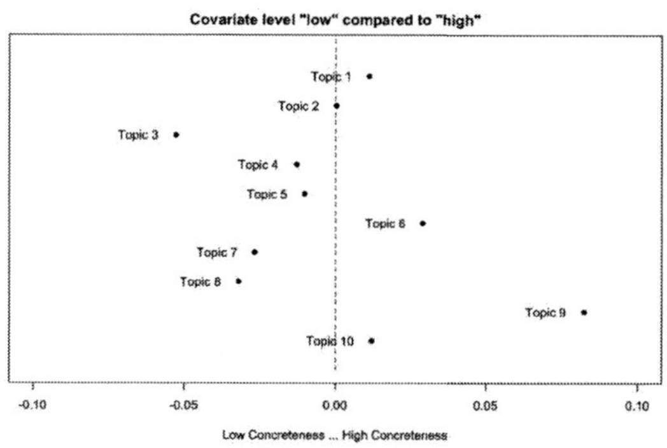

Figure 2: Measurement of concreteness of each topic

5 Results

After constructing a topic model, the patterns noticed among the topics and among the words that were most common in each topic can be used to explain the construal levels of the users.It is important to note that some of the topics produced, specifically Topic 2, 7, and 10 contained foul language, reflecting the harsh and opinionated nature of the tweets made regarding this event. We summarize our two main findings in this paper, while more in-depth analysis and contextualization within a larger research project is the main focus of an upcoming, larger publication.

Concreteness level differentiates between topics: Figure 2 shows the level of concreteness in each topic, arranged from Low to High Concreteness. For each individual post, a concreteness value above the mean was labelled as being "high concreteness", and below the mean was labelled as being "low concreteness". On a topic level, the concreteness value for each topic is determined internally by the STM library using prevalence, which based on the documentation[1] refers to how much of a document is associated with a topic taking into account the metadata provided. Figure 2 thus shows how the prevalence of topics differs across values of the categorical covariate which is the "concreteness" value.

As discussed above, concrete terms refer to specific tangible objects, while abstract terms can be general ideas or emotions. Topics 3 and 9 stand out as the least and most concrete, resp. Other topics with high concreteness terms in the tweets are Topic 1, 6 and 10. Most topics are characterized by low concreteness values (Topics 3, 7, 8, 5 and 4). This makes sense due to the fact that most of our data relating to the event is collected *before*, in fact, months before the rally was scheduled to take place (our data collection starts in February while the main Charlottesville protests took place in August 2017). This means, on average, Topic 3 discusses the Charlottesville rally in more general ideas and terms, while Topic 9 discusses using specific people or more concrete objects. Terms that served as labels for topic 1 include "stand", "vote", and "quit", while topic labels for topic 3 include "outrage", "lead", and "nationalist". Frequent terms found in topic 1 are more easily visualized compared to terms in topic 3 that exhibit low concreteness and are considered more abstract. Terms in topics 6 and 10 include "america", "resist-trump", "assault", and "historic". These terms are imaginable and can present an image in the reader or tweeter's mind, showing the high concreteness of the tweets in the topics they belong to. Terms with low concreteness including "wrong", "praise", "civil", "approve", and "game" can be found in topics 4, 5, 7, and 8. These terms are (in contrast to those in topics 1, 6, and 10) less imaginable and do not clearly present a picture in the reader's mind, illustrating how the topics these terms belong to discuss more abstract ideas.

[1] https://tinyurl.com/37rwucpw

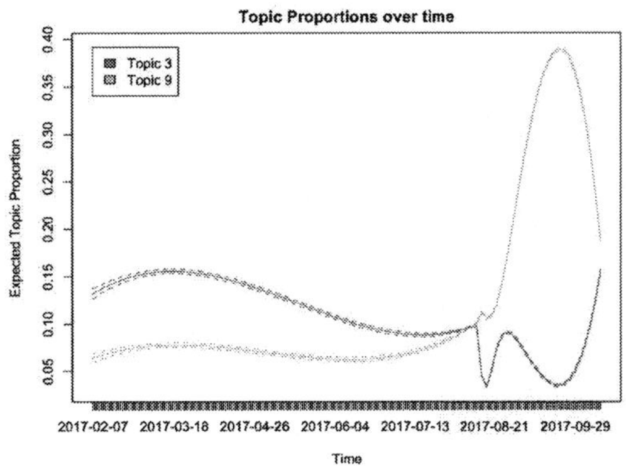

Figure 3: Change in Topic proportion over time: Topics 3 and 9

Topic proportions over time reflect construals: The discussion of Topics 3 and 9 is important because they are so widely dissimilar. To investigate further, we plot the difference between the two topics over time in terms of expected topic proportion in Figure 3. This figure shows how tweets in Topic 9 began to steadily increase immediately after the Charlottesville protests began in August, and peaked during the period *after* the events, while Topic 3 (characterized by low concreteness language, with terms such as "outrage", "attention", "nationalist", and "return") declined during the month of the protests and was less popular during the peak of Topic 9. At the time of the protests (August 11-12), Topic 9 had begun to increase while topic 3 had been declining and reached its lowest point yet. Topic 9 also contains terms that may be related to the aftermath of the protests because they illustrate the reaction

This suggests that topics associated with more concrete terms regarding the Charlottesville event, specifically Topic 9, were more prevalent *after* the event. Put differently, individuals were more likely to talk about the protests in concrete terms *after* the main protest event had passed (Aug 10-11). While the expected topic proportion of Topic 3 dips after the August time window, it does not dramatically differ from the previous expected topic proportion.

This suggests that the abstract construals are likely to appear both before and after the event but not during. This finding is consistent with prior research applying Construal Level Theory in lab settings.

6 Conclusion

The protests that took place in Charlottesville in August of 2017 caused an outsize reaction on social media. We investigate how individuals perceive an event during its occurrence and after it ends, through the lens of Construal Level Theory. Our main finding is that adding concreteness values as covariates during topic modeling can help distinguish which topics were prevalent before, during and after the event. We find that during the ongoing discussion surrounding the protests (time period of Feb through Oct 2017 in our corpus), it was more likely that abstract terms that refer to ideas and emotions were used.

Notably, we found that language using more concrete terms was used to describe the events *after* they occurred. This finding is not surprising — it is easier to discuss an event in concrete terms after it occurs, because individuals will have specific objects (like `car` and `torch`) to refer to, in addition to proper nouns like specific names or places. However, a significant dip in the expected topic proportion after the event (c.f. Figure 3 Topic 9 trajectory) suggests that the this effect is attenuated over time. Our research can be used to gain insight into how to measure construals of events over time, and can be used to show what elements of an event people focus on as they react to it. Thus, our methodology showcases the use of quantitative methods which could be used to study how Construal Level Theory is reflected during crisis events. For future work, we also aim to study how our approach could be applied towards different crisis events.

Limitations: We acknowledge several limitations of our work:

- **Single Event:** Our analysis is focused on a single event: the Charlottesville protest rally. As such, we cannot yet claim generalizability of our findings. We offer our research as a first foray into a series of analyses focusing on construals across varying events and contexts. For example, one direction for future work is suggested in analysis of construals about the COVID-19 pandemic at different stages of an ongoing, global event.
- **Deeper Analysis of Concrete Terms:** In this work, we do not present an in-depth study for the concrete vs. abstract words associated with each topic. Certainly, interesting questions to ask would be whether the frex terms (highest ranking frequent and exclusive words) or the highest probability words in each topic are correlated in any way with the concreteness values. We address this limitation as part of our future work.
- **Language Limitations:** Our study is focused on an event that occurred in the United States. As such, all of our data are in English. As part of addressing the question of generalizability of findings, we further aim to replicate our findings in multiple languages given appropriate data. Concreteness lexicons now exist in multiple languages, including Dutch (Brysbaert et al., 2014b) and French (Bonin et al., 2020), which makes this future analysis a viable option.

Acknowledgments

This research is part of a multi-phase study funded by the Department of Defense's Army Research Office through federal grant 72487-RT-REP.

References

Paul C Bauer, Pablo Barberá, Kathrin Ackermann, and Aaron Venetz. 2017. Is the left-right scale a valid measure of ideology? *Political Behavior*, 39(3):553–583.

Sudeep Bhatia and Lukasz Walasek. 2016. Event construal and temporal distance in natural language. *Cognition*, 152:1–8.

David M Blei and John D Lafferty. 2006. Dynamic topic models. In *Proceedings of the 23rd international conference on Machine learning*, pages 113–120.

David M Blei, John D Lafferty, et al. 2007. A correlated topic model of science. *The annals of applied statistics*, 1(1):17–35.

Francesca Bonin, Martin Gleize, Ailbhe Finnerty, Candice Moore, Charles Jochim, Emma Norris, Yufang Hou, Alison J. Wright, Debasis Ganguly, Emily Hayes, Silje Zink, Alessandra Pascale, Pol Mac Aonghusa, and Susan Michie. 2020. HBCP corpus: A new resource for the analysis of behavioural change intervention reports. In *Proceedings of the 12th Language Resources and Evaluation Conference*, pages 1967–1975, Marseille, France. European Language Resources Association.

M. Brysbaert, Amy Beth Warriner, and V. Kuperman. 2014a. Concreteness ratings for 40 thousand generally known english word lemmas. *Behavior Research Methods*, 46:904–911.

Marc Brysbaert, Michaël Stevens, Simon De Deyne, Wouter Voorspoels, and Gert Storms. 2014b. Norms of age of acquisition and concreteness for 30,000 dutch words. *Acta psychologica*, 150:80–84.

Scott A Crossley, Stephen Skalicky, Mihai Dascalu, Danielle S McNamara, and Kristopher Kyle. 2017. Predicting text comprehension, processing, and familiarity in adult readers: New approaches to readability formulas. *Discourse Processes*, 54(5-6):340–359.

Biraj Dahal, Sathish AP Kumar, and Zhenlong Li. 2019. Topic modeling and sentiment analysis of global climate change tweets. *Social Network Analysis and Mining*, 9(1):1–20.

Dorottya Demszky, Nikhil Garg, Rob Voigt, James Zou, Matthew Gentzkow, Jesse Shapiro, and Dan Jurafsky. 2019. Analyzing polarization in social media: Method and application to tweets on 21 mass shootings. *arXiv preprint arXiv:1904.01596*.

Kentaro Fujita, Marlone D Henderson, Juliana Eng, Yaacov Trope, and Nira Liberman. 2006. Spatial distance and mental construal of social events. *Psychological Science*, 17(4):278–282.

Thomas Hofmann. 2001. Unsupervised learning by probabilistic latent semantic analysis. *Machine learning*, 42(1):177–196.

Matthew Honnibal, Ines Montani, Sofie Van Landeghem, and Adriane Boyd. 2020. spaCy: Industrial-strength Natural Language Processing in Python.

Bennett Kleinberg, Isabelle van der Vegt, and Maximilian Mozes. 2020. Measuring emotions in the covid-19 real world worry dataset. *arXiv preprint arXiv:2004.04225*.

Nira Liberman, Yaacov Trope, and Cheryl Wakslak. 2007. Construal level theory and consumer behavior. *Journal of consumer psychology*, 17(2):113–117.

Sean M McCrea, Nira Liberman, Yaacov Trope, and Steven J Sherman. 2008. Construal level and procrastination. *Psychological Science*, 19(12):1308–1314.

Sean M McCrea, Frank Wieber, and Andrea L Myers. 2012. Construal level mind-sets moderate self-and social stereotyping. *Journal of personality and social psychology*, 102(1):51.

Marta Ponari, Courtenay Frazier Norbury, and Gabriella Vigliocco. 2018. Acquisition of abstract concepts is influenced by emotional valence. *Developmental science*, 21(2):e12549.

M. E. Roberts, Brandon M Stewart, and D. Tingley. 2019. stm: R package for structural topic models. *Journal of Statistical Software*, 91:1–40.

Margaret E Roberts, Brandon M Stewart, Dustin Tingley, Christopher Lucas, Jetson Leder-Luis, Shana Kushner Gadarian, Bethany Albertson, and David G Rand. 2014. Structural topic models for open-ended survey responses. *American Journal of Political Science*, 58(4):1064–1082.

Sohaib R Rufai and Catey Bunce. 2020. World leaders' usage of twitter in response to the covid-19 pandemic: a content analysis. *Journal of Public Health*, 42(3):510–516.

Leila Scannell and Robert Gifford. 2013. Personally relevant climate change: The role of place attachment and local versus global message framing in engagement. *Environment and Behavior*, 45(1):60–85.

Bryor Snefjella and Victor Kuperman. 2015. Concreteness and psychological distance in natural language use. *Psychological science*, 26(9):1449–1460.

Elena Stephan, Nira Liberman, and Yaacov Trope. 2011. The effects of time perspective and level of construal on social distance. *Journal of experimental social psychology*, 47(2):397–402.

Chenhao Tan, Vlad Niculae, Cristian Danescu-Niculescu-Mizil, and Lillian Lee. 2016. Winning arguments: Interaction dynamics and persuasion strategies in good-faith online discussions. In *Proceedings of the 25th international conference on world wide web*, pages 613–624.

Yaacov Trope and Nira Liberman. 2010. Construal-level theory of psychological distance. *Psychological review*, 117(2):440.

Zeynep Tufekci. 2014. Big questions for social media big data: Representativeness, validity and other methodological pitfalls. In *Proceedings of the International AAAI Conference on Web and Social Media*, volume 8.

Hanna Megan Wallach. 2008. *Structured topic models for language*. Ph.D. thesis, University of Cambridge Cambridge, UK.

Lawrence E Williams, Randy Stein, and Laura Galguera. 2014. The distinct affective consequences of psychological distance and construal level. *Journal of Consumer Research*, 40(6):1123–1138.

Cross-lingual Evidence Improves Monolingual Fake News Detection

Daryna Dementieva and Alexander Panchenko
Skolkovo Institute of Science and Technology, Moscow, Russia
{daryna.dementieva,a.panchenko}@skoltech.ru

Abstract

Misleading information spreads on the Internet at an incredible speed, which can lead to irreparable consequences in some cases. Therefore, it is becoming essential to develop fake news detection technologies. While substantial work has been done in this direction, one of the limitations of the current approaches is that these models are focused only on one language and do not use multilingual information. In this work, we propose a new technique based on cross-lingual evidence (CE) that can be used for fake news detection and improve existing approaches. The hypothesis of the usage of cross-lingual evidence as a feature for fake news detection is confirmed, firstly, by manual experiment based on a set of known true and fake news. Besides, we compared our fake news classification system based on the proposed feature with several strong baselines on two multi-domain datasets of general-topic news and one newly fake COVID-19 news dataset showing that combining cross-lingual evidence with strong baselines such as RoBERTa yields significant improvements in fake news detection.

1 Introduction

After the manipulation of opinions on Facebook during the 2016 U.S. election (Allcott and Gentzkow, 2017), the interest in the topic of fake news has increased substantially. Unfortunately, the distribution of fakes leads not only to misinformation of readers but also to more severe consequences such as shooting in Washington Pizzeria (Kang and Goldman, 2016) that was caused by the spreading of fake news about Hillary Clinton leading a child sex trafficking. Also, due to the global pandemic in 2020, there was a simultaneous emergence of infodemic (Alam et al., 2020) that could lead to an even worse epidemiological situation and harm people's health dramatically.

As a result, fake news received tremendous public attention, as well as drawn increasing interest from the academic community. Multiple supervised fake news detection models were proposed based on linguistic features (Pérez-Rosas et al., 2018; Patwa et al., 2020); deep learning models (Barrón-Cedeño et al., 2019; Glazkova et al., 2020; Kaliyar et al., 2021); or signals from social networks (Nguyen et al., 2020; Cui et al., 2019). One of the directions of the supervised approaches is to use additional information from the Web (Popat et al., 2017; Karadzhov et al., 2017; Ghanem et al., 2018). However, in these works only monolingual signals were taken into account.

In our work, we assume that viral spreading of (fake) information may naturally hit the "language barrier" and cross-checking of facts across media in various languages (supposed to be strongly independent) could yield an additional signal. We aim to close this gap and perform an exploration of cross-lingual Web features to fake news detection.

The contribution of our work is a new **cross-lingual evidence** feature for fake news detection based on multilingual news verification.[1] We conduct a manual experiment based on cross-lingual dataset markup to evaluate if the user can use such a feature for misinformation identification. After that, we implement the proposed feature showing that adding cross-lingual evidence consistently improves the results of strong baselines including large pre-trained transformers. We release publicly all code and data.[2]

2 Related Work

Firstly, several datasets have been collected for different sub-tasks of fake news detection pipeline:

[1]This work is a substantially extended version of the preliminary experiment by Dementieva and Panchenko (2020).

[2]https://github.com/skoltech-nlp/multilingual-fake-news

Proceedings of the Joint Conference of the 59th Annual Meeting of the Association for Computational Linguistics and the 11th International Joint Conference on Natural Language Processing: Student Research Workshop, pages 310–320
August 5–6, 2021. ©2021 Association for Computational Linguistics

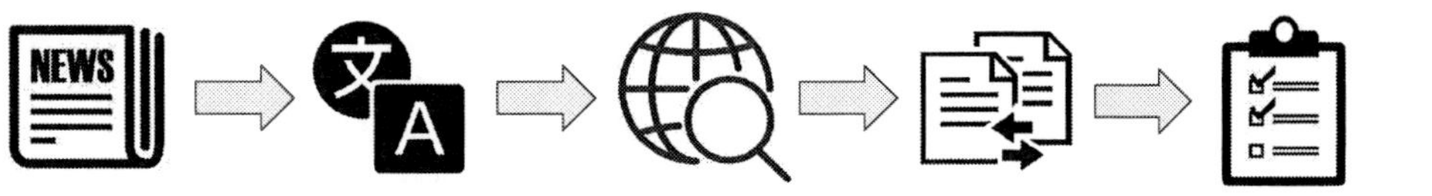

Figure 1 – Overview of our approach: checking for fake news based on cross-lingual evidence (CE).

dataset from *The Fake News Challenge*[3] for stance detection; *LIAR* (Wang, 2017), *FakeNewsNet* (Shu et al., 2018), FakeNewsDatasets (Pérez-Rosas et al., 2018), and *NELA-GT-2018* (Norregaard et al., 2019) for fake news classification tasks; *FEVER* (Thorne et al., 2018) for fact checking tasks. Responding to current events in 2020, COVID-19 fake news classification datasets *COVID-19 Fake News* (Patwa et al., 2020), *ReCOVery* (Zhou et al., 2020) have been already created.

Several supervised models were previously explored. Some of the works focused on exploring internal features of news. In (Pérez-Rosas et al., 2018; Patwa et al., 2020) different linguistic features extracted from news texts were used. In (Ghanem et al., 2020) the perspective of the usage of emotional signals extracted from the news text for detecting fakes was shown. In addition to internal features, a set of external features can add more confidence in fake news detection model decision reasoning. For instance, user interaction signals were explored in (Nguyen et al., 2020; Cui et al., 2019). Another quite strong signal can be additional information extracted from the Web. In (Popat et al., 2017; Karadzhov et al., 2017; Ghanem et al., 2018; Li and Zhou, 2020) the authors referred to the Web search (Google or Bing) to collect relevant articles and use such scraped information as an external feature to build a fake news classifier.

Seeking information via some search engine to find evidence is a quite natural feature motivated by real users' behaviour. Several studies tried to figure out how users authenticate the information from the Web. Jr. et al. (2018) showed that individuals rely on both their judgment of the source and the message, and when this does not adequately provide a definitive answer, they turn to external resources to authenticate news. The intentional and institutional reaction was seeking confirmation from institutional sources (some respondents answered simply "Google"). Moreover, participants that received messages across different media platforms (Zhao, 2019) and different perspectives of the information (Geeng et al., 2020) showed greater awareness about news evidence. Consequently, the information from the external search is an important feature for news authenticity evaluation and evidence seeking. While the idea of multilingualism was already explored for hate speech (Aluru et al., 2020) and rumors (Wen et al., 2018) detection, however, previous works did not fully use multilingual information of fake news detection. In our study, we explore fake news spread on the Web for different languages and extend evidence retrieval to cross-lingual news verification.

3 Detection of Fake News using Cross-lingual Evidence (CE)

Our approach is based on the following **hypothesis**: if the news is *true*, then it will be widespread in different languages and also across media with different biases, and the facts mentioned should be identical. On the other hand, if it is *fake* news, it will receive a lesser response in the foreign press than true news. The step-by-step process, schematically represented in Figure 1, is as follows:

Step 1. Text extraction: As a new article arrives, title and content are extracted from it.

Step 2. Text translation: The title is translated into target languages and new search requests are generated.

Step 3. Cross-lingual news retrieval: Search is executed based on the translated titles in multiple languages.

Step 4. Cross-lingual evidence impact computation Top-N articles from search results are used to evaluate the authenticity of the initial news. The information described in the news is compared with the information in the articles from the search result. The number of articles that confirms or disproves the original news is estimated.

Step 5. News classification: Based on the information from the previous step, the decision is made about the authenticity of the news. If the majority of results support the original news, then it is more

[3] http://www.fakenewschallenge.org

likely to be true; if there are contradictions – it is a signal to consider the news as fake.

To confirm the hypothesis that cross-lingual evidence can be used for fake news detection we conducted two experiments. The first one (Section 4) is a manual small-scale study confirming the hypothesis that a person can distinguish fake news based on such cross-lingual evidence. The second one (Section 5) is an automated fake news detection system tested on several fake news datasets: we implemented our cross-lingual evidence feature and compared it with several baselines achieving SOTA on all datasets.

4 Experiment 1: Manual Verification

First, we conducted a manual experiment on a small dataset to test the hypothesis in "ideal conditions".

4.1 Dataset

For fake news examples, we used the list of top 50 fake news from 2018 according to BuzzFeed.[4]. For true news, we used NELA-GT-2018 dataset (Norregaard et al., 2019). We manually selected 10 fake and true news and manually executed all steps of our approach (Section 3) on this dataset. This dataset featuring 20 news is provided in Table 2 in the Appendix A: the dataset is combined by news from several fields – celebrities, science, politics, culture, and world.

4.2 Experimental Setup

We precalculated **Step 2** and **Step 3** for annotators convenience and reproducibility. We generated cross-lingual requests in five languages – English, French, German, Spanish, and Russian. For translation from English, Google Translation service was used. As all news are of 2018, the time range of every search was limited only by this year. From search results, we used the first page of the search which consisted of 10 news. As a result, for 20 news for each of languages we got 1000 pairs of "original news ↔ scraped news" to markup.

We asked 6 annotators to take part in the experiment: manually conduct **Step 4**: cross-lingual evidence impact computation. For each news, we provide information about its title, content, and link of the source. Every annotator got 10 randomly selected news, as a result, we got each news cross-checked by 3 annotators. All non-English news were translated into English. For each pair "original news ↔ scraped news" the annotator provided one of three answers: 1) **Support**: the information in the scraped news supports the original news; 2) **Refute**: the information is opposite or differ from the original news or there is an explicit refutation; 3) **Not enough info**: the information is not relevant or not sufficient to support/refute the original news. Finally, at the end of the annotation of a sample, the annotator was asked to conduct **Step 5** of the pipeline and classify the news as fake or true.

The used interface for manual markup is presented in Appendix A Figure 3.

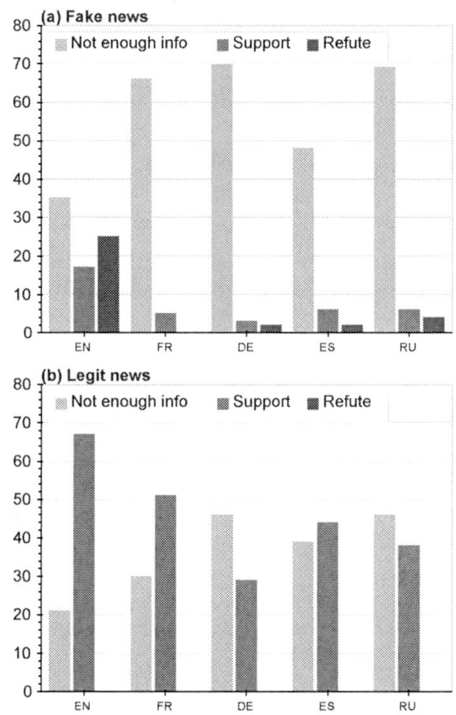

Figure 2 – The results of manual annotation: the distribution of annotators answers for fake (a) and legit (b) news.

4.3 Discussion of Results

Based on the collected annotations, for each news we chose the final label based on the majority voted. We estimated confidence in the annotators' agreement with Krippendorff's alpha ($\alpha = 0.83$). After that, we calculated the distribution of each type of annotators' answers for the top 10 search results by language for fake and true news separately. The results are provided in Figure 2.

As we can see, the distribution of labels for true news significantly differs from the distribution for fake ones: the number of supporting articles is

[4] `https://github.com/BuzzFeedNews/2018-12-fake-news-top-50`

	FakeNewsAMT			Celebrity			ReCOVery		
	Pre.	Rec.	F1	Pre.	Rec.	F1	Pre.	Rec.	F1
TextCNN	0.276	0.250	0.260	0.641	0.703	0.664	0.733	0.913	0.805
LSTM	0.614	0.614	0.614	0.745	0.740	0.740	0.800	0.803	0.793
ME Sim + ME AlexaRank	0.539	0.593	0.592	0.552	0.550	0.550	0.794	0.798	0.793
CE AlexaRank	0.541	0.541	0.541	0.605	0.605	0.605	0.768	0.773	0.765
CE Sim + CE AlexaRank	0.872	0.864	0.864	0.631	0.620	0.619	0.829	0.829	0.829
BERT	0.586	0.586	0.586	0.800	0.800	0.800	0.868	0.868	0.866
BERT + CE AlexaRank	0.541	0.541	0.541	0.810	0.728	0.915	0.768	0.773	0.765
BERT + CE Sim + CE AlexaRank	**0.884**	**0.885**	**0.894**	**0.982**	**0.982**	**0.982**	**0.870**	**0.863**	**0.884**
RoBERTa	0.895	0.548	0.656	0.856	0.690	0.731	0.986	0.936	0.956
RoBERTa + CE AlexaRank	0.930	0.820	0.872	0.799	**0.890**	0.822	0.949	**0.986**	0.966
RoBERTa + CE Sim + CE AlexaRank	**0.973**	**0.938**	**0.953**	**0.952**	0.784	**0.856**	**0.992**	0.960	**0.975**
Ngrams	0.573	0.572	0.572	0.730	0.730	0.730	0.878	0.879	0.877
Ngrams + CE AlexaRank	0.655	0.655	0.655	0.740	0.740	0.740	0.891	0.891	0.891
Ngrams + CE Sim + CE AlexaRank	**0.864**	**0.854**	**0.853**	**0.789**	**0.790**	**0.789**	**0.931**	**0.932**	**0.931**
Punctuation	0.239	0.489	0.321	0.211	0.460	0.289	0.433	0.658	0.522
Punctuation + CE AlexaRank	0.741	0.741	0.741	0.605	0.600	0.600	0.668	0.673	0.665
Punctuation + CE Sim + CE AlexaRank	**0.872**	**0.864**	**0.864**	**0.631**	**0.620**	**0.619**	**0.829**	**0.829**	**0.829**
LIWC	0.597	0.593	0.592	0.630	0.610	0.605	0.768	0.771	0.756
LIWC + CE AlexaRank	0.646	0.645	0.644	0.712	0.700	0.690	0.846	0.846	0.842
LIWC + CE Sim + CE AlexaRank	**0.894**	**0.885**	**0.884**	**0.692**	**0.680**	**0.679**	**0.894**	**0.894**	**0.894**
Readability	0.729	0.729	0.729	0.478	0.470	0.468	0.732	0.741	0.724
Readibility + CE AlexaRank	0.760	0.760	0.760	0.592	0.590	0.590	0.796	0.798	0.790
Readability + CE Sim + CE AlexaRank	**0.928**	**0.927**	**0.927**	**0.674**	**0.670**	**0.670**	**0.828**	**0.829**	**0.828**
Syntax	0.626	0.625	0.624	0.639	0.630	0.629	0.812	0.809	0.797
Syntax + CE AlexaRank	0.677	0.677	0.677	0.721	0.720	0.720	0.844	0.841	0.834
Syntax + CE Sim + CE AlexaRank	**0.902**	**0.895**	**0.895**	**0.754**	**0.750**	**0.750**	**0.886**	**0.886**	**0.886**
All linguistic	0.739	0.739	0.739	0.750	0.750	0.750	0.875	0.874	0.870
All linguistic + CE AlexaRank	0.641	0.641	0.641	0.605	0.600	0.600	0.868	0.868	0.868
All linguistic + CE Sim + CE AlexaRank	**0.940**	**0.937**	**0.937**	**0.801**	**0.800**	**0.800**	**0.916**	**0.917**	**0.916**

Table 1 – Results: adding our Cross-lingual Evidence (CE) improves various baseline systems and yields state-of-the-art results. The proposed feature is used in two parts: (i) content similarity score based on embeddings distance (Sim); (ii) AlexaRank score of the scraped news source (AlexaRank). ME stands for Monolingual Evidence. The statistical significance of the baselines improvements was tested with paired t-test over 5-fold cross-validation.

enough for almost every language. At the same time, for fake news we got more refuting signals than supporting for the English language and little or no evidence or relevant information dissemination for other languages. The average accuracy of annotators classification is 0.95. Thus, a person can distinguish fake based on cross-lingual evidence.

5 Experiment 2: Automatic Verification

We implemented cross-lingual evidence (CE) feature, as described below. We tested its performance on fake news detection on three multi-domain datasets comparing it with strong baselines.

5.1 Cross-lingual Evidence (CE) Feature

Cross-lingual evidence retrieval As in manual setup, for translation and search we used Google services via Python APIs. In our setup for the automated feature we focused as well on five languages: English, French, German, Spanish, and Russian. We extracted only the first page of the search result that gave us 10 articles for each language.

Cross-lingual text similarity For unsupervised cross-lingual relevance computation between original news and scraped one, we chose cosine similarity between sentence embeddings. To get sentence vector representation, we averaged the both title and content sentence's tokens' embeddings extracted from M-BERT (Devlin et al., 2019). For the sample news the similarity score is extracted for all 10 pairs "original news ↔ scraped news" for each of 5 languages.

Source credibility Also, we took into account the credibility of the source. Following Popat et al. (2016) we used AlexaRank for source assessment.

Cross-lingual evidence (CE) feature is constructed of two parts: content similarity score based on embeddings distance (Sim) and AlexaRank score of the scraped news source (AlexaRank).

5.2 Datasets

Firstly, we evaluate the systems on a multi-domain dataset by Pérez-Rosas et al. (2018) which consist of two parts: *FakeNewsAMT* dataset (240 fake and 240 legit articles) and *CelebrityDataset* dataset (250 fake and 250 legit articles). *FakeNewsAMT* dataset consists of news from six topics: sports, business, entertainment, politics, technology, and education. *CelebrityDataset* is dedicated to rumors, hoaxes, and fake reports about famous actors, singers, socialites, and politicians. Secondly, we ran experiments on COVID-19 fake news dataset *ReCOVery* (Zhou et al., 2020). It consists of 2029 (665 fake and 1364 true news). All datasets are originally in English. We used 70%-20%-10% proportion for train-test-validation split.

5.3 Baselines

We compare to both linguistic-based fake news detection models and SOTA deep neural networks:

Linguistic Features: In (Pérez-Rosas et al., 2018) a baseline fake news classification model was trained based on Ngrams, punctuation, psycholinguistic features extracted with LIWC, readability, syntax, and concatenation of all these set of features. In (Zhou et al., 2020) LIWC features were also used as one of the proposed baselines. We tested these features separately, grouped them all, and in combination with our proposed feature. We experimented with SVM, RandomForest, LogRegression, and LightGBM. The best models based on LightGBM are presented.

Text-CNN, LSTM: Following (Zhou et al., 2020), we tested TextCNN and LSTM models on all datasets. We fined-tuned models hyperparameters and report the best ones in the results.

BERT, RoBERTa: BERT (Devlin et al., 2019) based models were used for fake news detection by Kaliyar et al. (2021) and specifically for COVID-19 fake news classification (Gundapu and Mamidi, 2021; Glazkova et al., 2020). We used pretrained models and fine-tuned them. The combination with CE feature was done as a concatenation with `[CLS]` token embedding before Linear layer.

Monolingual Evidence (ME): In addition, we compared our feature with the case when only monolingual English evidence was used. The LightGBM classification model was used as well.

5.4 Discussion of Results

Table 1 compares results of our model based on cross-lingual evidence (CE) with the baselines on three datasets. The statistical significance of the baselines improvements was tested with paired t-test over 5-fold cross-validation. The CE feature by itself outperforms all baseline for *FakeNewsAMT* and better than some linguistic features for *Celebrity* and *ReCOVery*. The monolingual English evidence (ME) works worse than the cross-lingual one. The usage of only rank feature improves the baselines, but the best scores are achieved by adding full CE features set. The combinations of CE feature with BERT and RoBERTa gains SOTA results for all dataset. At the same time, despite linguistic features did not outperform Transformer-based baselines, the combination of our CE feature and different linguistic features showed competitive results that can be more explainable than the transformer model. Examples how retrieved cross-lingual results can be used to explain the classification results are illustrated in Appendix B.

6 Conclusion

We presented an approach for fake news detection based on cross-lingual evidence (CE) which provides a different perspective on the event across languages verified in two experiments. A fake news classification model with CE significantly improves performance over various baselines and compares favorably to SOTA. Besides, the CE is interpretable as a user can check in which and how many languages a piece of given news was found.

A promising direction to explore is to increase the number of languages used for cross-lingual information retrieval. In addition to this, the general distribution of news in the world should be taken into account – for instance, US news tend to be covered in European presses more than European news are covered in the US press. Also, in our work the language of original news was English. The analogous experiments for other original languages of news should be conducted.

Acknowledgments

We thank anonymous reviewers for their thorough comments and suggestions for future work. The work has been conducted in the framework of the joint MTS-Skoltech laboratory.

References

Firoj Alam, Fahim Dalvi, Shaden Shaar, Nadir Durrani, Hamdy Mubarak, Alex Nikolov, Giovanni Da San Martino, Ahmed Abdelali, Hassan Sajjad, Kareem Darwish, and Preslav Nakov. 2020. Fighting the COVID-19 infodemic in social media: A holistic perspective and a call to arms. *CoRR*, abs/2007.07996.

Hunt Allcott and Matthew Gentzkow. 2017. Social media and fake news in the 2016 election. *Journal of economic perspectives*, 31(2):211–36.

Sai Saketh Aluru, Binny Mathew, Punyajoy Saha, and Animesh Mukherjee. 2020. Deep learning models for multilingual hate speech detection. *CoRR*, abs/2004.06465.

Alberto Barrón-Cedeño, Israa Jaradat, Giovanni Da San Martino, and Preslav Nakov. 2019. Proppy: Organizing the news based on their propagandistic content. *Inf. Process. Manag.*, 56(5):1849–1864.

Limeng Cui, Kai Shu, Suhang Wang, Dongwon Lee, and Huan Liu. 2019. defend: A system for explainable fake news detection. In *Proceedings of the 28th ACM International Conference on Information and Knowledge Management, CIKM 2019, Beijing, China, November 3-7, 2019*, pages 2961–2964. ACM.

Daryna Dementieva and Alexander Panchenko. 2020. Fake news detection using multilingual evidence. In *7th IEEE International Conference on Data Science and Advanced Analytics, DSAA 2020, Sydney, Australia, October 6-9, 2020*, pages 775–776. IEEE.

Jacob Devlin, Ming-Wei Chang, Kenton Lee, and Kristina Toutanova. 2019. BERT: Pre-training of deep bidirectional transformers for language understanding. In *Proceedings of the 2019 Conference of the North American Chapter of the Association for Computational Linguistics: Human Language Technologies, Volume 1 (Long and Short Papers)*, pages 4171–4186, Minneapolis, Minnesota. Association for Computational Linguistics.

Christine Geeng, Savanna Yee, and Franziska Roesner. 2020. Fake news on facebook and twitter: Investigating how people (don't) investigate. In *CHI '20: CHI Conference on Human Factors in Computing Systems, Honolulu, HI, USA, April 25-30, 2020*, pages 1–14. ACM.

Bilal Ghanem, Manuel Montes-y Gòmez, Francisco Rangel, and Paolo Rosso. 2018. Upv-inaoe-autoritas-check that: An approach based on external sources to detect claims credibility. In *Proceedings of the Conference and Labs of the Evaluation Forum (CLEF'18)*.

Bilal Ghanem, Paolo Rosso, and Francisco M. Rangel Pardo. 2020. An emotional analysis of false information in social media and news articles. *ACM Trans. Internet Techn.*, 20(2):19:1–19:18.

Anna Glazkova, Maksim Glazkov, and Timofey Trifonov. 2020. g2tmn at constraint@aaai2021: Exploiting CT-BERT and ensembling learning for COVID-19 fake news detection. *CoRR*, abs/2012.11967.

Sunil Gundapu and Radhika Mamidi. 2021. Transformer based automatic COVID-19 fake news detection system. *CoRR*, abs/2101.00180.

Edson C. Tandoc Jr., Richard Ling, Oscar Westlund, Andrew Duffy, Debbie Goh, and Lim Zheng Wei. 2018. Audiences' acts of authentication in the age of fake news: *A conceptual framework. New Media Soc.*, 20(8):2745–2763.

Rohit Kumar Kaliyar, Anurag Goswami, and Pratik Narang. 2021. Fakebert: Fake news detection in social media with a bert-based deep learning approach. *Multim. Tools Appl.*, 80(8):11765–11788.

Cecilia Kang and Adam Goldman. 2016. In washington pizzeria attack, fake news brought real guns. *New York Times*, 5.

Georgi Karadzhov, Preslav Nakov, Lluís Màrquez, Alberto Barrón-Cedeño, and Ivan Koychev. 2017. Fully automated fact checking using external sources. In *Proceedings of the International Conference Recent Advances in Natural Language Processing, RANLP 2017*, pages 344–353, Varna, Bulgaria. INCOMA Ltd.

Qifei Li and Wangchunshu Zhou. 2020. Connecting the dots between fact verification and fake news detection. In *Proceedings of the 28th International Conference on Computational Linguistics*, pages 1820–1825, Barcelona, Spain (Online). International Committee on Computational Linguistics.

Van-Hoang Nguyen, Kazunari Sugiyama, Preslav Nakov, and Min-Yen Kan. 2020. FANG: leveraging social context for fake news detection using graph representation. In *CIKM '20: The 29th ACM International Conference on Information and Knowledge Management, Virtual Event, Ireland, October 19-23, 2020*, pages 1165–1174. ACM.

Jeppe Norregaard, Benjamin D. Horne, and Sibel Adali. 2019. NELA-GT-2018: A large multi-labelled news dataset for the study of misinformation in news articles. *CoRR*, abs/1904.01546.

Parth Patwa, Shivam Sharma, PYKL Srinivas, Vineeth Guptha, Gitanjali Kumari, Md. Shad Akhtar, Asif Ekbal, Amitava Das, and Tanmoy Chakraborty. 2020. Fighting an infodemic: COVID-19 fake news dataset. *CoRR*, abs/2011.03327.

Verónica Pérez-Rosas, Bennett Kleinberg, Alexandra Lefevre, and Rada Mihalcea. 2018. Automatic detection of fake news. In *Proceedings of the 27th International Conference on Computational Linguistics, COLING 2018, Santa Fe, New Mexico, USA, August 20-26, 2018*, pages 3391–3401. Association for Computational Linguistics.

Kashyap Popat, Subhabrata Mukherjee, Jannik Strötgen, and Gerhard Weikum. 2016. Credibility assessment of textual claims on the web. In *Proceedings of the 25th ACM International Conference on Information and Knowledge Management, CIKM 2016, Indianapolis, IN, USA, October 24-28, 2016*, pages 2173–2178. ACM.

Kashyap Popat, Subhabrata Mukherjee, Jannik Strötgen, and Gerhard Weikum. 2017. Where the truth lies: Explaining the credibility of emerging claims on the web and social media. In *Proceedings of the 26th International Conference on World Wide Web Companion, Perth, Australia, April 3-7, 2017*, pages 1003–1012. ACM.

Kai Shu, Deepak Mahudeswaran, Suhang Wang, Dongwon Lee, and Huan Liu. 2018. Fakenewsnet: A data repository with news content, social context and dynamic information for studying fake news on social media. *CoRR*, abs/1809.01286.

James Thorne, Andreas Vlachos, Christos Christodoulopoulos, and Arpit Mittal. 2018. FEVER: a large-scale dataset for fact extraction and VERification. In *Proceedings of the 2018 Conference of the North American Chapter of the Association for Computational Linguistics: Human Language Technologies, Volume 1 (Long Papers)*, pages 809–819, New Orleans, Louisiana. Association for Computational Linguistics.

William Yang Wang. 2017. "liar, liar pants on fire": A new benchmark dataset for fake news detection. In *Proceedings of the 55th Annual Meeting of the Association for Computational Linguistics (Volume 2: Short Papers)*, pages 422–426, Vancouver, Canada. Association for Computational Linguistics.

Weiming Wen, Songwen Su, and Zhou Yu. 2018. Cross-lingual cross-platform rumor verification pivoting on multimedia content. In *Proceedings of the 2018 Conference on Empirical Methods in Natural Language Processing*, pages 3487–3496, Brussels, Belgium. Association for Computational Linguistics.

Wenqing Zhao. 2019. Misinformation correction across social media platforms. In *2019 International Conference on Computational Science and Computational Intelligence (CSCI)*, pages 1371–1376. IEEE.

Xinyi Zhou, Apurva Mulay, Emilio Ferrara, and Reza Zafarani. 2020. Recovery: A multimodal repository for COVID-19 news credibility research. In *CIKM '20: The 29th ACM International Conference on Information and Knowledge Management, Virtual Event, Ireland, October 19-23, 2020*, pages 3205–3212. ACM.

A Manual Evaluation

News title	URL	Label
Lottery winner arrested for dumping $200,000 of manure on ex-boss' lawn	https://worldnewsdailyreport.com/lottery-winner-arrested-for-dumping-200000-of-manure-on-ex-boss-lawn/	Fake
Woman sues Samsung for $1.8M after cell phone gets stuck inside her vagina	https://worldnewsdailyreport.com/woman-sues-samsung-for-1-8m-after-cell-phone-gets-stuck-inside-her-vagina/comment-page-58/	Fake
BREAKING: Michael Jordan Resigns From The Board At Nike-Takes 'Air Jordans' With Him	https://www.newsbreak.com/news/944830700924/breaking-michael-jordan-resigns-from-the-board-at-nike-takes-air-jordans-with-him	Fake
Donald Trump Ends School Shootings By Banning Schools	https://www.8shit.net/donald-trump-ends-school-shootings-banning-schools/	Fake
New mosquito species discovered that can get you pregnant with a single bite	https://thereisnews.com/new-mosquito-species-discovered-can-make-you-pregnant/	Fake
Obama Announces Bid To Become UN Secretary General	https://www.pinterest.com/pin/465630048969491948/	Fake
Lil Tay Rushed To Hospital After Being Beat By Group Of Children At A Playground	https://www.huzlers.com/lil-tay-rushed-to-hospital-after-being-beat-by-group-of-children-at-a-playground/	Fake
Post Malone's Tour Manager Quits Says Post Malone Smells Like Expired Milk And Moldy Cheese	https://www.huzlers.com/post-malones-tour-manager-quits-says-post-malone-smells-like-expired-milk-and-moldy-cheese/	Fake
Putin: Clinton Illegally Accepted $400 Million From Russia During Election	https://newspunch.com/putin-clinton-campaign-400-million-russia/	Fake
Elon Musk: 99.9% Of Media Is Owned By The 'New World Order'	https://newspunch.com/elon-musk-media-owned-new-world-order/	Fake
Scientists Develop New Method to Create Stem Cells Without Killing Human Embryos	https://www.christianpost.com/news/scientists-develop-new-method-to-create-stem-cells-without-killing-human-embryos.html	Legit
Luis Palau Diagnosed With Stage 4 Lung Cancer	https://cnnw.com/luis-palau-diagnosed-with-stage-4-lung-cancer/	Legit
1st black woman nominated to be Marine brigadier general	https://edition.cnn.com/2018/04/12/politics/marine-corps-brigadier-general-first-black-female/index.html	Legit
Disney CEO Bob Iger revealed that he seriously explored running for president	https://www.businessinsider.com/disney-ceo-bob-iger-says-he-considered-running-for-president-oprah-pushed-2018-4	Legit
Trump Has Canceled Via Twitter His G20 Meeting With Vladimir Putin	https://www.buzzfeednews.com/article/emilytamkin/trump-g20-putin-russia	Legit
US Mexico and Canada sign new USMCA trade deal	https://www.dw.com/en/us-mexico-canada-sign-usmca-trade-deal/a-51613992	Legit
Afghanistan Women children among 23 killed in US attack UN	https://www.aljazeera.com/news/2018/11/30/afghanistan-women-children-among-23-killed-in-us-attack-un	Legit
UNESCO adds reggae music to global cultural heritage list	https://www.aljazeera.com/features/2018/11/29/unesco-adds-reggae-music-to-global-cultural-heritage-list	Legit
The Saudi women detained for demanding basic human rights	https://www.aljazeera.com/news/2018/11/29/the-saudi-women-detained-for-demanding-basic-human-rights/	Legit
Georgia ruling party candidate Zurabishvili wins presidential runoff	https://www.aljazeera.com/news/2018/11/30/ex-envoy-wins-georgia-presidency-vote-to-be-challenged	Legit

Table 2 – The manually selected 20 news dataset (10 fake and 10 true news) for manual experiment. Fake news were selected from the top 50 fake news of 2018 according to BuzzFeed. Legit news were selected from NELA-GT-2018 dataset.

	Original news:			Lottery winner arrested for dumping $200,000 of manure on ex-boss' lawn	https://worldnewsdailyreport.com/lottery-winner-arrested-for-dumping-200000-of-manure-on-ex-boss-lawn/		
	Title	**Title in EN**	**Link**	**Text of the content**	**Content in EN**	**Do you think it supports original news? Answer: 1 (Support), 0 (Refute), -1 (Not enough info)**	**Any comments**
0	Lottery winner arrested for dumping $200,000 of manure on ex-boss' lawn	—	https://worldnewsdailyreport.com/lottery-winner-arrested-for-dumping-200000-of-manure-on-ex-boss-lawn/	A man from Illinois was arrested for getting $224,000 worth of manure dumped on his former employer's property, only two weeks after he won $125 million at the lottery and quit his job. 54-year old Brian Morris, from the small town of Clarendon Hills in Dupage County, bought over 20,000 tons of manure and asked for it to be dumped on his former boss' property, pretending it was his residence.	—	—	
	Englsih query			https://www.google.com/search?cd_min:1/1/2018,cd_max:1/1/2019&q=Lottery+winner+arrested+for+dumping+$200000+of+manure+on+exbossâ€™+lawn&num=10			
	Title	**Title in EN**	**Link**	**Text of the content**	**Content in EN**	**Do you think it supports original news? Answer: 1 (Support), 0 (Refute), -1 (Not enough info)**	**Any comments**
1	PolitiFact - Viral post that lottery winner was arrested for dumping manure on former boss' lawn reeks of falsity	—	https://www.politifact.com/factchecks/2018/nov/05/worldnewsdailyreportcom/viral-post-lottery-winner-was-arrested-dumping-man/	A viral blog post claims that a man who won the lottery was arrested "for getting $224,000 worth of manure dumped on his former employer's property." Published on World News Daily Report, the post claims that a 54-year-old Clarendon Hills, Ill., resident named Brian Morris bought over 20,000 tons of manure after winning $125 million at Powerball Multi-state lottery two weeks before. This story was flagged as part of Facebook's efforts to combat false news and misinformation on its News Feed. (Read more about our partnership with Facebook.) The post received over 2.3 million interactions and had been shared over 285,000 times, CrowdTangle data show.	—		
						Finish!!!	
	Your decision:			Finally, how can you classifier the news: is it fake or true?			

Figure 3 – User interface that was used for annotators answer collection for manual verification. An annotator has to conduct **Step 4** and **Step 5** of the pipeline: (i) identify whether a cross-lingual scraped news supports, refutes or has not enough info with respect to the original one; (ii) classify the original news as a fake or a true one based on the provided cross-lingual evidence.

B Samples of Cross-lingual Evidence for News Items

Title	English translation
Original news (FAKE)	
Kate Middleton & Prince William Try To Save Crumbling Marriage?	–
English search results	
Prince William and Kate Middleton's Love Through the Years	–
How Princess Diana made desperate 'last-ditch attempt' to save marriage with Charles	–
Prince William of Wales — Economist - World News, Politics, Economics, Business & Finance	–
French search results	
Le jour où le prince William a demandé Kate Middleton en mariage	The day Prince William proposed to Kate Middleton
William et Kate, fiançailles avant le mariage royal	William and Kate, engagement before the royal wedding
Mariage William et Kate	William and Kate wedding
German search results	
Elternschaft, Babynamen, Prominente und königliche Nachrichten — CafeMom.com	Parenting, Baby Names, Celebrities, and Royal News — CafeMom.com
Kate Middletons umstrittenste Momente aller Zeiten	Kate Middleton's Most Controversial Moments of All Time
Wie Kate Middleton und Prinz William das Leben ihrer Kinder normal halten	How Kate Middleton and Prince William Keep Their Kids' Lives Normal
Spanish search results	
Príncipe William – Clarín.com	Prince William - Clarín.com
Con un comentario, Harry hizo llorar a Kate Middleton en el día de su boda	With a comment, Harry made Kate Middleton cry on his wedding day
El Príncipe Guillermo de Inglaterra se casará con su novia Kate Middleton en 2011 - RTVE.es	Prince William of England will marry his girlfriend Kate Middleton in 2011 - RTVE.es
Russian search results	
Факты о свадьбе Кейт Миддлтон и принца Уильяма, о которых вы могли не знать	Kate Middleton and Prince William's wedding facts you might not know
Кейт Миддлтон	Kate Middleton
Кэтрин, герцогиня Кембриджская — Википедия	Catherine, Duchess of Cambridge - Wikipedia
Original news (LEGIT)	
Amazon Prime Air drone completes its first US public delivery	–
English search results	
Amazon Prime Air drone completes its first US public delivery	–
Amazon's Prime Air drone delivery fleet gains FAA approval for trial commercial flights – TechCrunch	–
Amazon completes its first public US drone delivery	–
French search results	
E-commerce. Amazon autorisé à livrer par drone aux États-Unis	E-commerce. Amazon authorized to deliver by drone to the United States
Première livraison par drone réussie pour Amazon	First successful drone delivery for Amazon
Amazon a livré son premier colis par drone	Amazon delivered its first package by drone
German search results	
Prime Air: FAA erteilt Amazons Lieferdrohnen die Starterlaubnis	Prime Air: FAA gives Amazon's delivery drones permission to take off
Amazon Prime Air-Drohne schließt erste öffentliche Auslieferung in den USA ab	Amazon Prime Air drone completes first US public delivery
Amazon Prime Air: Amazon kündigt Lieferungen per Drohne binnen Monaten an	Amazon Prime Air: Amazon announces drone deliveries within months
Spanish search results	
Amazon hace su primera entrega por dron en Estados Unidos	Amazon makes its first delivery by drone in the United States
Amazon recibe autorización para operar entregas con drones	Amazon receives authorization to operate drone deliveries
Amazon recibe aprobación federal para arrancar Prime Air, su propuesta de entrega con drones	Amazon receives federal approval to launch Prime Air, its drone delivery proposal
Russian search results	
Amazon запускает дроны Prime Air для быстрой доставки	Amazon launches Prime Air drones for fast delivery
В США прошла первая публичная демонстрация доставки товара с помощью дронов Amazon Prime Air	First Public Demonstration of Amazon Prime Air Product Delivery Held in USA
Amazon показала новые гибридные дроны для доставки заказов сервиса Prime Air	Amazon Shows New Hybrid Drones To Deliver Prime Air Orders

Table 3 – The example of the cross-lingual evidence extraction for fake and legit news from **FakeNewsAMT**. For each target language (English, French, German, Spanish, Russian) search results are presented: titles of top 3 news. For every non-Enlgish title the English translation is provided. For **fake news** the search results across other languages are only mildly topically related to the original news while for **legit news** the search results across other languages are strongly related to the original news.

Title	English translation
Original news (FAKE)	
В Израиле создали лекарство от коронавируса: https://www.vesty.co.il/article/SJxK1wRF8	Israel invented a vaccine against coronavirus
English search results	
Israel isolates coronavirus antibody in 'significant breakthrough'	–
Israel is not releasing a coronavirus vaccine – The Forward	–
Hadassah treats COVID-19 patient with new concentrated passive vaccine	–
French search results	
Les Israéliens et le vaccin contre le coronavirus	The Israelis and the coronavirus vaccine
Pandémie de Covid-19 en Israël — Wikipédia	Covid-19 pandemic in Israel - Wikipedia
Vaccin contre la Covid-19 — Wikipédia	Vaccin contre la Covid-19 — Wikipédia
German search results	
Impfstoffe gegen Coronavirus – aktueller Forschungsstand	Coronavirus vaccines - current state of research
Warum es so lang dauert, einen Corona-Impfstoff zu entwickeln	Why it takes so long to develop a corona vaccine
Falschinformationen zur COVID-19-Pandemie – Wikipedia	Incorrect information about the COVID-19 pandemic - Wikipedia
Spanish search results	
Cuáles son y en qué estado están los esfuerzos israelíes para inventar una vacuna para el coronavirus	What are and in what state are Israeli efforts to invent a coronavirus vaccine
Sus mejores intentos ... - Consulado General H. de Israel	Your best attempts ... - Consulate General H. of Israel
Vacuna de Pfizer y BioNTech muestra resultados positivos	Pfizer and BioNTech vaccine shows positive results
Russian search results	
В Израиле заявили, что Covid-19 остановит лекарство от холестерина	Israel says cholesterol medication will stop Covid-19
Врач о Covid-19: «Мы не понимаем патогенез заболевания» — Израиль в фокусе	Doctor about Covid-19: ≪We do not understand the pathogenesis of the disease≫ - Israel in focus
Израильские технологии	Israeli technology
Original news (LEGIT)	
В Монголии произошла вспышка бубонной чумы: https://hightech.fm/2020/07/02/plague-outbreak	Bubonic plague outbreak in Mongolia
English search results	
Bubonic plague: Case found in China's Inner Mongolia - CNN	–
Teenager dies of Black Death in Mongolia	–
China bubonic plague: Inner Mongolia takes precautions after case	–
French search results	
Epidémie : des cas de peste détectés en Chine et en Mongolie	Epidemic: cases of plague detected in China and Mongolia
Craintes d'une épidémie de peste bubonique? Un adolescent de 15 ans est la première victime recensée en Mongolie	Fear of a bubonic plague epidemic? A 15-year-old is the first victim in Mongolia
Chine : Un cas de peste bubonique détecté en Mongolie intérieure	China: Bubonic plague case detected in Inner Mongolia
German search results	
Mongolei: 15-Jähriger an Beulenpest gestorben - DER SPIEGEL	Mongolia: 15-year-old died of bubonic plague - DER SPIEGEL
Beulenpest - Was über die Pest-Fälle in China bekannt	Bubonic plague - what is known about the plague cases in China
Bringen Murmeltiere die Pest zurück? Mongolei warnt vor Tier-Kontakt	Will marmots bring the plague back? Mongolia warns of animal contact
Spanish search results	
BROTE DE PESTE BUBÓNICA EN MONGOLIA	BUBONIC PLAGUE OUTBREAK IN MONGOLIA
Brote de peste negra provoca cuarentena en Mongola	Black plague outbreak causes quarantine in Mongolia
Brote de peste negra alarma en Mongolia y cierra frontera con Rusia	Black plague outbreak alarms Mongolia, closes border with Russia
Russian search results	
В Монголии произошла вспышка бубонной чумы ... - Гордон	There was an outbreak of bubonic plague in Mongolia ... - Gordon
В Монголии произошла вспышка бубонной чумы - Урал56.Ру	Bubonic plague outbreak in Mongolia - Ural56.Ru
Возвращение «Черной смерти»: главное о вспышке бубонной чумы в Монголии	Return of the "Black Death": the main thing about the outbreak of the bubonic plague in Mongolia

Table 4 – The result of the cross-lingual evidence extraction for real-life news. For each target language (English, French, German, Spanish, Russian) search results are presented: titles of top 3 news. For every non-Enlgish title the English translation is provided. For **fake news** the search results across other languages are only mildly topically related to the original news while for **legit news** the search results across other languages are strongly related to the original news.

Neural Machine Translation with Synchronous Latent Phrase Structure

Shintaro Harada **Taro Watanabe**
Nara Institute of Science and Technology (NAIST), Nara, Japan
`{harada.shintaro.hk4, taro}@is.naist.jp`

Abstract

It is reported that grammatical information is useful for machine translation (MT) task. However, the annotation of grammatical information requires the highly human resources. Furthermore, it is not trivial to adapt grammatical information to MT since grammatical annotation usually adapts tokenization standards which might not be suitable to capture the relation of two languages, and the use of subword tokenization, e.g., Byte-Pair-Encoding, to alleviate out-of-vocabulary problem might not be compatible with those annotations. In this work, we propose two methods to explicitly incorporate grammatical information without supervising annotation; first, latent phrase structure is induced in an unsupervised fashion from a multi-head attention mechanism; second, the induced phrase structures in encoder and decoder are synchronized so that they are compatible with each other using constraints during training. We demonstrate that our approach produces better performance and explainability in two tasks, translation and alignment tasks without extra resources. Although we could not obtain the high quality phrase structure in constituency parsing when evaluated monolingually, we find that the induced phrase structures enhance the explainability of translation through the synchronization constraint.

1 Introduction

Although machine translation (MT) has achieved improved performance using neural machine translation (NMT), the translation qualities for distant languages are still poor (Johnson et al., 2017). As a way to tackle the problem, statistical MT (SMT) incorporates synchronous grammar to achieve more linguistically accurate translations, in which complex structural relations between source and target languages are expressed using phrase structure (Wong et al., 2005). The synchronous grammar expresses the complex relationships between source and target languages and incorporates phrase structure to enable more linguistically accurate translation. A similar idea could be employed for NMT to achieve improved performance on those distant language pairs. However, grammatical information annotation demands high human resources. In addition, such grammatical annotation is done on word-level granularities, which might not be the best tokenization for MT tasks due by language mismatch or out-of-vocabulary problem, and often sub-word tokenization, e.g., Byte-Pair-Encoding (BPE) (Sennrich et al., 2016), is employed to alleviate the problem. As a result, it is difficult to incorporate grammatical information into NMT that handle multiple languages simultaneously.

Recently, there have been researches on unsupervised learning of phrase structure without relying on human annotations. Although these phrase structures learned in an unsupervised fashion are very close to the human annotation (Shen et al., 2018a,c), there exists no model which incorporates phrase structures as latent information to improve the performance and explainability of translation.

In this work, we introduce an approach to incorporate the phrase structure explicitly into Transformer (Vaswani et al., 2017). The approach can split into two steps; first, latent phrase structures are induced in an unsupervised fashion for the source and target sides (Shen et al., 2018a); second, the two induced latent phrase structures are synchronously agreed with each other through an attention mechanism (Deguchi et al., 2021). Experiments on German-English and Japanese-English show that our synchronous latent structures have achieved better performance on translation and alignment tasks. We also show that the induced phrase structures and synchronous structures can enhance the explainability of translation through

Proceedings of the Joint Conference of the 59th Annual Meeting of the Association for Computational Linguistics and the 11th International Joint Conference on Natural Language Processing: Student Research Workshop, pages 321–330
August 5–6, 2021.

our detailed analysis in word alignment task.

2 Related Work

2.1 NMT with Supervised Tree Structure

In the previous work, it is reported that supervised phrase structures (Eriguchi et al., 2017; Nguyen et al., 2020) and dependency structures (Ma et al., 2019; Deguchi et al., 2019) can help the performance of MT. However, these approaches require an annotated corpus of syntactic structures. In addition, such syntactic annotation is done on word-level granularities, which might not be the best tokenization for MT tasks due by language mismatch or out-of-vocabulary problem, and often BPE (Sennrich et al., 2016), is employed to alleviate the problem. However, the application of BPE to grammatical information might require a different approach for each language.

2.2 Latent Grammar Induction with Neural Machine Translation

Shen et al. (2018a) introduce the concept called "syntactic distance" which represents the syntactic relation of word pairs. Similarly, Shen et al. (2018c) introduce ordered neurons which allows to learn long-term or short-term information by a novel gating mechanism and activation function. Kim et al. (2019) apply amortized variational inference for recurrent neural network grammar to learn the phrase structures in an unsupervised fashion. Wang et al. (2019) add an extra constraint to the multi-head self-attention mechanism in order to encourage the attention heads to follow phrase structures. Shen et al. (2020) introduce the constrained multi-head self-attention mechanism that allows to induct phrase and dependency structure at the same time.

These works successfully learn to induce phrase structure from language modeling task without extra linguistic resources. It is described in (Htut et al., 2019) that translation task is a conditional language modeling task with many supervisory signals and is suitable for deriving phrase structure. Unfortunately, despite grammatical information helps the understanding model work, previous work has not explicitly used induced phrase structures.

2.3 Transformer NMT

We employ the Transformer (Vaswani et al., 2017) as our base model, which is an encoder-decoder model that relies on an attention mechanism for computing the contextual representations of source and target text. Both the encoder and decoder are composed of multiple layers, each of which includes a multi-head attention (MHA) and a feed-forward sub-layer. To compute the MHA output, three inputs, query $\mathbf{Q}$, key $\mathbf{K}$, and value $\mathbf{V}$ are projected into N different sub-spaces, namely heads, with each output computed in each subspace, then, projected back to the original space after aggregation:

$$\hat{\mathbf{Q}}^{1:N} = \mathbf{Q}\mathbf{W}_Q, \hat{\mathbf{K}}^{1:N} = \mathbf{K}\mathbf{W}_K, \hat{\mathbf{V}}^{1:N} = \mathbf{V}\mathbf{W}_V \tag{1}$$

$$\mathbf{H}^n = \mathbf{A}\hat{\mathbf{V}}^n = \mathrm{softmax}\left(\frac{\hat{\mathbf{Q}}^n \hat{\mathbf{K}^n}^\top}{\sqrt{d_h}}\right)\hat{\mathbf{V}}^n \tag{2}$$

$$\mathrm{MHA}(\hat{\mathbf{Q}}, \hat{\mathbf{K}}, \hat{\mathbf{V}}) = \mathrm{concat}\left(\mathbf{H}^1, ..., \mathbf{H}^N\right)\mathbf{W}_O \tag{3}$$

where $\mathbf{W}_Q \in \mathbb{R}^{d_o \times d_h}$, $\mathbf{W}_K \in \mathbb{R}^{d_o \times d_h}$, $\mathbf{W}_V \in \mathbb{R}^{d_o \times d_h}$, $\mathbf{W}_O \in \mathbb{R}^{d_o \times d_h}$ are projection parameters. d_o is dimension of original space. $d_h = d_o/N$ is the dimension of subspace. The value $\mathbf{A}$ denotes the attention probability for the jth target token overall the ith source token, computed by nth head.

In the translation task, Transformer is frequently used for its translation accuracy and efficiency. Transformer decoder employs the autoregressive model which guesses the next token having read all the previous ones. Also, since attention represents relationship the between source and target tokens, it is used in the alignment task (Garg et al., 2019).

2.4 Synchronous syntactic attention

Deguchi et al. (2021) find that NMT performance can be improved by synchronizing the encoder attention to decoder attention, which is called "synchronous syntactic attention". The dependency information is embedded in these attention by supervised learning task. The encoder-decoder attention can be viewed as a soft word alignment, which is a weight that can project the source vector into the target vector space without additional model parameters. This work synchronize the source and target attentions that be embedded dependency information by supervision task. To match the attention of encoder and decoder, they project the encoder attention to the target one, and incorporate constraints such that the source and target attention agree with each other.

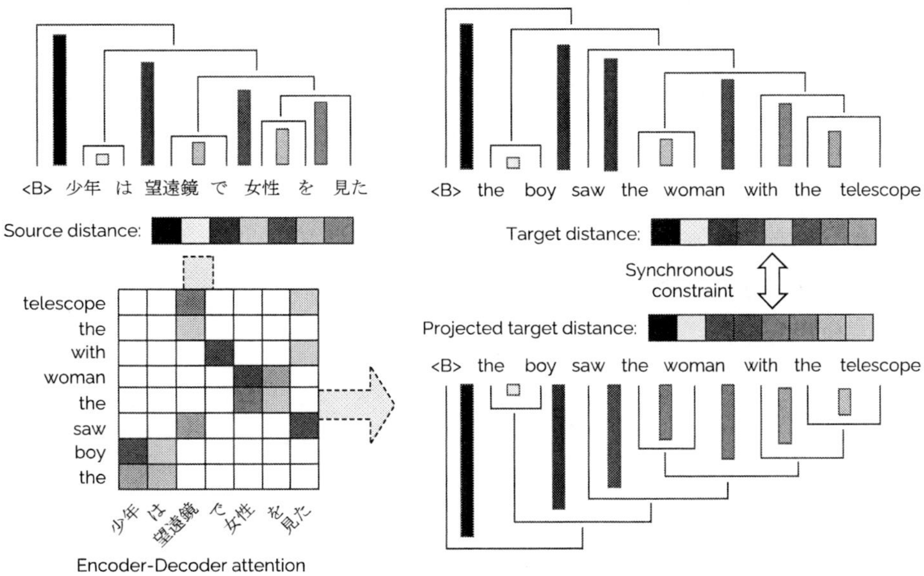

Figure 1: The example of relation between syntactic distances and synchronous constraint on Japanese to English translation task. Starting from induction of source and target syntactic distances, we project the source distance to the target one through encoder-decoder attention weight. By measuring the difference between the projected target syntactic distance and target one with the synchronous constraint. It can embed the syntactic correspondences of source and target language into the encoder-decoder attention weight.

3 Synchronous Latent Phrase Structure

In this section, we present the Synchronous Latent Phrase Structure. This proposed method is split into two steps. One is Latent Phrase Structure Induction (LPSI) and the other is Synchronous Constraint. Figure 1 shows the flow of synchronizing Japanese source and English target syntactic distances.

3.1 Latent Phrase Structure Induction

We employ syntactic distance (Shen et al., 2018a) as a way to induce phrase structure. Each syntactic distance d_i is associated with each span $(i, i+1)$ which indicates the relative order of hierarchically splitting a sentence into smaller components. For example, Figure 1 shows that the target syntactic distance between 'woman' and 'with' covers the phrase 'the woman with the telescope'. Mathematically, syntactic distance d_i is computed through the convolution-based network:

$$d_i = \tanh(\mathbf{W_D} \begin{bmatrix} \boldsymbol{k}_{i-M} \\ \boldsymbol{k}_{i-M+1} \\ \cdots \\ \boldsymbol{k}_i \end{bmatrix} + b_D) \quad (4)$$

where $\mathbf{W}_D$ and b_D are convolution kernel parameter, kernel size M represents a look-back range to calculate syntactic distance $\boldsymbol{d}$. $\boldsymbol{k}_i \in \hat{\mathbf{K}}^n$ is same as key used in MHA. The attention gate values are computed as follows:

$$g_{i,t} = P(b_t \leq i) = \prod_{j=i+1}^{t-1} \alpha_{j,t} \quad (5)$$

$$\alpha_{j,t} = \frac{\text{hardtanh}((d_t - d_j) \cdot \tau) + 1}{2}$$

where t is the current time step. $\alpha_{j,t}$ is a probability value that represents the syntactic relationship of distance d_j and d_t, and $\text{hardtanh}(x) = \max(-1, \max(1, x))$. τ is the temperature hyper parameter that controls the sensitivity of $\alpha_{j,t}$ to the differences between syntactic distances. b_t is a variable that indicates the position of break in the phrase structure. This α is sharper than softmax function, which allows to separate the constituents more easily. The phrase structured MHA is defined based on the gates:

$$\tilde{a}_{i,t} = \frac{g_{i,t} \cdot a_{i,t}}{\sum_i g_{i,t} \cdot a_{i,t}} \quad (6)$$

where a is an element of attention $\mathbf{A}$. The gate $g_{i,t}$ is a weight that constrains attention to only the same hierarchy in the phrase structure. Here, $\tilde{a}$ is used in place of the elements of $\mathbf{A}$ in Equation 2.

3.2 Synchronous Constraint

In the MT model, encoder and decoder learn separate phrase structures, which are not necessarily synchronized in that two structures may not be compatible with each other in terms of vector representations. Therefore, synchronizing each phrase structure learned in encoder and decoder, inspired by synchronous grammar in SMT, may improve the performance of translation by the synchronous structure. Inspired by synchronous syntactic attention (Deguchi et al., 2021), we project the structure expressed by the encoder syntactic distance to the target one, and incorporate constraints such that the source and target syntactic distances agree with each other. In Figure 1, the source syntactic distance is projected to the target syntactic distance through the attention weight, and the syntactic correspondence between Japanese and English is learned from the target and projected syntactic distances of the phrase 'saw the woman with the telescope'.

The synchronous constraint can be represented by using the Mean Squared Error (MSE) of the syntactic distance between the source and target languages:

$$\mathcal{L}_{sync} = \sum_{l}^{L} \sum_{i} \left(d_i^{(l)} - \tilde{d}_i^{(l)} \right)^2 \quad (7)$$

$\tilde{\boldsymbol{d}}^{(l)}$ is projected syntactic distance in lth decoder layer and computed as:

$$\tilde{\boldsymbol{d}}^{(l)} = \mathbf{C}^{(l)} \boldsymbol{e}^{(l)} \quad (8)$$

where $\boldsymbol{e}^{(l)}$ is syntactic distance in lth encoder layer. $C^{(l)} \in \mathbf{R}^{J \times I}$ is the lth encoder-decoder attention weight, which represents the relationships of encoder and decoder representations, works just like MHA. Here, I and J are length of source and target sentence. The lth encoder-decoder attention weight is computed as:

$$\mathbf{C}^{(l)} = \mathrm{softmax}\left(\frac{\hat{\mathbf{Q}}_{dec}^{(l)} \hat{\mathbf{K}}_{enc}^{(l)\top}}{\sqrt{\delta_h}}\right) \quad (9)$$

where $\mathbf{Q}_{dec}^{(l)}$ and $\mathbf{K}_{enc}^{(l)}$ are lth decoder and encoder hidden weights.

The important element in phrase structure is the hierarchical positional relationship derived from syntactic distance. However, MSE over-penalizes the models, because it results in the exact distance prediction task. Therefore, we use the rank loss (Burges et al., 2005) as proposed by Shen et al. (2018b), which takes hierarchical positioning into account. Applying the rank loss to the synchronous constrict, we obtain the following:

$$\mathcal{L}_{sync} = \sum_{l}^{L} \sum_{i,j>i} \mathrm{hinge}\left(d_i^{(l)} - d_j^{(l)}, \tilde{d}_i^{(l)} - \tilde{d}_j^{(l)} \right) \quad (10)$$

where $\mathrm{hinge}(x_1, x_2) = \max(0, 1 - \mathrm{sign}(x_1) \cdot x_2)$ and $\mathrm{sign}(x)$ is sign function. Therefore, the overall objective $\mathcal{L}$ is represented by:

$$\mathcal{L} = \mathcal{L}_{trans} + \lambda \mathcal{L}_{sync} \quad (11)$$

where $\mathcal{L}_{trans} = -\sum_i^J \log p(y_i | \boldsymbol{x}, \boldsymbol{y}_{<i})$ where $\mathcal{L}_{trans}$ is the objective of machine translation task and $\lambda \geq 0$ is hyper parameter to control the degree of the synchronous constraint $\mathcal{L}_{sync}$. $\boldsymbol{x}$ and $\boldsymbol{y}$ are source and target sentences, respectively.

4 Experiments

We train our proposed models using the training objective in Equation 11 and evaluate them on three tasks: translation, constituency parsing, and word alignment. We implement models within the Fairseq sequence modeling toolkit (Ott et al., 2019).

4.1 Training Details

We employ the `transformer_iwslt_de_en_align` fairseq configuration for German-English dataset and the `transformer_align` fairseq configuration for Japanese-English dataset. We use two MHA layers from the bottom to induct the phrase structures, and two encoder-decoder MHA layers from the top to synchronize the encoder and decoder syntactic distances [1]. The hyper parameters are set as look back range $M = 5$ and temperature $\tau = 1.0$ [1]. The synchronous constrain hyper parameter is set by $\lambda = 0.01$ for MSE and Rank loss.

4.2 Tasks

4.2.1 Translation Task

We evaluated the effectiveness of the synchronous latent phrase structures for MT tasks on IWSLT'14 German-English and ASPEC Japanese-English

[1] We tried various settings in our preliminary experiments, and this setting achieved the best performance.

	Train	Valid	Test
IWSLT'14	160,239	7,283	6,750
ASPEC	1,255,372	1,790	1,812
Europarl v7	1,905,695	997	508

Table 1: Number of sentences in each dataset.

datasets. We train the translation models on the IWSLT'14 German-English and ASPEC Japanese-English (Nakazawa et al., 2016) datasets. We use the `prepare_iwslt14.sh` for IWSLT'14 German-English and follow the instruction of constructing the baseline system of WAT [2], but KyTea (Neubig et al., 2011) is used as the tokenizer for Japanese sentences. These datasets are applied BPE. Table 1 shows the detailed data statistics. To compare the effectiveness of synchronous latent phrase structure, we run additional baselines without latent phrase induction but with synchronous constraints applied to the attention weights. We run inference with a beam size of 5 and report the quality of translation of our models with BLEU (Papineni et al., 2002).

4.2.2 Constituency Parsing Task

In this experiment, we did not apply BPE and English data was parsed using `Stanford CoreNLP version 4.1.0` [3], and thus the number of tokens in each sentence is preserved.

The latent phrase structure is obtained by force decoding; we feed the gold target sentences from the test set into the word-wise trained MT models. We report unlabeled F-measure (UF) as the quality of English latent phrase structures, inducted from the bottom syntactic distances, with scoring script `Evalb` [4]. Here, UF is an F-measure that ignores constituency tags and evaluates only by bracketing.

4.2.3 Alignment Task

We also measure the impact of the alignment qualities represented by our synchronous grammar against other models including a statistical model FAST-ALIGN (Dyer et al., 2013) [5]. We use the same experimental setup as described in (Chen et al., 2020) and use the scripts [6] for pre-processing and evaluation. The scripts provide three different

[2]http://lotus.kuee.kyoto-u.ac.jp/WAT/WAT2019/baseline/dataPreparationJE.html

[3]https://stanfordnlp.github.io/CoreNLP/

[4]https://nlp.cs.nyu.edu/evalb/

[5]https://github.com/clab/fast_align

[6]https://github.com/lilt/alignment-scripts

	BLEU[%]	
	De→En	**Ja→En**
Transformer	34.42	29.48
w/. Synchronous Attn	34.54	29.56
Transformer + LPSI	34.83	29.44
w/. SynchMSE	34.79†	**29.79**†
w/. SynchRank	**35.05**†	29.62†

Table 2: Results on translation task in IWSLT'14 German to English (De→En) and ASPEC Japanese to English (Ja→En). Translation quality is reported in BLEU and its values in bold indicate the best performance. The numbers with † are significantly different from the Transformer baseline measured by approximate randomization test ($\alpha = 1\%$).

datasets, but we only use German-English Europarl v7 training data and the gold alignments [7] provided by (Vilar et al., 2006). Table 1 shows the detailed data statistics. We report the alignment quality in the penultimate layer following (Garg et al., 2019) with Alignment Error Rate (AER) introduced in (Vilar et al., 2006). In this task, the trained model is BPE-wise, but the reported AER is word-wise. Furthermore, we report the quality of symmetrized alignments that combined both unidirectional alignments. The combination method is employed the `grow-diagonal` heuristic (Koehn et al., 2005), in which alignments are greedily enlarged from the intersected alignments.

4.3 Results

4.3.1 Translation Task

Table 2 compares the performance of our methods against baselines. The NMT models with synchronous latent phrase structures have better translation performance. In IWSLT'14 German-English dataset, the NMT model with synchronous latent phrase structure by rank loss improves 0.63 BLEU point. In ASPEC Japanese-English dataset, the NMT model with synchronous latent phrase structure by MSE loss improves 0.31 BLEU point. These results show that the use of explicit latent phrase structures can be useful in MT tasks involving syntactically distant languages like Japanese-English.

However, the Rank synchronous constraint model performed worse than the MSE synchronous constraint model in the ASPEC Japanese-English dataset. This probably is because that the phrase

[7]https://www-i6.informatik.rwth-aachen.de/goldAlignment/

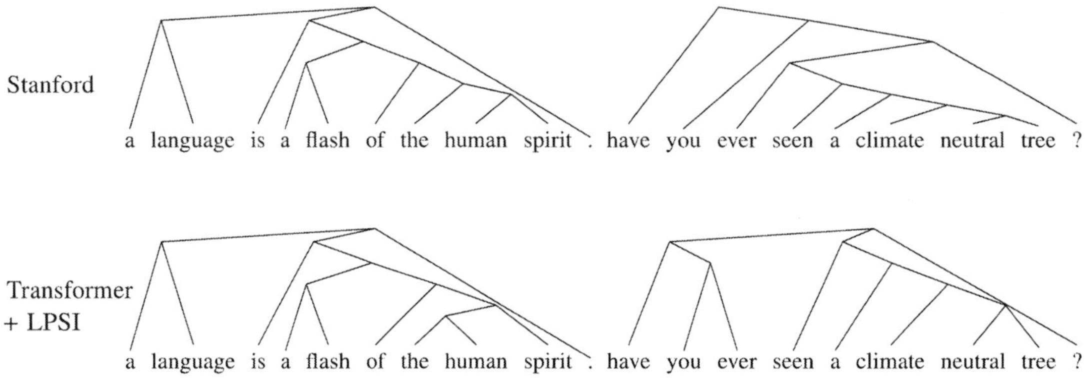

Figure 2: The top parse trees are obtained from the Stanford parser. The bottom parse trees are inducted from our transformer with LPSI (first layer) trained on IWSLT'14 German to English.

	UF[%]	BLEU[%]
	De→En	
(Hent et. al., 2019)	**56.1**	30.2
Transformer + LPSI	37.40	30.69
w/. SynchMSE	14.33	30.41
w/. SynchRank	33.75	**30.80**

Table 3: Results on constituency parsing task in IWSLT'14 German to English (De→En). Latent phrase structure quality is reported in UF and its values in bold indicate the best performance.

structure is not well inducted from the Japanese-English dataset and the advantage of Rank synchronous constraint is not utilized. The difficulty of induction phrase structure in the Japanese-English dataset can also be read from the results of Transformer with LPSI.

The synchronous syntactic attention model (Deguchi et al., 2021) also have good translation performance, but we can improve it further by incorporating the syntactic distance into the attention.

Although not shown in previous work (Htut et al., 2019), Table 2 shows that the use of explicit latent phrase structure is useful for the MT task. Interestingly, we found that the effective synchronous constrain differed between syntactically close, i.e., German-English, and distant languages, i.e., Japanese-English.

4.3.2 Constituency Parsing Task

Table 3 compares the performance of our methods against baselines. The results show that the synchronous constraint hurt the quality of latent phrase structures. Especially, in MSE synchronous constraint, UF is drooped 17.01 points from the result of Transformer with latent phrase structure induction. This is because the MSE synchronous constraints induct a synchronous grammar that is different from the phrase structure being evaluated. In other words, synchronous constrain hinders the derivation of the latent phrase structures. However, the decrease in UF by synchronous constrain by rank loss is small, whereas synchronous constrain by MSE greatly reduced UF. It suggests that synchronous constrain by MSE derives an exact synchronization grammar and synchronous constrain by rank loss derives a minimal synchronization grammar.

As with prior study (Htut et al., 2019), we did not find any correlation between the phrase structure qualities and translation qualities especially when two structures are synchronized in encoder and decoder. This indicates that our induced grammatical structures using synchronous constraints might capture bilingual correspondence better than non-constrained models.

Figure 2 shows examples of parse tree from Stanford Parser and our Transformer with LSPI. In the first example "a flash of the human spirit", our model almost correctly inducts phrase structure in comparison with Stanford Parser. The only mistake is grouping "the" and "human" first in the noun phrase "the human spirit". This mistake can be unique to concepts of syntactic distance, as it is the same as in the prior study (Htut et al., 2019). In the second example "have you ever seen a climate neutral tree ?", our model correctly inducts the verb phrase "ever seen a climate neutral tree", but fails to induct the phrase "have you ever" correctly.

	AER[%] (precision[%], recall[%])			BLEU[%]	
	De→En	**En→De**	**Symmetrized**	**De→En**	**En→De**
FAST-ALIGN	30.8 (68.2, 70.3)	32.4 (66.8, 68.4)	27.7 (81.4, 65.0)	-	-
Transformer	46.2 (51.0, 57.1)	47.5 (49.5, 56.1)	35.8 (84.9, 51.3)	33.62	26.59
Transformer + LPSI	43.4 (53.5, 60.1)	**45.9 (51.1, 57.6)**	34.3 (84.6, 53.4)	33.25	26.98
w/. SynchMSE	**42.4 (54.5, 61.2)**	46.3 (50.8, 57.2)	**34.1** (84.5, **53.8**)	33.96	26.61
w/. SynchRank	44.4 (52.7, 58.9)	50.1 (47.3, 52.9)	36.1 (**86.5**, 50.5)	**34.13**	**27.03**

Table 4: Results on the alignment and translation task in Europarl v7 German to English (De→En) and English to German (En→De). 'Symmetrized' indicates the alignments combined both unidirectional alignments De→En and En→De. Alignment quality is reported in AER, translation quality in BLEU and its values in bold indicate best performance.

	AER[%] (Precision[%], Recall[%])		
Layer	**Transformer**	**w/. SynchMSE**	**w/. SynchRank**
1	92.2 (62.7, 4.1)	95.0 (25.6, 2.7)	93.2 (26.0, 3.9)
2	92.1 (28.3, 4.5)	91.1 (34.9, 5.0)	90.8 (28.9, 5.4)
3	84.0 (42.7, 9.8)	88.6 (34.1, 6.8)	81.5 (37.2, 12.2)
4	49.3 (79.7, 37.0)	53.2 (75.2, 33.8)	40.7 (81.4, 46.4)
5	35.8 (84.9, 51.3)	**34.1** (84.5, **53.8**)	36.1 (**86.5**, 50.5)
6	47.2 (86.9, 37.7)	52.1 (87.7, 32.8)	56.9 (87.5, 28.4)

Table 5: Results of AER on each layer. The value in bold indicates the best performance.

	De→En	**Ja→En**
Transformer	34.42	29.48
w/o. Positional Embedding	17.01	15.40
Transformer + LPSI	34.83	29.44
w/o. Positional Embedding	33.94	28.89
Transformer + Local Attn	34.77	30.19
w/o. Positional Embedding	33.84	29.58

Table 6: Results on IWSLT'14 German to English (De→En) and ASPEC Japanese to English (Ja→En) for effectiveness of learning word order. 'w/o. Positional Embedding' indicates removing positional embedding from the models. The local attention mask is applied only to the encoder following a prior study (Cui et al., 2019).

4.3.3 Alignment Task

Table 4 compares the performance of our methods against statistic and neural baseline approaches. Compared with Transformer, the model with latent phrase structure show better translation performance and quality of alignments. Furthermore, synchronizing source and target latent phrase structure decreases the AER, which indicates that synchronous constrain improves the interpretability of translation. However, synchronous constrain by Rank loss resulted in a deterioration in AER, despite improving the translation performance BLEU. Therefore, the relationship between BLEU and AER does not seem to be significantly correlated.

Table 5 shows that the effectiveness of synchronous latent phrase structure for two layers from the top in terms of AER. In the penultimate layer, while synchronous constrain by MSE contributed to the improvement of AER, but synchronous constrain by rank loss conversely worsened AER. However, rank loss resulted in a significant improvement AER in the third and fourth layers. In the final layer, both synchronous constraints by MSE and rank loss result in the worse AER. It suggests that the quality of the latent phrase structure derived from the second layer from the bottom is poor and this may have affected the results adversely.

5 Analysis

5.1 Effectiveness of Attention Gate

We realize that our gated multi-head attention (GMHA), without synchronous constraint, is very similar to local attention within mixed multi-head attention (MMHA) (Cui et al., 2019). MMHA encourages each head to acquire different features by masking them differently and allows the model to be aware of the order of the sequence. Table 6 show that Transformer without position embedding decrease of 17.41 BLEU point in IWSLT'14

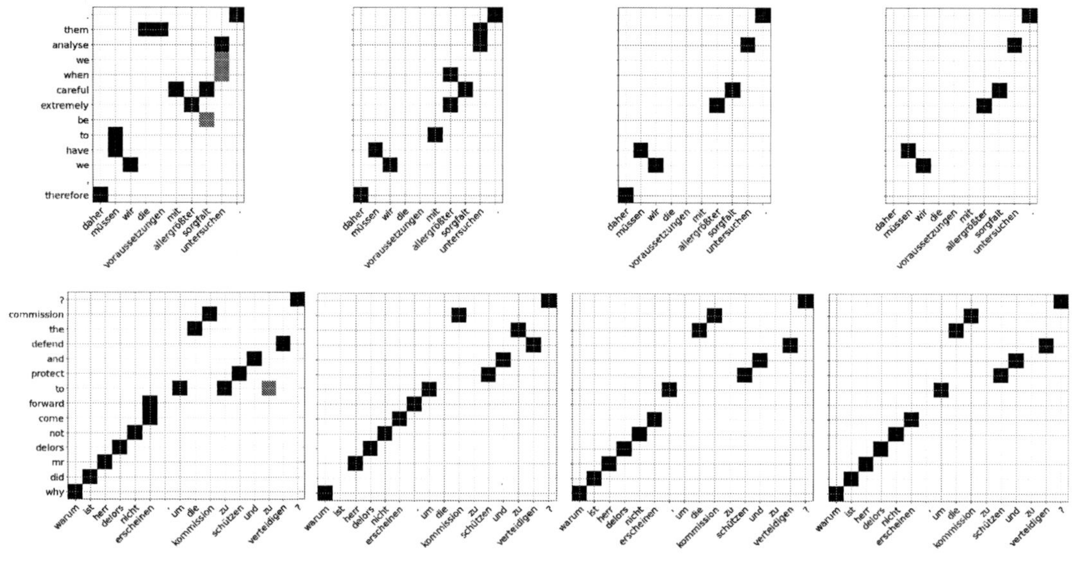

(a) Reference (b) FastAlign (c) SyncMSE (d) SyncRank

Figure 3: The symmetrized examples from the German-English alignment test set. Gold Alignment is shown in (a). Alignment in (b) show the output from FastAlign (BPE-wise trained), (c) from synchronized MSE model, and (d) from synchronized Rank model. Black squares and gray squares in the reference represent sure and possible alignments, respectively.

German-English and 14.08 BLEU point in ASPEC Japanese-English. In the Transformer with latent phrase structure induction (LPSI), the performance is only reduced by 0.89 BLEU point in IWSLT'14 German-English and 0.55 BLEU point in ASPEC Japanese-English without position embedding. For a fair comparison, we employ local attention with 2 window in the two bottom layers of encoder. Similarly, in the Transformer with local attention, the performance is only reduced by 0.93 BLEU point in IWSLT'14 German-English and 0.61 BLEU point in ASPEC Japanese-English without position embedding. It indicates that local constraints on attention mechanisms help learning the order of the sequence rather than latent phrase structure induction.

5.2 Effectiveness of Synchronous Latent Phase Structure

Figure 3 shows examples from the German-English alignment test set. In the first example, we find that there are no false alignments in our models with synchronous constraints. However, in rank loss, the alignment between 'Therefore' and 'Daher', which was captured by MSE, is lost. In the second example, duplicated our model correctly aligns them with 'um' compared with FastAlign. Therefore, The synchronous constraints by MSE and rank loss indicate that only alignments with high confidence are provided. Furthermore, as can be seen from the precision values in this Table 4, there are no false alignments in synchronous constrain by rank loss, and definite explainability of translation is achieved. In other words, the synchronization constraint favors precision over recall, which may make the AER worse, but it can provide a reliable explanation for human. The prior study (Jain and Wallace, 2019; Serrano and Smith, 2019) conclude that the attentions have not explainability. However, our attention is constrained by the syntactic distance, it can explain the relation between source and target sentence following the constituency tree. We will work it as the future works.

6 Conclusion

This paper introduces the approach to improve the performance and explainability of MT. In the MT task, our model improves the quality of translation even through distant language pairs. In the alignment task, we demonstrate that synchronous constraint for syntactic distance can produce high precisional alignments to interpret MT hypothesis. Currently, our approach induces the poor latent phrase structure constructed with the previous work. To achieve the more high performance and explainability of MT, we would like to investigate other syntactic structures and a translation model which can induce better latent phrase structure.

References

Chris Burges, Tal Shaked, Erin Renshaw, Ari Lazier, Matt Deeds, Nicole Hamilton, and Greg Hullender. 2005. Learning to rank using gradient descent. In *Proceedings of the 22nd international conference on Machine learning*, pages 89–96.

Yun Chen, Yang Liu, Guanhua Chen, Xin Jiang, and Qun Liu. 2020. Accurate word alignment induction from neural machine translation. In *Proceedings of the 2020 Conference on Empirical Methods in Natural Language Processing (EMNLP)*, pages 566–576, Online. Association for Computational Linguistics.

Hongyi Cui, Shohei Iida, Po-Hsuan Hung, Takehito Utsuro, and Masaaki Nagata. 2019. Mixed multi-head self-attention for neural machine translation. In *Proceedings of the 3rd Workshop on Neural Generation and Translation*, pages 206–214, Hong Kong. Association for Computational Linguistics.

Hiroyuki Deguchi, Akihiro Tamura, and Takashi Ninomiya. 2019. Dependency-based self-attention for transformer NMT. In *Proceedings of the International Conference on Recent Advances in Natural Language Processing (RANLP 2019)*, pages 239–246, Varna, Bulgaria. INCOMA Ltd.

Hiroyuki Deguchi, Akihiro Tamura, and Takashi Ninomiya. 2021. Synchronous syntactic attention for transformer nmt. In *The Joint Conference of the 59th Annual Meeting of the Association for Computational Linguistics and the 11th International Joint Conference on Natural Language Processing (ACL-IJCNLP 2021)*.

Chris Dyer, Victor Chahuneau, and Noah A Smith. 2013. A simple, fast, and effective reparameterization of ibm model 2. In *Proceedings of the 2013 Conference of the North American Chapter of the Association for Computational Linguistics: Human Language Technologies*, pages 644–648.

Akiko Eriguchi, Yoshimasa Tsuruoka, and Kyunghyun Cho. 2017. Learning to parse and translate improves neural machine translation. In *Proceedings of the 55th Annual Meeting of the Association for Computational Linguistics (Volume 2: Short Papers)*, pages 72–78, Vancouver, Canada. Association for Computational Linguistics.

Sarthak Garg, Stephan Peitz, Udhyakumar Nallasamy, and Matthias Paulik. 2019. Jointly learning to align and translate with transformer models. In *Proceedings of the 2019 Conference on Empirical Methods in Natural Language Processing and the 9th International Joint Conference on Natural Language Processing (EMNLP-IJCNLP)*, pages 4453–4462, Hong Kong, China. Association for Computational Linguistics.

Phu Mon Htut, Kyunghyun Cho, and Samuel R Bowman. 2019. Inducing constituency trees through neural machine translation. *arXiv preprint arXiv:1909.10056*.

Sarthak Jain and Byron C. Wallace. 2019. Attention is not Explanation. In *Proceedings of the 2019 Conference of the North American Chapter of the Association for Computational Linguistics: Human Language Technologies, Volume 1 (Long and Short Papers)*, pages 3543–3556, Minneapolis, Minnesota. Association for Computational Linguistics.

Melvin Johnson, Mike Schuster, Quoc V. Le, Maxim Krikun, Yonghui Wu, Zhifeng Chen, Nikhil Thorat, Fernanda Viégas, Martin Wattenberg, Greg Corrado, Macduff Hughes, and Jeffrey Dean. 2017. Google's multilingual neural machine translation system: Enabling zero-shot translation. *Transactions of the Association for Computational Linguistics*, 5:339–351.

Yoon Kim, Alexander Rush, Lei Yu, Adhiguna Kuncoro, Chris Dyer, and G'abor Melis. 2019. Unsupervised recurrent neural network grammars. In *Proceedings of the 2019 Conference of the North American Chapter of the Association for Computational Linguistics: Human Language Technologies, Volume 1 (Long and Short Papers)*, pages 1105–1117, Minneapolis, Minnesota. Association for Computational Linguistics.

Philipp Koehn, Amittai Axelrod, Alexandra Birch Mayne, Chris Callison-Burch, Miles Osborne, and David Talbot. 2005. Edinburgh system description for the 2005 iwslt speech translation evaluation. In *International Workshop on Spoken Language Translation (IWSLT) 2005*.

Chunpeng Ma, Akihiro Tamura, Masao Utiyama, Eiichiro Sumita, and Tiejun Zhao. 2019. Improving neural machine translation with neural syntactic distance. In *Proceedings of the 2019 Conference of the North American Chapter of the Association for Computational Linguistics: Human Language Technologies, Volume 1 (Long and Short Papers)*, pages 2032–2037, Minneapolis, Minnesota. Association for Computational Linguistics.

Toshiaki Nakazawa, Manabu Yaguchi, Kiyotaka Uchimoto, Masao Utiyama, Eiichiro Sumita, Sadao Kurohashi, and Hitoshi Isahara. 2016. Aspec: Asian scientific paper excerpt corpus. In *Proceedings of the Ninth International Conference on Language Resources and Evaluation (LREC 2016)*, pages 2204–2208, Portorož, Slovenia. European Language Resources Association (ELRA).

Graham Neubig, Yosuke Nakata, and Shinsuke Mori. 2011. Pointwise prediction for robust, adaptable Japanese morphological analysis. In *Proceedings of the 49th Annual Meeting of the Association for Computational Linguistics: Human Language Technologies*, pages 529–533, Portland, Oregon, USA. Association for Computational Linguistics.

Xuan-Phi Nguyen, Shafiq Joty, Steven CH Hoi, and Richard Socher. 2020. Tree-structured attention with hierarchical accumulation. *arXiv preprint arXiv:2002.08046*.

Myle Ott, Sergey Edunov, Alexei Baevski, Angela Fan, Sam Gross, Nathan Ng, David Grangier, and Michael Auli. 2019. fairseq: A fast, extensible toolkit for sequence modeling. In *Proceedings of NAACL-HLT 2019: Demonstrations*.

Kishore Papineni, Salim Roukos, Todd Ward, and Wei-Jing Zhu. 2002. Bleu: a method for automatic evaluation of machine translation. In *Proceedings of the 40th Annual Meeting of the Association for Computational Linguistics*, pages 311–318, Philadelphia, Pennsylvania, USA. Association for Computational Linguistics.

Rico Sennrich, Barry Haddow, and Alexandra Birch. 2016. Neural machine translation of rare words with subword units. In *Proceedings of the 54th Annual Meeting of the Association for Computational Linguistics (Volume 1: Long Papers)*, pages 1715–1725, Berlin, Germany. Association for Computational Linguistics.

Sofia Serrano and Noah A. Smith. 2019. Is attention interpretable? In *Proceedings of the 57th Annual Meeting of the Association for Computational Linguistics*, pages 2931–2951, Florence, Italy. Association for Computational Linguistics.

Yikang Shen, Zhouhan Lin, Chin wei Huang, and Aaron Courville. 2018a. Neural language modeling by jointly learning syntax and lexicon. In *International Conference on Learning Representations*.

Yikang Shen, Zhouhan Lin, Athul Paul Jacob, Alessandro Sordoni, Aaron Courville, and Yoshua Bengio. 2018b. Straight to the tree: Constituency parsing with neural syntactic distance. In *Proceedings of the 56th Annual Meeting of the Association for Computational Linguistics (Volume 1: Long Papers)*, pages 1171–1180, Melbourne, Australia. Association for Computational Linguistics.

Yikang Shen, Shawn Tan, Alessandro Sordoni, and Aaron Courville. 2018c. Ordered neurons: Integrating tree structures into recurrent neural networks. *arXiv preprint arXiv:1810.09536*.

Yikang Shen, Yi Tay, Che Zheng, Dara Bahri, Donald Metzler, and Aaron Courville. 2020. Structformer: Joint unsupervised induction of dependency and constituency structure from masked language modeling.

Ashish Vaswani, Noam Shazeer, Niki Parmar, Jakob Uszkoreit, Llion Jones, Aidan N Gomez, Lukasz Kaiser, and Illia Polosukhin. 2017. Attention is all you need. *arXiv preprint arXiv:1706.03762*.

David Vilar, Maja Popović, and Hermann Ney. 2006. Aer: Do we need to "improve" our alignments? In *International Workshop on Spoken Language Translation (IWSLT) 2006*.

Yaushian Wang, Hung-Yi Lee, and Yun-Nung Chen. 2019. Tree transformer: Integrating tree structures into self-attention. In *Proceedings of the 2019 Conference on Empirical Methods in Natural Language Processing and the 9th International Joint Conference on Natural Language Processing (EMNLP-IJCNLP)*, pages 1061–1070, Hong Kong, China. Association for Computational Linguistics.

Fai Wong, Dong-Cheng Hu, Yu-Hang Mao, Ming-Chui Dong, and Yi-Ping Li. 2005. Machine translation based on constraint-based synchronous grammar. In *International Conference on Natural Language Processing*, pages 612–623. Springer.

Zero Pronouns Identification based on Span Prediction

Sei Iwata[1], **Taro Watanabe**[1], and **Masaaki Nagata**[2]
[1]Nara Institute of Science and Technology
[2]NTT Communication Science Laboratories, NTT Corporation
{iwata.sei.is6,taro}@is.naist.jp
masaaki.nagata.et@hco.ntt.co.jp

Abstract

The presence of zero-pronoun (ZP) greatly affects the downstream tasks of NLP in pro-drop languages such as Japanese and Chinese. To tackle the problem, the previous works identified ZPs as sequence labeling on the word sequence or the linearlized tree nodes of the input. We propose a novel approach to ZP identification by casting it as a query-based argument span prediction task. Given a predicate as a query, our model predicts the omission with ZP. In the experiments, our model surpassed the sequence labeling baseline.

1 Introduction

Pro-drop languages, such as Japanese, Chinese, or Arabic, allow omissions of essential phrases or arguments, e.g., nouns, which could be easily inferred by humans given contexts in a sentence. The omitted argument is called zero-pronoun (ZP), or (small) "pro", which is an instance of empty categories in linguistics.

JA このケーキは美味しい。私は (pro-OBJ) 気に入った.

EN This cake is delicious. I like (it).

In the Japanese example above, the object argument (OBJ) is omitted from the second sentence because Japanese speakers can predict from the context that the OBJ is "it", and the omission is natural for the Japanese speakers.

Downstream tasks involving pro-drop languages could easily suffer from the existence of ZPs. In the machine translation task, it has been reported that supplementing the ZP information when translating from pro-drop languages to non-pro-drop languages improves the performance (Wang et al., 2019).

When identifying a ZP from the sentence where the argument is omitted, the predicate information is the key. The ZP identification is solved in many previous works as a labeling task for input sentence tokens (Aloraini and Poesio, 2020; Song et al., 2020) or nodes in a parse tree (Xiang et al., 2013; Takeno et al., 2015).

In this study, we treat ZP identification as an instance of span prediction tasks inspired by the QA method proposed in Devlin et al. (2019). There are two steps to solve the ZP identification in our approach. 1) Given a predicate as a query, our model extracts each argument, such as subject or object, as the answer from the input sentence. 2) If our model cannot extract any corresponding argument from the input sentence, the model predicts whether or not it is a ZP. In the above example, given a predicate 気に入った "like", our model should predict that the subject argument is 私は "I" in the sentence and the object argument is a ZP. By explicitly providing predicates as queries in this way, our approach allows the model to capture information about the ZP cue from the input sentence, thereby improving the ZP identification performance.

Our contributions are as follows: 1)We proposed a novel approach for ZP identification. 2)The improvement from the sequence labeling baseline was confirmed on two different language datasets.

2 Related work

Most of the researchers considered the ZP detection or ZP identification as a labeling task. Xiang et al. (2013) and Takeno et al. (2015) used parse trees as input and detected empty categories, including ZPs, by labeling a node representing the maximal projection of a predicate, namely IP or VP. Song et al. (2020) proposed jointly learning

Proceedings of the Joint Conference of the 59th Annual Meeting of the Association for Computational Linguistics and the 11th International Joint Conference on Natural Language Processing: Student Research Workshop, pages 331–336
August 5–6, 2021. ©2021 Association for Computational Linguistics

ZP resolution and ZP identification by treating it as sequence labeling on every word boundary. Aloraini and Poesio (2020) considered word positions before or after each VP node as ZP location candidates and predicted whether the candidate has ZP or not as a binary classification task. To the best of our knowledge, our approach is the first work that formalizes ZP identification as a QA task.

In recent years, approaches for solving various tasks as QA-based span prediction problems have been proposed. Li et al. (2020) made questions corresponding to NER entity tags. Then, their model predicted the entity span giving the question and a sentence as QA tasks to tackle the nested NER problem. In the coreference resolution task, Wu et al. (2020) generated queries based on each mention and extracted the text spans of coreferences as answers to given queries. Nagata et al. (2020) improved the performance of word alignment task by giving a word in the source language sentence as a question and predicting its corresponding word span in the target language sentence.

3 Span-based ZP identification

Treebanks have phrase structure tree information, and in some treebanks, empty categories are also annotated as null terminal nodes (Butler et al., 2012; Xue et al., 2005). However, we focused only on ZP identification, not dealing with other empty categories, such as trace and PRO, in this paper.

We formally define the ZP identification as span-based prediction as follows: Given a tokenized sentence $\boldsymbol{x} = x_1, ..., x_{|\boldsymbol{x}|}$, we denote a span of the sentence as $x_{qs:qe}$ $(1 \leq qs \leq qe \leq |\boldsymbol{x}|)$ that corresponds to the head of predicate of the sentence, i.e., verb or adjective. The task is to identify the span of the sentence $\boldsymbol{x}$ corresponding to the argument required by the predicate $x_{qs:qe}$. When no span is detected, there are three possible cases: (i) the argument is dropped as a kind of ZP; (ii) the argument is not dropped as a ZP, but as another empty category such as trace or PRO; (iii) it is not required by the predicate at all. We grouped the latter two cases into one class, the non-ZP class. Therefore, our model predicts one of the ZP classes or the non-ZP class for the required but omitted argument. The prediction is applied for each grammatical function of the argument, such as SBJ, OBJ, etc.

Our argument span prediction is inspired by BERT fine-tuning for the QA task (Devlin et al., 2019). Inputs follow a BERT style formulated as "[CLS] query [SEP] sentence [SEP]", where [CLS] is a special token to output the classification result and [SEP] denotes the boundary of "query" and "sentence." The query in the input is defined as follows:

$$\{\ x_{qs-C:qs-1},\ \text{[Predicate1]},\ x_{qs:qe},\ \text{[Predicate2]},\ x_{qe+1:qe+C}\ \}$$

where C is the size of the context windows before and after the span $x_{qs:qe}$ in the sentence. [Predicate1] and [Predicate2] [1] are used as boundary markers to specify the start and end of the predicate in the query.

(1) (ϕ) 大学 へ 着き まし た
(pro)-SBJ university at VB AX AXD
' (pro) arrived at the university. '

In the example sentence (1) , there are five words in the tokenized input sentence excluding a null token ϕ [2]. Given "着き" as a predicate with $C = 1$, the query is represented as follows:

{"へ", [Predicate1], "着き", [Predicate2], "まし" }

Given the inputs, our model is expected to predict that SBJ is a required argument belonging to "pro" class and OBJ is a non-ZP argument because the predicate is an intransitive verb.

3.1 Argument Span Prediction

Two independent linear layers are added to BERT for predicting the start and end positions of an argument type for an input predicate. We dealt with three arguments, which are subject, object, and indirect object, for a predicate and added six layers in total.

Using hidden size H, $\boldsymbol{h}_a \in \mathbb{R}^H$ is the embedding of the final BERT encoder layer, corresponding to a token a in the input, and $f^{arg}_{start}(\cdot)$ and $f^{arg}_{end}(\cdot)$ are linear layers to calculate start and end probabilities. Given x_i, the ith word in a sentenece $\boldsymbol{x}$, let $p^{arg}_{start}(x_i) = f^{arg}_{start}(\boldsymbol{h}_{x_i})$ and $p^{arg}_{end}(x_i) = f^{arg}_{end}(\boldsymbol{h}_{x_i})$ denote the probabilities that the ith word is the start and end of the span of arg, argument e.g., SBJ, OBJ, etc.

[1] These words are implemented using unused words in the BERT vocabulary, "[UnusedX]".

[2] ϕ is a null token indicating "pro", which does not appear in the actual input sentence.

The score that the span $x_{i:j}$ is the span of arg is defined as the product of the ith word start probability and the jth word end probability of arg. We define $\hat{\imath}$ and $\hat{\jmath}$ as the start and the end positions that maximize $score_{arg}(i,j)$.

$$score_{arg}(i,j) = p^{arg}_{start}(x_i) \cdot p^{arg}_{end}(x_j) \quad (1)$$

$$(\hat{\imath},\hat{\jmath}) = \underset{1 \le i \le j \le |\boldsymbol{x}|}{\arg\max}\ score_{arg}(i,j) \quad (2)$$

When there is no arg span in the predicate, we assume its start and end positions equal to that of [CLS] and define the score as follows:

$$score_{null} = p^{arg}_{start}(\text{[CLS]}) \cdot p^{arg}_{end}(\text{[CLS]}) \quad (3)$$

There are two cases for $score_{null}$ and $score_{arg}(\hat{\imath},\hat{\jmath})$:

$$score_{null} \le score_{arg}(\hat{\imath},\hat{\jmath}) \quad (4)$$

$$score_{null} > score_{arg}(\hat{\imath},\hat{\jmath}) \quad (5)$$

When Equation 4 holds, our model predicts that the span between the $\hat{\imath}$th and $\hat{\jmath}$th in $\boldsymbol{x}$ is the argument arg for the given predicate. Otherwise, the argument for the given predicate does not exist in $\boldsymbol{x}$ denoted by Equation 5, which implies ZP exists in the argument or the argument is a non-ZP state.

The loss of a single example is calculated by the cross-entropy loss of correct positions i' and j':

$$loss_{span} = \sum_{arg} -\log p^{arg}_{start}(x_{i'}) - \log p^{arg}_{end}(x_{j'}) \quad (6)$$

3.2 ZP classification

The difference between ZP detection and ZP identification is whether there are one or more classes of ZPs for arguments. In the ZP detection task, ZP classification is binary classification whether the argument is either ZP class or non-ZP class. When there are multiple ZP classes to solve the ZP identification task, the ZP classification is a multi-class classification.

To classify, we add an independent layer for each predicted argument type into BERT. The arg class probabilities are as follows:

$$p^{arg}_{class} = softmax(\boldsymbol{h}_{\text{[CLS]}}\mathbf{W}_{arg} + \boldsymbol{b}_{arg}) \quad (7)$$

where $\mathbf{W}_{arg} \in \mathbb{R}^{H \times num_{class}}$, and $\boldsymbol{b}_{arg} \in \mathbb{R}^{num_{class}}$ are parameters. num_{class} is the number of classes including the non-ZP class.

The loss $loss_{label}$ is calculated by cross-entropy function and the correct label probability.

$$loss_{label} = -\log p^{arg}_{class}(index_{correct}) \quad (8)$$

Datasets	Category	Train	Dev	Test
NPCMJ	docs(all)		261	
	sents	29,796	3,724	3,726
	preds	76,892	9,595	9,450
OntoNotes 5.0	docs	1,391	172	166
	sents	32,358	5,435	9,450
	preds	135,241	19,538	16,556

Table 1: Statistics on NPCMJ and OntoNotes5.0. In the "Category" column, "docs", "sents", and "preds" represent documents, senteneces, and predicates, respectively. In NPCMJ, "all" means the total number of documents in train, dev, and test.

Datasets	argument	SBJ	OB1	OB2
NPCMJ	ZP ratio(%)	20.58	3.67	0.24
	ZP number	15,824	2,823	184
OntoNotes 5.0	ZP ratio(%)	21.59	0.05	0.00
	ZP number	29,195	61	1

Table 2: The ratio and the number of ZPs to queries in train datasets of NPCMJ and Chinese subsets OntoNotes.

3.3 Training

The training objective is defined using $loss_{span}$ and $loss_{label}$ in 3.1 and 3.2 as follows:

$$loss_{total} = \alpha loss_{span} + (2-\alpha) loss_{label} \quad (9)$$

α is a hyperparameter that weights the loss function of each task by taking a value between $0 < \alpha < 2$ [3].

4 Experiments

4.1 Datasets

We take two Datasets: NPCMJ[4] for Japanese ZP identification and OntoNotes5.0[5] for Chinese ZP detection. The dataset statistics are shown in Tables 1 and 2.

NPCMJ is an extension of the Keyaki Treebank (Butler et al., 2012), which contains empty category information including ZP, and has 40,831 sentences with trees in the March 2020 version. ZPs are annotated at the first position of a predicate head phrase (inflectional phrase, IP). In the Japanese experiments, let $x_{qs:qe}$ in a query be a word tagged either with the verb or the adjective that constitutes a predicate.

The verb tags are "VB", "VB0", "VB2", and "AX", and the adjective tags are "ADJN" and

[3] We first run our preliminary experiments by setting $\alpha = 1$, and then, run further experiments using linear interpolation

[4] http://npcmj.ninjal.ac.jp

[5] https://catalog.ldc.upenn.edu/LDC2013T19

"ADJI". The phrase tagged with "-SBJ", "-OB1", or "-OB2", which is at the same depth of the query, is selected as the argument. In training, we used "pro" and its derived tags, i.e., "speaker" and "hearer", as ZP classes for ZP classification.

OntoNotes5.0 is used in the official CoNLL-2012 shared task. The rate of phrase tags of "pro" nodes in train datasets is composed of "-SBJ" with more than 99%, "-OBJ" with less than 0.5%, and others. The phrases tagged with "-SBJ", "-OBJ", or "-IO" are treated as arguments. The head word of the phrase with VP is considered as a predicate, and let the head word be $x_{qs:qe}$ in a query.

In Japanese and Chinese, there are nominal predicate phrases which do not have verbs and copulas. Such phrases were tagged with "-PRD" tags in both datasets, but we did not deal tagged with "-PRD" in this paper.

4.2 Model and Setting

We used NICT BERT Japanese pre-trained model without BPE[6] for NPCMJ, and "bert-base-chinese"[7] models in HuggingFace's Transformers (Wolf et al., 2019) for OntoNotes5. Japanese texts are tokenized by MeCab with Juman dic[8], and Chinese texts are tokenized by BERT Tokenizer, i.e., WordPiece.

The following are the hyperparameters: batch_size = 16, learning_rate = 3e-5, training_epoch = 4, C = 2, $\alpha = 1$ in training objective.

4.3 Baseline

The sequence labeling model with BERT is used as a baseline model, referring to the method of Devlin et al. (2019). The entire sentence is used as input, and the predicate tokens with ZP argument in the sentence are labeled with a particular ZP class using the BIOES format.

For each argument, we use a different model for each argument type prediction.

4.4 Results

We evaluate the results in terms of precision, recall, and F-score. For example, in case the SBJ argument has "pro", one of the ZP classes, it is defined as follows,

$$Precision^{pro}_{SBJ} = \frac{\text{correct number of predicted ``pro'' SBJ}}{\text{number of predicted ``pro'' SBJ}}$$

$$Recall^{pro}_{SBJ} = \frac{\text{correct number of predicted ``pro'' SBJ}}{\text{number of gold ``pro'' SBJ}}$$

[6]https://alaginrc.nict.go.jp/nict-bert/index.html

[7]https://huggingface.co/bert-base-chinese/tree/main

[8]https://taku910.github.io/mecab/

Model	argument	Arg span accuracy	ZP F1	ZP pre	ZP recall
Baseline	SBJ	-	61.5	62.3	60.8
	OB1	-	58.0	62.3	54.2
	ALL	-	**60.9**	62.2	59.6
QAZP	SBJ	90.8	66.0	66.2	65.8
	OB1	88.5	59.7	60.6	59.0
	ALL	89.3	**64.9**	65.4	64.5

Table 3: Argument span accuracy and ZP identification on NPCMJ for each argument. The row of ALL indiciataes the value for SBJ, OB1 and OB2.

label	Model	F1	pre	recall
pro	baseline	60.8	61.3	60.2
	QAZP	65.1	64.2	66.0
speaker	baseline	62.2	66.2	58.8
	QAZP	65.4	68.7	62.5
hearer	baseline	65.1	60.9	70.0
	QAZP	68.7	65.3	72.7

Table 4: ZP identification on NPCMJ for each ZP class. This values are the result for three arguments.

The same calculation applies to the other arguments and the other labels. The accuracy for required arguments that appear in the sentence is evaluated with the accuracy of whether the prediction span matches exactly with the gold span.

Table 3 and Table 4 show the results of ZP identification on NPCMJ for each argument and each ZP class. In Table 3 and Table 4, QAZP indicates our proposal method, and the baseline is left blank because the argument span is not predicted by the baseline. Compared to the baseline, the proposed method outperformed for each argument and each ZP class. The lower F1 value of ZP identification for OB1 in Table 3 can be attributed to the fact that ZPs occur only about 18% as often in OB1 as in SBJ.

Table 5 shows the result of the Chinese ZP detection. Compared to the baseline, the proposed method outperformed for both argument cases. Although it is not directly comparable with (Aloraini and Poesio, 2020) in that their task definition is slightly different and their targets are only anaphoric ZPs, our model achieves about 80% F1 values, which is higher than their F1 of 68.5%.

4.5 Examples

Figure 1 shows the three prediction examples of the baseline and our proposal model, QAZP. Example 1 is the case when the the QAZP's prediction is correct and the baseline's prediction is incorrect. In this example, the model needs to recognize that the SBJ arguments of the two predi-

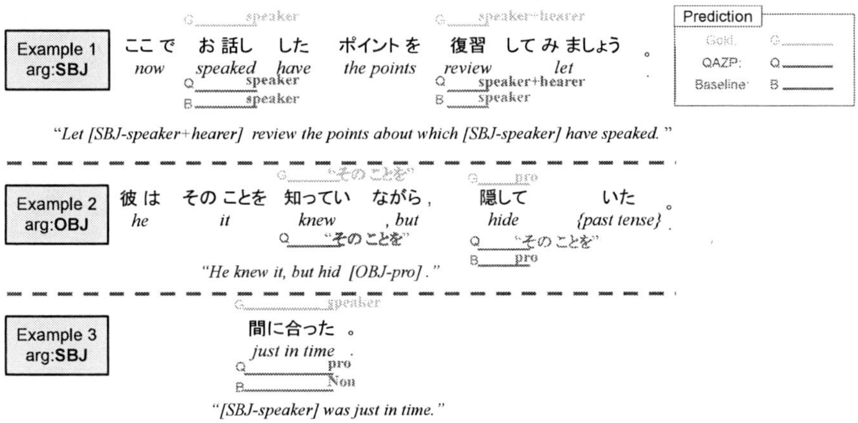

Figure 1: Prediction examples of the baseline and QAZP, our proposal model for three sentences in a Japanese ZP identification task. Each line represents either the prediction of one of the both models, or the Gold data for the argument of a predicate covered by the lines. The first and third examples are predictions for SBJ arguments, and the second example is a prediction result for the OBJ arguments by the baseline and QAZP.

Model	Arg	Arg span accuracy	ZP F1	ZP pre	ZP recall
Baseline	SBJ	-	71.5	72.5	70.5
	ALL	-	**71.4**	72.6	70.3
QAZP	SBJ	88.7	80.6	81.2	80.6
	ALL	88.3	**80.5**	81.0	80.4

Table 5: Argument(Arg) span accuracy and ZP detection on OntoNotes5.0. for "pro" class. The row of ALL indiciataes the value for SBJ, OBJ and IO2 arguments.

cates お 話し "speak" and 復習 "review" are different. While the proposed model predicted a different SBJ argument for each predicate, the baseline predicted the same SBJ item for both predicates. Therefore, we consider that the proposed model is more context-aware than the baseline.

Example 2 is the case when the QAZP's prediction is incorrect and the baseline's prediction is correct. In this example, その ことを "it" is the OBJ argument for the first predicate 知ってい "know", but it is also the referent of the omitted object argument, which is ZP, for the second predicate 隠して "hide". Our model predicted the first predicate 知ってい has その ことを as an OBJ argument. It also predicted the same span その ことを as the OBJ argument for the second predicate 隠して, which results in failing to detect that the OBJ argument is dropped. The reason is that our model predicts an OBJ argument span for each predicate independently. To alleviate such errors, we need to add a constraint to the model that no span in the input sentence can be the argument for more than one predicate at the same time, using Integer Linear Programming as in the method of (Iida and Poesio, 2011).

Example 3 is the case when the predictions of both models are incorrect. In this example sentence, the gold ZP class is the first person "speaker", but it is impossible to identify the ZP without knowing the context before and after the input sentence. We expect our model will capture context information by extending the input unit to multiple sentences instead of a single sentence.

5 Conclusion

We proposed a ZP identification method based on span prediction and evaluate it on Japanese and Chinese datasets. Our model is the first approach to consider ZP detection as a QA task. In experiments, the F1 values of our method were higher than the baseline method using sequence labeling for both Japanese and Chinese.

Future works include to analyze arguments that appeared overtly in tasks such as semantic role labeling. As a setting closer to the real problem, we will use a tagger to create queries instead of using Gold data. The other future work is comparison with a baseline which predicts all arguments at once by sharing the model parameters of BERT as our proposal model. We also consider extending our proposed method to coreference resolution tasks in pro-drop languages.

References

Abdulrahman Aloraini and Massimo Poesio. 2020.

Anaphoric zero pronoun identification: A multilingual approach. In *Proceedings of the Third Workshop on Computational Models of Reference, Anaphora and Coreference*, pages 22–32, Barcelona, Spain (online). Association for Computational Linguistics.

Alastair Butler, Tomoko Hotta, Ruiko Otomo, Kei Yoshimoto, Zhen Zhou, and Hong Zhu. 2012. Keyaki treebank : phrase structure with functional information for japanese. In *In Proceedings of Text Annotation Workshop*.

Jacob Devlin, Ming-Wei Chang, Kenton Lee, and Kristina Toutanova. 2019. BERT: Pre-training of deep bidirectional transformers for language understanding. In *Proceedings of the 2019 Conference of the North American Chapter of the Association for Computational Linguistics: Human Language Technologies, Volume 1 (Long and Short Papers)*, pages 4171–4186, Minneapolis, Minnesota. Association for Computational Linguistics.

Ryu Iida and Massimo Poesio. 2011. A cross-lingual ILP solution to zero anaphora resolution. In *Proceedings of the 49th Annual Meeting of the Association for Computational Linguistics: Human Language Technologies*, pages 804–813, Portland, Oregon, USA. Association for Computational Linguistics.

Xiaoya Li, Jingrong Feng, Yuxian Meng, Qinghong Han, Fei Wu, and Jiwei Li. 2020. A unified MRC framework for named entity recognition. In *Proceedings of the 58th Annual Meeting of the Association for Computational Linguistics*, pages 5849–5859, Online. Association for Computational Linguistics.

Masaaki Nagata, Katsuki Chousa, and Masaaki Nishino. 2020. A supervised word alignment method based on cross-language span prediction using multilingual BERT. In *Proceedings of the 2020 Conference on Empirical Methods in Natural Language Processing (EMNLP)*, pages 555–565, Online. Association for Computational Linguistics.

Linfeng Song, Kun Xu, Yue Zhang, Jianshu Chen, and Dong Yu. 2020. ZPR2: Joint zero pronoun recovery and resolution using multi-task learning and BERT. In *Proceedings of the 58th Annual Meeting of the Association for Computational Linguistics*, pages 5429–5434, Online. Association for Computational Linguistics.

Shunsuke Takeno, Masaaki Nagata, and Kazuhide Yamamoto. 2015. Empty category detection using path features and distributed case frames. In *Proceedings of the 2015 Conference on Empirical Methods in Natural Language Processing*, pages 1335–1340, Lisbon, Portugal. Association for Computational Linguistics.

Longyue Wang, Zhaopeng Tu, Xing Wang, and Shuming Shi. 2019. One model to learn both: Zero pronoun prediction and translation. In *Proceedings of the 2019 Conference on Empirical Methods in Natural Language Processing and the 9th International Joint Conference on Natural Language Processing (EMNLP-IJCNLP)*, pages 921–930, Hong Kong, China. Association for Computational Linguistics.

Thomas Wolf, Lysandre Debut, Victor Sanh, Julien Chaumond, Clement Delangue, Anthony Moi, Pierric Cistac, Tim Rault, Rémi Louf, Morgan Funtowicz, and Jamie Brew. 2019. Huggingface's transformers: State-of-the-art natural language processing. *CoRR*, abs/1910.03771.

Wei Wu, Fei Wang, Arianna Yuan, Fei Wu, and Jiwei Li. 2020. CorefQA: Coreference resolution as query-based span prediction. In *Proceedings of the 58th Annual Meeting of the Association for Computational Linguistics*, pages 6953–6963, Online. Association for Computational Linguistics.

Bing Xiang, Xiaoqiang Luo, and Bowen Zhou. 2013. Enlisting the ghost: Modeling empty categories for machine translation. In *Proceedings of the 51st Annual Meeting of the Association for Computational Linguistics (Volume 1: Long Papers)*, pages 822–831, Sofia, Bulgaria. Association for Computational Linguistics.

Naiwen Xue, Fei Xia, Fu-Dong Chiou, and Marta Palmer. 2005. The penn chinese treebank: Phrase structure annotation of a large corpus. *Natural language engineering*, 11(2):207.

On the differences between BERT and MT encoder spaces and how to address them in translation tasks

Raúl Vázquez
raul.vazquez@helsinki.fi

Hande Celikkanat
hande.celikkanat@helsinki.fi

Mathias Creutz
mathias.creutz@helsinki.fi

Jörg Tiedemann
jorg.tiedemann@helsinki.fi

University of Helsinki
Department of Digital Humanities

Abstract

Various studies show that pretrained language models such as BERT cannot straightforwardly replace encoders in neural machine translation despite their enormous success in other tasks. This is even more astonishing considering the similarities between the architectures. This paper sheds some light on the embedding spaces they create, using average cosine similarity, contextuality metrics and measures for representational similarity for comparison, revealing that BERT and NMT encoder representations look significantly different from one another. In order to address this issue, we propose a supervised transformation from one into the other using explicit alignment and fine-tuning. Our results demonstrate the need for such a transformation to improve the applicability of BERT in MT.

1 Introduction

Contextualized token representations produced by pretrained language models (LMs), in particular BERT (Devlin et al., 2019), have ushered in a new era, allowing the separation of unsupervised pretraining of powerful representation spaces, from the supervised training of task-specific, comparatively shallow classifiers on top of these representations. BERT-based models have consistently shown state-of-the-art performance in a variety of tasks, which is largely attributed to the rich information captured by the representations. These capabilities and its Transformer-based architecture suggest that BERT could improve neural machine translation (NMT) as well. However, as shown by Clinchant et al. (2019), although useful, information encoded by BERT is not sufficient by itself for successful MT. The reason for this is still an open question. Some of the most widely accepted hypotheses to date argue that either there is a fundamental discrepancy between the masked language modeling training objective of BERT compared to the generative, left-to-right nature of the MT objective (Song et al., 2019; Lewis et al., 2020) ; or that catastrophic forgetting (Goodfellow et al., 2015) takes place when learning the MT objective on top of the pretrained LM (Merchant et al., 2020). The latter could be caused by the large size of the training data typically used in MT,and by the high capacity decoder network used in MT because to fit the high-capacity model well on massive data requires a huge number of training steps. However, since on the one hand, the left-to-right constraint in MT is potentially more relevant for the decoders than the typically bidirectional encoder that has access to the entire input sequence, and on the other hand, BERT and other pre-trained LMs have been successfully used for other complex problems with large training data and high capacity classifiers (Liu and Lapata, 2019; Witteveen and Andrews, 2019; Huang et al., 2021), it is reasonable to assume there may be further reasons for these discrepancies.

We take a complementary stance and analyze the differences between the representation spaces produced by BERT and those produced by the MT objective. We therefore attempt to *align* these spaces, and investigate whether such an explicit alignment would reshape the BERT representation space to enable its use as an NMT encoder. To the best of our knowledge, this is the first study to investigate the intrinsic differences of pretrained LM and MT spaces, as well as the first attempt to explicitly align them. For reproducing our experiments, we make our code available at `https://github.com/Helsinki-NLP/Geometry`

2 Methodology

2.1 Comparing the Representation Spaces

Measures of Isotropy and Contextuality. We investigate how the embedding spaces of BERT

Proceedings of the Joint Conference of the 59th Annual Meeting of the Association for Computational Linguistics and the 11th International Joint Conference on Natural Language Processing: Student Research Workshop, pages 337–347
August 5–6, 2021. ©2021 Association for Computational Linguistics

and MT differ by making a layer-by-layer comparison of these spaces. First, we measure the *level of isotropy* of these spaces using the average cosine similarity (*AvgSim*) between the representations of uniformly randomly sampled words from different contexts (Ethayarajh, 2019). (An)isotropy corresponds to the degree of directional (non)uniformity in an embedding space, where perfect isotropy implies directional uniformity in the distribution word vectors. It is important to consider (an)isotropy when discussing contextuality since cosine similarity is relative to the directional uniformity of the sample space. Then, we also generalize *AvgSim* to using the Euclidean distance as our distance metric. Understanding how cosine similarity and the Euclidean distance interact allows for a more complete understanding of the space.

We also make a layer-wise comparison using two of the anisotropy-adjusted contextuality metrics presented in Ethayarajh (2019): *SelfSim:* average cosine similarity between the contextualized representations of a word across its occurrences in the dataset, and *IntraSim:* average cosine similarity between representations of words in a sentence and the sentence mean vector. Both metrics are corrected for anisotropy via subtracting the corresponding *AvgSim*, assuming *AvgSim* as a measure of anisotropy.

Measures of Representational Similarity. We measure the similarities between pairs of layers of both models using Representational Similarity Analysis (RSA) (Laakso and Cottrell, 2000; Kriegeskorte et al., 2008) and Projection-Weighted Canonical Correlation Analysis (PWCCA) (Morcos et al., 2018) as task-agnostic measures.

RSA, originally developed for neuroscience, and later adopted for quantifying the similarity between neural networks (Chrupała and Alishahi, 2019; Abnar et al., 2019) works by taking a set of input stimuli of size n, and running them through the models to be compared. For each model, the activations to each of the n stimuli points are pairwise compared to each other using a similarity metric to compute a an adjacency matrix of size $[n \times n]$ between the stimuli points obtained. These matrices are then contrasted against each other using the Pearson's correlation coefficient, giving a measure of the "representational similarity".

PWCCA is an extension over the SVCCA (Singular Value Canonical Correlation Analysis) distance measure (Raghu et al., 2017), which combines Singular Value Decomposition (SVD) and Canonical Correlation Analysis (CCA) (Hotelling, 1936). CCA is invariant to linear transforms, hence, it is useful for finding shared structures across representations which are superficially dissimilar, making it a good tool for comparing the representations across groups of networks and for comparing representations. Specifically, given the two sets of n corresponding representations from two models, PWCCA performs (1) SVD over the dimension space to prune redundant dimensions, (2) CCA to find linear transformations of the two spaces' dimensions, which are maximally correlated to each other, and (3) a weighted average of the resulting correlation coefficients, which favor the ones that are more relevant to the underlying representations.

2.2 Aligning the Representation Spaces

We present two methods to align the BERT space to that of the MT encoder: *(i)* an explicit alignment transformation that forces BERT representations to better match those of the MT encoder, and *(ii)* an implicit alignment effect achieved by a fine-tuning process which uses translation as its objective.

Explicit Alignment Transformation. We build upon Cao et al. (2020), maximizing the *contextual alignment* the model can achieve via the average accuracy on the *contextual word retrieval task.* This method presents several advantages that can be leveraged in our work. It is multilingual, it respects contextuality of the embeddings, and it makes use of rather reliable, widely used and not-memory intensive alignment algorithms (Brown et al., 1993; Och and Ney, 2003)

The task, as originally posed by Cao et al. (2020) is as follows. Given a parallel pre-aligned corpus C of source-target pairs (s, t), and one word within a source sentence, the objective is to find the corresponding target word. Let each sentence pair (s, t) have word pairs, denoted $a(s, t) = (i_1, j_1), ..., (i_m, j_m)$, containing position tuples (i, j) such that the words s_i and t_j are translations of each other. We use a regularized loss function $Loss = L + \lambda R$ so that L aligns the embeddings from one model, $f_1(i, s)$, to the ones of the other model $f_2(j, t)$:

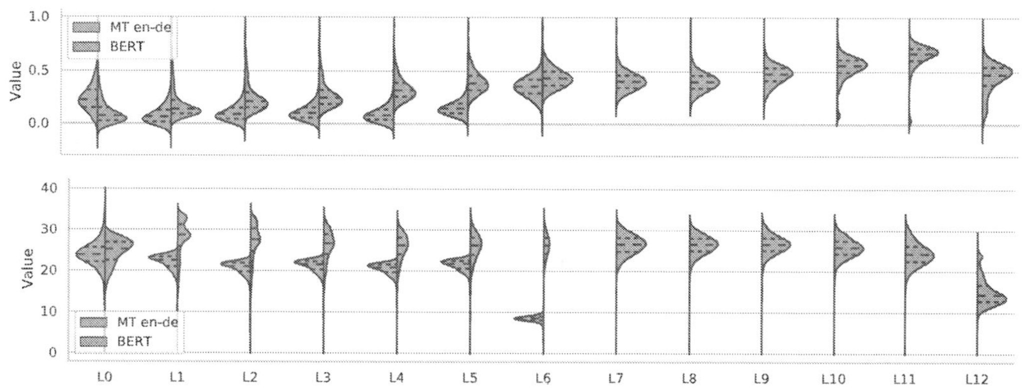

Figure 1: Cosine similarity *(top)* and Euclidean distance *(bottom)* distributions between randomly sampled words. Note that BERT has 12 layers and MT encoder has 6 layers, so the layers should be compared according to their relative positions, such as comparing the final layer of BERT to the final layer of MT encoder.

$$L(f_1, f_2; C) = -\sum_{(s,t)\in C} \sum_{(i,j)\in a(s,t)} \mathrm{sim}\left(f_1(i,s), f_2(j,t)\right)$$

$$R(f; C) = \sum_{s\in C} \sum_{i=1}^{len(t)} \|f_1(i,s) - f_1^{\circ}(i,s)\|_2^2$$

where f_1° denotes the pretrained model 1 before alignment and R is the regularization term that imposes a penalty if the target embeddings stray too far from their initialization. We validate using a version of Cao et al. (2020) word retrieval task using a nearest neighbor retrieval function:

$$N(i, s|f_1, f_2) = \underset{t\in C, 0\geq j\geq len(t)}{\arg\max}\ \mathrm{sim}\left(f_1(i,s), f_2(j,t)\right)$$

We propose to modify the regularized loss function $Loss = L + \lambda R$ so that L aligns the embeddings from one model, $f_1(i,s)$, to the ones of another model, $f_2(j,t)$, and also use a regularization term R to impose a penalty if the aligned embeddings stray too much. In contrast with Cao et al. (2020), this allows for alignment between embeddings produced by different models. Specifically, we align the representations in the final layer of the pretrained language model, to that of the encoder of the MT model. Although in this work, we focus on aligning the different representations for the same word to each other, aligning embedding spaces of different languages and different models is also an interesting future direction.

Implicit Alignment via Fine-tuning. We fine-tune a hybrid model consisting of BERT in the encoder side that sends its representations to a pre-trained MT decoder. We then use smoothed cross entropy loss as our training objective to fine-tune BERT representations for performing MT. The outputs of BERT are passed through a linear projection layer to match the dimension of the MT decoder and then fed into the decoder in the same way as in the standard Transformer architecture.

3 Comparing The Embedding Spaces.

We compare the representation spaces produced by BERT and the encoder of a Transformer trained on the MT task. BERT is composed of 12 layers, plus an initial input embedding layer, with a dimension of 768. The MT system we apply consists of an input embedding layer followed by 6 Transformer layers with a hidden dimension of 512. We use the pretrained `bert-base-uncased` model, as well as the pretrained English-German translation model `opus-mt-en-de`, both from the HuggingFace library (Wolf et al., 2019). Following Ethayarajh (2019), we extract embeddings using data from the SemEval Semantic Textual Similarity tasks from 2012 to 2016 (Agirre et al., 2016).

Average similarity between random tokens. Figure 1 presents the layer-wise cosine similarity *(top)* and the Euclidean distance *(bottom)* distributions of randomly sampled words.The behavior of BERT in Figure 1*(top)* is consistent with the findings of Ethayarajh (2019). The level of anisotropy of the embedding representations throughout layers of BERT increases towards higher layers, with the exception of a slight drop at the last layer (L12), considering the average cosine similarity of the representations as a proxy measure of anisotropy. Further, we notice Figure 1*(bottom)* that BERT embeddings follow an inverted U-shape. This, together with the *AvgSim* trend, means that the embedding space starts by stretching out and becoming narrower, later on to spread out shorter embeddings in layer 12, in line with (Voita et al., 2019).

The MT-based representations, however, look significantly different. The cosine-based *AvgSim* follows an almost U-like trend: it starts from a relatively high level at layer 0, then immediately drops and stays low throughout the middle layers, before a sudden increase at the final layer (L6). In particular:

1. a high average similarity of the MT embeddings in layer 0 is striking since the representations are not yet that "contextualized" this early in the model, and

2. the gradual increase of average similarity in BERT layers, versus the very steep increase at the last layer of MT model.

Behavior (1) might be caused by the shared source-target vocabularies and the embedding layer in the MT model in the encoder and the decoder being shared. Such shared processing can result in a seeming inflation of the cosine similarity of randomly selected vectors, which actually belong to two different language spaces. To test for this hypothesis, we check the average Euclidean distance between randomly selected tokens in Figure 1-*bottom*. Interestingly, we do not observe considerable high levels of closeness between random words in layer 0, and the distribution is widespread. That is, the embeddings are organized in a narrow cone but have a wide range of lengths. This behaviour might arise from the system needing to represent both languages in the same space, and the interplay between training the embeddings layer at the target side while needing to keep source embeddings apart enough - future work is necessary to confirm this. Motivated by these findings, we emphasize that using both metrics and observing how they interact allows for a more complete understanding of the representation spaces. [1]

Finding (2) is more relevant to our main question of the differences between the geometries of BERT and MT. Both metrics show a more gradual increase in the closeness of random tokens in the BERT over layers, as compared to an abrupt increase in the MT space. Therefore, we can deduce that the MT model can keep random representations successfully apart for all but the uppermost of the layers. We hypothesize that this monotonously increasing levels of closeness of random token embeddings in BERT may be contributing to its sub-optimal machine translation performance. To verify this hypothesis, in section 4 we present results on MT performance after alignment and in section 4.1 we show how the alignment method changes the embeddings distributions.

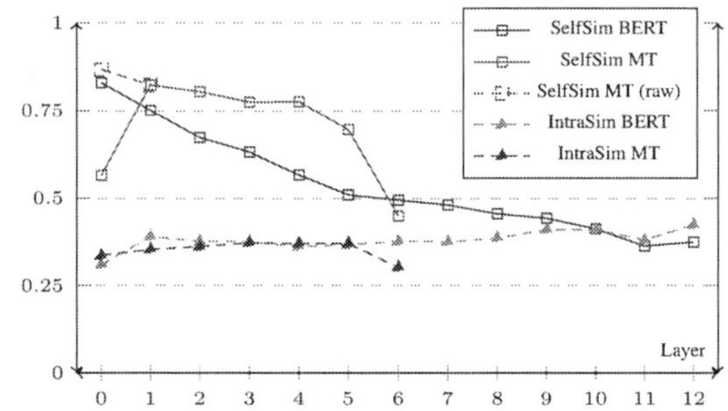

Figure 2: Comparison of contextualization for BERT and MT spaces using *SelfSim* and *IntraSim*. We also present the raw *SelfSim* before anisotropy correction.

Similarity between tokens of the same form. *SelfSim* will be high in less contextualized models, because such models use similar representations for each occurrence of the same token. Highly contextualized models will have lower *SelfSim* since every occurrence of the word will have a different representation. Comparing the two spaces (Figure 2), we again observe different trends. *SelfSim* steadily drops for BERT except for the last layer, showing an increase in the contextuality of the representations. For the MT model, on the other hand, we observe a steep drop at layer 6, indicating a sudden increase in contextuality here. All in all, BERT gradually increases contextualization whereas the MT encoder tends to model individual lexical concepts in most layers before adding a strong contextual influence in the last one.

Once again, we see a different behavior in layer 0 of the MT model, which is characterized by low *SelfSim* in the embedding layer. This a direct result of the high *AvgSim* value at the embeddings layer (due to the shared vocabulary space) which is the anisotropy correction factor for *SelfSim*. We

[1]Cosine similarity does not take into account the magnitude of the vectors at play, making it susceptible to the existence a large value in one of the entries of a high-dimensional vector, while Euclidean distance is hard to interpret in high-dimensional spaces and it is unbounded from above.

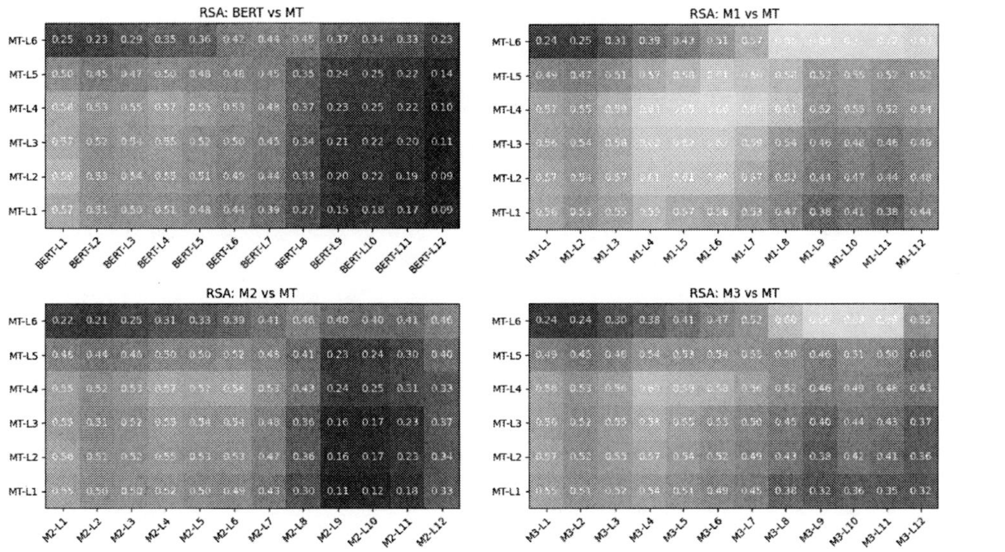

Figure 3: Representation similarity analysis between of out-of-box BERT, as well as the aligned models M1/M2/M3, with MT model from HuggingFace.

deduce that anisotropy-corrected *SelfSim* cannot straightforwardly be interpreted as a measure of contextuality in the embeddings layer of MT models with a shared source-target vocabulary. For comparison, we, therefore, also present the uncorrected *SelfSim (raw)* value (dashed line) for this layer, which confirms this reasoning.

Similarity between tokens within the same sentence. We check the average similarity between tokens in the same sentence (*IntraSim*). Figure 2 reveals different behavior between the two models. In particular, we see a smooth increase over the layers for both models until the penultimate layer, pointing to an increasing level of in-sentence contextualization, as shown by the embeddings of the words in the same sentence gradually coming together. However, the behavior at the final layer is different between the two models. We observe an increase in *IntraSim* for the BERT model at the last layer, in contrast to the drop at the last layer of the MT model. In other words, the MT model is suddenly discriminating between the words in the sentence at layer 6, just before passing information to the decoder. We hypothesize that it may be useful for the MT decoder to have access to representations that are less contextualized at a source sentence level, since it still needs to add semantic information for decoding into the target language. Notice that *SelfSim* and *IntraSim* decrease for final

	Encoder	Explicit alignment	Fine-tuning
MTbaseline	Trf	✗	✗
huggingface en-de	(6-layers)	✗	✗
M1:align	BERT (12-layers)	✓	✗
M2:fine-tune		✗	✓
M3:align+fine-tune		✓	✓

Table 1: Model setups. **MTbaseline** and **huggingface en-de** are baseline models which use Transformer ("Trf") as encoder. **M1**, **M2** and **M3** utilize various combinations of the proposed alignment strategies.

layer of the MT model. That is, similarity of word forms in different contexts is decreasing greatly and similarity of words to the mean sentence vector is (to a smaller degree) also decreasing. This might be an indication of the different constraints MT models have on contextualization. For example, the model may have a tendency to pay strong attention to syntactic and positional information, instead of focusing on shared semantics of the sentence.

Layer-wise similarity analysis between models. Figures 3-*top left* and 4-*top-left* present the results of the representational similarity analysis (RSA) and projection-weighted canonical correlation analysis (PWCCA) between out-of-the-box BERT and the MT model representational spaces. Both analyses depict higher similarity values between the lower layers of the models. At the lower layers, the

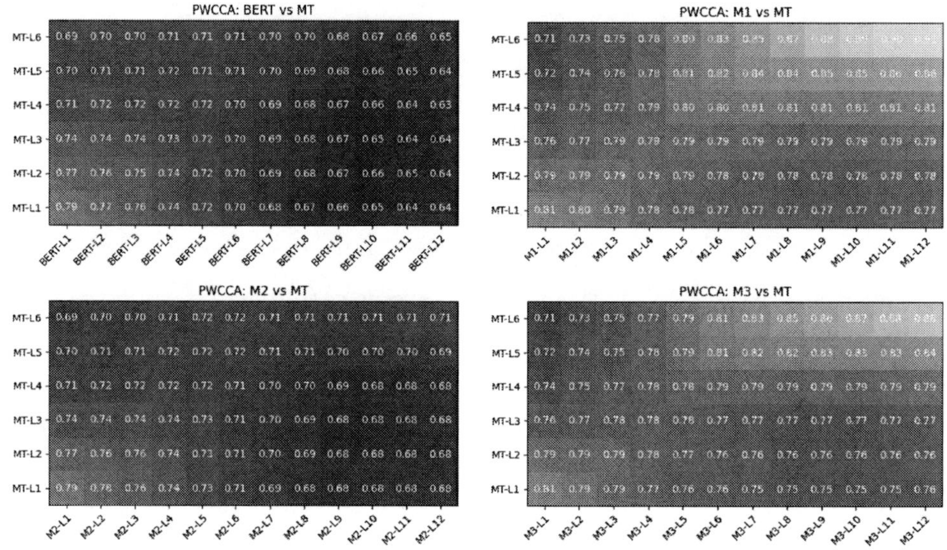

Figure 4: Representational similarity analysis of BERT, HuggingFace MT model, and aligned models M1/M2/M3.

representations are not yet changed so much from their initial starting point, so it is to be expected that they are more similar between the models. Towards the higher levels, though, the similarity decreases. The BERT representations gain distance from the MT representations, reaching the lowest similarity between the BERT-L12 and the MT layers.

	Train		Val.
	Explicit Alignment	Fine-Tuning	
Europarl	45K	150K	1.5K
MuST-C	45K	150K	1.5K
newstest	13K	13K	500
Total	102K	313K	3.5K

Table 2: Train and validation splits for the datasets.

4 Aligning the Representation Spaces

To address the discrepancies observed in the BERT and the MT encoder embedding spaces, we use the transformations from section 2.2. We use five different setups (Table 1). Two of these use 6-layered Transformer encoders and serve as baselines: the **MTbaseline** model, a transformer-based MT model trained from scratch with the fine-tuning data (Table 2), and **Huggingface en–de** a state-of-the-art, pretrained Transformer model. We compare the proposed alignment methods using **M1**, which uses only the explicit alignment transformation strategy, **M2**, which uses the implicit alignment via fine-tuning strategy, and the hybrid **M3**, which combines the two strategies.

Data. We use data from the English-German sections of the MuST-C dataset (Di Gangi et al., 2019), Europarl (Koehn, 2005), extracted using OpusTools (Aulamo et al., 2020) and the development tarball from the WMT2019 news translation shared task (Bojar et al., 2019) in the proportions indicated in Table 2. We test using the MuST-C provided test-split, newstest2014 (Bojar et al., 2014) and newstest2015 (Bojar et al., 2015), which were excluded from the train data. All of the data splits are attainable using our repository.

We purposefully restrict the data amount used for training the alignments. Such aligned systems should be able to work under less intensive resource requirements. The size of the training data for both methods varies, because we try to keep the explicit alignment comparable to what was originally proposed for mBERT (Cao et al., 2020), whereas the implicit alignment via fine-tuning requires more data since the MT decoder is also to be fine-tuned.

Results. Table 3 presents the BLEU scores for five setups. Notably, we see that by explicitly aligning the embedding spaces in a supervised way (**M1**) the system is already able to perform translation reasonably well. Besides being data efficient, due to its simplicity, the alignment method used for **M1** is also memory efficient and fast to train. We think that this shows how applying the simple alignment procedure described in section 2.2 can be

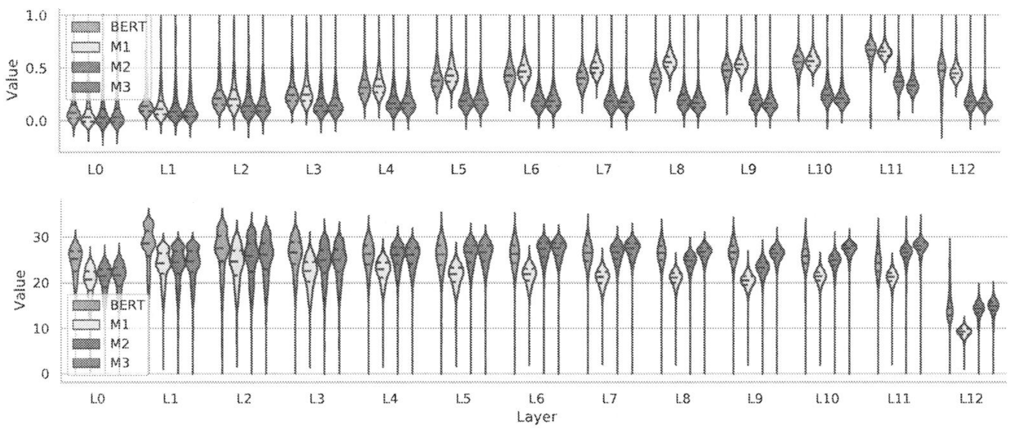

Figure 5: Comparison of out-of-box BERT and MT models, against the aligned models M1/M2/M3, in terms of the Cosine similarity *(top)* and Euclidean distance *(bottom)* distributions between randomly sampled words.

	MuST-C	newstest	
		2014	2015
MTbaseline	29.9	14.5	17.6
huggingface en-de	33.7	28.3	31.1
M1:align	21.4	18.1	18.9
M2:fine-tune	33.8	23.9	28.0
M3:align+fine-tune	34.1	25.0	29.2

Table 3: BLEU scores for EN-DE test sets.

used to make the rich world-knowledge captured by BERT accessible for NMT by making the embedding spaces compatible. In section 4.1, we investigate the distributional changes in the embeddings spaces caused by the alignments.

We also notice that fine-tuning in **M2** works quite well. We highlight how data efficient this method is. After training for 1 epoch we obtain already over 30 BLEU points for MuST-C and after 3 epochs of fine-tuning we achieve results comparable with the **huggingface en-de model**. On MuST-C data, **M3** yields similar results, notably however, it converges much faster. At only 1% of the 1st epoch ($\sim$ 3K utterances) it achieves already 85% of its performance in both test sets, and with 10K utterances it starts to converge. The results obtained with **newstest 2014** and **newstest 2015** follow a similar trend, yet fail to surpass the huggingface model – a state-of-the-art MT model trained with all available EN-DE resources ($\sim$ 350.7M parallel sentences) from OPUS (Tiedemann, 2012). However, in all cases, we observe a better performance than the **MTbaseline**, an MT model trained with the same restricted data. These results indicate that BERT can indeed be used as an MT encoder, but only with a careful alignment procedure that overcomes the incompatibilities between the encoders.

4.1 The Aligned BERT Space

Finally, we check the effects of the alignment schemes on the geometry of the BERT space. Here, our specific question of interest is in which ways the BERT-produced embedding space became more similar (or not) to the MT space after applying the alignment methods.

AvgSim. Figure 5 shows layer-wise cosine similarity *(top)* and Euclidean distance *(bottom)* distributions of random words of the aligned models.

While all three distributions are different from the original BERT, **M1** is the least different in terms of where the distribution is centered, but even here the distributions are less skewed/more symmetrical, with respect to the cosine similarity. However, the Euclidean distance results show that **M1** consistently produces shorter word vectors. This aligned model is hence creating a space that is as narrow as BERT's, but not as elongated. This might be due to the regularization term in the supervised alignment not allowing the embeddings to drift too far from its pre-optimized setting, as well as the alignment being explicitly done for the last layer.[2] For both metrics, **M2** and **M3** are noticeably different compared to the original BERT and similar to each other. This indicates that aligning via fine-tuning propagates information in such a way that the space

[2]We see changes in the distributions of all layers due to backpropagation of information at training time.

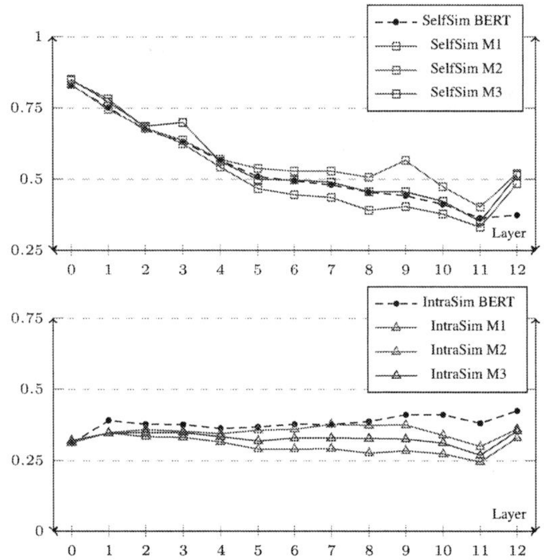

Figure 6: Comparison of BERT and the aligned models M1/M2/M3, in terms of *SelfSim* and *IntraSim*.

is reshaped drastically. The increase in the BLEU scores discussed above correlates with the amount of change we observe in the distance distributions.

SelfSim and IntraSim. Figure 6-*top* shows considerable change in the *SelfSim* of M1/M2/M3 following the alignment. Now all three models show an abrupt increase in the similarity of tokens of the same form in the ultimate layer. In other words, these models are retrieving information related to the specific word form, just before passing the information to the decoder. This finding is in line with (Voita et al., 2019), who find that the MT decoder seems to require more information about the specific word form's representation, as compared to the overly contextual representations that the pretrained language models tend to produce.

Figure 6-*bottom* compares the after-alignment *IntraSim* with before-alignment case. Note that the M1/M2/M3 values in general are lower than the BERT, throughout the layers. This confirms the previous findings that the word forms seem to retain their original representations more, and adjusting to the sentence context less.

Layer-wise similarity analysis between models. Figures 3 and 4 show how the responses of M1/M2/M3 become significantly similar to that of the MT model post-alignment. Note that interestingly the explicit alignment method is particularly successful in achieving similarity to the MT model, in terms of similarities between responses to pairs of stimuli (as measured by RSA) and correlation of model responses over changing stimuli (as measured by PWCCA). However, as shown in Table 3, model M1 is outperformed by M2 and M3, which might be related to the anisotropy levels of M1 being similar to those of BERT (Figure 5).

5 Related Work

Analysis of contextualized representations. While there has been huge efforts to analyze word representations, most of it has been conducted using probing tasks (McCann et al., 2017; Conneau and Kiela, 2018; Conneau et al., 2018; Hewitt and Manning, 2019). Similarly, Merchant et al. (2020) study the effects of fine-tuning BERT representations on a specific set of probing tasks and analyse the change in the contextual representations using similarity analysis. Mimno and Thompson (2017) quantitatively studied static word representations produced with skip-gram with negative sampling. Their work was extended by Ethayarajh (2019) for contextualized embeddings, in which they use word level measures of contextuality to contrast ELMo (Peters et al., 2018), GPT-2 (Radford et al., 2019) and BERT (Devlin et al., 2019). Voita et al. (2019) present a comparison of contextualized representations trained with different objectives, using CCA and and mutual information to study information flow across networks. They conclude that although MT-produced representations do get refined with context, the change in those is not as extreme as for masked LM-produced representations (BERT-like), which is in line with our observations of higher *SelfSim* and lower *IntraSim* (i.e. not ultra-contextualized embeddings) for MT and aligned models as compared to BERT.

Pretrained LMs in NMT. Clinchant et al. (2019) present a systematic comparison of methods to integrate BERT into NMT models, including using BERT at the embedding level or for initializing an encoder. Zhu et al. (2020) propose a BERT-fused MT system that uses additional attention modules between the outputs of BERT and the encoder and decoder of the Transformer, increasing the model parameters by the number of parameters the chosen BERT flavour has. Yang et al. (2020) proposes a similar strategy, though using BERT outputs only in the encoder, and a three-fold training technique. Imamura and Sumita (2019) propose a simple yet effective two-stage optimization technique that first freezes BERT, and then fine-tunes over the full model parameters set. We argue that this is similar to the align and fine-tune approach we propose for incorporating BERT into MT. Finally, a number of studies leverage pretraining techniques. MASS (Song et al., 2019) is partly inspired by BERT, but it is pretrained in NMT and is tailored to match the way prediction is done in NMT (left-to-right). Liu et al. (2020) enhance transformer-based MT systems performance by using a BART pretraining technique (Lewis et al., 2020) in a multilingual fashion to initialize an NMT system.

Alignment. Numerous methods have been proposed for aligning (contextualized) word representations (Och and Ney, 2003; Ruder et al., 2019). Wang et al. (2019) learn an optimal linear transformation between embedding spaces. Schuster et al. (2019) propose a similar approach using the centroids of the instances of the same word in different contexts. Our work is closer to Cao et al. (2020), which use a resource-efficient algorithm that takes into account the contextuality of embeddings.

6 Conclusion

This paper provides an analysis of the intrinsic differences between BERT and machine translation encoders. We compare the representation spaces of both models and pinpoint discrepancies between them. We show that this mismatch can be remedied through an alignment strategy, which successfully reshapes BERT into an effective MT encoder. We also study the effects that the alignment methods have on the geometry of the embeddings spaces.

Acknowledgments

This work is part of the FoTran project, funded by the European Research Council (ERC) under the European Union's Horizon 2020 research and innovation programme (grant agreement № 771113).

We also acknowledge the CSC – IT Center for Science Ltd., for computational resources.

References

Samira Abnar, Lisa Beinborn, Rochelle Choenni, and Willem Zuidema. 2019. Blackbox meets blackbox: Representational similarity and stability analysis of neural language models and brains. In *Proceedings of the 2019 ACL Workshop BlackboxNLP: Analyzing and Interpreting Neural Networks for NLP*, pages 191–203, Florence, Italy. Association for Computational Linguistics.

Eneko Agirre, Carmen Banea, Daniel Cer, Mona Diab, Aitor Gonzalez-Agirre, Rada Mihalcea, German Rigau, and Janyce Wiebe. 2016. SemEval-2016 task 1: Semantic textual similarity, monolingual and cross-lingual evaluation. In *Proceedings of the 10th International Workshop on Semantic Evaluation (SemEval-2016)*, pages 497–511, San Diego, California. Association for Computational Linguistics.

Mikko Aulamo, Umut Sulubacak, Sami Virpioja, and Jörg Tiedemann. 2020. OpusTools and parallel corpus diagnostics. In *Proceedings of The 12th Language Resources and Evaluation Conference*, pages 3782–3789. European Language Resources Association.

Ondřej Bojar, Christian Buck, Christian Federmann, Barry Haddow, Philipp Koehn, Christof Monz, Matt Post, and Lucia Specia, editors. 2014. *Proceedings of the Ninth Workshop on Statistical Machine Translation*. Association for Computational Linguistics, Baltimore, Maryland, USA.

Ondřej Bojar, Rajen Chatterjee, Christian Federmann, Mark Fishel, Yvette Graham, Barry Haddow, Matthias Huck, Antonio Jimeno Yepes, Philipp Koehn, André Martins, Christof Monz, Matteo Negri, Aurélie Névéol, Mariana Neves, Matt Post, Marco Turchi, and Karin Verspoor, editors. 2019. *Proceedings of the Fourth Conference on Machine Translation (Volume 2: Shared Task Papers, Day 1)*. Association for Computational Linguistics, Florence, Italy.

Ondřej Bojar, Rajen Chatterjee, Christian Federmann, Barry Haddow, Matthias Huck, Chris Hokamp, Philipp Koehn, Varvara Logacheva, Christof Monz, Matteo Negri, Matt Post, Carolina Scarton, Lucia Specia, and Marco Turchi. 2015. Findings of the 2015 workshop on statistical machine translation. In *Proceedings of the Tenth Workshop on Statistical Machine Translation*, pages 1–46, Lisbon, Portugal. Association for Computational Linguistics.

Peter F. Brown, Stephen A. Della Pietra, Vincent J. Della Pietra, and Robert L. Mercer. 1993. The mathematics of statistical machine translation: Parameter estimation. *Computational Linguistics*, 19(2):263–311.

Steven Cao, Nikita Kitaev, and Dan Klein. 2020. Multilingual alignment of contextual word representations. In *International Conference on Learning Representations*.

Grzegorz Chrupała and Afra Alishahi. 2019. Correlating neural and symbolic representations of language. In *Proceedings of the 57th Annual Meeting of the Association for Computational Linguistics*, page 2952–2962, Florence, Italy.

Stephane Clinchant, Kweon Woo Jung, and Vassilina Nikoulina. 2019. On the use of BERT for neural machine translation. In *Proceedings of the 3rd*

Workshop on Neural Generation and Translation, pages 108–117, Hong Kong. Association for Computational Linguistics.

Alexis Conneau and Douwe Kiela. 2018. Senteval: An evaluation toolkit for universal sentence representations. *arXiv preprint arXiv:1803.05449*.

Alexis Conneau, Germán Kruszewski, Guillaume Lample, Loïc Barrault, and Marco Baroni. 2018. What you can cram into a single vector: Probing sentence embeddings for linguistic properties. In *Proceedings of the 56th Annual Meeting of the Association for Computational Linguistics (Volume 1: Long Papers)*, pages 2126–2136, Melbourne, Australia. Association for Computational Linguistics.

Jacob Devlin, Ming-Wei Chang, Kenton Lee, and Kristina Toutanova. 2019. BERT: Pre-training of deep bidirectional transformers for language understanding. In *Proceedings of the 2019 Conference of the North American Chapter of the Association for Computational Linguistics: Human Language Technologies, Volume 1 (Long and Short Papers)*, pages 4171–4186, Minneapolis, Minnesota. Association for Computational Linguistics.

Mattia A. Di Gangi, Roldano Cattoni, Luisa Bentivogli, Matteo Negri, and Marco Turchi. 2019. MuST-C: a Multilingual Speech Translation Corpus. In *Proceedings of the 2019 Conference of the North American Chapter of the Association for Computational Linguistics: Human Language Technologies, Volume 1 (Long and Short Papers)*, pages 2012–2017, Minneapolis, Minnesota. Association for Computational Linguistics.

Kawin Ethayarajh. 2019. How contextual are contextualized word representations? comparing the geometry of BERT, ELMo, and GPT-2 embeddings. In *Proceedings of the 2019 Conference on Empirical Methods in Natural Language Processing and the 9th International Joint Conference on Natural Language Processing (EMNLP-IJCNLP)*, pages 55–65, Hong Kong, China. Association for Computational Linguistics.

Ian J. Goodfellow, Mehdi Mirza, Da Xiao, Aaron Courville, and Yoshua Bengio. 2015. An empirical investigation of catastrophic forgetting in gradient-based neural networks.

John Hewitt and Christopher D. Manning. 2019. A structural probe for finding syntax in word representations. In *Proceedings of the 2019 Conference of the North American Chapter of the Association for Computational Linguistics: Human Language Technologies, Volume 1 (Long and Short Papers)*, pages 4129–4138, Minneapolis, Minnesota. Association for Computational Linguistics.

Harold Hotelling. 1936. Relations between two sets of variates. *Biometrika*, 28:321–337.

Wen-Chin Huang, Chia-Hua Wu, Shang-Bao Luo, Kuan-Yu Chen, Hsin-Min Wang, and Tomoki Toda. 2021. Speech recognition by simply fine-tuning bert.

Kenji Imamura and Eiichiro Sumita. 2019. Recycling a pre-trained BERT encoder for neural machine translation. In *Proceedings of the 3rd Workshop on Neural Generation and Translation*, pages 23–31, Hong Kong. Association for Computational Linguistics.

Philipp Koehn. 2005. Europarl: A parallel corpus for statistical machine translation. In *MT summit*, volume 5, pages 79–86. Citeseer.

Nikolaus Kriegeskorte, Marieke Mur, and Peter A. Bandettini. 2008. Representational similarity analysis-connecting the branches of systems neuroscience. *Frontiers in systems neuroscience*, 2(4).

Aarre Laakso and Garrison Cottrell. 2000. Content and cluster analysis: assessing representational similarity in neural systems. *Philosophical psychology*, 13(1):47–76.

Mike Lewis, Yinhan Liu, Naman Goyal, Marjan Ghazvininejad, Abdelrahman Mohamed, Omer Levy, Veselin Stoyanov, and Luke Zettlemoyer. 2020. BART: Denoising sequence-to-sequence pre-training for natural language generation, translation, and comprehension. In *Proceedings of the 58th Annual Meeting of the Association for Computational Linguistics*, pages 7871–7880, Online. Association for Computational Linguistics.

Yang Liu and Mirella Lapata. 2019. Text summarization with pretrained encoders. In *Proceedings of the 2019 Conference on Empirical Methods in Natural Language Processing and the 9th International Joint Conference on Natural Language Processing (EMNLP-IJCNLP)*, pages 3730–3740, Hong Kong, China. Association for Computational Linguistics.

Yinhan Liu, Jiatao Gu, Naman Goyal, Xian Li, Sergey Edunov, Marjan Ghazvininejad, Mike Lewis, and Luke Zettlemoyer. 2020. Multilingual denoising pre-training for neural machine translation. *Transactions of the Association for Computational Linguistics*, 8:726–742.

Bryan McCann, James Bradbury, Caiming Xiong, and Richard Socher. 2017. Learned in translation: Contextualized word vectors. In *Advances in Neural Information Processing Systems*, volume 30, pages 6294–6305. Curran Associates, Inc.

Amil Merchant, Elahe Rahimtoroghi, Ellie Pavlick, and Ian Tenney. 2020. What happens to BERT embeddings during fine-tuning? In *Proceedings of the Third BlackboxNLP Workshop on Analyzing and Interpreting Neural Networks for NLP*, pages 33–44, Online. Association for Computational Linguistics.

David Mimno and Laure Thompson. 2017. The strange geometry of skip-gram with negative sampling. In *Proceedings of the 2017 Conference on Empirical*

Methods in Natural Language Processing, pages 2873–2878, Copenhagen, Denmark. Association for Computational Linguistics.

Ari S. Morcos, Maithra Raghu, and Samy Bengio. 2018. Insights on representational similarity in neural networks with canonical correlation. In *Advances in Neural Information Processing Systems*, pages 5727–5836. Curran Associates, Inc.

Franz Josef Och and Hermann Ney. 2003. A systematic comparison of various statistical alignment models. *Computational Linguistics*, 29(1):19–51.

Matthew Peters, Mark Neumann, Mohit Iyyer, Matt Gardner, Christopher Clark, Kenton Lee, and Luke Zettlemoyer. 2018. Deep contextualized word representations. In *Proceedings of the 2018 Conference of the North American Chapter of the Association for Computational Linguistics: Human Language Technologies, Volume 1 (Long Papers)*, pages 2227–2237, New Orleans, Louisiana. Association for Computational Linguistics.

Alec Radford, Jeffrey Wu, Rewon Child, David Luan, Dario Amodei, and Ilya Sutskever. 2019. Language models are unsupervised multitask learners. *OpenAI blog*, 1(8):9.

Maithra Raghu, Justin Gilmer, Jason Yosinski, and Jascha Sohl-Dickstein. 2017. SVCCA: Singular vector canonical correlation analysis for deep learning dynamics and interpretability. In *Advances in Neural Information Processing Systems*. Curran Associates, Inc.

Sebastian Ruder, Ivan Vulić, and Anders Søgaard. 2019. A survey of cross-lingual word embedding models. *Journal of Artifical Intelligence Research*, 65:569–631.

Tal Schuster, Ori Ram, Regina Barzilay, and Amir Globerson. 2019. Cross-lingual alignment of contextual word embeddings, with applications to zero-shot dependency parsing. In *Proceedings of the 2019 Conference of the North American Chapter of the Association for Computational Linguistics: Human Language Technologies, Volume 1 (Long and Short Papers)*, pages 1599–1613, Minneapolis, Minnesota. Association for Computational Linguistics.

Kitao Song, Xu Tan, Tao Qin, Jianfeng Lu, and Tie-Yan Liu. 2019. Mass: Masked sequence to sequence pre-training for language generation. In *International Conference on Machine Learning (ICML)*.

Jörg Tiedemann. 2012. Parallel data, tools and interfaces in opus. In *Proceedings of the Eight International Conference on Language Resources and Evaluation (LREC'12)*, Istanbul, Turkey. European Language Resources Association (ELRA).

Elena Voita, Rico Sennrich, and Ivan Titov. 2019. The bottom-up evolution of representations in the transformer: A study with machine translation and language modeling objectives. In *Proceedings of the 2019 Conference on Empirical Methods in Natural Language Processing and the 9th International Joint Conference on Natural Language Processing (EMNLP-IJCNLP)*, pages 4396–4406, Hong Kong, China. Association for Computational Linguistics.

Yuxuan Wang, Wanxiang , Jiang Guo, Yijia Lui, and Ting Liu. 2019. Cross-lingual bert transformation for zero-shot dependency parsing. In *Proceedings of the 2019 Conference on Empirical Methods in Natural Language Processing and the 9th International Joint Conference on Natural Language Processing (EMNLP-IJCNLP)*, pages 5721–5727, Hong Kong, China. Association for Computational Linguistics.

Sam Witteveen and Martin Andrews. 2019. Paraphrasing with large language models. In *Proceedings of the 3rd Workshop on Neural Generation and Translation*, pages 215–220, Hong Kong. Association for Computational Linguistics.

Thomas Wolf, Lysandre Debut, Victor Sanh, Julien Chaumond, Clement Delangue, Anthony Moi, Pierric Cistac, Tim Rault, R'emi Louf, Morgan Funtowicz, and Jamie Brew. 2019. Huggingface's transformers: State-of-the-art natural language processing. *ArXiv*, abs/1910.03771.

Jiacheng Yang, Mingxuan Wang, Hao Zhou, Chengqi Zhao, Yong Yu, Weinan Zhang, and Lei Li. 2020. Towards making the most of bert in neural machine translation. In *Proceedings of the AAAI Conference on Artificial Intelligence*, New York, USA.

Jinhua Zhu, Yingce Xia, Lijun Wu, Di He, Tao Qin, Wengang Zhou, Houqiang Li, and Tieyan Liu. 2020. Incorporating bert into neural machine translation. In *International Conference on Learning Representations*.

Synchronous Syntactic Attention for Transformer Neural Machine Translation

Hiroyuki Deguchi
Nara Institute of Science and Technology
deguchi.hiroyuki.db0@is.naist.jp

Akihiro Tamura
Doshisha University
aktamura@mail.doshisha.ac.jp

Takashi Ninomiya
Ehime University
ninomiya@cs.ehime-u.ac.jp

Abstract

This paper proposes a novel attention mechanism for Transformer Neural Machine Translation, "Synchronous Syntactic Attention," inspired by synchronous dependency grammars. The mechanism synchronizes source-side and target-side syntactic self-attentions by minimizing the difference between target-side self-attentions and the source-side self-attentions mapped by the encoder-decoder attention matrix. The experiments show that the proposed method improves the translation performance on WMT14 En-De, WMT16 En-Ro, and ASPEC Ja-En (up to +0.38 points in BLEU).

1 Introduction

The Transformer Neural Machine Translation (NMT) model (Vaswani et al., 2017) has achieved state-of-the-art performance and become the focus of many NMT studies. One of its characteristics is the self-attention mechanism, which computes the strength of relationships between two words in a sentence. Transformer NMT has been improved by extending the self-attention mechanism to incorporate syntactic information (Wang et al., 2019b; Omote et al., 2019; Deguchi et al., 2019; Wang et al., 2019a; Bugliarello and Okazaki, 2020). In particular, Deguchi et al. (2019) and Wang et al. (2019a) have proposed dependency-based self-attentions, which are trained to attend to the syntactic parent for each token under constraints based on the dependency relations, for capturing sentence structures. Existing syntax-based NMT models, including their ones, use only monolingual syntactic information on either side or both.

By contrast, synchronous grammars such as synchronous context-free grammars and synchronous dependency grammars, which are defined in two languages and generate sentence structures aligned across them, have been introduced into many SMT models with the result of improving their translation performances (Jiang et al., 2009; Ding and Palmer, 2005; Chiang, 2005; Zhang et al., 2006). Figure 1 shows an example of the dependency structures of source and target language sentences and their alignments[1]. Inspired by synchronous dependency grammars, we aim to improve the performance of Transformer NMT by incorporating the main idea of the synchronous dependency grammars (i.e., synchronizing sentence structures across two languages). As far as we know, neither the synchronous dependency grammars themselves nor their basic idea has yet been incorporated into NMT.

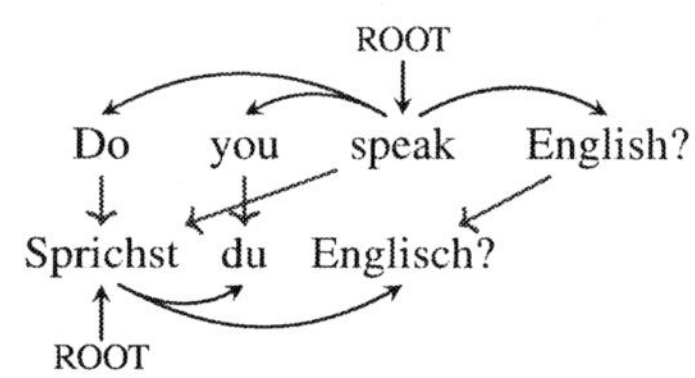

Figure 1: An example of dependency structures and alignments

This paper proposes a novel attention mechanism for Transformer NMT, called "Synchronous Syntactic Attention," which captures sentence structures aligned across two languages by the aligned self-attentions on the source- and target-side. The mechanism uses encoder-decoder attentions to map source-side syntactic self-attentions into a target language space based on Garg et al. (2019)'s observation that encoder-decoder attentions represent the alignments of source and target words. The mechanism is trained to maintain consistency between source- and target-side syntactic self-attentions according to an objective

[1]In this paper, an arrow is drawn from a head to its dependent.

Proceedings of the Joint Conference of the 59th Annual Meeting of the Association for Computational Linguistics and the 11th International Joint Conference on Natural Language Processing: Student Research Workshop, pages 348–355
August 5–6, 2021.

loss function that incorporates the difference between the target-side syntactic self-attentions and the mapped source-side syntactic self-attentions. We use *dependency-based self-attention* (Deguchi et al., 2019) as source- and target-side syntactic self-attentions.

2 Transformer NMT Model

The Transformer NMT model (Vaswani et al., 2017) is an encoder-decoder model composed of the encoder that encodes source tokens $\boldsymbol{f} = (f_1, f_2, \dots, f_I)$ into hidden vectors and the decoder that generates target tokens $\boldsymbol{e} = (e_1, e_2, \dots, e_J)$ from the outputs of the encoder. The encoder and decoder consist of N_{enc} encoder layers and N_{dec} decoder layers, respectively. Both the encoder layers and decoder layers are composed of multiple sub-layers, each of which includes a self-attention layer and a feed forward layer. The decoder layers additionally apply an encoder-decoder attention layer between the self-attention layer and the feed forward layer.

The self-attention and encoder-decoder attention are calculated by a multi-head attention mechanism. The multi-head attention $\mathrm{MHA}(Q, K, V)$ maps the d_{emb}-dimension embedding space into H subspaces of the d_k $(= \frac{d_{emb}}{H})$ dimension and calculates attention in each subspace as shown in Equations 1 to 3:

$$\mathrm{MHA}(Q, K, V) = [M_1; \dots; M_H]W^M, \quad (1)$$

$$M_h = A_h V_h, A_h = \mathrm{softmax}\left(\frac{Q_h K_h^\top}{\sqrt{d_k}}\right), \quad (2)$$

$$Q_h = QW_h^Q, K_h = KW_h^K, V_h = VW_h^V, \quad (3)$$

where W_h^Q, W_h^K, $W_h^V \in \mathbb{R}^{d_{emb} \times d_k}$ and $W^M \in \mathbb{R}^{d_{emb} \times d_{emb}}$ are parameter matrices. In the self-attention, the previous layer's output is used as Q, K, and V. In the encoder-decoder attention, the previous layer's output is used as Q and the last encoder layer's output is used as K and V. Note that, in training, the decoder's self-attention masks future tokens.

3 Dependency-Based Self-Attention

This section describes *dependency-based self-attention (DBSA)* (Deguchi et al., 2019), which is the baseline of our syntactic self-attention. DBSA captures dependency structures by extending the multi-head self-attention of the l_{dep}-th layer of the encoder or decoder. Let h be one of head of the l_{dep}-th encoder layer's self-attention or the l_{dep}-th decoder layer's self attention. An attention weight matrix A_h, where each value indicates the dependency relationship between two words, is calculated by using the bi-affine operation in Equation 4:

$$A_h = \mathrm{softmax}\left(\frac{Q_h U K_h^\top}{\sqrt{d_k}}\right), U \in \mathbb{R}^{d_k \times d_k}. \quad (4)$$

In A_h, the probability of token q being the head of token t in a source/target sentence S (i.e., $P(q = \mathrm{head}(t)|S)$) is modeled as $A_h[t, q]$. Then, a weighted representation matrix M_h, which includes dependency relationships in the source sentence or target sentence, is obtained by multiplying A_h and V_h (i.e., $M_h = A_h V_h$). Finally, M_h is concatenated with the other heads and mapped to a d_{emb}-dimensional matrix. In the decoder-side DBSA, future information is masked to prevent attending to unpredicted tokens in inference.

The Transformer NMT model with DBSA learns translation and dependency parsing at the same time by minimizing the objective function $\mathcal{L} = \mathcal{L}_t + \lambda_{dep}\mathcal{L}_{dep}$, where $\mathcal{L}_t$ is the translation loss and $\mathcal{L}_{dep}$ is computed in Equation 5:

$$\mathcal{L}_{dep} = -\sum_{i=1}^{I} \log P(\mathrm{head}(f_i) \mid \boldsymbol{f}) - \sum_{j=1}^{J} \log P(\mathrm{head}(e_j) \mid \boldsymbol{e}). \quad (5)$$

$\lambda_{dep} > 0$ is a hyperparameter to control the influence of the dependency parsing loss $\mathcal{L}_{dep}$.

DBSA has been extended to deal with subword tokens. For details, see the original paper by Deguchi et al. (2019).

4 Proposed Method: Synchronous Syntactic Attention

This section proposes a novel attention mechanism for Transformer NMT, "Synchronous Syntactic Attention," which captures sentence structures aligned across source and target languages. A Transformer NMT model with the proposed attention is trained according to the objective function presented below as Equation 6:

$$\mathcal{L} = \mathcal{L}_t + \lambda_{dep}\mathcal{L}_{dep} + \lambda_{sync}\mathcal{L}_{sync}, \quad (6)$$

where $\mathcal{L}_{sync}$ is the loss to keep consistency between source-side and target-side syntactic self-

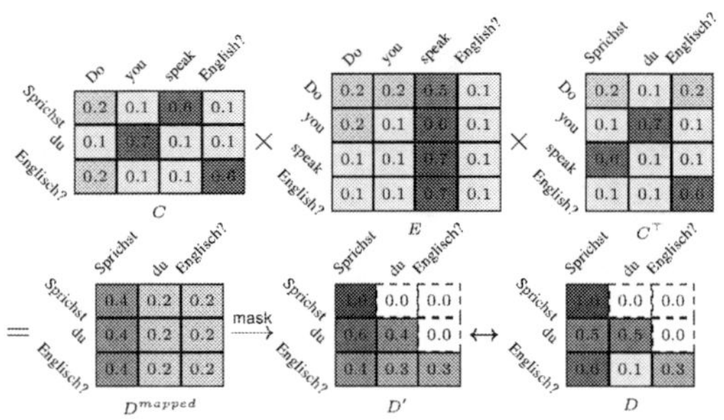

Figure 2: An example of synchronous syntactic attention

attention (i.e., DBSA) and λ_{sync} is a hyperparameter to control the influence of $\mathcal{L}_{sync}$. In particular, $\mathcal{L}_{sync}$ is the differences between the encoder's self-attention, which is mapped into target language space by the encoder-decoder attention, and the decoder's self-attention.

Let E and D be the attention matrix A_h of the l_{dep}-th encoder layer's syntactic self-attention and that of the l_{dep}-th decoder layer's syntactic self attention, respectively. The proposed method first maps E into the target language space by the encoder-decoder attention as shown by Equation 7:

$$D^{mapped} = CEC^{\top}, \quad (7)$$

where D^{mapped} is the mapped encoder's syntactic self attention matrix, and C is the encoder-decoder attention weight matrix of the l_{sync}-th decoder's layer. Then, D^{mapped} is masked to prevent attending to future tokens, and a softmax function is applied to the masked D^{mapped} as follows in Equation 8:

$$D' = \mathrm{softmax}(\mathrm{mask}(D^{mapped})). \quad (8)$$

Next, the proposed method computes the mean squared error between D' and D as $\mathcal{L}_{sync}$ as follows in Equation 9:

$$\mathcal{L}_{sync} = \sum_{t,q}(D'_{t,q} - D_{t,q})^2. \quad (9)$$

Figure 2 shows an example of the synchronous syntactic attention. The value in each cell indicates an attention score (i.e., an element of an attention weight matrix), and the darker cell represents a higher attention score. In all matrices, each row represents an attention distribution for each token (i.e., scores are normalized in a row direction). As can be seen in Figure 2, the English encoder's syntactic self-attentions E is mapped into the German encoder's syntactic self-attentions D' using the encoder-decoder attentions C and $C^{\top}$. Then, the loss between the German encoder's syntactic self-attentions D' and the German decoder's syntactic self-attentions D is measured. When calculating the loss, the values of the masked elements in D' and D, such as $D_{\text{Sprichst,du}}$ and $D_{\text{du,Englisch?}}$, are assigned to zero.

5 Experiments

5.1 Setup

We compared the proposed model with a conventional Transformer NMT model and a Transformer NMT with DBSA (Transformer+DBSA), which do not synchronize between source- and target-side self attentions, to confirm the effectiveness of the proposed synchronous syntactic attention. The Transformer *base* model (Vaswani et al., 2017) was used as the baseline model.

We evaluated translation performance in the WMT14 En-De translation task, WMT16 En-Ro translation task, and WAT ASPEC Ja-En translation task (Nakazawa et al., 2016). In ASPEC Ja-En, we used the first 1.5 million translation pairs of the training data in training. We used Moses Tokenizer to tokenize English, German, and Romanian sentences and KyTea (Neubig et al., 2011) to tokenize Japanese sentences. Byte Pair Encoding (BPE) was applied to create subword tokens. We used dependency structures generated by `Stanza` (Qi et al., 2020) for English, German, and Romanian sentences, and `EDA`[2] for Japanese sentences as the supervisions in the training of source- and target-side DBSA (i.e., calculation of $\mathcal{L}_{dep}$ in Transformer+DBSA and the proposed model). Note that `Stanza` and `EDA` are not used in testing. The details of the dataset and preprocessing are shown in the Appendix.

All models were trained for 100,000 updates. We used label smoothed cross entropy (Szegedy et al., 2016) as the $\mathcal{L}_t$ of the objective function and set label smoothing ϵ to 0.1. In the proposed model, the hyperparameter λ_{sync} was tuned for each development set and set to 0.5 for WMT14 En-De, 0.1 for WMT16 En-Ro, and 10.0 for ASPEC Ja-En. In all experiments, λ_{dep} and l_{dep} were set to 0.5 and 1, respectively. l_{sync} was set to 5 according to Garg et al. (2019)'s finding that the

[2] `http://www.ar.media.kyoto-u.ac.jp/tool/EDA`

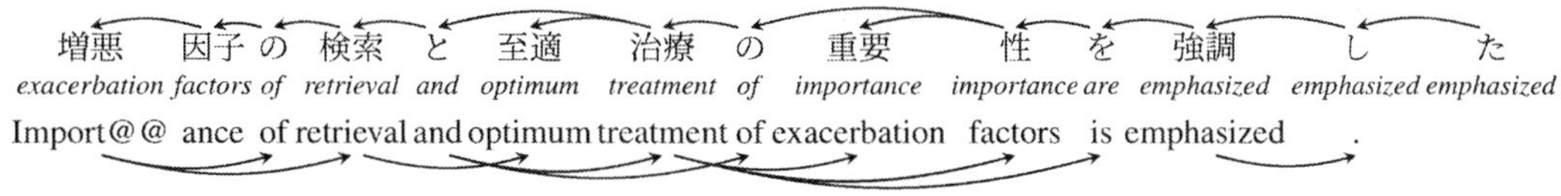

(a) Dependency structures captured by DBSA's attentions

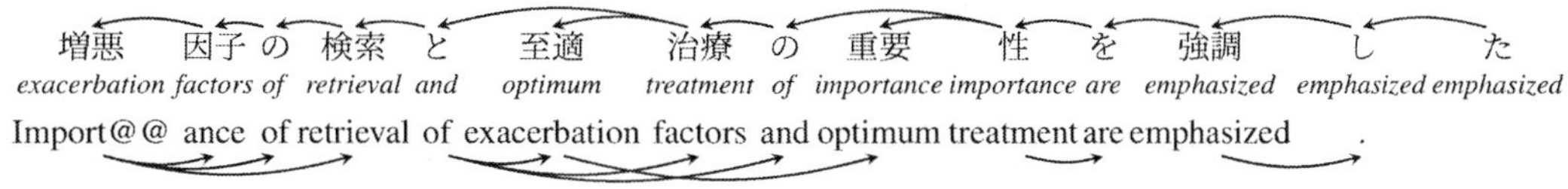

(b) Dependency structures captured by SyncAttn's attentions

Figure 3: Dependency structures of the examples in Figure 4

Model	WMT14 En→De	WMT16 En→Ro	ASPEC Ja→En
Transformer	27.23	23.83	28.94
DBSA	27.31	24.13	29.57
SyncAttn	**27.69**	**24.33**	**29.84**

Table 1: Experimental results (BLEU(%))

Input	増悪因子の検索と至適治療の重要性を強調した
DBSA	*Importance of **retrieval and optimum treatment of exacerbation factors** is emphasized.*
SyncAttn	*Importance of **retrieval of exacerbation factors and optimum treatment** are emphasized.*
Reference	*The importance of finding out exacerbation factors and optimum treatment are emphasized.*

Figure 4: Translation examples of DBSA and SyncAttn in the ASPEC Ja-En task

alignment performance of the encoder-decoder attention in the penultimate layer is the best among all layers. In decoding, we used beam search with length penalty and set the beam size to 4. The details of the hyperparameters are shown in the Appendix.

5.2 Results

Table 1 shows the experiment results. In the table, "DBSA" and "SyncAttn" indicate Transformer NMT with DBSA and Transformer NMT with the proposed synchronous syntactic attention, respectively. Translation performance was evaluated by BLEU (Papineni et al., 2002).

As Table 1 illustrates, the proposed model SyncAttn outperforms the baseline models Transformer and DBSA on all the tasks. In particular, SyncAttn improved by 0.38, 0.20, and 0.27 BLEU points in the WMT14 En-De, WMT16 En-Ro, ASPEC Ja-En tasks, respectively, compared to DBSA. These results demonstrate the effectiveness of our synchronous syntactic attention.

5.3 Case Study

This section compares translation examples of the baseline model DBSA and the proposed model SyncAttn to show the effectiveness of the synchronous syntactic attention. Figure 4 shows translation examples of the two models for the Ja-En task. The bold words are the differences between the translations by the two models. As can be seen in Figure 3, in both models, the encoder's self-attentions correctly find that "因子 (*factors*)" attends to "の (*of*)". However, DBSA does not correctly find the head of "factors" on the English side, while SyncAttn does. This is because SyncAttn synchronizes the source- and target-side dependency structures between "因子" and "factors" identified by the encoder-decoder attentions while DBSA does not. Figure 3 and 4 show that the correct analysis for the target-side dependency structures led to the correct translation.

6 Related Work

The main characteristic of Transformer NMT is attention mechanisms (i.e., self-attentions and encoder-decoder attentions). Some researches have analyzed and/or improved the attention mechanisms of Transformer NMT. For instance, Tang et al. (2018b) analyzed encoder-decoder attentions in terms of word sense disambiguation, and Tang et al. (2018a) analyzed self-attentions in terms of subject-verb agreement and word sense disambiguation. Raganato and Tiedemann (2018) and Voita et al. (2019) revealed the behaviors of attention heads in terms of dependency relations. Namely, Raganato and Tiedemann (2018) observed that specific attention heads of the encoder's self-attentions mark syntactic dependency relations. Voita et al. (2019) found that the confident heads play linguistically-interpretable roles like dependency relations. Garg et al. (2019) proposed a method for jointly learning to produce translations and alignments with a single Transformer model and showed that encoder-decoder attentions emulate word alignments. Based on their observations, our method maps the encoder's syntactic self-attentions into the target language space by using encoder-decoder attentions.

Shaw et al. (2018) extended a self-attention mechanism to encode the relative positions between two words in a sentence. Omote et al. (2019) and Wang et al. (2019b) proposed a self-attention mechanism to encode relative positions on source-side dependency trees.

Some researchers proposed syntax-aware self-attentions that are trained using dependency-based constraints. For instance, Wang et al. (2019a) and Bugliarello and Okazaki (2020) proposed source-side dependency-aware Transformer NMT. Wang et al. (2019a) created a constraint based on dependency relations between tokens to encoder self-attentions. Bugliarello and Okazaki (2020) also proposed *Parent-Scaled Self-Attention*, which multiplies an attention weight matrix by scores based on dependency relations. Deguchi et al. (2019) proposed *DBSA*, which is applicable to both the encoder's and decoder's self-attentions and is extended to subword units. We used DBSA to implement source- and target-side syntactic attentions in Transformer NMT. The main difference from the above-mentioned studies is that our work focuses on the incorporation of bilingual syntactic information into NMT.

Harada and Watanabe (2021) incorporated synchronous phrase structure grammar into NMT. Specifically, they proposed a syntactic NMT model that induces latent phrase structure and synchronizes the source- and target-side sentence structures. The difference with our model is that we synchronize dependency structures while they synchronize phrase structures.

7 Conclusions

In this paper, we proposed a novel attention mechanism for Transformer NMT, "Synchronous Syntactic Attention," which captures sentence structures aligned across source and target languages by aligned self-attention. The synchronous attention mechanism trains syntactic self-attentions (DBSA) under a constraint that minimizes the loss between encoder's and decoder's self attentions, where the encoder's self attentions are mapped into the target language space by encoder-decoder attentions. Since this method relies only on the constraint induced from the encoder's and decoder's self-attentions and encoder-decoder attentions, it does not require additional model parameters. The experiments show that the proposed method improves Transformer NMT's translation performance (up to a 0.38 BLEU point improvement).

Acknowledgments

The research results are achieved by "Research and Development of Deep Learning Technology for Advanced Multilingual Speech Translation," the Commissioned Research of National Institute of Information and Communications Technology (NICT), JAPAN. This work was partially supported by JSPS KAKENHI Grant Number JP20K19864 and JP21K12031.

References

Emanuele Bugliarello and Naoaki Okazaki. 2020. Enhancing machine translation with dependency-aware self-attention. In *Proceedings of the 58th Annual Meeting of the Association for Computational Linguistics*, pages 1618–1627, Online. Association for Computational Linguistics.

David Chiang. 2005. A hierarchical phrase-based model for statistical machine translation. In *Proceedings of the 43rd Annual Meeting of the Association for Computational Linguistics (ACL'05)*, pages 263–270, Ann Arbor, Michigan. Association for Computational Linguistics.

Hiroyuki Deguchi, Akihiro Tamura, and Takashi Ninomiya. 2019. Dependency-based self-attention for transformer nmt. In *Proceedings of Recent Advances in Natural Language Processing*, pages 239–246.

Yuan Ding and Martha Palmer. 2005. Machine translation using probabilistic synchronous dependency insertion grammars. In *Proceedings of the 43rd Annual Meeting of the Association for Computational Linguistics (ACL'05)*, pages 541–548, Ann Arbor, Michigan. Association for Computational Linguistics.

Sarthak Garg, Stephan Peitz, Udhyakumar Nallasamy, and Matthias Paulik. 2019. Jointly learning to align and translate with transformer models. In *Proceedings of the 2019 Conference on Empirical Methods in Natural Language Processing and the 9th International Joint Conference on Natural Language Processing (EMNLP-IJCNLP)*, pages 4453–4462, Hong Kong, China. Association for Computational Linguistics.

Shintaro Harada and Taro Watanabe. 2021. Neural machine translation with synchronous latent phrase structure. In *Proceedings of the Joint Conference of the 59th Annual Meeting of the Association for Computational Linguistics and the 11th International Joint Conference on Natural Language Processing: Student Research Workshop (ACL-IJCNLP SRW 2021) (to appear)*.

Hongfei Jiang, Muyun Yang, Tiejun Zhao, Sheng Li, and Bo Wang. 2009. A statistical machine translation model based on a synthetic synchronous grammar. In *Proceedings of the ACL-IJCNLP 2009 Conference Short Papers*, pages 125–128, Suntec, Singapore. Association for Computational Linguistics.

Diederik P. Kingma and Jimmy Ba. 2014. Adam: A method for stochastic optimization. *CoRR*, abs/1412.6980.

Marco Lui and Timothy Baldwin. 2012. langid.py: An off-the-shelf language identification tool. In *Proceedings of the ACL 2012 System Demonstrations*, pages 25–30, Jeju Island, Korea. Association for Computational Linguistics.

Toshiaki Nakazawa, Manabu Yaguchi, Kiyotaka Uchimoto, Masao Utiyama, Eiichiro Sumita, Sadao Kurohashi, and Hitoshi Isahara. 2016. Aspec: Asian scientific paper excerpt corpus. In *Proc. of LREC 2016*, pages 2204–2208.

Graham Neubig, Yosuke Nakata, and Shinsuke Mori. 2011. Pointwise prediction for robust, adaptable Japanese morphological analysis. In *Proceedings of the 49th Annual Meeting of the Association for Computational Linguistics: Human Language Technologies*, pages 529–533. Association for Computational Linguistics.

Nathan Ng, Kyra Yee, Alexei Baevski, Myle Ott, Michael Auli, and Sergey Edunov. 2019. Facebook FAIR's WMT19 news translation task submission. In *Proceedings of the Fourth Conference on Machine Translation (Volume 2: Shared Task Papers, Day 1)*, pages 314–319, Florence, Italy. Association for Computational Linguistics.

Yutaro Omote, Akihiro Tamura, and Takashi Ninomiya. 2019. Dependency-based relative positional encoding for transformer nmt. In *Proceedings of the International Conference Recent Advances in Natural Language Processing 2019 (RANLP 2019)*, pages 854–861.

Kishore Papineni, Salim Roukos, Todd Ward, and Wei-Jing Zhu. 2002. Bleu: a method for automatic evaluation of machine translation. In *Proceedings of the 40th Annual Meeting of the Association for Computational Linguistics*, pages 311–318, Philadelphia, Pennsylvania, USA. Association for Computational Linguistics.

Peng Qi, Yuhao Zhang, Yuhui Zhang, Jason Bolton, and Christopher D. Manning. 2020. Stanza: A python natural language processing toolkit for many human languages.

Alessandro Raganato and Jörg Tiedemann. 2018. An analysis of encoder representations in transformer-based machine translation. In *Proceedings of the 2018 EMNLP Workshop BlackboxNLP: Analyzing and Interpreting Neural Networks for NLP*, pages 287–297, Brussels, Belgium. Association for Computational Linguistics.

Peter Shaw, Jakob Uszkoreit, and Ashish Vaswani. 2018. Self-attention with relative position representations. In *Proceedings of the 2018 Conference of the North American Chapter of the Association for Computational Linguistics: Human Language Technologies, Volume 2 (Short Papers)*, pages 464–468. Association for Computational Linguistics.

C. Szegedy, V. Vanhoucke, S. Ioffe, J. Shlens, and Z. Wojna. 2016. Rethinking the inception architecture for computer vision. In *2016 IEEE Conference on Computer Vision and Pattern Recognition (CVPR)*, pages 2818–2826.

Gongbo Tang, Mathias Müller, Annette Rios, and Rico Sennrich. 2018a. Why self-attention? a targeted evaluation of neural machine translation architectures. In *Proceedings of the 2018 Conference on Empirical Methods in Natural Language Processing*, pages 4263–4272, Brussels, Belgium. Association for Computational Linguistics.

Gongbo Tang, Rico Sennrich, and Joakim Nivre. 2018b. An analysis of attention mechanisms: The case of word sense disambiguation in neural machine translation. In *Proceedings of the Third Conference on Machine Translation: Research Papers*, pages 26–35, Brussels, Belgium. Association for Computational Linguistics.

Ashish Vaswani, Noam Shazeer, Niki Parmar, Jakob Uszkoreit, Llion Jones, Aidan N Gomez, Ł ukasz Kaiser, and Illia Polosukhin. 2017. Attention is all you need. In *Advances in Neural Information Processing Systems 30*, pages 5998–6008. Curran Associates, Inc.

Elena Voita, David Talbot, Fedor Moiseev, Rico Sennrich, and Ivan Titov. 2019. Analyzing multi-head self-attention: Specialized heads do the heavy lifting, the rest can be pruned. In *Proceedings of the 57th Annual Meeting of the Association for Computational Linguistics*, pages 5797–5808, Florence, Italy. Association for Computational Linguistics.

Chengyi Wang, Shuangzhi Wu, and Shujie Liu. 2019a. Source dependency-aware transformer with supervised self-attention. *arXiv preprint arXiv:1909.02273*.

Xing Wang, Zhaopeng Tu, Longyue Wang, and Shuming Shi. 2019b. Self-attention with structural position representations. In *Proceedings of the 2019 Conference on Empirical Methods in Natural Language Processing and the 9th International Joint Conference on Natural Language Processing (EMNLP-IJCNLP)*, pages 1403–1409, Hong Kong, China. Association for Computational Linguistics.

Yonghui Wu, Mike Schuster, Zhifeng Chen, Quoc V Le, Mohammad Norouzi, Wolfgang Macherey, Maxim Krikun, Yuan Cao, Qin Gao, Klaus Macherey, et al. 2016. Google's neural machine translation system: Bridging the gap between human and machine translation. *arXiv preprint arXiv:1609.08144*.

Hao Zhang, Liang Huang, Daniel Gildea, and Kevin Knight. 2006. Synchronous binarization for machine translation. In *Proceedings of the Human Language Technology Conference of the NAACL, Main Conference*, pages 256–263, New York City, USA. Association for Computational Linguistics.

A Dataset and Preprocessing Details

We used Moses Tokenizer with the aggressive hyphen splitting option[3] for English, German, and Romanian sentences and KyTea for Japanese sentences. In English, German, and Romanian sentences, we used `normalize-punctuation.perl`, contained in the Moses toolkit, to normalize the characters. In WMT14 En-De, we also applied language identification filtering to the training data using `langid`[4] (Lui and Baldwin, 2012), keeping only the sentence pairs with correct languages on both sides (Ng et al., 2019). In ASPEC Ja-En, we used the first 1.5 million translation pairs of the training data in training. We trained Byte Pair Encoding (BPE) with 37,000 joint operations for WMT14 En-De and 40,000 joint operations for WMT16 En-Ro and trained BPE separately on the source and target sides with 16,000 merge operations for ASPEC Ja-En. We set the batch size to 25,000 tokens for WMT14 En-De, 6,000 tokens for WMT16 En-Ro, and 12,000 tokens for ASPEC Ja-En. Before applying BPE, we removed sentences longer than 100 words in all the training datasets and sentence pairs with a source/target length ratio exceeding 1.5 for WMT14 En-De and WMT16 En-Ro and 2.0 for ASPEC Ja-En.

Dataset	# Sentence pairs Train	Dev	Test
WMT14 En→De	3,772,107	3,000	3,003
WMT16 En→Ro	599,208	1,999	1,999
ASPEC Ja→En	1,428,181	1,790	1,812

Table 2: Statistics of evaluation dataset

Table 2 shows the number of parallel sentence pairs in the training, development, and test sets.

B Model and Training Details

We used the Transformer *base* model (Vaswani et al., 2017) as the baseline model. We used the Adam optimizer (Kingma and Ba, 2014) with $\beta_1 = 0.9$, $\beta_2 = 0.98$. The learning rate was warmed up over the first 4,000 steps to a peak value of 7e-4, and then it was decreased proportionally to the inverse square root of the step number (Vaswani et al., 2017). All models were trained for 100,000 updates. The dropout probability was set to 0.1. We used label smoothed cross entropy (Szegedy et al., 2016) as the $\mathcal{L}_t$ of the objective function and set label smoothing ϵ to 0.1. In all experiments, λ_{dep} was set to 0.5, the l_{dep}-th layer that captures source or target side's sentence structures was set to the 1st (bottom) layer, and the encoder-decoder attention for mapping the encoder's self-attention was obtained from the 5th layer (i.e., l_{sync}=5) according to Garg et al. (2019)'s finding that the alignment performance of the encoder-decoder attention in the penultimate layer is the best among all layers. In decoding, we used beam search with a beam size of 4 and length penalty $\alpha = 0.6$ (Wu et al., 2016).

We performed all the training on 2 V100 GPUs for WMT14 En-De, and a single V100 GPU for WMT16 En-Ro and ASPEC Ja-En. For all the models, training took about 7 hours for WMT14 En-De, about 3 hours for WMT16 En-Ro, and about 4 hours for ASPEC Ja-En. The number of model parameters of all models is about 64M for WMT14 En-De and WMT16 En-Ro, and about 72M for ASPEC Ja-En. In WMT14 En-De and WMT16 En-Ro, the encoder-side embedding layer and the decoder-side embedding layer are shared.

[3] `https://github.com/moses-smt/mosesdecoder/blob/master/scripts/tokenizer/tokenizer.perl`

[4] `https://github.com/saffsd/langid.c`

C Hyperparameter Search

In the proposed model, the hyperparameter λ_{sync} was tuned on each development set. We tuned λ_{sync} by trying different $\lambda_{sync} \in \{0.01, 0.05, 0.1, 0.5, 1.0, 5.0, 10.0\}$.

D Evaluation Details

In all experiments, translation performance was evaluated by BLEU (Papineni et al., 2002). As for the ASPEC Ja-En task, we followed the WAT Automatic Evaluation Systems[5].

[5]http://lotus.kuee.kyoto-u.ac.jp/WAT/evaluation/index.html#automatic_evaluation_systems.html

Author Index

Association for Computational Linguistics
209 N. Eighth Street
Stroudsburg, Pennsylvania 18360

ISBN 978-1-7138-3311-6

CURRAN ASSOCIATES INC.
proceedings.com